"The notion of a critical juncture has become a key idea in social science to capture the interaction of structure and agency in ways that open up new intellectual horizons and free us from outdated frameworks. This volume brings together the leading scholars on the topic and will become the standard reference work."

—**Daron Acemoglu**, Massachusetts Institute of Technology

"Social scientists have a growing interest in historical explanation and in the dramatic events that shape subsequent history, but that research tradition has often suffered from theoretical imprecision and insufficient methodological self-consciousness. Collier and Munck's volume marks a sharp break, giving historical researchers important new tools to sharpen their arguments. Other equally distinguished scholars have added chapters laying out the full range of methods and controversies in the study of critical junctures. This is a must-have book."

—**Christopher H. Achen**, Princeton University

"Critical junctures implicitly or explicitly inform much social science research. Collier, Munck, and a top-notch roster of authors, provide the definitive treatment of this vital conceptual, methodological, and substantive tool. Collectively, the volume's contributors convincingly assess what has endured, which refinements and critiques are most compelling, and new directions for the development and application of the critical junctures approach. The book is a must-read for social scientists from diverse disciplines."

—**Melani Cammett**, Harvard University

"In merging the frameworks of critical junctures with that of historical legacy, this volume provides substantive insights into how we have come to be where we are. A heuristic which allows the scholar to combine structural deterministic accounts with the agency of chance and choice. It represents a much-needed alternative to current approaches."

—**Miguel Centeno**, Princeton University

"At last, we have the definitive work on critical junctures. Ranging widely across time, continents and methodological issues, this stellar volume considers and advances the many debates about how political systems change, setting new research agendas for the field. With a wide ambit and a distinguished set of contributors, this book will be indispensable reading for all scholars interested in how politics evolves over time."

—**Peter Hall**, Harvard University

Critical Junctures
and Historical Legacies

Critical Junctures and Historical Legacies

Insights and Methods for Comparative Social Science

Edited by David Collier and Gerardo L. Munck

ROWMAN & LITTLEFIELD
Lanham • Boulder • New York • London

Published by Rowman & Littlefield
An imprint of The Rowman & Littlefield Publishing Group, Inc.
4501 Forbes Boulevard, Suite 200, Lanham, Maryland 20706
www.rowman.com

86-90 Paul Street, London EC2A 4NE, United Kingdom

British Library Cataloguing in Publication Information Available

Library of Congress Cataloging-in-Publication Data

Names: Collier, David, 1942– editor. | Munck, Gerardo L. (Gerardo Luis),
  1958– editor.
Title: Critical junctures and historical legacies : insights and methods
  for comparative social science / edited by David Collier and Gerardo L. Munck.
Description: Lanham : Rowman & Littlefield, [2022] | Includes bibliographical
  references and index.
Identifiers: LCCN 2021047005 (print) | LCCN 2021047006 (ebook) |
  ISBN 9781538166147 (cloth) | ISBN 9781538166154 (paperback) |
  ISBN 9781538166161 (epub)
Subjects: LCSH: Social sciences—Comparative method. | Social change. |
  Social structure. | Critical theory.
Classification: LCC H61 .C75 2022 (print) | LCC H61 (ebook) | DDC 300.72—dc23
LC record available at https://lccn.loc.gov/2021047005
LC ebook record available at https://lccn.loc.gov/2021047006

Contents

III. Substantive Applications I: States and Political Regimes

IV. Substantive Applications II: Neoliberalism and Political Parties

V. Conclusion

Figures and Tables

FIGURES

TABLES

Preface

The importance of historically oriented analysis in the social sciences is increasingly recognized. Research on critical junctures and their historical legacies is part of a broad intellectual movement that addresses the historical evolution of societies and international orders and studies the way historical events impact the present. To understand the contemporary world and to think seriously about how it might change, it is indispensable to understand how social orders are created, become entrenched, and are transformed. Thus, carefully scrutinizing the theoretical framework and research methods used in historically oriented research and proposing, refining, and testing arguments about the historical origins of the current world are central to the mission of the social sciences.

This book is a collective enterprise that originated in a roundtable at the 2016 Annual Meeting of the American Political Science Association (APSA), convened to recognize the twenty-fifth anniversary of the publication of Ruth Berins Collier and David Collier's 1991 book *Shaping the Political Arena*. The initiative quickly became much more than that. Discussion at the roundtable itself—and ongoing exchanges at subsequent APSA meetings—sparked important questions and disagreements, and other scholars joined the debate. This exchange led initially to a symposium on critical junctures and historical legacies published as a special issue of *Qualitative and Multi-Method Research* (*QMMR*) in 2017. We reached out to more scholars working on critical junctures, and we organized further panels and roundtables at APSA meetings (in 2017, 2018, and 2019) and a working dinner at APSA 2019. Kenneth M. Roberts graciously organized a panel at the 2021 Congress of the Latin American Studies Association (LASA). Thus, the present volume is the result of a long and fruitful series of discussions with a group of scholars who have been thinking about critical junctures in an open way. In parallel, we launched a website intended to be a resource for scholars, teachers, and the general public who are interested in critical junctures. This website can be accessed at http://www.critical-juncture.net.

We would like to acknowledge the extensive help we received from many colleagues as we prepared the *QMMR* Symposium, constructed the website, and edited the chapters in this book: Pamela Carey, Christopher Chambers-Ju, Louise Curtis, Laura Deneckere, Sondra Jensen, William Ryan, Patti Smolian, and Emma Soldon. Exceptional assistance with the logistics of manuscript preparation and other project initiatives was provided by Jennifer Collier Jennings and Ben Harper. Finally, we thank Tulia Falleti for serving as discussant on the APSA 2018 panel; her comments were very helpful.

David Collier began to analyze critical junctures in his book, *Shaping the Political Arena*, co-authored with Ruth Berins Collier. The analysis posed many methodological challenges: How can we make analytically valid comparisons across a diverse set of countries and time periods? How can we use qualitative methods to tease out the causal processes and analyze the partial explanations that are central to arguments about critical junctures? Stimulated by such questions, in subsequent work he turned his attention to laying out tools for qualitative and multi-method research, including the analysis of concepts, comparison, and causal assessment. He became actively involved in the American Political Science Association and the International Political Science Association, organizing initiatives to support this kind of analysis. The collaborative work on the *QMMR* symposium, the website, and this volume have been a gratifying extension of these efforts. Above all, he would like to thank Ruth Berins Collier for her insight and engagement in these issues over many years.

Gerardo L. Munck worked on this project in parallel with his study on the evolution of knowledge in the social sciences since the late eighteenth century. Starting with Kuhn's work on paradigms and paradigm shifts, research on the evolution of knowledge has debated many of the same issues addressed in discussions about the evolution of societies and international orders. These issues include the relative role of discontinuous and incremental change, the impact on change of endogenous and exogenous factors. Thus, Gerardo's thinking about critical junctures was informed by his related research on how social science knowledge evolves. He wishes to acknowledge the support and encouragement he received throughout from Claudia Luera. Gracias.

David Collier
Gerardo L. Munck

Berkeley and Santa Monica,
California

Introduction

Tradition and Innovation in Critical Juncture Research

David Collier and Gerardo L. Munck

For half a century, the study of critical junctures and their legacies has been an influential and fruitful research tradition within the broader enterprise of comparative social science. Launched by Lipset and Rokkan in 1967, it is traceable to Weber's (1946 [1922–1923]: 280) idea of historical "switchmen" who select the "tracks along which action is pushed."

This tradition is based on a theoretical framework centered on the idea that critical junctures are major, macro-level episodes of change that yield enduring legacies. It has been closely associated with comparative historical research and the use of qualitative methods. And it has explored fundamental substantive questions about a broad array of topics, including state formation, political regimes and democracy, party systems, public policy, government performance, economic development, and cultural norms.[1] Research on critical junctures has been and remains a vibrant tradition in the social sciences.

At the same time, the field has undergone important changes and several questions have been raised about this tradition. Interest in the critical juncture framework has led to many valuable refinements. However, the growing literature has created confusion about some of its central ideas. For example, scholars hold different views regarding whether critical junctures are only big changes, necessarily involve contingent events, always comprise institutional changes, and consistently lead to divergent outcomes. Further, scrutiny of this framework has led to some critiques. Most importantly, students of incremental change argue that critical juncture research is flawed because it underplays the role of agency, focuses excessively on exogenous shocks to explain change, and neglects gradual change.

---

1. For a comprehensive list of works in this tradition, see Appendix III.

Questions have also been raised regarding how claims about critical junctures are empirically assessed. Discussions about the use of qualitative methods have introduced both improvements and critiques of these methods. Moreover, a literature using quantitative methods that is relevant to the study of critical junctures—in that it tests hypotheses about long-term, persistent effects—has begun to take shape in recent years. As with discussions about the framework used in this research, new and not always compatible ideas have been introduced about how empirical research should be conducted.

This volume contributes to research on critical junctures by offering a critical review of the key theoretical and methodological ideas used in this field. As we will show, some old ideas are still useful, while others are not and should be discarded. Some recent proposals are genuine advances and should be incorporated into the tradition's repertoire, whereas others should be discarded. Some critiques are valid and should be taken seriously, but others should not. Also, some new ideas that are not part of the recent discussion merit consideration. Thus, based on a careful, balanced assessment of the field, this volume reaffirms the value of many traditional practices and specifies how the field can build on proven ideas, while embracing the need for innovation and opening new frontiers.

We will also place a strong emphasis on substantive research. Debates about theory and methods are necessary and important. However, when delinked from substantive concerns they become sterile. Moreover, research on substantive questions offers the clearest indication of the value of a research tradition. Thus, this volume presents many examples of substantive research. These examples illustrate how researchers draw on the critical juncture framework in developing arguments and rely on various methods in assessing these claims. They also show how this research produces knowledge about how big structures originate, endure, and change, using a macro-historical perspective to elaborate original explanations that are crucial to an understanding of the world's past and current problems.

This chapter introduces the volume. We first situate research on critical junctures within the historically oriented social sciences and identify its key aims and characteristics. We then consider debates and disagreements concerning the framework and methods, and spell out the book's approach to contrasting views about this research. Finally, we present a detailed overview of the book, mapping out its organization and briefly discussing each chapter.

AIMS AND CHARACTERISTICS
OF CRITICAL JUNCTURE RESEARCH

Research on critical junctures is part of a larger social science agenda that focuses on temporality and challenges presentism or short-termism, i.e., the assumption that patterns of the current world can be explained by causes in the recent past (Pierson

2004: 45–46, Ch. 3; Rueschemeyer 2009: 147–51; Guldi and Armitage 2014).[2] This agenda is advanced in broad fields of research that have been identified by the labels of (1) comparative historical analysis, a tradition launched in the 1960s that bridges sociology, political science, and history;[3] (2) historical institutionalism, a newer tradition begun in the 1990s and based largely in political science;[4] and (3) the new institutional economics, an approach pioneered by economists that achieved prominence throughout the social sciences in the 1990s.[5] Thus, research on critical junctures is not a self-contained field. Many concerns that motivate this research, and many of its ideas and methods, are shared by a larger community of scholars. This research is part of a large intellectual movement.[6]

The critical juncture tradition itself is wide and diverse. However, it can be characterized in terms of three features: (1) a theoretical framework, (2) research methods, and (3) substantive questions.

(1) *Framework*. Research in this tradition relies on a framework that is built around two key ideas. One is that critical junctures are a distinct kind of change,

---

2. See also Rueschemeyer et al. (1992: 7, 23, 35), Reid (2011), and Akyeampong et al. (2014).

3. For overviews of comparative historical analysis, see Skocpol (1984), Collier (1998), Mahoney and Rueschemeyer (2003), Ritter (2014), Mahoney and Thelen (2015), and Møller (2017). On the temporal concepts used in comparative historical analysis, see Kreuzer (2013, forthcoming).

4. Historical institutionalism overlaps in part with comparative historical analysis and some scholars (e.g., Skocpol) play a key role in both traditions. In addition, many of the works cited as examples of historical institutionalism are also routinely treated as part of comparative historical analysis. Indeed, there is considerable overlap in the works discussed in two texts on comparative historical analysis (Mahoney and Rueschemeyer 2003; Mahoney and Thelen 2015) and two texts on historical institutionalism (Steinmo 2008; Fioretos et al. 2016). For overviews of historical institutionalism, see Steinmo et al. (1992), Thelen and Steinmo (1992), Thelen (1999), Pierson and Skocpol (2002), Steinmo (2008), Fioretos et al. (2016), Rixen et al. (2016), and Fioretos (2017).

5. For overviews of the new institutional economics, see Richter (2005), Bates (2014), Levi and Menaldo (2015), and Alston et al. (2018). The new institutional economics is an encompassing field, much of which has little resonance with critical juncture research. However, the strand of the new institutional economics associated with North is certainly part of the historical turn in the social sciences. On North's contribution, see Galiani and Sened (2014).

6. Three strands of this literature, which might be fit under the three broader traditions just noted, are American Political Development (APD), which adopts a historical perspective to the study of U.S. politics; legacies research, which has focused among other things on postcommunist and postcolonial societies; and historical political economy, which combines economic theories and quantitative historical research. On American Political Development, see Mayhew (2002) and Orren and Skowronek (2004). On legacies research, see Simpser et al. (2018). On historical political economy, see Gailmard (2021).

an idea that has been conveyed in different terms. Some authors conceive of these as "periods of radical change" (Rokkan 1970, in Flora 1999: 37), "crucial founding moments" (Thelen 1999: 387; see also Ikenberry 2016: 541), or "large-scale change" (Katznelson 2003: 282). Others see them as "discontinuous . . . macro transformations" (Collier and Collier 1991: 11), "discontinuous . . . massive changes" (Weingast 2005: 164–65), or "changes that are . . . abrupt [and] discontinuous" (Roberts 2014: 43). Although using different terms, scholars have generally understood critical junctures as large, rapid, discontinuous changes.

The other main idea in the framework is that critical junctures produce a distinct kind of causal effect, usually called a historical legacy. One basic point is that the effect of critical junctures is "frozen over long periods of time" (Rokkan 1970, quoted in Flora 1999: 36) or, more simply, is "durable" (Roberts 2014: 42). A related point is that this effect "reproduces itself without requiring the recurrence of the original cause" (Scully 1992: 12) and does so through distinct "mechanisms . . . that reproduce the legacy" (Collier and Collier 1991: 35, 37). Thus, a critical juncture is a change that produces an effect that persists over a long time, through mechanisms of reproduction, after the initial cause has ceased to operate.

Not all authors conceive of critical junctures and historical legacies in the same way. However, there is considerable consensus in the literature on these basic points.[7]

(2) *Methods.* Research on critical junctures has relied heavily on qualitative methods. All of the twentieth-century exemplars are based fully or largely on qualitative research (e.g., Moore 1966; Lipset and Rokkan 1967; Collier and Collier 1991; Baumgartner and Jones 1993; Putnam 1993). Furthermore, inasmuch as this research has been methodologically self-conscious, it has drawn on general discussions about qualitative methodology (Smelser 1976; King et al. 1994; Brady and Collier 2010) and on reflections regarding the study of historical processes (Collier and Collier 1991: Ch. 1; Grzymała-Busse 2011; Mahoney and Thelen 2015: Parts III and IV).[8]

(3) *Substantive Questions.* Finally, research on critical junctures is characterized by its focus on big, fundamental, questions or what has been described as first-order historically enduring questions (Rule 1997: 45–48; Laitin 2004: 33–36) or, more simply, "big problems" (Lichbach 2009: 29–31). The following examples of actual research give a sense of the centrality and range of the substantive questions addressed in critical juncture research.

---

7. For an overview and comparison of different conceptions of critical junctures and their historical legacies, see Appendix I.

8. See also Mahoney and Rueschemeyer (2003: Part III), George and Bennett (2005), Capoccia and Kelemen (2007), Bennett and Checkel (2015), and Møller and Skaaning (2021).

- Why do some countries have weak states and others have greater state capacity?[9]
- Why do some countries have democratic regimes and others authoritarian regimes?[10]
- Why do some countries have high-quality democracies and others low-quality democracies?[11]
- Why do countries have different party systems?[12]
- Why do some countries have governments that perform well and others governments that perform poorly?[13]
- Why do policy monopolies—the dominance of public policy by the same group of policymakers and organizations—develop and endure in the U.S. government?[14]
- Why do some countries have legally enforced racial segregation and others do not?[15]
- Why are some countries prosperous and others are poor?[16]
- Why were developmental states established in some Asian countries and not others?[17]
- Why did the West become dominant in the world?[18]
- Why have international orders varied in character over time?[19]

In short, a considerable body of research in this field has been produced since the 1960s. This research has relied on a framework centered on the idea of critical junctures and historical legacies. It has been strongly associated with qualitative research and has addressed many key substantive questions in the social sciences. As a result of the work of a large community of scholars, critical juncture research has become an established tradition in the historically oriented social sciences (Thelen 1999; Pierson 2004: Ch. 2; Capoccia 2015; 2016).[20]

---

9. Skocpol (1979), Mann (1986), Tilly (1990), Waldner (1999), Kurtz (2013), Soifer (2015), and Mazzuca (2021).

10. Moore (1966), Collier and Collier (1991), Jalal (1995), Yashar (1997), Gould (1999), López-Alves (2000), Mahoney (2001), and Tudor (2013).

11. della Porta (2016), Fishman (2019), and Mazzuca and Munck (2020).

12. Lipset and Rokkan (1967), Collier and Collier (1991), Scully (1992), Bartolini (2000), Riedl (2014), Roberts (2014), and Caramani (2015).

13. Putnam (1993).

14. Baumgartner and Jones (2009).

15. Marx (1998).

16. Waisman (1987), North and Weingast (1989), Engerman and Sokoloff (2012), and Acemoglu and Robinson (2012).

17. Chibber (2003), Kohli (2004), and Vu (2010).

18. Diamond (1997), Mitterauer (2010), and Acemoglu and Robinson (2019).

19. Ikenberry (2001).

20. See also Fioretos (2017: Ch. 1) and Berntzen (2020).

DEBATES AND DISAGREEMENTS ABOUT
THE FRAMEWORK AND METHODS

The growing literature on critical junctures has also given rise to some new discussions. Since around 2000, many scholars have advanced several ideas about the framework and methods used in this research. Some have made proposals for changes that neatly supplement and clearly add to the repertoire of ideas associated with this tradition. However, others have made suggestions that are not compatible with earlier ideas or are themselves mutually incompatible. This new literature reflects strong interest in the study of critical junctures. It also has created some confusion, controversy and, ultimately, uncertainty about the framework and methods used in critical juncture research.

Weighing in on these discussions is crucial in a volume that seeks to suggest how this research should move forward. Here we preview the key issues this volume will address. We lay out contrasting views presented in the literature and briefly anticipate the specific positions supported by the authors in the following chapters. We likewise offer a more general statement about how these issues and debates are approached in the book.

Theoretical Framework

Some key disagreements concern the framework used in substantive research. Until the 1990s, this research relied on a set of ideas introduced by Lipset and Rokkan (1967) and others, that collectively shaped a distinctive approach to historical causation.[21] These ideas provided useful guidance for research. However, as the literature on these ideas has expanded, questions have arisen about the core components of the critical juncture framework. The idea of a tradition relying on a common theoretical

---

21. Lipset and Rokkan (1967: 3, 50–53) presented the concepts of critical juncture and cleavage structure, and a somewhat vague notion of the "freezing" and "entrenchment" of outcomes of critical junctures. Stinchcombe (1968: 101–25) specified the distinctive causal structure—a self-replicating causal loop—that reproduces an outcome over time. David (1985) launched the related idea of path dependence, and both David (1985) and Arthur (1989; 1994) supplemented this general idea with the more specific idea of increasing returns that lock in past choices. North (1990) linked the idea of path dependence to the study of institutions and institutional change. And Collier and Collier (1991: Ch. 1) offered a synthesis that integrates the ideas of antecedent conditions, cleavage or crisis, critical juncture, aftermath, and historical legacy.

Some researchers use the cognate idea of punctuated equilibrium, drawn from research in evolutionary biology pioneered by Eldredge and Gould (1972) and developed extensively by Gould (2007). Krasner (1984; 1988) played a central role in introducing these ideas in political science. Other researchers use what Gellner (1964: 42–49) calls a neo-episodic model of change. These various frameworks share some core ideas.

structure has also in some respects been cast in doubt. Even the value of this research has sometimes been questioned.[22]

Critical Junctures and Legacies

One source of uncertainty involves the basic idea of a critical juncture and its legacy, the core concepts in this field. Although we find substantial consensus about how critical junctures and legacies should be understood, different views are defended in the literature.

First, scholars disagree on whether critical junctures are large-scale, rapid, discontinuous changes. Most hold that critical junctures are only macro-level events that introduce discontinuous change, that is, some new property or a qualitative novelty (Lipset and Rokkan 1967: 13–15, 47; Collier and Collier 1991: 11; Katznelson 2003: 282).[23] However, an influential view, especially among scholars who draw on the idea of path dependence, is that small rather than big changes can be critical junctures (Mahoney 2000: 526; Pierson 2004: 44, 50–52; Greer 2008: 220–21).[24]

Second, scholars also diverge on whether critical junctures are wholly contingent events, that is, events in which actors are not constrained by antecedent conditions. Numerous authors hold that critical junctures are often strongly shaped by precisely such antecedent conditions (Collier and Collier 1991: 27; Katznelson 2003: 282–83, 291–92; Pierson 2004: 51–52).[25] They also stress that the extent to which critical junctures inherently entail contingency is best treated as a variable factor to be addressed in the context of substantive research.

However, growing attention to how path-dependent processes originate has generated an interest in the decisive role of actors' choices. Several authors claim that critical junctures are a distinct kind of cause—one in which actors' choices cause outcomes but are themselves not caused—and that such fully contingent choices

---

22. The new literature includes, among others, Thelen (1999; 2003; 2004), Mahoney (2000; 2001), Pierson (2000; 2004), Katznelson (2003), Orren and Skowronek (2004), Streeck and Thelen (2005b), Hogan (2006), March and Olsen (2006), Boas (2007), Capoccia and Kelemen (2007), Djelic and Quack (2007), Greer (2008), Howlett (2009), Sydow et al. (2009), Mahoney and Thelen (2010), Slater and Simmons (2010), Soifer (2012), Bernhard (2015), Capoccia (2015; 2016a; 2016b), Hacker et al. (2015), Rixen and Viola (2015), Sarigil (2015), Wittenberg (2015), Conran and Thelen (2016), Fioretos et al. (2016), Hall (2016), Collier and Munck (2017), Acharya et al. (2018), García-Montoya and Mahoney (2020), and Gerschewski (2021).

23. See also Roberts (2014: 43) and Ikenberry (2016: 540–41).

24. See also David (1985: 332) and Arthur (1989: 117).

25. See also Weingast (2005: 165–66), Martin and Sunley (2006: 402–03), Slater (2010: 55), Slater and Simmons (2010: 887–90), and Soifer (2012: 1574, 1593).

should be treated as a defining characteristic of critical junctures (Mahoney 2000: 507–08, 511, 513; Capoccia and Kelemen 2007: 343, 348; Bernhard 2015: 978).[26]

A third source of disagreement concerns the causal structure through which a critical juncture generates a legacy. The classic position, articulated by Stinchcombe (1968: 101–25), holds that the historical legacy of a critical juncture is, in causal terms, a persistent or enduring effect that is created by a self-replicating causal loop (Howlett 2009: 252–53; Sydow et al. 2009: 697–98; Rixen and Viola 2015: 317). In contrast, a more recently formulated position is that a legacy can also be produced by a distinct kind of path dependence, one involving "reactive sequences" that generate a long-term effect but not one that reinforces a prior outcome and involves persistence (Mahoney 2000: 509, 526–35; Arestis and Sawyer 2009: 11; Beyer 2010: 4–5; Martin and Sunley 2010: 84–85).

A well-vetted and precise understanding of critical junctures and their legacies is a basic requirement for this field of research. These controversies are addressed in this volume, by D. Collier (Chapter 1), Munck (Chapters 5 and 19), Riedl and Roberts (Chapter 6), and Waldner (Chapter 7). On the first source of disagreement, D. Collier (Chapter 1) and Munck (Chapter 5) defend the traditional conception of critical junctures as rapid, discontinuous, macro-level changes. On the second point, D. Collier (Chapter 1), Riedl and Roberts (Chapter 6), Waldner (Chapter 7), and Munck (Chapter 19) make a case for not treating contingent choices as a defining feature of critical junctures. Finally, on the third point, Munck (Chapter 5) defends the standard conception of critical junctures as changes that create a persistent effect through a self-replicating causal loop. This volume thus argues that many earlier ways of thinking about this field definitely remain useful.

However, as stressed by Munck (Chapter 5), the current discussion shows that we need a better theoretical foundation for critical juncture research. Indeed, the diversity of views regarding essential concepts is a sign that basic issues have not been properly addressed and that the framework should be given stronger foundations. Thus, Munck provides a thorough discussion of key issues and shows why some views about critical junctures and legacies should be adopted while other (earlier and newer) ideas should be discarded. Regarding erroneous ideas that should be dismissed, see also Chapter 19.

Agency, Exogenous Shocks, and Incremental Change

Additional issues are raised by analysts of incremental change, who express serious reservations both about some building blocks, and also the overall value, of critical

---

26. See also Greer (2008: 219), Calder and Ye (2010: 42), Capoccia (2015: 148, 150–51, 156–60, 165), and García-Montoya and Mahoney (2020).

juncture research (Thelen 1999, 2003, 2004; Streeck and Thelen 2005a, 2005b; March and Olsen 2006).[27]

According to this view, critical juncture research does not explain change properly. This limitation is seen as flowing from Mahoney's (2000: 507) view that "path dependence characterizes specifically those historical sequences in which contingent events set into motion institutional patterns or event chains that have deterministic properties." Indeed, this deterministic conception of path dependence is seen as underpinning a static approach to change—one that disregards the ever-present role of agency and contentious actions that challenge established orders and necessarily invokes exogenous shocks as a source of change (Crouch and Farrell 2004; Thelen 2004: xii–xiii, 8, 25–31; Streeck and Thelen 2005a; 2005b: 6–9).[28]

These critics also maintain that critical juncture research offers an inadequate overall portrayal of how societies change. In their view, this research depicts history in terms of sudden big jumps followed by long periods of continuity and ignores the pervasive and impactful role of gradual change. Further, this research is seen as overlooking a key insight: that much change is incremental, and that such change can actually lead, cumulatively, to major social change (Thelen 2004: 28; Streeck and Thelen 2005a; 2005b: 6, 8–9; March and Olsen 2006: 12; Mahoney and Thelen 2010: 2–3).

Responding to these strong critiques, D. Collier (Chapter 1), Munck (Chapter 5), and Riedl and Roberts (Chapter 6) show that they are largely unwarranted. With some exceptions, critical juncture research offers an explanation of change that draws on endogenous and exogenous factors, as well as the interplay between structural factors and actors. Moreover, rather than denying the importance of incremental change, researchers acknowledge the need to consider critical junctures as one among various possible kinds of change and to explore ways in which the study of big, discontinuous changes and incremental changes might be combined. Many substantive chapters (see especially Chapters 2, 4, 12, and 14) provide further evidence that critical juncture research avoids the various pitfalls discussed by these critics.

At the same time, this debate again points to the need for an explicit discussion of the theoretical foundations of critical juncture research, a challenge taken up by Munck (Chapter 5). He discusses two basic issues in the study of social change: the problem of deciding how the analysis of endogenous and exogenous sources of change should be combined, and the problem of integrating structure and agency. He also argues that insights about these problems developed more broadly in social theory, yet largely ignored by critical juncture research, should be used to reconstruct the critical juncture framework.

---

27. See also Crouch and Farrell (2004), Orren and Skowronek (2004), Deeg (2005), Djelic and Quack (2007), Mahoney and Thelen (2010), Hacker et al. (2015), and Conran and Thelen (2016).

28. See also Arthur (1994: 27, 118), Thelen (1999: 387; 2004: 8, 31, 34), Pierson (2004: 51–52), Martin and Sunley (2006: 402), Greer (2008: 219), and Fioretos (2017: 12).

The critique made by analysts of incremental change also highlights the need to bridge approaches focused on rapid, discontinuous change and on gradual adjustments, a task addressed by Riedl and Roberts (Chapter 6). They make a case for treating critical junctures and incremental changes as two potentially complementary kinds of change, and they specify the conditions under which one or the other will occur. More broadly, Riedl and Roberts show that a focus on the relationship between critical junctures and other types of transformation opens up new, barely explored avenues for future research.

Research Methods

The methods used to assess claims about critical junctures and their legacies have also become the focus of discussion. Until the 1990s, critical juncture research relied almost entirely on qualitative methods, and these methods continue to predominate. But some changes are evident. A concern with causal inference has long been part of the qualitative tradition, yet given the heightened interest in inferring causation—especially in the disciplines of economics and political science (Gerring 2017)—this has become a stronger focus in qualitative research on critical junctures. Further, since the turn of the century, we see a growing body of literature that could be called quantitative history that places a distinctive focus on quantitative methods specifically designed to identify causal effects (Angrist and Pischke 2008, 2015; Morgan and Winship 2015; see also Goodrich et al. 2012 and Wawro and Katznelson 2014).

In this changing situation, the relative value of qualitative and quantitative research has become a matter of some controversy.[29] Many scholars hold that qualitative methods should continue to be used in the study of critical junctures (Collier 1998; Mahoney and Rueschemeyer 2003; Mahoney and Thelen 2015; Fioretos et al. 2016). Moreover, although these scholars are open to quantitative methods, they have reservations about their use. This position is clearly formulated by Kurtz (2013: 50), who states that

> [i]n principle, given data sets of long historical sweep, it might be possible to adequately model theories . . . [about critical junctures and legacies] in large-N quantitative data. But even so, it would imply complicated functional forms and would pose a series of econometric and data challenges.

---

29. Researchers have largely taken it as a given that, in terms of the choice between experimental and observational research, the latter is the most viable and useful. There is a silent consensus in the field, articulated by Diamond and Robinson (2010: 1), that controlled experiments are not possible in the study of historical causation because "one cannot manipulate the past." Even though real experiments, that is, randomized controlled trials, on certain aspects of claims about critical junctures, could be designed, experimental research has practically not even been discussed (for an exception, see Steinmo 2016).

Other scholars, who work within the new institutional economics tradition and use quantitative methods to study critical junctures, offer a different perspective. At times these scholars articulate a critique of qualitative research, stating that this research is useful, at most, for the purpose of collecting data (Nunn 2014: 351, 354). They also make a case that quantification is an unambiguous sign of progress (Nunn 2009: 71, 81). Thus, the rise of quantitative history has introduced a methodological divide in historically oriented analysis.[30]

The controversy about methods used in critical juncture research is more circumscribed than the debate about the theoretical framework employed. However, addressing this discussion is essential. All research traditions need to scrutinize their methodological foundations and be open to incorporating new methods into their repertoire. Moreover, as the social sciences in general place more attention on causal inference, all research traditions need to consider their practices in light of new standards. Consequently, matters of method are dealt with in this volume, by D. Collier (Chapter 1), Waldner (Chapter 7), and Munck (Chapter 8).

Taken together, these chapters argue that qualitative methods continue to have value—a point forcefully demonstrated by the substantive studies in this volume. However, some chapters make a case for innovation. Qualitative research on critical junctures should focus more intently on problems of causal inference. Quantitative analysis should be embraced and improved through greater reliance on qualitative data and methods. Finally, a dialogue that bridges these traditions, and avoids a ranking of methods, is indispensable.

These three chapters address diverse issues and emphasize distinct ideas. D. Collier (Chapter 1) places a heavy emphasis on long-standing concerns in qualitative research. He highlights the need for description that carefully establishes conceptual equivalence across domains. He also endorses the use of process tracing and analysis of mechanisms.

Waldner (Chapter 7) focuses squarely on causal inference in qualitative research. He provides a critical review of methodological issues and underscores the problem of backdoor paths that emerges when there is a common cause of a posited cause and a posited effect. He argues that this problem has not been recognized and addressed in discussions about qualitative methods. Waldner further stresses that qualitative research on critical junctures needs to go beyond its usual focus on the connection between a posited cause and a posited effect—the central concern of process tracing studies—and consider the bias possibly introduced by backdoor paths.

Lastly, Munck (Chapter 8) provides a critical assessment of the newer quantitative literature. He shows that quantitative history is relevant to research on critical junctures—its interest in persistent effects is consistent with the focus on legacies in

---

30. This divide runs through the new institutional economics itself. Indeed, some researchers identified with this tradition make a strong case in favor of case studies (Alston 2008; Poteete et al. 2010) and "analytical narratives" (Bates et al. 1998; Rodrik 2003).

the literature on critical junctures—and he argues that it makes an important contribution due to its attention to causal inference. However, Munck also holds that quantitative history has important limitations as a tool to study historical causation and that it ignores the distinct contribution to causal inference provided by qualitative research on mechanisms.

Addressing Divergent Positions

Contrasting views about the framework and methods used in a research tradition can block progress in knowledge. Inasmuch as the positions defended in debates are problematic, they can lead substantive analysts astray, inducing them to develop and test theories inappropriately. Inasmuch as critiques are unfounded, they can dissuade scholars from following potentially fruitful avenues of research. Thus, when disagreements concern central issues in a research tradition—as is currently the case in critical juncture work—they are best confronted head-on. And that is what this volume does.

It is equally important to confront contrasting views in a way that is mindful of the dangers of change for the sake of change. Change should always be welcome. Indeed, to be successful, every tradition needs to be open to innovation regarding its framework and methods. However, change should be managed carefully. Dispensing with established ideas of proven value is reckless. In turn, new ideas should be carefully introduced, after they have been closely scrutinized and their value is substantiated. That is, progressive change should be selective. It should not discard old but useful ideas. It should also avoid incorporating new but flawed ideas.

Of course, as Kuhn notes, progress in the production of knowledge sometimes comes through more radical change—paradigm change. However, as he argues (1970 [1962]: Chs. 6 and 7), such cognitive revolutions occur and could even be said to be needed when serious anomalies—phenomena that cannot be explained in terms of a theoretical framework—add up and an epistemic crisis ensues. And this is not the current situation with the critical juncture tradition. Indeed, the task at hand is better understood in terms of Otto Neurath's (1944: 47) metaphor of the ship of science, which is summarized as follows:

> Imagine sailors, who, far out at sea, transform the shape of their clumsy vessel from a more circular to a more fishlike one. They make use of some drifting timber, besides the timber of the old structure, to modify the skeleton and the hull of their vessel. But they cannot put the ship in dock in order to start from scratch. During their work they stay on the old structure and deal with heavy gales and thundering waves. In transforming their ship they take care that dangerous leakages do not occur.

In brief, innovation is always desirable. Yet, given the current state of the critical juncture tradition, progress is more likely when risky innovations are pursued for good reason and with deliberate care.

OVERVIEW OF THE BOOK

This book is divided into four parts, with a concluding chapter that emphasizes the power and promise of critical juncture research.

Basics: Core Concepts and Big Substantive Questions

The first part starts by introducing the core concepts of the critical juncture framework. David Collier (Chapter 1) proposes a working definition of a critical juncture and a five-step template that synthesizes the basic sequence on which scholars routinely focus. The heart of this framework is the critical juncture-legacy nexus. To these two core concepts, Collier adds three more: antecedent conditions, cleavage or shock, and aftermath.

Antecedent conditions stand prior to a posited critical juncture, and encompass diverse features of economy, society, and politics that set the parameters for subsequent change. The cleavage or shock precedes and precipitates critical junctures. Cleavages grow out of a fundamental societal or political division, and shocks— sometimes international, sometimes domestic—may likewise be the triggering event. Finally, during the aftermath, the transformations introduced during a critical juncture may be contested, and are either rolled back or gain acceptance.

This framework extends Lipset and Rokkan's (1967) approach and updates the framework presented in *Shaping the Political Area* (Collier and Collier 1991: Ch. 1). It also comments on methodological issues. It is intended to anchor research in this tradition, yet is sufficiently flexible to be valuable for scholars who approach this topic in different ways.

The volume turns next to some examples of substantive research. Indeed, before delving into detailed discussions of theory and methods, it presents three chapters that showcase the richness of critical juncture analysis and illustrate how the concepts presented in Chapter 1 are employed in comparative historical studies.

James A. Robinson (Chapter 2) analyzes Europe's colonization of the Americas, which he interprets as a shock of global significance that opened new opportunities for power and wealth, along with the resulting critical juncture, i.e., the complex patterns of institution-formation triggered by this shock. In tracing the long-term economic trajectories produced by different types of colonialism, he tackles two analytical tasks.

Robinson first focuses on antecedent conditions to explain the differential response to this shock. In Europe, these involve institutional differences: constitutional monarchy in Britain versus absolutism in Spain and Portugal. In the Americas, they involve contrasts in the density and organization of indigenous peoples. Adding even further historical depth to this analysis, Robinson traces the origins of the institutional differences among Britain, Spain, and Portugal to a prior critical juncture— the collapse of the Western Roman Empire.

Second, Robinson spells out why the institutions created with colonization yielded contrasting economic trajectories, thereby providing a compelling explanation for the different long-term patterns of economic development followed by North America and Spanish America. His explanation is strengthened by his analysis of how institutions founded in the colonial period are reproduced, generating path dependence. Robinson thus connects successive links in a causal chain that extends over several centuries. Although the analysis makes strong explanatory claims, he concludes by speculating about the possible role of agency in these transformations—an important recurring theme in this literature.

G. John Ikenberry (Chapter 3) applies the critical juncture framework to key questions in the study of international relations. Why do international orders vary in character—i.e., take the form of a balance of power, have a hegemon, or are constitutional in form? Why do international orders vary in terms of stability and durability? He analyzes four potential critical junctures: the order-building attempts by leading states in the wake of four major wars, after 1815, 1919, 1945, and 1989. And he provides a multipart argument.

According to Ikenberry's multistep argument, wars destroy established orders and open opportunities for states to build new orders. However, a key antecedent condition, whether the states that are part of a postwar settlement are democratic or not, determines the type and stability of the international order that emerges. The postwar order is also shaped by the magnitude of the shock of war and whether power disparities after the war are great or small. For example, the international order takes on a "constitutional" form, as it did after World War II, when more of the states are democracies and the power disparities among the leading states emerging from the war are great. Ikenberry also explains the stability and durability of the post–World War II order in terms of the logic of increasing returns. The chapter concludes by drawing implications from this analysis for a possible change in the current international order due to the rise of China.

Finally, Sidney Tarrow (Chapter 4) analyzes the wave of mobilization, protest, and conflict that erupted in and around 1968 in France, Italy, and the United States. Drawing on the critical juncture framework, Tarrow argues that these protests were a shock that triggered policy innovations conditioned by antecedent conditions. However, Tarrow underscores that policy innovations do not necessarily have a lasting effect, and that in France—the case where the shock was the most explosive—a conservative reaction was largely successful at rolling back changes. Indeed, in France, 1968 left few legacies. In Italy and the United States, the movements of the late 1960s helped to transform institutional politics and contributed to the "movementization" of politics. Thus, Tarrow argues that, somewhat surprisingly, the legacy was more extensive and enduring in countries where the shock was less explosive—Italy and the United States. In short, Tarrow shows how the study of social movements and their impact can benefit from the deployment of concepts from the critical juncture framework.

Framework and Methods: Historical Causation and Causal Inference

The second part of this volume discusses the theoretical framework and methods used in research on critical junctures. It addresses the challenges faced in the critical juncture tradition, tackling various debated issues and proposing solutions to controversies. It also introduces ideas relevant to this field that have not been discussed within this tradition. Jointly, the chapters in this part provide a justification for retaining classic ideas and practices, but also for introducing significant innovations.

First, starting with the theoretical foundations of critical juncture research, Gerardo L. Munck (Chapter 5) provides a critical review and proposes various refinements and reformulations of the framework. First, Munck focuses on the way critical juncture analysis should provide a historical explanation of social order. He argues that this research must confront two foundational issues that inevitably emerge in the study of historical causation: the problems of infinite regress and distal (i.e., distant) nonrecurring causes. And he holds that these problems should be addressed by conceptualizing critical junctures as rapid, discontinuous, macro-level changes that generate a persistent effect. In addition to clarifying these core ideas, he makes a case for greater attention to causal mechanisms that stabilize the legacy.

Second, Munck discusses how critical juncture research should explain social change. Again, he highlights two foundational issues: the challenges of integrating endogenous and exogenous sources of change, and also structure and agency. He claims, most basically, that critical juncture research should avoid pitfalls by considering both endogenous and exogenous factors as well as the interplay of structural factors and actors. He also argues for attention to the limits of endogenous drivers of change, a more careful analysis of agency, and for theorizing mechanisms of change. Overall, this chapter suggests how the critical juncture framework can be reconstructed on stronger foundations.

Rachel Beatty Riedl and Kenneth M. Roberts (Chapter 6) examine the extent to which outcomes are explained by antecedent conditions and differentiate between two types of critical junctures: generative, in which contingent choice plays a greater causal role; and activating, in which antecedent conditions play a more important causal role. They treat the weight of antecedent conditions and contingent choices as a matter to be theorized and also treated as an empirical question rather than being settled by definitional fiat.

Riedl and Roberts also tackle a further challenge: to explain whether institutional change is likely to take the form of a critical juncture or some other form (e.g., incremental change, serial replacement). To this end, they focus on two key variables: strength of the institutional environment and the role of contingent choices. The result is a novel synthesis that pinpoints the circumstances under which different kinds of change—critical junctures, incremental changes, and serial replacements—are more likely.

The book then moves to methods. New ideas about methods regularly play a key role in energizing research programs. Two chapters scrutinize the use of qualitative analysis and quantitative methods in critical juncture studies.

David Waldner (Chapter 7) calls for greater attention to causal inference in qualitative research on critical junctures. He draws on ideas from the fields of causal inference and causal graphs, and focuses on bias introduced by backdoor paths—an issue when a posited cause and a posited effect have a common cause. Waldner then diagnoses several limitations of qualitative research. He argues that treating contingency as a defining attribute of critical junctures—a view he finds problematic—does not solve the problem of backdoor paths. More broadly, he shows that some well-known studies on critical junctures have not adequately addressed the possibility of backdoor paths. Finally, he offers some methodological recommendations for dealing with these challenges.

Waldner maintains that qualitative researchers must rely on strict procedures to properly analyze a causal path between a cause and an outcome—the front-door path in the language of graph theory. However, as he notes, the possibility of backdoor paths is a distinctive threat to causal inference that qualitative researchers have largely ignored.

Gerardo L. Munck (Chapter 8) examines a new line of quantitative historical research by economists and political scientists that is relevant to the critical juncture tradition. He notes that this new literature does not generally use the language of critical junctures, but shares an interest in distant causes and persistent effects. Although it primarily seeks to estimate causal effects, it also studies causal mechanisms and even uses some qualitative tools. Munck sees this new literature as a welcome addition to a field that, until recently, relied entirely on qualitative research.

Munck's overall assessment of quantitative history is mixed, however. Although a major strength of this literature is its keen focus on causal inference, Munck argues that quantitative researchers sometimes mistakenly suggest that analysts must choose between qualitative and quantitative methods, and that quantitative research is always preferable. In fact, he holds that quantitative history would benefit from a greater use of qualitative tools and, in particular, from taking advantage of a strength of qualitative research, the careful tracing of processes connecting distal causes with much later outcomes. Thus, he recommends developing mixed-methods strategies that better marshal the strengths of both traditions.

Substantive Applications I: States and Political Regimes

Part III of the book continues with chapters that exemplify the range of substantive questions and the kind of arguments advanced in this literature. These chapters focus on critical junctures associated with state formation, the state's response to religious authorities, labor's political incorporation, communist rule, and democratization. They span Europe, Latin America, and postcommunist countries, and developments from the nineteenth to the early twenty-first centuries. Some chapters focus more on theory generation, others on hypothesis testing. One addresses the distinctive challenge of theoretical integration, based on bridging the perspectives of multiple authors.

Sebastián L. Mazzuca's (Chapter 9) study of nineteenth-century state formation in Latin America is an example of theory generation. He develops a novel argument, connecting political transformations in the nineteenth century with twentieth-century patterns. He begins by examining the outcome to be explained: the inefficient combination of populations and natural resources, together with relatively poor governance and economic performance, that characterizes Latin America in the twentieth century. Thus, while many studies begin with a critical juncture and work forward, he begins with the outcome to be explained and works backward.

Mazzuca then turns to explaining this outcome by leveraging comparisons both across and within regions to analyze the antecedent conditions leading to distinctive patterns of nineteenth-century state formation. Whereas in Europe this process was driven by war, in Latin America it took place in the context of global capitalism and the dynamics and legacies of colonialism. Within Latin America, a combination of geographic factors (proximity to seaports), political factors (coalition building), and the mode of incorporation of peripheries created commonalities and differences in state formation. These factors together created perverse relationships between core and periphery, and hindered the long-run economic development of the two largest states—Brazil and Argentina—and by extension, of their smaller neighbors. Mazzuca concludes by briefly noting the relationship between his analysis and other work that seeks to explain some of these same outcomes.

Andrew C. Gould (Chapter 10) provides an overview of his book, *Origins of Liberal Dominance: State, Church, and Party in Nineteenth-Century Europe* (Gould 1999). He conceptualizes liberal forces as those that favor a secular, representative government that places constitutional checks on the monarchy, while not involving democracy. He also explains the contrasting fate of liberal parties and liberal regimes in nineteenth-century Belgium, France, Germany, and Switzerland in terms of the evolution of church-state relations.

Gould shows that the church's role in liberal reforms and the ultimate success or failure of liberal regimes was shaped by two closely connected critical junctures. In the elite phase, the cleavage between liberalism and the clerical elite led to a critical juncture—the liberal reform of political institutions—in which the church's support for these reforms depended on its potential to gain political authority. In the mass phase, institutions created in the first juncture were the antecedent conditions for the next liberal reform period. Here, the church's role depended on the support derived from a substantial expansion of the suffrage. Gould offers a novel argument for the failure of democracy in Germany. He also offers some observations on how the study of critical junctures has evolved.

Ruth Berins Collier (Chapter 11) addresses a key issue in empirical research: How should a critical juncture hypothesis be empirically assessed against alternative hypotheses involving temporally proximate causes? Focusing on Brazil, Chile, Mexico, and Venezuela, she juxtaposes (1) a thesis about the legacy of the critical juncture of labor incorporation during the first half of the twentieth century with (2) hypotheses rooted in a set of temporally proximate international events and policies that had an immediate impact on domestic politics in Latin America in the 1940s.

R. Collier's analysis suggests that, although international events left a clear imprint, they did not deflect internal dynamics and they yielded some mistaken predictions. However, she argues that the two perspectives can usefully be integrated, because international factors help explain some patterns and account for the timing and intensity of the steps that reflected internal trajectories.

Robert M. Fishman (Chapter 12) tackles a key debate in the study of democratization—whether the mode of transition has a long-term effect—and uses a comparison of Portugal and Spain to support the view that the mode of democratic transition can leave an enduring legacy for the post-transition regime. He also shows that the critical juncture framework need not be restricted to formal institutions. Rather, drawing on ideas from the sociology of culture, he applies it to uncodified, yet exceedingly important, political practices.

Fishman argues that an inclusionary democratic practice emerged in Portugal, where actors in positions of authority acknowledged and interacted with mobilizations and demands that occurred outside of formal institutions. By contrast, a segmented and exclusionary democratic practice arose in Spain, where similar mobilizations and demands were not legitimated and accepted. By applying the critical juncture framework, he cogently demonstrates the steps through which this contrast between Spain and Portugal was generated and subsequently consolidated. Further, by employing a cultural perspective, Fishman teases out a fundamental contrast in post-transition regimes that is rarely acknowledged in studies of political institutions.

Danielle N. Lussier and Jody LaPorte (Chapter 13) reconstruct the literature on legacies in post-communist countries initiated with Jowitt's (1992) work and, using the critical juncture approach and Waldner's (Chapter 7) methodological framework, cast a new light on the study of historical legacies in the postcommunist world. Evaluating three important studies of postcommunism, Lussier and LaPorte map out alternative causal pathways. Legacies may be shaped by the critical juncture itself (Wittenberg 2006), by the critical juncture in combination with antecedent conditions (Pop-Eleches and Tucker 2017), or by a chain of multiple critical junctures (Grzymała-Busse 2002).

Lussier and LaPorte establish a fruitful dialogue between critical juncture research and the influential analysis of postcommunist legacies. They show that the concepts of the critical juncture framework facilitate a comparison of these three studies and help to pinpoint agreements and disagreements. Moreover, they derive an important conclusion: the idea of a universal critical juncture that explains postcommunist outcomes is not valid.

Substantive Applications II: Neoliberalism and Political Parties

Part IV of the volume consists of an exchange about the possibility that the neoliberal reforms in Latin America in the 1990s are a critical juncture that has transformed party systems. The dialogue is centered on Roberts's major book *Changing Course in Latin America* (2014), which treats neoliberalism as a critical juncture in Latin

America. One of the methodological issues raised by such a claim—and addressed by several chapters—is whether this thesis can be supported without the benefit of considerable hindsight.

Kenneth M. Roberts (Chapter 14) discusses the problems he faced in writing his book on the impact of the neoliberal reforms of the 1990s on party politics. He notes that in carrying out this research, the challenge of achieving adequate hindsight was daunting, and he was pushed to recast the argument several times over a number of years. He stresses the value of distinguishing between the crisis or shock of the 1980s—along with even earlier antecedent conditions—and the neoliberal reforms of the 1990s. Moreover, he notes that divergent institutional legacies, i.e., different configurations of party systems, did not begin to be identifiable until the "left turn" in Latin America that occurred in the early twenty-first century.

Only at that point did Roberts formulate his hypothesis that divergent party outcomes resulted from two key differences in the critical juncture proper—that is to say, from the neoliberal reforms: whether conservative actors directed the process of market reform, and whether a major left party was available to channel resistance to market orthodoxy. However, Roberts argues that, by the time he published his book, the consequences for party systems of neoliberal reforms were sufficiently resilient to validate, if still tentatively, the claim that these reforms had indeed produced an enduring legacy and hence were a critical juncture.

Samuel Handlin (Chapter 15) further addresses this problem of hindsight based on a comparison between Roberts's (2014) book and his own book, *State Crisis in Fragile Democracies* (2017). He argues that, even though scholars should proceed with caution in making claims about recent events, some questions can be addressed with confidence. Moreover, he holds that knowledge is advanced by juxtaposing different arguments about a hypothesized critical juncture, such as Robert's claim about the impact of neoliberal reforms on party politics and Handlin's thesis about relative state weakness.

Handlin argues that, based on these alternative perspectives, it is possible to formulate arguments about potential critical junctures and refine them in light of the evidence, even before the dust has settled. Moreover, he holds that explicit comparisons of the duration and a hypothesized legacy of a critical juncture may provide a basis for inferring whether it in fact occurred. It is possible, even with limited hindsight, to formulate arguments about potential critical junctures and assess these arguments in light of evidence.

Timothy R. Scully (Chapter 16) evaluates the hypothesis that dramatic transformations introduced under the Pinochet dictatorship (1973–1990) are a critical juncture that reshaped the Chilean party system. Scully shows that during Chile's three prior critical junctures, which extend back to the mid-nineteenth century, the Chilean party system had a distinctive feature that is unique in Latin America: a strong political center. Thus, for the post-Pinochet period, a key question is whether the Pinochet dictatorship was a critical juncture whose legacy was the destruction of the political center. As Scully shows, answering this question is complex, given ambiguities resulting from recent shifts in electoral laws and other short- to medium-term dynamics. However, he argues that Chile continues to have a viable center. Therefore, he concludes that his specific hypothesis about a critical juncture in Chile in the 1970s and 1980s is not supported.

This section concludes with two brief commentaries on the potential of critical juncture research to understand contemporary politics in Latin America. Taylor C. Boas (Chapter 17) explores the problem of hindsight through a dialogue with Roberts's book. He holds that, for critical junctures that have occurred in the recent past, it might be impossible to establish that a legacy is enduring. Notwithstanding this constraint, he identifies certain kinds of limited analytic claims that can be productively assessed. Preliminary evidence can rule out claims that a change was *not* a critical juncture. For example, he shows that Roberts was able to offer two negative findings: that shifts in party alignments were *not* incremental and did *not* occur in the same way in different countries. The latter would have undermined the hypothesis that the critical juncture was a point of differentiation among countries, which is crucial to Roberts's argument. Additionally, Boas suggests that the analysis of sequential critical junctures—as exemplified by Ikenberry's chapter (Chapter 3)—provides additional leverage in thinking about recent transformations. Thus, Boas highlights the value of critical juncture analysis in the study of contemporary politics, while urging care in drawing conclusions.

Finally, Robert R. Kaufman (Chapter 18) closes Part IV of the volume with some brief reflections on the appropriate way to analyze contemporary Latin American politics. He suggests that in the past few decades, the region has experienced so many crises and upheavals that analysts should recognize the challenge of achieving agreement on what transformations have and have not occurred. Correspondingly, he emphasizes that it is difficult to establish whether recent changes constitute critical junctures. Overall, Kaufman underscores the need for caution in using the critical juncture framework to study recent or ongoing developments.

Conclusion

In the conclusion to the volume, Gerardo L. Munck (Chapter 19) clarifies why critical juncture research should be encouraged, and dispels some common misconceptions about this field. This chapter argues that critical juncture analysis excels in addressing big, substantive questions, recognizing qualitative breaks, analyzing the social world with a sense of historical depth, and theorizing with an expansive vision. This chapter also makes a case that several claims about critical juncture research—for example, that it involves a change in an entire system and that it only produces institutional legacies—are erroneous and costly, and shows how the agenda and possibilities of this field are expanded when these misconceptions are rejected.

In short, this chapter encapsulates one of the overarching messages of the volume: critical juncture research has great power and promise, and it is key that it not be curtailed due to flawed views about the theory and methods used in this tradition.

Appendices

Appendix I lists alternative conceptions of a critical juncture and cognate terms, underscoring points of agreement and disagreement. Consistent use of key concepts is an important desideratum in the social sciences, and one of the issues addressed in several chapters is how the core concepts of the critical juncture framework should be understood. This appendix is thus a valuable point of departure for ongoing discussions of concepts and definitions.

Appendix II is a glossary of the broader set of terms used in critical juncture research. Over the years, many concepts have been introduced, and even a researcher who works in this tradition may sometimes have difficulty holding to their precise meaning. The glossary offers brief definitions and pinpoints cases in which terms are given more than one meaning.

Appendix III is a comprehensive bibliography. It includes studies that, while not explicitly framed in terms of critical junctures, adopt a similar approach to comparative historical analysis. The bibliography is organized thematically, and it demonstrates the remarkable range of substantive topics addressed by this body of research.

Appendix IV offers brief discussions of eight books that exemplify critical juncture research. The core arguments of these works are summarized, and their contribution to multiple fields of research is noted. This appendix illustrates, in a synoptic fashion, the kind of work that is done in the critical juncture tradition.

BIBLIOGRAPHY

Acemoglu, Daron, Simon Johnson, and James Robinson. 2001. "The Colonial Origins of Comparative Development: An Empirical Investigation." *American Economic Review* 91(5): 1369–401.

Acemoglu, Daron, and James A. Robinson. 2012. *Why Nations Fail: Origins of Power, Poverty and Prosperity*. New York, NY: Crown.

———. 2019. *The Narrow Corridor: States, Societies, and the Fate of Liberty*. New York, NY: Penguin.

Acharya, Avidit, Matthew Blackwell, and Maya Sen. 2016. "The Political Legacy of American Slavery." *Journal of Politics* 78(3): 621–41.

———. 2018. *Deep Roots: How Slavery Still Shapes Southern Politics*. Princeton, NJ: Princeton University Press.

Akyeampong, Emmanuel, Robert H. Bates, Nathan Nunn, and James A. Robinson (eds.). 2014. "Introduction. Africa—The Historical Roots of Its Underdevelopment." In *Africa's Development in Historical Perspective* (pp. 1–29). New York, NY: Cambridge University Press.

Alston, Eric, Lee J. Alston, Bernardo Mueller, and Tomas Nonnenmacher. 2018. *Institutional and Organizational Analysis: Concepts and Applications*. New York, NY: Cambridge University Press.

Alston, Lee J. 2008. "The 'Case' for Case Studies in New Institutional Economics." In Éric Brousseau and Jean-Michel Glachant (eds.), *New Institutional Economics: A Guidebook* (pp. 103–21). New York, NY: Cambridge University Press.

Angrist, Joshua D., and Jörn-Steffen Pischke. 2008. *Mostly Harmless Econometrics: An Empiricist's Companion.* Princeton, NJ: Princeton University Press.

———. 2015. *Mastering 'Metrics: The Path from Cause to Effect.* Princeton, NJ: Princeton University Press.

Arestis, Philip, and Malcolm Sawyer. 2009. "Path Dependency and Demand-Supply Interactions in Macroeconomic Analysis." In Philip Arestis and Malcolm Sawyer (eds.), *Path Dependency and Macroeconomics* (pp. 1–36). New York, NY: Palgrave Macmillan.

Arthur, W. Brian. 1989. "Competing Technologies, Increasing Returns, and Lock-In by Historical Events." *Economic Journal* 99(394): 116–31.

———. 1994. *Increasing Returns and Path Dependence in the Economy.* Ann Arbor, MI: University of Michigan Press.

Bartolini, Stefano. 2000. *The Political Mobilization of the European Left, 1860–1980: The Class Cleavage.* New York, NY: Cambridge University Press.

Bates, Robert H. 2014. "The New Institutionalism." In Sebastian Galiani and Itai Sened (eds.), *Institutions, Property Rights, and Economic Growth: The Legacy of Douglass North* (pp. 50–65). New York, NY: Cambridge University Press.

Bates, Robert H., Avner Greif, Margaret Levi, Jean-Laurent Rosenthal, and Barry Weingast. 1998. *Analytic Narratives.* Princeton, NJ: Princeton University Press.

Baumgartner, Frank R., and Bryan D. Jones. 1993. *Agendas and Instability in American Politics.* Chicago, IL: University of Chicago Press.

———. 2009. *Agendas and Instability in American Politics* (2nd ed.). Chicago, IL: University of Chicago Press.

Bennett, Andrew, and Jeffrey Checkel (eds.). 2015. *Process Tracing: From Metaphor to Analytic Tool.* New York, NY: Cambridge University Press.

Bernhard, Michael. 2015. "Chronic Instability and the Limits of Path Dependence." *Perspectives on Politics* 13(4): 976–91.

Berntzen, Einar. 2020. "Historical and Longitudinal Analyses." In Dirk Berg-Schlosser, Bertrand Badie, and Leonardo Morlino (eds.), *The SAGE Handbook of Political Science* (pp. 390–405). Thousand Oaks, CA: SAGE.

Beyer, Jürgen. 2010. "The Same or Not the Same. On the Variety of Mechanisms of Path Dependence." *International Journal of Social Sciences* 5(1): 1–11.

Boas, Taylor C. 2007. "Conceptualizing Continuity and Change: The Composite-Standard Model of Path Dependence." *Journal of Theoretical Politics* 19(1): 33–54.

Brady, Henry E., and David Collier (eds.). 2010. *Rethinking Social Inquiry: Diverse Tools, Shared Standards* (2nd ed.). Lanham, MD: Rowman & Littlefield.

Calder, Kent, and Min Ye. 2010. *The Making of Northeast Asia.* Stanford, CA: Stanford University Press.

Capoccia, Giovanni. 2015. "Critical Junctures and Institutional Change." In James Mahoney and Kathleen Thelen (eds.), *Advances in Comparative-Historical Analysis* (pp. 147–79). New York, NY: Cambridge University Press.

———. 2016a. "Critical Junctures." In Orfeo Fioretos, Tulia G. Falleti, and Adam Sheingate (eds.), *The Oxford Handbook of Historical Institutionalism* (pp. 89–106). New York, NY: Oxford University Press.

———. 2016b. "When Do Institutions 'Bite'? Historical Institutionalism and the Politics of Institutional Change." *Comparative Political Studies* 49(8): 1095–127.

Capoccia, Giovanni, and R. Daniel Kelemen. 2007. "The Study of Critical Junctures: Theory, Narrative, and Counterfactuals in Historical Institutionalism." *World Politics* 59(3): 341–69.

Caramani, Daniele. 2015. *The Europeanization of Politics: The Formation of a European Electorate and Party System in Historical Perspective*. New York, NY: Cambridge University Press.

Chibber, Vivek. 2003. *Locked in Place: State-Building and Late Industrialization in India*. Princeton, NJ: Princeton University Press.

Collier, David. 1998. "Comparative-Historical Analysis: Where Do We Stand?" *APSA-CP. Newsletter of the APSA Organized Section in Comparative Politics* 9(2): 1–2, 4–5.

Collier, David, and Gerardo L. Munck. 2017. "Building Blocks and Methodological Challenges: A Framework for Studying Critical Junctures." *Qualitative and Multi-Method Research* 15(1): 2–9.

Collier, Ruth Berins, and David Collier. 1991. *Shaping the Political Arena: Critical Junctures, the Labor Movement, and the Regime Dynamics in Latin America*. Princeton, NJ: Princeton University Press.

Conran, James, and Kathleen Thelen. 2016. "Institutional Change." In Orfeo Fioretos, Tulia G. Falleti, and Adam Sheingate (eds.), *The Oxford Handbook of Historical Institutionalism* (pp. 51–70). New York, NY: Oxford University Press.

Crouch, Colin, and Henry Farrell. 2004. "Breaking the Path of Institutional Development? Alternatives to the New Determinism." *Rationality and Society* 16(1): 5–43.

David, Paul A. 1985. "Clio and the Economics of QWERTY." *American Economic Review* 75(2): 332–37.

Deeg, Richard. 2005. "Change from Within: German and Italian Finance in the 1990s." In Wolfgang Streeck and Kathleen Thelen (eds.), *Beyond Continuity: Institutional Change in Advanced Political Economies* (pp. 169–202). Oxford, UK: Oxford University Press.

Dell, Melissa. 2010. "The Persistent Effects of Peru's Mining Mita." *Econometrica* 78(6): 1863–903.

della Porta, Donatella. 2016. *Where Did the Revolution Go?: Contentious Politics and the Quality of Democracy*. New York, NY: Cambridge University Press.

Diamond, Jared. 1997. *Guns, Germs and Steel: The Fate of Human Societies*. New York, NY: Norton.

Diamond, Jared, and James A. Robinson. 2010. "Prologue." In Jared Diamond and James A. Robinson (eds.), *Natural Experiments of History* (pp. 1–14). Cambridge, MA: The Belknap Press of Harvard University Press.

Djelic, Marie-Laure, and Sigrid Quack. 2007. "Overcoming Path Dependency: Path Generation in Open Systems." *Theory and Society* 36(2): 161–86.

Eldredge, Niles, and Stephen Jay Gould. 1972. "Punctuated Equilibria: An Alternative to Phyletic Gradualism." In Thomas J. M. Schopf (ed.), *Models in Paleobiology* (pp. 82–115). San Francisco, CA: Freeman, Cooper.

Engerman, Stanley L., and Kenneth L. Sokoloff. 2012. *Economic Development in the Americas since 1500: Endowments and Institutions*. New York, NY: Cambridge University Press.

Fioretos, Orfeo (ed.). 2017. *International History and Politics in Time*. Oxford, UK: Oxford University Press.

Fioretos, Orfeo, Tulia G. Falleti, and Adam Sheingate (eds.). 2016. *The Oxford Handbook of Historical Institutionalism*. New York, NY: Oxford University Press.

Fishman, Robert M. 2019. *Democratic Practice: Origins of the Iberian Divide in Political Inclusion*. Oxford, UK: Oxford University Press.

Flora, Peter. 1999. "Introduction and Interpretation." In Peter Flora (ed.), *State Formation, Nation-Building, and Mass Politics in Europe: The Theory of Stein Rokkan* (p. 1–91). Oxford, UK: Oxford University Press.

Gailmard, Sean. 2021. "Theory, History, and Political Economy." *Journal of Historical Political Economy* 1(1): 69–104.

Galiani, Sebastian, and Itai Sened (eds.). 2014. *Institutions, Property Rights, and Economic Growth: The Legacy of Douglass North.* New York, NY: Cambridge University Press.

García-Montoya, Laura, and James Mahoney. 2020. "Critical Event Analysis in Case Study Research." *Sociological Methods and Research.* doi:10.1177/0049124120926201

Gellner, Ernest. 1964. *Thought and Change.* Chicago, IL: University of Chicago Press.

George, Alexander L., and Andrew Bennett. 2005. *Case Studies and Theory Development in the Social Sciences.* Cambridge, MA: MIT Press.

Gerring, John. 2017. *Case Study Research: Principles and Practices* (2nd ed.). New York, NY: Cambridge University Press.

Gerschewski, Johannes. 2021. "Explanations of Institutional Change. Reflecting on a 'Missing Diagonal.'" *American Political Science Review* 115(1): 218–33.

Goodrich, Benjamin King, Gregory Wawro, and Ira Katznelson. 2012. "Designing Quantitative Historical Social Inquiry: An Introduction to Stan (2012)." Paper presented at the Annual Meeting of the American Political Science Association (APSA), New Orleans, LA.

Gould, Andrew C. 1999. *Origins of Liberal Dominance: State, Church, and Party in Nineteenth-Century Europe.* Ann Arbor, MI: University of Michigan Press.

Gould, Stephen Jay. 2007. *Punctuated Equilibrium.* Cambridge, MA: Harvard University Press.

Greer, Scott L. 2008. "Choosing Paths in European Union Health Services Policy: A Political Analysis of a Critical Juncture." *Journal of European Social Policy* 18(3): 219–31.

Grzymała-Busse, Anna M. 2002. *Redeeming the Communist Past: The Regeneration of Communist Parties in East Central Europe.* New York, NY: Cambridge University Press.

———. 2011. "Time Will Tell? Temporality and the Analysis of Causal Mechanisms and Processes." *Comparative Political Studies* 44(9): 1267–97.

Guldi, Jo, and David Armitage. 2014. *The History Manifesto.* New York, NY: Cambridge University Press.

Hacker, Jacob S., Paul Pierson, and Kathleen Thelen. 2015. "Drift and Conversion: Hidden Faces of Institutional Change." In James Mahoney and Kathleen Thelen (eds.), *Advances in Comparative-Historical Analysis* (pp. 180–210). New York, NY: Cambridge University Press.

Hall, Peter A. 2016. "Politics as a Process Structured in Space and Time." In Orfeo Fioretos, Tulia G. Falleti, and Adam Sheingate (eds.), *The Oxford Handbook of Historical Institutionalism* (pp. 31–50). New York, NY: Oxford University Press.

Handlin, Samuel. 2017. *State Crisis in Fragile Democracies: Polarization and Political Regimes in South America.* New York, NY: Cambridge University Press.

Hogan, John. 2006. "Remoulding the Critical Junctures Approach." *Canadian Journal of Political Science* 39(3): 657–79.

Howlett, Michael. 2009. "Process Sequencing Policy Dynamics: Beyond Homeostasis and Path Dependency." *Journal of Public Policy* 29(3): 241–62.

Ikenberry, G. John. 2001. *After Victory: Institutions, Strategic Restraint, and the Rebuilding of Order after Major Wars.* Princeton, NJ: Princeton University Press.

———. 2016. "The Rise, Character, and Evolution of International Order." In Orfeo Fioretos, Tulia G. Falleti, and Adam Sheingate (eds.), *The Oxford Handbook of Historical Institutionalism* (pp. 738–52). New York, NY: Oxford University Press.

Jalal, Ayesha. 1995. *Democracy and Authoritarianism in South Asia: A Comparative and Historical Perspective.* New York, NY: Cambridge University Press.

Jowitt, Ken. 1992. "The Leninist Legacy." In Ken Jowitt, *New World Disorder: The Leninist Extinction* (pp. 284–305). Berkeley, CA: University of California Press.

Katznelson, Ira. 2003. "Periodization and Preferences: Reflections on Purposive Action in Comparative Historical Social Science." In James Mahoney and Dietrich Rueschemeyer (eds.), *Comparative Historical Analysis in the Social Sciences* (pp. 270–303). New York, NY: Cambridge University Press.

King, Gary, Robert O. Keohane, and Sidney Verba. 1994. *Designing Social Inquiry: Scientific Inference in Qualitative Research*. Princeton, NJ: Princeton University Press.

Kohli, Atul. 2004. *State-Directed Development: Political Power and Industrialization in the Global Periphery*. New York, NY: Cambridge University Press.

Krasner, Stephen D. 1984. "Approaches to the State: Alternative Conceptions and Historical Dynamics." *Comparative Politics* 16(2): 223–46.

———. 1988. "Sovereignty: An Institutional Perspective." *Comparative Political Studies* 21(1): 66–94.

Kreuzer, Marcus (ed.). 2013. "Symposium: Conceptions of Historical Time: Looking Beyond Time on the Clock." *Qualitative & Multi-Method Research* 11(2): 2–21.

———. Forthcoming. *The Grammar of Time: Using Comparative Historical Analysis to Study the Past*. New York, NY: Cambridge University Press.

Kuhn, Thomas S. 1970 [1962]. *The Structure of Scientific Revolutions* (2nd ed.). Chicago, IL: University of Chicago Press.

Kurtz, Marcus. 2013. *Latin American State Building in Comparative Perspective: Social Foundations of Institutional Order*. New York, NY: Cambridge University Press.

Laitin, David D. 2004. "The Political Science Discipline." In Edward Mansfield and Richard Sisson (eds.), *The Evolution of Political Knowledge: Democracy, Autonomy, and Conflict in Comparative and International Politics* (pp. 11–40). Columbus, OH: Ohio State University Press.

Laitin, David D., Joachim Moortgat, and Amanda Lea Robinson. 2012. "Geographic Axes and the Persistence of Cultural Diversity." *PNAS (Proceedings of the National Academy of Sciences)* 109(26): 10263–68.

Levi, Margaret, and Victor Menaldo. 2015. "The New Economic Institutionalism in Historical Perspective." In Jennifer Gandhi and Rubén Ruiz-Rufino (eds.), *Routledge Handbook of Comparative Political Institutions* (pp. 15–30). London: Routledge.

Lichbach, Mark Irving. 2009. "Thinking and Working in the Midst of Things: Discovery, Explanation, and Evidence in Comparative Politics." In Mark Irving Lichbach and Alan S. Zuckerman (eds.), *Comparative Politics: Rationality, Culture and Structure* (2nd ed.; pp. 18–71). New York, NY: Cambridge University Press.

Lipset, Seymour M., and Stein Rokkan. 1967. "Cleavage Structures, Party Systems, and Voter Alignments: An Introduction." In Seymour M. Lipset and Stein Rokkan (eds.), *Party Systems and Voter Alignments: Cross-National Perspectives* (pp. 1–64). New York, NY: Free Press.

López-Alves, Fernando. 2000. *State Formation and Democracy in Latin America, 1810–1900*. Durham, NC: Duke University Press.

Mahoney, James. 2000. "Path Dependence in Historical Sociology." *Theory and Society* 29(4): 507–48.

———. 2001. *The Legacies of Liberalism: Path Dependence and Political Regimes in Central America*. Baltimore, MD: Johns Hopkins University Press.

Mahoney, James, and Dietrich Rueschemeyer (eds.). 2003. *Comparative Historical Analysis in the Social Sciences*. New York, NY: Cambridge University Press.

Mahoney, James, and Kathleen Thelen. 2010. "A Theory of Gradual Institutional Change." In James Mahoney and Kathleen Thelen (eds.), *Explaining Institutional Change: Ambiguity, Agency, and Power* (pp. 1–37). New York, NY: Cambridge University Press.

Mahoney, James, and Kathleen Thelen (eds.). 2015. *Advances in Comparative-Historical Analysis*. New York, NY: Cambridge University Press.

Mamdani, Mahmood. 1996. *Citizen and Subject: Contemporary Africa and the Legacy of Late Colonialism*. Princeton, NJ: Princeton University Press.

Mann, Michael. 1986. *The Sources of Social Power*. Vol. 1: *A History of Power from the Beginning to A.D. 1760*. New York, NY: Cambridge University Press.

March, James G., and Johan P. Olsen. 2006. "Elaborating the 'New Institutionalism.'" In R. A. W. Rhodes, Sarah A. Binder, and Bert A. Rockman (eds.), *The Oxford Handbook of Political Institutions* (pp. 3–20). New York, NY: Oxford University Press.

Martin, Ron, and Peter Sunley. 2006. "Path Dependence and Regional Economic Evolution." *Journal of Economic Geography* 6(4): 395–437.

Marx, Anthony W. 1998. *Making Race and Nation: A Comparison of the United States, South Africa, and Brazil*. New York, NY: Cambridge University Press.

Mayhew, David R. 2002. *Electoral Realignments: A Critique of an American Genre*. New Haven, CT: Yale University Press.

Mazzuca, Sebastián. 2021. *Latecomer State Formation: Political Geography and Capacity Failure in Latin America*. New Haven, CT: Yale University Press.

Mazzuca, Sebastián L., and Gerardo L. Munck. 2020. *A Middle-Quality Institutional Trap: Democracy and State Capacity in Latin America*. New York, NY: Cambridge University Press.

Mitterauer, Michael. 2010. *Why Europe? The Medieval Origins of Its Special Path*. Chicago, IL: University of Chicago Press.

Møller, Jørgen. 2017. *State Formation, Regime Change, and Economic Development*. London, UK: Routledge Press.

Møller, Jørgen, and Svend-Erik Skaaning. 2021. "The Ulysses Principle: A Criterial Framework for Reducing Bias When Enlisting the Work of Historians." *Sociological Methods and Research* 50(1): 103–34.

Moore, Jr., Barrington. 1966. *Social Origins of Dictatorship and Democracy. Lord and Peasant in the Making of the Modern World*. Boston, MA: Beacon Press.

Morgan, Stephen L., and Christopher Winship. 2015. *Counterfactuals and Causal Inference: Methods and Principles for Social Research* (2nd ed.). New York, NY: Cambridge University Press.

Neurath, Otto. 1944. *Foundations of the Social Sciences*. Chicago, IL: University of Chicago Press.

North, Douglass C. 1990. *Institutions, Institutional Change and Economic Performance*. New York, NY: Cambridge University Press.

North, Douglass C., and Barry W. Weingast. 1989. "Constitutions and Commitment: The Evolution of Institutional Governing Public Choice in Seventeenth-Century England." *Journal of Economic History* 49(4): 803–32.

Nunn, Nathan. 2008. "The Long-Term Effects of Africa's Slave Trades." *Quarterly Journal of Economics* 123(1): 139–76.

———. 2009. "The Importance of History for Economic Development." *Annual Review of Economics* 1(1): 65–92.

———. 2014. "Historical Development." In Philippe Aghion and Steven N. Durlauf (eds.), *Handbook of Economic Growth* (Vol. 2; pp. 347–402). North-Holland: Elsevier.

Nunn, Nathan, and Leonard Wantchekon. 2011. "The Slave Trade and the Origins of Mistrust in Africa." *American Economic Review* 101(7): 3221–52.

Orren, Karen, and Stephen Skowronek. 2004. *The Search for American Political Development.* New York, NY: Cambridge University Press.

Pierson, Paul. 2000. "Increasing Returns, Path Dependence, and the Study of Politics." *American Political Science Review* 94(2): 251–67.

———. 2004. *Politics in Time: History, Institutions, and Social Analysis.* Princeton, NJ: Princeton University Press.

Pierson, Paul, and Theda Skocpol. 2002. "Historical Institutionalism in Contemporary Political Science." In Ira Katznelson and Helen V. Milner (eds.), *Political Science: The State of the Discipline* (pp. 693–721). New York, NY and Washington, DC: W. W. Norton & Co. and the American Political Science Association.

Pop-Eleches, Grigore, and Joshua Tucker. 2017. *Communism's Shadow: Historical Legacies and Contemporary Political Attitudes.* Princeton, NJ: Princeton University Press.

Poteete, Amy R., Marco A. Janssen, and Elinor Ostrom. 2010. *Working Together: Collective Action, the Commons, and Multiple Methods in Practice.* Princeton, NJ: Princeton University Press.

Putnam, Robert D., with Robert Leonardi and Raffaella Nanetti. 1993. *Making Democracy Work: Civic Traditions in Modern Italy.* Princeton, NJ: Princeton University Press.

Reid, Richard. 2011. "Past and Presentism: The Precolonial and the Foreshortening of African History." *Journal of African History* 52(2): 135–55.

Richter, Rudolf. 2005. "The New Institutional Economics: Its Start, Its Meaning, and Its Prospects." *European Business Organization Law Review* 6(2): 161–200.

Riedl, Rachel Beatty. 2014. *Authoritarian Origins of Democratic Party Systems in Africa.* New York, NY: Cambridge University Press.

Ritter, Daniel P. 2014. "Comparative Historical Analysis." In Donatella della Porta (ed.), *Methodological Practices in Social Movement Research* (pp. 97–116). Oxford, UK: Oxford University Press.

Rixen, Thomas, and Lora Anne Viola. 2015. "Putting Path Dependence in its Place: Toward a Taxonomy of Institutional Change." *Journal of Theoretical Politics* 27(2): 301–23.

Rixen, Thomas, Lora Viola, and Michael Zuern (eds.). 2016. *Historical Institutionalism and International Relations.* Oxford, UK: Oxford University Press.

Roberts, Kenneth M. 2014. *Changing Course in Latin America: Party Systems in the Neoliberal Era.* New York, NY: Cambridge University Press.

Rodrik, Dani (ed.). 2003. *In Search of Prosperity: Analytic Narratives on Economic Growth.* Princeton, NJ: Princeton University Press.

Rokkan, Stein. 1970. "Nation-Building, Cleavage Formation and the Structuring of Mass Politics." In Stein Rokkan, with Angus Campbell, Per Torsvik, and Henry Valen, *Citizens, Elections, and Parties: Approaches to the Comparative Study of the Processes of Development* (pp. 72–144). New York, NY: David McKay.

Rueschemeyer, Dietrich. 2009. *Usable Theory: Analytic Tools for Social and Political Research.* Princeton, NJ: Princeton. University Press.

Rueschemeyer, Dietrich, Evelyne Huber Stephens, and John D. Stephens. 1992. *Capitalist Development and Democracy.* Chicago, IL: University of Chicago Press.

Rule, James B. 1997. *Theory and Progress in Social Science.* New York, NY: Cambridge University Press.

Sarigil, Zeki. 2015. "Showing the Path to Path Dependence: The Habitual Path." *European Political Science Review* 7(2): 221–42.

Scully, Timothy R. 1992. *Rethinking the Center. Party Politics in Nineteenth- and Twentieth-Century Chile*. Stanford, CA: Stanford University Press.

Simpser, Alberto, Dan Slater, and Jason Wittenberg. 2018. "Dead but Not Gone: Contemporary Legacies of Communism, Imperialism, and Authoritarianism." *Annual Review of Political Science* 21: 419–39.

Skocpol, Theda. 1979. *States and Social Revolution*. New York, NY: Cambridge University Press.

Skocpol, Theda (ed.). 1984. *Vision and Method in Historical Sociology*. New York, NY: Cambridge University Press.

Slater, Dan. 2010. *Ordering Power: Contentious Politics and Authoritarian Leviathans in Southeast Asia*. New York, NY: Cambridge University Press.

Slater, Dan, and Erica Simmons. 2010. "Informative Regress: Critical Antecedents in Comparative Politics." *Comparative Political Studies* 43(7): 886–917.

Smelser, Neil J. 1976. *Comparative Methods in the Social Sciences*. Englewood Cliffs, NJ: Prentice Hall.

Soifer, Hillel David. 2012. "The Causal Logic of Critical Junctures." *Comparative Political Studies* 45(12): 1572–97.

———. 2015. *State Building in Latin America*. New York, NY: Cambridge University Press.

Steinmo, Sven. 2008. "Historical Institutionalism." In Donatella della Porta and Michael Keating (eds.), *Approaches and Methodologies in the Social Sciences* (pp. 118–38). New York, NY: Cambridge University Press.

———. 2016. "Historical Institutionalism and Experimental Methods." In Orfeo Fioretos, Tulia G. Falleti, and Adam Sheingate (eds.), *The Oxford Handbook of Historical Institutionalism* (pp. 107–23). New York, NY: Oxford University Press.

Steinmo, Sven, Kathleen Thelen, and Frank Longstreth (eds.). 1992. *Structuring Politics: Historical Institutionalism in Comparative Analysis*. New York, NY: Cambridge University Press.

Stinchcombe, Arthur L. 1968. *Constructing Social Theories*. New York, NY: Harcourt, Brace, and World.

Streeck, Wolfgang, and Kathleen A. Thelen. 2005a. "Preface." In Wolfgang Streeck and Kathleen Thelen (eds.), *Beyond Continuity: Institutional Change in Advanced Political Economies* (p. i). Oxford, UK: Oxford University Press.

———. 2005b. "Introduction: Institutional Change in Advanced Political Economies." In Wolfgang Streeck and Kathleen Thelen (eds.), *Beyond Continuity: Institutional Change in Advanced Political Economies* (pp. 1–39). Oxford, UK: Oxford University Press.

Sydow, Jörg, Georg Schreyögg, and Jochen Koch. 2009. "Organizational Path Dependence: Opening the Black Box." *Academy of Management Review* 34(4): 689–709.

Thelen, Kathleen. 1999. "Historical Institutionalism in Comparative Politics." *Annual Review of Political Science* 2: 369–404.

———. 2003. "How Institutions Evolve: Insights from Comparative Historical Analysis." In James Mahoney and Dietrich Rueschemeyer (eds.), *Comparative Historical Analysis in the Social Sciences* (pp. 208–40). New York, NY: Cambridge University Press.

———. 2004. *How Institutions Evolve: The Political Economy of Skills in Germany, Britain, the United States and Japan*. New York, NY: Cambridge University Press.

Thelen, Kathleen, and Sven Steinmo. 1992. "Historical Institutionalism in Comparative Politics." In Sven Steinmo, Kathleen Thelen, and Frank Longstreth (eds.), *Structuring Politics: Historical Institutionalism in Comparative Analysis* (pp. 1–32). New York, NY: Cambridge University Press.

Tilly, Charles. 1990. *Coercion, Capital, and European States, AD 990–1990.* Oxford, UK: Basil Blackwell.

Tudor, Maya. 2013. *The Promise of Power: The Origins of Democracy in India and Autocracy in Pakistan.* New York, NY: Cambridge University Press.

Vu, Tuong. 2010. *Paths to Development in Asia: South Korea, Vietnam, China, and Indonesia.* New York, NY: Cambridge University Press.

Waisman, Carlos H. 1987. *Reversal of Development in Argentina. Postwar Counter-Revolutionary Policies and Their Structural Consequences.* Princeton, NJ: Princeton University Press.

Waldner, David. 1999. *State Building and Late Development.* Ithaca, NY: Cornell University Press.

Wawro, Gregory J., and Ira Katznelson. 2014. "Designing Historical Social Scientific Inquiry: How Parameter Heterogeneity Can Bridge the Methodological Divide between Quantitative and Qualitative Approaches." *American Journal of Political Science* 58(2): 526–46.

Weber, Max. 1946 [1922–1923]. "The Social Psychology of the World Religion." In H. H. Gerth and C. Wright Mills (eds.), *From Max Weber* (pp. 267–301). New York, NY: Oxford University Press.

Weingast, Barry R. 2005. "Persuasion, Preference, Change, and Critical Junctures: The Microfoundations of a Macroscopic Concept." In Ira Katznelson and Barry R. Weingast (eds.), *Preferences and Situations: Points of Intersection Between Historical and Rational Choice Institutionalism* (pp. 129–60). New York, NY: Russell Sage Foundation.

Wittenberg, Jason. 2006. *Crucibles of Political Loyalty: Church Institutions and Electoral Continuity in Hungary.* New York, NY: Cambridge University Press.

———. 2015. "Conceptualizing Historical Legacies." *East European Politics & Societies* 29(2): 366–78.

Yashar, Deborah J. 1997. *Demanding Democracy: Reform and Reaction in Costa Rica and Guatemala, 1870s–1950s.* Stanford, CA: Stanford University Press.

I

BASICS
Core Concepts and Big Substantive Questions

1

Critical Juncture Framework and the Five-Step Template

David Collier

The basic idea of critical junctures and historical legacies is both simple and complex. It is simple because it captures a framing that is quite standard, both in the social sciences and in ordinary language. We have a rich vocabulary for discussing major transitions seen as having a long-term impact. Examples of common terms include historical turning point, pivotal episode, choice point, watershed, and point of inflection—and at least six others are readily identified.[1] The core idea is familiar.

Yet this idea is also complex. Adequately conceptualizing and describing these presumably major transitions can be a daunting challenge. Further, these expressions all entail a causal claim: that this turning point does indeed have an impact, producing an enduring legacy. The complexity therefore centrally arises in the task of evaluating this causal claim.

With the goal of cutting through this complexity, the present chapter proposes a critical juncture framework, based on a working definition and a five-step template that synthesizes the basic historical sequence on which scholars routinely focus. The framework draws on a spectrum of ideas employed in the analysis of critical junctures. It serves to anchor research, yet is sufficiently flexible to be valuable for scholars who approach this topic in different ways. It provides a common language, establishing and delimiting the field, and its value is well illustrated by its fruitful application in the many chapters of this book.

Taylor Boas and Samuel Handlin made valuable suggestions on this chapter. Ruth Collier and Gerardo L. Munck each offered several rounds of comments that were exceptionally helpful. Ben Harper, Patti Smolian, and Ananya Narayanan provided crucial assistance with the manuscript and bibliography.

1. Breakpoint, critical event, defining episode, forking path, founding moment, and point of differentiation.

This chapter is organized as follows. It first proposes a working definition of critical juncture, together with a specification of related properties[2] that are important features, but are more productively not included in the definition. We then review an important scholarly disagreement as to whether the criterion of "contingency" should be part of the definition, or treated as a related property. We favor the latter choice. Next, we explore the five-step template in substantial detail, specifying the opportunities for arriving at interesting findings, along with some of the many pitfalls encountered in studying critical junctures. The chapter concludes by evaluating the template, focusing on how much analytic leverage is gained with the analysis of each step.

WORKING DEFINITION AND RELATED PROPERTIES

We start with a parsimonious working definition that seeks to nail down the most important features of critical junctures. Our definition is as follows:

> A critical juncture is (1) a concentrated, macro episode of innovation that (2) generates an enduring legacy.[3]

Two points should immediately be addressed. First, the fundamental requirement posited by this definition is that for an episode of innovation to be a critical juncture, it must generate an enduring legacy. No legacy, no critical juncture. In a spirit of healthy skepticism, scholars should recognize that the negative finding that a given episode of innovation *is not* a critical juncture is just as valuable as the positive finding that it *is* one.

Second, we discuss four key attributes of critical junctures, about which scholars may sometimes disagree regarding whether they should be included in the definition, or are better seen as related properties. These involve differentiation, institutions, level of analysis, and contingency.

a. Differentiation

In a great many studies, the critical juncture occurs in contrasting ways across cases, and the analyst asks whether parallel contrasts emerge in the legacy. Yet in research on single cases, such contrasts do not play a role. Hence, differentiation is treated as an important related property, and not part of the definition.[4]

---

2. This approach is a modified version of that proposed by Sartori (2009 [1985]).

3. Our own prior definitions—Collier and Collier (1991: 782) and Collier and Munck (2017: 2)—treated differentiation as a defining property, whereas here it is a related property. The Collier and Munck definition also refers to *institutional* innovation. See the discussion under "b. Institutions."

4. A further point about differentiation: it may subsequently be followed by convergence. In addition, cases that are different *prior* to the critical juncture might converge at the critical juncture.

b. Institutions

The definition could potentially refer to *institutional* innovation, with institutions understood as formal and informal rules that structure behavior. However, the idea of institutions evokes specific literatures that are not a point of reference for some scholars—for example, those who study culture and political practices. Hence, the definition refers simply to innovation.

c. Level of Analysis

In defining a critical juncture as a macro episode of innovation, we follow the framing in Appendix I. If the outcome being explained is the transformation of national political regimes, then the political regimes are at the macro level. The analysis will also routinely focus on the micro-foundations of this transformation. An example of the micro focus is the mechanisms of reproduction of the legacy, which is sustained by the behavior of individual actors.

This framing is readily applied to quite different domains, including subnational comparisons. For example, Rast (2009) adopts the critical juncture framework in a comparison of urban redevelopment policy in Chicago and Milwaukee. Here, the overall policies are understood to be at the macro level, and the micro-foundations involve the behavior of individuals who shape and sustain the policies.

d. Contingency

A further issue concerns the role of contingency as a property of critical junctures, with a contingent event understood as one that is not anticipated, based on available theoretical frameworks.[5] It is ". . . not expected to take place, given certain theoretical understandings of how causal processes work" (Mahoney 2000: 513). It involves, as Capoccia and Kelemen (2007: 343) put it, ". . . a situation in which the structural (that is, economic, cultural, ideological, organizational) influences on political action are significantly relaxed."

The prevailing view in the literature is that contingency is so fundamental to understanding critical junctures that it should be part of the definition.[6] However, some scholars[7] do not favor including it, and this issue therefore merits close attention.

---

5. Mahoney (2000: 507–08).

6. Mahoney (2000: 513; 2001: 268), Katznelson (2003: 277), Capoccia and Kelemen (2007: 343), Greer (2008: 219), Calder and Ye (2010: 42), Gerring (2012: 418), Soifer (2012: 1573–74), Roberts (2014: 43), Bernhard (2015: 978), and Capoccia (2015: 148; 2016: 6, 33). García-Montoya and Mahoney (2020) make basically this same argument—using the term "critical event," which they treat as a synonym for critical juncture.

7. Pierson (2004: 89), Slater and Simmons (2010), Collier and Collier (1991: 27).

CONTINGENCY AS A DEFINING PROPERTY:
GOALS AND PROBLEMS

Scholars who advocate making contingency part of the definition have the goal of identifying a break in the causal chain leading up to the hypothesized critical juncture, with the objective of establishing its novelty and addressing the problem of infinite regress.[8] By establishing novelty, they seek to show that it is the real, i.e., the "most critical,"[9] critical juncture. If it is not the real critical juncture, then the scholar is vulnerable to fundamental errors of descriptive and causal inference. Contingency breaks the causal chain, blocks infinite regress, establishes novelty, and thereby addresses these shortcomings.

Demonstrating novelty is indeed a worthy goal. However, (1) pursuing this goal by making contingency a defining property is problematic, and (2) better criteria are available for demonstrating novelty.

We first develop the argument that contingency is a problematic criterion. Let us accept the idea, noted above, that establishing contingency does indeed depend on theory. However, some theories are deterministic and structural, whereas others emphasize uncertainty, including the relatively unconstrained choices of individual political actors.

In a given context of research, one or the other theory may be in vogue, thereby upending efforts to have consistent criteria for establishing contingency. A new structural theory might provide a strong explanation for episodes previously seen as deriving from agency, with the consequence that what were initially viewed as critical junctures would turn out not to be. Alternatively, a prior theory that offers a structural explanation might be discredited, potentially leading scholars to treat more cases as resulting from contingency. Episodes considered not to be critical junctures would be reclassified in the opposite direction.

A further issue arises with the idea of individual choice. One way to analyze choice is provided by a game-theoretic framework. This framework usefully posits that individual choice is motivated by—and may be interpreted as strongly shaped by—the larger context of strategic interaction. Hence, "choice" may be structured and does not necessarily involve discretion and contingency.

Contingency is also a problematic criterion, given sharply contrasting views of probabilities. Some scholars view contingency as ubiquitous. Alker (1973: 307) quite some time ago stated pointedly that "actualities are low probability events." Here again, based on the contingency definition, the number of critical junctures would expand. At the other end of the spectrum, Mahoney (2008: 415) has suggested that once an event has occurred, its probability is 1.0. It is inevitable. This approach has been characterized by Dunning (2017: 45) as the "ex-post inevitability" framework.

---

8. Mahoney (2000: 527), Capoccia (2015: 170).
9. Capoccia (2015: 170).

In this view, the idea of varying degrees of inevitability applies only to future events. For scholars who embrace the definitional stipulation of contingency, adopting this approach would mean that critical junctures cannot be found in the past, because the probability of 1.0 precludes contingency. Again, a sweeping reclassification of cases might be called for.

A striking example of the potential need to reclassify hypothesized critical junctures is Lipset and Rokkan (1967: 36–38), who frame their analysis in strongly deterministic terms. If we take their argument at face value, then the definitional requirement of contingency is not satisfied, and the study that founded the field is not an analysis of critical junctures.[10] Yet what if their assessment of deterministic causal patterns is mistaken, and many of the patterns they analyze entail contingency? If so, their study would be about critical junctures after all, which would push us further toward confusion.

The vicissitudes of inferring contingency, along with the potential need to classify and reclassify hypothesized critical junctures, suggest that contingency is not a reliable criterion for establishing novelty.

However, a simple alternative is available. The criterion of "innovation" is, after all, part of the definition of a critical juncture. If one looks across many studies, it is evident that the innovations are rarely trivial, and in fact routinely involve striking novelty. Based on that novelty—assuming other criteria are met, such as generating an enduring legacy—they are definitely "real" critical junctures, and the further criterion of contingency is not needed to establish this.

Consider an example in which novelty is strikingly evident: innovations in church-state relations—for example in nineteenth-century Chile—that included secularization in domains of great social and political importance: education, marriage, and control of cemeteries. Scully (1992) interprets this as a critical juncture. A pivotal episode of innovation occurred under President Montt between 1851 and 1861. He succeeded in outmaneuvering the powerful Archbishop of Santiago and increasingly established the preeminence of the state in all three spheres (Scully 1992: 31–43). From the perspective of the state, religious authorities, and the lived experience of individual Catholics, these are fundamental transformations.[11] The criterion of contingency is not needed to establish their novelty.

Another example is the legalization and incorporation of organized labor movements in Latin America during the first half of the twentieth century, which created new legal and political institutions. Collier and Collier (1991) likewise interpret this

---

10. Rokkan's (1970) subsequent, closely related book likewise advances a deterministic formulation of the argument. See pp. 79, 82, 96, 103, 112, 114, 116, 120, and 129. Here, the same issues would arise. Did Rokkan overlook key steps in the analysis where causation was not deterministic? Correspondingly, is this or is it not a critical juncture study?

11. See also Gould (1999).

as a critical juncture. Against the backdrop of what had often been fierce resistance to the very existence of labor organizations, this period saw the active promotion of unions, typically within the framework of innovative labor law and the corporatist structuring of relations among unions, political parties, and the state.

Of course, innovations in church-state relations and labor law were not invented for the first time in each country, but rather were often borrowed in a process of international diffusion and national imitation. They were novel because, within each national context, they often represented a sharp disjuncture in relation to earlier political, economic, and social patterns.

This brings us back to the basic point. Scholars who advocate giving contingency definitional status are definitely seeking to advance an important objective. Yet balanced against the vicissitudes of relying on the criterion of contingency, the straightforward approach to novelty suggested by these examples is far more reliable.

FIVE-STEP TEMPLATE

A central component in the critical juncture framework is the five-step template (Figure 1.1). This is basically a temporal chain, and also a causal chain. The idea of five steps extends Lipset and Rokkan's (1967) approach, which involves three steps: cleavage, critical juncture, and the resulting party system—i.e., the legacy. As will become clear, adding two more—antecedent conditions and aftermath—deepens the historical analysis and increases leverage for sorting out rival explanations.

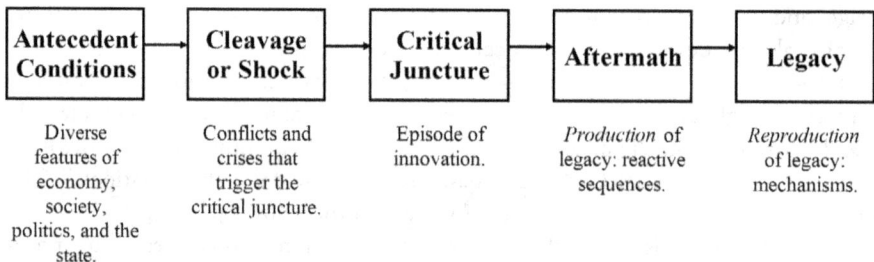

Antecedent Conditions	→	Cleavage or Shock	→	Critical Juncture	→	Aftermath	→	Legacy
Diverse features of economy, society, politics, and the state.		Conflicts and crises that trigger the critical juncture.		Episode of innovation.		*Production* of legacy: reactive sequences.		*Reproduction* of legacy: reproduction mechanisms.

Figure 1.1 Five-Step Template. *Note*: Arrows are intended to reflect the idea of historical sequence. They also represent potential causal connections that must be tested with great care.

In the five-step template, the core causal connection is from critical juncture to legacy, and we begin there. We then analyze the step located *between* critical juncture and legacy, i.e., the aftermath period. Finally, we reach back to the first two steps in the temporal sequence: antecedent conditions, along with the cleavage or shock that triggers the critical juncture.

FROM CRITICAL JUNCTURE TO LEGACY

The nexus of critical juncture and legacy is the heart of the matter. Among many kinds of change social scientists address, the central characteristics of a critical juncture are condensed change, followed by enduring consequences.

A memorable example of this concept of major, discontinuous change leading to considerable continuity is Moore's (1966) *Social Origins of Dictatorship and Democracy*, although it is not couched in the language of critical junctures. The central argument is that revolutions (the critical junctures) occurred in different ways—he distinguishes among bourgeois revolutions, revolutions from above, and revolutions from below. This difference led to contrasting political regimes in the long term (the legacy)—democracy, fascism, and communism, respectively.

A further example of the critical juncture-legacy nexus is Acemoglu et al.'s (2001) study of colonialism and its legacy in sixty-four former colonies throughout the world. These authors argue that the imposition of colonial rule (the critical juncture) occurred in different ways. They distinguish between settler and non-settler colonies, arguing that this difference led to contrasting institutions and economic outcomes in the long term (the legacy): inclusive institutions and strong economic growth, versus extractive institutions and poor economic growth, respectively.

Analyzing the critical juncture-legacy nexus involves two basic questions of causal assessment: (1) Does the critical juncture indeed *generate*—i.e., cause—the legacy? (2) How do we explain the *endurance* of the legacy?

Of course, meaningful causal inference must build on careful description of the critical juncture and legacy. Drawing on the definition presented above, we first consider three elements that pose a challenge of description: *concentrated*, *legacy*, and *enduring*.

Concentrated

Is the critical juncture indeed a concentrated episode of innovation? One major challenge here is to distinguish carefully between episodes of concentrated innovation, versus the more extended pattern that is the focus of the important literature on incremental change.[12] Analysis of critical junctures is incomplete if researchers are unable to recognize extended, incremental change, just as analysis of incremental change is incomplete if researchers are unable to recognize the concentrated change of critical junctures. In this sense, these two traditions stand not in a relationship of conflicting interpretation, but rather of mutual indispensability.

---

12. For an elegant new formulation of these issues, see Gerschewski (2021). See also Collier and Collier (1991: 403–04).

Legacy

The task of identifying the legacy is sometimes relatively straightforward. For example, in the United States the most important reforms of the 1960s, such as the Voting Rights and Civil Rights Acts, persisted in the same form for many years (see Tarrow, this volume, Chapter 4). By contrast, in the context of powerful political reactions and counterreactions, the innovations of a critical juncture may be fundamentally transformed, and analysis of the legacy requires careful judgement about how this transformation has played out.

Enduring

Analysts must demonstrate that the legacy is enduring. Capoccia and Kelemen (2007: 361) provide an example of meeting this challenge. They construct an equation for establishing the significance of a critical juncture, based on the criterion that the legacy should last many years longer than the critical juncture itself. In this equation, a descriptive characterization of the legacy's duration plays a key role.

In the assessment of whether the legacy is enduring, a further point concerns the dilemma of scholars who seek to analyze the legacy while it is still unfolding, and who therefore cannot know how long it will ultimately last. They must ask: How much hindsight is needed to evaluate the legacy? This issue is addressed, for example, by Tarrow's (2017) analysis of the 9/11 terrorist attacks, in which he sought to evaluate an enormous event that had occurred quite recently.

We now return to the two basic issues of causal inference.

Does the Critical Juncture Cause the Legacy?

This is a paradigmatic question. The definitional requirement is that the legacy is indeed caused by the critical juncture. If the legacy follows soon after the critical juncture and is plausibly connected to it, that might appear to settle the matter. Yet this may involve a classic and simple fallacy of causal inference: *post hoc ergo propter hoc*—i.e., because event Y follows event X, event Y must have been caused by event X. The post hoc fallacy is certainly familiar, and is highly relevant here.

In fact, the legacy may result from some other cause, which could originate prior to the hypothesized critical juncture or simultaneously with it. This alternative cause may directly produce the legacy, or it may interact with the critical juncture, yielding potentially complex interconnections among these causal factors. One of the conundrums of critical juncture analysis is how to disentangle these relationships.

The challenge of teasing out the effect of a hypothesized critical juncture versus another causal factor is illustrated in the analysis of political stalemate in Argentina during the 1950s and 1960s. It can be argued that this stalemate is a legacy of the convulsive rise of Peronism in the 1940s, that is, of a critical juncture (Collier and Collier 1991: 37–38). Alternatively, stalemate may be due to underlying structural features of the Argentine economy. O'Donnell (1978) has argued that Argentina's particular configuration of primary products is conducive to zero-sum policy conflicts between rural and urban sectors, which in turn can contribute to political stalemate. Both before and after the rise of Peronism, this may well have been an ongoing cause of stalemate, and hence it is an alternative explanation vis-à-vis the critical juncture hypothesis.

A reasonable conclusion is that the incorporation period and the structure of the economy are both partial causes of the legacy, and this finding of partial causation should be understood as satisfying the definition of critical juncture (Collier and Collier 1991: 20, 38–39).[13] Hence, the analysis supports the argument that the incorporation period is indeed a critical juncture.

In this example, the conclusion may be relatively clear. However, the discussion below points to more complicated situations in which reaching an appropriate conclusion may be a daunting task. Correspondingly, achieving analytic closure on the critical juncture-legacy nexus is an ongoing challenge.

How Do We Explain Duration of the Legacy?

This is a second paradigmatic question. If the critical juncture generates a legacy that endures over a long period, we must ask: Why does it endure so long? Lipset and Rokkan (1967: 50) use the term "frozen" to characterize long-term continuity in the party systems they analyze. Yet underlying this continuity, legacies are in a sense dynamic. This is Stinchcombe's (1968) focus in his analysis of historical causes. We must identify the *mechanisms of reproduction* that account for a legacy's duration.[14]

Close analysis of mechanisms is valuable in evaluating all forms of explanation,[15] and it is certainly crucial here, given the temporal distance between cause and long-term effect. The definitional requirement is that the critical juncture has enduring consequences. Yet if the mechanisms of reproduction fail, the legacy will end, and the criterion that it is enduring will not be met. Hence, it will not be a critical juncture after all. Mechanisms of reproduction are crucial.

Pierson (2000) identifies three such mechanisms: increasing returns, the norms and cognitive frameworks of actors who favor perpetuation of existing structures, and the empowerment of actors who obstruct further change to protect their positions. It may be added that countless works invoke path dependence—and the ideas about mechanisms associated with this concept—to account for the endurance of the legacy.[16] Mechanisms of reproduction are illustrated by Acemoglu et al.'s (2001:

---

13. This idea of a partial cause could be taken too far. It must be an *important* partial cause; i.e., not one that, in the margin, makes little difference. Otherwise it could become too easy to affirm a particular critical juncture hypothesis.

14. Stinchcombe (1968: 101–25), Collier and Collier (1991: 30–31, 35–37).

15. On the role of causal mechanisms in explanations, see Elster (2015: Part I). Waldner (2012; 2015) presents an incisive discussion of the contribution of process tracing and mechanisms in this kind of causal assessment.

16. David (1985), Putnam (1993), Ikenberry (2001), Mahoney (2001), Lieberman (2003), and Kurtz (2013).

1376–77) large-*n* analysis. They argue that the imposition of colonial rule produces a long-term legacy. To account for this causal relationship, they suggest that the legacy is sustained because once inclusive or extractive institutions are adopted, they will persist due to the cost of modifying them.

In sum, carefully analyzing mechanisms of reproduction is crucial for understanding the legacy of critical junctures.

AFTERMATH

The aftermath period is an intervening step connecting critical juncture and legacy. An exceedingly important type is a pattern of "reactions and counterreactions" (Collier and Collier 1991: passim), which Mahoney (2000: 509) has more concisely called a "reactive sequence." The hypothesized critical juncture may involve "progressive" institutional innovations, and conservative political forces who oppose these innovations may overthrow the government that introduced them, producing a period of regime shifts and political turbulence—in sum, a reactive sequence. In Chile, by contrast, where the Pinochet period is sometimes interpreted as a critical juncture, it was *progressive* political forces that brought the Pinochet dictatorship to an end with the plebiscite of 1988. This was followed by a long period of shifts in the rules of the game and in the party system.

Overall, in the midst of this turbulence and these shifts—regardless of whether the episode of innovation was to the left or the right—the consequences of the critical juncture may be sustained, transformed, or completely reversed, and these linking processes are a key to understanding the subsequent legacy. Given this reactive sequence, the consolidation of the legacy may not be completed for a number of years, in some cases for nearly a decade.

In other cases, the critical juncture does not lead to political polarization, this reactive sequence does not occur (Mahoney 2000: 508), and the critical juncture may be followed by a direct transition to the legacy. For example, as Mazzuca (this volume, Chapter 9) argues, once early state formation had occurred in Latin America, territorial boundaries remained stable for a substantial period. In contrast to the pattern of reactive sequences, in such cases the aftermath period is not an analytically meaningful step within the template.

Does this mean that researchers should not look for an aftermath period in the second group of cases? The best way to deal with these cases is to focus on the potential aftermath period, so as to discover if there is a direct transition. This follows the standard norm that the best way of establishing that something does *not occur* is to look closely for its *potential occurrence*. In this sense, looking for the aftermath period is always important.

Exploring the aftermath is valuable for making a judgement about when the legacy begins: immediately for the second group of cases, versus delayed in the others. Demarcating the onset of the legacy is, in turn, important for the adequate analysis of the juncture-legacy nexus. For the reactive sequence cases, analysis of the aftermath also helps bring into focus distinctive features of the legacy—sometimes referred to as "pact-making"—that are created by political actors to overcome the prior trajectory of conflict.

ANTECEDENT CONDITIONS

Diverse features of economy, society, politics, and the state are routinely analyzed as antecedent conditions that can set parameters for subsequent change. They may be important to the contextual understanding that is essential to evaluating long-term processes, and they are often a point of entry for exploring the dilemmas of causal inference that arise in the analysis of the critical juncture and legacy.

Antecedent conditions have been a concern of critical juncture scholars for some time.[17] Against this backdrop, Slater and Simmons (2010) formulated a valuable typology that differentiated among: (1) Descriptive context, involving factors that are causally irrelevant; (2) Background similarities, which allow "controlled comparison" and are a step towards causal inference; (3) Critical antecedents, which set into motion a causal chain that connects antecedent conditions, critical juncture, and legacy; and (4) Alternative explanations, which directly influence the legacy and are rival explanations vis-à-vis the critical juncture.

The typology was a major, and deservedly influential, stride forward in strengthening our understanding of antecedent conditions. Yet a decade later, it would be surprising if additional insights could not be added, and the present discussion proceeds in that spirit (see Table 1.1).

(1) Descriptive Context

Slater and Simmons argue that this component of the antecedent conditions has no causal importance for subsequent steps in the template. As they put it, "for those seeking to uncover historical causation, attention to such *descriptive context* sacrifices parsimony without any gain in explanatory leverage" (2010: 889).

In fact, careful description is more important and more complicated than this. The complexity of description is central to the longstanding concern with establishing analytic equivalence that is fundamental to comparative research, and we will make reference to two strands of work here: the "contextualized comparison" tradition, and the partially overlapping interpretive tradition. The analyst of critical junctures routinely undertakes complex comparisons across policy domains, national

---

17. Collier and Collier (1991: 30), Mahoney (2001: 15).

Table 1.1 Types of Antecedent Conditions Formulated by Slater and Simmons (2010)

Type of Antecedent Condition	Slater and Simmons's Assessment of Causal Status	Supplementary Discussion
1. Descriptive Context	Causally irrelevant.	Contextualized comparison, interpretive understanding.
2. Background Similarities	Control variables. Can be set aside as explanations.	Cautionary observations about interpretation, and about comparison with a small N.
3. Critical Antecedents	Influence the critical juncture, and thereby indirectly the legacy.	Scholars face severe challenges in sorting out alternative causal paths.
4. Alternative Explanations	Directly influence legacy. Rival explanations vis-à-vis the critical juncture.	If they are the cause of the legacy, then the posited critical juncture does not cause the legacy and is not a critical juncture. But also possibility of partial explanation.

Note: The first two columns in this table summarize Slater and Simmons's (2010) analysis. The right-hand column identifies supplementary ideas presented in the discussion below.

settings, historical periods, and sometimes regional contexts. Establishing analytic equivalence across domains can be a challenge, and in the wider literature scholars have explored this challenge in great detail.[18]

Within this big topic, it is valuable to focus on an exemplar study that provides concrete guidance for critical juncture scholars: Locke and Thelen's (1995) "Apples and Oranges Revisited." These authors explore the diverse responses of organized labor in Europe and the United States to a major economic transformation: growing pressure for the "flexibilization" of production.

In a carefully grounded discussion, Locke and Thelen show that across national contexts, labor processes previously described as *different* are in fact relatively *similar*; and based on a closer look, other processes described as *similar* are in fact *different* (359–60). In research on critical junctures, claims about similarities and contrasts among cases are ubiquitous, and the validity of these claims is essential to achieving meaningful causal inference.

---

18. The classic literature includes Bendix (1964), Sartori (1970), and Przeworski and Tenue (1970). More recent work includes Locke and Thelen (1995), Adcock and Collier (2001), Pierson (2003, 2004), Chen and Sil (2007), Christopherson (2010), Locke, Rissing, and Pal (2013), Simmons and Smith (2017, 2021), and Sil (2018). With reference to critical junctures, see Collier and Collier (1991: 31–32).

With regard to interpretive analysis, Simmons, in collaboration with Smith (2017, 2021), has extended this line of work, proposing to increase descriptive leverage in this kind of comparative research based on what they call "ethnographic sensibility." This entails probing the meaning of political action, symbols, and rituals with far greater attention to context. As with the analysis of Locke and Thelen, this may lead scholars to rethink the categories and comparisons that frame their analysis. Overall, the goal is to use the diverse tools of contextual analysis to strengthen descriptive claims that are a foundation of this research tradition.

(2) Background Similarities

Slater and Simmons (2010: 889) view these as "control variables" that, within the framework of the method of controlled comparison, permit the rejection of some explanations. This is an important analytic procedure for critical juncture scholars, yet some warnings are needed.

Both standard work on contextualized comparison and Simmons and Smith's interpretive approach have important implications for causal assessment. The revision of categories that may occur can lead to reconsidering whether what had been presumed to be background similarities are in fact similar, and whether they serve as control variables.

Again with regard to controlled comparison, Collier et al. (2010: 10) argue that it is risky to treat this method as a basis for causal inference. It is, after all, correlation analysis with an extremely small N. Rather, it is more productive to view it as a tool for using small-N comparison as a source of causal ideas.

(3) Critical Antecedents and (4) Alternative Explanations

The final two parts of the typology are closely connected. *Critical antecedents* are those involving "factors or conditions preceding a critical juncture that combine with causal forces during a critical juncture to produce long-term divergence in outcomes" (Slater and Simmons 2010: 889). These authors discuss the sometimes complex intertwining of causal paths, influencing both the critical juncture and the legacy. By contrast, *alternative explanations* directly influence the legacy, bypassing the critical juncture. One possibility is that these alternative explanations fully account for the legacy, leading to rejection of the hypothesis that this really is a critical juncture. Alternatively, both the alternative explanation and the critical juncture may be partial causes of the legacy, in which case the critical juncture hypothesis is supported (see O'Donnell example above).

With regard to critical antecedents and alternative explanations, Slater and Simmons provide good insight—with examples—into how these factors interact with the critical juncture. Certainly in both qualitative and quantitative research, sorting out these causal paths is hard. It is true that an earlier tradition of quantitative research had treated this as a tractable problem, yet more recently methodologists have argued that untangling these alternatives with statistical tools is difficult.[19] For qualitative researchers it is likewise a challenge, yet Waldner (this volume, Chapter 7) has offered a more encouraging option of special relevance for critical juncture scholars—by formulating a new framework of qualitative analysis that aims to sort out these causal paths.

And of course, these issues are important not just in reference to antecedent conditions. The hypothesized causal paths extend through the entire template, and evaluating them is a fundamental challenge in research on critical junctures.

CLEAVAGE/SHOCK

A central idea in this literature is that a cleavage or shock is the immediate trigger for the critical juncture. The antecedent conditions are further in the background and play diverse roles vis-à-vis critical juncture and legacy, whereas the cleavage/shock is an immediate, triggering condition.

The first phase of this literature focused on the role of cleavages in precipitating critical junctures. For example, in seeking to account for the long-term evolution of European party systems, Lipset and Rokkan (1967) focus on four cleavages that emerged across five centuries: center-periphery, state-church, land-industry, and owner-worker.

More recently, scholars have shown that the critical juncture may be triggered not by a cleavage, but instead by a shock. Acemoglu and Robinson (2012: Ch. 1) analyze the European "discovery"[20] of the Americas at the end of the fifteenth century as a shock that opened new opportunities for power and wealth and led to major episodes of institutional innovation. In parallel, Tarrow (2017) analyzes the 9/11 terrorist attacks as a shock. Both cleavages and shocks are important.

Exogenous vs. Endogenous Sources of Change

In ongoing discussions of critical junctures versus incremental change, a standard argument is that the cause of critical junctures is exogenous: i.e., it comes from *outside* the domain where change occurs. By contrast, the cause of incremental change is seen as endogenous: i.e., it originates *inside* the domain where change occurs.[21] This distinction certainly applies to the role of external shocks in triggering critical junctures. However, a critical juncture resulting from a cleavage may sometimes be an intermediate case.

---

19. Green et al. (2009) are among many authors who argue that sorting out alternative causal paths is exceedingly difficult.

20. Obviously, the Americas had been discovered many times before.

21. Once again, Gerschewski (2021) provides a helpful overview of this discussion.

For instance, taking the example of working-class incorporation in Latin America analyzed by Collier and Collier (1991), conflicts surrounding the working-class cleavage involved in part workers' struggles to achieve precisely the gains subsequently institutionalized in labor law. External forces and influences may well have played a role in intensifying the cleavage. However, the immediate battles involving the cleavage occurred close to the domain that was subsequently transformed by the critical juncture.

Overall, the identification of critical junctures with external sources of change, and of incremental transformation with internal sources, should not be overdrawn.

Frequency

Cleavages/shocks on a scale likely to precipitate a critical juncture are relatively rare. Lipset and Rokkan's (1967) four cleavages extend over almost five centuries, and Scully (1992) analyzes three cleavages and critical junctures in Chile that extend over more than a century. Many authors view cleavages as fundamental developmental conflicts that one would not expect to occur with great frequency. Hence, scholars should avoid looking with excess eagerness for the "next critical juncture." At the same time, they must keep a sharp eye out for the large-scale conflicts and macro processes of change that characterize the emergence of these major historical discontinuities.

Conflation

A final point should be made about labelling. It is important not to confound cleavage/shock and critical juncture. For example, let us posit that in the United States at the state and local level, major innovation in public health infrastructure—i.e., a critical juncture—occurs in the wake of the 2020–21 pandemic. Seeing the pandemic as a turning point, an analyst might refer to the pandemic as the critical juncture, yet it is not. Rather, it is the triggering shock. Pandemic and critical juncture stand in a relationship of cause and effect, and they should not be conflated. This might appear to be a minor point, but the problem of conflating them arises more frequently than one might expect.

EVALUATING THE TEMPLATE

How have the five steps in the template been addressed in published studies? Important contrasts in the number of steps analyzed point to a further question: What contribution is made by each step to the more adequate analysis of critical junctures?

Table 1.2 presents twenty examples from the literature, fifteen[22] of which explicitly use the language of critical junctures. The other five do not make the connection explicit, yet in the structure of their analysis they are part of this tradition. All twenty studies analyze the two steps that are most fundamental: critical juncture and legacy.

Application of the template differs notably among these studies. With regard to the number of steps addressed, six of the twenty studies analyze all five steps,[23] seven more encompass four steps, six focus on three, and one study on the two central steps, critical juncture and legacy.

All twenty studies examine critical juncture and legacy, yet six of these analyze the legacy only in passing. Only six address the aftermath; sixteen address antecedent conditions, although eight do so only in passing. Finally, the cleavage or shock receives detailed attention in fourteen studies, with another two examining it in passing.

Scholars have thus made diverse choices in analyzing the steps. What is the payoff derived from focusing on each step? What criteria should be applied in making these choices? Is a focus on more steps necessarily better?

As already stated, the critical juncture-legacy nexus is the heart of the matter. These two steps are of paramount importance.

What can be said about the other steps? Regarding antecedent conditions, analysis of this step strengthens efforts at contextualized comparison, which in turn improves the analysis at subsequent steps. Further, examination of this period can contribute to parsing out complex paths of causation that extend throughout the template. This step is important.

The cleavage/shock that triggers the critical juncture is of great historical interest, and understanding it is valuable for gaining insight into the onset and substance of the critical juncture. As noted above, analysis of this step addresses the debate on exogenous versus endogenous causation. This is an interesting debate, yet perhaps a secondary issue compared to the challenge of evaluating the basic critical juncture hypothesis. Hence, notwithstanding its historical significance, the cleavage/shock is definitely not the most important step.

Analysis of the aftermath plays a key role in demarcating the onset of the legacy. The researcher will encounter cases of reactive sequences in which the onset may be substantially delayed, as well as instances of immediate transition to the legacy, where there is no delay at all. The aftermath is thus a useful step in the template, and in some cases it is very important. But overall, it is likewise not the most important step.

The number of steps analyzed should be guided by other criteria as well, including the amount and quality of data available for each step and the analytic tools employed. With the addition of these further criteria, scholars do indeed face trade-offs.

Two types of studies employ contrasting combinations of these criteria. One is conventional qualitative analysis, which routinely relies on secondary and archival sources and occasionally quantitative data sets. Here, the additional cost in terms of research time of focusing on all five steps may not be great. In addition, given the

---

22. Not shown in table.

23. These numbers include studies that focus on a given step "in passing," whereas these are differentiated in the following paragraph.

Table 1.2 Five-Step Template: Substantive Examples

| | Components of the Framework | | | | |
| | Antecedent Conditions | Cleavage or Shock | Critical Juncture | Aftermath | Legacy |
Works					
Collier and Collier (1991) †	●●	●●	●●	●●	●●
Mahoney (2001) †	●●	●●	●●	●●	●●
Riedl (2014) †	●●	●●	●●	●●	●●
Roberts (2014) †	●●	●●	●●	●●	●●
Yashar (1997) †	●●	●●	●●	●●	●
Gould (1999) †	●	●●	●●	●●	●
Scully (1992) †	●●	●●	●●		●●
Kurtz (2013) †	●	●●	●●		●●
Tudor (2013) †	●	●●	●●		●●
Moore (1966)	●●	●●	●●		●
Lipset and Rokkan (1967) †	●	●●	●●		●
Ikenberry (2001) †	●	●	●●		●●
Calder and Ye (2010)	●	●●	●●		●
Mamdani (1996)	●●		●●		●●
Lieberman (2003) †		●●	●●		●●
Acharya, et al. (2018) †		●●	●●		●●
Acemoglu, et al. (2001)	●		●●		●●
Chibber (2003) †		●	●●		●●
Putnam (1993)	●		●●		●
Lange (2009) †			●●		●●

Note: ●● = addressed in detail; ● = addressed in passing; blank = not addressed.
† = Studies that explicitly use the concepts of the critical juncture framework. For others, the connection is not explicit, but the structure of the analysis is the same.
Studies are in descending order according to the degree to which they address all steps in the template.

forms of fine-grained inferential leverage that are crucial in qualitative analysis, these studies can productively benefit from addressing all five steps.

A second type is the specific kind of quantitative work analyzed in this volume by Munck (Chapter 8). Some of these studies focus only on critical juncture and legacy, often building on impressive data sets and employing econometric tools. Given this data and these tools, the focus on these two steps is more viable than it otherwise might be.

Of course, scholars hold different views on the strengths and limitations of qualitative versus quantitative analysis. Hence, they may have contrasting opinions about the best match-up among number of steps, form of data, and analytic tools. Trade-offs are unavoidable here.

CONCLUSION

This chapter has offered a working definition of critical juncture, addressed the idea of related properties, and shown how the five-step template serves to organize research and strengthen causal inference. In evaluating the template, we have identified opportunities for gaining analytic leverage, but also pitfalls and trade-offs.

As formulated here, the template seeks to encourage healthy skepticism. It provides criteria appropriate for validating the claim that a given episode of innovation is indeed a critical juncture; and of course, these same criteria can lead to rejecting this claim. Further, given debates on pitfalls and trade-offs, the definitive acceptance of a critical juncture hypothesis may sometimes require exceedingly careful assessment. Yet fortunately, a good deal of the time it is more straightforward.

Overall, the important substantive topics addressed make this a compelling line of research. Yet the goal here is definitely not to promote an undisciplined search for new critical junctures. Rather, it is to encourage appropriate caution in identifying and understanding this distinctive form of historical discontinuity.

BIBLIOGRAPHY

Acemoglu, Daron, Simon Johnson, and James Robinson. 2001. "The Colonial Origins of Comparative Development: An Empirical Investigation." *American Economic Review* 91(5): 1369–1401.

Acemoglu, Daron, and James A. Robinson. 2012. *Why Nations Fail: Origins of Power, Poverty and Prosperity*. New York, NY: Crown.

Acharya, Avidit, Matthew Blackwell, and Maya Sen. 2018. *Deep Roots: How Slavery Still Shapes Southern Politics*. Princeton, NJ: Princeton University Press.

Adcock, Robert, and David Collier. 2001. "Measurement Validity: A Shared Standard for Qualitative and Quantitative Research." *American Political Science Review* 95(3): 529–46.

Alker, Hayward R. 1973. "On Political Capabilities in a Schedule Sense: Measuring Power, Integration, and Development." In Hayward R. Alker, Karl W. Deutsch, and A. M. Stoetzel (eds.), *Mathematical Approaches to Politics* (pp. 307–73). San Francisco, CA: Jossey-Bass.

Bendix, Reinhard. 1964. "Concepts and Generalizations in Comparative Sociological Studies." *American Sociological Review* 28(4): 532–39.

Bernhard, Michael. 2015. "Chronic Instability and the Limits of Path Dependence." *Perspectives on Politics* 13(4): 976–91.

Calder, Kent, and Min Ye. 2010. *The Making of Northeast Asia*. Stanford, CA: Stanford University Press.

Capoccia, Giovanni. 2015. "Critical Junctures and Institutional Change." In James Mahoney and Kathleen Thelen (eds.), *Advances in Comparative-Historical Analysis* (pp. 147–79). New York, NY: Cambridge University Press.

———. 2016. "Critical Junctures." In Orfeo Fioretos, Tulia G. Falleti, and Adam Sheingate (eds.), *The Oxford Handbook of Historical Institutionalism* (pp. 89–106). New York, NY: Oxford University Press.

Capoccia, Giovanni, and Daniel Kelemen. 2007. "The Study of Critical Junctures: Theory, Narrative and Counterfactuals in Institutional Theory." *World Politics* 59(3): 341–69.

Chen, Cheng, and Rudra Sil. 2007. "Stretching Postcommunism: Diversity, Context, and Comparative Historical Analysis." *Post-Soviet Affairs* 23(4): 275–301.

Chibber, Vivek. 2003. *Locked in Place: State-Building and Late Industrialization in India*. Princeton, NJ: Princeton University Press.

Christopherson, Susan. 2010. "Afterword: Contextualized Comparison in Local and Regional Economic Development: Are United States Perspectives and Approaches Distinctive?" *Regional Studies* 44(2): 229–33.

Collier, David, Henry E. Brady, and Jason Seawright. 2010. "Introduction to the Second Edition: A Sea Change in Political Methodology." In Henry E. Brady and David Collier (eds.), *Rethinking Social Inquiry: Diverse Tools, Shared Standards* (2nd ed.) (pp. 1–10). Lanham, MD: Rowman & Littlefield.

Collier, David, and Gerardo L. Munck. 2017. "Building Blocks and Methodological Challenges: A Framework for Studying Critical Junctures." *Qualitative and Multi-Method Research* 15(1): 2–9.

Collier, Ruth Berins, and David Collier. 1991. *Shaping the Political Arena: Critical Junctures, the Labor Movement, and the Regime Dynamics in Latin America*. Princeton, NJ: Princeton University Press.

David, Paul A. 1985. "Clio and the Economics of QWERTY." *American Economic Review* 75(2): 332–37.

Dunning, Thad. 2017. "Contingency and Determinism in Research on Critical Junctures: Avoiding the 'Inevitability Framework.'" *Qualitative & Multi-Method Research* 15(1): 41–47.

Elster, Jon. 2015. *Explaining Social Behavior: More Nuts and Bolts for the Social Sciences* (2nd. ed.). New York: Cambridge University Press.

García-Montoya, Laura, and James Mahoney. 2020. "Critical Event Analysis in Case Study Research." *Sociological Methods and Research*. doi:10.1177/0049124120926201.

Gerring, John. 2012. *Social Science Methodology: A Unified Framework*. Cambridge, UK: Cambridge University Press.

Gerschewski, Johannes. 2021. "Explanations of Institutional Change: Reflecting on a 'Missing Diagonal.'" *American Political Science Review* 115(1): 218–33.

Gould, Andrew C. 1999. *Origins of Liberal Dominance: State, Church, and Party in Nineteenth-Century Europe*. Ann Arbor, MI: University of Michigan Press.

Green, Donald P., Shang E. Ha, and John G. Bullock. 2010. "Enough Already about 'Black Box' Experiments: Studying Mediation Is More Difficult than Most Scholars Suppose." *The Annals of the American Academy of Political and Social Science* 628(1): 200–08.

Greer, Scott L. 2008. "Choosing Paths in European Union Health Services Policy: A Political Analysis of a Critical Juncture." *Journal of European Social Policy* 18(3): 219–31.

Ikenberry, G. John. 2001. *After Victory: Institutions, Strategic Restraint, and the Rebuilding of Order after Major Wars*. Princeton, NJ: Princeton University Press.

Katznelson, Ira. 2003. "Periodization and Preferences: Reflections on Purposive Action in Comparative Historical Social Science." In James Mahoney and Dietrich Rueschemeyer (eds.), *Comparative Historical Analysis in the Social Sciences* (pp. 270–303). New York, NY: Cambridge University Press.

Kurtz, Marcus. 2013. *Latin American State Building in Comparative Perspective: Social Foundations of Institutional Order*. New York, NY: Cambridge University Press.

Lange, Matthew. 2009. *Lineages of Despotism and Development: British Colonialism and State Power*. Chicago, IL: University of Chicago Press.

Lieberman, Evan S. 2003. *Race and Regionalism in the Politics of Taxation in Brazil and South Africa*. New York, NY: Cambridge University Press.

Lipset, Seymour M., and Stein Rokkan. 1967. "Cleavage Structures, Party Systems, and Voter Alignments: An Introduction." In Seymour M. Lipset and Stein Rokkan (eds.), *Party Systems and Voter Alignments: Cross-National Perspectives* (pp. 1–64). New York, NY: Free Press.

Locke, Richard M., Ben A. Rissing, and Timea Pal. 2013. "Complements or Substitutes? Private Codes, State Regulation and the Enforcement of Labour Standards in Global Supply Chains." *British Journal of Industrial Relations* 51(3): 519–52.

Locke, Richard M., and Kathleen Thelen. 1995. "Apples and Oranges Revisited: Contextualized Comparisons and the Study of Comparative Labor Politics." *Politics & Society* 23(3): 337–67.

Mahoney, James. 2000. "Path Dependence in Historical Sociology." *Theory and Society* 29(4): 507–48.

———. 2001. *The Legacies of Liberalism: Path Dependence and Political Regimes in Central America*. Baltimore, MD: Johns Hopkins University Press.

———. 2008. "Toward a Unified Theory of Causality." *Comparative Political Studies* 41(4–5): 412–36.

Mamdani, Mahmood. 1996. *Citizen and Subject: Contemporary Africa and the Legacy of Late Colonialism*. Princeton, NJ: Princeton University Press.

Moore, Jr., Barrington. 1966. *Social Origins of Dictatorship and Democracy: Lord and Peasant in the Making of the Modern World*. Boston, MA: Beacon Press.

O'Donnell, Guillermo. 1978. "State and Alliances in Argentina, 1956–1976." *Journal of Development Studies* 15(1): 30–33.

Pierson, Paul. 2000. "Increasing Returns, Path Dependence, and the Study of Politics." *American Political Science Review* 94(2): 251–67.

———. 2003. "Epilogue: From Area Studies to Contextualized Comparisons." In Grzegorz Ekiert and Stephen E. Hanson (eds.), *Capitalism and Democracy in Central and Eastern Europe: Assessing the Legacy of Communist Rule* (pp. 353–66). New York, NY: Cambridge University Press.

———. 2004. *Politics in Time: History, Institutions, and Social Analysis*. Princeton, NJ: Princeton University Press.

Przeworski, Adam, and Henry Teune. 1970. *The Logic of Comparative Social Inquiry*. New York, NY: Wiley-Interscience.

Putnam, Robert D., with Robert Leonardi and Raffaella Nanetti. 1993. *Making Democracy Work: Civic Traditions in Modern Italy*. Princeton, NJ: Princeton University Press.

Rast, Joel. 2009. "Critical Junctures, Long-Term Processes: Urban Redevelopment in Chicago and Milwaukee, 1945–1980." *Social Science History* 33(4): 393–426.

Riedl, Rachel Beatty. 2014. *Authoritarian Origins of Democratic Party Systems in Africa*. New York, NY: Cambridge University Press.

Roberts, Kenneth M. 2014. *Changing Course in Latin America: Party Systems in the Neoliberal Era*. New York, NY: Cambridge University Press.

Rokkan, Stein. 1970. *Citizens, Elections, Parties*. Oslo, Norway: Universiteforlaget.

Sartori, Giovanni. 1970. "Concept Misformation in Comparative Politics." *American Political Science Review* 64(4): 1033–53.

———. 2009 [1985]. "The Tower of Babel." In David Collier and John Gerring (eds.), *Concepts and Method in Social Science: The Tradition of Giovanni Sartori* (pp. 61–96). New York, NY: Routledge.

Scully, Timothy R. 1992. *Rethinking the Center: Party Politics in Nineteenth- and Twentieth-Century Chile*. Stanford, CA: Stanford University Press.

Sil, Rudra. 2018. "Triangulating Area Studies, Not Just Methods: How Cross-Regional Comparison Aids Qualitative and Mixed-Method Research." In Ariel Ahram, Patrick Köllner, and Rudra Sil (eds.), *Comparative Area Studies: Methodological Rationales and Cross-Regional Applications* (pp. 225–46). Oxford, UK: Oxford University Press.

Simmons, Erica, and Nicholas Rush Smith. 2017. "Comparison with an Ethnographic Sensibility." *PS: Political Science & Politics* 50(1): 126–30.

———. 2021. *Rethinking Comparison: Innovative Methods for Qualitative Political Research*. New York, NY: Cambridge University Press.

Slater, Dan, and Erica Simmons. 2010. "Informative Regress: Critical Antecedents in Comparative Politics." *Comparative Political Studies* 43(7): 886–917.

Soifer, Hillel David. 2012. "The Causal Logic of Critical Junctures." *Comparative Political Studies* 45(12): 1572–97.

Stinchcombe, Arthur L. 1968. *Constructing Social Theories*. New York, NY: Harcourt, Brace, and World.

Tarrow, Sidney. 2017. "'The World Changed Today!' Can We Recognize Critical Junctures When We See Them?" *Qualitative & Multi-Method Research* 15(1): 9–11.

Tudor, Maya. 2013. *The Promise of Power: The Origins of Democracy in India and Autocracy in Pakistan*. New York, NY: Cambridge University Press.

Waldner, David. 2012. "Process Tracing and Causal Mechanisms." In Harold Kincaid (ed.), *The Oxford Handbook of Philosophy of Social Science* (pp. 65–84). Oxford, UK: Oxford University Press.

———. 2015. "What Makes Process Tracing Good? Causal Mechanisms, Causal Inference, and the Completeness Standard in Comparative Politics." In Andrew Bennett and Jeffrey Checkel (eds.), *Process Tracing: From Metaphor to Analytic Tool* (pp. 126–52). New York, NY: Cambridge University Press.

Yashar, Deborah J. 1997. *Demanding Democracy: Reform and Reaction in Costa Rica and Guatemala, 1870s–1950s*. Stanford, CA: Stanford University Press.

2

Critical Junctures and Developmental Paths

Colonialism and Long-Term Economic Prosperity

James A. Robinson

> The discovery of America, the rounding of the Cape, opened up fresh ground for the rising bourgeoisie. The East-Indian and Chinese markets, the colonization of America, trade with the colonies, the increase in the means of exchange and in commodities generally, gave to commerce, to navigation, to industry, an impulse never before known, and thereby, to the revolutionary element in the tottering feudal society, a rapid development.
>
> —Marx and Engels (1992: 18–19).

In the assessment of Marx and Engels, Europe's "discovery" of the Americas—a major economic shock—helped to polish off feudalism, while ushering in capitalism. But paradoxically, the bourgeoisie of the country whose mariners had "discovered" America (Spain, and soon after Portugal) subsequently went into a long economic decline (Álvarez-Nogal and Prados de la Escosura 2013; Costa et al. 2015). Instead, it was the politically and economically marginal country of Britain that ended up as the ultimate beneficiary of the economic opportunities in the new world, notably the Atlantic slave trade (Williams 1944), the flow of new resources such as cotton (Pomeranz 2000), and the expanded world demand for industrial goods (Habbakuk and Deane 1963). Why?

This chapter argues that the critical juncture framework (see Chapter 1) provides a powerful model for explaining these divergent outcomes and understanding these facts. It does so by incorporating not just the critical juncture itself, i.e., the sustained period of institution-building in the New World; but also the triggering shock, i.e., Europe's "discovery" of the new world; the critical antecedent conditions that produced this differentiation, specifically initial institutional differences; and finally the longer-term legacies of the juncture (Collier and Collier 1991). These steps are summarized in Table 2.1.

Table 2.1. Colonialism and Its Legacy: Spain and Britain in the Americas*

Country	Spain	Britain
Antecedent Conditions	• Absolutist monarchy. Weak representative institutions. • Long history of the Reconquest of most of Iberian Peninsula. This strengthened absolutism and weakened representation. • Large indigenous population in territories that would later become colonies.	• Much weaker monarchy. Power to legitimate state-building initiatives lay in Parliament, not king. • Long history of building representative institutions. • More sparse indigenous population in territories that would later become colonies.
Transformative Shock	**European "Discovery" of the Americas** Opened vast new opportunities for power and wealth. Obviously, they had been discovered before. However, for Europe this new discovery "gave to commerce, to navigation, to industry, an impulse never before known, and thereby, to the revolutionary element in the tottering feudal society, a rapid development" (Marx and Engels 1992: 18–19).	
Critical Juncture	**Creation of Institutions** **Type of Colony** **Interaction:** Type of colony depends on interplay between type of monarchy and kind of indigenous population. • Strategy of conquering, controlling, and exploiting indigenous populations was a natural extension of absolutism and of earlier military success in reconquering most of Iberian Peninsula. It was also well suited, given the concentrated populations of the Aztec and Inca empires. Military and state officials played preeminent role, and European settlement was not needed and was discouraged. • **Non-settler colonies**	• Colonizers had to some degree (e.g., Virginia) intended to follow Spanish model. Yet this was ill suited, given the sparser indigenous population of colonized territories. To make colonies profitable, colonial authorities adopted settlement model, creating institutions that would attract settlers from Britain. Expansion of settlements accompanied by major, often coercive, displacement of Indigenous groups. • **Settler colonies**

(continued)

Table 2.1. Colonialism and Its Legacy: Spain and Britain in the Americas* (*continued*)

Country	Spain	Britain
	Property Rights and Class Formation	
	• Strong monarchs asserted property rights over revenue from colonies. • Emergence of smaller, less wealthy commercial class.	• Weaker British monarchy unable to assert property rights over revenue from colonies. • Emergence of larger, wealthier commercial class.
	Institutions of Trade	
	• Restricted trade and limited opportunities for merchants.	• Unrestricted trade and good economic opportunities for merchants.
	Representative Institutions	
	• Limited representative institutions. • Fewer institutional constraints on exercise of power by monarchy. • Weaker commercial and merchant class less able to challenge monarchical power.	• Stronger representative institutions. • Greater institutional constraints on exercise of power by monarchy. • Stronger commercial and merchant class more able to challenge monarchical power.
	Overall Institutional Quality	
	Poor	Good
Legacy	**Institutional Legacy: The Colonies**	
	• In the colonies, narrow distribution of resources—as well as of political and economic power—contributed to a period of relative economic decline. • Frontier lands in colonies concentrated in hands of powerful elites in the eighteenth and nineteenth centuries.	• More egalitarian institutions and stronger merchant and commercial class in the colonies contributed to sustained economic growth. • Frontier lands in colonies far more widely distributed in the eighteenth and nineteenth centuries; more egalitarian.
	Interaction: Relationship between open frontier and growth in the colonies may be positive or negative, depending on quality of colonial institutions (econometric finding).	
	• With poor institutions, open frontier has negative impact on growth in the colonies.	• With good institutions, open frontier has positive impact on growth in the colonies.

(continued)

Table 2.1. Colonialism and Its Legacy: Spain and Britain in the Americas* (*continued*)

Country	Spain	Britain
	Institutional Legacy: Spain and Britain	
	• Institutional features of monarchy enumerated above had a dramatic negative impact on Spain. • Relative economic decline between 1600 and roughly 1800, due in part to the narrow distribution of resources from the colonies and the more limited development of a merchant and commercial class.	• Institutional features of colonies enumerated above had a dramatic positive impact on Britain. • Long-term economic growth after 1600, based in part on economic resources gained from the colonies and a wider sharing of these resources that yielded expansion of a merchant and commercial class.
	1500 1600 1700 1820 GDP** 4,744 7,416 7,893 12,975	1500 1600 1700 1820 GDP 2,815 6,007 10,709 36,232
	Interaction: For Spain and Britain, relationship between colonialism and growth may be positive or negative, depending on quality of institutions in the colonies (econometric finding).	
	• Given the poor institutions in the colonies, colonial expansion yields slower growth in Spain.	• Given the good institutions in the colonies, colonial expansion yields faster growth in Britain.

*This chapter discusses other colonizers and other world regions, but the central focus is on Spain and Britain in the New World.

**Maddison 2001: 261. GDP is in 1990 international dollars.

For those familiar with the history of colonization in the Americas, on one level this is a familiar story. The critical juncture framework makes the fundamental contribution of adding a focus on causal sequences and causal mechanisms. Further, in the analysis presented below, econometric tests provide leverage for teasing out key interactions among explanatory factors.

THE EARLY-MODERN EUROPEAN DIVERGENCE

The "discovery" of the Americas was a huge shock, one aspect of which was a vast set of new economic opportunities. This shock created new possibilities for European societies, but it did not predetermine what would happen next. This was because the impact was filtered through initial conditions, in particular the preexisting institutions of different societies. In Spain a period of consolidation of absolutist rule over society had been initiated by the "Reconquest" of the south of the country from the "Moors," which ended in the late fifteenth century. Monarchs, such as Charles V (1516–1556) and Philip II (1556–1598), took advantage of the property rights the crown could assert over the mineral wealth in the Americas to undermine the functioning of representative institutions such as the Cortes of Castile. Flush with silver revenue from the Americas, the monarchy did not need to summon representative institutions to raise taxes. Monarchs were also able to restrict entry by Spanish merchants into trading activities with the Americas. The increased absolutism of the crown pushed the economic institutions of Spain in a much more extractive direction (Acemoglu and Robinson 2012), undermining opportunities and property rights, and tipped the country into a long decline, both relative and absolute. Urbanization, for example, decreased between the sixteenth and eighteenth centuries and real wages were substantially lower in the eighteenth century than they had been in the fifteenth.

In Britain, the situation was different. After having narrowly escaped being invaded by Spain in 1588, Britain tentatively launched her own model of colonial expansion in the Americas. Yet when she did so the monarchy was weaker than in Spain and was unable to assert property rights over income streams generated by colonization or restrict access to trade and economic opportunities. Thus, just as Marx and Engels discussed, the shock of "the discovery of America" did indeed create a huge impulse toward a much larger and wealthier bourgeoisie. This new class was frustrated by incipient absolutism and threats both to property rights and to economic opportunities emanating from the crown (Jha 2015). The bourgeoisie therefore sided with Parliament in the English Civil War of the 1640s and stopped the first attempt of the Stuart monarchs to create absolutism in its tracks. The second attempt, by James II in the 1680s, ended in the same way with the Glorious Revolution. Rather than leading to economic decline, these institutional dynamics led to the industrial revolution and a period of sustained economic growth. Even today, income per-capita in Britain is one third higher than in Spain, and close to double that of Portugal, while at the time of the "discovery" of the Americas the three countries likely had very similar average living standards (Bolt et al. 2018).

Hence, there was one shock with two very different outcomes depending on small differences in initial circumstances. Econometrically, Acemoglu et al. (2005) modeled the opening of commerce with the new world by looking at interactions between explanatory variables. To do this they had to deal with the fact that some countries, like Spain or Britain, were much more involved in Atlantic commerce than others, like Italy or Germany. This created an empirical problem—because involvement in trade was "endogenous," decided by the individuals in the countries themselves, there could be some omitted factor that influenced both the extent of involvement in the trade and any likely consequence. Therefore, it is very difficult to estimate the causal effect of trade involvement on economic growth or institutional change. The solution they came up with was to use the "Atlantic potential" of a country—the length of the Atlantic seaboard divided by its total geographic area—as an exogenous source of variation in the actual involvement in Atlantic commerce. The idea is that this potential predicts involvement in Atlantic trade but is not itself a determinant of growth or institutions. They then showed that in countries with Atlantic potential, the "discovery" of the Americas led to more rapid economic growth when initial political institutions placed constraints on executive power. Neither initial institutional quality nor Atlantic potential had this effect on its own, only their interaction. Indeed, when institutional quality was low, so that there were few constraints on the executive, the effect of greater Atlantic potential on growth was negative, capturing the dynamics of early modern Spain. Similarly, improvements in political institutions, or increases in constraints, arose in the same circumstances—the juxtaposition of initially high levels of executive constraints *with* high Atlantic potential. Just as with economic growth, with low levels of executive constraints and high Atlantic potential, institutional quality actually deteriorated over time, again as in Spain.

COLONIAL DIVERGENCE

Economic and institutional divergence did not just happen in Europe as a consequence of the "discovery" of the Americas. It also happened in the colonies themselves. Europeans entered the colonial world with similar ideas and intentions, but they faced different contexts. For example, Acemoglu and Robinson (2012) document that the colonizing strategy of the U.S.'s initial "founding fathers" (and mothers), in Jamestown, Virginia, was modeled on successful Spanish models of colonization further south. Yet this model—to, in effect, take over, control, and exploit indigenous society—was not feasible in the far less densely populated Virginia tidewater. Instead, for the Virginia Company to make profits Europeans had to be incentivized to work and voluntarily migrate to the Americas. In order for this to happen, the Virginia Company eventually had to create a society based on economic incentives with political institutions to make these incentives credible. North America got onto the path of being a settler colony. In Latin America, the ability to exploit indigenous peoples meant that no such incentives or political institutions were necessary. Indeed, settlement from Spain was discouraged.

Here again relatively small differences in the density and organization of indigenous peoples led to the emergence of very different types of societies with huge long-term consequences for economic development (Acemoglu et al. 2002). Sometimes, of course, the initial conditions were radically different. West Africa was the "white man's graveyard," where the disease environment was so adverse for Europeans that it made the creation of settler colonies impracticable (Acemoglu et al. 2001). Nevertheless, even here the same logic of divergence—of the interaction between a shock (i.e., the opportunity for colonization) and initial conditions (i.e., the disease environment)—is the same. Different initial conditions led colonization to have dramatically different long-term economic and political consequences. Where Europeans could settle, there was more chance that a society based on economic incentives and inclusive political institutions could emerge. This was not by design. Like the history of early Virginia, the history of New South Wales in Australia shows that, rather, this equilibrium emerged as a consequence of contestation and the desire by the colonizing power—in both cases Britain—to make colonialism economically profitable.

The interaction between the antecedent conditions, in terms of indigenous population density or disease environment, and the shock of colonialism led to a divergence of a far greater magnitude than we saw in Europe. While at the time of colonization, Mexico or Andean South America probably had higher levels of income per-capita, and certainly had more advanced technology and organization than North America, today they are substantially poorer. Income per-capita in Perú, for example, is a little over 10 percent of the U.S. level.

Could this colonial divergence be explained by the fact that there were institutional differences within Europe? Could these have been projected into the colonial world? This is a clear possibility, but it is not what econometric analysis of the data suggests (Acemoglu et al. 2001). And history supports these findings. When British people and institutions, like Cecil Rhodes and the British South Africa Company, got the chance to exploit indigenous people, as they did in the Rhodesias in Southern Africa, they ended up creating societies that looked remarkably like Latin American ones, with very high levels of exclusion and inequality.

The power of the critical junctures approach therefore is that it doesn't just help to organize our thinking about the impact of the "discovery" of the Americas on Europe. It also helps us understand the impact of the shock on the Americas, and the broader colonial world itself.

THE MEDIEVAL ROOTS OF THE
ANTECEDENT CONDITIONS

But where do these different initial institutional differences come from? Why was it that Britain had initially better political institutions than Spain at the time the Americas were "discovered"? One can treat this as something idiosyncratic, perhaps as a result of the Spanish crown gaining more power during the Reconquest. Or, perhaps it was a consequence of the delegitimation of central authority in England during the long War of the Roses between the House of York and the House of Lancaster.

But one can also see this as an outcome of previous critical junctures such as the collapse of the Western Roman Empire (Acemoglu and Robinson 2019). There, the legacy of Roman state institutions merged with the democratic institutions of Germanic tribes, described during Roman times by the historian Tacitus, in such a way as to create a centralized state with institutionalized representative institutions. This was particularly the case after the founding by Clovis of the Merovingian dynasty of the Franks in the early sixth century. The evidence suggests that the sorts of representative institutions Clovis adapted to a centralized state were far less strong in Visigothic Spain (Wickham 2017), where they ended up having a narrower and different composition in which only towns were represented (as emphasized by Ertman 1997). It also seems likely that the Reconquest did influence their relative power; Navarre, León, and Castile had a Cortes, but Andalucía did not.

Though Britain was not part of the Frankish empire, it imported many of the same Germanic representative institutions via the Saxons. In the words of abbot Ælfric of Eynsham, who lived in the late tenth and early eleventh centuries,

> No man can make himself king, but the people has the choice to choose as king whom they please. (Quoted in Williams 2003: 17)

The best surviving description we have of a *witan* from this period, the English version of a Germanic assembly, comes from the writings of the monk Byrhtferth of Ramsey. He describes the second coronation of King Edgar ("the Peaceful") at Bath in 973. Byrhtferth recorded that

> in accordance with custom, the archbishops and all the other distinguished bishops and the glorious abbots and religious abbesses, and all the ealdormen, reeves and judges—or rather everyone whom it is fitting to describe as the nobility of this wide and spacious realm—were all to assemble. . . . This splendid and glorious army his realm did not assemble thus in order to depose him, or to take the decision to put him to death or hang him . . . but rather they came for the entirely plausible reason . . . that the venerable bishops should bless, anoint, and consecrate him. (Byrthtfert 2009: 105, 107)

This remarkable account makes it clear that the assembly, composed of people like the ealdormen, high-ranking royal officials usually in charge of a shire, and the reeves who were their subordinates, could have deposed Edgar rather than crowned him. After the religious components took place the king made various promises, for example to dispense justice and mercy. Only then did Bishop Dunstan, who was in charge of the proceedings, place a crown on his head.

The idea of the crown symbolizing royal authority was a German import, and it was not the only one. According to the famous contemporary historian the Venerable Bede, Saxons brought their political institutions with them from Germany. In his *Ecclesiastical History of the English People* he reports that the

> Old Saxons have no king, but several lords who are set over the nation. Whenever war is imminent, these cast lots impartially, and the one on whom the lot falls is followed and obeyed by all for the duration of the war, but as soon as the war ends, the lords revert to equality of status. (Bede 1991: 281)

Apart from such direct influences, Anglo-Saxon leaders travelled in Europe and borrowed freely from the institutional models they knew about. King Alfred the Great had a Carolingian adviser, Grimbald of St. Bertin. The *witan* became the same sort of participatory institution that characterized the Frankish state. Byrhtferth also describes another assembly held in 965, which was also attended by "an incalculable number of the populace" in addition to "all the important leading men, and the outstanding ealdormen, and powerful *thegns* from all the boroughs and towns and cities and territories" (Byrthtfert 2009: 73).

State-building in the late Saxon period therefore had to be legitimated by participation, and Maddicott (2010) has argued that in this legitimacy lies the origins of the English Parliament. Though William the Conqueror and the Normans invaded in 1066 and imposed feudalism, William's first act was to reconfirm the laws of Edward the Confessor, since his claim to the throne was based on Edward having adopted him as heir. Direct evidence for the continuity between Saxon institutions and subsequent English ones comes from the fact that King John and the English barons negotiated the Magna Carta in Runnymede, which was a site for Anglo-Saxon *witans* and therefore a traditional place for deliberation and accountability (for such persistence in England and Europe more generally, see Pantos and Semple 2004). Even the imposition of feudalism did not eradicate the notion that kings had to consult. In this way, the deep history of England diverged from that of Spain, which only had representation in the north of the Iberian peninsula, in contrast to the former lands of the Moors, where the monarchy held more sway. This long, slow divergence created the difference in initial conditions that was to have profound consequences once the "discovery" of the Americas played out.

MECHANISMS OF REPRODUCTION AND PATH DEPENDENCE

Returning to the Americas, the notion of critical junctures helps us understand not just the reason that North and South America got into such different development trajectories, it also helps us to understand why they stayed on those trajectories. Consider the nineteenth century. The industrialization of Western Europe suddenly created a huge demand for tropical products and resources that Latin America had or could produce. In many cases these were land intensive and suddenly vast amounts of land that were either vacant or occupied by indigenous peoples became potentially valuable.

Everywhere countries had to decide on property rights in these lands—who had access and on what terms? In the United States this process had already started with the Northwest Ordinances of 1784, 1785, and 1787, a legal train that came to fruition with the Homestead Act of 1862. These laws opened up the "frontier" to egalitarian homesteading. At the same time, most Latin American countries made very different decisions, typically dividing frontier lands between politically well-connected elites (Mahoney 2001, on the Central American case, and Solberg 1969, on Chile). These decisions reflected the initial institutional conditions in which political power was much more narrowly concentrated and there were far fewer constraints on the exercise of power in Latin America. Indeed, García-Jimeno and Robinson (2011) show econometrically that the consequences of having an open frontier in the nineteenth-century Americas was precisely conditional on initial institutional quality. For countries with poor political institutions, measured as in the research on Europe described above by constraints on the executive, the larger the amount of frontier land relative to the initial size of the territory, the worse economic growth has been over the past 150 years. For countries with relatively good institutions, however, having more frontier land has mapped into better economic outcomes.

Turner might therefore have been correct when he argued that in the U.S. case

> [t]hese free lands promoted individualism, economic equality, freedom to rise, democracy. . . . American democracy is fundamentally the outcome of the experiences of the American people in dealing with the West. (Turner 1920: 259, 266)

But elsewhere in the Americas the story was different:

> Latin American frontiers have not provided fertile ground for democracy. The concentration of wealth and the absence of capital and of highly motivated pioneers effectively blocked the growth of independent smallholders and a rural middle class. (Hennessy 1978: 129)

Again in this case the notion of a critical juncture, of large shocks interacting with antecedent conditions in the shape of initial institutional differences, provides a powerful way of understanding how Turner's famous thesis may be a useful explanation of nineteenth-century U.S. development, but at the same time the same physical circumstances and the same economic shock led to very different outcomes in Latin America. Critically in both cases the initial conditions were replicated; in the U.S., the initially high level of constraints on the exercise of political power led to an inclusive allocation of frontier rights that tended to reproduce the circumstances that led to the constraints on power. In Latin America, the weakness of constraints on power led to oligarchic frontier expansion that tended to concentrate frontier assets in the hands of the powerful, reproducing their relatively unconstrained power. The critical junctures approach therefore provides an important way of thinking about path dependence, not just initial divergence (for other examples, see Robinson and Torvik 2013).

CONCLUSION

Looking back over the *longue durée* of human societies since the Neolithic Revolution, we can conceive of different approaches to understanding their evolution. One, argued by Diamond (1997), is that the initial conditions are everything and they then determine the next 10,000 years of economic and political development. This view is central to the theory of economic growth in the economic profession (e.g., Rebelo 1991). Yet this view is hard to square with basic facts. It predicts, for example, that Mesopotamia ought to be the most economically advanced part of the globe. It isn't.

The critical junctures approach is an alternative. It suggests that the world changes over time, but in an understandable, not random, way. The "fundamentals" that made the ancient city of Uruk in the region of Mesopotamia the most successful society of its age may not be the same as those that facilitate success later. Technologies change. There is innovation and reorganization. Institutions and new ideas in one place spread elsewhere, fundamentally changing the nature of society.

But there is never a tabula rasa. The critical junctures concept provides a flexible way of thinking about this change, but grounded in the past, in path dependence. It suggests that the modern world has been shaped by large historical shocks and the way that people and societies have reacted to them.

It also allows, though this has not been the focus of my analysis, for the possibility of agency. I am not thinking here of the proposal to treat agency or contingency as a defining attribute of critical junctures. That is a bad idea that should be rejected.

Rather, I am thinking of agency/contingency as a *political opportunity*. At a critical juncture there can be greater fluidity, there are multiple possibilities, and individual projects and agendas can have lasting effects because they become institutionalized. It's not a coincidence that James Madison was from Virginia, in the U.S., rather than Cundinamarca, Colombia, but he still likely forged the way that the United States has evolved since 1787 by grasping the agenda at the Constitutional Convention in Philadelphia and persuading many people to go along with him. His Virginia Plan shaped the way that participants thought about the issues they faced, the problems and the solutions. People responded, with the New Jersey Plan, but by that point Madison had already seized the agenda with profound consequences. Trying to conceptualize this element of agency and how it interacts with initial conditions is one of the most exciting areas of the social sciences and the critical junctures approach gives us a way of thinking about just why it is so important.

BIBLIOGRAPHY

Acemoglu, Daron, Simon Johnson, and James A. Robinson. 2001. "The Colonial Origins of Comparative Development: An Empirical Investigation." *American Economic Review* 91(5): 1369–401.

———. 2002. "Reversal of Fortune: Geography and Institutions in the Making of the Modern World Income Distribution." *Quarterly Journal of Economics* 117(4): 1231–94.

———. 2005. "The Rise of Europe: Atlantic Trade, Institutional Change and Economic Growth." *American Economic Review* 95(3): 546–79.

Acemoglu, Daron, and James A. Robinson. 2012. *Why Nations Fail*. New York, NY: Crown.

———. 2019. *The Narrow Corridor: States, Societies, and the Fate of Liberty*. New York, NY: Penguin.

Álvarez-Nogal, Carlos, and Leandro Prados de la Escosura. 2013. "The Rise and Fall of Spain (1270–1850)." *Economic History Review* 66(1): 1–37.

Bede. 1991. *Ecclesiastical History of the English People.* New York, NY: Penguin.

Bolt, Jutta, Robert Inklaar, Herman de Jong, and Jan Luiten van Zanden. 2018. "Rebasing 'Maddison': New Income Comparisons and the Shape of Long-Run Economic Development." Maddison Project Working Paper, no. 10. www.ggdc.net/maddison.

Byrthtferth of Ramsey. 2009. "Vita S. Oswaldi." In Michael Lapidge (ed.), *Byrthtferth of Ramsey: The Lives of St. Oswald and St. Ecgwine* (pp. 1–204). New York, NY: Oxford University Press.

Collier, Ruth Berins, and David Collier. 1991. *Shaping the Political Arena: Critical Junctures, the Labor Movement, and Regime Dynamics in Latin America.* Princeton, NJ: Princeton University Press.

Costa, Leonor Freire, Nuno Palma, and Jaime Reis. 2015. "The Great Escape? The Contribution of the Empire to Portugal's Economic Growth, 1500–1800." *European Review of Economic History* 19(1): 1–22.

Diamond, Jared. 1997. *Guns, Germs and Steel. The Fate of Human Societies.* New York, NY: Norton.

Ertman, Thomas. 1997. *Birth of the Leviathan: Building States and Regimes in Medieval and Early Modern Europe.* New York, NY: Cambridge University Press.

García-Jimeno, Camilo, and James A. Robinson. 2011. "The Myth of the Frontier." In Dora L. Costa and Naomi R. Lamoreaux (eds.), *Understanding Long-Run Economic Growth* (pp. 49–88). Chicago, IL: University of Chicago Press.

Habakkuk, John H., and Phyllis Deane. 1963. "The Take-Off in Britain." In Walt W. Rostow (ed.), *The Take-Off into Sustained Growth* (pp. 63–82). London, UK: Macmillan.

Hennessy, C. Alistair M. 1978. *The Frontier in Latin American History.* London, UK: Edward Arnold.

Jha, Saumitra. 2015. "Financial Asset Holdings and Political Attitudes: Evidence from Revolutionary England." *Quarterly Journal of Economics* 130(3): 1485–545.

Marx, Karl, and Friedrich Engels. 1992. *The Communist Manifesto.* New York, NY: Bantam Books.

Maddicott, J. R. 2010. *The Origins of the English Parliament, 924–1327.* New York, NY: Oxford University Press.

Maddison, Angus. 2001. *The World Economy: A Millennial Perspective.* Paris, France: OECD.

Mahoney, James. 2001. *The Legacies of Liberalism: Path Dependence and Political Regimes in Central America.* Baltimore, MD: Johns Hopkins University Press.

Pantos, Aliki, and Sarah Semple (eds.). 2004. *Assembly Places and Practices in Medieval Europe.* Dublin, Ireland: Four Courts Press.

Pomeranz, Kenneth. 2000. *The Great Divergence: China, Europe, and the Making of the Modern World.* Princeton, NJ: Princeton University Press.

Rebelo, Sergio. 1991. "Long Run Policy Analysis and Long Run Growth." *Journal of Political Economy* 99(3): 500–21.

Robinson, James A., and Ragnar Torvik. 2013. "Institutional Comparative Statics." In Daron Acemoglu, Manuel Arellano, and Eddie Dekel (eds.), *Advances in Economics and Econometrics: Tenth World Congress,* Volume II: *Applied Economics* (pp. 97–134). New York, NY: Cambridge University Press.

Solberg, Carl E. 1969. "A Discriminatory Frontier Land Policy: Chile, 1870–1914." *The Americas* 26(2): 115–33.

Turner, Frederick Jackson. 1920. *The Frontier in American History.* New York, NY: H. Holt and Co.

Wickham, Christopher. 2017. "Consensus and Assemblies in the Romano-Germanic King-doms: A Comparative Approach." In Verena Epp and Christoph H. F. Meyer (eds.), *Recht und Konsens im Frühen Mittelalter* (pp. 389–424). Ostfildern, Germany: Jan Thorbecke Verlag.

Williams, Ann. 2003. *Athelred the Unready: The Ill-Counselled King*. New York, NY: St. Martin's Press.

Williams, Eric. 1944. *Capitalism and Slavery*. Chapel Hill, NC: University Of North Carolina Press.

3

Postwar Settlements and International Order

A Critical Juncture Perspective

G. John Ikenberry

Historical institutionalism offers original ways of thinking about the origins, evolution, and consequences of political institutions—including international order. This chapter argues that a "rise and decline" theory of international order based solely on the distribution of power is inadequate. The idea that leading states periodically have found themselves in a position to build or at least shape international order is not in dispute. But the explanation for the variations in the character of orders depends on more than simply the presence of a powerful lead state. Moments of opportunity for order building open up and close. The character of the state that finds itself with the opportunity to build order also matters. Employing insights from historical institutionalism and the critical juncture framework, this chapter directs attention to the temporal dynamics that shape international orders, including the timing and sequence of past events that set the stage for subsequent struggles over political institutions.

This chapter explores the transformation of international orders following major wars. It argues that major wars are periods of great discontinuity in which old international orders collapse and leading victorious powers are faced with choices regarding how to build a new one. Specifically, the analysis focuses on the role of institutions in generating longer-lasting orders as states have become more democratic and leading states have gained more economic and military power. Given these transformations, they have been more likely to engage in "strategic restraint" and create institutions that limit their power in the short-run and, through increasing returns and path dependence, reproduce themselves in the long-run.[1]

---

1. For a more elaborate version of the arguments presented here, along with full documentation and references, see Ikenberry (2001).

INTERNATIONAL ORDER
AND CRITICAL JUNCTURES

Across historical eras, international order has come and gone, risen and fallen.[2] International orders differ in character from one era and geographic area to another. Some have been more coherent and consent-based than others. Some have been organized and run "from the center" and others less so. Some have been imperial and others more liberal in character. The durability of orders has also varied. Some international orders—such as the post-1815 order—lasted for nearly a century, while the post-1919 order never fully took shape. The American-led order built after World War II has had a wide range of features—economic, political, and security-oriented. More than past international orders, it has been globally expansive, organized around layers of institutions and alliance partnerships—and it has endured into the current era.

They may also vary in the geographic extent included in the order. Throughout history, the settlements grew increasingly global in scope. The Westphalian settlement in 1648 was primarily a continental European settlement, whereas the Utrecht settlement of 1713 saw the beginning of Britain's involvement in shaping the European state system. The Vienna settlement of 1815 brought the wider colonial and non-European world into negotiations. In the twentieth century, the settlements were truly global. The peace agreements also expanded in scope and reach. They dealt with a widening range of security, territorial, economic, and functional issues and they became increasingly intrusive, entailing greater involvement in the internal structures and administration of the defeated states; they culminated in 1945 with the occupation and reconstruction of Germany and Japan.

Importantly, different types of international order may be distinguished. One is the "balance of power," in which states of roughly equal power form alliances and coalitions to ensure that no other state gains overwhelming power. When states exist in an anarchic system with no overarching security guarantee, order is based on the balancing actions of states—the necessary and inevitable outcome of states seeking

---

2. International order refers to "governing" arrangements among a group of states, including its fundamental rules, principles, and institutions. Political order is established when the basic organizing arrangements of the system are set up. When they are overturned, contested, or in disarray, order has broken down; when they are reestablished, order has been recreated. The focus is on the explicit principles, rules, and institutions that define the core relationship between the states that are party to the order. This limits the concept of order to settled arrangements between states that define their relationships to each other and mutual expectations about their ongoing interaction.

to ensure their security in an anarchic system. A second international order takes the form of "hegemony," where one state or group of states have dominant power. This establishes a sort of hierarchy in which political authority is centralized, although there may be a great deal of interdependence and functional differentiation among the units. Finally, international order may take on a "constitutional" form that is organized around agreed-upon legal and political institutions that operate to allocate rights and limit the exercise of power. Institutions, rules, and norms prevent any one state from exercising its power to dominate others.

The ability of these states to engage in what can be called "strategic restraint" has evolved over the centuries, and this has changed the way in which leading states have been able to create and maintain international order. The earliest postwar power restraint strategies of states primarily entailed the separation and dispersion of state power and later the counterbalancing of power. More recently, postwar states have dealt with the uncertainties and disparities in state power with institutional strategies that—to varying degrees—bind states together and circumscribe how and when state power can be exercised.

To explain the origins and changing character of international orders, a historical institutionalist approach and the idea of critical junctures are useful. International order-building exhibits a critical juncture logic. Moments open up, giving powerful states the opportunity to lay down the "tracks" along which interstate relations run. The moments after great power wars stand out as major turning points—1648, 1713, 1815, 1919, and 1945. At these junctures, newly powerful states have been given extraordinary opportunities to shape world politics. In the chaotic aftermath of war, leaders of these states have found themselves in unusually advantageous positions to put forward new rules and principles of international relations and by so doing remake international order.

To explain why critical junctures occur and what consequences they have for the *character* of international orders, that is, the type of international order that is created, and the *durability and stability* of international orders, what follows deploys the concepts of the critical juncture framework (see Chapter 1) and focuses on order-building by leading states in the wake of four major wars, after 1815, 1919, 1945, and 1989. The argument is summarized in Table 3.1. The following sections discuss each part of the argument in detail.

Table 3.1 Critical Junctures and International Orders

	Napoleonic Wars	*World War I*	*World War II*	*Fall of Berlin Wall and Collapse of Soviet Union*
Antecedent Conditions	Britain was the only democracy, and institutional commitments were limited by the "autocratic nature" of other states.	Major victorious powers were all democracies, allowing for more stable institutional structures.	European and American leaders voiced support for democracy and justified institutional commitments as necessary for democracy.	A majority of other Western powers had firmly established democracies, strengthening existing institutions.
Shock				
a. Scope of the shock	Complete overthrow of French hegemony.	Total collapse of old order and disintegration of many European empires.	Total breakdown of post–WWI order.	Only part of the post–WW II order collapsed (bipolar Cold War).
b. Other features of war critical for subsequent innovation	British aimed for a comprehensive peace, subsidized the Quadruple Alliance, and had few territorial ambitions in Europe.	U.S. did not enter the war until 1917 and had a smaller postwar military presence on the continent.	Most destructive war in human history. U.S. played a prominent part in securing the allied victory. Complete Axis surrender and postwar occupation by allies.	Breakdown not due to war but to internal contradictions and failures of the Soviet system.

(continued)

Table 3.1 Critical Junctures and International Orders (continued)

Critical Juncture	Napoleonic Wars *Vienna Settlement*	World War I *Treaty of Versailles*	World War II *Postwar Settlements (1944–1951)*	Fall of Berlin Wall and Collapse of Soviet Union *Post–Cold War Institution Building*
a. *Institutional innovation: Formal institutions constructed after war*	• Alliance system: Mutually restraining partnership. • Concert of Europe: System of dispute resolution that institutionalized periodic consultation between great powers. • However, no guarantees for mutual protection and enforcement due to undemocratic and "fickle" Russian leadership.	• Severe punishments for Germany, imposing responsibility for all war damages. • Establishment of League of Nations without United States and without sufficient security guarantees to satisfy France. • U.S. concessions were not far-reaching enough for European powers, but too extensive for approval by the U.S. Congress.	• Created a "layer cake" of international and regional institutions that aimed to establish open and plural Western order, free-trade, and European "third force" for security (e.g., Bretton Woods, UN, NATO). • U.S. used its power to manage openness and accepted limitations on its power to gain acquiescence from secondary states.	U.S. strengthened and expanded existing institutions like NATO, NAFTA, and WTO; strategy of "enlargement" used multilateral institutions to stabilize and integrate new emerging markets.
b. *Character of the postwar order*	*Combination of balance of power with semi-institutional order.*	*Weak institutional order.*	*Highly institutionalized order.*	*Post–WWII institutions largely remain.*
c. *The role of institutions in restraining leading state power*	Power restraints in institutions, but locking mechanism organized around consultation, democracy, and great-power norms.	U.S. did signal its restraint and created institutions, but these fell apart quickly because U.S. preeminence did not translate into leverage to maintain institutions.	A diverse array of institutions led to a stable and enduring postwar order, and institutions limited U.S. hegemonic power.	In face of a shift in the international balance of power, the liberal multilateral post–WWII institutions remained intact and even became stronger.

(continued)

Table 3.1 Critical Junctures and International Orders (continued)

	Napoleonic Wars	World War I	World War II	Fall of Berlin Wall and Collapse of Soviet Union
Legacy	*Stable, long-lasting order:* Lasted a century and war between great powers ceased for forty years.	*No stable, lasting legacy:* Institutions fell short of their goal and within decades the international order collapsed. Post–WWI legacy a total failure.	*Stable, long-term legacy:* Institutions became self-reproducing and continue to the present day.	*Legacy basically a continuation of post–WWII legacy:* The scope and array of international institutions has expanded since 1991.
a. Was it a critical juncture?	Yes, a critical juncture.	Not a critical juncture.	Yes, a critical juncture.	Probably not a critical juncture.
b. Mechanisms of reproduction	Joint powers acknowledged need to "lock in" some institutions, but also relied somewhat on the less stable balance of power logic, aggregating alliances to offset disparities.	The League of Nations was intended to lock in postwar order, but was undermined by the U.S. withdrawal, France's desire for strict security guarantees, and the absence of global democratic revolutions.	Increasing returns: • Binding institutions guaranteed commitment to the postwar order and were difficult to retract. • International order became more stable over time as rules and institutions became embedded in society as a whole.	Institution-building from post–WWII contributed to the stability of this order. Rules had become embedded enough for Soviet Union to acquiesce into existing order.

POSTWAR SETTLEMENTS AS CRITICAL JUNCTURES

Wars destroy established orders and open opportunities for states to build new orders. They eliminate the option of operating in the current international order. Moreover, wars and the struggles surrounding them delegitimate the rules and institutions of the old order. Indeed, the war itself is evidence of the failure of the old order. Wars also usher in a new distribution of power, creating new asymmetries between powerful and weak states. In effect, great power wars—like powerful storms—destroy and clear away the old rules and institutional structures. The slate is more or less wiped clean. A newly powerful state or group of states can now step forward to rethink and rebuild international order. The constraints of the old order are thrown off, at least temporarily and at least for the most powerful states.

A state that wins a war has acquired what can usefully be thought of as a sort of "windfall" of power assets. The winning postwar state is newly powerful—indeed, in some cases it is newly hegemonic, acquiring a preponderance of material power capabilities. The question is: What does this state do with its new abundance of power? It has three broad choices. It can *dominate*—use its commanding material capabilities to prevail in the endless conflicts over the distribution of gains. It can *abandon*—wash its hands of postwar disputes and return home. Or it can try to *transform* its favorable postwar power position into a durable order that commands the allegiance of the other states within the order. To achieve this outcome, it must overcome the fears of the weaker and defeated states that it will pursue the other options: domination or abandonment.

Though the opportunity to create a new international order is a fairly common impact of wars, the outcome of wars varies. Postwar settlements vary in their character, and in particular in whether they yield an international order that is "constitutional" in form. Some postwar settlements are more stable and endure longer than others. And, as I show next, the critical juncture framework provides tools to explain these differences.

ANTECEDENT CONDITIONS: DEMOCRACY AND INSTITUTIONAL CREDIBILITY

Antecedent conditions can set parameters for subsequent change. In building international order, some conditions prior to the war have a strong effect on the character and durability of the institutions that are ultimately created. The most important condition is the type of states that enter into an agreement. States' regime types can strongly shape their ability to partake in institutions that restrain their own power. In particular, democracies have the greatest credibility in their commitment to international institutions. Three characteristics of democracies contribute to this effect: their transparency, accessibility, and policy viscosity.

First, democracies have higher levels of political transparency than nondemocracies, which allows other states to make more exact determinations of the state's commitment to rules and agreements. Political transparency refers to the openness and visibility of the polity, and democracies have a variety of characteristics that promote such transparency, the most crucial of which is the decentralization of power and decision making. Because decision making is dispersed, more people and a more elaborate process are involved. Second, the openness and decentralization of democratic states also provides opportunities for other states to consult and make representations directly, thus increasing their willingness to make binding commitments. The multiple points of access allow other states to make direct assessments of policy commitments and to lobby on behalf of their interests. As a result, the credibility of commitments rises. Finally, democratic states have greater institutional checks on abrupt policy shifts than nondemocratic states, and this "policy viscosity" serves to reduce policy surprises. One type of check is simply that policy in a decentralized pluralistic democracy must usually pass through a series of veto points. Policy making is essentially a process of coalition building, and this makes it less likely that one individual can command policy unilaterally and move it abruptly in ways that are threatening to others.

In each of the postwar settlements analyzed, the regime type of the states entering into the agreement strongly influenced the character of the subsequent order. The limits to authoritarian commitments are clear in the 1815 negotiations following the Napoleonic Wars. As the only parliamentary democracy, Britain gave voice to the view that a representative government had more difficulty but ultimately greater credibility in making treaty commitments. However, Russian Tsar Alexander ultimately created a separate Holy Alliance based on his mystic Christian faith. The 1815 juncture provided Britain with a leading power position, but the establishment of binding institutions was limited by the nondemocratic character of the states involved. The proposed general security guarantee failed primarily because of the inability of the states involved to make binding commitments. Russian Tsar Alexander's highly personal and eccentric foreign policy was the most visible expression of this constraint. The 1815 case shows the leading state attempting to use institutions as a mechanism of power restraint, and there are some traces of constitutional order, but the episode also reveals the limits faced by nondemocratic states that seek to create binding institutions.

Conditions were significantly different following both world wars, with the greater presence of democracies allowing for stronger institutional commitments. In 1919, the prevalence of democracies among the Western postwar powers provided opportunities for institutional agreement, and Woodrow Wilson articulated ambitious institutional proposals. An institutional bargain was within reach, and the reasons for failure are more idiosyncratic than deeply rooted in the democratic character of the states entering into the agreement. Wilson's stubborn convictions about the sources of law and institutions, the poor exercise of American power, and missed opportunities were enough to doom the settlement despite the favorable conditions for institutional commitments created by the presence of democracies in the postwar settlement.

The 1945 juncture provided the most pronounced incentives and capacities for the leading and secondary states to move toward an institutionalized settlement. The democratic character of the states involved made the institutional agreements that resulted—however reluctantly they were initially entered into—more credible and effective in mitigating the severest implications of power asymmetry. The character of the American domestic system—which provided transparency and "voice opportunities"—and the extensive use of binding institutions served to limit the returns to power and provide assurances to states within the order that they would not be dominated or abandoned. This allowed the United States to build a diverse set of security, economic, and political institutions in the postwar settlements and to establish a more constitutional international order.

Finally, the continued spread of democracy contributed to the survival of this order following the end of the Cold War and the collapse of the Soviet Union. The Western democracies together formed a grouping of countries that made it very difficult for them individually or collectively to exploit or dominate the Soviet Union as it contemplated the transformation of its posture toward the outside world. As Russian Foreign Minister Andrei Kozyrev (1990: 7) noted subsequently, the Western countries are pluralistic democracies and this "practically rules out the pursuance of an aggressive foreign policy" (see also Kozyrev 1995). The widespread presence of democracies contributed to the peaceful integration of Russia into the international order, leading not to the destruction of old international institutions but the strengthening of existing ones.

SHOCK: SCOPE OF THE WAR AND COLLAPSE OF OLD ORDER

Characteristics of the shock of war also shape the critical juncture and the likelihood that the postwar order is constitutional in nature. While asymmetries prior to the war may influence the outcome of the war, it is ultimately the relative power of the leading state emerging from the war that has the biggest effect on the institutions and order it creates. The leading power may emerge as the dominant power, or there may be a closer balance of power among states. The more extreme the power disparities after the war, the greater the capacity of the leading state to employ institutions to lock in a favorable order. The specific way the war itself plays out, including the destruction of the old order, the decisiveness of the victory, and the role of the leading state in the victory, shapes the distribution of power among states entering into postwar negotiations and has an important impact on the stability of the order ultimately created.

The greater the asymmetries of power, the more the rebuilding of order after the war will turn on the resolution of issues relating to domination, abandonment, legitimacy, and strategic restraint. Put differently, the more that power is concentrated in the hands of a single state, the more the problem of order involves issues of compliance and domination between unequal states, and the more acute will be the problem of overcoming the strategic fears of subordinate states. Where the postwar distribution of power is less concentrated and where the winning coalition of states is larger and more equally constituted, settlement agreements will necessarily emerge from wider negotiations. It will be harder for one state to impose its conception of order on the others, and the specific advantages that an institutional settlement provides in muting the implications of power asymmetries are less acutely felt.

Postwar power disparities are themselves determined by specific circumstances related to the end of the war. These elements include the extent to which the old order was destroyed by the war, the decisiveness of the victory, and the degree to which the leading state was responsible for winning the war. The greater the breakdown of order, the greater the opportunities to recast the rules and principles of order. Where the breakdown is extensive, the postwar juncture is more path dependent, and this situation provides incentives for the leading states to seek far-reaching and principled agreements on postwar order. In effect, the extent to which the leading state can in fact lock in a favorable postwar order is greater when the degree of breakdown in the old order is greater. Extensive breakdown also tends to eliminate the default option; it makes it harder to accept a nonagreement.

The impact of the extent of the collapse of the old international order is clearly evident. The collapse of the Napoleonic empire completely and abruptly altered the distribution of power, shifting and magnifying the position of Britain and Russia. World War I saw an even bigger breakdown of the old order and left deep uncertainty of the future. The social and economic destruction that the war left in its wake was unprecedented and unanticipated. It was not possible to foresee at its start that the war would sweep away the Hohenzollern, Romanov, Habsburg, and Ottoman dynasties; lead to the dismemberment or disintegration of the German, Russian, Austro-Hungarian, and Turkish empires; introduce the principle of self-determination; or prompt the establishment of the League of Nations. More than in 1815, the breakdown of the old order was nearly complete. The resulting political disintegration of most of Europe rendered uncertain the basic features of the post-1919 world. Finally, the break after World War II was much more dramatic and complete than at earlier junctures. The war more thoroughly destroyed the old order and the power disparity between the United States and the other great powers was greater. This gave the United States truly unprecedented opportunities to purvey its order-building agenda. It amplified its influence and the ideas it wielded in postwar negotiations, putting the United States in a unique position to translate its dominance into the mostly deeply institutionalized and enduring order to date.

Some more contextual aspects of wars also affect the postwar distribution of power. When the war ends with a decisive victory, the terms of the peace can be more extensive and ambitious; the defeat of the losing states is associated with the defeat of the old order, and the opportunities to usher in new rules and principles of order increase. When the war ends in an armistice or a ceasefire, it is more difficult for the winning states to impose a comprehensive settlement. The role of the leading postwar state in winning the war also has a bearing on its power after the war. Bargaining over postwar order tends to begin even before the fighting stops, and if the lead state is a decisive presence in ensuring victory it is in a stronger position to dominate the postwar proceedings.

For example, during the Napoleonic Wars, Britain was critical not only in ensuring victory but also in using its wartime resources—particularly financial subsidies—to hold the coalition together and gain agreement on alliance cooperation after the war. Britain's leading role in the victory gave it a commanding position in building the postwar order. In contrast, the United States was not in a fully commanding position after 1918. The war ended in a somewhat indecisive armistice, and the United States played a less decisive role in ending the war. Although the United States played an important role in financing the allies, its late entrance into the war, small military presence in Europe following the war, and failure to pursue unconditional surrender gave it less of a voice in postwar negotiations. These conditions changed following World War II. Although the United States was not an early entrant into the war, by 1945 it was a leading military presence and played a critical role in ending the war in both Europe and Asia. Much as Britain did during the Napoleonic war, the United States used its resources during the war to orchestrate a definitive victory for the coalition states. The decision to seek an unconditional surrender in the war, and the resulting occupation of the defeated states, also increased the power position of the United States.

Taken together, these differences in postwar power disparities and positioning are crucial in explaining variations in the capacities and incentives for postwar states to move toward an institutionalized postwar settlement. The characteristics of the shock varied across each war, as did the extent of the collapse of the old order, the role of the leading states, and the extent of the victory. These differences had a big impact on the ensuing critical juncture of postwar negotiations and the international order that emerged.

CRITICAL JUNCTURE: CREATING INTERNATIONAL ORDERS

Following the shock of major power wars, the postwar negotiations among victorious powers serve as critical junctures in the history of international political order. In these periods, leading states can use their power to create new institutions to "lock in" their power. The character of these institutional innovations, including the capacity of the leading state to exercise "strategic restraint" and the incentives of secondary states to accept the agreements, varies greatly across critical junctures, and this in turn contributes to the relative stability of the ensuing postwar order.

Postwar ordering moments have changed over time in the degree to which the leading states had available institutional tools and used them. With the rise of liberal democracies over the past two centuries, the leading states have had options that did not exist previously. Particularly in the twentieth century, the United States was able to contemplate building order around quite complex forms of institutional cooperation. As states found ways to use institutions to restrain and bind themselves to each other, the possibilities for international order expanded enormously.

The institutions created in the four potential critical junctures exhibit this trend toward more institutionalized orders. The critical juncture year of 1815 witnessed the creation of a number of institutions to lock in the postwar order. Several different types of mutual restraint mechanisms were employed by Britain and the other great powers in their attempt to maintain stability in Europe after the war, by creating a series of mutually reinforcing institutional layers to European political order and moving it away from a simple balance-of-power system. Three mechanisms were most important. First, at the core of the settlement was the alliance itself, which the allies agreed would extend into peacetime. This was the mechanism that seemed to introduce some measure of restraint on power. Second, the congress system—the Concert of Europe—was also used as a process of institutional consultation among the great powers. It provided a mechanism for the joint management of conflict and the adjudication of territorial disputes. Finally, there was a diffuse promulgation of norms and rules of European public law, which together were intended to give the institutional, territorial, and great-power arrangements in Europe a certain sense of legal-based legitimacy and authority. However, the institutional settlement fell short of specific commitments of mutual protection and enforcement. These limits can be seen in the fate of the allied discussions of treaty guarantees.

Following World War I, the United States emerged as the leading world power, and it brought an ambitious institutional agenda aimed at binding democratic states together in a universal rule-based association. These institutional proposals were more sweeping than those that Britain brought to Vienna in 1815; they envisioned a worldwide organization of democracies—a League of Nations—operating according to more demanding rules and obligations. The great powers would still form the core of this democratic community, but power balancing would be replaced by more legal and rule-based mechanisms of power management and dispute resolution. However, these institutions fell short of their intended goal when the United States withdrew from the League of Nations, due to divergent great power interests and idiosyncrasies of American leadership. The dilemma that Wilson faced in crafting a settlement around the League of Nations was in providing European governments with enough of a commitment to their security to ensure their participation in the postwar liberal order, yet not too much to raise the resistance of the American Congress. Wilson failed on both counts.

In contrast, the aftermath of World War II resulted in successful international institutions that persist to the present day. Among the Western industrial countries, the settlement was particularly striking in its extensive use of multilateral institutions to organize a wide range of postwar relations, including the use of alliances to bind the United States and its European partners together. Between 1944 and 1951, the United States and the other advanced industrial democracies engaged in a flurry of institution building. The resulting institutionalization of postwar order was vastly greater in scope than in the past, dealing with issues of economic stabilization, trade, finance, and monetary relations as well as political and security relations among the postwar allies. The result was a "layer cake" of regional and global, multilateral and bilateral institutions. Whereas after World War I the United States sought to build a single universal institution with authority across all the realms of interstate relations, after World War II the United States and its partners created a diversified array of institutions, many of them organized more narrowly around the Western industrial democracies and the Atlantic region.

These institutions survived and were even strengthened following the collapse of the Soviet Union, when the United States responded to its favorable shift in power by seeking an expansion or the creation of a variety of security and economic institutions—such as the North Atlantic Treaty Organization (NATO), the North American Free Trade Agreement (NAFTA), the Asia Pacific Economic Cooperation (APEC) forum, and the World Trade Organization (WTO). Thus, the breadth and depth of the institutions created in the aftermath of World War II represented the clearest example of the leading postwar power exercising strategic restraint to lock in a constitutional international order.

LEGACY: ENDURANCE OF THE ORDER

Postwar international settlements do not necessarily endure and create stable orders. Orders may collapse instantly as they fail to manage changes in the balance of power, while others may persist for decades or even centuries as institutions adapt to changing conditions. And, since a defining feature of critical junctures is that they create stable and enduring legacies, it is key to ascertain whether each of the postwar settlements was a critical juncture based on the relative stability of its postwar order.[3]

---

3. A useful measure of stability is the ability of the political order to contain and overcome disturbances to order. Orders will differ in their ability to handle internal and external forces that threaten instability. Different governing rules, principles, and institutions will be better able to cope with disturbances—such as shifts in power distributions, the rise of new states, and changes in the goals and purposes of states—than other orders. But the simple durability or longevity of such an order is not in itself a complete measure of its stability. An order may last a long time, but not be put to the test in terms of its ability to contain disturbances, whereas an order that does have such characteristics may be overturned because of extraordinary circumstances (Jervis 1997: 95). Therefore, assessing the stability of a political order entails making judgments about how resilient it is in the face of disturbances. It is necessary to look at the durability of the order in the face of threatening forces from both within and outside. But it is also necessary to look within the order to see what sort of mechanisms are at work that allow it to adjust and stabilize in the face of such disturbances.

The Enduring Impact of Postwar Settlements

Based on this criterion, the Congress of Vienna in 1815 did in fact serve as a critical juncture that created an enduring legacy. By most measures the order was, in fact, quite successful. War among the great powers ceased for forty years and an entire century would pass before the international order was again consumed by a general European war. However, it did face limitations in the extent of institutions that could be created. The political order that emerged from the Vienna settlement combined elements of the old European balance of power logic with new legal-institutional arrangements meant to manage and restrain power. Its most important departure from previous peace agreements was that it sought to cope with problems of menacing states and strategic rivalry by tying states together through a treaty and a jointly managed security consultation process. It foreshadowed but fell short of the 1919 and 1945 settlements, which tackled a wider range of security, political, and functional problem areas, established semipermanent multilateral institutions, and created more invasive agreements that extended further into the domestic politics of the participating states.

The post–World War I negotiations resulted in the shortest international order. In fact, the postwar order envisioned by Wilson and other institution-builders failed to truly materialize. Despite the broad institutional ambitions, the failure of the United States to join the League of Nations and the divergent major-power interests undermined the ability to lock in any stable postwar order. Although gross power disparities favored the United States, the specific circumstances at the end of the war and Wilson's conduct of policy tended to undercut the American position. Within two decades the world fell into another global war, this time the bloodiest conflict in human history. Because an enduring legacy failed to crystallize, the Treaty of Versailles cannot be classified as a critical juncture.

In contrast, the institutions created after World War II triggered the longest-lasting legacy of the recent major power wars. The order created by the advanced industrial countries was distinctive and unprecedented. More than the early postwar orders, it had—and continues to have—constitutional characteristics. The Western industrial order was characterized by multilayered institutions and alliances, open and penetrated domestic orders, and reciprocal and largely legitimate mechanisms for dispute resolution and joint decision making. It was marked by wide disparities in power—after the war, the United States stood in an unparalleled superordinate position in relation to Europe and Japan. But despite these power differentials, a mutually agreeable order was devised after the war.

The endurance of this legacy is even more evident following the collapse of the Soviet Union. Only part of the post–World War II order—the bipolar order—was destroyed by the dramatic events of 1989–1991. The order among the democratic industrial powers was left intact. Indeed, many American and European observers were quick to argue that the Soviet collapse amounted to a triumph of Western institutions and policies. After past great wars, the old international order tended to be destroyed and discredited, and the way opened for sweeping negotiations over the basic rules and principles of postwar order. After 1989–1991, Western leaders were more likely to argue that the international order was working quite well. Western policy toward the Soviet Union had been vindicated, and the organization of relations among the industrial democracies remained stable and cooperative. The end of the Cold War might best be seen as the result of a fateful decision by Gorbachev in the late 1980s, as the Soviet system faltered around him, to seek accommodation and cautious integration with the West. The result was the collapse of one part of the postwar order and the continuing stability of the other. Because the end of the Cold War represented not a sharp break from the past but rather a strengthening of existing institutional order, it cannot be considered a critical juncture; rather, it is a continuation of the post–World War II legacy.

The Mechanisms of Reproduction

There are several reasons why institutions become "locked in." First, they exhibit the logic of increasing returns. An important way in which institutions take on binding characteristics occurs when adjacent institutions and groups become connected to the institution and dependent on it for their own functioning. Institutions can become embedded within the polity, which in turn makes institutional change more difficult. That is, more people and more of their activities are hooked into the institution and its operations. A wider array of individuals and groups, in more countries and more realms of activity, have a stake—or a vested interest—in the continuation of the institution. The costs of disruption or change in the institution grow over time. This means that "competing orders" or "alternative institutions" are at a disadvantage. The system is increasingly hard to replace. Indeed, an important reason why international order has path-dependent characteristics is the phenomenon of "increasing returns" to institutions (Arthur 1989: 116–31).

There are several aspects to increasing returns. First, large initial startup costs tend to exist in the creation of new institutions. Even when alternative institutions might be more efficient or accord more closely with the interests of powerful states, the gains for the new institutions must be overwhelmingly greater before they overcome the sunk costs of the existing institutions (Stinchcombe 1968: 108–18). Second, there tend to be learning effects that are achieved in the operation of the existing institution that give it advantages over a new institution. Finally, institutions tend to create relations and commitments with other actors and institutions that serve to embed the institution and raise the costs of change. Taken together, as Douglass North (1990: 95) concludes, "the interdependent web of an institutional matrix produces massive increasing returns."

The notion of increasing returns to institutions means that once a moment of institutional selection comes and goes, the cost of large-scale institutional change rises dramatically, even if potential institutions, when compared with existing ones, are more efficient and desirable. In terms of postwar settlements, this means that, short of another major war or a global economic collapse, it is very difficult to create the type of historical breakpoint needed to replace the existing order. At the post-war juncture, the institutions proposed by the leading state are not compared with an existing set of institutions. The war has eliminated—at least to a considerable degree—the old order, so the postwar institutional offering is not competing with an entrenched rival. But after the postwar institutions are in place, this cost logic changes. At these later moments, rival institutional orders must now compete with a preexisting order, with all the sunk costs and vested interests that it manifests.

Thus, institutions take on path dependence. Once they are in place, they are difficult to remove even as international conditions change. This is because there is some separation between the balance of power and the institutions themselves. When leading states implement institutions, they agree to restrain their own exercise of power, subordinating their exercise of power to rules and norms. Constitutional orders thus take on an "autonomous" nature, creating enduring changes in the relative power of states.

The institutional logic of increasing returns is useful in explaining the relative stability of each of the postwar orders examined. The post-1815 order represented a semi-institutional order that tied states together through a treaty system in order to lock in the postwar order. Because the settlement was based on the incorporation of many specific agreements and compromises, it had a cumulative impact. It provided an implicit enforcement mechanism that gave stability and durability to the postwar order. However, it did face some limitations in its institutional commitments because it relied in part on a balance of power logic. The absence of security guarantees, and the lack of credibility that democratic states could bring to the agreement, contributed to the eventual collapse of the order.

The post–World War I order failed to take root precisely because of the lack of mechanisms to lock in institutional arrangements. The United States' failure to ratify the League of Nations and the lack of security guarantees robbed the institution of legitimacy, preventing it from becoming embedded in wider society. Despite the aspirations of Wilson and the leaders of other powers, the institutional structure set up in the Treaty of Versailles failed to reproduce itself and to prevent the near-immediate collapse of the international order.

The logic of path dependency and increasing returns also helps to explain the remarkable stability of the post-1945 order among the industrial democracies—an order that has persisted despite the end of the Cold War and the huge asymmetries of power. More than in 1815 or 1919, the circumstances in 1945 provided opportunities for the leading state to move toward an institutionalized settlement. Once in place, the open and democratic character of the states facilitated the further growth of intergovernmental institutions and commitments, creating deeper linkages between these states and making it increasingly difficult for alternative orders to replace the existing one.

Indeed, the institutional logic of the post-1945 order explains both the way the Cold War ended and the persistence of this order after the Cold War. It tells us why the Soviet Union gave up with so little resistance and acquiesced in a united and more powerful Germany tied to NATO. Soviet leaders appreciated that the institutional aspects of political order in the West made it less likely that these states would take advantage of the Soviets as they pursued reform and integration. The institutional structure of the Western countries mitigated the security consequences of an adverse shift in power disparities and the rise of a united Germany, and this gave the Soviets incentives to go forward with their fateful decisions sooner and on terms more favorable to the West than they would have otherwise been. The expansive and sunk-cost character of the postwar American-led international order helps account for why it continued to persist—indeed to expand outward and deepen—despite the collapse of bipolarity. After the Cold War, this order remained the dominant reality of world politics.

CONCLUSION

Historical institutionalism and the critical juncture framework provide a useful way of explaining broad shifts in the political organization of interstate relations. The point of departure for this kind of analysis is the problem of order in world politics. How have states created order and how do we explain variations in the type of order that has emerged across historical eras and regions of the world? At least in the modern era, states have endeavored in various ways to build rules and institutions of order. Powerful states across the centuries have repeatedly found themselves in a position—typically after major wars—to establish the terms of order. International order is not simply the crystallization of the balance of power or a byproduct of states doing other things. It is a sort of political formation. International orders have differed greatly, but each has had at least implicit in it a logic of a rudimentary political system—manifesting authority relations, principles of sovereignty and intervention, and rules and institutions of diplomacy and commerce.

What is remarkable about these ordering moments is their episodic and varied nature. It is not simply a story of powerful states that use their growing strength to organize the arrangements of global governance. Rather, it is a story of openings, turning points, breakdowns, and temporally bound opportunities. The rules and institutions of governance do not "flex" in a simple and fluid way with the ebb and flow of power and interests. Like Weber's tracks, the ordering arrangements of the system get laid down at critical moments. Openings emerge to put in place basic rules and institutions, and those moments disappear, at least for a while. The notions of critical junctures and path dependence are therefore useful analytical tools to make sense of the punctuated nature and continuous trajectories of the world's governing institutions.

These observations about the logic and character of international order are visible on the world stage today. A cohort of non-Western states, led by China, is rising up within the global system. A global power transition is underway. The "old order" put in place by the United States and its Western allies over the last seventy-six years is under pressure. The distribution of power that was in place at the "moment of creation" of this American-led order has eroded, and states with different interests and values are seeking to exert influence and shape the international political order. This contemporary drama will put to the test the various arguments put forward in this chapter about the logic and character of international order. The old order will not exit the global stage easily. Rising states will be confronted with a complex array of constraints, opportunities, incentives, and legacies from the past that weigh on their capacities and interests.

There is also the issue of great power war—or its absence. In the past, the old order tended to be weakened, delegitimated, and ultimately swept away by major wars. But war as an instrument of global change has, in the age of nuclear weapons, been thankfully thrown into doubt. As a result, it is not clear that China and other rising states will be given the sort of critical juncture that past rising states have had and used to great effect. China and other rising states face an existing order with a more elaborate and world-spanning array of peoples and societies with a stake in keeping it going. As historical institutionalists suggest, change is episodic, contingent, complex, and full of unanticipated outcomes. The shifts underway in the global system today will no doubt confirm this view.

BIBLIOGRAPHY

Arthur, W. Brian. 1989. "Competing Technologies, Increasing Returns, and Lock-In by Historical Events." *Economic Journal* 99(394): 116–31.

Bairoch, Paul, 1982. "International Industrialization Levels from 1750 to 1980." *Journal of European Economic History* 11(2): 269–333.

Ikenberry, G. John. 2001. *After Victory: Institutions, Strategic Restraint, and the Rebuilding of Order after Major Wars*. Princeton, NJ: Princeton University Press.

Jervis, Robert. 1997. *Systems Effects: Complexity in Political and Social Life*. Princeton, NJ: Princeton University Press.

Kennedy, Paul. 1987. *The Rise and Fall of the Great Powers: Economic Change and Military Conflict from 1500 to 2000*. New York, NY: Random House.

Kozyrev, Andrei. 1990. "Building a Bridge along or across a River." *New Times* 43 (October 23–29): 6–8.

———. 1995. "Partnership or Cold Peace?" *Foreign Policy* 99 (Summer): 3–14.

North, Douglass. 1990. *Institutions, Institutional Change and Economic Performance*. New York, NY: Cambridge University Press.

Stinchcombe, Arthur L. 1968. *Constructing Social Theories*. New York, NY: Harcourt, Brace, and World.

4

Mobilization, Protest, and Conflicts of the 1960s

What Is the Legacy, and How Did It Unfold?

Sidney Tarrow

When it comes to the naming of ages "What is important are the *significant breaks*—where old lines of thought are disrupted, older constellations displaced, and elements, old and new, are regrouped around a different set of premises and themes" (Hall 1986: 33). But of what do Hall's "significant breaks" consist? Single episodes? Broad cultural changes? Political critical junctures? Or all of the above? Many observers have seen the entire decade of the 1960s as such a "break," while others have zeroed in on particular shocks—like the epochal year 1968—as constituting such a break. Still others—like this author—have focused on the institutional changes in the period that follow such a break (Tarrow 2021). Historian Daniel Rodgers seems to agree: "The 1960s," he writes, "were a moment of break, but *the regrouping around a different set of premises and themes, as Hall describes it, was the work of the era that followed*" (Rodgers 2011: 5–6, italics added).

Rodgers's extended notion of a significant break can serve as a useful introduction to this chapter. What he is really talking about is duration of "critical junctures," employing that term to encompass outcomes and institutional changes that arise from a historic shock. My starting point is his warning that the protagonists and antagonists of episodes of crisis—and, it might be added, some social scientists as well—may have had exaggerated expectations about the magnitude of change that follow the shock that is the most visible signal of a critical juncture. But the extent of a shock—however great—is no predictor of the degree of "regrouping" that follows. Developing appropriate expectations about these shocks and their "regroupings" is the theme of this chapter.

I am grateful to David Collier, Donatella della Porta, Gerardo L. Munck, Ken Roberts, and George Ross for comments on an earlier version of this chapter.

My empirical focus will be on the dramatic period of mobilization, protest, and conflict that erupted in and around 1968 in France, Italy, and the United States. The epicenter of the explosion, of course, was in France, as the French will quickly tell you. For two weeks, ten million workers went on strike, an abruptly born national student movement occupied universities and schools throughout the country, the economy ground to a halt, and the memory of that year looms large in visions of the country's subsequent history. The situation was so threatening that in the midst of the upheaval, President de Gaulle briefly left the country to consult his generals.

In Italy mass protest lasted longer, began in 1967 and extended well into the 1970s, while in the United States it began with the civil rights movement and spanned a much longer period. However, the events in France were so remarkable that the single year 1968 has become a benchmark in the construction of this momentous period.

In analyzing 1968 and its long-term effects, I draw on the tradition of research on critical junctures in comparative politics.[1] This literature has mainly focused on wars, economic crises, new stages of development, and on emerging social cleavages as triggering critical junctures, but has seldom focused on periods of mass protest (see, however, Capdeveille and Mouriaux 1988; Crouch and Pizzorno 1978; Miller 1987). "Such periods," notes Kenneth Roberts, "can bring new actors and issues onto the political stage in highly disruptive ways that can spawn massive institutional or policy change."[2] A major cycle of contention may well be a shock that brings on a critical juncture, brings new actors onto the stage, and lays the groundwork for institutional changes and for the formation of new and insurgent collective identities, as Pizzorno (1978) wrote in a signal essay on the cycle of the late 1960s in Western Europe.

In the literature on critical junctures, Rodgers's historic "breaks" are labeled "shocks"; and his "regroupings" are specified as subsequent episodes of institutional innovation. The distinction is an important one because, although some critical junctures emerge directly and dramatically from the shock—what Riedl and Roberts call "generative critical junctures" (see Chapter 6)—in others, the institutional innovation is strongly shaped by antecedent conditions—what Riedl and Roberts call "activating junctures." I will argue that in the three cases I will analyze, the "regrouping" depended not on the degree of shock, as in a "generative" juncture, but on the antecedent conditions, on the processing of the juncture, and on its legacy. The surprise finding is that in the country in which the shock was the most explosive—France—the legacy was least extensive, while in Italy and the United States—but in different ways and to different degrees—it was more enduring, due to a combination of antecedent conditions and how the original shock was processed.

---

1. See the symposium on critical junctures under the leadership of Collier and Munck (2017a). That symposium, in turn, was inspired by Ruth Berins Collier and David Collier's path-breaking 1991 book *Shaping the Political Arena*.

2. I am grateful to Ken Roberts for putting succinctly in a personal communication what was implicit—but never made explicit—in an earlier version of this chapter.

The analysis will focus on three main factors:

- First, on the antecedent conditions that shape the critical juncture. While French politics had sunk into a torpor after the de Gaulle Republic was initiated in 1958, in Italy, contention bubbled up throughout the 1960s (Tarrow 1989) while in the United States, the civil rights protests of the early 1960s bled into the anti-war movement.
- Second, on the immediate changes *produced by* the initial stages of the critical junctures. As we will see, often these changes do *not* reproduce themselves but are defeated in dramatic policy reversals.
- Third, on the degree to which the movements generated by such shocks were *reproduced* within institutional politics. One of the distinctive outcomes of this episode was the penetration of institutional politics by noninstitutional actors.[3]

Crucial to this discussion is the distinction between the *shock*—1968—and the *institutional innovations* that followed, i.e., the *critical juncture*. A shock either does or does not trigger a critical juncture, i.e. the episode of innovation, but crucially, it is distinct from it. Given this distinction, referring to a cycle of protest, however dramatic, as a critical juncture would confuse our understanding of what happened during the decade of the 1960s and in the years that followed. This distinction will prove particularly important in the case of France, where the shock was epochal in its intensity and its immediate impact, while its innovations were much less so. These are the issues that I want to take up a half century after the exceptionally dramatic episode of contentious politics—1968.

1968: SOME GUIDING QUESTIONS

The remarkable mobilizations and conflicts of 1968 were certainly one of the most important eruptions of contentious politics in twentieth century history. They gave rise to an enormous literature in all three countries and in the Global North in general. As noted above, this shock bracketed a longer time period in some countries more than in others, but the designation of "1968" at its core derives from the stunning mobilization occurring in May and June of that year in France. May 1968 in France was a shock—or a trigger—but its impact cannot be judged by the claims of

---

3. This "movementization" of the party system was a major legacy of the entire critical juncture, leading to the conversion of Western polities into what I have elsewhere called, with David Meyer, "social movement societies" (Meyer and Tarrow 1998; see also Tarrow 2018 and 2021).

its supporters or the fears of its detractors.[4] It was followed by a conservative reaction beginning with the reversal of the immediate labor and academic reforms that will be described below and, ultimately, by the legislative elections that followed (Wilson 1969).

In Italy, what came to be called "il sessantotto" ('68) is mainly remembered as a reflection of the French "soixante-huit," but it actually preceded it by a year (Tarrow 1989). And the most enduring part of the protest wave only arose in 1969, with a wave of industrial conflict that began in the "industrial triangle" of the North and expanded throughout the country (ibid.). Social and political conflict extended into the 1970s and was linked to a spectacular growth of political violence, culminating in the kidnapping and murder of Christian Democratic leader Aldo Moro in 1978. Taking his cue from the French "May," economist Salvati (1981) designated the entire period as a "sliding May."[5]

The American "'68" was different yet again, both because its major focus was the Vietnam War, a very minor theme in the other two countries, and because it came on the heels of—and drew inspiration from—a much longer cycle of protest, the civil rights movement (Hall 2005; Francis 2014; Milkis 1993). It was also marked by two key political assassinations—that of Robert F. Kennedy and Martin Luther King Jr.—and a catastrophic change of leadership in the Democratic Party, which led to that party's loss in the election the same year. As I will argue below, these differences between an explosive May (France), a "sliding" (Italy), and a concentrated wave of protest and political change rooted in a much longer movement (the United States) are the key descriptive differences that characterize the three "activating" critical junctures in these three countries.

This descriptive comparison is interesting in itself, but it takes on added usefulness for what it tells us about critical juncture theory. As we will see, that body of work draws attention not only to epochal shocks but to longer periods of institutional change and to their legacies in the reproduction of the innovations of those junctures. I will begin with a sketch of three important factors in these country's antecedent period: the shape of the state, the structure of the party system, and the path dependency of contentious politics that preceded the shock. Then I will survey some important differences in the character of the critical junctures and the policy innovations they produced, before turning to the reproduction of these innovations—especially with regard to the relations between social movements and parties.

---

4. In France, one thinks of the sharp turn in the work of Touraine, who, from a distinguished career studying the French working class, came, after May 1968, to the view that the new agent of history would be the student movement (Touraine 1971). With the virtues of time, more sober observers like Capdevielle and Mouriaux (1988) came to a more balanced conclusion.

5. Salvati's term is "maggio strisciante," which, according to Cassell's *Italian Dictionary*, means "creeping, crawling, or cringing." I draw here on my reconstruction of the Italian cycle in Tarrow (1989).

ANTECEDENT CONDITIONS

In the literature on critical junctures, antecedent structural cleavages are often portrayed as dominant causes, in contrast to the contingencies that turn the cleavages into conflict and change. For example, in Collier and Collier's (1991) classical study of Latin American corporatism, industrial conflict produced a militant labor movement to which different states responded in various ways, yielding a legacy of either authoritarian or democratic incorporation. But more recently, a strong dose of contingency has been added to the structural basis of critical juncture theory in many accounts (Slater and Simmons 2010; Roberts 2014; Dunning 2017).

Rather than take a position on the endless debate between structure and agency, this section will focus on three aspects of the antecedent conditions that helped lay the groundwork for the shocks of the period that will be examined.

The Shape of the State. As is well known, the French state in the 1960s was highly centralized, deeply penetrated French society, and—following the caesura of the Algerian War—gained political centrality in the towering figure and the political movement led by President Charles de Gaulle (Gourevitch 1980). The Italian state was equally centralized until the 1970s, when a major regional reform was instituted (Putnam 1993), but it was far less concentrated than the French one, and was marked by a high degree of clientelism and politicization (Tarrow 1977). In even greater contrast, the American state was highly decentralized by the federal system, although it shared the politicization of the Italian one (King and Milkis forthcoming). Of these three countries, the shape of the state would turn out to be the most determinative in France, where state elites were able to turn back several of the key policy innovations of the critical juncture.

The Stability of the Party System. As is also well known, the French electorate had been highly volatile during the years of the Fourth Republic (1946–1959), with a level of electoral volatility that was the highest in Western Europe (Pedersen 1979). But its volatility was sharply reduced after the coming of the Fifth Republic—from 21.8 on Pedersen's index to 11.9 after the Vth Republican was initiated.

From Pedersen's index of electoral volatility, we can see that the Italian system remained at roughly the same moderate level of volatility through the 1950s and 1960s. Italian voters appear to have been loyal to their chosen parties—or at least to the political subcultures that sustained them.

Because of its two-party system, as opposed to Europe's multiparty systems, American volatility is difficult to compare to France and Italy's, but it is notable that volatility increased sharply in the years leading up to 1968 (Boyd 1985: 518).

One other difference in the party systems would prove critical later: their degree of institutionalization. As Riedl and Roberts note, "[W]e find that weakly institutionalized domains provide exactly the conditions that make *activating* critical junctures likely. In periods of flux that relax prior restraints maintaining the previous system, antecedent conditions shape future trajectories in *new and divergent* ways" (see Chapter 6). Although the parties of the French Fourth Republic had been sent reeling by its fall, the French parties were highly institutionalized, while the Italian ones continued to shed splinter groups throughout the postwar period. And while the American two-party system remained rock-solid, the parties as organizations began to be "hollowed out" during the 1960s (Schlozman and Rosenberg 2019). These changes in the party system in the 1960s and early 1970s would prove crucial for the capacity of the movements that arose in that period to reshape it.

The Rise of Contentious Politics. Finally, while the level of contentious politics was so high in France in 1968 that it is impossible to find reliable quantitative measures for it, it is notable that this followed a period in which French society was unusually quiescent. But for those who cared to look, there were signs that France was less stable than it looked from a distance. First, in the aftermath of the Algerian war, there were a number of terrorist incidents arising from far-right groups that had been unwilling to see France's overseas empire decapitated. Second, while the economy was booming, inequality was growing, with a Gini coefficient of 48.0 in 1967.[6] This is compared to a Gini level of 40.9 in Italy and 40.0 in the United States in the same period.

As Figure 4.1 shows, in contrast to France, the cycle of contention in Italy began well before May 1968 with a series of student occupations—some of them quite disruptive. Mobilization actually began within existing student organizations as student militants, many of whom had come from Communist or Christian Democratic backgrounds, broke away from their party affiliations and formed a series of "little journals" and independent student organizations (Tarrow 1989). A key hinge in the move from party-dominated to independent student organizations was a small left-wing socialist party, the Italian Socialist Party of Proletarian Unity (PSIUP), that came out of the left wing of the Socialist Party (PSI).

Figure 4.1 shows that although the memories of these years focus on highly contentious events, in fact, the cycle of protest began—and would remain—for the most part driven by a majority of conventional events—strikes, marches, demonstrations, petitions, and assemblies. Nevertheless, the period was also marked by disruptive events, like the occupation of university buildings, symbolic acts against consumer society, and violence between scattered leftwing and extreme rightwing groups, which came out of the woodwork in these years.

Still more encompassing than Italy's experience with mass protest before 1968 was the "long" civil rights movement in the United States that had arisen early in the century and drew sustenance from the "Great Migration" northward and from Cold War politics (Hall 2005; McAdam 1988; Dudziak 2000). The first signs that change was afoot came through the "least dangerous branch," with court battles against educational segregation in the Supreme Court case of *Brown v. Board of Education*

---

6. http://stats.areppim.com/listes/list_gini_1960x2012.htm

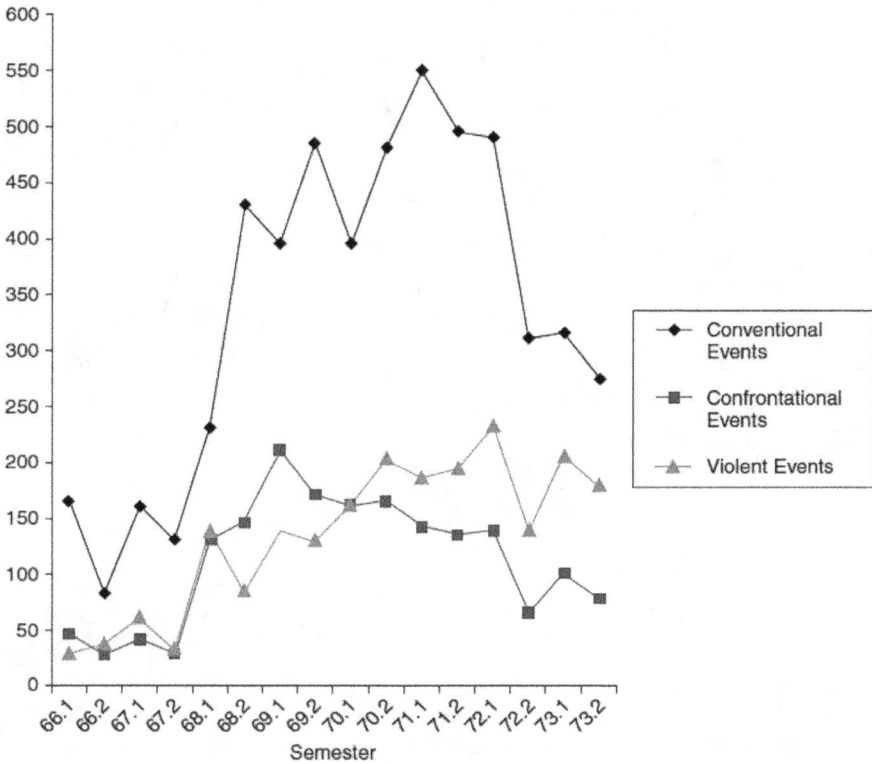

Figure 4.1 Italy: Yearly Number of Protest Events, 1966–1973, by Type of Event
Source: Tarrow (2012: 136)

in 1954.[7] The movement became more contentious with a series of Freedom Rides and student-led protests around the turn of the decade (Andrews and Biggs 2006).

The latter movement provided a template for a new repertoire of contention (Tilly 2006) in the form of the sit-in, which became "modular" in the protests against the Vietnam War and in other movements that emerged toward the end of the decade and in the 1970s. If 1968 was the keystone of the American cycle of contention, it drew heavily on the repertoire and forms of organization that it inherited (McAdam 1988; Milkis 1993).

To summarize, among the most important anticipatory conditions for these three "activating" critical junctures were the strength of the state, the degree of institutionalization of the party system, and the path dependency of the repertoire of

---

7. 347 US 483 (1954).

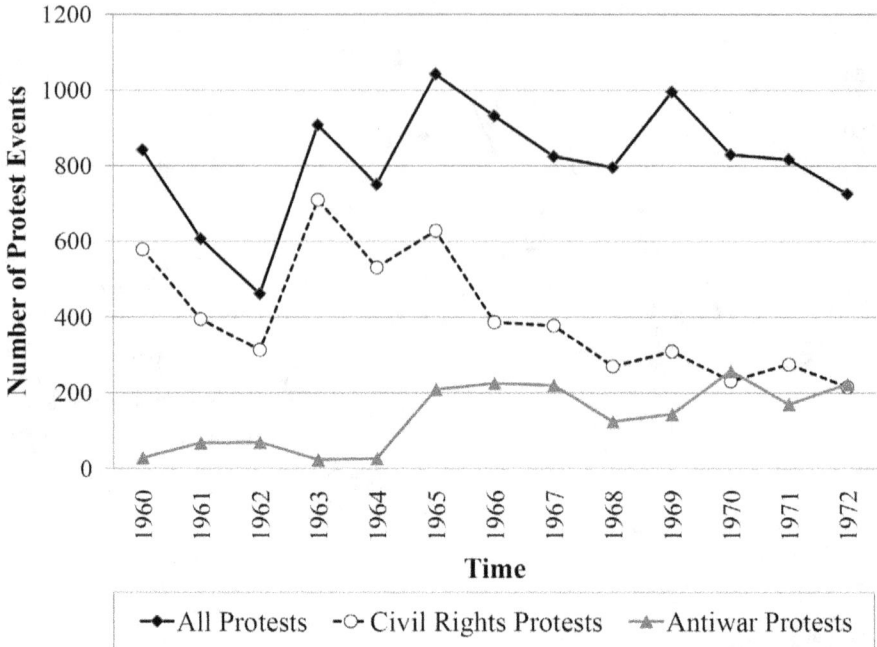

Figure 4.2 United States: Yearly Number of Protest Events, 1960 to 1972
Note: Civil rights protests include events that express any "civil rights" issue as one of their major claims. Antiwar protests include events that have "peace movement" as one of their main claims.
Source: The Dynamics of Collective Protests in the U.S., 1960–1995. Dataset downloaded from https://web.stanford.edu/group/collectiveaction/cgi-bin/drupal/ on August 2017. I am grateful to Chan Suh for carrying out the analysis for Figure 4.2 and to Sarah Soule for permission to access the dataset.

contention. The first factor will turn out to be most important for the French critical juncture, the second one for the Italian one, and the third for the United States.

AN OVERVIEW OF 1968

When scholars and historians talk about "1968," they are generally referring to a period of contentious politics that had its apogee in that year. The year "1968" has become a shorthand for that period mostly because the "Events" of May of that year in France were the most dramatic and the most compressed in time. Yet as we shall see below, the key lesson is that the degree of fire and brimstone of a shock may not predict the rapidity, intensity, and longevity of the changes that follow.

France: A Condensed Shock

Of the three cases that motivate this chapter, France had the most "condensed" shock, and for that reason, the Events of May 1968 have shaped scholarly accounts of that year. For not only were the protests that paralyzed that country concentrated into a few weeks; they spread like wildfire across the territory and social system, mobilizing social and professional groups who are seldom seen in the streets, as well as "the usual suspects" of students and workers. They paralyzed the French economy, produced a major improvement in the wages of lower-paid workers, led the towering founder of the Fifth Republic, Charles de Gaulle, to seek the support of the army against the insurgents, and were largely responsible for his resignation after his failed referendum the following year.

Italy: A "Sliding" Shock

More extended in time and more immediate in its effects was the Italian cycle of protest. First, as Figure 4.1 shows, the cycle of contention in Italy began before May 1968 with the student occupations of 1967. Second, the workers' movement peaked not in 1968 but in the "Hot Autumn" of the following year. Third, and most important, the cycle extended well into the 1970s, especially if we take into account one of the distinctive features that Italy experienced—a profound period of both violence and institutionalization of the movement (della Porta and Tarrow 1986; Tarrow 1989; della Porta 1995). Italy's cycle of contention was part of an extended episode of conflict that both preceded and followed the year 1968.

United States: A Shock Following a "Long Movement"

Still more encompassing than Italy's experience with mass protest was the period of contention in the United States. Here it began much earlier—with the civil rights protests of the early 1960s. Civil rights had been high on the public agenda since the key Supreme Court case of *Brown v. Board of Education* in 1954,[8] but it was in the early 1960s that the United States experienced a sustained period of contention, beginning with the sit-ins and Freedom Rides in the South. This period of contention continued with the urban uprisings of the mid-1960s, and exploded into the protests against the Vietnam War that peaked in the late 1960s and early 1970s.

Of course, 1968 was in many ways the peak of the cycle: that year saw the assassinations of Martin Luther King Jr. and Robert F. Kennedy, urban riots in over 100 cities, and a "police riot" in which over 20,000 police and National Guardsmen attacked anti-war protesters around the Democratic presidential convention. This episode contributed directly to subsequent reforms in the Democratic Party, and it

---

8. 347 US 483 (1954).

also marked a dividing line between support for, and opposition to, the mass politics of the decade, which was the origin of the deep political polarization of American politics (McAdam and Kloos 2014).

The antiwar movement declined as the government began to withdraw from Vietnam, but the new decade saw many former civil rights and antiwar protesters gravitating into the feminist and environmental movements (McAdam 1988). At the same time, spinoff movements arose among Latinos and Native Americans, the gay and lesbian movement began to stir, and a few extreme militants moved into armed struggle. Figure 4.2, drawn from the best existing dataset on the dynamics of collective action, charts the time flow in the 1960s of the two main sectors of contention in the United States—civil rights and the peace movement—as well as the dynamic of the cycle in general.

But it was not only the social movement surge of the 1960s that mattered for the future of American politics. Growing out of the internal struggles in the Democratic Party over race and representation at the party's 1968 Chicago convention, a series of campaign reforms were passed that limited the influence of party elites on their own nomination processes, making the support of mobilized citizen groups far more critical than they had been in the past (Berry 2000). From the ill-fated McGovern nomination in the 1972 presidential election to the infiltration of the Tea Party into the Republican congressional delegation after Barack Obama's election in 2008, mobilized minorities came to play a critical role in the nomination process and—because they are typically more extreme than the average party member—they helped lead to the polarization of the two major parties (Tarrow 2021).

Looking at the United States and Italy together, we see in their extended cycles of protest processes of both radicalization and institutionalization. While the French "May" did not endure even into the following year, In Italy, aboveground radical groups like *Lotta Continua* (the Fight Goes On) and *Potere Operaio* (Workers' Power) generated militant minorities that moved into armed struggle (Tarrow 1989). In the United States, black power groups emerged from the largely peaceful civil rights movement, and militant minorities melted away from mass movements like the Students for a Democratic Society (SDS) into underground groups like the Weathermen.

There were also significant conservative countermovements in both countries: in the United States, the libertarian thrust of the '60s movements led to the beginning of a conservative countermovement with a strong religious component, while in Italy, the excesses of the "extraparliamentary" movement added fuel to the recrudescence of far-right violent fascist organizations.

But at the same time, major elements that grew out of the movements of the late 1960s helped to transform institutional politics by entering the parties of the center-left. If the protest movements of the late 1960s were a shock that generated a critical juncture, that juncture was an extended episode of conflict that bridged institutional and noninstitutional politics, and triggered incremental mechanisms like radicalization, institutionalization, and party reform, rather than a single critical juncture that expanded synoptically across the society, as occurred in France.

THE LEGACIES OF "1968"

What was the legacy of those moments for the institutions of these three countries? Collier and Munck describe the mechanisms that produce a critical juncture's legacy. They write:

> The legacy is an enduring, self-perpetuating institutional inheritance of the critical juncture that persists and is stable for a substantial period. . . . In parallel with mechanisms of production that generate the legacy, scholars also analyze mechanisms of reproduction that account for its stability. (Collier and Munck 2017b: 6)

Of course, deciding exactly what are the major mechanisms at work in a critical juncture is no easy task. Given space concerns, I will limit myself to focusing on mechanisms of policy change that are produced in the immediate wake of a shock—and that may or may not be reproduced over the longer term. I will argue that the key to the reproducibility of significant change is not the shock itself but antecedent conditions like the strength of the state, and also the enduring strength of the social movements that are spawned by the initial shock. In some cases, movements decline rapidly after the disappointments of the initial shock are effectively repressed; in others, they remain active but often take more institutional form; and in still others, they become anchored to the party system, through which they are in a position to influence policy making over the long haul (Schlozman 2015; Milkis and Tichenor 2019; Tarrow 2021).

France: Rapid Change and Policy Reversal

From this point of view, the French case is the most interesting, because it led to rapid policy change after May, followed by a substantial return to the previous status quo. Capdevielle and Mouriaux focus on the initial impact. Writing on the twentieth anniversary of 1968, they argue that

> despite the retreat of the movement and its rejection in the ballot box, the Events were the carriers of potentialities that, by one means or another, durably mortgaged the French political system in a way that had to be immediately faced. (Capdevielle and Mouriaux 1988: 219, author's translation)

Capdevielle and Mouriaux are right about the *immediate production* of policy changes in the wake of May. But in my view, the changes they documented were not reproduced, because the French state was too resilient to be permanently "mortgaged." After May, the same political class retained power as before, while the social movement it generated collapsed too rapidly to have an enduring impact on policy. Three examples illustrate this combination of policy change and reversal.

First, as the result of its high-level summit meeting with the trade unions in late May, the Gaullist government made a number of policy concessions to labor—in particular, dramatically increasing the wages of the lowest-paid workers. Those results were rejected as too modest by part of the labor movement but were heralded by most of the left as a major success of the protests of the previous weeks. Yet only a few months later, the government executed a financial maneuver that sharply reduced the effect of its concessions (Salvati 1981). True, some labor reforms survived the end of the period of reform, but the gap in incomes between the lowest-paid workers and the rest of the French labor force persisted to the present day.

Second, nowhere more than in the universities were the hopes of May kindled. Shortly after the end of the 1968 mobilizations, a reformist Minister of Education, Edgar Faure, instigated negotiations with students, assistants, and professors toward the passage of a reform of the university system. The production of this reform was greeted with anticipation by reformists both inside the government and in the opposition, even if the residue of the student movement had doubts about its significance. Alas, the reform that emerged from the intricate gears of French politics was soon turned to the advantage of the academic mandarins of the old system.[9]

This institutional innovation, produced with great fanfare on the heels of the dramatic student revolt in May, could not deter the reproduction in new form of the traditional system of higher education. Building on the power of the academic mandarins, state and Gaullist party elites whittled down the reform until it looked nothing like what the students and their progressive supporters in the academy had called for. As in the case of the failure of the working class to narrow the wage differential created by the negotiations of May, the student movement and its political supporters lacked the ongoing strength to prevent this.

Thus, in two domains where one might most expect major innovation, there was neither synoptic nor incremental change, but rather dramatic policy shift followed by a conservative policy reversal. In a third area—reform of the centralized French state—reform was so minimal that it did not even warrant the term "decentralization" and was instead labeled "deconcentration" by observers (Gourevitch 1980).

Italy: Episodic and Diffuse Reform

In Italy, the policy effects of the movements of the late 1960s were episodic and diffuse, yet the impact of the movements on the party system was profound.

The first thing to note is that reformism in Italy began during the early 1960s, when, with an exquisitely political logic, the governing Christian Democracy Party (DC) maneuvered the previously oppositional Socialist Party (PSI) into a center-left coalition and separated it from its long-time Communist (PCI) ally. The reforms of this "opening to the left" remained unimpressive until the movements of the later part of the 1960s forced more vigorous reforms on the government. The most important was the modernization of industrial relations, which passed in 1969, giving

---

9. I rely here on Tarrow (1993) and the much more sustained study by Fomerand (1975).

union representatives access to the shop floor and unleashing a tidal wave of both organized and wildcat strikes (Tarrow 1989: Ch. 7).

As for the student movement—which had so rapidly disintegrated in France—it continued to foster new movement organizations long after the French movement declined, some of them sliding into clandestine organized violence, but most of them eventually blending into the party system (della Porta and Tarrow 1986). The most long-lasting effect on the university system was the recruitment of thousands of graduates into research and teaching positions and the virtual institutionalization of the repertoire of student mass assemblies (*assemblearismo*), which slowed governance of the universities to a standstill.

Within the Italian state, a major institutional reform, passed in 1970, created a new level of regional government that dispersed political power across the territory of the country, eventually absorbing an increasing share of national income (Putnam 1993). Here, the contrast with French "deconcentration" was most dramatic, for while the latter lodged new powers in regional prefects, the Italian system created a regional political elite around elected governors (Gourevitch 1980; Putnam 1993).

The United States: An Extended Period of Reform

In the United States, because the movements of the late 1960s built on the heroic phase of the civil rights movement, the policy response was both extended and diffuse (Milkis 1993). However, it did encompass dramatic policy innovations, beginning a half-decade earlier with the Civil Rights and Voting Rights Acts in 1964 and 1965 and extending well into the 1970s. Within the framework of twentieth-century U.S. history, these two pieces of legislation stand out for their singular importance— i.e., for their dramatic impact on race relations and for the representation and rights of African Americans. Although that agenda continues to evolve and may even be suffering reversals in the twenty-first century, these policy initiatives of the 1960s represent an extraordinary discontinuity, and a stride forward, in this domain of policy. Lyndon B. Johnson's War on Poverty, though partially eclipsed by the evolving calamity of the Vietnam War, was likewise a substantial innovation in social policy. With regard to Vietnam, the anti-war movement unquestionably hastened the withdrawal from Vietnam—thereby again reflecting a dramatic impact on public policy.

The United States perhaps did not experience the kinds of dramatic policy reversals that France did. But the civil rights and voting rights reforms and the shifts in the electorate that followed led to important changes in administrative practice. On the one hand, the failure of the Southern states to implement the *Brown* decision led to an increase in the national government's intervention into what had previously been state prerogatives (Klarman 2004). In some cases, this occurred through the intervention of the Supreme Court, and in others by implicit coalitions between movement organizations and the national state (Lieberman 2009).

Women's rights were another sector in which mobilized lobbies were able to put pressure on the national state to defend private rights (Costain 1992; Banaszek

2009). The strengthening of the national administrative state in the wake of the movements of the 1960s was in direct opposition to the decentralizing/deconcentrating reforms in France and Italy toward the end of that decade (King and Milkis forthcoming).

But not all the policy and institutional changes that followed the 1960s worked in favor of expanded rights. Weaver (2007) analyzes a different kind of reaction that merits the close attention of scholars concerned with critical junctures. She argues that opposition to progressive innovations such as the Civil Rights and Voting Rights Acts galvanized a broad conservative coalition that launched a remarkable cluster of initiatives, which both held up educational expansion for minorities and made punitive crime policy a hallmark of the U.S. system of criminal justice and social policy for decades. As is well known, these policies were especially disastrous for one of the key communities that benefited from the civil rights and voting rights policies—African Americans.[10] It was only after the turn of the new century that the "punitive turn" in the American justice system began to be reversed (Margulies 2013).

A key lesson emerges here: as scholars look for conservative reactions that seek to defeat policy initiatives growing out of critical junctures, they should not necessarily restrict their attention to exactly the same domains of policy. Although in some respects crime policy overlapped with civil rights and voting rights, this trend describes a separate policy trajectory. Any analysis of the reaction to the reform innovations that grew out of the 1960s would be incomplete if it did not consider this distinct domain of policy.

In sum, the French reforms in industrial relations and higher education emerged quickly in response to the earthquake of May, but were soon whittled away by continued center-right political control of a still-powerful centralized state. The movement that exploded in May was quickly dispersed and was unable to defend

---

10. Weaver (2007) reminds readers of the remarkable scope of these policies:

The death penalty was reinstated, felon disenfranchisement statutes from the First Reconstruction were revived, and the chain gang returned. State and federal governments revised their criminal codes, effectively abolishing parole, imposing mandatory minimum sentences, and allowing juveniles to be incarcerated in adult prisons. Meanwhile, the Law Enforcement Assistance Act of 1965 gave the federal government an altogether new role in crime control; several subsequent policies, beginning with the Crime Control and Safe Streets Act of 1968 and culminating with the Federal Sentencing Guidelines, "war on drugs," and extension of capital crimes, significantly altered the approach. These and other developments had an exceptional and long-lasting effect, with imprisonment increasing six-fold between 1973 and the turn of the century. Certain groups felt the burden of these changes most acutely. As of the last census, fully half of those imprisoned are black and one in three black men between ages 20 [to] 29 are currently [2007] under state supervision. Compared to its advanced industrial counterparts in western Europe, the United States imprisons at least five times more of its citizens per capita. (230)

the gains it had achieved. In Italy, by contrast, the immediate reforms were partial and contradictory, but the movements of the late 1960s changed the dynamic of the party system and instituted major reforms in industrial relations and the territorial structure of the state. In the United States, dramatic policy innovations emerged and were sustained: in civil rights, social policy, and the eventual withdrawal from Vietnam.

Non-Institutional Politics Penetrates Institutional Politics

As these reflections suggest, a key legacy of 1968—or, in the United States, of the entire decade of the 1960s—took the form of lasting changes in the structure of contentious politics. To some extent, from that period on, Western polities became "social movement societies," in which protest became both more common and took a wider variety of forms (Meyer and Tarrow 1998). But what happened most was not so much innovations in either institutional or noninstitutional politics, but rather a much greater impregnation of the latter with the former—that is, with a greater "movementization" of politics (McAdam and Kloos 2014; Schlozman 2015; Tarrow 2018, 2021).

Consider, first, the United States, where the party system at first resisted, and then absorbed, much of the energy of the movements of the period. By the beginning of the 1970s, when it had become clear that "the battle in the streets was an exercise in futility" (McAdam and Kloos 2014: 125), contention shifted to struggle for power within the Democratic Party, where a party reform movement developed out of the struggles of the previous decade. As many members of the Civil Rights and anti-war movements gravitated into that party, a set of internal party reforms increased the power of grassroots voters to shift the party's center of balance to the left and its racial content to favor African Americans and other minorities.

This was ultimately reflected in how that party nominates its candidates. In contrast to the party's 1968 convention, when party oligarchs brushed aside a challenge by anti-war dissidents, by the 1972 convention, insurgents were able to force through a reform of its nominating procedures to replace the traditional power of party elites with a more grassroots-influenced process. This amounted to a revolution in the way electoral politics was going to be organized for the next half century (Shafer 1983). As McAdam and Kloos (2014: 141) conclude, "the revolution was launched, sustained, and orchestrated primarily by self-identified *movement activists* rather than *party members*." Although the initial innovations were limited to the Democratic Party, the Republicans soon followed, allowing an opening for formally apolitical religious militants to enter the local and state levels of that party, ultimately transforming it into the white-based, nationalist party of today.

In Italy, the movements of the late 1960s also had a profound effect on opposition parties. By the middle of the next decade, a generation of activists who had earned their spurs in the student movement had entered the ranks of the trade unions and the Communist Party. Before 1968, the majority of local PCI activists came either from the Communist Youth Federation (FGCI) or from Communist family back-grounds, or both. After that, a majority of activists entered the party from either the student movement or the unions, an infusion of new blood that laid the groundwork for a reformist shift in the party's class base and its policy lines as it surpassed one-third of the vote in the middle of the 1970s (Lange et al. 1989). The Communist party was only prevented from entering a governing coalition in the mid-1970s by the Red Brigades' murder of its prospective ally in the ruling Christian Democrats, Aldo Moro.

In France the locus of innovation was not the Communist Party, but rather the Socialist Party—itself a product of the political shifts brought about in May. The French Communist Party experienced 1968 more as a challenge to Stalinist orthodoxy than as an opportunity for change (Jenson and Ross 1984). But it was actually within the non-Communist left that the old French Section of the Workers' International (SFIO) was taken over by a new generation of activists—many of them veterans of the May movement, who formed a new party, the *Parti Socialiste*—under the leadership of a non-Socialist, François Mitterrand.

Nonetheless, notwithstanding these achievements, of the three countries discussed in this chapter, France—the country that had put its stamp on the memory of 1968—experienced the least infusion of movement energy into its party system. For although de Gaulle left the scene in 1969, his coalition remained in power for the next decade and the opposition Socialists—under the leadership of Mitterrand—did not succeed it in power until 1981.

CONCLUSIONS

Since this chapter has ranged widely across both time and geography, a few words of caution are important: about what has been attempted and what was left out.

First, I limited the analysis to three Western countries that were each touched by the mass politics of the 1960s. A fuller account would have given attention to Germany and to two central European countries—Czechoslovakia and Poland—in which the year 1968 constituted a profound shock. It would also have examined Latin America, where Mexico experienced a major student movement around the Olympics and its violent repression in the same year.

Secondly, the chapter focused only on the most obvious innovations in policy and institutions during the period examined. Much could be gained from extending this analysis to additional policy domains that exhibit diverse outcomes. Alternatively, it could unearth instances in which meaningful innovation is reversed—like the growth of "law and order" legislation in the United States in the wake of the urban riots of the 1960s, which was followed by the massive growth of the prison population. This in turn raises questions about the hypothesized mechanisms of reproduction that failed to sustain the innovations. With a longer time horizon than is explored here, scholars might also look for trajectories of incremental change that add up to substantial transformations, as well as instances where such trajectories are deflected or defeated. For those interested in change *within* institutions, a key finding of the chapter concerns the penetration of institutional politics by noninstitutional politics. We have interpreted this as a greater "movementization" of politics and a shift to "social movement societies." This interpretation has profound implications for politics in Western societies in the twenty-first century.

In the time horizon considered here it is clear that even after the most dramatic political and social shocks, the institutional and policy innovations that follow may be attenuated and erratic and may trigger significant conservative reactions. As Riedl and Roberts point out in their contribution to this book (see Chapter 6), both antecedent factors and contingent choices must be taken into account when examining the degree and the nature of the critical juncture that follows a major shock.

For example, the 1960s in the American South saw the rise of a network of private academies designed to extract white students from the feared integration of the public school system following the *Brown* decision. This triggered the rise of the religious right around the issue of exemption from taxation, which the Internal Revenue Service refused to accord these schools. The long-term result was a blending of religious and white racial activism that has lasted to the present day (Milkis and Tichenor 2019: 205–06).

Another countermovement arose in the legal system. As Teles (2008) shows, a conservative legal movement was triggered by what conservatives saw as the successes of the liberal legal movement that peaked in the 1960s. To reiterate the argument of Rodgers (2011) with which this chapter began, the protagonists and antagonists of these innovations—and some social scientists as well—may have exaggerated expectations about the magnitude—and the homogeneity—of the changes that follow a major shock.

Stepping further back to consider the wider objectives of this chapter, one goal has been to place the French May in a comparative perspective. Many analysts have taken the French case of 1968 as their lodestar and then turned to other cases as if they were derivatives of what happened there. But that makes of a particularly dramatic shock both a determination of an entire critical juncture and a measuring rod for what happened in other countries during roughly the same period. This determination says both too much and too little about 1968. It says too much in that it neglects the fact that the innovations of the French May were far weaker than often imagined and were reversed soon after; and it says too little in that it gives short shrift to the distinctive properties of the corresponding periods of mass politics in other countries.

A closely related goal of this chapter has been to illustrate the virtues of the comparative method. Comparison across these three cases proved to be a fruitful approach to gaining new insight into both the nature of the shocks at the peak of this period of mass politics and to the nature and durability of the innovations that followed. Although the French Events were singularly dramatic and event-*ful*, the actors who triggered them soon disappeared from the streets, and the legacy was less dramatic and less enduring than what many observers predicted at the time (Touraine 1971). Conversely, although the Italian mass politics of the late 1960s had less transnational resonance than the French May, they turned into a "sliding May" that produced far greater changes in the shape of the state, in industrial relations, and in higher education. Finally, the American period of mass politics began earlier and lasted longer than in either European country. It led to the passage of civil rights and voting rights legislation, to a growth in the power of the central executive vis-à-vis the states, and to a partial "movementization" of the internal life of the two major political parties—a shift whose full implications would be felt in the Republican party as it was infiltrated first by the Tea Party (Blum 2020) and then by the Trumpian movement (Tarrow 2021: Ch. 8).

The contribution of comparison involves not only juxtaposing national cases, but also public policies. Policy innovation and policy reversal can differ greatly across different domains of policy, and a comparison with additional domains will be valuable for fleshing out the arguments presented above. Further, as we saw with the dramatic expansion of civil rights and voting rights in the United States, the political reaction—which was really a counterattack—occurred in a different domain, i.e., crime policy.

Among the lingering questions, one is certainly why the French labor and student movements did not mobilize again when key policy gains were reversed. The answer may be found in the idea of 1968 as a distinctive, condensed episode of mobilization that was not readily repeated, even in response to serious policy setbacks. This calls for further reflection on the nature of these intense episodes, as opposed to incremental politics in "normal times." There is still much work that remains to be done, which indicates the importance of both the "shock" of 1968 and the broader implications of the critical junctures that followed.

BIBLIOGRAPHY

Andrews, Kenneth T., and Michael Biggs. 2006. "The Dynamics of Protest Diffusion: Movement Organizations, Social Networks, and News Media in the 1960 Sit-Ins." *American Sociological Review* 71(5): 752–77.

Banaszek, Lee Ann. 2009. "Moving Feminist Activists Inside the American State: The Rise of a State-Movement Intersection and Its Effects on State Policy." In Larry Jacobs and Desmond King (eds.), *The Unsustainable American State* (pp. 223–54). New York, NY: Oxford University Press.

Berry, Jeffrey M. 2000. *The New Liberalism: The Rising Power of Citizen Groups.* Washington, DC: The Brookings Institution.

Blum, Rachel M. 2020. *How the Tea Party Captured the GOP: Insurgent Factions in American Politics.* Chicago IL: University of Chicago Press.

Boyd, Richard W. 1985. "Electoral Change in the United States and Great Britain." *British Journal of Political Science* 15(4): 517–28.

Capdevielle, Jacques, and René Mouriaux. 1988. *Mai 68: L'entre-deux de la modernité. Histoire de trente ans.* Paris: Presses de la Fondation Nationale des Sciences Politiques.

Collier, David, and Gerardo L. Munck (eds.). 2017a. "Symposium on Critical Junctures and Historical Legacies." *Qualitative and Multi-Method Research* 15(1): 2–47.

Collier, David, and Gerardo L. Munck. 2017b. "Building Blocks and Methodological Challenges: A Framework for Studying Critical Junctures." *Qualitative and Multi-Method Research* 15(1): 2–9.

Collier, Ruth Berins, and David Collier. 1991. *Shaping the Political Arena: Critical Junctures, the Labor Movement, and Regime Dynamics in Latin America.* Princeton, NJ: Princeton University Press.

Costain, Anne. 1992. *Inviting Women's Rebellion: A Political Process Approach to the Women's Movement.* Baltimore, MD: Johns Hopkins University Press.

Crouch, Colin, and Alessandro Pizzorno (eds.). 1978. *The Resurgence of Class Conflict in Western Europe.* 2 Vols. London, UK: MacMillan.

della Porta, Donatella. 1995. *Social Movements, Political Violence and the State: A Comparative Analysis of Italy and Germany.* New York, NY: Cambridge University Press.

della Porta, Donatella, and Sidney Tarrow. 1986. "Unwanted Children: Political Violence and the Cycle of Protest in Italy." *European Journal of Political Research* 14(5–6): 607–32.

Dudziak, Mary L. 2000. *Cold War Civil Rights: Race and the Image of American Democracy.* Princeton, NJ: Princeton University Press.

Dunning, Thad. 2017. "Contingency and Determinism in Research on Critical Junctures: Avoiding the Inevitability Framework." *Qualitative & Multi-Method Research* 15(1): 41–47.

Fomerand, Jacques. 1975. "Policy Formulation and Change in Gaullist France. The 1968 Orientation Act of Higher Education." *Comparative Politics* 8(1): 59–89.

Francis, Megan Ming. 2014. *Civil Rights and the Making of the Modern American State.* New York, NY: Cambridge University Press.

Gourevitch, Peter A. 1980. *Paris and the Provinces: The Politics of Local Government Reform in France.* Berkeley, CA: University of California Press.

Hall, Jacquelyne Dowd. 2005. "The Long Civil Rights Movement and the Political Uses of the Past." *Journal of American History* 91(4): 1233–63.

Hall, Stuart. 1986. "Cultural Studies: Two Paradigms." In Richard Collins (ed.), *Media, Culture, and Society: A Critical Reader* (pp. 277–94). Beverly Hills, CA: Sage.

Jenson, Jane, and George Ross. 1984. *The View from Inside: A French Communist Cell in Crisis.* Berkeley CA: University of California Press.

King, Desmond, and Sidney M. Milkis. Forthcoming. "Polarization, the Administrative State, and Executive-Centered Partisanship." In Robert Lieberman, Suzanne Mettler, and Kenneth M. Roberts (eds.), *Democratic Resilience: Can the United States Withstand Rising Polarization.* New York, NY: Cambridge University Press.

Klarman, Michael J. 2004. *From Jim Crow to Civil Rights: The Supreme Court and the Struggle for Racial Equality.* Oxford, UK: Oxford University Press.

Lange, Peter, Cynthia Irvin, and Sidney Tarrow. 1989. "Mobilization, Social Movements and Party Recruitment: The Italian Communist Party since the 1960s." *British Journal of Political Science* 20(1): 15–42.

Lieberman, Robert C. 2009. "Civil Rights and the Democratization Trap: The Public-Private Nexus and the Building of American Democracy." In Desmond King, Robert C. Lieberman, Gretchen Ritter, and Laurence Whitehead (eds.). *Democratization in America: A Comparative-Historical Analysis* (pp. 211–32). Baltimore MD: Johns Hopkins University Press.

Margulies, Joseph. 2013. *What Changed When Everything Changed: 9/11 and the Making of National Identity*. New Haven, CT: Yale University Press.

McAdam, Doug. 1988. *Freedom Summer*. New York, NY: Oxford University Press.

McAdam, Doug, and Karina Kloos. 2014. *Deeply Divided: Racial Politics and Social Movements in Post-War America*. New York, NY: Oxford University Press.

Meyer, David S., and Sidney Tarrow (eds.). 1998. *The Social Movement Society: Contentious Politics for a New Century*. Lanham, MD: Rowman & Littlefield.

Milkis, Sidney M. 1993. *The President and the Parties: The Transformation of the American Party System Since the New Deal*. New York, NY: Oxford University Press.

Milkis, Sidney M., and Daniel J. Tichenor. 2019. *Rivalry and Reform: Presidents, Social Movements, and the Transformation of American Politics*. Chicago, IL: University of Chicago Press.

Miller, James. 1987. *Power Is in the Streets: From Port Huron to the Streets of Chicago*. New York, NY: Simon and Shuster.

Pedersen, Mogens N. 1979. "The Dynamics of European Party Systems: Changing Patterns of Electoral Volatility." *European Journal of Political Research* 7(1): 1–26.

Pizzorno, Alessandro. 1978. "Political Exchange and Collective Identity in Industrial Conflict." In Colin Crouch and Alessandro Pizzorno (eds.), *The Resurgence of Class Conflict in Western Europe since 1968* (Vol. II; pp. 277–98). London, UK: Macmillan Press.

Putnam, Robert D. 1993 *Making Democracy Work: Civic Traditions in Modern Italy*. Princeton, NJ: Princeton University Press.

Roberts, Kenneth M. 2014. *Changing Course in Latin America: Party Systems in the Neoliberal Era*. New York, NY: Cambridge University Press.

Rodgers, Daniel T. 2011. *Age of Fracture*. Cambridge, MA: Harvard University Press.

Salvati, Michele. 1981. "May 1968 and the Hot Autumn of 1969: The Responses of Two Ruling Classes." In Suzanne Berger (ed.), *Organizing Interests in Western Europe* (pp. 329–63). New York, NY: Cambridge University Press.

Schlozman, Daniel. 2015. *When Movements Anchor Parties. Electoral Alignments in American History*. Princeton NJ: Princeton University Press.

Schlozman, Daniel, and Sam Rosenberg. 2019. "The Hollow Parties." In Frances Lee and Nolan McCarty (eds.), *Can America Govern Itself?* (pp. 120–52). New York, NY: Cambridge University Press.

Shafer, Byron E. 1983. *Quiet Revolution: The Struggle for the Democratic Party and the Shaping of Post-Reform Politics*. New York, NY: Russell Sage Foundation.

Slater, Dan, and Erica Simmons. 2010. "Informative Regress: Critical Antecedents in Comparative Politics." *Comparative Political Studies* 43(7): 886–917.

Tarrow, Sidney. 1977. *Between Center and Periphery: Grassroots Politicians in Italy and France*. New Haven, CT: Yale University Press.

———. 1989. *Democracy and Disorder: Protest and Politics in Italy, 1965–1974*. New York, NY: Oxford University Press.

———. 1993. "Social Protest and Policy Reform: May 1968 and the Loi d'Orientation in France." *Comparative Political Studies* 25(4): 579–607.

———. 2012. *Strangers at the Gates. Movements and States in Contentious Politics*. New York, NY: Cambridge University Press.

———. 2018. "Rhythms of Resistance: The Anti-Trumpian Movement in a Cycle of Contention." In David S. Meyer and Sidney Tarrow (eds.), *The Resistance: The Dawn of the Anti-Trump Opposition Movement* (pp. 187–20). New York, NY: Oxford University Press.

———. 2021. *Movements and Parties: Critical Connections in American Political Development.* New York, NY: Cambridge University Press.

Teles, Steven M. 2008. *The Rise of the Conservative Legal Movement: The Battle for Control of the Law.* Princeton NJ: Princeton University Press.

Tilly, Charles. 2006. *Regimes and Repertoires.* New York, NY: Cambridge University Press.

Touraine, Alain. 1971. *The May Movement: Revolt and Reform.* New York, NY: Random House.

Weaver, Velsa M. 2007. "Frontlash: Race and the Development of Punitive Crime Policy." *American Political Development* 21(2): 230–65.

Wilson, Frank L. 1969. "The French Left and the Elections of 1968." *World Politics* 21(4): 539–74.

Zolberg, Aristede. 1972. "Moments of Madness." *Politics and Society* 2(2): 183–207.

II

FRAMEWORK AND METHODS
Historical Causation and Causal Inference

5

The Theoretical Foundations of Critical Juncture Research

Critique and Reconstruction

Gerardo L. Munck

Research on critical junctures is a well-established tradition that sheds light on the historical origin, endurance, and change of social order. The core ideas used in this research have been systematized in the form of a recognizable theoretical framework.[1] This framework, or parts of it, has been used to study various topics, such as state formation, political regimes and democracy, party systems, public policy, government performance, and economic development. And the original arguments developed in this literature constitute important contributions to central areas of inquiry in the social sciences.[2] Critical juncture research can rightly be characterized as a progressive research program that offers a distinctive approach to history and historical causation.[3]

However, recent discussions about critical junctures have generated strife within the critical juncture tradition. Since around 2000, many authors have presented

I would like to acknowledge the useful comments and suggestions received from Richard Bensel, Erin Baggott Carter, Brett Carter, David Collier, Laura Deneckere, Tulia Falleti, Marcus Kreuzer, Sebastián Mazzuca, and David Waldner.

1. This framework draws on contributions by Kuhn (1970 [1962]), Lipset and Rokkan (1967), Stinchcombe (1968: Ch. 3), Eldredge and Gould (1972; see also Gould 2007), Krasner (1984; 1988), David (1985), Arthur (1989, 1994), North (1990), and Collier and Collier (1991: Ch. 1).

2. On the extensive substantive research on critical junctures, see Appendix III.

3. For sweeping overviews of key approaches to historical analysis, see Nisbet (1969) and Sanderson (1990). For approaches within distinct disciplines, see Ingold (1986) on anthropology; Smith (1973), Moore (1974), and Sztompka (1993) on sociology; Burke (1979; 1993: Ch. 5) on history; and Pierson (2004) and Grzymała-Busse (2011) on political science.

their views about key conceptual and theoretical matters in this research.[4] And this collective effort has helped to refine old ideas and introduce important innovations. At the same time, scholars have frequently defended counterposed views and thus sown doubts about a question as basic as, what are the building blocks of the critical juncture framework? There is even considerable disagreement about the nature of a critical juncture. In short, a problem facing this field of research is that the framework that should provide the common ideas for the research program—there is no research program without at least some agreement on core ideas—has been articulated in different, frequently incompatible ways.

This chapter reviews the theoretical foundations of critical juncture research and, based on a consideration of how foundational issues should be addressed, suggests that some changes to the core ideas used in this research are needed. The aim of the chapter is to show how the critical juncture framework can be reconstructed on stronger foundations.

The first section focuses on social statics, i.e., how and why order is maintained in a society, and discusses the way critical juncture research should account for the historical origins of social orders. It makes the case that all research on historical causation must address two problems: (1) the problem of infinite regress, i.e., the possibility that historically oriented research will constantly push back the analysis to earlier events and hence not find an adequate starting point; and (2) the problem of distal nonrecurring causes, i.e., the difficulty of arguing convincingly that a change that occurred in the distant past and has ceased to recur is the cause of a much later outcome. It claims that research on critical junctures should address these problems by studying rapid, discontinuous, macro-level, changes—i.e., critical junctures—and spells out how such changes generate persistent effects through a distinct causal chain that includes a repeated cause-effect pair. It also argues that greater attention to stabilizing causal mechanisms, micro-level processes that bridge macro-level variables, is needed.

The second section focuses on social dynamics, i.e., how and why societies change over time and, in particular, the task of explaining why critical junctures occur. It discusses two basic problems all explanations of change must confront: (1) the problem of endogenous and exogenous sources of change, i.e., the challenge of deciding whether to give primacy to endogenous or exogenous factors or, if both are treated

---

4. An incomplete list of recent works includes Thelen (1999; 2003; 2004), Mahoney (2000; 2001), Pierson (2000; 2004), Garud and Karnøe (2001), Katznelson (2003), Crouch and Farrell (2004), Orren and Skowronek (2004), Streeck and Thelen (2005b), Hogan (2006), Martin and Sunley (2006), Boas (2007), Capoccia and Kelemen (2007), Djelic and Quack (2007), Greer (2008), Baumgartner and Jones (2009), Ebbinghaus (2009), Howlett (2009), Sydow et al. (2009), Beyer (2010), Djelic (2010), Garud et al. (2010), Slater and Simmons (2010), Streeck (2010), Soifer (2012), Bernhard (2015), Capoccia (2015; 2016a; 2016b), Rixen and Viola (2015), Sarigil (2015), Fioretos et al. (2016), Acharya et al. (2018), García-Montoya and Mahoney (2020), and Gerschewski (2021).

as part of an explanation, how to combine them; and (2) the problem of structure and agency, i.e., the task of deciding whether to give primacy to structural factors or to actors and their choices or, if both factors and actors are used in an explanation, how to integrate them. Most basically, it maintains that research should account for the occurrence of critical junctures in a balanced way, avoiding both the pitfall of one-sided explanations that see change as driven by endogenous factors or exogenous shocks and the danger of historical and structural determinism. More specifically, it holds that research needs to recognize the limits of purely endogenous accounts of change more explicitly, move beyond a conception that treats agency as a matter of choosing between externally given alternatives and that equates agency with contingency, and fully appreciate the importance of theorizing change mechanisms.

This chapter engages with an ongoing discussion. Some of its arguments build on, support, and refine some views in the literature. Others imply that some ideas in the literature are erroneous and should be discarded. And yet others involve ideas that are new, at least with regard to the literature on critical junctures. Thus, to clarify how the reconstructed framework that is proposed coincides with and differs from ideas in the literature, the claims made here are compared to current thinking about critical junctures.

The conclusion of the chapter draws together its main arguments.

SOCIAL STATICS

Critical juncture research seeks to understand the historical origins of social orders and rejects presentism or short-termism, the assumption that patterns of the current world can be explained fully by reference to causes in the recent past (Rueschemeyer et al. 1992: 7, 23, 35; Rueschemeyer 2009: 147–51). That is, it puts the focus on temporally distal, as opposed to proximate, causes.[5] More specifically, it spotlights events (X) that lie in a distant past and have ceased to occur and hence do not directly cause a much later outcome (Y) (see Figure 5.1).

$$X_{t-n} \longrightarrow \cdots\cdots\cdots \longrightarrow Y_t$$

Figure 5.1 An (Incomplete) Model of a Distal Cause

---

5. This distinction is similar to Stinchcombe's (1968: 101–16) between historical and constant causes. However, Stinchcombe's definition of a historical cause is rather narrow, so it is preferable to use the more general term distant or distal causes. It is also convenient to contrast this distinction to the distinction between ultimate and proximate causes (Mayr 1961), given that the notion of ultimate cause conveys a sense of causal primacy rather than temporal distance.

Given this interest in distal causes, critical juncture research inevitably faces two problems. The first is the problem of infinite regress, which concerns the question: How far back must we go to find the event (X) that is seen as the historical source of a later outcome (Y)? That is, in terms of Figure 5.1, how is the value of "n" determined? The second is the problem of distal nonrecurring causes, which raises the question: How can an event in a distant past that has ceased to occur be considered as the cause of a much later effect? That is, in terms of Figure 5.1, how can the gap between initial cause (X) and ultimate outcome (Y) be filled or how can an unbroken causal chain joining cause and outcome be constructed?

These are long-standing problems in the study of distal causes. Yet scholars continue to disagree on whether they can be solved and, if so, how. A common view is that contiguity is essential to the relation of causation and hence that the idea of causation at a temporal distance is suspect (Hume 1896 [1739–1740]: 73–76). Some methodologists consider that the problem of infinite regress is unsolvable and thus doubt the viability of arguments based on distal causes (King et al. 1994: 86; Gerring 2007: 181–82). Moreover, even authors who treat these two problems as solvable do not offer consistent recommendations regarding how to solve them. A few authors suggest that critical junctures provide a solution to the problem of infinite regress but conceptualize critical junctures in different ways (Krasner 1984; Collier and Collier 1991: Ch. 1; Mahoney 2000; Pierson 2004; Capoccia and Kelemen 2007). Many authors argue that the problem of distal nonrecurring causes is solvable, but present different proposals to bridge distal causes and later outcomes (Stinchcombe 1968; Collier and Collier 1991: Ch.1; Mahoney 2000; Martin and Sunley 2010).

Therefore, a detailed discussion about how critical juncture research can and should tackle the problems of infinite regress and distal nonrecurring causes is called for.

Infinite Regress

The problem of infinite regress, briefly introduced above, can be formulated more fully as follows. Any research that suggests that an explanation of certain enduring structural features of contemporary societies (e.g., why do some societies have welfare states and other do not?) must address the historical origin of these features, and not only temporally proximate causes, which instantly invites the following questions: How far back is it necessary to go? Is it enough to reach back to a prior decade or maybe a prior century? Is it necessary to go back to the beginning of time or at least the birth of societies, an extremely demanding requirement? Is there any basis for cutting into the long flow of history by positing a meaningful and nonarbitrary starting point to what might be represented as a long causal chain?

A distinctive solution to this problem is provided by conceptualizing *critical junctures* as *rapid discontinuous changes* at the *macro-level* of society or the international system. When understood in these terms, critical junctures introduce a *qualitative novelty* that marks a before and after and provides a basis for identifying a point of entry into the stream of history and solving the problem of infinite regress.[6] It is imperative, therefore, to elucidate what a critical juncture is and is not.

Critical Junctures as Rapid Discontinuous Changes

The idea that a critical juncture is a rapid discontinuous change can be clarified by distinguishing discontinuous from continuous change. This contrast has been conveyed in different terms. Social theorists contrast change of a system—also called structural change—to change within a system (Parsons 1951: Ch. 11; Radcliffe-Brown 1957: 71–89).[7] Focusing on the sphere of knowledge, Kuhn (1970 [1962]: 181) distinguishes revolutionary paradigm change from the incremental, cumulative change that occurs within a paradigm. Yet the basic point is that not all change involves differences in degree or movement along some continuum and that discontinuous change differs from continuous change in that it involves the introduction of some new property or qualitative novelty.

To further explain the idea of a critical juncture, it is necessary to distinguish rapid from gradual discontinuous change. This difference corresponds to the contrast between Eldredge and Gould's (1972) saltationist (or punctuated equilibrium) model and Darwin's (1964 [1859]) gradualist model (see Figure 5.2). Both models are branching models of macroevolution and thus recognize the role of discontinuous changes in evolution—these changes are depicted by the nodes at which new branches sprout. However, the distinctiveness of a saltationist model is that it posits that change can involve a rapid discontinuous change—a critical juncture—that introduces a new property in a sudden burst, or what social scientists have variously characterized as a "leap-like change" (Schumpeter 2005 [1932]: 115), a "great spurt" (Gerschenkron 1962: 206–07), a "step-like" change (Gellner 1964: 45), or a "power jump" (Mann 1986: 3, 524–25).[8]

Critical Junctures as Macro-Level Changes

The second attribute of a critical juncture, that it is change at the macro-level, can be clarified in terms of the distinction between properties that are not possessed intrinsically by a unit—which can be identified as macro properties—and properties possessed intrinsically by a unit (e.g., individuals, groups, states) or micro properties

---

6. On discontinuous changes as a solution to the problem of infinite regress, see Bunge (2009: 125–47).

7. See also Dahrendorf (1959: Ch. 1) and Mann (1986: 3).

8. It is worth noting that such rapid discontinuous changes do not happen instantaneously. For example, punctuations in evolutionary biology typically lasted between 50,000 and 100,000 years or longer (Eldredge and Gould 1972). In turn, the critical junctures studied by Collier and Collier (1991: 32) unfolded over nine to twenty-three years.

Gerardo L. Munck

(a) Saltationism: Qualitative
novelty and episodic spurts

(b) Gradualism: Qualitative
novelty and slow, steady change

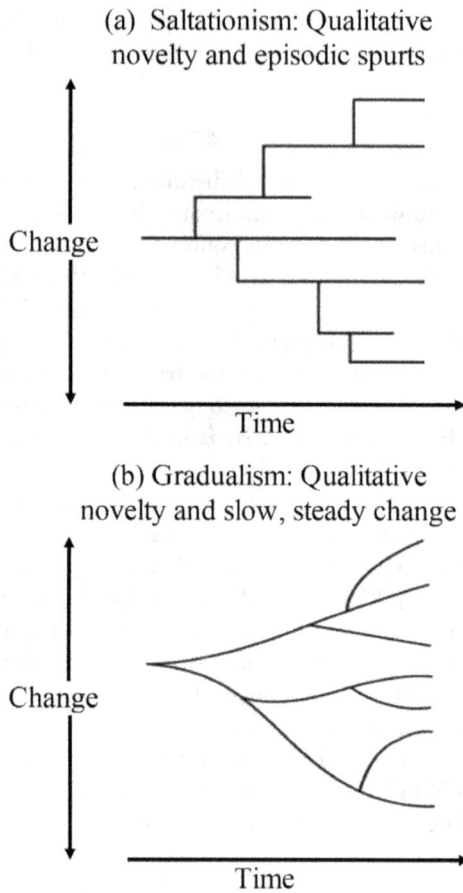

Figure 5.2 Two Kinds of Branching Macroevolution: Saltationism and Gradualism.
Note: New branches indicate discontinuous change or qualitative novelty.
"Saltationism" is the term used to describe the model of change associated with the
idea of punctuated equilibrium. Adapted from Eldredge and Gould (1972: 109, 113).

(Bunge 1996: 17–23).[9] Understood this way, a critical juncture can be a change in
a property units have by virtue of their relationship to other units. For example, it
could involve a change in the class structure of a society (e.g., the concentration of
wealth in the hands of the 1 percent) or the structure of the global economy (e.g., the

---

9. It is conventional to think of micro as related to persons and macro to a social system.
However, what may be regarded as macro in one context (e.g., the state) may be treated as
micro in another (e.g., in a discussion of the global order). What is crucial, then, is whether a
property is intrinsic to a unit or not.

emergence of a semi-periphery between the core and the periphery). A critical juncture can also be a change in properties possessed by wholes. For instance, it could involve the change from a socialist to a capitalist economy or from an authoritarian to a democratic political regime. Briefly, a critical juncture can be a change in either a structural or a systemic property—what is loosely seen as a big change.[10]

Because a critical juncture is a big change, it is also useful to distinguish it from a total revolution. A critical juncture can be a change in one aspect of society (e.g., the political system), one part of an aspect of society (e.g., the political regime, which is one part of the political system), or even one part of a part of an aspect of society (e.g., theories of physics, which is one discipline of the sciences, which is part of culture). Moreover, a critical juncture can change some structure partially rather than fully. As Kuhn (1970 [1962]: 49, 92) puts it, revolutions can change systems "in part" or "in whole" and hence "there can be small revolutions as well as large ones." But a critical juncture can never be a total revolution. Indeed, there are no changes that involve the replacement of an entire system and, if critical junctures are seen as total revolutions, the concept of a critical juncture would have no empirical referents and would cease to provide a solution to the problem of infinite regress.

In short, a critical juncture is a distinct kind of change. It is not a micro-level change, one that involves intrinsic properties of units. Yet it is also not a total revolution. Indeed, it can be a range of big changes that are structural or systemic in nature.[11]

Summary

Historically oriented research must address the problem of infinite regress. And a focus on critical junctures provides a solution to this problem. The search for distal causes of social outcomes does not have to reach back to some elusive first cause. Rather, it can cut into the stream of history where some rapid, discontinuous change at the macro level occurred (e.g., the formation of modern states, the transition to industrial capitalism, the introduction of multiparty elections). Prior events can be analyzed inasmuch as considering possible causes of a critical juncture is of substantive interest or of methodological value. Nonetheless, the identification of qualitative novelties introduced by critical junctures provides a well justified and practical criterion to anchor research on the historical origins of outcomes and to respond to the insinuation that the real starting point of a causal chain always lies further back in history.

---

10. The distinction between structural and systemic properties draws on Lazarsfeld and Menzel (1961: 426–29).

11. For a useful inventory of such changes in world history before 1760, see Mann's (1986: 524–25) list of "power jumps."

Distal Non-Recurring Causes

Any research suggesting that the cause of an effect lies in the distant past, and that such a cause has ceased to recur and thus does not directly cause an effect, must also confront the problem of distal nonrecurring causes. That is, it must address the following questions: How can a distant event have a long-term effect, that is, an effect many decades or even centuries after it occurred? How can the temporal gap between the initial event and the ultimate outcome be bridged? How can a credible claim be made about the effect of a nonrecurring event? This is a key burden that arguments involving distal causes must face.

Bridging Distal Causes and Later Outcomes with a Self-Replicating Loop

The way critical juncture research can confront this key problem in historical research is by treating a critical juncture as a distal cause that triggers what Stinchcombe (1968: 102) calls a self-replicating causal loop, a kind of causal chain that bridges a temporally distant cause and effect (see Figure 5.3). This basic causal model, also called a self-reinforcing positive feedback loop (Krasner 1988: 83; Thelen 1999: 392–96), is readily recognizable. It has been given content with various more specific ideas, which help to explain why certain outcomes are self-reinforcing. For example, scholars have argued that some processes entail "sunk costs" (Stinchcombe 1968: 120–30), have a "lock-in effect" (David 1985: 334; Arthur 1989), or yield "increasing returns" (Arthur 1989, 1994; Pierson 2000).[12] And it offers an elegant solution to the problem of distal nonrecurring causes.

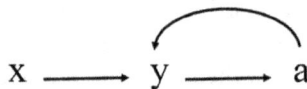

$$x \longrightarrow y \longrightarrow a$$

Figure 5.3 A Model of a Self-Replicating Causal Loop.
Note: The figure draws on Stinchcombe (1968: 103).

    Basically, this problem is overcome by positing that the outcome (Y) of a distal nonrecurring cause (X) persists due to reciprocal causation, whereby Y causes A and A causes Y in successive time periods. In other words, the claim that a critical juncture produces an outcome that persists over a considerable time, even after the

---

    12. See also Mahoney (2000: 515–26), Katznelson (2003: 291–92), Sydow et al. (2009: 698–701), Beyer (2010), Rixen and Viola (2015), and Sarigil (2015).

distal cause has ceased to recur, is sustained by specifying a causal chain that accounts for the reproduction of some outcome—an outcome commonly called the *historical legacy* of a critical juncture.

This building block of critical juncture research is clear and hardly needs any elaboration. However, two points help to complete the discussion.

Distinguishing Causal Cycles from Causal Series

To avoid a possible confusion between this kind of argument and other historical arguments about distal causes and long-term effects, it is useful to distinguish between causal chains that rely on the idea of causal cycles or causal series (see Figure 5.4).

a) Causal Cycles: Chain With a Repeated Cause-Effect Pair

$$X_{t1} \longrightarrow Y_{t2} \longrightarrow a_{t3} \longrightarrow Y_{t4} \longrightarrow a_{t5} \longrightarrow Y_{t6}$$

b) Causal Series: Chain Without a Repeated Cause-Effect Pair

$$X_{t1} \longrightarrow m_{t2} \longrightarrow n_{t3} \longrightarrow o_{t4} \longrightarrow p_{t5} \longrightarrow Y_{t6}$$

Figure 5.4 Two Kinds of Causal Chains: Causal Cycles and Causal Series. *Note:* The distinction between causal cycles and causal series is developed in Bunge (2009: 132, 155).

Using these terms, the distinctive feature of critical juncture research is that it always uses a model that includes a *causal cycle*. Indeed, the signature feature of critical junctures, the persistence of the same outcome, is the result of the defining feature of a causal cycle, the repetition of a cause-effect pair (see the A-Y pair in Figure 5.4, panel a). However, this is not the only way in which distal causes may be connected to later outcomes.

For example, a common way of arguing that a distant cause has a long-term effect is to posit what Weber (1978: 331) calls a "concatenation of circumstances," a kind of causal argument well exemplified by Weber's own theory of the origins of capitalism (Collins 1980: 929–35).[13] Such a concatenation of circumstances can be represented as a causal chain that bridges the temporal gap between a distal cause and

---

13. For another classic example, see Machiavelli (1996 [1531]: Book I, Ch. 39) on the history of Florence.

a later outcome. But this causal chain does not include any repeated cause-effect pair and is better represented as a *causal series* (see Figure 5.4, panel b).

In sum, it is necessary to recognize that not all arguments about distal causes account for the persistence of some effect over a long time—what critical juncture research calls a historical legacy. And it is useful to distinguish historical arguments that rely on different kinds of causal chains.[14]

Bridging Macro-Level Relations with Causal Mechanisms

More crucially, to fill out any claim about the historical legacy of a critical juncture, greater attention to the causal mechanisms that account for stability is needed. The literature refers to "mechanisms of reproduction" and "feedback mechanisms" that are key to the stability of the legacy (Collier and Collier 1991: 35–37; Thelen 1999: 387–96). However, if arguments about these mechanisms are to add something significant to claims about causal cycles, they must meet three basic requirements.

They must model mechanisms as processes that happen within the objects being studied, that is, at a lower level of organization than the variables in an X → Y hypothesis or, more precisely, at the level of actors and their actions (see Figure 5.5).[15] In other words, they must be arguments that do more than treat causal mechanisms as mere intervening variables.

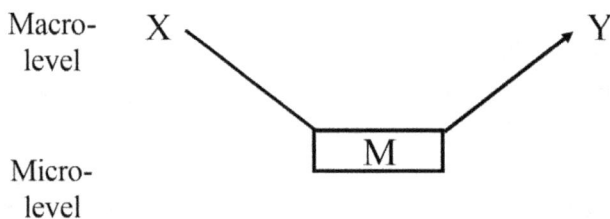

Macro-level   X ⟍   ⟋ Y

Micro-level   [M]

Figure 5.5 A Model of a Causal Mechanism. *Legend*: X: independent variable; M: mechanism; Y: dependent variable

---

14. To clarify, the point is not that an argument about critical junctures only involves a causal cycle but rather that it always contains a causal cycle. That is, a critical juncture might produce a legacy through a causal cycle combined with a causal series. For example, what is called the aftermath period (Collier and Collier 1991: 37) or the formation phase (Sydow et al. 2009: 692–94) could be modeled in terms of a causal series prior to the operation of a causal cycle.

15. This concept of causal mechanism is due to philosophers of science and sociologists (Boudon 1986: 30; Coleman 1986: 1322; 1990: 8; Bunge 1996: 123–24, 137–50; 1997; Elster 2015: Ch. 2) and contrasts with the understanding of mechanisms as any intervening variable.

Arguments about mechanisms should also be treated as central to explanations and not reducible to some minimal point (e.g., positing that some single generic mechanism, coordination among actors, establishes a connection between a macro-condition and a macro-outcome). Specifically, they should strive to meet various standards that have been elaborated for theories of mechanisms, such as spelling out a complete set of essential, system-specific mechanisms and addressing how they interact among each other.[16]

Lastly, any theory about the mechanisms used to explain why a social order endures needs to adequately consider agency. The mechanisms connecting two variables specify actors and their actions. And all actors cannot be assumed to act so as to stabilize the current order. Some actors will always be better off with a new order and hence favor change. Moreover, all actors have agency and need not reproduce a social order. In other words, actors that are part of a system can always try to change the system. And, inasmuch as these actors prevail, the mechanisms that reproduce a legacy would cease to operate. Thus, a complete theory of mechanisms must address the possibility of disequilibrium behavior.

Accounting for the persistence of an effect in terms of *stabilizing causal mechanisms* increases the value of arguments about persistent effects made in terms of macro-level variables.[17] Indeed, explanations involving only macro-level variables beg another question about bridging, in this case about how macro-level causes could produce macro-level effects (Coleman 1990: Ch. 1). Going beyond arguments about how the persistent effect of a critical juncture is produced through a causal cycle, the legacy of a critical juncture needs to be explained through a systematic account of causal mechanisms.

Summary

Critical junctures are distal causes that cease to recur. Thus, they do not directly generate outcomes that occur at a great temporal distance. Yet, research on critical junctures gets around the problem of distal nonrecurring causes by specifying how a critical juncture has a long-term, persistent effect—i.e., generates a historical legacy—through a causal chain involving a self-replicating causal loop or what has been called here, for sake of precision, a causal cycle. Moreover, inasmuch as the stabilizing causal mechanisms that bridge macro-level variables are spelled out, the claim to have connected a distal cause to a later, enduring outcome is even more credible.

---

16. On various ways in which mechanisms can be represented and assessed, see Bunge (1997: 454–58; 2006: 131), Craver and Darden (2013: Chs. 3 and 6), Elster (2015: Ch. 2), and Waldner (2015).

17. On the epistemic value of knowledge about causal mechanisms, see Thagard (1999: Ch. 7), Bunge (2006: Chs. 4 and 5), Darden (2006), Elster (2015: Part 1), and Craver and Darden (2013).

The Claims, Compared

The arguments presented here support some positions in the literature. They run counter to other positions. And they introduce some novel ideas.

Critical Junctures as Rapid, Discontinuous, Macro-Level Changes

The case made for conceptualizing critical junctures as rapid, discontinuous, macro-level changes provides a justification for what might be characterized as the consensus view in the literature. Some authors who draw on the idea of path dependence argue for a view not supported here: that small changes can be critical junctures (Mahoney 2000: 526; Pierson 2004: 44, 50–52; Greer 2008: 220–21).[18] However, a majority of authors define critical junctures as discontinuous and/or rapid changes (see Appendix I). Moreover, most scholars characterize critical junctures as "*macro transformations*" (Collier and Collier 1991: 11) or large-scale events (Ekiert 1996: xi; Hacker 2002: 58–59; Katznelson 2003: 282; Ikenberry 2016: 540–41), while specifying that such macro-level events encompass a range of big changes short of total revolutions.[19]

In contrast, the argument that rapid, discontinuous, macro-level changes solve the problem of infinite regress provides a basis for rejecting some common views in the literature. A few scholars explicitly acknowledge that major discontinuities can be used to tackle the problem of infinite regress (Hogan 2006: 663; Slater and Simmons 2010: 888). Nonetheless, some authors do not acknowledge the seriousness of the problem of infinite regress in the study of distal causes. For example, Diamond (1997: 9) simply urges scholars to "search for ultimate explanations" by "pushing back the chain of historical causation as far as possible." Others do not always confront the problem of infinite regress squarely, suggesting that an objective criterion is not needed and that the starting point of an analysis of historical causation "might merely be a point in the causal chain beyond which it is empirically difficult or theoretically less interesting to pursue causality" (Simpser et al. 2018: 420; see also Pierson 2004: 89).

And yet others address the problem of infinite regress but provide dubious solutions. Some authors propose to address this problem by focusing on moments when "contingent historical events . . . that cannot be explained on the basis of prior historical conditions [or] prior events" occur (Mahoney 2000: 507–09, 511; 2001: 7–8). However, critical junctures are not and could not be fully contingent events, i.e., uncaused causes. Other scholars suggest that this problem could be solved by identifying points "at which . . . cases begin to diverge in significant ways" (Pierson 2004: 89). However, critical junctures can send units (e.g., countries) on divergent,

---

18. See also David (1985: 332) and Arthur (1989: 117).

19. See the suggestions to treat changes in "partial regimes" (Collier and Chambers-Ju 2012: 565) and "policy subsystems" (Baumgartner and Jones 2009) as critical junctures.

convergent, or parallel paths. Thus, neither contingency nor differentiation are defining features of a critical juncture (see Chapter 19) and hence do not provide a basis for identifying critical junctures.[20] Various arguments in the literature are best discarded.

Finally, the argument about critical junctures presented here goes beyond the current literature in various ways. It explicitly treats the problem of infinite regress as a foundational issue in critical juncture research. And it clarifies key concepts commonly used somewhat loosely in much of the literature. To give but one example, authors who use the concept of punctuated equilibrium commonly rely on the metaphor of a branching tree to specify what is distinctive about a punctuated equilibrium, but fail to differentiate between the Darwinian and Gouldian branching models of evolution (Krasner 1984: 242; Capoccia and Kelemen 2007: 342). Thus, this discussion moves the literature forward by offering a precise conceptualization of critical junctures as rapid, discontinuous, macro-level changes and by proposing such qualitative novelties as a criterion for solving the problem of infinite regress.

Critical Junctures as Causes of Persistent Effects

The idea that critical junctures are causes that have persistent effects hardly requires discussion. All definitions of a critical juncture note that it produces a historical legacy (see Appendix I). Furthermore, many scholars clarify that arguments about a historical legacy must meet the burden of bridging an initial nonrecurring cause and an ultimate outcome by specifying what has been called "mechanisms of reproduction" (Collier and Collier 1991: 35–37; Acharya et al. 2018: Ch. 7), "feedback mechanisms" (Thelen 1999: 387–96), "transmission mechanisms" (Peisakhin 2015: 22; Acharya et al. 2016: 637; Simpser et al. 2018: 422), "channels" of "transmission" (Acharya et al. 2016: 633), or "conveyor belts for legacies" (Simpser et al. 2018: 427). The idea that critical juncture research rests on a causal claim about persistent effects is widely recognized.

This core idea is not accepted by all, however. One view presented in the literature that draws on the notion of path dependence is that the legacy of a critical juncture can be explained by a causal chain that involves "reactive sequences" that "are marked by backlash processes that *transform* and perhaps *reverse* early events" rather than by "processes of reproduction that *reinforce* early events" (Mahoney 2000:

---

20. Capoccia (2015: 169–70) discusses the problem of infinite regress but suggests a different criterion, one based on the size and duration of the impact of a critical juncture, for identifying critical junctures (Capoccia and Kelemen 2007: 360–63). However, it is not clear how this solution gets around the problem of infinite regress, in that it essentially calls for an assessment of the causal impact of all hypotheses about critical junctures before making any call regarding where to start the analysis. Furthermore, it is not clear how this solution could be consistent with Capoccia and Kelemen's (2007: 348, 352) claim that "change is not a necessary element of a critical juncture" (see also Capoccia 2015: 165).

509, 526–35; see also Arestis and Sawyer 2009: 11; Beyer 2010: 4–5; and Martin and Sunley 2010: 84–85). Yet, reactive sequences involve a causal sequence that resembles a causal series as opposed to a causal cycle (Mahoney 2000: 526–29; Falleti and Mahoney 2015: 220–23), and thus can account for a long-term effect but not for a persistent effect, the distinguishing feature of critical junctures. Therefore, the distinction between causal cycles and causal series introduced above provides a basis for both clarifying the distinctiveness of causal claims about historical legacies and for disposing of the view that reactive sequences are a kind of path dependence and can explain the persistence of some legacy.[21]

As a final point, the proposal made here adds something new to the literature. Discussions about mechanisms have not been based on an explicit definition of a causal mechanism and have not recognized that a theory that incorporates mechanisms is a cross-level theory. The distinct epistemic value of a theory that specifies causal mechanisms is also rarely recognized. Indeed, the literature has largely failed to acknowledge the need to bridge macro-level variables by spelling out causal mechanisms. Thus, adding the idea of stabilizing mechanisms to the repertoire of ideas used in critical juncture research is a significant innovation.

SOCIAL DYNAMICS

The study of social statics is central to critical juncture research. And the argument that critical junctures produce historical legacies is the most distinctive claim of this research. But the study of social statics is only half of the research agenda on critical junctures. This research also addresses the sources of social change and provides explanations of social dynamics, that is, of how and why societies change over time.[22] Moreover, it uses the classic distinction between the crisis of an old order and the creation of a new order (Kuhn 1970 [1962]: Chs. 7 and 8; Collier and Collier 1991: 773; Roberts 2014: xiii), and frequently analyzes two distinct questions about dynamics:

---

21. A similar conclusion is reached by Howlett (2009: 252–53), Sydow et al. (2009: 697–98), Rixen and Viola (2015: 317), and Sarigil (2015: 222–23).

22. Some key texts on the critical juncture framework suggest that an analysis of dynamics is not central to research in this tradition. For example, Stinchcombe (1968: 105) states that "the *interesting* part" of explanations that rely on what he calls "historical causes" is "the process creating the self-regenerating loop, not the original cause," i.e., the critical juncture. However, scholars have dedicated a lot of attention to the causes rather than the consequences of critical junctures. Actually, early works in this tradition focused more on explaining critical juncture than on accounting for the legacies of critical junctures; see, for example, Kuhn (1970 [1962]), Moore (1966), Lipset and Rokkan (1967), Skocpol (1979), and Mann (1986). And the interest in understanding why critical junctures occur continues (e.g., Ikenberry 2001; Kurtz 2013; Mazzuca 2021).

(1) The causes of the end of the legacy: Why does the legacy of a critical juncture erode and end?
(2) The causes of the critical juncture: Why does a critical juncture occur? Why does change occur through big, discontinuous leaps rather than small, incremental steps?[23]

Given this interest in social dynamics, critical juncture research again inevitably faces some problems. One is the problem of endogenous and exogenous sources of change or, more specifically, the challenge of deciding whether change should be explained mainly in terms of endogenous or exogenous factors or, if not, how these two sources should be combined. Another is the problem of structure and agency, which creates a similar challenge of deciding whether change should be explained mainly in terms of structural factors or actors and their choices or, if not, how factors and actors should be integrated in an explanation.

Compared to the problems of infinite regress and distal nonrecurring causes, these two problems are more general ones. In effect, although critical juncture research faces the specific challenge of explaining major discontinuous changes, the issues relevant to critical juncture studies of social dynamics are less distinctive than those it must confront in the study of social statics. What is more, unlike the problems of infinite regress and distal nonrecurring causes, these problems have been discussed extensively for a long time. They have been the focus of considerable attention in classical social theory (Nisbet 1969; Smith 1973; Sztompka 1993) and they continue to be the focus of reflection (Koning 2016; Emmenegger 2021; Gerschewski 2021).

However, it is not clear how these two problems should be tackled. Some scholars consider that critical juncture research has not solved (and possibly could not solve) these problems (Thelen 2003, 2004: 29–31; Streeck and Thelen 2005a, 2005b: 6–9; March and Olsen 2006: 11–13). Given that critical juncture research focuses to a great extent on how order is maintained in a society, it is seen as assuming that stability is the natural state of the world, that change is an anomaly, and that only exogenous shocks can account for major discontinuous changes. Further, given that this research traces the origins of social order back to distant macro-level or structural

---

23. The importance of these questions is stressed, among others, by Collier and Collier (1991: 33–34), Lee (2012: 94), Chibber (2003: Ch. 8), Roberts (2014: 44–46, 229), and Acharya et al. (2018: Part III). In addressing these questions, scholars commonly focus on one critical juncture and, looking backwards, seek to account for its origin (Collier and Collier 1991; Roberts 2014), and looking forward, consider why the legacy of the critical juncture erodes and/or comes to an end (Collier and Collier 1991: Ch. 8; Chibber 2003: Epilogue; Collier and Chambers-Ju 2012). Other scholars start their analysis at one critical juncture and, looking forward, analyze why the legacy of a critical juncture erodes and/or comes to an end and why a new critical juncture occurs (Rokkan 1970; Scully 1992; Ikenberry 2001; Kurtz 2013). This choice is largely dictated by research interests and is not consequential.

factors, it is portrayed as disregarding the role of agents as possible causal forces and exemplifying the pitfalls of historical and structural determinism. In short, critical juncture research is seen as having a static bias and providing an impoverished externalist and deterministic account of change.

Moreover, even authors who treat these problems as solvable offer different, not clearly reconcilable positions. Most of the discussion centers on the role of structure and agency in accounting for change—scholars have been largely silent about the analysis of endogenous and exogenous sources of change. And, while some authors focus on the various ways in which critical junctures are determined by antecedent conditions (Slater and Simmons 2010; Soifer 2012), others argue that critical junctures are determined by contingent choices, choices made by actors that are unconstrained by antecedent conditions (Mahoney 2000; Bernhard 2015).

Thus, this section discusses how critical juncture research can and should confront these two problems relevant to the study of social dynamics.

Endogenous and Exogenous Sources of Change

Social theory provides some useful guidance regarding how critical juncture research should approach the role of endogenous and exogenous sources of change. The discussion about endogenous and exogenous factors—also called internal and external factors—has gone through two phases. Initially, a debate was framed in terms of the extent to which social change should be explained by factors internal to a society or by intersocietal or international factors. Classic evolutionary theory focused on internal factors, and diffusionist theory on external factors. However, these two options were scrutinized and discussed. And, over time, both options were seen as limited and the need to integrate the two kinds of sources of change was recognized (Sanderson 1990; Smelser 1992).

A more recent iteration of this debate was framed in terms of the relationship among spheres or systems within a society—the economy, politics, and culture. In this context, the Marxist view that change originates in the economy offered a clear example of an externalist account, in that the economy was portrayed as the prime mover of society and hence as the cause of political and cultural change. Yet, again, over time the view that change is driven by developments in one sphere has been replaced by a pluralist view of social change, which recognizes that change can be driven by different spheres in different periods, that many times they operate jointly, and that at times they affect each other (Bunge 1985: 193–99; Mann 1986: Ch. 1). In short, a basic lesson of social theory that should be incorporated into research on critical junctures is that one-sided accounts of change should be avoided.

However, adding to this general point, the distinctive role of exogenous factors in explanations of discontinuous change should be recognized. It is key to stress that no system can be endogenously transformed into a new system, and that discontinuous change is always driven—at least in part—by exogenous factors.[24] Put differently, one of the distinguishing features of critical juncture research is that it rejects the view that all change can be immanent, that is, driven purely by endogenous factors (e.g., a change in political regime cannot be explained only in terms of tensions within the antecedent political regime). This is a common view, which is associated with the idea that change is always continuous. But it is erroneous.[25]

Thus, it is important to stress that critical juncture research should avoid explanations based largely or entirely on exogenous shocks. And it is equally essential to acknowledge that explanations of discontinuous change necessarily must address exogenous drivers of change and cannot focus only on endogenous factors.

Structure and Agency

Social theory also provides some useful guidance regarding the analysis of structure and agency. Indeed, the structure/agency problem has been the subject of a great amount of discussion in social theory (Giddens 1984; Ingold 1986: Ch. 5; Bunge 1996: Chs. 9 and 10). And this literature points to some obvious potential hazards for critical juncture research. This research places emphasis on macro-level or historical factors. Yet outcomes are never predetermined by macro-level or historical factors. Thus, it needs to take steps to avoid structural and historical determinism.

Critical juncture research also relies heavily on arguments about path dependence to explain the legacy of critical junctures. However, it is important to recognize that agency is possible "*all* the time and not just in the very rare moments when structures break down entirely" (Conran and Thelen 2016: 66; see also Thelen 2004: 28–31), and that "processes of path destruction and new path creation are always latent in the process of path dependence" (Martin and Sunley 2006: 408; see also Garud and Karnøe 2001 and Garud et al. 2010). Accordingly, critical juncture research must avoid what has been appropriately called "path dependence determinism" (Crouch and Farrell 2004) and recognize the possibility of "path generation" (Djelic and Quack 2007: 161–62, 167–68) and "path switching" (Crouch and Farrell 2004: 12).

Yet, again, it is important to go beyond this sound but basic advice to avoid determinisms. Critical juncture research should provide a full and nuanced analysis

---

24. This fundamental point has been made, in different ways, by various social theorists (Gellner 1964: 27–32; Nisbet 1969: 275–84; Smith 1973: Chs. 6–7; Touraine 1977: Ch. 7; and Giddens 1984: 163–64, 228–51; see also Schumpeter 2005 [1932]: 116–18). Yet this insight has largely been lost.

25. The view that all change is endogenous change does allow for external factors, but only inasmuch as they serve as a stimulus that works itself through a system (Smith 1973: 150). On immanent change and its connection to the idea that change is always continuous, see Nisbet (1969: 170–78). For a classic argument in favor of "immanent self-determination," a purely endogenous theory of change, see Sorokin (1941: Chs. 12–16). For a recent defense of a theory of change that eschews exogenous factors, see Crouch and Farrell (2004).

of actors and agency. Actors are always agents within a social system and agents are always conditioned. Yet actors always have the capacity for agency. Thus, actors do not have agency only when constrains on action are lifted. As Bunge (1998: 279) stresses, "history is made by individuals acting in and upon social systems that pre-exist and shape them" (see also Bunge 1996: Chs. 9 and 10). Moreover, the equation of agency and contingency is mistaken. Indeed, it is worth recalling Weber's (1946 [1919]: 120–27) moving depiction of the responsible politician who is called upon to make a choice, and says "here I stand, I can do no other."

In other words, researchers should not provide an account of agents as causes by equating agency with moments of contingency allowed by structural factors. This view reduces agency to a choice regarding the unconditioned remainder left after the impact of structural factors has been accounted for. Rather, they should explore the many ways in which actors shape history, even when the circumstances are not favorable, sometimes by choosing between externally given alternatives, other times by creating new conditions, and yet other times by controlling conditions.[26]

More to the point, as in the analysis of statics, the study of dynamics should specify *change causal mechanisms*, i.e., the mechanisms that produce change. In this regard, it is important to recognize that the mechanisms that generate system change are not the same ones as those that underpin the stability of a system. Further, as noted above, theorizing mechanisms involves several things. It requires the specification of the actors and the actions of actors that produce change. It calls for spelling out all essential, system-specific mechanisms and their interaction. And, key to the question of agency, it entails considering whether, rather than assuming that, all actors support change.

Summary

To address social dynamics, that is, why orders come to an end and critical junctures occur, critical juncture research needs to rely on an integrative approach that avoids some common extremes in theories of social change. It should also go further and incorporate some less obvious ideas. It should avoid both excessively internalist and externalist accounts. Yet it should also recognize that one of the distinctive features of critical juncture research is its rejection of the view that all change can be driven by endogenous factors. It should escape macro-reductionism, the view that actors play no role in determining social outcomes. But it should also avoid micro-reductionism, the view that actors are not part of a system. Indeed, critical juncture research requires an understanding of agency that does not treat it as a matter of contingent,

---

26. The impact of actors on social processes is sometimes analyzed as an example of self-determination, which is contrasted to causal determination by factors or conditions external to actors. But self-determination does not imply causal indeterminacy nor is it an escape from external conditions. On self-determination, see Bunge (2009: 17–21, Ch. 7) and Wehmeyer et al. (2017: Part I).

unconditioned choice that opens up when structural factors do not fully determine outcomes. And it needs to theorize causal mechanisms of change.

The Claims, Compared

These arguments are consistent with and provide a justification for much thinking about critical juncture research. Scholars regularly explain critical junctures in terms of both endogenous and exogenous sources of change. They recognize that a "crisis may be generated internally or externally" (Krasner 1984: 234; see also Bulmer and Burch 1998: 605; and Ikenberry 2001: 44–48). And they go to some length to draw attention to the role of "endogenous social strains or pressures" and to show how exogenous shocks are actually associated with endogenous processes (Roberts 2014: 47–48; see also Collier and Collier 1991: 768–72; and Kurtz 2013: 42–43).[27] The need to avoid one-sided accounts of change is largely reflected in substantive research on critical junctures.[28]

The literature on critical junctures offers an even more elaborate discussion about the role of structure and agency and stresses the importance of averting determinisms. The idea that critical junctures must be explained in terms of structural factors and agents is explicitly endorsed by most scholars (Sabel and Zeitlin 1985: 162–63; Collier and Collier 1991: 27; Katznelson 2003: 282–83).[29] Moreover, a rich discussion focuses on how structure and agency might be integrated. In particular, many authors consider how antecedent conditions (i.e., the exogenous and endogenous factors that precede a critical juncture) affect the discretion of actors during critical junctures (Collier and Collier 1991: 27, 771; Roberts 2014: 48–49), and they have proposed distinctions to think about the relationship between antecedent conditions and actor choices.[30] To a large extent, the proposed approach coincides with and provides support for current practices.

---

27. Relatedly, in debates between internalists and externalists in studies of knowledge—a debate that maps on to the one about endogenous and exogenous factors addressed here—Kuhn is frequently depicted as a radical externalist (Barnes 1982). However, Kuhn's analysis of the crisis of paradigms puts great weight on an internal factor, the anomalies that emerge within a reigning paradigm, as a driver of paradigm change (Kuhn 1970 [1962]: Chs. 6–8).

28. For examples of substantive research that addresses the interplay between endogenous and exogenous factors, and avoids treating exogenous (international) shocks as the main or only driver of change, see Collier and Collier (1991: Chs. 3 and 4), Collier (1993), Roberts (2014: 47–48, Ch. 4), and Mazzuca (2021).

29. See also Pierson (2004: 51–52), Weingast (2005: 165–66), Martin and Sunley (2006: 402–03), Soifer (2012: 1574, 1593), Slater (2010: 55), and Slater and Simmons (2010: 887–90).

30. Soifer (2012: 1573, 1575–76) distinguishes permissive conditions, which ease "the constraints of structure and make change possible," from productive conditions, which "determine the outcome that emerges from the critical juncture." Riedl and Roberts (see Chapter 6) distinguish between activating and generative critical junctures.

Nonetheless, the positions articulated here are not shared by all. It does not coincide with the critical view that most research on critical junctures relies on a deterministic account of path dependence and hence is forced to explain change by invoking exogenous shocks (Thelen 2004: xii–xiii, 8, 25–31; Streeck and Thelen 2005a; 2005b: 6–9). This is not an accurate depiction of the tradition of critical juncture research as a whole. Even though research could be more explicit about which factors are endogenous and which are exogenous, they routinely explain change in terms of both endogenous and exogenous factors. Even though research could provide a more nuanced analysis of actors, it has avoided the pitfall of various determinisms. This critique rightly pushes researchers to be more attentive to agency. Nonetheless, critical juncture research does not provide a static account of dynamics.

The views presented here also do not coincide with some common practices in critical juncture research. Many explanations of critical junctures are couched in terms of antecedent conditions, cleavages, and shocks. However, the discussion here suggests that a focus on the distinction between endogenous and exogenous drivers of change would lead to clearer theorizing about possible sources of change. Some antecedent conditions are endogenous, and others are exogenous. Some cleavages are internal to a system (e.g., the cleavage between hardliners and soft-liners in a study of regimes), and others are external to a system (e.g., the owner-worker cleavage in a study of political regimes). Thus, a focus on the theoretically fundamental distinction between endogenous and exogenous factors is seen as preferable to the somewhat cumbersome terminology of antecedent conditions, cleavages, and shocks used in many explanations of critical junctures.

In turn, even though the literature on critical junctures has sought to combine the analysis of structure and agency, most scholars conceive of agency as a choice between externally given alternatives. Indeed, a commonly voiced idea is that "at critical junctures . . . many constraints on agency are broken or relaxed and opportunities expand so that purposive action may be especially consequential" (Katznelson 2003: 282–83; see also Sabel and Zeitlin 1985: 162; Capoccia and Kelemen 2007: 342; Greer 2008: 219; and Roberts 2014: 43). Additionally, scholars regularly equate agency and contingency, seeing agency as manifested through the contingent choices of actors—choices seen as unaffected by or independent from prior conditions (Mahoney 2000: 511; Bernhard 2015: 978), and even make a case for treating contingency as a hallmark of critical junctures (Capoccia and Kelemen 2007: 343, 348; Greer 2008: 219; Calder and Ye 2010: 42; Capoccia 2015: 148, 150–51, 156–60, 165). Thus, the analysis of actors and agency supported above differs from the way in which agency is analyzed in the literature on critical junctures.

Finally, the discussion in this section goes beyond the existing literature in several ways. Beyond suggesting that critical juncture research should explicitly build on basic insights in social theory, it has introduced three key points. It has clarified what is distinctive about explanations of big, discontinuous changes—their rejection of the view that all change can be immanent, i.e., endogenously driven. It has pointed to the need to broaden the scope for agency beyond the choice between externally given alternatives and to break the equation between agency and contingency. And it has called for specifying change mechanisms, an important gap in current theorizing.

Additionally, the most sweeping innovation in this discussion has been its treatment of the matters of the endogenous and exogenous sources of change, and the relationship between structure and agency, as foundational issues in critical juncture research. Such a focus on fundamentals is needed to justify decisions about the critical juncture framework. And, as the critical review of the basic building blocks of critical juncture research in this section (and the first section) shows, it provides a basis for the introduction of several new ideas to the critical juncture framework (for a graphic representation of the proposed reconstruction of this framework that combines the ideas on statics and dynamics presented in this chapter, see Figure 5.6).

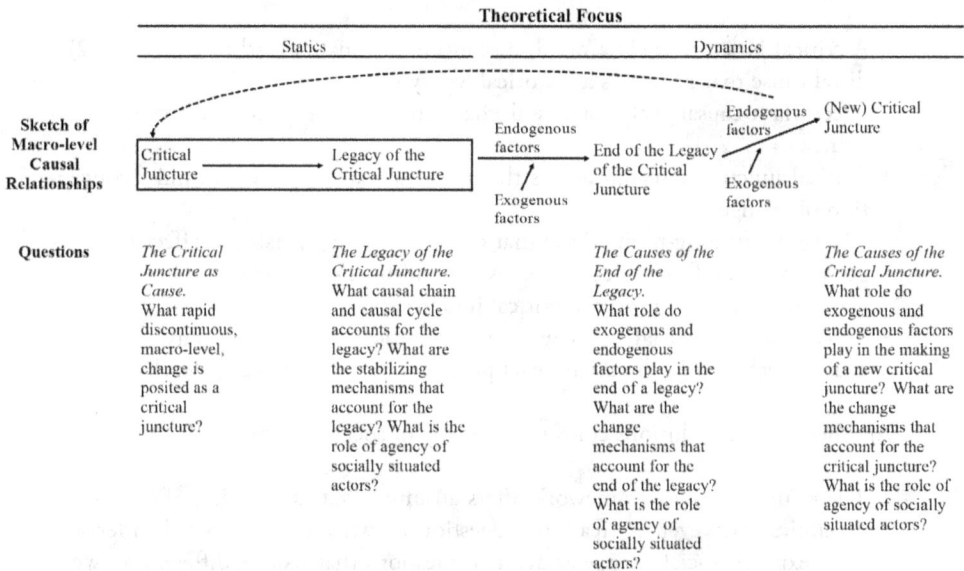

	Theoretical Focus			
	Statics		Dynamics	
Sketch of Macro-level Causal Relationships	Critical Juncture → Legacy of the Critical Juncture	Endogenous factors / Exogenous factors → End of the Legacy of the Critical Juncture	Endogenous factors / Exogenous factors →	(New) Critical Juncture
Questions	*The Critical Juncture as Cause.* What rapid discontinuous, macro-level, change is posited as a critical juncture?	*The Legacy of the Critical Juncture.* What causal chain and causal cycle accounts for the legacy? What are the stabilizing mechanisms that account for the legacy? What is the role of agency of socially situated actors?	*The Causes of the End of the Legacy.* What role do exogenous and endogenous factors play in the end of a legacy? What are the change mechanisms that account for the end of the legacy? What is the role of agency of socially situated actors?	*The Causes of the Critical Juncture.* What role do exogenous and endogenous factors play in the making of a new critical juncture? What are the change mechanisms that account for the critical juncture? What is the role of agency of socially situated actors?

Note: To indicate that the *critical juncture-legacy* nexus anchors the study of critical junctures—from a methodological perspective, the study of dynamics takes a certain order as its point of reference—it is highlighted in a box. *Endogenous factors* are internal to the system under consideration; *exogenous factors* are external to the system under consideration. Thus, the meaning of the term "exogenous" varies according to the subject matter. Economic factors may be considered as exogenous in research on politics, and vice versa. Exogenous can also be taken to mean, more strictly, factors that are not themselves traceable back to a critical juncture. The dotted line connecting the (new) critical juncture to the prior critical juncture is not a causal arrow; rather, it indicates that, with a new critical juncture, the analysis moves next to the effect of the critical juncture. *Causal mechanisms* are actions of entities at a lower level of organization than the ultimate outcome that is being explained.

Figure 5.6 The Critical Juncture Framework: An Approach to the Study of Statics and Dynamics

CONCLUSIONS

Discussions about critical junctures during the past two decades have revealed considerable disagreement about the building blocks of critical juncture research. This situation is not necessarily problematic. Debates and controversies are a common feature in successful research programs. However, when serious doubts are raised about the core ideas of a research program, its momentum is weakened. Thus, this chapter has sought to reconstruct the critical juncture framework on stronger foundations. And, to this end, it has offered a review of the theoretical foundations of critical juncture research and, following a discussion about how various foundational issues should be handled, proposed various changes to the critical juncture framework. It suggested that some ideas should be clarified and refined, that other ideas should be discarded, and that yet other ideas should be introduced.

The foundational issues addressed in this chapter are complex, and some questions are best treated as open. Nonetheless, the discussion has yielded several conclusions.

One set of conclusions concern the study of social statics:

- A critical juncture is (1) a rapid, discontinuous, macro-level change, and (2) a distal cause that generates a historical legacy or, more precisely, has a persistent effect via a causal cycle—a causal chain that includes a repeated cause-effect pair.
- Critical juncture research rejects the universal validity of a continuist conception of change.
- Claims about long-term effects that do not involve a persistent effect (e.g., arguments in the form of causal series) should be distinguished from arguments about the historical legacy of critical junctures.
- Explanations of social order are more credible when they specify stabilizing causal mechanisms, the micro-level processes that bridge macro-level variables.

Another set of conclusions concern the study of social dynamics:

- The critical juncture framework offers an integrated explanation of statics and dynamics. However, it treats the question of what explains social order and what explains social change as distinct questions that require different answers.
- Critical juncture research should avoid the shortcomings of extreme internalism and externalism, and not privilege either endogenous or exogenous sources of change. Nonetheless, it does reject the view that all change can be endogenously driven.
- Critical juncture research should avoid the shortcomings of macro-reductionism and micro-reductionism, and address the impact of structural factors and agency. Yet, it requires a better understanding of agency that does not equate agency with moments of contingency allowed by structural factors.
- Explanations of social change are more credible when they specify change causal mechanisms that bridge macro-level variables.

The critical juncture framework systematizes one approach to historically oriented research. Indeed, it certainly is not the only approach that makes use of temporal concepts and addresses how history matters. It is not even the only approach that links the study of social statics to that of social dynamics. Nonetheless, this framework is a rather unique synthesis of well-vetted ideas that avoids a number of possible pitfalls. It provides a useful guide to researchers seeking to encompass and combine the study of statics and dynamics, of social order and social change.

BIBLIOGRAPHY

Acemoglu, Daron, and James A. Robinson. 2012. *Why Nations Fail: Origins of Power, Poverty and Prosperity.* New York, NY: Crown.

Acharya, Avidit, Matthew Blackwell, and Maya Sen. 2016. "The Political Legacy of American Slavery." *Journal of Politics* 78(3): 621–41.

———. 2018. *Deep Roots: How Slavery Still Shapes Southern Politics.* Princeton, NJ: Princeton University Press.

Arestis, Philip, and Malcolm Sawyer. 2009. "Path Dependency and Demand-Supply Interactions in Macroeconomic Analysis." In Philip Arestis and Malcolm Sawyer (eds.), *Path Dependency and Macroeconomics* (pp. 1–36). New York, NY: Palgrave Macmillan.

Arthur, W. Brian. 1989. "Competing Technologies, Increasing Returns, and Lock-In by Historical Events." *Economic Journal* 99(394): 116–31.

———. 1994. *Increasing Returns and Path Dependence in the Economy.* Ann Arbor, MI: University of Michigan Press.

Barnes, Barry. 1982. *T. S. Kuhn and Social Science.* New York, NY: Columbia University Press.

Baumgartner, Frank R., and Bryan D. Jones. 2009. *Agendas and Instability in American Politics* (2nd ed.). Chicago, IL: University of Chicago Press.

Bernhard, Michael. 2015. "Chronic Instability and the Limits of Path Dependence." *Perspectives on Politics* 13(4): 976–91.

Beyer, Jürgen. 2010. "The Same or Not the Same. On the Variety of Mechanisms of Path Dependence." *International Journal of Social Sciences* 5(1): 1–11.

Boas, Taylor C. 2007. "Conceptualizing Continuity and Change: The Composite-Standard Model of Path Dependence." *Journal of Theoretical Politics* 19(1): 33–54.

Boudon, Raymond. 1986. *Theories of Social Change: A Critical Appraisal.* Berkeley, CA: University of California Press.

Bulmer, Simon, and Martin Burch. 1998. "Organising for Europe: Whitehall, the British State and the European Union." *Public Administration* 76(4): 601–28.

Bunge, Mario. 1985. *Treatise on Basic Philosophy.* Vol. 7: *Epistemology and Methodology III: Philosophy of Science and Technology.* Part II: *Life Science, Social Science and Technology.* Dordrecht, Holland: D. Reidel Publishing Company.

———. 1996. *Finding Philosophy in Social Science.* New Haven, CT: Yale University Press.

———. 1997. "Mechanism and Explanation." *Philosophy of the Social Sciences* 27(4): 410–65.

———. 1998. *Social Science Under Debate.* Toronto: University of Toronto Press.

———. 2006. *Chasing Reality: Strife over Realism.* Toronto: University of Toronto Press.

———. 2009. *Causality and Modern Science* (4th ed.). New Brunswick, NJ: Transaction Publishers.

Burke, Peter. 1979. "Introduction: Concepts of Continuity and Change in History." In Peter Burke (ed.), *The New Cambridge Modern History* (pp. 1–14). New York, NY: Cambridge University Press.

————. 1993. *History and Social Theory*. Ithaca, NY: Cornell University Press.

Calder, Kent, and Min Ye. 2010. *The Making of Northeast Asia*. Stanford, CA: Stanford University Press.

Capoccia, Giovanni. 2015. "Critical Junctures and Institutional Change." In James Mahoney and Kathleen Thelen (eds.), *Advances in Comparative-Historical Analysis* (pp. 147–79). New York, NY: Cambridge University Press.

————. 2016a. "Critical Junctures." In Orfeo Fioretos, Tulia G. Falleti, and Adam Sheingate (eds.), *The Oxford Handbook of Historical Institutionalism* (pp. 89–106). New York, NY: Oxford University Press.

————. 2016b. "When Do Institutions 'Bite'? Historical Institutionalism and the Politics of Institutional Change." *Comparative Political Studies* 49(8): 1095–127.

Capoccia, Giovanni, and R. Daniel Kelemen 2007. "The Study of Critical Junctures: Theory, Narrative, and Counterfactuals in Historical Institutionalism." *World Politics* 59(3): 341–69.

Chibber, Vivek. 2003. *Locked in Place State-Building and Late Industrialization in India*. Princeton, NJ: Princeton University Press.

Coleman, James Samuel. 1986. "Social Theory, Social Research, and a Theory of Action." *The American Journal of Sociology* 91(6): 1309–35.

————. 1990. *Foundations of Social Theory*. Cambridge, MA.: Harvard University Press.

Collier, David, and Gerardo L. Munck. 2017. "Building Blocks and Methodological Challenges: A Framework for Studying Critical Junctures." *Qualitative and Multi-Method Research* 15(1): 2–9.

Collier, Ruth Berins. 1993. "Combining Alternative Perspectives: Internal Trajectories versus External Influences as Explanations of Latin American Politics in the 1940s." *Comparative Politics* 26(1): 1–29.

Collier, Ruth Berins, and Christopher Chambers-Ju. 2012. "Popular Representation in Contemporary Latin American Politics: An Agenda for Research." In Peter Kingstone and Deborah J. Yashar (eds.), *Routledge Handbook of Latin American Politics* (pp. 564–78). New York, NY: Routledge.

Collier, Ruth Berins, and David Collier. 1991. *Shaping the Political Arena: Critical Junctures, the Labor Movement, and the Regime Dynamics in Latin America*. Princeton, NJ: Princeton University Press.

Collins, Randall. 1980. "Weber's Last Theory of Capitalism: A Systematization." *American Sociological Review* 45(6): 925–42.

Conran, James, and Kathleen Thelen. 2016. "Institutional Change." In Orfeo Fioretos, Tulia G. Falleti, and Adam Sheingate (eds.), *The Oxford Handbook of Historical Institutionalism* (pp. 51–70). New York, NY: Oxford University Press.

Craver, Carl F., and Lindley Darden. 2013. *In Search of Mechanisms: Discoveries across the Life Sciences*. Chicago, IL: University of Chicago Press.

Crouch, Colin, and Henry Farrell. 2004. "Breaking the Path of Institutional Development? Alternatives to the New Determinism." *Rationality and Society* 16(1): 5–43.

Dahrendorf, Ralf. 1959. *Class and Class Conflict in Industrial Society*. Palo Alto, CA: Stanford University Press.

Darden, Lindley. 2006. *Reasoning in Biological Discoveries: Essays on Mechanisms, Interfield Relations, and Anomaly Resolution*. Cambridge, MA: Cambridge University Press.

Darwin, Charles. 1964 [1859]. *On the Origin of Species.* Cambridge, MA: Harvard University Press.

David, Paul A. 1985. "Clio and the Economics of QWERTY." *American Economic Review* 75(2): 332–37.

Diamond, Jared. 1997. *Guns, Germs and Steel. The Fate of Human Societies.* New York, NY: W. W. Norton.

Djelic, Marie Laure. 2010. "Institutional Perspectives—Working Towards Coherence or Irreconcilable Diversity?" In Glenn Morgan, John L. Campbell, Colin Crouch, Ove Kaj Pedersen, and Richard Whitley (eds.), *The Oxford Handbook of Comparative Institutional Analysis* (pp. 15–40). New York, NY: Oxford University Press.

Djelic, Marie-Laure, and Sigrid Quack. 2007. "Overcoming Path Dependency: Path Generation in Open Systems." *Theory and Society* 36(2): 161–86.

Ebbinghaus, Bernhard. 2009. "Can Path Dependence Explain Institutional Change? Two Approaches Applied to Welfare State Reform." In Lars Magnusson and Jan Ottosson (eds.), *The Evolution of Path Dependence* (pp. 191–212). Cheltenham, UK: Edward Elgar.

Ekiert, Grzegorz. 1996. *The State against Society: Political Crises and Their Aftermath in East Central Europe.* Princeton, NJ: Princeton University Press.

Eldredge, Niles, and Stephen Jay Gould. 1972. "Punctuated Equilibria: An Alternative to Phyletic Gradualism." In Thomas J. M. Schopf (ed.), *Models in Paleobiology* (pp. 82–115). San Francisco, CA: Freeman, Cooper.

Elster, Jon. 2015. *Explaining Social Behavior: More Nuts and Bolts for the Social Sciences* (2nd ed.). New York: Cambridge University Press.

Emmenegger, Patrick. 2021. "Agency in Historical Institutionalism: Coalitional Work in the Creation, Maintenance, and Change of Institutions." *Theory and Society* 50(4): 607–26.

Falleti, Tulia G., and James Mahoney. 2015. "The Comparative Sequential Method." In James Mahoney and Kathleen Thelen (eds.), *Advances in Comparative-Historical Analysis* (pp. 211–39). New York, NY: Cambridge University Press.

Fioretos, Orfeo, Tulia G. Falleti, and Adam Sheingate. 2016. "Historical Institutionalism in Political Science." In Orfeo Fioretos, Tulia G. Falleti, and Adam Sheingate (eds.), *The Oxford Handbook of Historical Institutionalism* (pp. 3–28). New York, NY: Oxford University Press.

García-Montoya, Laura, and James Mahoney. 2020. "Critical Event Analysis in Case Study Research." *Sociological Methods and Research.* doi:10.1177/0049124120926201

Garud, Raghu, and Peter Karnøe. 2001. "Path Creation as a Process of Mindful Deviation." In Raghu Garud and Peter Karnøe (eds.), *Path Dependence and Creation* (pp. 1–40). Mahwah, NJ: Lawrence Erlbaum Associates.

Garud, Raghu, Arun Kumaraswamy, and Peter Karnøe. 2010. "Path Dependency or Path Creation?" *Journal of Management Studies* 47(4): 760–74.

Gellner, Ernest. 1964. *Thought and Change.* Chicago, IL: University of Chicago Press.

Gerring, John. 2007. *Case Study Research: Principles and Practices.* New York, NY: Cambridge University Press.

———. 2012. *Social Science Methodology: A Unified Framework.* New York, NY: Cambridge University Press.

Gerschenkron, Alexander. 1962. "On the Concept of Continuity in History." *Proceedings of the American Philosophical Society* 106(3): 195–209.

Gerschewski, Johannes. 2021. "Explanations of Institutional Change. Reflecting on a 'Missing Diagonal.'" *American Political Science Review* 115(1): 218–233.

Giddens, Anthony. 1984. *The Constitution of Society: Outline of the Theory of Structuration.* Berkeley, CA: University of California Press.

Gould, Stephen Jay. 2007. *Punctuated Equilibrium.* Cambridge, MA: Harvard University Press.

Greer, Scott L. 2008. "Choosing Paths in European Union Health Services Policy: A Political Analysis of a Critical Juncture." *Journal of European Social Policy* 18(3): 219–31.

Grzymała-Busse, Anna. 2011. "Time Will Tell? Temporality and the Analysis of Causal Mechanisms and Processes." *Comparative Political Studies* 44(9): 1267–297.

Hacker, Jacob S. 2002. *The Divided Welfare State: The Battle over Public and Private Social Benefits in the United States.* New York, NY: Cambridge University Press.

Hogan, John. 2006. "Remoulding the Critical Junctures Approach." *Canadian Journal of Political Science* 39(3): 657–79.

Howlett, Michael. 2009. "Process Sequencing Policy Dynamics: Beyond Homeostasis and Path Dependency." *Journal of Public Policy* 29(3): 241–62.

Hume, David. 1896 [1739–1740]. *A Treatise of Human Nature.* Oxford, UK: Clarendon Press.

Ikenberry, G. John. 2001. *After Victory: Institutions, Strategic Restraint, and the Rebuilding of Order after Major Wars.* Princeton, NJ: Princeton University Press.

———. 2016. "The Rise, Character, and Evolution of International Order." In Orfeo Fioretos, Tulia G. Falleti, and Adam Sheingate (eds.), *The Oxford Handbook of Historical Institutionalism* (pp. 738–52). New York, NY: Oxford University Press.

Ingold, Tim. 1986. *Evolution and Social Life.* New York, NY: Cambridge University Press.

Janos, Andrew C. 1986. *Politics and Paradigms: Changing Theories of Change in Social Science.* Stanford, CA: Stanford University Press.

Johnson, Juliet. 2001. "Path Contingency in Postcommunist Transformations." *Comparative Politics* 33(3): 253–74.

Katznelson, Ira. 2003. "Periodization and Preferences: Reflections on Purposive Action in Comparative Historical Social Science." In James Mahoney and Dietrich Rueschemeyer (eds.), *Comparative Historical Analysis in the Social Sciences* (pp. 270–303). New York, NY: Cambridge University Press.

King, Gary, Robert O. Keohane, and Sidney Verba. 1994. *Designing Social Inquiry: Scientific Inference in Qualitative Research.* Princeton, NJ: Princeton University Press.

Koning, Edward Anthony. 2016. "The Three Institutionalisms and Institutional Gynamics: Understanding Endogenous and Exogenous Change." *Journal of Public Policy* 36(4): 639–64.

Krasner, Stephen D. 1984. "Approaches to the State: Alternative Conceptions and Historical Dynamics." *Comparative Politics* 16(2): 223–46.

———. 1988. "Sovereignty: An Institutional Perspective." *Comparative Political Studies* 21(1): 66–94.

Kuhn, Thomas S. 1970 [1962]. *The Structure of Scientific Revolutions* (2nd ed.). Chicago, IL: University of Chicago Press.

Kurtz, Marcus. 2013. *Latin American State-Building in Comparative Perspective: Social Foundations of Institutional Order.* New York, NY: Cambridge University Press.

Lazarsfeld, Paul F., and Herbert Menzel. 1961. "On the Relation between Individual and Collective." In Amitai Etzioni (ed.), *Complex Organizations: A Sociological Reader* (pp. 422–40). New York: Holt, Rinehart and Winston.

Lee, Taek-Ku. 2012. "Rethinking Path Dependency and Regional Innovation. Policy Induced 'Government Dependency': The Case of Daedeok, South Korea." *World Technopolis Review* 1(2): 92–106.

Lewis, Orion A., and Sven Steinmo. 2012. "How Institutions Evolve: Evolutionary Theory and Institutional Change." *Polity* 44(3): 314–39.

Lipset, Seymour M., and Stein Rokkan. 1967. "Cleavage Structures, Party Systems, and Voter Alignments: An Introduction." In Seymour M. Lipset and Stein Rokkan (eds.*), Party Systems and Voter Alignments: Cross-National Perspectives* (pp. 1–64). New York, NY: Free Press.

Lustick, Ian. 2011. "Taking Evolution Seriously: Historical Institutionalism and Evolutionary Theory." *Polity* 43(2): 179–209.

Machiavelli, Niccoló. 1996 [1531]. *Discourses on Livy*. Chicago, IL: University of Chicago Press.

Mahoney, James. 2000. "Path Dependence in Historical Sociology." *Theory and Society* 29(4): 507–48.

———. 2001. *The Legacies of Liberalism: Path Dependence and Political Regimes in Central America*. Baltimore, MD: Johns Hopkins University Press.

Mann, Michael. 1986. *The Sources of Social Power*. Vol. 1: *A History of Power from the Beginning to A.D. 1760*. New York, NY: Cambridge University Press.

March, James G., and Johan P. Olsen. 2006. "Elaborating the 'New Institutionalism.'" In R. A. W. Rhodes, Sarah A. Binder, and Bert A. Rockman (eds.), *The Oxford Handbook of Political Institutions* (pp. 3–20). New York, NY: Oxford University Press.

Martin, Ron, and Peter Sunley. 2006. "Path Dependence and Regional Economic Evolution." *Journal of Economic Geography* 6(4): 395–437.

———. 2010. "The Place of Path Dependence in an Evolutionary Perspective on the Economic Landscape." In Ron Boschma and Ron Martin (eds.), *The Handbook of Evolutionary Economic Geography* (pp. 62–92). Chichester, UK: Edward Elgar.

Mayr, Ernst. 1961. "Cause and Effect in Biology." *Science*, New Series, 134(3489): 1501–506.

Mazzuca, Sebastián. 2021. *Latecomer State Formation. Political Geography and Capacity Failure in Latin America*. New Haven, CT: Yale University Press.

Moore, Jr., Barrington. 1966. *Social Origins of Dictatorship and Democracy: Lord and Peasant in the Making of the Modern World*. Boston, MA: Beacon Press.

Moore, Wilbert E. 1974. *Social Change* (2nd ed.). Englewood Cliffs, NJ: Prentice-Hall, Inc.

Nisbet, Robert A. 1969. *Social Change and History. Aspects of the Western Theory of Development*. New York, NY: Oxford University Press.

North, Douglass C. 1990. *Institutions, Institutional Change and Economic Performance*. New York, NY: Cambridge University Press.

Nunn, Nathan. 2012. "Culture and the Historical Process." *Economic History of Developing Regions* 27(1): 108–26.

Orren, Karen, and Stephen Skowronek. 2004. *The Search for American Political Development*. New York, NY: Cambridge University Press.

Palier, Bruno. 2005. "Ambiguous Agreement, Cumulative Change: French Social Policy in the 1990s." In Wolfgang Streeck and Kathleen Thelen (eds.), *Beyond Continuity: Institutional Change in Advanced Political Economies* (pp. 127–44). Oxford, UK: Oxford University Press.

Parsons, Talcott. 1951. *The Social System*. Glencoe, IL: The Free Press.

Peisakhin, Leonid. 2015. "Cultural Legacies: Persistence and Transmission." In Norman Schofield and Gonzalo Caballero (eds.), *The Political Economy of Governance: Institutions, Political Performance and Elections* (pp. 21–39). Basel, Switzerland: Springer.

Pierson, Paul. 2000. "Increasing Returns, Path Dependence, and the Study of Politics." *American Political Science Review* 94(2): 251–67.

———. 2004. *Politics in Time: History, Institutions, and Social Analysis*. Princeton, NJ: Princeton University Press.

Radcliffe-Brown, A. R. 1957. *A Natural Science of Society*. Chicago, IL: Free Press.

Rixen, Thomas, and Lora Anne Viola. 2015. "Putting Path Dependence in its Place: Toward a Taxonomy of Institutional Change." *Journal of Theoretical Politics* 27(2): 301–23.

Roberts, Kenneth M. 2014. *Changing Course in Latin America: Party Systems in the Neoliberal Era*. New York, NY: Cambridge University Press.

Rokkan, Stein. 1970. "Nation-Building, Cleavage Formation and the Structuring of Mass Politics." In Stein Rokkan, with Angus Campbell, Per Torsvik, and Henry Valen, *Citizens, Elections, and Parties: Approaches to the Comparative Study of the Processes of Development* (pp. 72–144). New York, NY: David McKay.

Rossi, Federico M. 2017. *The Poor's Struggle for Political Incorporation: The Piquetero Movement in Argentina*. New York, NY: Cambridge University Press.

Rueschemeyer, Dietrich. 2009. *Usable Theory: Analytic Tools for Social and Political Research*. Princeton, NJ: Princeton. University Press.

Rueschemeyer, Dietrich, Evelyne Huber Stephens, and John D. Stephens. 1992. *Capitalist Development and Democracy*. Chicago, IL: University of Chicago Press.

Sabel, Charles F., and Jonathan Zeitlin. 1985. "Historical Alternatives to Mass Production: Politics, Markets and Technology in Nineteenth-Century Industrialization." *Past and Present* 108: 133–76.

Sanderson, Stephen K. 1990. *Social Evolutionism: A Critical History*. Oxford, UK: Blackwell Publishers.

Sarigil, Zeki. 2015. "Showing the Path to Path Dependence: The Habitual Path." *European Political Science Review* 7(2): 221–42.

Schumpeter, Joseph, A. 2005 [1932]. "Development." *Journal of Economic Literature* 43(1): 108–20.

Scully, Timothy R. 1992. *Rethinking the Center. Party Politics in Nineteenth- and Twentieth-Century Chile*. Stanford, CA: Stanford University Press.

Simpser, Alberto, Dan Slater, and Jason Wittenberg. 2018. "Dead but Not Gone: Contemporary Legacies of Communism, Imperialism, and Authoritarianism." *Annual Review of Political Science* 21: 419–39.

Skocpol, Theda. 1979. *States and Social Revolution*. New York, NY: Cambridge University Press.

Slater, Dan. 2010. *Ordering Power: Contentious Politics and Authoritarian Leviathans in Southeast Asia*. New York, NY: Cambridge University Press.

Slater, Dan, and Erica Simmons. 2010. "Informative Regress: Critical Antecedents in Comparative Politics." *Comparative Political Studies* 43(7): 886–917.

Smelser, Neil J. 1992. "External and Internal Factors in Theories of Social Change." In Hans Haferkamp and Neil J. Smelser (eds.), *Social Change and Modernity* (pp. 369–94). Berkeley, CA: University of California Press.

Smith, Anthony D. 1973. *The Concept of Social Change: A Critique of the Functionalist Theory of Social Change*. London, UK: Routledge and Kegan Paul.

Soifer, Hillel David. 2012. "The Causal Logic of Critical Junctures." *Comparative Political Studies* 45(12): 1572–597.

Sorokin, Pitirim A. 1941. *Social and Cultural Dynamics*. Vol. IV: *Basic Problems, Principles, and Methods*. New York, NY: American Book Co.

Steinmo, Sven. 2010. *The Evolution of Modern States: Sweden, Japan, and the United States.* New York, NY: Cambridge University Press.

Stinchcombe, Arthur L. 1968. *Constructing Social Theories.* New York, NY: Harcourt Brace.

Streeck, Wolfgang. 2010. "Institutions in History: Bringing Capitalism Back In." In Glenn Morgan, John L. Campbell, Colin Crouch, Ove Kaj Pedersen, and Richard Whitley (eds.), *The Oxford Handbook of Comparative Institutional Analysis* (pp. 659–86). New York, NY: Oxford University Press.

Streeck, Wolfgang, and Kathleen A. Thelen. 2005a. "Preface." In Wolfgang Streeck and Kathleen Thelen (eds.), *Beyond Continuity: Institutional Change in Advanced Political Economies* (pp. i). Oxford, UK: Oxford University Press.

———. 2005b. "Introduction: Institutional Change in Advanced Political Economies." In Wolfgang Streeck and Kathleen Thelen (eds.), *Beyond Continuity: Institutional Change in Advanced Political Economies* (pp. 1–39). Oxford, UK: Oxford University Press.

Sydow, Jörg, Georg Schreyögg, and Jochen Koch. 2009. "Organizational Path Dependence: Opening the Black Box." *Academy of Management Review* 34(4): 689–709.

Sztompka, Piotr. 1993. *The Sociology of Social Change.* Oxford, UK: Blackwell Publishers.

Thagard, Paul. 1999. *How Scientists Explain Disease.* Princeton, NJ: Princeton University Press.

Thelen, Kathleen. 1999. "Historical Institutionalism in Comparative Politics." *Annual Review of Political Science* 2: 369–404.

———. 2003. "How Institutions Evolve: Insights from Comparative Historical Analysis." In James Mahoney and Dietrich Rueschemeyer (eds.), *Comparative Historical Analysis in the Social Sciences* (pp. 208–40). New York, NY: Cambridge University Press.

———. 2004. *How Institutions Evolve: The Political Economy of Skills in Germany, Britain, the United States and Japan.* New York, NY: Cambridge University Press.

Touraine, Alain. 1977. *The Self-Production of Society.* Chicago, IL: University of Chicago Press.

Waldner, David. 2015. "What Makes Process Tracing Good? Causal Mechanisms, Causal Inference, and the Completeness Standard in Comparative Politics." In Andrew Bennett and Jeffrey Checkel (eds.), *Process Tracing: From Metaphor to Analytic Tool* (pp. 126–52). New York, NY: Cambridge University Press.

Weber, Max. 1946 [1919]. "Politics as a Vocation." In H. H. Gerth and C. Wright Mills (eds.), *From Max Weber: Essays in Sociology* (pp. 77–128). New York, NY: Oxford University Press.

———. 1978. *Max Weber. Selections in Translation,* edited by W.G. Runciman. New York, NY: Cambridge University Press.

Wehmeyer, Michael L, Karrie A. Shogren, Todd D. Little, and Shane J. Lopez (eds.). 2017. *Development of Self-Determination through the Life-Course.* Dordrecht, The Netherlands: Springer.

Weingast, Barry R. 2005. "Persuasion, Preference, Change, and Critical Junctures: The Microfoundations of a Macroscopic Concept." In Ira Katznelson and Barry R. Weingast (eds.), *Preferences and Situations: Points of Intersection between Historical and Rational Choice Institutionalism* (pp. 129–60). New York, NY: Russell Sage Foundation.

Yashar, Deborah J. 1997. *Demanding Democracy: Reform and Reaction in Costa Rica and Guatemala, 1870s–1950s.* Stanford, CA: Stanford University Press.

6

Critical Junctures, Contingency, and Models of Institutional Change

Rachel Beatty Riedl and Kenneth M. Roberts

While there are multiple models of institutional change, critical juncture frameworks are particularly effective in illuminating distinct pathways that follow from episodes of distinct and divergent institutional innovation (Collier and Munck 2017). These elements of the critical juncture are definitional: the institutional change or innovation, the divergence, and the resulting enduring and contrasting legacies that follow (ibid.). Yet some definitions of critical junctures require a high degree of contingency that locates the actual source of differentiation in a relatively small and contingent occurrence that has outsized and long-term impact (Capoccia and Kelemen 2007): a butterfly flapping its wings creates a ripple in the wind current that ultimately contributes to a tornado on another continent (Lorenz 1993). In the political world, an agent's choices in moments of great uncertainty will affect the outcome of interest, such as the fate of the regime or future penetration of state capacity. This is in contrast to definitions that allow the possibility that antecedent conditions may structure how new institutions are crafted in the critical juncture, with the key focus on the period and process by which institutional change and subsequent, enduring divergence occurred (Slater and Simmons 2010; Collier and Munck 2017; Slater and Soifer 2020).

We argue that real-world events always have some combination of contingency and determinism from past sequences (as allowed in the definitions of the latter group of authors), and that attention to the *degree* of contingency versus determinism can help us to understand exactly how critical junctures work in two distinct ways. All critical junctures share enduring *variation* in the outcomes of interest from this particular period. But some critical junctures *generate* differences from largely similar conditions or previously parallel trajectories due to contingent choices of actors in this particular moment. Other critical junctures *activate* latent differences, those which were preexisting in social cleavages, the organization of the ruling party, the nature of state building, prior alliance-making, and on and on, but would *not* have had a causal impact on the outcome of interest were it not for the moment itself, a temporary relaxation on the structural influences that had maintained the previous equilibrium. We leverage this distinction in degrees of contingency to further probe various models of institutional change in a unified framework, to better understand what type of institutional change is likely under what conditions.

Although the critical juncture framework is generally adopted to explain policy or institutional changes that are contingent outcomes of actors' choices, it has also been used to explain basic shifts in the configuration or competitive alignments of national party systems. Indeed, the concept of a "crucial juncture" was first introduced to the political science lexicon in Lipset and Rokkan's (1967: 37) seminal study of party system cleavage structures. Basic shifts in the structure of partisan competition may not be a direct or intentional result of actors' strategic choices; they may, instead, reflect deep-seated changes in the competitive balance and relative mobilizational capacities of rival collective actors. Accounting for such changes across a range of similar cases with divergent outcomes can pose formidable challenges to causal inference. However, it also can shed light on the causal logic undergirding a critical juncture framework and its relationship to other models of institutional change.

Drawing on recent work by the authors on party system change in Africa (Riedl 2014) and Latin America (Roberts 2014), this chapter addresses both of these analytical questions. We start with an exploration of the locus of causal attribution in critical juncture approaches—that is, the extent to which divergent institutional outcomes are explained by variation in antecedent conditions, as opposed to variation in the strategic choices or alignments of actors during the critical juncture itself. This exploration leads us to differentiate two distinct subtypes of critical junctures— those that activate (and often accentuate) latent differences across cases, and those that generate differences across otherwise similar cases. Both activating and generative subtypes require the disjunctive influence of the critical juncture to produce divergent outcomes, but their sources of variation are differentially located in the temporal and analytical chain of causality.

Second, we argue that a critical juncture framework can shed considerable light on patterns of institutional change that do not conform to punctuated equilibrium models—that is, models of discontinuous institutional change followed by the lock-in and reproduction of a new institutional equilibrium (Krasner 1988: 77–86). When properly viewed across a range of cases subjected to similar environmental shocks or disruptions, it is readily apparent that a punctuated equilibrium is not the only possible outcome; institutions can experience patterns of incremental or gradual change (Thelen 2004; Mahoney and Thelen 2010), as well as patterns of serial replacement (Levitsky and Murrillo 2014), or what Bernhard (2015) calls "chronic instability." Neither incremental change nor serial replacement produces a new, punctuated equilibrium, and they lack the conventional hallmarks of a critical juncture, since incremental change is not discontinuous, and serial replacement does not produce durable institutional arrangements. However, a critical juncture framework provides conceptual and analytical tools to assess the conditions under which these different models of institutional change are more or less likely to unfold, thus helping to explain why some outcomes are more discontinuous or gradual than others, as well as more durable or fleeting. In short, punctuated equilibriums, incremental change, and serial replacement may be alternative institutional trajectories derivative of common environmental shocks or disruptions that are differentially experienced across a number of cases. Our analysis, then, explores variation in both the sources and the outcomes of institutional change from a critical juncture perspective.

SOURCES OF VARIATION: LOCATING CAUSALITY IN A CRITICAL JUNCTURE FRAMEWORK

As Krasner (1988: 72) emphasizes, institutionalist approaches to the study of politics are predicated on the notion of persistence—that is, the assumption that "institutional arrangements perpetuate themselves across time." The institutionalization or "persistence over time" of party systems, however, has distinctive properties—and challenges—when compared to the institutionalization of political rules, procedures, policies, or regimes. At a minimum, party system institutionalization requires continuity in a system's constituent actors—that is, the major party organizations that define a country's electoral alternatives and compete for support within the electorate. More ambitiously, it requires relative stability in the competitive balance among these rival actors, and not simply stability in the rules of the game. Institutionalization thus depends on supply-side decisions by political entrepreneurs to pursue their objectives (whether policy, personal, or organizational) within the parameters of established parties, as well as myriad micro-level decisions by voters on the demand side to support those parties in relatively stable proportions over time.

To be sure, established parties boast a wide range of competitive advantages over newcomers in the electoral marketplace, and they typically aim to sort the electorate into stable blocs of like-minded or organizationally-loyal voters to whom they are bound by programmatic, clientelistic, or charismatic linkages (see Lipset and Rokkan 1967; Converse 1969; Bartolini and Mair 1990; Kitschelt 2000). However, such linkages can fray over time, or even fail to congeal at all when competitive party systems are in gestation in new democratic regimes. Since individual vote choices under democracy are voluntary and potentially mobile, any competitive balance is susceptible to disruption by large-scale shifts in voter preferences or loyalties across election cycles. Such shifts can be driven by a wide range of factors, including performance failures, corruption scandals, economic crises, policy "betrayals," and the mobilization of new voters into the electorate with preferences that diverge from those of existing voters.

Not surprisingly, then, party systems in developing regions during the so-called "third wave of democratization" (Huntington 1991) have varied widely in their levels of electoral stability or institutionalization. To what extent does the critical juncture framework provide analytical leverage for explaining such variation? As stated by Collier and Collier (1991: 29), a critical juncture is "a period of significant change, which typically occurs in distinct ways in different countries (or in other units of analysis) and which is hypothesized to produce distinct legacies." So conceived, the critical juncture framework is intrinsically comparative, as it is designed to explain patterns of change that vary across cases in systematic ways.

A key question to be asked, however, is where the source (or sources) of such variation is located. The critical juncture framework traces patterns of change in a sequential process across four distinct periods of time: (1) an antecedent period that establishes the baseline conditions and institutional arrangements prior to the onset of a critical juncture; (2) the period in which the critical juncture occurs, typically in response to some sort of environmental shock or endogenous strains that challenge the reproduction of the institutional baseline; (3) an aftermath period in which the institutional changes of the critical juncture are contested and the legacy emerges; and (4) the legacy of enduring institutions. Analysis of these sequential periods and their causal connections can buttress claims that a critical juncture in institutional development has occurred.

As Collier and Collier (1991) emphasize, the critical juncture is typically experienced in different ways across a range of cases, producing divergent institutional outcomes with path-dependent development trajectories in the legacy period. A graphic depiction of such divergence across two cases is provided in Figure 6.1. In this figure, A—B represents the baseline antecedent conditions under a preexisting institutional equilibrium—the persistence noted by Krasner (1988). Point B depicts the onset of a critical juncture attributable to some type of exogenous shock or disruption that impedes the reproduction of the institutional baseline. The dashed lines B—C and B—D thus represent the period of the critical juncture when institutional arrangements in the two cases depart—in different directions—from the baseline trajectory. The two cases reach a new institutional equilibrium at points C and D, respectively, which is then reproduced in the legacy period (C—E and D—F). This simplified model captures the basic logic of a punctuated equilibrium, or equilibriums, with diverging institutional legacies. So conceived, the critical juncture is a period in which forking paths emerge, as the two cases experience the critical juncture in different ways.

In this descriptive model, the juncture is critical because the cases cannot arrive at E or F without passing through B—C or B—D, and the legacies are path dependent because the route to E passes through B—C and C—E, and the route to F passes through B—D and D—F. In other words, there is no path that leads to E through the critical juncture of B—D, and no path that leads to F through the critical juncture of B—C. As depicted, neither is there what Waldner (see Chapter 7) characterizes as a "backdoor" path that leads directly from the antecedent conditions (A—B) to either E or F without passing through one of the critical junctures (B—C or B—D). It is incumbent on any critical juncture account to explain why such backdoor pathways were not plausible—that is, why the institutional legacies could not have emerged

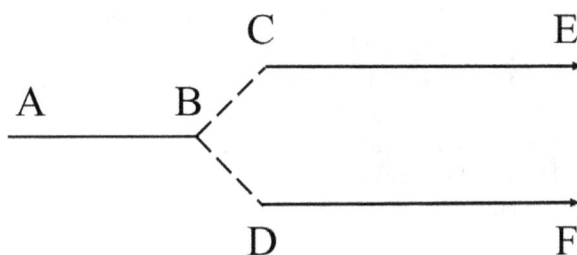

Figure 6.1 Critical Junctures and Punctuated Equilibriums

without passing through the critical juncture. We believe such backdoor pathways, where they exist, are more appropriately analyzed through the models of incremental institutional change (Thelen 2004; Mahoney and Thelen 2010) discussed below, as they lack the punctuated, crisis-induced, and period-specific institutional discontinuities that are the hallmark of the critical juncture framework.

The model in Figure 6.1, however, does not tell us *why* the two cases diverge during the critical juncture, or where the source of that variation is located. Explaining this variation—the forking paths, so to speak—is a basic task of the critical juncture framework, as it helps to account for distinct institutional legacies.

Nevertheless, the source of variation—or the locus of causal attribution—is treated differently by scholars who employ the critical juncture framework. In part, these differences reflect variation in the perceived levels of contingency associated with critical junctures, and thus the latitude they provide for political agency and choice to influence outcomes. It is widely recognized that the exogenous shocks or strains that bring about a critical juncture challenge the reproduction of antecedent institutional baselines and, in the process, make possible dramatic breaks in institutional rules and arrangements, policy orientations, or actor alignments. For some authors, the essence of a critical juncture is the heightened level of contingency and uncertainty that exists during a period of institutional disruption, and the resulting space that is opened for political agency—the strategic choices and behavior of different actors—to chart a new course. As stated by Soifer (2012: 1574), it is "the reduced importance of structural constraints that opens up space for divergence to emerge." This relaxation of structural constraints creates "permissive conditions" that "increase the causal power of agency or contingency and thus the prospects for divergence" (Soifer 2012: 1574).

Although Soifer (2012: 1593, fn. 2) is "agnostic" about the "relative importance" of agency and contingency in a critical juncture, other scholars see them as central to the framework. Capoccia and Kelemen (2007: 348, 352), for example, identify "structural fluidity and heightened contingency" as the "defining traits of critical junctures," as they create a "*substantially* heightened probability that agents' choices will affect the outcome of interest" (emphasis in the original). For this reason,

Mahoney (2001b: 112) characterizes critical junctures as a "key choice point" in which "a particular option is selected from among two or more alternatives" (see also Mahoney 2001a). Such choices can be seen as the outcome of what Soifer (2012: 1575) calls the "productive conditions" that "operate within the possibility space bounded by the permissive conditions" during a critical juncture.

Soifer (2012: 1576–77) takes care to differentiate these permissive and productive conditions from baseline antecedent conditions. To what extent, however, do the latter weigh on the operation of productive conditions during a critical juncture and thus influence its outcome? The strong emphasis of Capoccia and Kelemen (2007: 342) on contingency and choice—on the "actions and decisions that occur during the critical juncture itself"—relegates "structural, antecedent conditions" to a clearly secondary plane (if not a purely descriptive one) in an explanatory account of institutional change. The source of variation, then, is the strategic behavior and decisions made by political actors along B—C and B—D in Figure 6.1. Mahoney shares this emphasis on choice, but nonetheless recognizes a significant role for antecedent conditions in constraining choice by determining what options are available to the relevant political actors. So conceived, antecedent conditions along A—B in Figure 6.1 do not simply provide a baseline against which to measure change; they provide a "starting point" for causal explanation by defining "a range of options available to actors at a key choice point" (Mahoney 2001b: 112). Actors may be free to choose between B—C and B—D, but the delineation of those options—and the foreclosure of others—would be structured by A—B.

Collier and Collier go even further in attributing potential causal significance to antecedent conditions, suggesting that there is a high degree of variation in their influence on outcomes. Whereas some critical junctures "may entail considerable discretion," in others "the presumed choice appears deeply embedded in antecedent conditions" (Collier and Collier 1991: 27). A similar interpretation is found in Slater and Simmons's (2010: 889) insightful discussion of "critical antecedents"—that is, "factors or conditions preceding a critical juncture that combine with causal forces during a critical juncture to produce long-term divergence in outcomes." The combinatory logic is crucial, as critical antecedents cannot produce the outcome in question directly without experiencing the shock or disruption of the critical juncture. As stated above, it must be demonstrated that A—B cannot lead directly to C—E or D—F; there is, in Waldner's terminology (see Chapter 7), no backdoor path that leads directly from the antecedent conditions to the divergent outcomes. In that sense, the juncture is surely still critical. But neither will actor choices in the critical juncture produce the divergence without the conditioning effects of critical antecedents. It is the latter that often lead cases to experience the critical juncture in different ways. In so doing, they "predispose (but do not predestine) cases to diverge as they ultimately do" (Slater and Simmons 2010: 891)—that is, to embark along either B—C or B—D. For this reason, Slater and Simmons (2010: 890) caution against the treatment of crisis periods as "blank slates" with untrammeled political agency; critical junctures, they argue, are "typically moments of expanding agency, not complete contingency." Divergence, not contingency, is their analytical hallmark, as critical junctures activate or reformulate latent antecedent differences, magnify their effects, and propel cases along divergent evolutionary pathways.

Our own research suggests that an analysis of antecedent conditioning effects is likely to be important in explanations of party system divergence during critical junctures in political development. Antecedent conditions not only define the range of viable options available to different players, as Mahoney suggests, but also determine who those players are likely to be, how their interests are defined, and what the distribution of power and resources among them will be. Such factors heavily condition the strategic choices and behavior of actors in a critical juncture, even if they do not predetermine them. Likewise, antecedent conditions may cause one or more cases to experience a common crisis or shock in more or less extreme ways than others, with important implications for the political choice set, strategic alignments, and actor decisions.

Although antecedent conditioning effects may not be a universal property of critical junctures, we agree with Slater and Simmons (2010) that they are common, and the critical juncture framework should be flexible enough to accommodate them. Indeed, both the level of contingency and the degree of antecedent conditioning should be treated as *variable properties* rather than binary categories that establish defining features of critical junctures. This variation can be conceptualized as a spectrum or analytical dimension that has a high level of contingency (or choice) on one pole, and high levels of analytical conditioning on the other (see Figure 6.2). Most critical junctures are likely to involve elements of each, in different combinations, making it possible to identify subtypes of critical junctures based on their locus or primary source of divergence. A critical juncture can be considered *generative* when it is characterized by a high degree of contingency, such that divergence is largely a product of actor choices and strategic behavior located within the critical juncture itself. Alternatively, a critical juncture is *activating* when it is characterized by strong antecedent conditioning effects, such that latent differences across cases are activated to predispose cross-case divergence during a critical juncture. Predisposition, however, is not fully determinative, as political actors can still make choices within a set of opportunities and constraints structured by the antecedent conditions.

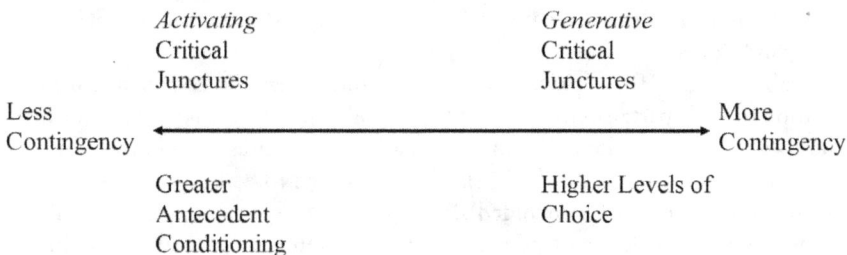

Figure 6.2 Activating and Generative Critical Junctures

Such patterns of activation are readily apparent in our own work on critical junctures in party system development. In Latin America, the collapse of state-led development in the debt crisis of the 1980s and the subsequent process of market-based structural adjustment posed formidable challenges to party systems across the region (Roberts 2013; 2014). This exogenous shock, however, was not equally shared by all countries, and it hardly created a blank slate for actor choices and institutional change. The economic crisis was more severe and prolonged—and thus politically disruptive—in the subset of countries whose antecedent conditions included ambitious statist development models, labor-based forms of political representation, and widespread social mobilization. Although every country in the region shifted in the direction of market liberalism, they did not enter the period of transition—the critical juncture—on equal footing.

Antecedent conditions associated with the military dictatorships of the 1960s and 1970s also shaped the competitive balance between conservative and populist or leftist actors in party systems during the critical juncture. Such conditioning effects weighed heavily on political alignments around the market reform process—the decisive "choice" in Latin America's neoliberal critical junctures (Roberts 2014). Where antecedent conditions empowered conservative actors to lead the process of neoliberal reform over staunch labor and leftist opposition, the critical juncture was more likely to assume activating properties and to align and stabilize partisan competition along a left-right axis of programmatic contestation. Brazil and Uruguay provide examples of such activating critical junctures during the period of neoliberal reform. Alternatively, where antecedent conditions left conservative actors too weak or cautious to lead the process of neoliberal reform, severe inflationary crises often induced labor-based populist or center-left parties to "swallow the bitter pill" (Weyland 1998)—that is, to impose austerity and adjustment measures that clashed with their campaign promises and traditional policy commitments. Such "bait-and-switch" patterns of neoliberal reform were characterized by high levels of contingency and choice, as in the generative critical junctures depicted in Figure 6.2. Not surprisingly, they de-aligned party systems programmatically and, as explained below, left them vulnerable to destabilizing "reactive sequences" (Mahoney 2001a) in the aftermath period. Strategic choices to implement neoliberal reforms thus had divergent political effects, depending on partisan alignments around the reform process—alignments that were not strictly predetermined by antecedent factors, but surely conditioned by them.

In sub-Saharan Africa, party systems were fundamentally reshaped during the transition to multipartyism in the early 1990s, following the breakdown of the Soviet Union and ascendant domestic and international pressures for political and economic neoliberal reform (Riedl 2014). What appeared to be largely similar baseline conditions in period A—B included single-party authoritarian regimes, significant state weakness, high levels of patronage, ethnic heterogeneity, and the "politics of permanent economic crisis" (van de Walle 2001). Strategic choices of key political elites during the transition (Point B) appeared very similar as well. Incumbent parties and their top officeholders sought to stay in power by managing the institutional reforms necessary to introduce multiparty competition and win founding elections. High levels of overall political uncertainty undoubtedly characterized the transition, given that actors during the transition were not clear about the durability of the new regime, economic repercussions, and the longevity of the institutional reforms proposed (Lupu and Riedl 2013). This uncertainty created opportunities for contingency, and political elites demonstrated shrewd calculations to react to the unfolding transitions and craft new solutions, such as dissolving an authoritarian incumbent party and running as independent candidates (as in Benin), crafting new ethnic or religious alliances to build a national constituency (as in Ghana), and partnering with trade unions and other civil society activists to form a democratic movement-turned-party (as in Zambia).

Yet the dominant force in determining the nature of the new multiparty systems was based on a latent antecedent condition, the varied strategies of support and power accumulation pursued by the single-party authoritarian regimes during the prior decades. In most African authoritarian regimes, incumbents consolidated their power in one of two ways: broad-based incorporation of social and economic authorities at the local level, or state substitution—attempting to neutralize local power brokers and replace them with state-sponsored organizations. Both strategies were useful for authoritarian control and maintenance. But they provided unequal transferrable assets when unforeseen transitions to multiparty competition required that these incumbent parties win majorities in founding elections in order to stay in power. These foundations of authoritarian power accumulation structured the strategic calculations of key political agents throughout the transition period, activating unequal potential to control the transition period, set new rules of electoral competition to lock in future patterns of party competition, and shape strategic interparty alignments and organization.

Where authoritarian incumbents were strong at the moment of transition, they restricted entry by new challengers and compelled opposition parties to coalesce in order to compete. These pressures forced party organizations to emulate the incumbent's party, leading to fewer effective parties and discrete incumbent and opposition camps. These pressures made the party system more institutionalized in the democratic era. On the other hand, where authoritarian incumbents were weak, they lost control of the transition agenda, allowing new players to contribute in uncoordinated ways to press for more open participation. New parties organized along different lines in a party system open to reinvention and party proliferation. The result in these countries was that weakly institutionalized party systems persisted. During democratic transitions, these existing relations between national and local power brokers condition whether or not incumbents can maintain power and set the new rules of the game. These rules in turn influence how party systems develop. In the end, party systems exist along a range of levels of institutionalization—from well organized, durable, and coherent parties in the most institutionalized systems to highly volatile, scarcely organized, and fleeting parties in the weakly institutionalized systems. What this sequence of factors highlights is that democratization is not a blank slate: legacies from the past, specifically strategies for maintaining power, play a major role in determining how party systems develop and endure over time, as in the activating critical junctures outlined above.

EXPLAINING DIFFERENT KINDS OF CHANGE: LEVELS OF CONTINGENCY AND THE INSTITUTIONAL ENVIRONMENT

Attention to the degree of contingency versus antecedent conditioning can also help us to understand critical junctures in relation to other types of institutional change and, therefore, what type of change is likely depending on the existing institutional environment. In the standard model of a highly institutionalized political environment, a great deal of contingency introduced by an exogenous shock is likely to *generate* a new equilibrium around reconfigured institutions. Given this conceptual anchor, we may not expect critical junctures to be likely in conditions of weak institutionalization. Yet we find that weakly institutionalized domains provide exactly the conditions that make *activating* critical junctures likely. In periods of flux that relax prior constraints maintaining the previous system, antecedent conditions shape future trajectories in *new and divergent* ways. The congruence between the new institutional outcomes and the previously constructed social cleavages, party organization, elite alliances, or other conditioning factor, is what undergirds the equilibrium moving forward, despite the broader context of weak institutionalization. Without that congruence from the past (e.g., in a scenario instead defined by changes generated from high contingency), recurring institutional instability is the much more likely outcome.

To differentiate among the broader set of modes of institutional change, critical junctures are known to produce outcomes of institutional change and stasis through path dependence, in that outcomes during a crucial transition establish distinct trajectories (David 1985; Collier and Collier 1991: 27; Capoccia 2015), also referred to as a punctuated equilibrium (Krasner 1988: 77–86).[1] Yet other models of political change also exist without experiencing a critical juncture, including incremental change (Thelen 2004; Mahoney and Thelen 2010) and serial replacement, or chronic instability (Levitsky and Murillo 2014; Bernhard 2015; Riedl 2016).

Through attention to the *strength of the overarching institutional environment* and the *degree of contingency*, we propose an analytical framework to explain different models of institutional change. That is, by extending the insights of the first section regarding a spectrum from weak to strong antecedent conditioning (or high

---

1. Punctuated equilibrium can be defined as a discontinuity during the transition phase followed by the lock-in and reproduction of a new institutional equilibrium.

to low contingency), we can also shed light on later patterns of institutional stasis and change along a given pathway. Such a framework is important to understanding how recent critical junctures in party system development in both Africa and Latin America created a punctuated equilibrium in some countries, whereas others experienced patterns of incremental change (Thelen 2004; Mahoney and Thelen 2010) or serial replacement (Levitsky and Murillo 2014; Bernhard 2015; Riedl 2016).

As Levitsky and Murillo (2014) note, much of the literature on institutions suggests that they maintain equilibrium because they are designed in line with power distributions and existing social and political norms. Either actors initially accept the rules or lack the power to overturn them. Mahoney and Thelen (2010) add that subsequent drift or conversion may occur when gaps between formal rules and compliance create opportunities for contestation and serve as sources of incremental change. What these views of equilibrium and gradual institutional change generally assume is a strong institutional environment, one in which the state has the power to enact the rules and enforce compliance.

In contrast, in a weak institutional environment, there is greater likelihood of incongruence between formal rule-making processes and *de facto* power holders, creating the conditions for serial replacement (Levitsky and Murillo 2014). Electoral rules, constitutions, economic reforms, and decentralization are many domains in which countries with a weak institutional environment have experienced chronic instability: frequent constitutional crises and constituent assemblies to rewrite them; redrawing decentralized boundaries and redistribution of resources from the center to the periphery and back again; changing electoral rules to determine which parties and candidates are eligible and under what conditions citizens' votes are transferred to representative outcomes; and the pace and direction of economic liberalization have varied dramatically within countries across short historical time spans.

In addition to the strength of the overarching institutional environment, the degree of contingency can also shape the process of institutional change (Figure 6.3). A high degree of uncertainty or contingency characterizing a process of institutional change is more likely to lead to later patterns of serial replacement (lower right quadrant). Rapid institutional design can reduce institutional durability because actors are more likely to miscalculate potential consequences and key power holders may be temporarily excluded during a transition period (Elkins et al. 2009; Grzymała-Busse 2011; Levitsky and Murillo 2014; Riedl 2014). By the same logic, high levels of contingency regarding the major actors and their strategic behavior or choices can create uncertainty about power distributions, the impact of institutions for future power distributions, and ongoing reconfigurations of alliances between groups. As stated by Levitsky and Murillo (2014: 12): "When uncertainty is high, those in control of the rule-writing process are more likely to misjudge the preferences and/or strength of powerful actors, leaving newly-designed institutions vulnerable to displacement." The combination of a weak institutional environment and a high level of contingency, therefore, is the most likely to lead to serial replacement (or chronic instability), as seen in the lower right quadrant of Figure 6.3.

Contingency

		Low (Strong Antecedent Conditioning)	High (Weak Antecedent Conditioning)
Institutional Environment	Strong	Incremental Change	Critical Juncture
	Weak	Critical Juncture	Serial Replacement

Figure 6.3 Contingency and Institutional Environment

Alternatively, a standard critical juncture framework would suggest a reasonably strong institutional environment with an established equilibrium that is disrupted by a shock or severe strain, followed by a generative transition characterized by a contingent process of institutional design that creates a high degree of uncertainty. The strategic choices and alignments of key actors, however, would reflect new configurations of power and interest that are locked in and reproduced, generating new patterns of institutional continuity (upper right quadrant). In the rationalist approach, institutional stasis follows the new power and preference distributions established through the contingent transition process (Greif and Laitin 2004), and in a historical institutionalist approach, mechanisms of reproduction continue to generate the legacy, producing continuity (Steinmo et al. 1992; Streeck and Thelen 2005; Mahoney and Thelen 2010).

Yet patterns of punctuated equilibrium are also common in weakly institutionalized environments (lower left quadrant), as our own work on party systems has demonstrated. In these contexts, punctuated equilibrium is more likely when latent antecedent conditions are activated during a critical juncture to shape varied institutional pathways going forward. When institutions are crafted over longer time horizons, key power holders have time to assess and evaluate their impact and organize alliances to defend their interests. Furthermore, when informal institutions are significant, the slower pace allows for building in complementarity between *de facto* practices and formal rules. Activating critical junctures that draw upon critical antecedents may be more prone to maintaining a correspondence between key stakeholders and new institutional formations.

Finally, moments of low contingency may sow the seeds for later incremental change when the institutional environment is strong and new challenges are addressed through gradual processes of conversion, drift, layering, or displacement (Mahoney and Thelen 2010). Whereas a rapid and contingent transition may also create these forms of friction to be addressed through later reforms, transitions activating latent underlying conditions provide particularly productive pathways for actors to calculate how the rules affect their interests and redeploy their uses during a period of relatively relaxed structural constraints to reform (upper left quadrant). An extended transition also allows for the difficult work of collective mobilization, for either displacement or layering, as those impacted by the new rules of the transition recognize their newly shared interests in reform. A relatively strong institutional environment may stimulate an extended period of reorientation when underlying disjunctures between the rules and the power distribution are addressed. Underlying social cleavages may be expressed through new institutional forms as actors slowly subvert, build around, or redirect the existing rules through conversion (in which rules remain formally the same but are interpreted and enacted in new ways) and layering (the creation of new rules alongside old ones, thereby changing the way original rules structure behavior) (Mahoney and Thelen 2010: 15–18).

These combinations are not deterministic, but they suggest that critical junctures can be analyzed alongside other models of institutional change, providing comparative leverage to identify the conditions that are most conducive to discontinuous or gradual change, as well as more durable or fleeting institutional legacies. They also suggest that a range of cases may experience common environmental shocks or disruptions in different ways, producing alternative institutional trajectories of punctuated equilibrium, incremental change, and serial replacement. Attention to antecedent conditioning effects may help to explain why exogenous shocks are more severe in some cases than others, or why some institutional configurations are better positioned to weather common shocks than others. When viewed across a large number of cases, limiting an analysis to those that experience high levels of contingency through a critical juncture with punctuated equilibrium may truncate the sample and introduce the well-known inferential biases associated with selection on the dependent variable (Collier and Mahoney 1996). Examining cases that also experience incremental change or serial replacement—that is, cases on the "low" and "high" ends of the spectrum of institutional change, respectively—can provide crucial analytical leverage for identifying causal mechanisms of change and continuity (Roberts 2014: 44–45). Such mechanisms are central to our understanding of complex social processes and relationships (McAdam et al. 2001).

A broader comparative perspective focusing on the existing institutional environment and the degree of contingency can also help to explain why a common shock generates a new equilibrium with positive feedback or increasing returns in some cases, thus spawning enduring and resilient institutional legacies, whereas institutional outcomes in other cases may be susceptible to negative feedback effects that are sources of ongoing institutional change. As Grief and Laitin (2004: 649) argue, institutional equilibria "are more or less sensitive to exogenous shocks" and "environmental changes," as the behavior of rational actors is self-reinforcing "in larger or smaller sets of situations." So conceived, some cases may exit a common transition with an institutional equilibrium that is far more susceptible to the types of destabilizing "reactive sequences" analyzed by Mahoney (2001a) than others. Such was the case in Latin America's neoliberal critical junctures, where societal resistance to market reforms in the post-adjustment "aftermath" period reinforced or "locked in" party systems that had been programmatically aligned during the critical juncture, but thoroughly disrupted those that had been de-aligned (Roberts 2014). Indeed, a broader comparative perspective may suggest that some cases exit the transition period with no institutional equilibrium at all, along the lines of Levitsky and Murillo's (2014) serial replacement model. As they argue, such forms of chronic instability or deinstitutionalization can also follow a self-reinforcing, path-dependent logic, with initial institutional failures fostering expectations and strategic behavior that reproduce institutional fluidity. Political actors, in short, may adopt short time horizons, hedge their bets, and invest resources in extra-institutional arenas that undermine more formal types of institutions.

As Collier and Collier (1991: 27) eloquently described with reference to "The Road Not Taken," the character of critical junctures varies greatly, with some entailing great discretion by actors, even contingent uncertainty, and others belying deeply embedded antecedent conditions *which activate different pathways* going forward. Here we extend this variation in levels of contingency to explain how the institutional legacies will vary more broadly. The comparative analysis of party systems in Africa and Latin America suggests that institutional outcomes include models of punctuated equilibrium, gradual institutional change, and serial replacement.

High Contingency and Weak Institutional Environment: Serial Replacement

In sub-Saharan Africa, transitions to multiparty competition in the early 1990s were frequently characterized by a weak institutional environment, in which the state lacked the ability to enforce rules across the complete national territory. Frequently, this resulted in a security void, as in Mali's northern region, where the Tuareg population sought autonomy and independence. Combined with a rapid institutional design process of a National Conference in 1991, the transition excluded many key political actors from the prior regime, and created the foundations for ongoing regime instability, or serial replacement, as seen in the lower right quadrant of Figure 6.3 (Bingen 2000; Wing 2013; Riedl 2016). The combined effects of a highly uncertain institutional crafting process and rapid transition with an overarching security threat limited the utility of the democratic institutional arena as the center of conflict resolution and contestation. Instead, political battles were waged through precipitous institutional reforms including electoral systems and decentralization, coup attempts, military factions, and citizen disengagement from the formal arena. In short, the transition produced a durable pattern of serial replacement and chronic institutional instability.

In Latin America, Peru provides a paradigmatic example of serial replacement that followed this basic logic of a weak institutional environment and a highly contingent set of actors and policy choices. A weak state and relatively inchoate party system were buffeted by a severe economic crisis and a civil war in the 1980s, while the party system virtually collapsed in the early 1990s when the populist outsider

Alberto Fujimori implemented "bait-and-switch" neoliberal reforms and a "presidential coup" against legislative and judicial institutions. Thereafter neither Fujimori nor his opposition organized stable party organizations, allowing a series of largely independent presidential candidates to cycle into office under a pattern that Roberts (2014: 58) labeled "serial populism."

High Contingency and Strong Institutional Environment: Critical Juncture

Africa's independence-era period of party building demonstrated punctuated equilibrium in those countries where the decolonization process arose rapidly in the postwar withdrawal by the imperial powers (Keller 1995), and colonial electoral institutions of contestation were transferred and quickly dismantled by the emerging political elite, overlaid on strong informal institutions of neopatrimonialism. These conditions generated high levels of uncertainty and contingency in the founding era of multiparty competition. This process stands in stark contrast to intransigent colonial powers and homegrown revolutionary parties that had to fight for independence, such as in the former Portuguese colonies and white settler concentrations (Levitsky and Way 2012). In the former set of cases of rapid decolonization, the strong informal institutions of neopatrimonialism linked political elites at the center with a vast network of brokers and citizens, fostering a legacy of punctuated equilibrium in which a relatively cohesive political elite emerged and established single-party regimes (Collier 1982).

In Latin America, Chile's neoliberal critical juncture provides an example of strong institutions with high levels of contingency. A military coup followed by comprehensive neoliberal "shock treatment" created considerable uncertainty and disruption in one of Latin America's most institutionalized party systems. Nevertheless, this generative critical juncture fostered a new regime and programmatic cleavage around which partisan competition could be realigned and stabilized following a transition to democracy, a process with many of the hallmarks of a punctuated equilibrium.

Low Contingency and Weak Institutional Environment: Critical Juncture

In sub-Saharan Africa, the pathway to stable electoral democracy as well as stable competitive authoritarianism proceeded through rather prolonged transitions, activating latent antecedent conditions that could allow a ruling incumbent party either to transition to democracy through strength, as in Ghana (as well as in Taiwan, South Korea, and Indonesia; see Slater and Wong 2013), or to maintain power through a shift to multiparty competition in a newly designed authoritarian regime, as in Uganda and Tanzania (Riedl 2016). Despite an overall weakly institutionalized environment, ruling parties were able to align new institutional innovations with underlying power distribution and maintain stability. In Uganda's authoritarian ruling party, the National Resistance Movement (NRM) pursued a carefully controlled transition to multipartyism, first constraining opposition parties and then slowly legislating their existence and conduct while steering the constitutional reform process according to its own preferences (Tripp 2004; Makara et al. 2008). By shaping the rules of party registration, civil liberties, and the role of state forces, the NRM further institutionalized their broad-based coalition for long-term electoral success and durability.

The Brazilian case in Latin America also provides an example of an activating critical juncture in party system development that unfolded in a context of weak institutions but strong antecedent conditioning effects. Although Brazil's party system was highly inchoate in the 1980s, the political balance of power bequeathed by the country's military dictatorship positioned conservative forces to lead the process of market reform. As such, the party system became increasingly structured along a central cleavage between a center-right bloc and the leftist Workers Party (PT), which channeled labor and popular resistance to market liberalization policies. The progressive strengthening of the PT was grounded in labor and social movement currents that emerged under the prior military dictatorship but found newfound partisan representation under the democratic regime.

Low Contingency and Strong Institutional Environment: Incremental Change

Finally, a process of gradual incremental change through displacement shaped Senegal's party system over time in a context of strong antecedent conditioning. Given the strength of the authoritarian successor party, based on antecedent conditions of deep social linkages established under the prior regime, the ruling party had the capacity to undertake sequential changes to the electoral rules, attempting to engineer short-term advantages. Ultimately the displacement created conditions for gradual deinstitutionalization of the party system despite the continuity of core parties, joined by new personalist parties and movements (Riedl 2018).

Similarly, in Latin America, Uruguay provides an example of incremental change in a party system in a context of strong institutions and high levels of antecedent conditioning. Following Uruguay's democratic transition in the 1980s, two long-standing conservative parties were positioned to lead the process of market reform, but the party system was progressively transformed by the strengthening of a major leftist alternative that channeled societal opposition to market orthodoxy. The strengthening of the leftist Broad Front over time transformed the competitive balance and dynamics of the party system, while leaving its principal units intact.

CONCLUSION: CONTINGENCY AND DETERMINISM IN THE CRITICAL JUNCTURE FRAMEWORK

One of the central questions in the critical juncture framework is the extent to which contingency or determinism is an inherent feature in its model of institutional change (Collier and Munck 2017). Our work suggests that contingency is a variable property of critical junctures, one that is always present, but in greater or lesser degrees. The same could probably be said of antecedent conditioning. These two elements of critical junctures combine in complex ways that largely determine the locus of causal attribution for institutional divergence and differentiate activating from generative critical junctures. For this reason, critical junctures can be identified as "(1) a major episode of institutional innovation, (2) occurring in distinct ways, (3) and generating an enduring legacy" (Collier and Munck 2017: 2).

Further, activating and generative critical junctures suggest that there is less of an opposition between contingency and determinism in the overall framework than might be assumed. Critical antecedents can strongly shape the distinct forms taken by a critical juncture, while still not being completely deterministic (Dunning 2017). Critical junctures often emerge from some type of exogenous shock that introduces a changed environment. The antecedent conditions influence institutional innovation during the critical juncture, yet take on new values and shape possibilities in new ways given the transformed context. For Collier and Collier (1991), the contrasting degrees of rural elites' control over work relations in the agrarian sector were antecedent conditions that could be mapped onto differences in the labor incorporation period in each country. Roberts (2014) demonstrates that even within generative critical junctures, where contingent choices and political alignments produced institutional outcomes that could have been different, antecedent factors played a role in conditioning the competitive balance between competing actors, the type of actor making key strategic choices, and the set of choices available to them. Although some of these institutional outcomes were stable equilibria with durable legacies, others were susceptible to destabilizing reactive sequences and chronic instability.

Consequently, when viewed comparatively across a wide range of cases undergoing similar shocks or strains, a critical juncture framework provides analytical tools to explore different patterns of institutional change, facilitating comparison of the dynamics that produce punctuated equilibriums, serial replacement, and incremental change. Rather than treating these alternative models as analytic rivals, it might be more fruitful to compare and contrast their differential generative conditions and causal mechanisms, such as the strength of overarching institutional environments and the level of antecedent conditioning.

Even given self-reinforcing mechanisms of endurance, the probability of staying on a distinct path decreases with each cumulative step (Lieberson 1997). For party systems, a host of factors contribute to demand-side stability among voters, and the absence of any of them creates challenges to endurance, as noted above. In this way, the self-replicating causal structure of the legacy need not be seen as fully deterministic. By treating contingency as a variable property, we show how it is possible to address a range of processes that generate and activate institutional divergence and produce institutional endurance and change.

BIBLIOGRAPHY

Bartolini, Stefano, and Peter Mair. 1990. *Identity, Competition, and Electoral Availability: The Stabilisation of European Electorates 1885–1985*. New York, NY: Cambridge University Press.

Bernhard, Michael. 2015. "Chronic Instability and the Limits of Path Dependence." *Perspectives on Politics* 13(4): 976–91.

Bingen, R. James. 2000. "The Malian Path to Democracy and Development." In R. James Bingen, David Robinson, and John M. Staatz (eds.), *Democracy and Development in Mali* (pp. 245–51). East Lansing, MI: Michigan State University Press.

Capoccia, Giovanni. 2015. "Critical Junctures and Institutional Change." In James Mahoney and Kathleen Thelen (eds.), *Advances in Comparative-Historical Analysis* (pp. 147–79). New York, NY: Cambridge University Press.

Capoccia, Giovanni, and R. Daniel Kelemen. 2007. "The Study of Critical Junctures: Theory, Narrative, and Counterfactuals in Historical Institutionalism." *World Politics* 59(3): 341–69.

Collier, David, and James Mahoney. 1996. "Insights and Pitfalls: Selection Bias in Qualitative Research." *World Politics* 49(1): 56–91.

Collier, David, and Gerardo L. Munck. 2017. "Building Blocks and Methodological Challenges: A Framework for Studying Critical Junctures." *Qualitative and Multi-Method Research* 15(1): 2–9.

Collier, Ruth Berins. 1982. *Regimes in Tropical Africa: Changing Forms of Supremacy, 1945–1975*. Berkeley, CA: University of California Press.

Collier, Ruth Berins, and David Collier. 1991. *Shaping the Political Arena: Critical Junctures, the Labor Movement and Regime Dynamics in Latin America*. Princeton, NJ: Princeton University Press.

Converse, Philip E. 1969. "Of Time and Partisan Stability." *Comparative Political Studies* 2(2): 139–71.

David, Paul A. 1985. "Clio and the Economics of QWERTY." *American Economic Review* 75(2): 332–37.

Dunning, Thad. 2017. "Contingency and Determinism in Research on Critical Junctures: Avoiding the Inevitability Framework." *Qualitative & Multi-Method Research* 15(1): 41–47.

Elkins, Zachary, Tom Ginsburg, and James Melton. 2009. *The Endurance of National Constitutions*. New York, NY: Cambridge University Press.

Grief, Avner, and David D. Laitin. 2004. "A Theory of Endogenous Institutional Change." *American Political Science Review* 98(4): 633–52.

Grzymała-Busse, Anna. 2011. "Time Will Tell? Temporality and the Analysis of Causal Mechanisms and Processes." *Comparative Political Studies* 44(9): 1267–97.

Huntington, Samuel P. 1991. *The Third Wave: Democratization in the Late Twentieth Century*. Norman, OK: University of Oklahoma Press.

Keller, Edmond J. 1995. "Decolonization, Independence, and the Failure of Politics." In Phyllis Martin and Patrick O'Meara (eds.), *Africa* (3rd ed.; pp. 156–71). Bloomington, IN: Indiana University Press.

Kitschelt, Herbert. 2000. "Linkages between Citizens and Politicians in Democratic Politics." *Comparative Political Studies* 33(6/7): 845–79.

Krasner, Stephen D. 1988. "Sovereignty: An Institutional Perspective." *Comparative Political Studies* 21(1): 66–94.

Levitsky, Steven, and María Victoria Murillo. 2014. "Building Institutions on Weak Founda-tions: Lessons from Latin America." In Daniel Brinks, Marcelo Leiras, and Scott Main-waring (eds.), *Reflections on Uneven Democracies: The Legacy of Guillermo O'Donnell* (pp. 189–213). Baltimore, MD: Johns Hopkins University Press.

Levitsky, Steven, and Lucan A. Way. 2012. "Beyond Patronage: Violent Struggle, Ruling Party Cohesion and Authoritarian Durability." *Perspectives on Politics* 10(4): 869–89.

Lieberson, Stanley. 1997. "The Big Broad Issues in Society and Social History: Applications of a Probabilistic Perspective." In Vaughn McKim and Stephen Turner (eds.), *Causality in Crisis? Statistical Methods and the Search for Casual Knowledge in the Social Sciences* (pp. 359–85). Notre Dame, IN: University of Notre Dame Press.

Lipset, Seymour M., and Stein Rokkan. 1967. "Cleavage Structures, Party Systems, and Voter Alignments: An Introduction." In Seymour M. Lipset and Stein Rokkan (eds.), *Party Sys-tems and Voter Alignments: Cross-National Perspectives* (pp. 1–64). New York, NY: Free Press.

Lorenz, Hans-Walter. 1993. *Nonlinear Dynamical Economics and Chaotic Motion*. Berlin: Springer.

Lupu, Noam, and Rachel Beatty Riedl. 2013. "Political Parties and Uncertainty in Developing Democracies." *Comparative Political Studies* 46(11): 1339–65.

Mahoney, James. 2001a. *The Legacies of Liberalism: Path Dependence and Political Regimes in Central America*. Baltimore, MD: Johns Hopkins University Press.

_____. 2001b. "Path-Dependent Explanations of Regime Change: Central America in Com-parative Perspective." *Studies in Comparative International Development* 36(1): 111–41.

Mahoney, James, and Kathleen Thelen. 2010. "A Theory of Gradual Institutional Change." In James Mahoney and Kathleen Thelen (eds.), *Explaining Institutional Change: Ambiguity, Agency, and Power* (pp. 1–37). New York, NY: Cambridge University Press.

McAdam, Doug, Sidney Tarrow, and Charles Tilly. 2001. *Dynamics of Contention*. New York, NY: Cambridge University Press.

Makara, Sabiti, Lise Rakner, and Lars Svasand. 2008. "Turnaround: The National Resistance Movement and the Reintroduction of a Multiparty System in Uganda." *International Politi-cal Science Review* 30(2): 185–204.

Riedl, Rachel Beatty. 2014. *Authoritarian Origins of Democratic Party Systems in Africa*. New York, NY: Cambridge University Press.

_____. 2016. "Strong Parties, Weak Parties: Divergent Pathways to Democracy in Sub-Saharan Africa." In Nancy Bermeo and Deborah J. Yashar (eds.), *Parties, Movements, and Democracy in the Developing World* (pp. 122–56). New York, NY: Cambridge University Press.

_____. 2018. "Authoritarian Successor Parties in Sub-Saharan Africa: Into the Wilderness and Back Again?" In James Loxton and Scott Mainwaring (eds.), *Life after Dictatorship: Authoritarian Successor Parties Worldwide* (pp. 175–205). New York, NY: Cambridge Uni-versity Press.

Roberts, Kenneth M. 2013. "Market Reform, Programmatic (De-)Alignment, and Party Sys-tem Stability in Latin America." *Comparative Political Studies* 46(11): 1394–421.

_____. 2014. *Changing Course in Latin America: Party Systems in the Neoliberal Era*. New York, NY: Cambridge University Press.

Slater, Dan, and Erica Simmons. 2010. "Informative Regress: Critical Antecedents in Com-parative Politics." *Comparative Political Studies* 43(7): 886–917.

Slater, Dan, and Hillel Soifer. 2020. " The Indigenous Inheritance: Critical Antecedents and State Building in Latin America and Southeast Asia." *Social Science History* 44(2): 251–74.

Slater, Dan, and Joseph Wong. 2013. "The Strength to Concede: Ruling Parties and Democratization in Developmental Asia." *Perspectives on Politics* 11(3): 717–33.

Soifer, Hillel David. 2012. "The Causal Logic of Critical Junctures." *Comparative Political Studies* 45(12): 1572–97.

Steinmo, Sven, Kathleen Thelen, and Frank Longstreth (eds.). 1992. *Structuring Politics: Historical Institutionalism in Comparative Analysis.* New York, NY: Cambridge University Press.

Streeck, Wolfgang, and Kathleen A. Thelen (eds.). 2005. *Beyond Continuity: Institutional Change in Advanced Political Economies.* New York, NY: Oxford University Press.

Thelen, Kathleen. 2004. *How Institutions Evolve: The Political Economy of Skills in Germany, Britain, the United States, and Japan.* New York, NY: Cambridge University Press.

Tripp, Aili. 2004. "The Changing Face of Authoritarianism in Africa: The Case of Uganda." *Africa Today* 50(3): 3–26.

Van de Walle, Nicolas. 2001. *African Economies and the Politics of Permanent Crisis, 1979–1999.* New York, NY: Cambridge University Press.

Weyland, Kurt. 1998. "Swallowing the Bitter Pill: Sources of Popular Support for Neoliberal Reform in Latin America." *Comparative Political Studies* 31(5): 539–68.

Wing, Susanna. 2013. "Mali's Precarious Democracy and the Causes of Conflict." *Special Report* 331. Washington, DC: United States Institute of Peace.

7

Qualitative Causal Inference and Critical Junctures

The Problem of Backdoor Paths

David Waldner

The critical juncture literature has proceeded along two paths. Travelers along one path have produced path-breaking and classic studies of political change involving relatively compressed periods of institutional change followed by much longer periods of institutional continuity. Pioneering work in macro-historical analyses of political development, from Seymour Martin Lipset and Stein Rokkan (1967) and Barrington Moore (1966) to Ruth Berins Collier and David Collier (1991) and Gregory Luebbert (1991) can be found here. Travelers along the second and more recently trodden path have produced insightful and valuable commentary attempting to refine and systematize the key elements of the critical juncture framework by carefully considering the nature of the critical juncture and of the path-dependent processes that define historical legacies. Central to this conceptual literature are debates about whether critical junctures are inherently contingent.

   In this chapter, I argue that we need a third path that considers the methodological underpinnings of the critical juncture literature. The current literature places too much emphasis on contingency and path dependency, and too little emphasis on causal identification. The main problem of causal inference is that any associations we observe (for comparative historical approaches, these associations are sequences of events) are potentially an unknown mixture of causal and noncausal relationships. Noncausal relationships can be induced by confounding, or the existence of a pretreatment common cause, and by selection, or the restriction of the analysis to

An earlier version of this chapter was prepared for presentation at the Annual Meeting of the American Political Science Association, Boston, MA, August 30–September 2, 2018. David Collier and Gerardo L. Munck have been my intellectual partners as I wrote this chapter and their contributions have improved it in innumerable ways.

a subset of a population exhibiting a common effect. Confounding and selection interfere with our ability to make causal inferences by introducing bias, or systematic error, into an estimate of a causal effect; this is true whether we use quantitative or qualitative methods. Causal identification refers to the strategy we employ to remove sources of bias, so that observed associations can be interpreted as causal effects.

I focus here on noncausal associations due to common causes—the existence of some variable, Z, or some prior event that is causally related to both the hypothesized cause, X, and the outcome to be explained, Y.[1] This is a very common causal structure and it has been widely recognized for a long time as a source of potentially invalid causal claims. The problem I see in the current literature on critical junctures is a tendency to treat claims about contingency, implicitly or explicitly, as claims about causal identification. One problem with this claim is that the relationship of contingency to critical junctures is debated, with some scholars viewing contingency as constitutive of critical junctures and others denying this claim; there are no grounds to adjudicate this dispute on *a priori* theoretical grounds. A second problem with this claim is that even if we were to all agree that critical junctures are inherently contingent, no claim about contingency necessarily implies the absence of pretreatment common causes and hence the absence of potential biases in our causal claims. Contingency does not serve the methodological function needed for valid causal inference.

This chapter thus joins with David Collier's chapter in this volume (see Chapter 1) in arguing that contingency should not be a defining attribute of critical junctures. My reasons for taking this position are purely methodological; the assumption of contingency at the critical juncture does not address important components of causal inference. I agree with Collier, however, that eliminating contingency as a definitional attribute does not make critical junctures any less critical, in terms of their production of sharply discontinuous change with long-term consequences. The purpose of this chapter is to give scholars a better set of tools to make causal inferences about critical junctures.

The first section of this chapter introduces some concepts from the fields of causal inference and causal graphs, especially the concept of a *backdoor path*. The second section explains why the concept of contingency is inadequate to discriminate between causal and noncausal associations, while a third section provides illustrative examples from the existing literature on critical junctures. The fourth section pivots toward applied qualitative methodology, arguing that current approaches overemphasize inference via the elimination of alternative hypotheses, which are not equivalent to backdoor paths. The fifth section briefly discusses some methodological practices for better analyzing backdoor paths and their implications for causal inference. A sixth section concludes the chapter.

---

1. There is a parallel literature on bias due to selection effects; see Collier and Mahoney (1996) for discussion in the context of case-study research.

THE PROBLEM OF CAUSAL IDENTIFICATION

To discuss the problem of causal identification, I use an instrument called a causal graph, a simple representation of a causal model in which (1) nodes or vertices—denoted by text or text boxes—represent variables or types of events, and (2) arrows represent our testable beliefs about causal relationships. Causal graphs are useful because they simultaneously represent causal relationships and noncausal relationships. Causal graphs thus follow rules that distinguish them from more informal representations that also use boxes and arrows; these rules make causal graphs particularly valuable because they simultaneously represent causal models and statistical models.[2] Causal graphs are not identical with statistical analysis, however; causal graphs are *qualitative and nonparametric representations of causal models*. Their value is that they help us distinguish causal relationships from noncausal sources of associations.

Figure 7.1 below represents the most basic causal graph possible. It represents the claim—our testable belief, based on theory and prior research—that X is a cause of Y.

Figure 7.1 A Basic Causal Graph

Notice that by convention, the direction of causality is from left to right (from parent to descendent, in the language of graph theory) and that arrows also represent the passage of time. But it is not just the arrow from X to Y that is important; equally important is the *absence* of any other arrows and any other nodes. Interpreting the missing nodes and arrows of the causal graph in Figure 7.1 thus also represents the claim that Y does not cause X and that there are no common causes of X and Y. Finally, the causal graph in Figure 7.1 omits two other types of causes: intermediary causes between X and Y (mediators, in the language of graph theory) and other causes of Y that are unrelated to X, including error terms.[3]

The most basic rule of causal graph theory is that graphs must include all common causes of X and Y. Graphs that include all common causes are called complete graphs. Common causes are denoted by Z in Figure 7.2.[4]

---

2. The most important rules are the Causal Markov Condition and the rules governing d-separation. For discussion, see Pearl (2000) and Pearl and Mackenzie (2018), while Rosenbaum (2017) is an excellent resource on causal inference.

3. There is no prohibition against including either intervening causes on the path between X and Y or other causes of Y; their inclusion would be based on pragmatic context-specific considerations.

4. Note that we can distinguish between Z, measured common causes, and U, unobserved common causes, and that both Z and U could refer to a vector of causes.

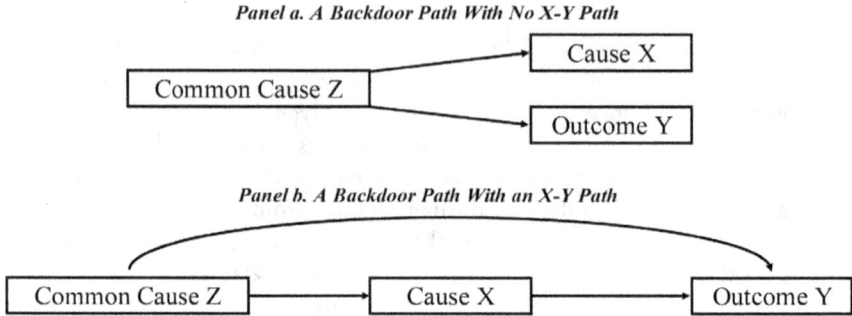

Figure 7.2 Common Causes and Backdoor Paths. *Note*: The backdoor path runs from X back to Z and then to Y.

The models in panels a and b of Figure 7.2 represent two distinct and basic ways that common causes can be represented. In panel a, Z is a cause of X and Z is a cause of Y, but X is not a cause of Y. This structure represents the classic case of a "spurious association," a well-known example being that smoking causes lung cancer and smoking causes yellowed fingertips; but yellowed fingertips do not cause lung cancer. In contrast, in panel b, Z is a cause of X, Z is a cause of Y, and X is also a cause of Y.

Each of the two graphs in Figure 7.2 contains multiple paths, one of which is called a backdoor path. A path is any arrow-based route between two variables, regardless of the direction of the arrows. Paths follow the edges that connect nodes, regardless of the direction represented by the arrowheads. Paths that follow the direction of arrows are causal paths; paths that at any point run backwards against the direction of the arrows are noncausal paths. In particular, a backdoor path from X to Y is a path from X to Y that does not follow an arrow out of X. In both graphs in Figure 7.2, the backdoor path runs from X to Z to Y.

The basic problem is that noncausal paths create associations that do not reflect causal relationships and hence bias our inferences about the causal effect of X on Y. In panel a of Figure 7.2, the association between X and Y completely disappears when we adjust for Z, while in panel b, the graph represents our belief that the association between X and Y does not disappear after adjusting for Z; instead, the remaining association represents the unbiased causal relationship. If we did not adjust for Z in panel b of Figure 7.2, however, then the observed association between X and Y would not represent the causal effect of X on Y; rather, the observed association would be a mixture of unknown proportions of the true causal relationship and the noncausal source of association induced by the backdoor path. Without some form of correction for this noncausal source of association, any causal claim of the effect of X on Y would be biased.[5]

Return now to Figure 7.1, the simple graph X → Y. If this graph is correctly specified—if we have not omitted any common causes and hence there are no backdoor paths from X to Y—then any observed association between X and Y represents an unbiased causal effect: there are no potential sources of bias.[6] Figure 7.1 would be accurate if it represented an experimental data-generating process, such that assignment to values of X was randomly assigned. Under this data-generating process, the values of all covariates would be balanced in expectation among all groups and a simple difference-of-means would be an unbiased estimate of the causal effect. Outside of the experimental setting, Figure 7.1 might be correct under the conditions of a natural experiment, in which some naturally occurring process, outside of the control of the researcher, assigns units to values of X "as-if" randomly or haphazardly.[7] If units are assigned to values of X as if by chance, then by definition, there can be no backdoor paths. But notice that the natural-experiment framework requires an explicit argument about as-if randomization, an argument that typically requires highly detailed and context-specific information about the assignment mechanism. These arguments will always be more or less plausible depending upon the degree of evidentiary support. The absence of a backdoor path, in other words, is an empirically testable claim, not an *a priori* proposition.

If causal identification cannot be justified by explicit randomization by the researcher or an argument about plausible as-if randomization, then unbiased causal inferences require a strategy of causal identification that eliminates the bias induced by the backdoor path; in the language of graph theory, backdoor paths must be blocked. There is a large literature on these strategies of causal identification, which I will draw on in the latter part of this chapter. For now, the important question is whether the concept of contingency could function as a satisfactory strategy of causal identification.

CONTINGENCY

Recent discussions of the critical juncture framework have not emphasized the problems of causal inference discussed above; rather, some prominent recent discussions

---

5. This source of bias goes by many discipline-specific names: it is known as endogeneity bias, bias induced by nonrandom assignment to treatment, selection bias, omitted variable bias, and confounding bias.

6. For completeness, we might add a prior node with a single arrow into X and label that node "ideal intervention" or "random assignment" to clarify the absence of any threat of an unobserved pretreatment common cause.

7. See Dunning (2012) for a clear exposition of research designs based on natural experiments.

have emphasized the contingent nature of critical junctures. James Mahoney (2000) was the first scholar to make contingency a defining feature of a critical juncture. Contingency, he argued,

> refers to the inability of theory to predict or explain, either deterministically or probabilistically, the occurrence of a specific outcome. A contingent event is therefore an occurrence that was not expected to take place, given certain theoretical understandings of how causal processes work. (513)

Giovanni Capoccia and Daniel Kelemen (2007: 348) concur with Mahoney, defining a critical juncture as a relatively short period of time "during which there is a *substantially* heightened probability that agents' choices will affect the outcome of interest." This definition, they argue, implies first that structural factors have been temporarily relaxed and second that political actors face an expanded feasible choice set, the selection from which will have momentous consequences for the long-term future. "Contingency," they conclude, "becomes paramount" (Capoccia and Kelemen 2007: 343).

Suppose, temporarily, that we all agreed that contingency was a definitional attribute of a critical juncture, such that we could not predict the critical event from antecedent conditions, perhaps because actors were liberated from structural conditions that had previously constrained their choice set or perhaps because multiple independent causes happened to coincide, or perhaps for both reasons. Would our analysis of the critical juncture and its long-term outcome satisfy the conditions for unbiased causal inferences? For two reasons, I would argue that contingency cannot be equated with the absence of backdoor paths.

First, there is enormous diversity of opinion about the contingent nature of a critical juncture, even among those who believe that to some degree, contingency should be a defining feature. Dan Slater and Erica Simmons (2010: 890) agree that the degree of contingency inherent in the concept of a critical juncture should be handled definitionally, but they differ on the semantic details. "Critical junctures," they state in their brief for some form of constrained contingency, "are typically moments of expanded agency, not complete contingency." Hillel Soifer (2012) seeks a different means to square this particular circle by distinguishing permissive conditions, or the suspension of prior mechanisms of reproduction that expands the scope of agency, and productive conditions that determine outcomes. Critical junctures thus feature a sequence in which initial contingency is followed by determinism. Rachel Riedl and Kenneth Roberts (see Chapter 6) argue that the balance between structure and agency will differ across cases and can only be discovered through careful research and analysis: therefore, no *a priori* claim about contingency is defensible. Finally, Ruth Berins Collier and David Collier (1991: 29), David Collier and Gerardo Munck (2017: 2), and David Collier (Chapter 1) define critical junctures without any reference to contingency at all; in their treatment, critical junctures may or may not be "deeply embedded in antecedent conditions" and actors may have very different degrees of discretion in different settings (Collier and Collier 1991: 27).

Therefore, it would be a mistake to make any version of contingency a definitional attribute of a critical juncture.

Given this diversity of opinion, even if we wanted to make contingency a definitional attribute of critical junctures, we would have to decide which version of contingency was the appropriate one. Inevitably, this decision would be arbitrary, to some extent at least, because there are no objective criteria that would guide our selection of the best version of contingency.

Second, contingency does not imply the absence of a potential backdoor path; it does not imply deliberately random or haphazardly random assignment to values of the treatment. *Merriam-Webster* gives five definitions of contingency. The first and primary definition is that contingency means dependent on or conditioned by something else. Clearly, this definition would not fulfill the necessary methodological function. The second definition is that a contingent event is likely but not certain to happen; it is a possible event. But this is true of virtually all causal relationships: when we say that smoking causes lung cancer, we mean that the probability of lung cancer is higher for smokers than for nonsmokers. We do not mean that every smoker will have lung cancer with absolute certainty. Debates about probabilism versus determinism are interesting, but they are irrelevant to the question of backdoor paths.[8] The third definition is that a contingent event is not logically necessary; contingent events are empirical. This is of course true for all empirical social sciences and so provides no methodological leverage. A fourth definition is that a contingent event is not necessitated, but rather determined by free choice. But free choice does not mean the absence of prior causes. Smoking may be heavily influenced by both genetic and environmental factors that make some people more likely to become smokers than other people. But people with a higher likelihood of becoming smokers still exercise choice; they are influenced by other factors, including the price of cigarettes. The argument that free choice is equivalent to randomness would imply that not only is choice free, it is chaotic and unstructured.

The fifth definition of contingency is perhaps the most interesting: happening by chance or unforeseen causes and hence unpredictable. Obviously, this particular definition is most relevant to our discussion. Contingency would serve the necessary methodological function *if and only if contingency always meant unpredictable because of randomness*—a genuine randomizing device or a haphazard or arbitrary assignment mechanism. But according to the definition, contingent events can also be unpredictable because of *unexpected causes*, which is not the same as randomness: it directly implies the existence of a cause of the critical juncture, a cause that may potentially be a pretreatment common cause, with one path to the treatment or independent variable and a second path to the outcome that does not pass through the treatment. This is precisely the source of a backdoor path. Unpredictability, then, can be an attribute of critical junctures because of discretionary choice by actors,

---

8. Dunning (2017) is relevant and instructive to this discussion.

because of unforeseen causes, or because of randomness; only the third reason is methodologically relevant and there is no justification for assuming a random or haphazard assignment mechanism.

Two implications follow: if by contingency, scholars intend randomness, then they should substitute the word random for the term contingency, given the connotative ambiguity of contingency. Second, randomness cannot be derived from unpredictability, for there are other sources of unpredictability that do not imply randomness. Randomness, then, *must be demonstrated empirically*; it is not a logical implication of any claims about contingency or unpredictability. Indeed, Mahoney (2000: 513) explicitly acknowledges this point, writing "To argue that an event is contingent is not the same thing as arguing that the event is truly random and without antecedent causes." Thus, contingency offers no solution at all to the problem of backdoor paths.

POTENTIAL BACKDOOR PATHS
IN CRITICAL JUNCTURES SCHOLARSHIP

In observational data, true randomness is exceedingly rare, and when scholars invoke it as a source of unbiased causal inference, they do so only after very careful empirical scrutiny of the assignment mechanism, the process by which units are assigned to values of the treatment variable. In this section, I briefly review a handful of landmark scholarly works in the critical juncture tradition to demonstrate the *potential* existence of a backdoor path. It is not my intention to criticize these works or to reject their claims; my purpose is exclusively to demonstrate the possibility that unblocked backdoor paths are present and that the analysis has not fully accounted for their potential to induce bias. To recall a point made earlier, one of the most basic rules of graph theory is that we include all potential common causes absent strong empirical or theoretical reasons to omit the backdoor path.

Example I. Mahoney's *Legacies of Liberalism*

In *Legacies of Liberalism: Path Dependence and Political Regimes in Central America*, Mahoney (2001a; see also 2001b) attributes varieties of twentieth-century political regimes in the five Central American countries to the critical juncture of the liberal reform period in the late nineteenth and early twentieth centuries. Mahoney insists that antecedent conditions did not determine the choices made during the liberal reform period; instead, small events, random processes, and human agency set these countries onto their path of long-term development. But to understand this argument, it is important to understand how Mahoney distinguishes antecedent conditions from agency-based decisions:

Liberals pursued a radical policy option in those countries (Guatemala, El Salvador, and Nicaragua) that were characterized by more developed agrarian economies and state structures at the beginning of the liberal reform period. By contrast, countries marked by lower levels of development (Costa Rica and Honduras) at the beginning of the reform saw the enactment of a reform policy option. Nevertheless, preexisting socioeconomic structures *did not make the adoption of a particular policy inevitable.* Liberals' choices were most immediately influenced by political considerations, especially threats from conservative rivals and other groups that sought to win state power. In Guatemala, El Salvador, and Nicaragua, liberals faced significant political challenges and were consequently led to build powerful militaries that made it structurally possible to pursue radical policy outcomes. By contrast, liberals in Costa Rica and Honduras faced fewer political challenges and never constructed the military and bureaucratic infrastructure necessary for the effective implementation of radical policy options. (Mahoney 2001a: 13; emphasis added)

Mahoney does not believe that preexisting socioeconomic structures made any subsequent choices *inevitable*; but inevitability is not our concern. Our concern is whether preexisting socioeconomic and political structures may have opened up a backdoor path. Furthermore, the strength of the conservative challenge to liberals appears to be correlated with prior socioeconomic structures: Guatemala, El Salvador, and Nicaragua all had more developed agrarian economies, more developed state structures, and a stronger conservative challenge to liberal elites. One might wish to consider, therefore, whether the nature of splits among the political elite, possibly induced by prior causes, might also have opened a backdoor path.

Figure 7.3 reproduces Mahoney's representation of his path-dependent argument (see panel a), and my recreation of his argument using a causal graph (see panel b). Panels a and b differ in two ways. First, panel b suggests that the strength of conservatives may itself be influenced by prior political-economic structures; this claim is at least consistent with Mahoney's argument. Second, panel b adds an arrow from "Strength of Conservatives" to "Regime Outcome," thus opening up a backdoor path from "Liberal Policy Choices" to "Establishment of Military" to "Strength of Conservatives" and terminating with "Regime Outcome."[9] This is a noncausal path—note how it runs counter to the direction of the arrows in panel a—linking liberal policy choices to regime outcomes by way of the strength of conservatives.[10]

---

9. The backdoor path is not simply the path from "Strength of Conservatives" to "Regime Outcomes." The backdoor path begins with the treatment variable and then runs "backwards" or against the direction of the arrow, into the pretreatment common cause and then to the outcome variable. It is the inclusion of the treatment, the pretreatment common cause, and the outcome variable that produces the noncausal association between treatment and outcome.

10. Figure 7.3 does not include a backdoor path running from political-economic structures to regime outcomes; surely this is plausible as well, however. Mahoney argues that these factors do not make liberal policy choices inevitable; he does not argue that these factors are unrelated to regime outcomes by any other path.

Panel a. Mahoney's Depiction of a Path-Dependent Process

	Liberal Reform Period		Legacy of Liberal Reform	
Antecedent Conditions	**Critical Juncture**	**Structural Persistence**	**Reactive Sequence**	**Outcome**
Nature of liberal-conservative cleavage; level of modernization	Adoption of radical or reform policy option by liberals	Production and reproduction of radical, reformist, or aborted liberalism	Relative prominence and success of democratizing movements	Military-authoritarian, democratic, or traditional-democratic regime

Presence or absence of serious foreign intervention

Panel b. Causal Graph, With a Backdoor Path

Political-economic Structures	→	Strength of Conservatives	→	Establishment of Military	→	Liberal Policy Choices	→	Regime Outcome

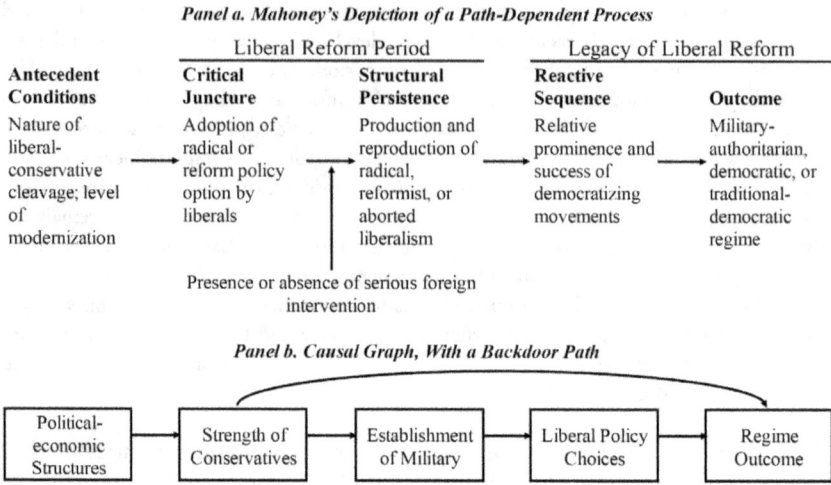

Figure 7.3 Mahoney's *Legacies of Liberalism. Source*: "Panel a." is an adaptation of Mahoney (2001a: 15, 2001b: 115).

I consider this a plausible backdoor path because countries with a deep divide in the political-economic elite might have regime outcomes distinct from those countries that have a relatively unified and cohesive political-economic elite for reasons other than those adduced by Mahoney as the path-dependent sequence. The claim is not that Mahoney's path-dependent sequence is spurious; the claim is that the observed association between liberal reform policies and regime outcomes *may be a mixture of unknown proportions containing the true causal relationship along the path-dependent sequence and the independent effect of the strength of the conservative elite on political outcomes that occurs through a distinct pathway.* The possibility of a backdoor path means that the observed association between liberal reformist policies and regime outcomes is compatible with more than one causal story.

Example II. Brownlee's *Authoritarianism in an Age of Democratization*

Consider next Jason Brownlee's (2007) *Authoritarianism in an Age of Democratization*, an enormously influential and admirably rigorous theory of how ruling political parties bolster authoritarian survival. For Brownlee (2007: 35), the critical juncture consists of "moments of regime formation," which in the authoritarian context he studies refers to whether ruling elites of new authoritarian regimes create a dominant party binding a cohesive, multifaction coalition or whether elites eschew strong parties and rely on tactical alliances instead of a cohesive coalition. Having a dominant or ruling party matters for regime survival, the outcome variable, because these parties can bind together elites who might otherwise defect and create a democratizing moment. In keeping with a contemporary approach that blends structuralism and voluntarism, Brownlee does not assume that the critical juncture was fully contingent. He traces moments of regime formation back to a prior causal variable: whether foundational social conflicts among the political elite were resolved or whether they lingered into the new authoritarian period. Graphically, the skeleton of the argument is depicted in Figure 7.4, in which I have added an arrow representing a *potential* backdoor path.

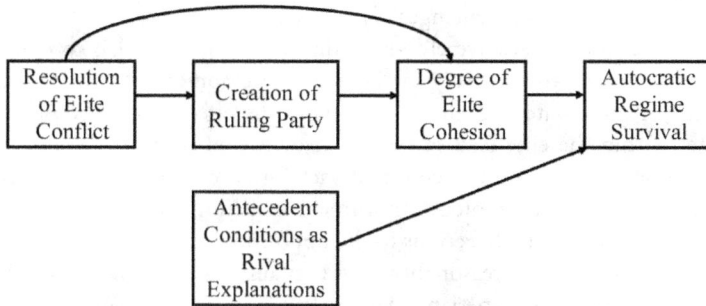

Figure 7.4 Causal Graph of Brownlee's *Authoritarianism in an Age of Democratization*, with a Backdoor Path

Figure 7.4 includes a backdoor path that begins with the creation of a ruling party, runs backwards to the resolution of elite conflict, then continues to the degree of elite cohesion and ends with autocratic regime survival. Brownlee's book analyzes two contrasting types of countries. In one set of countries, initial elite conflict is resolved as a dominant elite suppresses or co-opts its rivals, the unified elite creates a ruling-party system supported by a robust social coalition, and elites remain cohesive into the future. In the contrasting set of countries, elite conflict persists, challengers maintain broad social support, political parties are weak or nonexistent, and deep divisions continue into the future. The backdoor path in Figure 7.4 represents the reasonable concern that levels of elite cohesion at time t_0 fully account for levels of elite cohesion at t_1. It is possible, in other words, that initial elite cohesion is maintained only in the presence of a ruling party, but it is also possible that initial elite cohesion is a steady-state outcome. It is thus possible that the presence or absence of a dominant ruling party is more of a symptom of prior levels of elite consensus than a cause of future levels of elite consensus.[11]

Brownlee counters that dominant parties play a crucial role, nonetheless. He states that "[d]eveloped to meet the exigencies of regime formation, parties in which elite

---

11. Pepinsky (2014: 641–42) makes the identical critique.

conflicts have been resolved soon acquire a second use: They curb leaders' ambitions and bind together political coalitions" (Brownlee 2007: 37). Thus, when new disputes arise, as they inevitably do, ruling parties in systems of ruling elite cohesiveness prevent new disputes from escalating. Ruling parties thus reflect elite cohesiveness at one point in time and maintain that cohesiveness at future points in time, while autocracies without ruling parties exhibit a fragmented and contentious political elite at all points in time.

The argument is ingenious and quite plausibly correct. But note that Brownlee must confront two distinct challenges. The first is to demonstrate that parties have emergent properties that resolve elite-level disputes. The second is to demonstrate that the elite cohesion that initially catalyzes the development of a ruling party does not influence regime outcomes independently of the effect of parties. After all, not all disputes within the elite lead to regime change. Sometimes a disputatious elite faction is suppressed coercively or co-opted back into the ruling bloc, sometimes disputes within the elite lead to inter-authoritarian transitions, and sometimes disputes within the elite lead to elite defections to the opposition and the possibility of democratic transitions. We might reasonably posit that autocracies founded on initial elite cohesion will subsequently experience a lower level of elite factionalism that does not typically result in democratic openings. If this is true—and my claim is simply that it is plausible—then the observed association between ruling parties and authoritarian durability represents a mixture of causal effects and noncausal associations.

Example III. Collier and Collier's *Shaping the Political Arena*

As a third illustration of the potential for bias from unblocked backdoor paths, let's examine Ruth Berins Collier and David Collier's (1991) *Shaping the Political Arena* (henceforth *SPA*). Figure 7.5 represents the main causal argument, with the addition of a *potential* backdoor path.[12]

In general, *SPA* treats antecedent conditions as diverse features of economy, society, and politics that may provide rival hypotheses that explain outcomes that would otherwise be attributed to the critical juncture. But *SPA* also recognizes that the critical juncture—the timing and mode of labor incorporation—does not appear *ex nihilo*. Collier and Collier thus argue carefully that differences in labor incorporation can be partially traced back to corresponding differences in the nature of the oligarchic state, especially the strength of the oligarchy within the state and over the rural working class. With reference to this prior relationship and to contingency, *SPA* makes "no claim of a deterministic relationship, but maintain[s] that this is an

---

12. Unlike the other figures, Figure 7.5 includes the categories Antecdent Conditions, Critical Juncture, Legacy, and Additional Legacy. I include these here to faithfully represent the argument made in *Shaping the Political Arena* that has become the core representation of the critical junctures framework.

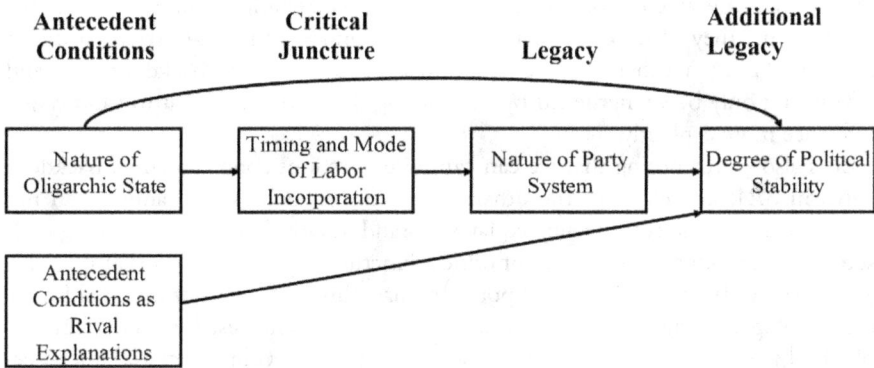

Figure 7.5 Causal Graph of Collier and Collier's *Shaping the Political Arena*, with a Backdoor Path

important source of insight into why labor incorporation occurred the way it did in each country" (Collier and Munck 2017: 5).

In most respects, the research design is exemplary. *SPA* eliminates two alternative hypotheses: one related to level of economic development, the other related to degree of ethnic homogeneity, through an ingenious set of paired comparisons. Collier and Collier identify four distinct modes of labor incorporation. They associate each mode with two countries. Within each pair of countries, they match a relatively wealthy country with a relatively poor country and a relatively homogeneous country with a relatively heterogeneous country. On the core principle that variation in treatment cannot explain similarity in outcome, they eliminate these rival hypotheses.

But the elimination of alternative hypotheses, while an important ingredient of causal analysis, is not sufficient. For our purposes, the critical question is whether the initiate node—the nature of the oligarchic state, which at least partially causes the critical juncture—generates a distinct causal path to the outcome node, regime stability. If so, there will be a backdoor path from labor incorporation to political stability that runs against the direction of the arrows and hence produces some degree of noncausal association between labor incorporation and political stability. Recent literature has suggested that state strength is directly related to political stability. Dan Slater et al. (2014) argue that contemporary democratic breakdowns in postcolonial states are caused by weak states, and Slater (2010) and Smith (2007) link state strength to autocratic durability.

Though Collier and Collier do not explicitly address the possibility of a backdoor path, some of their evidence suggests reasons why the backdoor path may not exist, at least in terms of state strength. Their two cases with the highest level of political stability, authoritarian Mexico and democratic Venezuela, are coded as having the weakest oligarchies of the eight countries they study. Thus, if we treat the strength of the oligarchy as conceptually equivalent to the strength of the state, then the relationships they observe run counter to the argument that state strength causes political stability. Yet there is more to be said about this potential backdoor path, and *SPA* would only be strengthened by considering this potential threat to valid causal inference more explicitly.

It is also worth noting that we can can raise questions about potential backdoor paths in *SPA*, as well as in the other two examples, because the authors do not simply assume that contingency equates to randomness. That each author spends some time thinking about causes of critical junctures raises questions that motivate an analysis of backdoor paths and potential bias: this is the penalty incurred by the methodologically righteous. Moreover, to reiterate a point raised earlier: I am emphatically not claiming that any of these works suffer from biased causal inferences induced by unblocked backdoor paths. I offer these examples only to illustrate the claim that backdoor paths remain an undiagnosed problem in the literature on critical junctures. My claim is that it is highly plausible that such backdoor paths exist, that any claim about contingency does not eliminate the threat of bias induced by the backdoor path, and that any work that successfully demonstrates the absence of a backdoor path will be methodologically more credible than an otherwise similar study that neglected the possibility of a backdoor path.

ALTERNATIVE HYPOTHESES

I have claimed that the problem of backdoor paths is an undiagnosed problem in the critical juncture literature—and, I would venture to say, in the larger literature on qualitative methodology. The current literature largely considers qualitative methodology to consist of an evaluation of the consistency of evidence with a research hypothesis relative to a set of alternative hypotheses, where alternative hypotheses are treated as independent hypotheses about the potential cause of an outcome. Causal claims are then based on efforts to falsify alternative hypotheses by showing that the evidence is not consistent with predictions derived from them and to confirm the research hypothesis by showing that the evidence is consistent with its predictions.[13]

---

13. There are two strands of this literature. In an earlier literature adopting a classical framework, a hypothesis would be definitively eliminated by failing a "hoop test," or a test that was a necessary implication of the hypothesis, while a research hypothesis could be corroborated by passing a "smoking-gun" test, such that the evidence was consistent with that hypothesis and no other. In more recent iterations, Bayesian reasoning replaces this categorical logic, such that evaluations are based upon the comparison of likelihoods. In both approaches, evidence is conceived of as some form of "causal process observation" that gives direct insight into the relevant causal relationships. Bennett and Checkel (2015) provide a recent statement of these positions.

Consider Figure 7.6, which reproduces a figure in Dan Slater and Erica Simmons's (2010) analysis of four types of antecedent conditions. The first two types, descriptive context and background similarities, are properly deemed causally irrelevant because they involve no connection to either the critical juncture or the outcome variable. The third type is what Slater and Simmons call a critical antecedent: notice that while this antecedent exerts influences on the critical juncture itself, it exerts no independent influence on the dependent variable; therefore, there is no backdoor path. In contrast, the fourth type of antecedent condition is an alternative explanation that is hypothesized to have an effect on the dependent variable but has no effect on the critical juncture itself.[14]

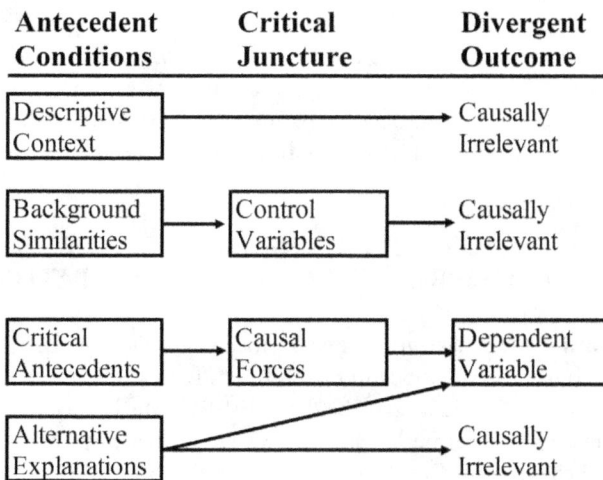

Figure 7.6 Critical Antecedents
Source: Adaptation of Slater and Simmons (2010: 890)

Notice that none of the four types of antecedent conditions generates a backdoor path: one of the most basic problems in the field of causal inference has not been considered here. And, I would claim further, Slater and Simmons are building on the conventional wisdom that ignores the problem of backdoor paths. This is true not only of the critical juncture framework but of the broader literature on qualitaive methods and process tracing.

---

14. The arrows in Figure 7.6 should not be interpreted in graph-theoretic terms.

It is therefore important to emphasize why the backdoor path is not just another alternative hypothesis. In the standard approach, the alternative explanation is a *rival explanation*, distinct from the research hypothesis. Therefore, as mentioned above, the basic research protocol is to find evidence disconfirming rival explanations and confirming one's research hypothesis.[15]

This basic procedure is not adequate for the problem of backdoor paths. As we saw in Figure 7.2, there are two basic formats for including a common cause, Z, in a causal graph that contains only a single cause, X, and an outcome, Y. One possibility represents spurious association: there is no arrow linking X and Y and any observed association between them is solely due to their being common effects of the cause, Z. The other possibility is the far more vexing one in which there is an arrow representing a causal relationship of X and Y, but there is also an arrow linking Z and Y that does not pass through X. This second causal relationship of Z and Y creates the backdoor path, X—Z—Y.[16] As a result, we should expect to find evidence linking X and Y. However, *the observed association of X and Y is a mixture of their true causal relationship and an unknown quantity of noncausal association induced by the backdoor path.* If this is the correctly specified causal model, then the nature of the problem is different: adducing evidence of the X → Y relationship will not be sufficient for unbiased causal inference.

QUALITATIVE CAUSAL INFERENCE AND THE PROBLEM OF BACKDOOR PATHS

In some previous work, I have articulated a procedure, called the completeness standard, for using qualitative methods to establish a causal path between a cause and an outcome (Waldner 2012, 2015a, 2015b, 2016, 2019). In the language of graph theory, most of this prior work has dealt with analysis along the "front-door path," or the extended causal chain from X to Y. To complement this prior work, I offer here some brief methodological recommendations for dealing with potential backdoor paths.[17]

Scenario I. The Absence of a Systematic Cause of the Cause

A first possibility corresponds to the standard natural experiment in which units are randomly assigned to the values of the treatment—i.e., pathways through the criti-

---

15. Zaks (2017) offers important insights into the common but mistaken belief that alternative hypotheses are necessarily rival hypotheses.

16. Undirected edges—as those in this example—denote the noncausal nature of the path from X to Y.

17. Dunning (2012) and Seawright (2016) offer extensive and vitally important commentary on how to use qualitative evidence in support of causal inference using various statistical techniques and research designs. My work is intended to support qualitative research as the primary method of causal inference.

cal juncture—by a process that is essentially haphazard or "as-if" random. In this case, the observed association between X and Y will be an unbiased estimate of the causal effect. As Thad Dunning (2012) makes abundantly clear, however, the "as-if" or haphazard assignment to values of the treatment variable can only be established by an argument based on carefully collected and scrutinized evidence about the assignment mechanism, or the "cause of the cause." Indeed, it is imperative to collect and consider evidence to back up a claim about random assignment rather than assume this is the case on the basis of the mere assertion that critical junctures are contingent events.[18]

Abhijit Banerjee and Lakshmi Iyer (2005) provide a compelling example of using qualitative evidence to establish the absence of a backdoor path. As Britain expanded its imperial control over the subcontinent, colonial officials selected which colonial land revenue system to put into place, with one system giving proprietary rights to landlords and another giving those rights directly to cultivators. Banerjee and Iyer study the possible long-term consequences of the critical juncture in which one or the other system was implemented.[19] Their expectation, based on the literature on the institutional foundations of development, is that land controlled by direct cultivators should exhibit higher rates of investment and higher levels of productivity in the postindependence period, many decades after the critical decisions were made. The methodological problem they confront is that colonial officials had great discretion in the choices they made, and one of the inputs into that discretionary choice may have been attributes of the land that would influence its long-term productivity.[20] The decision of which land revenue system to implement might have been endogenous to other causes of future productivity; if so, an observed association between institutions and outcomes would be a mixture of causal and noncausal sources of association. Figure 7.7 represents this methodological problem, with the potential backdoor path running from the revenue system to prior causes (against the direction of the arrow) and terminating with postcolonial outcomes, accompanying the hypothesized relationship between institutions and agricultural outcomes.

---

18. The phrase "cause of the cause" might trigger fears about infinite regress, forcing us to recursively consider the cause of the cause of the cause, *ad infinitum*. I consider this fear unfounded. On the one hand, there is no *a priori* reason to believe that the procedure of moving backwards along the causal chain must continue indefinitely. On the other hand, I know of no empirical research that has ever reported this problem. Readers who disagree with me should ask themselves whether they are willing to accept the very real and observable threat of biased causal inferences in order to avoid the purely theoretical threat of infinite regress.

19. There was a third system of collective village-based proprietary rights, but in practice, this system converged with either landlord-based or cultivator-based systems.

20. To reiterate a point made earlier: just because officials had discretion does not mean there was no prior cause unless it can be demonstrated that the officials made their decision without any influence from any potential prior cause. Furthermore, a prior cause is not necessarily the generator of a backdoor path.

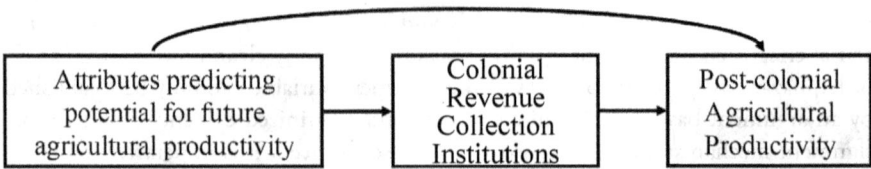

Figure 7.7 Causal Graph of Banerjee and Iyer's "Legacy of Colonial Land Tenure Systems in India"

The methodological challenge for Banerjee and Iyer is to demonstrate that the backdoor path cannot exist because, at different times and places, British colonial officials selected institutions for a wide variety of reasons, none of which appear, based on careful scrutiny of archival and other forms of evidence, to be related to any information about the agricultural potential of the land in question. The primary concern for officials was revenue collection, not productivity, and different officials in different places worked with different theories about whether small cultivators or large landlords would more reliably pay their taxes. In general, officials lacked accurate information about the territories under their control, based their decisions on *a priori* arguments that happened to be current at the time of the decision, and frequently misread Indian history. Add to these factors the idiosyncrasies of individual administrators and seemingly random events, and there is a strong case to be made that the selection of colonial land institutions was essentially haphazard: different regions were not assigned different revenue systems based on any expectation about the future productivity of the land. As such, there is no threat of a backdoor path inducing bias; it is highly plausible that variations in colonial institutions are determined exogenously, so that the simple causal graph Institutions → Outcomes represents the unbiased causal relationship.[21]

Note that the claim of "as-if" random assignment (assignment was not truly randomized, but it was sufficiently haphazard to produce approximately the same treatment assignment that true random assignment would have taken) is based upon careful evidence-based arguments; it is not based on the claim that critical junctures are inherently contingent. Furthermore, that colonial officials exercised agency or discretion in their choices does not itself imply as-if random. The haphazardness of assignment is an implication of the specific reasons that specific decisions were made.[22] Of crucial importance appears to be that British colonial officials lacked the

---

21. Here, as elsewhere, we could add a prior node representing the ideal intervention that constitutes as-if randomization.

22. Dunning (2012: 236–39) includes an incisive discussion of the specific conditions under which decision-making can be interpreted as haphazard. It is abundantly clear from this discussion that agent discretion over decision-making is emphatically not sufficient to assume as-if randomization.

information needed to base their decisions on the productivity of land and that British colonial officials were primarily motivated to maximize the reliable flow of revenue, not to maximize agricultural production per se. Therefore, while the decisions made at the critical juncture might have been unpredictable and not structurally determined, that fact in itself does not imply as-if randomization and the absence of a backdoor path.

Scenario II. The Absence of Backdoor Path Bias

A second scenario is to establish the cause of a cause that does not generate a backdoor path because the prior cause has no influence on the outcome variable that does not run through the hypothesized cause or critical juncture. We can draw on instrumental variable analysis to develop this procedure.[23] In the econometrics literature, Z is an instrument for X if Z is correlated with X, but Z's influence on Y travels only through X. Formally, $Corr(Z,X) \neq 0$, while $Corr(Z,\varepsilon) = 0$. The former condition, often called the relevance condition, will be true if Z is a cause of X; the latter condition, often called the exclusion restriction, is equivalent to saying that there is no path from Z to Y that does not pass through X; in other words, there is no independent causal pathway and hence no backdoor path. But note that the exclusion condition cannot be demonstrated statistically; the condition states that Z is not correlated with any unobserved elements of the disturbance term. Since they are unobserved, we cannot measure their correlation with Z. As in the case of natural experiment, we must exploit our local knowledge of the assignment mechanism.

For qualitative-historical researchers, the challenge is to argue on behalf of the absence of evidence. There are two possible procedures to follow. The first procedure would be purely theoretical: one would argue on purely theoretical grounds that there are no plausible pathways $Z \rightarrow M \rightarrow Y$, where M represents one or more intervening variables, excluding X or any variable descending from X, creating a path from Z to Y.[24] If this path is ruled out for sound theoretical reasons, there can be no backdoor path. The second procedure would be to acknowledge the theoretical possibility of a backdoor path running X—Z—M—Y, but to falsify this hypothesis by showing that on our best available evidence, the evidence does not support the claim that this is an unblocked path.

Arguing for the absence of a link between Z and Y that does not pass through X or any of X's descendants will be challenging, and the argument will always be more or less plausible, not incontrovertibly decisive. Edward Miguel et al. (2004) provide an illustration of this challenge. They wish to estimate the causal effect of economic shocks on the likelihood of civil war, but they recognize the strong likelihood that

---

23. Angrist and Pischke (2015) include an excellent and accessible introduction to instrumental variable analysis.

24. In the language of graph theory, M is a mediator, a variable along a path with only one arrow entering it and one arrow leaving it.

early events in a civil war or anticipation of heightened violence may cause capital flight and economic shocks. Economic shocks, in other words, may be endogenous to civil wars and they thus need an exogenous source of variation in economic shocks to yield an unbiased estimate of the causal effects of shocks on the likelihood of civil war. They propose rainfall as an instrument to study African civil wars. Rainfall is highly relevant because African economies are highly dependent on rain-fed agriculture. Years of relatively scarce rain should be correlated with economic shocks but not directly with the prospect of civil war—in other words, with no second causal pathway from rainfall to civil wars, there is no backdoor path. This is a highly plausible argument, yet the authors argue that the exclusion restriction may be violated in Africa because high levels of rainfall would make roads impassable and hence preclude government-insurgent conflict that would lead to battlefield deaths constitutive of a civil war; hence, rainfall could in principle affect civil wars through a channel that is independent of economic activity. The authors attempt to test this hypothesis, estimating the effect of higher-than-average rainfall on the extent of the usable road network and finding no statistically significant relationship. Yet even after this test and considering other possible violations of the exclusion restriction, they acknowledge their inability to "to definitively rule out the possibility that rainfall could have some independent impact on the incidence of civil conflict beyond its impact working through economic growth, though we believe that these other effects are likely to be minor" (Miguel et al. 2004: 746).

Scenario III. The Inevitability of Backdoor Path Bias

The third and final scenario to consider here is that a backdoor path is theoretically plausible, and the best available evidence does not definitively rule out the existence of an independent causal pathway. Given that qualitative research often involves big, macro-level questions that we try to answer by roaming widely across time and space, we should all acknowledge explicitly and transparently that we may not be able to rule out the possibility of a backdoor path with a high degree of confidence. Such claims are routinely made by authors of quantitative research, and qualitative researchers should drop the pretense that our extensive and fine-grained knowledge automatically eliminates the threat of bias. Acknowledging bias is surely better than ignorance of knowable bias or (self-) deception about known bias.

Assuming we have taken the appropriate steps to corroborate the direct $X \rightarrow Y$ relationship and we have reason to believe that this is not a fully spurious relationship, the nature of our analysis shifts.[25] Methodologically, our goal must now be to learn all that we can about the proportion of causal ($X \rightarrow Y$) and noncausal ($X—Z—Y$) sources of observed association. Notice how Miguel and his collaborators conclude

---

25. Typically, we establish the $X \rightarrow Y$ relationship via process tracing, or what I would like us to call "analysis of the front-door path."

their acknowledgement by stating that "we believe that these other effects are likely to be minor." To follow their lead, we should think in terms of the sign and magnitude of the relevant coefficients. In effect, we can develop a qualitative analogue to sensitivity analysis that examines "how fragile a result is against the possibility of unobserved confounding" (Cinelli and Hazlett 2020: 40).

Consider first the sign of the implicit coefficients. One possibility is that the $X \rightarrow Y$ relationship has a positive coefficient, while the $Z \rightarrow Y$ relationship has a negative coefficient: X raises the likelihood of Y while Z depresses that likelihood. This would allow us to make claims of the form "Despite the negative influence of Z, X still raises the likelihood of Y." We would not know the extent of the bias, but we would have reason to believe that observed associations underestimate the causal effect of X on Y.

The worst-case scenario, of course, is that the backdoor path is unblocked, and the causal effect of Z on Y has the same sign as the causal effect of X on Y. Now we have no choice but to exploit all of our available theoretical and empirical resources to make judgments about the relative magnitudes of the two causal effects. We might conclude that the causal effect along the backdoor path is relatively minor; then the backdoor path is little more than a nuisance. We might conclude that the causal effect along the backdoor path is of major significance that vastly outweighs the causal effect of our hypothesized cause, X. From the perspective of the collective advancement of knowledge, this should be considered an epistemological victory, as we as a community have learned more about how the world works. Finally, we may be highly uncertain about relative magnitudes of the two causal effects. We have still learned about the world, nonetheless, and our worst-case scenario will be a call for "more research in the future." This seems to me to be a more than reasonable price to pay for increasing our confidence in the basic validity of many of our causal claims.

CONCLUSION

This chapter has tried to establish that much work in the critical juncture tradition has ignored a basic source of biased causal inferences, the existence of a backdoor path induced by a pretreatment common cause. In retrospect, this might seem obvious; all of us know that causation is not equivalent to correlation. Yet, as I have demonstrated here, the possibility of backdoor path bias has been largely ignored in the qualitative literature. I have suggested that the misplaced emphasis on contingency has been one source of this error. Another possible source of this error might be that some contributions to qualitative methodology have construed the problem of causal inference too narrowly as a contest between a research hypothesis and its rivals. Backdoor path analysis shows why this approach is potentially misleading. Providing abundant evidence for some linkage between X and Y does not even begin to address the basic problem; in the presence of potential backdoor paths, the observed association between X and Y will reflect a mixture of unknown proportions of causal and noncausal sources of associations, with the former following the path of the arrows and the latter running against the direction of the arrows.

Much more needs to be said about how to conduct backdoor or front-door analysis, some of which can be found in previous publications and a book manuscript in process. As more qualitative researchers grapple more openly with backdoor path bias, I expect our collective knowledge of how to proceed to grow rapidly.[26]

BIBLIOGRAPHY

Angrist, Joshua D., and Jörn-Steffen Pischke. 2015. *Mastering 'Metrics: The Path from Cause to Effect*. Princeton, NJ: Princeton University Press.

Banerjee, Abhijit, and Lakshmi Iyer. 2005. "History, Institutions and Economic Performance: The Legacy of Colonial Land Tenure Systems in India." *American Economic Review* 95(4): 1190–213.

Bennett, Andrew. 2015. "Appendix: Disciplining Our Conjectures: Systematizing Process Tracing with Bayesian Analysis." In Andrew Bennett and Jeffrey Checkel (eds.), *Process Tracing: From Metaphor to Analytic Tool* (pp. 276–98). New York, NY: Cambridge University Press.

Bennett, Andrew, and Jeffrey Checkel (eds.). 2015. *Process Tracing: From Metaphor to Analytic Tool*. New York, NY: Cambridge University Press.

Brownlee, Jason. 2007. *Authoritarianism in an Age of Democratization*. New York, NY: Cambridge University Press.

Capoccia, Giovanni, and R. Daniel Kelemen. 2007. "The Study of Critical Junctures: Theory, Narrative, and Counterfactuals in Historical Institutionalism." *World Politics* 59(3): 341–69.

Cinelli, Carlos, and Chad Hazlett. 2020. "Making Sense of Sensitivity: Extending Omitted Variable Bias." *Journal of the Royal Statistical Society* 82(1): 39–67.

Collier, David, and James Mahoney. 1996. "Insights and Pitfalls: Selection Bias in Qualitative Research." *World Politics* 49(1): 56–91.

Collier, David, and Gerardo L. Munck. 2017. "Building Blocks and Methodological Challenges: A Framework for Studying Critical Junctures." *Qualitative and Multi-Method Research* 15(1): 2–9.

Collier, Ruth Berins, and David Collier. 1991. *Shaping the Political Arena: Critical Junctures, the Labor Movement, and the Regime Dynamics in Latin America*. Princeton, NJ: Princeton University Press.

Dunning, Thad. 2012. *Natural Experiments in the Social Sciences: A Design-Based Approach*. New York, NY: Cambridge University Press.

———. 2017. "Contingency and Determinism in Research on Critical Junctures: Avoiding the Inevitability Framework." *Qualitative & Multi-Method Research* 15(1): 41–47.

---

26. We will also need to develop qualitative responses to other sources of biased causal inference: measurement error and endogenous selection bias due to selection on collider variables.

Lipset, Seymour M., and Stein Rokkan. 1967. "Cleavage Structures, Party Systems, and Voter Alignments: An Introduction." In Seymour M. Lipset and Stein Rokkan (eds.), *Party Systems and Voter Alignments: Cross-National Perspectives* (pp. 1–64). New York, NY: Free Press.

Luebbert, Gregory M. 1991. *Liberalism, Fascism, or Social Democracy: Social Classes and the Political Origins of Regimes in Interwar Europe.* New York, NY: Oxford University Press.

Mahoney, James. 2000. "Path Dependence in Historical Sociology." *Theory and Society* 29(4): 507–48.

———. 2001a. *The Legacies of Liberalism: Path Dependence and Political Regimes in Central America.* Baltimore, MD: Johns Hopkins University Press.

_____. 2001b. "Path-Dependent Explanations of Regime Change: Central America in Comparative Perspective." *Studies in Comparative International Development* 36(1): 111–41.

Miguel, Edward, Shanker Satyanath, and Ernesti Sergenti. 2004. "Economic Shocks and Civil Conflict: An Instrumental Variables Approach." *Journal of Political Economy* 112(4): 725–53.

Moore, Jr., Barrington. 1966. *Social Origins of Dictatorship and Democracy: Lord and Peasant in the Making of the Modern World.* Boston, MA: Beacon Press.

Pearl, Judea. 2000. *Causality: Models, Reasoning, and Inference.* New York, NY: Cambridge University Press.

Pearl, Judea, and Dana Mackenzie. 2018. *The Book of Why: The New Science of Cause and Effect.* New York, NY: Basic Books.

Pepinsky, Thomas. 2014. "The Institutional Turn in Comparative Authoritarianism." *British Journal of Political Science* 44(3): 631–53.

Rosenbaum, Paul R. 2017. *Observation and Experiment: An Introduction to Causal Inference.* Cambridge, MA: Harvard University Press.

Seawright, Jason. 2016. *Multi-Method Social Science: Combining Qualitative and Quantitative Tools.* New York, NY: Cambridge University Press.

Slater, Dan. 2010. *Ordering Power: Contentious Politics and Authoritarian Leviathans in Southeast Asia.* New York, NY: Cambridge University Press.

Slater, Dan, and Erica Simmons. 2010. "Informative Regress: Critical Antecedents in Comparative Politics." *Comparative Political Studies* 43(7): 886–917.

Slater, Dan, Benjamin Smith, and Gautam Nair. 2014. "Economic Origins of Democratic Breakdown: The Redistributive Model and the Postcolonial State." *Perspectives on Politics* 12(2): 353–74.

Smith, Benjamin. 2007. *Hard Times in the Land of Plenty: Oil Politics in Iran and Indonesia.* Ithaca, NY: Cornell University Press.

Soifer, Hillel David. 2012. "The Causal Logic of Critical Junctures." *Comparative Political Studies* 45(12): 1572–597.

Waldner, David. 2012. "Process Tracing and Causal Mechanisms." In Harold Kincaid (ed.), *The Oxford Handbook of Philosophy of Social Science* (pp. 65–84). Oxford, UK: Oxford University Press.

———. 2015a. "What Makes Process Tracing Good: Causal Mechanisms, Causal Inference, and the Completeness Standard in Comparative Politics." In Andrew Bennett and Jeffrey T. Checkel (eds.), *Process Tracing: From Metaphor to Analytic Tool* (pp. 126–52). New York, NY: Cambridge University Press.

————. 2015b. "Process Tracing and Qualitative Causal Inference." *Security Studies* 24(2): 239–50.

————. 2016. "Invariant Causal Mechanisms." *Qualitative and Multi-Method Research* 14(1–2): 28–34.

————. 2019. "Causal Mechanisms and Qualitative Causal Inference in the Social Sciences." In Michiru Nagatsu and Attilla Ruzzene (eds.), *Contemporary Philosophy and Social Science: An Interdisciplinary Dialogue* (pp. 270–300). London, UK: Bloomsbury Press.

Zaks, Sherry. 2017. "Relationships among Rivals (RAR): A Framework for Analyzing Contending Hypotheses in Process Tracing." *Political Analysis* 25(3): 344–62.

8

Quantitative Methods and Critical Junctures

The Strengths and Limits of Quantitative History

Gerardo L. Munck

The classic literature on critical junctures used qualitative methods to assess causal claims. However, there is a quantitative tradition in economic history called cliometrics that gained prominence in the 1960s due to the work of North (1961) and Fogel (1964) and that has experienced a revival since the late 1990s (Nunn 2009, 2014; Haupert 2017). Moreover, this quantitative tradition has spread beyond economics, as political scientists have studied political history with quantitative methods (e.g., Pop-Eleches and Tucker 2017; Rozenas et al. 2017; Acharya et al. 2018). Thus, it is important to recognize that, alongside the literature using qualitative methods to assess arguments about critical junctures and historical legacies, there is another literature that uses quantitative methods to test historical arguments and, more specifically, claims about the persistent effects of distant causes.

This quantitative literature—we shall call it quantitative history—makes some strong methodological claims. It purports to bring the strengths of statistical analysis to a field not long ago entirely dominated by qualitative researchers (Diamond and Robinson 2010a: 5; 2010b: 270–74; see also Nunn 2014: 350). It also suggests that quantification is an unambiguous sign of progress, and that quantitative research is preferable to qualitative research (Nunn 2009: 71, 81; Diamond and Robinson 2010a: 2; 2010b: 270–72). That is, this literature frames methodological choices as one between either qualitative or quantitative research, and argues that quantitative research supersedes qualitative research.

This chapter places this new research on quantitative history in the context of the literature on critical junctures and considers its key methodological claims. It focuses

I would like to acknowledge useful comments and suggestions received from Taylor Boas, Sebastián Mazzuca, Ken Roberts, and David Waldner.

on theory testing as opposed to theory development.[1] Moreover, since quantitative history is an addition to an older and more voluminous qualitative literature, and since there has been no real dialogue between researchers working within quantitative and qualitative traditions, what follows also considers existing and possible combinations of quantitative and qualitative methods.

To anticipate the argument of this chapter, it holds that quantitative history is relevant to the study of critical junctures and historical legacies and makes an important contribution. In particular, it places a keen focus on causal inference and exemplifies how a concern with research design can be brought to bear on the kind of questions that are common in research on critical junctures. However, it also argues that this literature's sweeping claim in favor of quantification and its dismissal of qualitative research are not justified.

First, counter to the claim that it is best to move beyond qualitative analysis, the literature on quantitative history actually uses qualitative methods for the purpose of checking assumptions made in the quantitative analysis, that is, for providing qualitative diagnostics of quantitative tests. Indeed, one limitation of current quantitative history is that it does not use qualitative diagnostics more fully and in a self-conscious manner.

Second, and more fundamentally, the literature on quantitative history fails to acknowledge that the contribution of qualitative research to causal inference is not exhausted by its use in qualitative diagnostics, a secondary role. The attention in qualitative research to the processes through which effects persist, and the recognition that causal mechanisms are a distinctive kind of knowledge about causation, has not been matched in quantitative research. Yet quantitative history shows virtually no appreciation of this essential source of knowledge about the persistent effect of distant causes.

Quantitative history is a valuable addition to the methodological repertoire used in research on critical junctures. Yet, it does not supersede qualitative research. Thus, it is important to acknowledge both the promise and the limits of quantitative history.

THE RELEVANCE OF QUANTITATIVE HISTORY TO CRITICAL JUNCTURE RESEARCH

Quantitative history is a diverse field, and its relevance to the study of critical junctures and historical legacies is not obvious. However, part of this literature can be located within the new institutional economics most closely associated with North

---

1. A common point made in discussions about qualitative research concerns its contributions to theory development (George and Bennett 2005; Bennett and Checkel 2015). This is a broadly recognized point and is not discussed here.

(1990), which has many points of convergence with the critical juncture framework (Acemoglu et al. 2001: 1370; 2005: 389–96; Diamond and Robinson 2010b: 257–62; Besley and Reynal-Querol 2014: 321–22).[2] This literature occasionally uses the concept of critical juncture,[3] and frequently employs the concept of "legacy" and "historical legacy."[4] Moreover, the causal language used in quantitative history and in the critical juncture framework is similar (see Chapter 5).

Concerning causes, quantitative history focuses on causal factors that are temporally distant, and have ceased to recur, rather than on proximate causes (Acemoglu et al. 2005: 388–89; Besley and Reynal-Querol 2014: 321; Mukherje 2018a: 2233). Thus, in the common example of research on the legacies of colonialism, the causes are events during colonial times and the effects are outcomes that are manifested decades or even centuries after the end of colonial rule. Moreover, the kind of events this literature typically treats as potential distant causes resemble the big, discontinuous changes that are routinely considered as critical junctures. Quantitative history refers to "cataclysmic events" (Acharya et al. 2016: 622), "massive perturbations" (Diamond and Robinson 2010a: 10), and "historical shocks" (Acemoglu and Robinson 2006: 691) rather than to big, discontinuous changes.[5] However, the examples of such distant causes addressed in this literature—e.g., the imposition of colonial rule (Acemoglu et al. 2001),[6] the slave trade (Nunn 2008), and revolutions (Acemoglu et al. 2011)—are similar to those studied in the literature on critical junctures. Although the terminology in the literatures on quantitative history and on critical junctures is not always the same, there is considerable overlap.

Concerning effects, quantitative history focuses on "long-term effects" (Nunn 2009: 65; Dell 2010: 1864; Iyer 2010), "long-term outcomes" (Banerjee and Iyer 2005: 1192), and the "long-run impact" of causes (Acemoglu et al. 2012: 535). And such effects are not always consistent with the effects posited in critical juncture research. Indeed, it is important to stress that the claim "history matters" is consistent with many kinds of historical arguments and that what is distinctive about the critical juncture framework is that it focuses on persistent effects (see Chapter 5). However, the literature on quantitative history frequently does address "persistent

---

2. For the influence of North, see Acemoglu et al. (2001: 1369), Nunn (2009: 67), and Galiani and Sened (2014).

3. Acemoglu et al. (2008), Akee et al. (2015), Fontana et al. (2017), García-Ponce and Wantchékon (2017), Acharya et al. (2018).

4. Banerjee and Iyer (2005), Nunn (2007), Grosjean (2011), Lee and Schultz (2012), Acharya et al. (2016), Besley and Reynal-Querol (2014), Lupu and Peisakhin (2017), Pop-Eleches and Tucker (2017), Mukherjee (2018b).

5. See also Nunn (2012), Guiso et al. (2016: 1401), and Pierce and Snyder (2018: 142).

6. See also Iyer (2010), Lee and Schultz (2012), and Mukherjee (2018a; 2018b).

effects" (Banerjee and Iyer 2005: 1190),[7] "historical persistence" (Nunn 2014: 347), "long-term persistence" (Nunn 2009: 67; 2014: 349; Guiso et al. 2016), and "persistent impacts" (Dell 2010: 1865; Nunn 2014: 364; Acharya et al. 2016: 621). That is, the kind of effect studied in quantitative history and in research on critical junctures is frequently the same.

Finally, moving beyond reduced-form causal models, the literature on quantitative history focuses on causal mechanisms connecting distant causes and persistent effects (Nunn 2009: 75–85; 2014: 376–87). The concept of causal mechanism deserves closer scrutiny (as will be noted below). However, there is a resemblance between what in the literature on critical junctures is called "mechanisms of reproduction" (Collier and Collier 1991: 35–37) and what in quantitative history is called "mechanisms of persistence" (Acemoglu et al. 2012: 536), "transmission mechanisms" (Nunn 2009: 70; Guiso et al. 2016: 1428), "channels of causality" (Nunn 2008: 141; Grosjean 2011: 13), "historical channels" (Pierce and Snyder 2018), and "channels of persistence" (Dell 2010: 1863, 1887).[8]

In sum, there are differences between the critical juncture framework as used in the mainly qualitative literature on critical junctures, and the concepts employed in quantitative history. Nonetheless, research on critical junctures undeniably shares with quantitative history an interest in discontinuous changes that are treated as temporally distant causes that generate persistent effects. Quantitative history is relevant to critical juncture research, and hence it is important to consider it alongside the qualitative literature on critical junctures.

METHODS IN QUANTITATIVE HISTORY

Turning to substantive research on quantitative history, what follows focuses mainly but not exclusively on the methods of causal inference used in nine articles that are representative of this literature (see Table 8.1). This is a relatively new literature. Thus, the discussion highlights the new tools this literature has brought to bear on the kind of questions that have been a staple of research on critical junctures. It also notes that although quantitative history—true to its name—relies essentially on quantitative methods, it somewhat surprisingly also uses qualitative research for various purposes.

---

7. See also Dell (2010), Iyer (2010: 693), Acemoglu et al. (2012: 535), Besley and Reynal-Querol (2014: 320), Acharya et al. (2016: 638), and Lupu and Peisakhin (2017: 848).

8. See also Nunn (2014: 350) and Acharya et al. (2018).

Table 8.1 Methods of Causal Inference in Quantitative History

| Study | Argument — Causal Effect | | | | Quantitative Method** | Method of Causal Inference* — Causal Effect — Quantitative Diagnostic | | Method of Causal Inference* — Causal Effect — Qualitative Diagnostic | | Causal Mechanism — Quantitative Method | Causal Mechanism — Qualitative Diagnostic (Mechanism CPOs) |
	Cause, Distant	Effect, Persistent	Causal Mechanism	Cases		Model-Validation	Treatment-Assignment	Model-Validation CPOs	Treatment-Assignment CPOs		
Acemoglu, Johnson, and Robinson (2001)	Colonial institutions (extractive or non-extractive institutions)	Economic development	Sunk costs, size of the ruling elite, irreversible complementary investments	Ex-colonies around the world	Instrumental variable	First-stage regression, overidentification test	None	Secondary qualitative sources, to assess exclusion restriction	None	None	None
Nunn (2008)	Slave trade	Economic development	Intervillage ties, state capacity	Countries in Africa	Instrumental variable	First-stage regression	None	None	None	Mechanism as dependent variable in regressions	Secondary qualitative sources
Dell (2010)	Forced labor system	Human welfare	Land tenure, public goods provision, market participation	Peru, Bolivia	Regression discontinuity	NA	Balance test	NA	Historical documents and secondary qualitative sources, to assess statistical independence	Mechanism as dependent variable, measured at multiple points in time, in regressions	Secondary qualitative sources, interviews
Iyer (2010)	Colonial institutions (direct or indirect colonial rule)	Economic development	Colonial extraction, good governance of colonial local administrators, postcolonial institutions	India	Instrumental variable	First-stage regression, falsification test	None	Secondary qualitative sources, to assess exclusion restriction	Archival data, to assess statistical independence	Mechanism as control variable in instrumental variable regressions	None
Acemoglu, García-Jimeno, and Robinson (2012)	Slavery	Economic development	Sectoral specialization, state presence	Colombia	Instrumental variable	First-stage regression	Balance test	None	None	Mechanism as dependent variable in regressions	None

(continued)

Table 8.1 Methods of Causal Inference in Quantitative History (*continued*)

	Argument				Method of Causal Inference*						
	Causal Effect				Causal Effect					Causal Mechanism	
						Quantitative Diagnostic		Qualitative Diagnostic			
Study	Cause, Distant	Effect, Persistent	Causal Mechanism	Cases	Quantitative Method**	Model-Validation	Treatment-Assignment	Model-Validation CPOs	Treatment-Assignment CPOs	Quantitative Method	Qualitative Diagnostic (Mechanism CPOs)
Lee and Schultz (2012)	Colonial institutions (British or French colonial rule)	Economic development, public goods	Religion, educational system, forced labor, indirect rule	Cameroon	Regression discontinuity	NA	Placebo tests	NA	Secondary qualitative sources, to assess statistical independence	Mechanism as control variable in regressions	None
Bandopadhyay and Green (2013)	Precolonial centralization	Economic development	Prior economic development, local accountability	Uganda	Instrumental variable	First-stage regression	None	Secondary qualitative sources, to assess exclusion restriction	Secondary qualitative sources, to assess statistical independence	Mechanism as dependent variable in regressions	None
Acharya, Blackwell, and Sen (2016)	End of slavery	Racist attitudes	Institutional path dependence, intergenerational socialization	United States	Instrumental variable	First-stage regression, falsification test	None	None	None	Mechanism as dependent variable in regressions, and correlation of attitudes across generations	Secondary qualitative sources
Mukherje (2018a)	Colonial institutions (direct or indirect colonial rule)	Civil conflict	Ethnic and land inequality, state capacity, tribal alienation	India	Instrumental variable	First-stage regression, overidentification test	None	Secondary qualitative sources, to assess exclusion restriction	Archival and interview data, to assess statistical independence	Mechanism as dependent variable in instrumental variable regressions	Secondary qualitative sources, interviews

*Note: The concept of "causal process observations" (CPOs) is drawn from Collier, Brady, and Seawright (2010: 184–96). The distinction between treatment-assignment CPOs, model-validation CPOs, and mechanism CPOs is due to Dunning (2012: 243–44).

**The works discussed here routinely rely on various quantitative methods, and commonly start with OLS regressions. Here the focus is on their use of natural experiments. Thus, inasmuch as natural experiments are used, the discussion focuses on that part of the analysis.

CPOs: causal process observations. NA: not applicable

As a preface to this discussion, it is worth mentioning that scholars present different kinds of arguments and tests about *causal effects* involving distant causes and persistent effects. In the terminology used by Diamond and Robinson (2010b: 260), some arguments involve a "comparison of a perturbation . . . (referred to as 'treatments' in . . . the literature on experiments) . . . with a nonperturbation," while other arguments involve a comparison of "different types of perturbation." An example of the first kind of argument is provided by Dell (2010), who argues that the *mita*, a forced labor system used in colonial times in the Andes, is a distant cause of economic development that has a negative persistent effect still felt in the early twenty-first century. An example of the second kind of argument is offered by Iyer (2010), who claims that direct colonial rule by Britain in India is a distant cause of economic development that had a negative persistent effect still felt in the second half of the twentieth century compared to indirect colonial rule by Britain in India.

It is also noteworthy that this literature offers, as a supplement to claims about causal effects, arguments and tests about *causal mechanisms* that connect distant causes and persistent effects. For example, Dell (2010: 1863) argues that the *mita* has a lasting effect through two "channels of institutional persistence [or] mechanisms . . . its impacts on land tenure and public goods provision." In turn, Iyer (2010: 694) posits that there are several possible "intervening mechanisms" that could explain the long-term impact of different kinds of colonial rule, including "colonial extraction . . . local institutions, such as the prevalent land tenure system . . . [and] good governance in the colonial period." Although the discussion of causal mechanisms is given less prominence than the discussion of causal effects, it is rather conventional for this literature to make claims about mechanisms.

Thus, to offer a comprehensive discussion of quantitative history, what follows first focuses on the methods used to test hypotheses about causal effects, and then turns to the methods used to assess claims about causal mechanisms. Since researchers have different views about the epistemic value of knowledge about causal mechanisms, an additional section on mechanisms addresses this epistemological question. In each section, a description of research practices and approaches to research is followed by an evaluation.

CAUSAL EFFECTS IN QUANTITATIVE HISTORY

The core goal of quantitative history is an estimation of the effect of distant causes, in which the concept of causal effect is understood as the difference between a unit's potential outcome under treatment and under control.[9] To this end, quantitative

---

9. The literature on quantitative history rarely discusses its concept of causation. However, the methodological literature it draws on relies centrally on the potential outcomes approach to causation (Angrist and Pischke 2008; Dunning 2012: Ch 5).

history relies on quantitative tests to generate estimates of causal effects, and on diagnostic tests—both quantitative and qualitative in nature—to check the assumptions made in the core quantitative tests.

Quantitative Tests and Diagnostics

The main characteristic of this literature is the testing of the effect of distant causes through natural experiments, and instrumental variable and regression discontinuity designs in particular (see column 6 in Table 8.1).[10] Indeed, although some works rely fully on standard regression analysis (Pop-Eleches 2007; Besley and Reynal-Querol 2014), most of this research tackles the problem of confounders and reverse causation head-on and adopts a design-based approach to deal with unobserved covariates. Moreover, these works are crafty in the discovery of natural designs—in many instances demonstrating an impressive, nuanced knowledge of history—and methodical in the collection and analysis of quantitative data. The analysis of natural experiments is the heart of this literature.

This literature also takes steps to check assumptions by conducting quantitative diagnostics (see columns 7 and 8 in Table 8.1).[11] Two causal model assumptions in instrumental variable designs have been scrutinized. The assumption that the instrument affects the cause—called the inclusion restriction or the relevance requirement—is regularly checked with simple "first-stage regressions" in which the cause is treated as the dependent variable.[12] The assumption that an instrument affects the outcome only by influencing the cause being studied and thus does not affect the outcome directly—called the exclusion restriction—is not directly and easily verifiable. Nonetheless, some scholars have conducted "falsification tests" or "overidentification tests" to assess the plausibility of the exclusion restriction.[13]

The treatment-assignment assumption that the treatment is as good as or "as-if" randomly assigned, an assumption applicable to both instrumental variable and regression discontinuity designs, has been addressed less consistently. This assumption—called the assumption of independence or of statistical independence between

---

10. On these designs, see Dunning (2012), Lee and Lemieux (2015), and Muller et al. (2015).

11. On the assumptions in instrumental variable and regression discontinuity designs, and quantitative tests of these assumptions, see Angrist and Pischke (2015: Chs. 3 and 4), Pizer (2016), and Hartman (2021).

12. Acemoglu et al. (2001), Nunn (2008: 162–63), Iyer (2010: 701–02), Acemoglu et al. (2012: 549–52), Bandopadhyay and Green (2013: 488–89), Acharya et al. (2016: 629), Mukherje (2018a: 2259–61).

13. Acemoglu et al. (2001: 1372, 1393–95), Iyer (2010: 693–94, 705), Nunn and Wantchekon (2011: 3223, 3241–43), Acharya et al. (2016: 628), Guiso et al. (2016: 1427), Mukherje (2018a: 2256–58, 2262). On overidentification tests of instruments as tests of the exclusion restriction, see Kiviet (2017). On falsification tests, see Pizer (2016).

treatment assignment and confounders—has been rarely tested in instrumental variable designs (for an exception, see Acemoglu et al. 2012: 548–49). In contrast, the plausibility of the as-if-random assignment assumption has been frequently checked in regression discontinuity designs through "placebo tests" (Lee and Schultz 2012: 38) and "balance tests" (Dell 2010: 1871–75; Michalopoulos and Papaioannou 2016: 1816; Fontana et al. 2017: 20).

In sum, the literature on quantitative history uses a battery of quantitative tests to estimate, and shore up claims about, causal effects. Most distinctively, this literature relies heavily on natural experiments and offers some quantitative checks of causal model and treatment-assignment assumptions.

Qualitative Diagnostics

The literature on quantitative history does not explicitly present qualitative diagnostics of natural experiments. It disregards the research on qualitative methods that highlights the distinctiveness of "causal process observations" (CPOs) in contrast to "data set observations" (DSOs) (Collier et al. 2010: 184–96). It also neglects specific suggestions concerning how different kinds of CPOs might be used, as supplements of the more recognizable quantitative diagnostics, to check assumptions made in the analysis of natural experiments (Dunning 2012: 243–44, 248–49, Ch. 7; Seawright 2016: Ch. 6). However, it is important to highlight the relevance of qualitative tools to the tests presented in quantitative history and to note that, at times at least, they are implicitly used (see columns 9 and 10 in Table 8.1).

One relevant qualitative tool is *model-validation CPOs*. These CPOs consist of "knowledge about [the] causal process that support[s] or invalidate[s] core assumptions of causal models" and can be used, in the context of instrumental variable designs, to validate the credibility of the exclusion restriction (Dunning 2012: 209–10, 227–28).[14] A few studies have made some use of qualitative research to this end. However, scholars rarely take advantage of this opportunity by using process tracing, a common practice in qualitative research (Bennett and Checkel 2015), to assess whether or not the instrument is directly linked to the outcome. Indeed, the few uses of such a qualitative diagnostic are rather cursory.[15]

Another relevant qualitative tool is *treatment-assignment CPOs*. These CPOs are "pieces or nuggets of information about the process by which units were assigned to treatment and control conditions in a natural experiment" and can be used to validate the plausibility of the as-if-random assignment assumption (Dunning 2012:

---

14. On model-validation CPOs in the context of instrumental variable designs, see Dunning (2012: 209–10, 225–28) and Seawright (2016: 146–48).

15. Bandopadhyay and Green (2013: 488–89), Mukherje (2018a: 2255), Mukherjee (2018b: 120); for partial exceptions, see Acemoglu et al. (2001: 1371–72, 1380–83, 1391) and Iyer (2010: 703–06).

209).[16] This tool has been used rather frequently and to good effect in many works on quantitative history. Indeed, it is common that discussions of "the problem of selection" (Iyer 2010: 693; Nunn 2008: 157) draw on qualitative research to offer insight into the process through which units are assigned values on the variable of interest and to ascertain whether the assignment of "treatments" could be considered as-if-random.

Treatment-assignment CPOs have been used in research that relies on instrumental variables. For example, Iyer (2010: 693, 700–01, 704–05) uses "historical evidence" to show that even though the British in colonial India did not annex areas for direct colonial control at random, Iyer's instrument—the death of a ruler without a natural heir between 1848 and 1856—gets around this problem. Specifically, Iyer argues that the as-if-random assignment assumption is justified because the British Governor-General Lord Dalhousie had a policy during those years of annexing states under indirect rule when a ruler died without a natural heir, and the death of rulers without natural heirs and the annexation of these states was "likely to be a matter of circumstance rather than caused by systematic factors" (Iyer 2010: 693). Further bolstering the argument, Iyer notes that Lord Dalhousie's policy was not "put in place in order to obtain any specific states" and "the historical evidence does not indicate [that] the British deliberately caused the death of certain rulers" (Iyer 2010: 704–05). In another example, Mukherje (2018a: 2253–55) uses "historical documents" and secondary sources written by historians to offer a rather detailed account of the decision of British officers leading to the placement of territories in colonial India under direct or indirect rule, and to make a case that external warfare is a good instrument, in that the choice of annexation or signing of treaties of indirect rule with Indian states "was random and not related to the possibility of leftist rebellion," the study's outcome.

Treatment-assignment CPOs have also been used in regression discontinuity studies. Dell's (2010: 1868–69, 1876–77) work relies on "historical documents and scholarship" and secondary qualitative sources to grasp which variables affect the assignment to the *mita*, to ascertain whether these variables might be systematically linked with her outcome, and to check whether there is any "selective sorting across the treatment threshold" due to migration. In another example, Lee and Schultz (2012: 3, 8–10) use secondary qualitative sources and information about the negotiations between the British and the French regarding the drawing of the Picot line through Cameroon to show that a comparison of neighboring villages near the boundary dividing British and French regions of Cameroon offers a good basis for estimating the causal effect of colonialism. Indeed, they use qualitative evidence to show that the decision regarding the border dividing these two regions was

---

16. On treatment-assignment CPOs in the context of instrumental variable and regression discontinuity designs, see Dunning (2012: 209–19, 243–44, 248) and Seawright (2016: 138–42).

"unrelated to local conditions" and hence that "it is unlikely that . . . [local] units differed systematically in ways that have affected contemporary outcomes."

Assessment

The contribution of quantitative history is undoubtedly important. It uses a range of quantitative tests and diagnostics to address the kind of questions that are common in research on critical junctures. It exemplifies how a concern with research design can be brought to bear on historically oriented research. It adds rigor to the analysis of historical processes. Quantitative history is a valuable addition to the methodological repertoire used in research on critical junctures.

It is also worth noting that part of the strength of quantitative history is due to its use of qualitative research. Many works have made good use of qualitative research to supplement their quantitative analysis, by checking assumptions related to the statistical model and the assignment to treatment. In particular, qualitative research has been used creatively and effectively to validate the plausibility of the as-if-random assignment assumption. However, in part because quantitative history tends to play down the importance of qualitative research and does not self-consciously draw on qualitative methods, it has not seized on some opportunities to better combine quantitative and qualitative research.

Better use could be made of model-validation CPOs in the context of instrumental variable designs, so as to validate the credibility of the exclusion restriction. Within the quantitative literature, instruments are largely a matter of methodological interest. In contrast, within the qualitative literature, the relationship between antecedent conditions and critical junctures is a matter of substantive interest and considerable attention is given to the role of antecedent conditions (Collier and Collier 1991; Chibber 2003; Roberts 2014). Thus, even though qualitative researchers have not been as self-conscious as they should about the possible impact of antecedent conditions on the outcome of interest,[17] the kind of research that is rather typical in qualitative research could strengthen quantitative history.

In turn, although quantitative history has made good use of treatment-assignment CPOs, some important opportunities have not been considered. One of the main points of interest in qualitative research on critical junctures is the study of critical junctures proper, that is, of how critical junctures unfold, and what factors influence why critical junctures happen and unfold as they do.[18] This knowledge is key to an assessment of the plausibility of the as-if-random assignment assumption, especially

---

17. The chapters by Waldner (Chapter 7) and Lussier and LaPorte (Chapter 13) offer examples of qualitative research that would benefit from a more explicit and rigorous analysis of the potential impact of antecedent conditions.

18. For examples, see Collier and Collier (1991), Scully (1992), Ekiert (1996), Mahoney (2001), Chibber (2003), Kurtz (2013), and Roberts (2014).

in the case of regression discontinuity designs, and is typically a lot more detailed than comparable discussions in quantitative history.

In brief, the estimation of causal effects is a strength of quantitative history. However, various opportunities to bring substantive knowledge to bear on methodological questions, a sound principle (Freedman 1991, 2008), have not been seized as fully as they should. And these missed opportunities are not a small matter. As Dunning (2012: 216, 218) notes, qualitative diagnostics can be "a critical and often indispensable complement" to quantitative tests and diagnostics, and for certain purposes may even be considered "a near-*sine qua non* of successful natural experiments."

CAUSAL MECHANISMS IN QUANTITATIVE HISTORY

Beyond its focus on causal effects, a ubiquitous feature of quantitative history is its discussion of causal mechanisms. Research on quantitative history makes claims about causal mechanisms or the "mechanisms of persistence" linking distant cause to persistent effect. This research also takes some steps to test such claims (see columns 4, 11, and 12 in Table 8.1).

Quantitative Tests

Works in quantitative history commonly offer quantitative tests of hypotheses about causal mechanisms. These tests mainly rely on standard regression analysis, in which the hypothesized mechanism is treated as a dependent variable. For example, Dell's (2010: 1887–99) research—which offers one of the most elaborate tests of "mechanisms" or "channels of persistence"—focuses on the effect of the *mita* on economic development and, after focusing on this relationship, tests arguments about three causal mechanisms—land tenure, public goods provision, and market participation—by treating these mechanisms as potential effects of the *mita*.

Likewise, Acemoglu et al. (2012: 536, 556, 559, 563) go beyond testing whether slavery has a persistent effect on economic development by assessing their hypotheses that two possible "mechanisms of persistence"—sectoral specialization and state presence—link slavery to economic development. Furthermore, as Dell does, they test their hypotheses about mechanisms through a standard regression analysis that treats slavery as the independent variable, and sectoral specialization and state presence as dependent variables. Indeed, most tests of mechanisms simply regress the mechanism on the distant cause.

An additional characteristic of these tests concerns the number of data points used in the study of mechanisms. In this regard, Dell's (2010) work is somewhat of a model. To assess whether her hypothesized mechanisms recur over time, she tests the relationship between the *mita* and her mechanisms at multiple points in time. Specifically, while Dell (2010) tests her main hypothesis about the effect of the *mita* on economic development using data on the boundaries of the *mita* as instituted in

1573 and on economic development from the 2000s, she tests her mechanisms using data on the *mita* in 1573; on land tenure in 1689, 1845, and 1940; and on public goods in 1876, 1940, and 2001.

However, the use of data about mechanisms at multiple points in time is not standard practice. More common are tests such as Acemoglu et al.'s (2012: 553, 563), which assesses the causal effect of slavery on economic development using data on slavery from 1843 and on economic development from the 1990s, and tests their mechanisms using data on slavery from 1843 and on sectoral specialization and state presence—their two mechanisms—from the 2000s.

In brief, most tests of mechanisms simply regress the mechanism on the distant cause using a measure of the mechanism at a single point in time, at roughly the same year as the dependent variable in the core test about causal effects. That is, these quantitative tests simply do not assess explanations of the persistence proper of an effect by studying the recurring operation of some mechanism over a considerable time.

Qualitative Diagnostics

The relevance of qualitative tools to the testing of hypotheses about causal mechanisms is even more obvious than it is in relation to claims about causal effects. One relevant qualitative tool is *mechanism CPOs*, "information not just about whether an intervening event posited by a theory is present or absent but also about the kinds of causal processes that may produce an observed effect" (Dunning 2012: 209, 222; see also Seawright 2016: 55–67). However, quantitative history makes little use of such a tool.

A case can be made that a few studies in quantitative history make some use of qualitative evidence about mechanisms. For example, Dell (2010: 1887–99) relies on "the historical literature and fieldwork," including evidence drawn from interviews, to bolster her quantitative test. Mukherje (2018a: 2243–46) relies on secondary qualitative sources and "qualitative data collected during fieldwork" to go beyond his quantitative test of mechanisms and actually draw a link between his mechanisms and his outcome of interest, civil conflict. Nonetheless, such studies are rare. Indeed, qualitative analyses of causal mechanisms are seldom provided and, when offered, consist of rather brief discussions.

Assessment

Quantitative history largely assumes the repetition of the cause-effect pair that makes an effect persist and does not recognize the importance of verifying the recurrence of certain processes by analyzing data over time. That is, in terms of the model in Figure 8.1, the standard analysis in quantitative history focuses on the causal effect of X on Y by considering X at t_1 and Y at t_8, and typically an intervening variable (A) at one time period late in the process (e.g., at t_7). Quantitative history is largely silent about the signature feature of persistent effects, the repetition of A-Y pairs (see Chapter 5).

$$X_{t1} \longrightarrow Y_{t2} \longrightarrow a_{t3} \longrightarrow Y_{t4} \longrightarrow a_{t5} \longrightarrow Y_{t6} \longrightarrow a_{t7} \longrightarrow Y_{t8}$$

Figure 8.1 A Model of a Persistent Effect

Moreover, the discussion of mechanisms that is offered does not add anything of much significance. Some scholars who contribute to quantitative history make a case for studying mechanisms. For example, Diamond and Robinson (2010b: 266–67) argue that statistical analysis does not "demonstrate a . . . mechanism" and that "even if one has obtained convincing evidence that A causes B, further evidence is often required to establish the mechanism by which A causes B." However, current practice in quantitative history shows that the mechanisms that are actually studied are additional macro-variables (i.e., of the same nature of A and B) and hence the results of tests do not have a distinctive value.

Quantitative history also overlooks the possible contribution of qualitative research to the analysis of persistent effects and causal mechanisms. The analysis of the multiple steps in the causal chain linking a critical juncture to a much later effect and, more specifically, of the repetition of some cause-effect pair, is key to the credibility of claims about persistent effects. The analysis of causal mechanisms understood as more than an intervening macro-level variable (as clarified next) is key to causal inference. And much qualitative research of critical junctures focuses precisely on such persistent effects and causal mechanisms. Thus, it is significant that this is the area in which quantitative history is weak relative to the qualitative literature and, furthermore, that quantitative history largely ignores the potential contribution of qualitative research.

THE EPISTEMIC VALUE OF CAUSAL MECHANISMS

Ultimately, the role assigned to causal mechanisms in quantitative history follows from an epistemological rather than a methodological commitment. All quantitative researchers and all qualitative researchers do not rely on one concept of causation or even an explicit concept of causation. Moreover, qualitative research on critical junctures has used the concept of mechanism loosely. However, the methodological literatures that quantitative and qualitative research draws on largely differ in their understanding of what a causal mechanism is and what value should be assigned to knowledge about mechanisms.[19] And, to properly frame the discussion regarding

---

19. This difference is rooted in two general approaches to causation, the difference-making approach that is generally used in quantitative research, and the production approach that is used in qualitative research (Illari and Russo 2014). For statements that exemplify the approach in much recent quantitative literature, see Angrist and Pischke (2008, 2015) and Morgan and Winship (2015). For the qualitative perspective, see Waldner (2012, 2016) and Kaidesoja (2019).

how quantitative and qualitative research might be combined, it is necessary to grasp this difference.

Mechanisms in Quantitative Research

The literature on quantitative history routinely invokes the concept of causal mechanism. At times, it offers suggestive comments that indicate that the role of mechanisms in causal inference is distinctive. For example, Nunn claims that, in moving beyond reduced-form causal models, the literature on quantitative history has not only addressed "*whether* history matters" but also sought to "explain exactly *how* and *why* specific historic events can continue to matter today" (Nunn 2009: 66, emphasis added). However, a review of the examples of mechanisms discussed in the literature suggests that quantitative history does not treat hypotheses about causal mechanisms as qualitatively different from hypotheses about causal effects.

To give some examples, Nunn (2008: 164–68) links the slave trade to economic development through two mechanisms: intervillage ties and state capacity. Acemoglu et al. (2012: 543, 556, 559) consider two mechanisms linking slavery to economic development: sectoral specialization and state presence. Mukherje (2018a: 2239–46) connects colonial institutions to civil conflict through three mechanisms: ethnic and land inequality, state capacity, and tribal alienation. That is, although quantitative history uses the terms "causal effect" and "causal mechanism," there seems to be no loss of meaning by treating claims about causal mechanisms as claims about causal effects related to an intervening variable between a distant cause and a persistent effect.

In turn, although the literature on quantitative history regularly indicates that addressing causal mechanisms is important, it treats such an inquiry as secondary. Arguments that invoke mechanisms as understood within quantitative history are certainly more complete, in that they add a link in the causal argument and propose a causal chain that could be a more adequate representation of causal relations. However, the epistemic value of causal mechanisms understood as intervening variables is not great. It adds something marginal to the knowledge about causal effects—that is, it adds more of the same.

Thus, it is not surprising that the meticulous attention given to arguments about the relationship between a distant cause and a persistent effect in quantitative history is not replicated with an equally critical consideration of causal mechanisms (compare the columns on "method of causal inference" in Table 8.1). Indeed, because quantitative history relies on an approach to causation that does not offer a strong rationale for taking causal mechanisms seriously, it puts knowledge about causal effects at the center of its inquiry and sidelines the study of causal mechanisms.

Mechanisms in Qualitative Research

Qualitative research is not always based on a clear concept of causal mechanism. However, in line with a well-established view about mechanisms, qualitative research commonly distinguishes mechanisms from intervening variables, and does not consider that the analysis of mechanisms can be subsumed under the analysis of causal effects (Waldner 2012: 67; Beach and Pedersen 2016: Ch. 2; see also Kaidesoja 2019: 28). Moreover, the view of mechanisms in this research largely corresponds to the one proposed in Chapter 5, in that it understands mechanisms as necessarily involving the actions of actors or, more elaborately, as *processes* that happen *within* the objects being studied, that is, at a *lower level* of organization than the variables in an X → Y hypothesis (see Figure 8.2).[20]

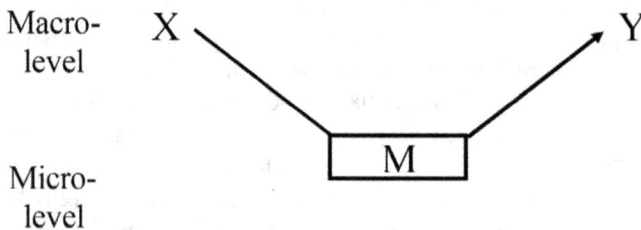

Figure 8.2 A Model of a Causal Mechanism. *Legend*: X: independent variable; M: mechanism; Y: dependent variable.

Qualitative research also assigns great value to knowledge about causal mechanisms. Again, in line with a well-established view about the value of mechanisms, qualitative research assumes that *whether* some relationship is causal can only be known inasmuch as evidence is provided to show *how* an effect is *produced*.[21] That is, knowledge about causal mechanisms is not simply more knowledge about the difference a change in one variable makes on another variable but, rather, qualitatively different knowledge that is decisive in establishing that the relationship between variables is indeed causal.

Consequently, qualitative research places causal mechanisms at the center of inquiry. For example, in his multi-method study on the long-term effects of

---

20. This concept of causal mechanism is due to philosophers of science and sociologists (Boudon 1986: 30; Coleman 1986: 1322; 1990: 8; Bunge 1996: 123–24, 137–50; 1997; Elster 2015: Ch. 2) and is connected to process tracing, a key tool of qualitative research, in discussions about qualitative methods (Waldner 2012, 2016; Bennett and Checkel 2015; Runhardt 2015; Beach and Pedersen 2016: Ch. 3; Kaidesoja 2019).

21. On the epistemic value of knowledge about causal mechanisms, see Thagard (1999: Ch. 7), Bunge (2006: Chs. 4 and 5), Darden (2006), Elster (2015: Part 1), and Craver and Darden (2013).

colonialism on development, Lange (2009: 68–69) argues that only by exploring the mechanisms between colonialism and development is it possible to establish "whether or not the relationship between the two is causal." Moreover, consistent with this view, after finding a statistical relationship between colonialism and development, Lange sets out to find whether "the statistical relationship . . . is causal" by collecting and analyzing "qualitative evidence" on mechanisms and dedicates the bulk of his book to studying causal mechanisms through process tracing.

Assessment

In short, both quantitative and qualitative researchers tackle the challenge of causal inference. Moreover, both traditions converge in making a case for studying causal mechanisms. However, these traditions largely rely on different views about causal mechanisms that are grounded in different approaches to causation.

Quantitative history assumes that the idea of causal effect it relies on offers a unified approach to causation—in a nutshell, it treats variables and mechanisms as the same thing. Thus, it essentially subsumes the study of causal mechanisms under the study of causal effects, does not consider that research on causal mechanisms can produce knowledge that is qualitatively different from the knowledge generated by the study of causal effects, and treats the study of causal mechanisms as a secondary matter.

Quantitative history also fails to recognize the validity of alternative epistemologies. Thus, it does not appreciate the distinctive and central contribution that qualitative research can provide to causal explanation. In short, the epistemological position adopted by quantitative history places a key limit on its contributions and, furthermore, leads it to ignore a potentially fundamental contribution of qualitative research.

CONCLUSIONS

The literature on quantitative history is a recent addition to a body of research on critical junctures and historical legacies that has until recently relied entirely on qualitative research. Thus, this chapter has discussed the relevance of quantitative history and the methodological tools used to assess claims about critical junctures and historical legacies in the literature on quantitative history.

In assessing the promise of quantitative history, it is also important to consider whether and how it uses qualitative research. As methodologists argue, there are good grounds for relying on the tools of qualitative research (Freedman 2008; Collier et al. 2010). Moreover, research on critical junctures using qualitative methods since the 1960s has shown that it has been the source of insights that are important to an assessment of causal hypotheses about critical junctures. Thus, this chapter considered the use of both quantitative and qualitative tools in quantitative history.

Several conclusions from this discussion deserve to be highlighted. The new literature on quantitative history is a valuable addition to a body of research on critical junctures and historical legacies that has until recently relied nearly entirely on qualitative research. Quantitative history addresses many of the same questions that are at the heart of research on critical junctures. It has brought new tools to bear on these questions. And it has shown that these tools should be incorporated into the repertoire of tools used in research on critical junctures. The promise of quantitative research is undeniable.

Nonetheless, it is important to distinguish this recognition of the value of quantitative history from an embrace of the view of promoters of quantitative history who suggest that the study of historical legacies should rely exclusively on quantitative research and that gains in quantification will supersede qualitative research (Nunn 2009: 71, 81). Indeed, this view disregards the well-established contributions of qualitative research.

Qualitative research has a role to play, as an adjunct to quantitative history, by offering qualitative diagnostics of quantitative tests. The literature on quantitative history includes scattered references to "qualitative evidence" (Nunn 2008: 157), "qualitative accounts" (Acharya et al. 2016: 623), and "qualitative data" (Mukherje 2018a: 2265). However, the reliance on qualitative research is both rather unsystematic and rare. Thus, the promise of quantitative history will be more fully realized inasmuch as this literature draws explicitly on the methodological work that addresses in some detail how qualitative research could be used in combination with quantitative research and more fully exploits the possibilities of qualitative diagnostics (Dunning 2012; Seawright 2016).

Additionally, qualitative research has a more central role to play through its emphasis on the actual persistence of effects and on causal mechanisms. The tools used in qualitative research do not play, at best, a supporting role in the challenge of causal inference. Most obviously, process tracing can be used to ascertain whether the operation of so-called mechanisms of reproduction or mechanisms of persistence actually sustain an effect over a period of time. In this way, qualitative research can fill a key gap in quantitative tests of persistent effects.

Qualitative research can also offer evidence about causal mechanisms that plays an even more important role in causal inference. Qualitative research commonly relies on a distinctive understanding of a causal mechanism that is not shared by quantitative history. Although the concept of causal effect used in quantitative history is assumed to be based on a unified approach to causation, much qualitative research questions this view and reverses the priority that quantitative research gives to causal effect and causal mechanisms. In this way, qualitative research casts the discussion about causal inference in a whole new light.

In sum, the potential of qualitative research on critical junctures and historical legacies is not exhausted by its use in qualitative diagnostics to quantitative tests and, more broadly, the contributions of qualitative research are not subsidiary to the contributions of quantitative research. Multi-method research should harness the strengths of quantitative research in estimating causal effects and the strengths of qualitative research in validating causal mechanisms. Moreover, discussions of multi-method research should recognize that there are important open questions regarding how the contributions of quantitative and qualitative research should be combined, especially given that qualitative researchers treat hypotheses about causal mechanisms as qualitatively distinct arguments compared to hypotheses about causal effects. Indeed, this discussion will only advance inasmuch as scholars embrace the spirit of multi-method research and openly acknowledge that no single methodological tradition offers all the answers to the important methodological challenges faced in historically oriented research.

BIBLIOGRAPHY

Acemoglu, Daron, Davide Cantoni, Simon Johnson, and James A. Robinson. 2011. "The Consequences of Radical Reform: The French Revolution." *American Economic Review* 101(7): 3286–307.

Acemoglu, Daron, Camilo García-Jimeno, and James A. Robinson. 2012. "Finding Eldorado: Slavery and Long-Run Development in Colombia." *Journal of Comparative Economics* 40(4): 534–64.

Acemoglu, Daron, Simon Johnson, and James A. Robinson. 2001. "The Colonial Origins of Comparative Development: An Empirical Investigation." *American Economic Review* 91(5): 1369–401.

———. 2005. "Institutions as a Fundamental Cause of Long-Run Growth." In Philippe Aghion and Steven Durlauf (eds.), *Handbook of Economic Growth*. Volume 1, Part A (pp. 385–472). Amsterdam: North Holland: Elsevier.

Acemoglu, Daron, Simon Johnson, James A. Robinson, and Pierre Yared. 2008. "Income and Democracy." *American Economic Review* 98(3): 808–42.

Acemoglu, Daron, and James A. Robinson. 2006. "Paths of Economic and Political Development." In Barry R. Weingast and Donald A. Wittman (eds.), *The Oxford Handbook of Political Economy* (pp. 673–92). Oxford, UK: Oxford University Press.

Acharya, Avidit, Matthew Blackwell, and Maya Sen. 2016. "The Political Legacy of American Slavery." *Journal of Politics* 78(3): 621–41.

———. 2018. *Deep Roots: How Slavery Still Shapes Southern Politics*. Princeton, NJ: Princeton University Press.

Akee, Randall, Miriam Jorgensen, and Uwe Sunde. 2015. "Critical Junctures and Economic Development. Evidence from the Adoption of Constitutions among American Indian Nations." *Journal of Comparative Economics* 43(4): 844–61.

Angrist, Joshua D., and Jörn-Steffen Pischke. 2008. *Mostly Harmless Econometrics: An Empiricist's Companion*. Princeton, NJ: Princeton University Press

———. 2015. *Mastering 'Metrics: The Path from Cause to Effect*. Princeton, NJ: Princeton University Press.

Bandopadhyay, Sanghamitra, and Elliott Green. 2013. "Precolonial Political Centralization and Contemporary Development in Uganda." *Economic Development and Cultural Change* 64(3): 471–508.

Banerjee, Abhijit, and Lakshmi Iyer. 2005. "History, Institutions and Economic Performance: The Legacy of Colonial Land Tenure Systems in India." *American Economic Review* 95(4): 1190–213.

Bates, Robert H., Avner Greif, Margaret Levi, Jean-Laurent Rosenthal, and Barry Weingast. 1998. *Analytic Narratives*. Princeton, NJ: Princeton University Press.

Beach, Derek, and Rasmus Brun Pedersen. 2016. *Causal Case Studies: Foundations and Guidelines for Comparing, Matching and Tracing*. Ann Arbor, MI: University of Michigan Press.

Bennett, Andrew, and Jeffrey Checkel (eds.). 2015. *Process Tracing: From Metaphor to Analytic Tool*. New York, NY: Cambridge University Press.

Besley, Timothy, and Marta Reynal-Querol. 2014. "The Legacy of Historical Conflict: Evidence from Africa." *American Political Science Review* 108(2): 319–36.

Boudon, Raymond. 1986. *Theories of Social Change: A Critical Appraisal*. Berkeley, CA: University of California Press.

Bunge, Mario. 1996. *Finding Philosophy in Social Science*. New Haven, CT: Yale University Press.

———. 1997. "Mechanism and Explanation." *Philosophy of the Social Sciences* 27(4): 410–65.

———. 2006. *Chasing Reality: Strife over Realism*. Toronto: University of Toronto Press.

Chibber, Vivek. 2003. *Locked in Place: State-Building and Late Industrialization in India*. Princeton, NJ: Princeton University Press.

Coleman, James Samuel. 1986. "Social Theory, Social Research, and a Theory of Action." *The American Journal of Sociology* 91(6): 1309–35.

———. 1990. *Foundations of Social Theory*. Cambridge, MA.: Harvard University Press.

Collier, David, Henry E. Brady, and Jason Seawright. 2010. "Sources of Leverage in Causal Inference: Toward an Alternative View of Methodology." In Henry E. Brady and David Collier (eds.), *Rethinking Social Inquiry: Diverse Tools, Shared Standards* (2nd ed.; pp. 161–99). Lanham, MD: Rowman & Littlefield.

Collier, Ruth Berins, and David Collier. 1991. *Shaping the Political Arena: Critical Junctures, the Labor Movement, and the Regime Dynamics in Latin America*. Princeton, NJ: Princeton University Press.

Craver, Carl F., and Lindley Darden. 2013. *In Search of Mechanisms: Discoveries across the Life Sciences*. Chicago, IL: University of Chicago Press.

Darden, Lindley. 2006. *Reasoning in Biological Discoveries: Essays on Mechanisms, Interfield Relations, and Anomaly Resolution*. Cambridge, MA: Cambridge University Press.

Dell, Melissa. 2010. "The Persistent Effects of Peru's Mining Mita." *Econometrica* 78(6): 1863–903.

Diamond, Jared, and James A. Robinson. 2010a. "Prologue." In Jared Diamond and James A. Robinson (eds.), *Natural Experiments of History* (pp. 1–14). Cambridge, MA: The Belknap Press of Harvard University Press.

———. 2010b. "Afterword: Using Comparative Methods in Studies of Human History." In Jared Diamond and James A. Robinson (eds.), *Natural Experiments of History* (pp. 257–76). Cambridge, MA: The Belknap Press of Harvard University Press.

Dunning, Thad. 2012. *Natural Experiments in the Social Sciences: A Design-Based Approach*. New York, NY: Cambridge University Press.

Ekiert, Grzegorz. 1996. *The State against Society: Political Crises and Their Aftermath in East Central Europe*. Princeton, NJ: Princeton University Press.

Elster, Jon. 2015. *Explaining Social Behavior: More Nuts and Bolts for the Social Sciences* (2nd ed.). New York: Cambridge University Press.

Fogel, Robert W. 1964. *Railroads and American Economic Growth: Essays in Econometric History*. Baltimore, MD: Johns Hopkins University Press.

Fontana, Nicola, Tommaso Nannicini, and Guido Tabellini. 2017. "Historical Roots of Political Extremism: The Effects of Nazi Occupation of Italy." *IZA Discussion Paper* No. 10551.

Freedman, David A. 1991. "Statistical Analysis and Shoe Leather." *Sociological Methodology* 21: 291–313.

———. 2008. "On Types of Scientific Reasoning: The Role of Qualitative Reasoning." In Janet M. Box-Steffensmeier, Henry E. Brady, and David Collier (eds.), *Oxford Handbook of Political Methodology* (pp. 300–18). Oxford, UK: Oxford University Press.

Galiani, Sebastian, and Itai Sened (eds.). 2014. *Institutions, Property Rights, and Economic Growth: The Legacy of Douglass North*. New York, NY: Cambridge University Press.

García-Ponce, Omar, and Léonard Wantchékon. 2017. "Critical Junctures: Independence Movements and Democracy in Africa." Unpublished paper, May 2017.

George, Alexander L., and Andrew Bennett. 2005. *Case Studies and Theory Development in the Social Sciences*. Cambridge, MA: MIT Press.

Grosfeld, Irena, and Ekaterina Zhuravskaya. 2015. "Cultural vs. Economic Legacies of Empires: Evidence from the Partition of Poland." *Journal of Comparative Economics* 43(1): 55–75.

Grosjean, Pauline. 2011. "The Institutional Legacy of the Ottoman Empire: Islamic Rule and Financial Development in South Eastern Europe." *Journal of Comparative Economics* 39(1): 1–16.

Guiso, Luigi, Paola Sapienza, and Luigi Zingales. 2016. "Long Term Persistence." *Journal of the European Economic Association* 14(6): 1401–36.

Hartman, Erin. 2021. "Equivalence Testing for Regression Discontinuity Designs." *Political Analysis* 29(4): 505–21.

Haupert, Michael. 2017. "The Impact of Cliometrics on Economics and History." *Revue d'économie politique* 127(6): 1059–81.

Illari, Phyllis, and Federica Russo. 2014. *Causality: Philosophical Theory Meets Scientific Practice*. Oxford, UK: Oxford University Press.

Iyer, Lakshmi. 2010. "Direct versus Indirect Colonial Rule in India: Long-Term Consequences." *Review of Economics and Statistics* 92(4): 693–713.

Kaidesoja, Tuukka. 2019. "Building Middle-Range Theories from Case Studies." *Studies in History and Philosophy of Science* Part A 78(1): 23–31.

Kiviet Jan F. 2017. "Discriminating between (In)valid External Instruments and (In)valid Exclusion Restrictions." *Journal of Econometric Methods* 6(1): 1–9.

Kurtz, Marcus. 2013. *Latin American State-Building in Comparative Perspective: Social Foundations of Institutional Order*. New York, NY: Cambridge University Press.

Laitin, David D., Joachim Moortgat, and Amanda Lea Robinson. 2012. "Geographic Axes and the Persistence of Cultural Diversity." *PNAS (Proceedings of the National Academy of Sciences)* 109(26): 10263–68.

Lange, Matthew. 2009. *Lineages of Despotism and Development: British Colonialism and State Power*. Chicago, IL: University of Chicago Press.

Lee, Alexander, and Kenneth A. Schultz. 2012. "Comparing British and French Colonial Legacies: A Discontinuity Analysis of Cameroon." *Quarterly Journal of Political Science* 7(4): 365–410.

Lee, David S., and Thomas Lemieux. 2015. "'Regression Discontinuity Designs in Social Sciences." In Henning Best and Christof Wolf (eds.), *The SAGE Handbook of Regression Analysis and Causal Inference* (pp. 301–26). London: Sage Publications.

Lupu, Noam, and Leonid Peisakhin. 2017. "The Legacy of Political Violence across Generations." *American Journal of Political Science* 61(4): 836–51.

Mahoney, James. 2001. *The Legacies of Liberalism: Path Dependence and Political Regimes in Central America*. Baltimore, MD: Johns Hopkins University Press.

Michalopoulos, Stelios, and Elias Papaioannou. 2016. "The Long-Run Effects of the Scramble for Africa." *American Economic Review* 106(7): 1802–48.

Morgan, Stephen L., and Christopher Winship. 2015. *Counterfactuals and Causal Inference: Methods and Principles for Social Research* (2nd ed., Revised and Enlarged). New York, NY: Cambridge University Press.

Mukherjee, Shivaji. 2018a. "Colonial Origins of Maoist Insurgency in India: Historical Institutions and Civil War." *Journal of Conflict Resolution* 62(10): 2232–74.

———. 2018b. "Historical Legacies of Colonial Indirect Rule: Princely States and Maoist Insurgency in Central India." *World Development* 111: 113–29.

Muller, Christopher, Christopher Winship, and Stephen L. Morgan. 2015. "Instrumental Variables Regression." In Henning Best and Christof Wolf (eds.), *The SAGE Handbook of Regression Analysis and Causal Inference* (pp. 281–304). London: Sage Publications.

North, Douglass C. 1961. *The Economic Growth of the United States, 1790–1860*. Englewood Cliffs, NJ: Prentice-Hall, Inc.

———. 1990. *Institutions, Institutional Change and Economic Performance*. New York, NY: Cambridge University Press.

Nunn, Nathan. 2007. "Historical Legacies: A Model Linking Africa's Past to Its Current Underdevelopment." *Journal of Development Economics* 83(1): 157–75.

———. 2008. "The Long-Term Effects of Africa's Slave Trades." *Quarterly Journal of Economics* 123(1): 139–76.

———. 2009. "The Importance of History for Economic Development." *Annual Review of Economics* 1(1): 65–92.

———. 2010. "Shackled to the Past: The Causes and Consequences of Africa's Slave Trade." In Jared Diamond and James A. Robinson (eds.), *Natural Experiments of History* (pp. 142–84). Cambridge, MA: The Belknap Press of Harvard University Press.

———. 2012. "Culture and the Historical Process." *Economic History of Developing Regions* 27(1): 108–26.

———. 2014. "Historical Development." In Philippe Aghion and Steven N. Durlauf (eds.), *Handbook of Economic Growth* (Vol. 2; pp. 347–402). North-Holland: Elsevier.

Nunn, Nathan, and Leonard Wantchekon. 2011. "The Slave Trade and the Origins of Mistrust in Africa." *American Economic Review* 101(7): 3221–52.

Pierce, Lamar, and Jason A. Snyder. 2018. "The Historical Slave Trade and Firm Access to Finance in Africa." *The Review of Financial Studies* 31(1): 142–74.

Pizer, Steven D. 2016. "Falsification Testing of Instrumental Variables Methods for Comparative Effectiveness Research." *Health Services Research* 51(2): 790–811.

Pop-Eleches, Grigore. 2007. "Historical Legacies and Post-Communist Regime Change." *Journal of Politics* 69(4): 908–26.

Pop-Eleches, Grigore, and Joshua Tucker. 2017. *Communism's Shadow: Historical Legacies and Contemporary Political Attitudes*. Princeton, NJ: Princeton University Press.

Roberts, Kenneth M. 2014. *Changing Course in Latin America: Party Systems in the Neoliberal Era*. New York, NY: Cambridge University Press.

Rodrik, Dani (ed.). 2003. *In Search of Prosperity: Analytic Narratives on Economic Growth*. Princeton, NJ: Princeton University Press.

Rozenas, Arturas, Sebastian Schutte, and Yuri Zhukov. 2017. "The Political Legacy of Violence: The Long-Term Impact of Stalin's Repression in Ukraine." *The Journal of Politics* 79(4): 1147–61.

Runhardt, Rosa. 2015. *Causal Inquiry in the Social Sciences: The Promise of Process Tracing.* PhD thesis, The London School of Economics and Political Science (LSE).

Scully, Timothy R. 1992. *Rethinking the Center: Party Politics in Nineteenth- and Twentieth-Century Chile.* Stanford, CA: Stanford University Press.

Seawright, Jason. 2016. *Multi-Method Social Science. Combining Qualitative and Quantitative Tools.* New York, NY: Cambridge University Press.

Thagard, Paul. 1999. *How Scientists Explain Disease.* Princeton, NJ: Princeton University Press.

Waldner, David. 2012. "Process Tracing and Causal Mechanisms." In Harold Kincaid (ed.), *The Oxford Handbook of Philosophy of Social Science* (pp. 65–84). Oxford, UK: Oxford University Press.

———. 2016. "Invariant Causal Mechanisms." *Qualitative & Multi-Method Research* 14(1/2): 28–34.

Wawro, Gregory J., and Ira Katznelson. 2014. "Designing Historical Social Scientific Inquiry: How Parameter Heterogeneity Can Bridge the Methodological Divide between Quantitative and Qualitative Approaches." *American Journal of Political Science* 58(2): 526–46.

III

SUBSTANTIVE APPLICATIONS I

States and Political Regimes

9

Nineteenth-Century State Formation and Long-Term Economic Performance in Latin America

Sebastián L. Mazzuca

In South America, income per capita—the standard measure of material prosperity—is five times larger than in tropical Africa but five times smaller than in the advanced economies of the North Atlantic. If we applied the distinction that economists usually draw between geography and politics as opposite fundamental factors of long-run development, a simple but powerful picture about the division of causal labor would emerge. Geography would explain why South American economies are ahead of those in Africa, whereas politics would explain why South America lags behind the United States and Western Europe. All relevant geographic factors in South America, including proportion of fertile land and number of navigable rivers and disease environment, are far superior to those in Africa. By contrast, political factors, including state capacity, types and stability of public institutions, viable political coalitions, and social and economic policies in South America are far inferior to those in Western Europe and North America.

What this distinction based on geography versus politics misses is the crucial role of a hybrid combination—namely, political geography. Some countries in South America could have followed the economic path that Australia and New Zealand initiated in the mid-nineteenth century. Such a path was not followed because of the way in which national boundaries were demarcated. The key legacy of the process of border demarcation was twofold: on the one hand, the creation of two territorial colossuses, Argentina and Brazil, that were *dysfunctional combinations of subnational economies*; on the other, the emergence of smaller countries that were not powerful enough to become the engine of development for South America. Even though some small countries originally had viable economies, as was the case of Chile and Uruguay, they were hurt by the dysfunctional economic nature of their giant neighbors.

The national territories of Argentina and Brazil included vast economic areas for which international trade promised enormous material rewards. The Pampa Húmeda of Argentina—similar to the American Midwest in terms of size and natural productivity—and the Paraíba Valley in Brazil—the undisputed world leader in coffee production—would typically be sources of growth with enough power to set in motion a process of economic modernization that would eventually produce a high-income national economy and potentially a prosperous continent. However, both subnational regions were united in the same country with a larger backward periphery that thwarted the path toward prosperity. The interaction between the regional economies can be characterized as "perverse." In this interaction, the periphery, through political means, became an insurmountable burden for the development of the center; the center, through unintended economic mechanisms, prevented the periphery from finding a comparative advantage that would help them upgrade their development chances. Perverse relations are worse than parasitic relations. Whereas in parasitic relations, one unit is negatively affected by the interaction with the other, in perverse relations the damage is reciprocal.

A dysfunctional territorial configuration not only caused the failure of Argentina and Brazil to fulfill their takeoff potential as individual countries. Because of their continental influence, it also caused the underdevelopment of the entire subcontinent. If Argentina and Brazil did not become Australia, Chile and Uruguay did not become New Zealand. Both Chile and Uruguay had similarly productive core areas, the Central Valley and the agricultural hinterland of the Montevideo port-city, respectively. However, these areas were too small compared to the Argentine Pampas or the Brazilian Paraíba Valley to play the role of South American dynamos. Eventually the small economies, especially Uruguay, suffered from recurrent economic crises that originated in their giant neighbors. Regional economies outside the Southern Cone of South America, with the exception of Antioquia and the *Eje Cafetero* in Colombia, lacked the natural endowments with which to initiate sustained economic growth. Hence, two specific subnational economies, the Argentine and Brazilian peripheries, had extraordinary repercussions. Their perverse effects scaled up from the purely local dimension to the continental one, as they stalled the two national economies with the potential to lead the entire region toward mature economic development.

An imaginary South American country combining the Argentine Pampa Húmeda, the entire territory of Uruguay, and the state of Rio Grande do Sul in Brazil—all three were world leaders in the production of cereals and cattle—would have been an economic powerhouse similar to Australia, and perhaps even stronger, and it would be free from the drag of a backward periphery. Such a country was not in the plans of any political elite, although at different times a combination of Uruguay and the Pampas on the one hand, and of Uruguay and Rio Grande do Sul on the other, were seriously considered. The Australia of South America, although fictional, illustrates how important borders and the associated composition of national economies are for long-term development. The fact that large countries in South America were economically dysfunctional combinations of subnational units, and the fact that small countries were not endowed with sufficiently strong regional economies to change the developmental fate of the continent, are both a direct outcome of the demarcation of national borders during the state formation process.

This chapter traces the sources of economic underdevelopment in South America to the critical juncture of state formation in the mid-nineteenth century, the period during which the physical space of the national economic and political arenas were defined and countries emerged as distinct combinations of subnational regions.[1] The first section specifies the main *legacies* of state formation, connecting the outcomes of the process of state formation in South America to the long-term economic performance of the region. The second section takes a step back and accounts for the *critical juncture* of state formation through an analysis of commonalities and differences in the solutions to the process of border demarcation in South and Central America. The concluding section summarizes my argument and contrasts it to two common historical explanations of economic underdevelopment in Latin America.

THE LEGACIES OF STATE FORMATION: FROM BORDER DEMARCATION TO ECONOMIC PERFORMANCE

The process of state formation in Latin America yielded three legacies. The main legacy of state formation was the demarcation of national borders. Two subsidiary legacies, which were created jointly with the national borders and affected especially the large countries of South America, were the formula of territorial power-sharing and the type of national administration. Finally, the ultimate legacy was the trajectory of economic development, a combined effect of the national borders, the formula of territorial power-sharing, and the type of national administration.

National Borders

National borders are the most prominent legacy of the state formation process. State formation was a true *critical juncture*, involving a common pattern of change as well as intraregional variations (Mazzuca 2021). The state formation process in South America, like in all Latin America, took place between the Wars of Independence (1810–1825) and the first decade of the twentieth century.[2] Although state formation is customarily defined as a process of violence monopolization, an analytically

---

1. State formation also has distinct legacies in terms of regime trajectories. Mazzuca and Munck (2020) show that Latin America's contemporary poor quality democracies are in part a consequence of the way states were formed in the nineteenth century.

2. Chile was an exceptionally early case of state formation (1830s) by Latin American standards, and Colombia was the latest one (1900s). Brazil consolidated its state around 1850, and Argentina's critical juncture spanned from 1850 to 1880.

distinct but intimately connected process is *border demarcation*—that is, the definition of the regions included and excluded from the emerging national territory. If
the rise of mass politics can largely be viewed as a process of labor incorporation, the
state formation process can be seen as a process of periphery incorporation into (or
exclusion from) national borders.

Rather than shaping national arenas (Collier and Collier 1991), the demarcation
of borders *created* them, at least in a physical sense, for it produced the geographic
space within which a national economy and a national polity would be hosted. From
an economic perspective, border demarcation defined countries as specific combinations of regional economies and associated endowments. Whether a dynamic region
was included and a backward periphery was excluded, the relative size of the regions,
as well as the relations of complementarity, competition, and conflict among them—
these were all at stake during state formation and subsequently became root causes
shaping the prospects of national economic development.

State formation in Latin America produced a variety of territorial outcomes.
Compared to the Western Europe pioneers in state formation, contrasts across
Latin American countries are staggering in terms of size and composition of the
national economic arena. The range spans from mini-republics like El Salvador and
Costa Rica, where most productive land is best suited for plantation ventures, to
geographical colossuses like Brazil and Argentina, which combine multiple urban
centers, dynamic agrarian hinterlands and large, relatively unproductive peripheries. Nevertheless, the variety of sizes and compositions of economic arenas in Latin
America did not include a single case that combined a large dynamic sector and a
vast periphery in a sustainable long-run relationship.

From a political perspective, border demarcation shaped almost every component
of subsequent dynamics. Crucially, it circumscribed the population on the basis of
which future coalitions would be built through political entrepreneurship, cleavage
activation, and alliance-making. Variations in size and composition of political arenas across Latin American countries are among the largest in the world. The range
spans from small countries like Chile and Uruguay, which are largely dominated by
the capital city, to colossuses like Argentina, Brazil, and Mexico, where a coalition
among multiple oligarchies in distant peripheries are an inescapable component of
any ruling alliance, both under democracy and dictatorship.

The national borders that were the primary legacy of the state formation juncture
in Latin America have been distinctively durable. For at least half a century after
independence, most national political arenas in Latin America had been fluid, ill-
defined spaces. In some cases, like Argentina and Colombia, the juncture was still
open in 1860 and 1900. However, the travails of the state-formation juncture in
Latin America left an extremely resilient legacy of political borders. State formation
was a watershed for Latin American history, and its durable legacy contrasts sharply
with the pioneering experience of Western Europe, where borders suffered substantial changes until as recently as 1991. Once national borders were defined in Latin
America, no posterior shock, no matter how big, ever altered them—not even the

deep economic crises that in part were the perverse effect of the very composition of the territorial units defined by such borders.[3]

Contrasts in size and composition of national territories reflect the variety of solutions to the state-formation juncture adopted by the emerging national ruling elites in different contexts. Coupled with the enduring legacy of stable borders, this interaction makes state formation a true critical juncture. As we will see, solutions to the state-formation process in Latin America were ultimately rooted in the economic revolution that shocked the region, especially its temperate areas, around the mid-nineteenth century. A new economic scenario dramatically changed the balance of power between central elites and peripheral oligarchies. The economic revolution provided central elites with new resources and opportunity costs to continue conflicts with peripheral regions. In different contexts, central elites combined different packages of co-optation, repression, and exclusion in order to settle the political and economic arena of the emerging countries. In the process, in addition to the physical legacy of national borders, two subsidiary institutional legacies were created.

Rentier Federalism and Patrimonial Administration

In large countries like Argentina and Brazil, in addition to borders, state formation produced a *formula for territorial governance*, that is, a division of political power between subnational governments and the central state, as well as among the subnational units. The geographic legacy of borders and the institutional legacy of the formula for territorial governance are joint creations. Boundary demarcation depended on the specific terms of territorial governance. A region's decision to accept or resist incorporation into a broader territory was a function of its expected position within the formal and informal hierarchies established by the emerging state.

A major novelty of the process of state formation in Argentina and Brazil (as well as in Mexico) was the creation of a unique structure of territorial governance: "rentier federalism." In contrast to the "competitive" type of federalism of the United States, rentier federalism involves a distinct set of incentives and induces a peculiar dynamic in the interaction among subnational governments. Instead of competing for private investment, subnational units in rentier federalism collude with each other and with national leaders in search of financial aid from the central government.

The second subsidiary legacy of state formation is the rudiments of a *national administration*, which is especially relevant in the larger countries. With few exceptions, public administrations in Latin America have been marked since inception by the twin features of low "infrastructural power," and a high propensity to "patrimonial rule." The former is the ability of the state to provide public goods and build social infrastructure in an economically efficient and territorially even manner. The latter is the probability that the state will be captured by patronage machines and predatory rulers. State formation in South America produced two giant countries—Argentina

---

3. One exception is Bolivia, which lost considerable territory in the War of the Pacific (1879–1883) and the Chaco War (1932–1935).

and Brazil—that were fundamentally underequipped to produce an effective rule over their vast territories (beyond South America, the same applies to Mexico). Peripheries in both countries had been ruled by local elites in a patrimonial fashion since time immemorial. The participation of peripheral rural oligarchies in national ruling coalitions transmitted patrimonialism from the local level to the emerging national level. The privileged position that peripheral oligarchies were able to secure for themselves in national coalitions reflects the concessions that state builders found necessary to make during the critical juncture of state formation in order to stabilize the national borders and pacify the territories within them.

Long-Run Economic Development

Rentier federalism, patrimonial rule, and low state capacity are important political outcomes. Additionally, in the cases of Argentina and Brazil they combined with the dysfunctional nature of their territories to create large obstacles to the economic development of the entire continent.

As a result of the way national borders were demarcated, Argentina and Brazil (and to a lesser extent Mexico) combined economic regions with different endowments of natural resources, which in turn induced a variety of local productivity rates. During the decades after state formation, the central regions of Argentina and Brazil could produce between three and six times more output per capita than the Northern regions. Monetary union, a direct corollary of territorial unification, meant that the dynamism of the central regions, by strengthening the exchange rate, hurt the international competitiveness of the backward regions, in a pattern that a century later, in a different context, economists would call "Dutch disease." The sugar and cotton industries of the Brazilian Northeast, once the jewel of Portuguese imperial finances, never recovered from the emergence of the coffee economy in the Paraíba Valley around the mid-nineteenth century (Leff 1982). Similarly, the manufacturing potential of the Argentine Northwest (textiles) and Northeast (shipyards, woodworks) was largely aborted after the string of export booms produced in the Pampas (wool, beef, and finally wheat) starting in the mid-1840s. At the moment of their formation, the territories of Argentina and Brazil included large backward areas. Subsequently, due to the stark contrast with the dynamic regions with which they were united, these backward areas were not able to establish a productive profile. The Dutch disease, a structural consequence of the physical space occupied by the new states, hurt the economies of the periphery in Argentina and Brazil.

The institutional legacies of rentier federalism and patrimonial rule were harmful both to the peripheries and the central economic regions. Rentier federalism was the main channel through which peripheral oligarchies secured regular transfers of economic resources from the dynamic center to the poor interior regions. Given the underlying local economy, peripheral oligarchies had a short-run incentive to grow the local bureaucracy so as to generate an implicit unemployment insurance for their followers in exchange for clientelist/partisan support. The long-run effect of this choice for peripheral regions was a low-quality trap that combined political inefficiency and poor economic productivity. Thus, in the peripheries, relatively unproductive employment opportunities in provincial governments crowded out private investment, further increasing the natural productivity gap between the sectors of the national economy. In turn, from the perspective of the center, redistribution to the periphery simply syphoned off the resources necessary to upgrade the economy beyond the level afforded by its natural advantages (Sawers 1996).

Finally, patrimonial rule and low infrastructural power contributed to economic failure because the lack of administrative capacity and the use of public resources for private or partisan gain led to an undersupply of growth-enhancing public goods, from contract enforcement to communications infrastructure. In both Argentina and Brazil, the engineering of winning political coalitions in the context of Dutch disease, rentier federalism, and subnational patrimonialism resulted in the transformation of the national state into a large-scale patronage machine, which was remarkably resistant to posterior economic shocks, regime changes, and other large-scale transformations. Hence, the effects of the original dysfunctional economic nature of the territories of Argentina and Brazil was aggravated and perpetuated by the joint institutional legacies of rentier federalism and patrimonial rule.

THE CRITICAL JUNCTURE OF STATE FORMATION: CONTRASTING SOLUTIONS TO BORDER DEMARCATION

The process and outcomes of the state formation process in Latin America can be analyzed through two sets of contrasts. First, factors can explain (1) the transition from ill-defined and unstable political units in the 1820s and 1830s to clearly demarcated, stable national political arenas in the 1890s and 1900s; and (2) the contrasts between Latin America and the pioneering cases of Western Europe in terms of the formula of territorial governability (the incidence of rentier federalism in Latin America) and the type of national administration (much weaker and more patrimonial in Latin America). Second, crucial differences in antecedent conditions across South and Central America explain variations within Latin America, especially contrasts across countries in terms of size and composition of the national territory.[4]

Contrasts between Latin America and Western Europe

State formation in Latin America and Western Europe occurred in drastically different political and economic international contexts. Politically, whereas Western European states formed in a context of international anarchy, Latin American states were built under an international hierarchy, at the peak of which was Great Britain and France. Adapting Gerschenkron's (1962) argument, the latecomer states in Latin

---

4. This argument is developed in much greater detail in Mazzuca (2021).

America came into existence in an international arena already populated by the Western European pioneers. Latin American latecomer states faced a new set of opportunities and constraints. The existence of well-established global powers outside the region attenuated the weight of security considerations in state-formation ventures. Great Britain's role was key. Concerned about disruptions in its trade relations with the region, Great Britain was a virtual referee in, and a strong sponsor of peaceful solutions to, disputes between Latin American countries. An informal outside umpire was an unimaginable form of conflict resolution in the original European setting of state formation.

Economically, whereas states in Western Europe were built before the rise of modern capitalism, states in Latin America were formed when capitalism, already half a century old in Western Europe, was quickly expanding throughout the Western hemisphere. A different context provided state builders in Latin America with an option not available to their European counterparts. In a capitalist world, international trade could provide governments with the revenues that in a precapitalist world could only be obtained through politically costly and contentious efforts at domestic extraction. More specifically, Latin American elites could count on the customhouse close to the main port to fund their state-formation projects and, indeed, with very few exceptions (Bolivia, Paraguay, and to a lesser extent Mexico), all states in Latin America were built on the revenues generated by a seaport.

Thus, in direct contrast to the main cases of state formation in Continental Europe (France, Prussia, and Spain), where the political center that took the initiative of state formation was an interior city, the vast majority of state formation centers in Latin America were port cities (Buenos Aires, Montevideo, and Rio de Janeiro) or cities closely connected to a major seaport (Santiago/Valparaíso and Lima/Callao). Very much like in Smith's *doux commerce* thesis, the role of foreign commerce in state formation in Latin America further attenuated the weight of geopolitical considerations, as military conflict would disrupt trade and interrupt the regular flow of revenues.

These differences played a key role in outcomes of the state formation process in Western Europe and Latin America. In early modern Europe, geopolitical pressures from foreign powers forced every central ruler into a direct clash with a large array of local powers. In order to mobilize the necessary financial and human resources to wage war, European state builders incorporated the surrounding peripheries by building state capacity throughout the territory. The emerging central state penetrated the countryside, destroyed recalcitrant local oligarchies, and upgraded public administrations, making the transition from patrimonial to bureaucratic rule. As a result of a Darwinian geopolitical game, Western European countries converged on the formation of modern bureaucratic states. Rulers who failed to engineer this political modernization were absorbed by those who succeeded. State formation in Western Europe also set in motion a reactive sequence by which future generations of the subject population, in exchange for sustaining the central state, would obtain different forms of political representation and a relatively uniform supply of public goods and services.

Although war and preparation for war had been the main occupation of the inchoate Latin American sovereignties for the first few decades after independence, starting around 1840 the relatively sudden rise of big economic opportunities in international trade drastically changed the political priorities of the emerging national elites. The new economic opportunities originated in a sustained boom in the demand for primary commodities, especially from temperate areas, and a massive reduction in transportation costs, due to the replacement of older vessels with steamboats in transatlantic navigation. From Buenos Aires to Mexico, Latin American political and economic elites began to see that a commercial revolution would provide the basis for a distinct political economy of state formation. Trade switched the state formation track that Latin American countries had originally taken. By the middle of the nineteenth century, Latin American rulers were responding to the incentives offered by world capitalism and relying on the taxation from foreign commerce to pursue a novel strategy of state formation quite inconceivable in early modern Europe.

Latin American state formation was a distinct process. Instead of fighting against local powers resisting the emergence of the territorial state, central rulers in Latin America could co-opt them, an option that in Western Europe would have meant the loss of international sovereignty. Decisive military penetration of the peripheries in Latin America became not only unnecessary, as it would have yielded little revenue compared to international trade, but also counterproductive, as it would have disrupted the peaceful environment needed to engage in world capitalism. If incorporation of peripheries into the national territory resulted in the destruction of local oligarchies in Western Europe, incorporation of peripheries preserved and usually reinforced the power of local oligarchies in Latin America. Patrimonial rulers in backward areas in Argentina, Brazil, and Mexico offered their support to national projects of state formation in the center in exchange for a wide variety of concessions, including institutional power, economic transfers, and informal favors.

Creatures of war and preparation for war in a precapitalist, Hobbesian international context, the pioneering states of Western Europe transformed their peripheries, enforced strict rules for territorial governance, and created highly professionalized national administrations, which were originally designed to maximize domestic extraction and eventually mutated into highly efficient agencies of public goods provision. Creatures of trade and preparation for trade in a capitalist, post-Hobbesian international context, the latecomer states of Latin America incorporated their peripheries without transforming their patrimonial institutions, created states with low capacities to provide public goods and social infrastructure in a territorially even and economically efficient fashion, and, in the case of the three largest countries, fostered the emergence of the rentier type of federalism.

Contrasts within Latin America

The commercial revolution of the mid-nineteenth century did not have uniform effects across Latin American countries. The boom helped all of them build or consolidate national states. Yet when the shock of prices hit the region, preexisting local conditions, rooted in geography and politics, led to differences in the process of state formation and the eventual size, composition, and capacity of the new countries. Geography (i.e., seaports) is enough to explain the emergence and evolution of the small states with simple economies, including Chile, Uruguay, and the five Central American republics. Political factors need to be added to understand the emergence of more complex states encompassing diverse regional economies such as Argentina and Brazil.

The key geographic factor for successful state formation in small, medium, and large states was the availability of a seaport from which to draw the essential fiscal resources. However, seaports varied along two key dimensions: proximity to a major producing regional economy, and separability from a backward, relatively unproductive periphery. With only the two partial exceptions of Bolivia and Paraguay, every new state had a major seaport, which in almost every case was the main source of public revenue.[5] Thus, availability of ports during the commercial revolution was far more important than borders inherited from colonial times in creating new states and defining their territorial jurisdictions. It is not an exaggeration to claim that seaports became a necessary condition for successful state formation. Bolivia and Paraguay did not have important seaports and are the only two countries that, after state consolidation in Latin America, suffered serious territorial losses to other Latin American countries.

Seaports were the main driver of state formation in the small countries of the region, including Chile and Uruguay, as well as the five original Central American republics. The seven cases share two common features. First, the proximity of the seaport to a large export-producing region secured the finances of state formation. Exports of cereals in Chile, wool and hides in Uruguay, and bananas and coffee in the Central American republics formed the economic basis that consolidated the rudiments of a government into a fully formed national state.

A second commonality was the absence of a less productive economic region within "predatory distance" of the port or its productive hinterland. Isolation from potential attackers exempted elites in Chile, Uruguay, and Central America from major security considerations, and allowed them to focus on the virtuous cycle of market formation and state formation. In Chile, isolation was a direct consequence of a physical barrier, the Andes mountain chain. In Uruguay, it was a mix of a physical barrier, the Uruguay River, and geopolitical protection afforded directly by Great Britain and indirectly by the balance of power between Argentina and Brazil. In Central America, the closest neighbor to each mini-republic was another mini-republic with an almost identical productive profile. The availability of an export outlet for

---

5. Bolivia had a minor seaport but lost its maritime coast in the War of the Pacific, decades after the core of its state was formed. Paraguay had a major river port in Asunción, from which it gained easy access to the South Atlantic.

each of the five republics generated a regional equilibrium in which all preferred growing their own state and economy to the military risks of attempting to capture wealth from the others.

Political factors need to be considered alongside geography to understand the state formation process in what eventually became the largest countries of South America. Brazil and Argentina combined economic regions that benefited greatly from the commercial revolution and vast peripheral areas characterized by low economic productivity and entrenched patrimonial domination of local oligarchies. Why did the centers in Brazil and Argentina incorporate into their national territories large backward peripheries? In a post-Hobbesian geopolitical context, country size was not a relevant consideration. Periphery incorporation cannot be attributed to international security motives. It cannot be explained by the search for material prosperity either, given the large productivity differences between the regions, and the fact that, from a fiscal point of view, peripheries were net beneficiaries of incorporation. Indeed, to answer this question we must look beyond geopolitical competition and economic advantage to strictly political considerations of the state builders.

The peripheries of Brazil and Argentina were not separated from the center by large natural barriers. Peripheries could threaten, with military power, to disrupt the process of economic modernization undertaken by the center. However, neither the Paraíba Valley nor the Pampa Húmeda chose to build a physical or military border against the Brazilian and Argentine peripheries. On the contrary, oligarchic elites in the peripheries became active political players in the national arena.

The reason for incorporation was, most likely, *coalitional*. Divisions in the center in both Brazil (conservatives versus liberals) and Argentina (Buenos Aires versus Entre Ríos) prompted an "arena expanding" type of conflict. Local conflict for primacy *within* the central area led opposing factions to search for allies *outside* it, sponsoring in the process the incorporation of peripheral oligarchies into a national arena. In exchange for their support, peripheral oligarchies were not only able to secure a range of short-term material rewards—crucially, they were also able to lock in a variety of institutional privileges that were vastly out of proportion to their underlying economic strength. Paradoxically, local conflict caused national unification. National unification provided short-term allies to factions in the center at the cost of patrimonial concessions and, ultimately, long-term economic stagnation.

There were also some contrasts between the process of state formation in Brazil and Argentina. For instance, Brazil and Argentina differ in the timing of the state-formation process. The process of incorporation of the backward periphery was completed in Brazil around 1830, when the commercial revolution was only showing the first signs of its potential magnitude. By contrast, in Argentina, it occurred four decades later, when economic modernization in the center was advancing at full steam. This difference helps explain why Brazil is larger in size than Argentina. Moreover, Brazil provides an exception to the rule of "one port, one state" that characterizes Spanish America.

In addition, the central elites of Rio de Janeiro also incorporated a dynamic periphery in the South, Rio Grande do Sul. In contrast to the Paraíba Valley, the center of coffee, Rio Grande do Sul was ideally endowed for cattle-ranching activities, comparable in size and productivity to neighboring Uruguay. Additionally, Rio Grande had its own Atlantic coastline, and could easily build a customhouse from where to derive the resources for independent state formation. Indeed, when the commercial revolution of the mid-century hit the continent, ranching elites in Rio Grande do Sul strove for secession in order to secure an autonomous trade, monetary, and fiscal policy. For an entire decade (1835–1845), Rio Grande do Sul was a separate country, the *República de Piratini*. Thus, whereas the commercial revolution provided central elites in Brazil and Argentina with the incentives and resources to incorporate backward peripheries through co-optation, in Brazil it also created a dynamic periphery that had its own state formation aspirations and that threatened territorial unification. For the first and only time in Latin American history, in Brazil in the mid-1830s, a dynamic periphery challenged territorial union and the center had a firm economic and fiscal incentive to fight back. Rio de Janeiro responded to secession with a combination of military action—of a scale and duration unimaginable in Spanish America—and massive policy, institutional, and economic concessions. The eventual success of the Rio elite was due in part to the fortunes of war, but also to the fact that Brazil had settled its dealings with its backward periphery to the North at an earlier stage, and had secured the rudiments of a consolidated central civil and military bureaucracy by the time of the commercial revolution.

CONCLUSION

This chapter traced economic underdevelopment in South America to the juncture of state formation, which created two large countries that were dysfunctional combinations of subnational economic regions, and several countries whose economies were not big enough to produce the economic takeoff of the continent. State formation in Argentina and Brazil created national territories with the birth defect of structural Dutch disease, which in turn was deepened and perpetuated by the joint institutional legacies of rentier federalism and patrimonial rule. The two areas with the potential to become continental economic engines, the Pampa Húmeda and the Paraíba Valley, were strangled by political subsumption within a wider economic and political arena, marked by systematic fiscal transfers from economically dynamic subnational regions to economically unproductive but politically profitable peripheries.

This perspective about the long-run development of South American countries in part complements, and in part rectifies, two dominant historical visions. The dominant visions attribute foundational power either to the colonial period of institution building in the seventeenth and eighteenth centuries (Sokoloff and Engerman 2000; Mahoney 2010), or to the emergence of mass politics and labor mobilization in the mid-twentieth century (Germani 1971; Dornbusch and Edwards 1991). However, the sources of underdevelopment in South America are younger than colonial legacies and older than mass politics. To a large extent, independence revolutions wiped away the colonial institutional legacy, and the rise of mass politics in Latin America occurred where obstacles to economic takeoff were already formidable.

By emphasizing the role of political and economic geography, this chapter also advances one way of integrating root causes of long-run development, which economists usually divide into competing institutional and geographic factors. As we have seen, the fundamental geographic features of Argentina and Brazil, including centrally the demarcation of natural assets contained in the national arena and the configuration of subnational economies, were *political* creations. National economic and political arenas were defined during the crucial state-formation juncture of the mid-nineteenth century.

State formation in South America—and Latin America more generally—was a fundamental episode of change, which transformed ill-defined political units into durable, sovereign territories. Although state formation showed different patterns in the different emerging national contexts, the unique international context of the mid-nineteenth century furnished Latin American countries with many commonalities that were unimaginable in the pioneering cases of Western Europe. Latin American states were formed when the international geopolitical arena had already crystallized into a hierarchy of national powers, led by Great Britain and France, as well as after the Western economy became dominated by capitalism. Faced with much less demanding international security constraints, and much more attractive opportunities for international trade, state-building rulers in Latin America had the incentives and the resources to forego investments in Weberian meritocratic administrations and infrastructural capacities, and constructed instead the minimal territorial and political institutions required to take advantage of international commercial opportunities.

Differences within Latin America in terms of size and composition of national territories are much larger than in Western Europe. In Latin America, every region endowed with the assets for a primary-export economy and a viable seaport was willing and able to create an independent state—the cases of Chile, Uruguay, and the Central American republics. What set apart Argentina and Brazil was not only the existence of the largest and most powerful subnational economies, but also the proximity between the dynamic regions and backward peripheries dominated by patrimonial rulers. Argentine and Brazilian state-builders did not deal with peripheral powers as the Western European state-builders did. Instead of transforming or repressing peripheral powers, they co-opted them into emerging national coalitions. Short-term coalitional gains were obtained at the cost of heavy obstacles to economic development for generations to come.

BIBLIOGRAPHY

Collier, Ruth Berins, and David Collier. 1991. *Shaping the Political Arena: Critical Junctures, the Labor Movement and Regime Dynamics in Latin America*. Princeton, NJ: Princeton University Press.

Dornbusch, Rudiger, and Sebastián Edwards (eds.). 1991. *The Macroeconomics of Populism in Latin America*. Chicago, IL: University of Chicago Press.

Germani, Gino. 1971. *Política y sociedad en una época de transición: De la sociedad tradicional a la sociedad de masas*. Buenos Aires, Argentina: Paidós.

Gerschenkron, Alexander. 1962. *Economic Backwardness in Historical Perspective: A Book of Essays*. Cambridge, MA: Belknap Press of Harvard University Press.

Leff, Nathaniel H. 1982. *Underdevelopment and Development in Brazil*. New York, NY: Routledge.

Mahoney, James. 2010. *Colonialism and Postcolonial Development: Spanish America in Comparative Perspective*. New York, NY: Cambridge University Press.

Mazzuca, Sebastián. 2021. *Latecomer State Formation: Political Geography and Capacity Failure in Latin America*. New Haven, CT: Yale University Press.

Mazzuca, Sebastián L., and Gerardo L. Munck. 2020. *A Middle-Quality Institutional Trap: Democracy and State Capacity in Latin America*. New York, NY: Cambridge University Press.

Sawers, Larry. 1996. *The Other Argentina: The Interior and National Development*. Boulder, CO: Westview Press.

Sokoloff, Kenneth L., and Stanley L. Engerman. 2000. "History Lessons: Institutions, Factors Endowments, and Paths of Development in the New World." *Journal of Economic Perspectives* 14(3): 217–32.

10

Religion and Critical Junctures

Divergent Trajectories of Liberalism in Modern Europe

Andrew C. Gould

Half a century ago, Lipset and Rokkan (1967) launched the study of cleavages, critical junctures, and resulting trajectories in the evolution of politics and party systems. In their classic study of Western Europe, they focused on four fundamental societal cleavages: center-periphery, church-state, land-industry, and owner-worker. According to their argument, the resolution of these cleavages crystallized in critical junctures, which in turn set countries on distinctive historical paths. In the intervening decades since 1967, numerous studies have extended, refined, and in some ways corrected their arguments about Western Europe, and a substantial body of research has applied this framework to other regions.

This chapter discusses my work on critical junctures, presented in *Origins of Liberal Dominance: State, Church, and Party in Nineteenth-Century Europe* (Gould 1999). This study focused on the politics of liberalism in France, Belgium, Switzerland, and Germany, from the restoration of conservative monarchies in 1815 to the outbreak of World War I in 1914. In this historical context, liberals sought to build representative and constitutional government, to develop national economic systems, and to confine clerical authority to religious affairs (Gould 1999: 3). Most scholars viewed nineteenth-century liberals through a prism that emphasized battles over private property and socialism; my work took the interaction between liberalism and religious institutions as equally decisive.

LINES OF INFLUENCE

The lines of influence that shaped my book on religion and politics reach back to Lipset and Rokkan's (1967) framework, which provided a powerful, fresh, and welcome new perspective on the study of religion and politics. This framework helped to move the discussion beyond what was too often a rather limited analysis of secularization in the context of modernization. Attention shifted instead to how, at critical junctures, religion played a crucial and complex role in shaping European politics.

Institutional ties played a key role in keeping Lipset and Rokkan's work at the forefront of my thinking. My book began as a dissertation at Berkeley, where Ruth and David Collier were leading scholars of comparative politics. Their work on critical junctures, eventually published as *Shaping the Political Arena* (Collier and Collier 1991), influenced many graduate students in comparative politics, including those of us outside the Latin American field. In 1982, Berkeley hired the young scholar who became my principal academic mentor, Gregory Luebbert. He had done his graduate work with Lipset at Stanford, and in his short career, Luebbert published two remarkable books that fit squarely in the critical juncture tradition. In the first book, *Comparative Democracy: Policymaking and Governing Coalitions in Europe and Israel*, Luebbert (1986, xiii) acknowledged his "great intellectual debt" to Lipset and Rokkan. Their cleavage theory became the core of Luebbert's (1986: 53–60) own account of how policy preferences shaped party leaders' decisions about whether to participate in coalition governments. In Luebbert's analysis, party leaders cared primarily about the policies at the core of a party's programmatic profile, and he interpreted this profile as determined by the societal cleavage that was most salient when the party was founded. This was a classic Lipset and Rokkan analysis: commitments undertaken at a critical juncture had long-lasting consequences that set parties on different paths into the future.

Luebbert thus offered a deterministic view of critical juncture theory. In *Comparative Democracy*, he argued that parties acquired profiles "by translating societal cleavages into lines of party conflict during the years before and just after the adoption of universal suffrage and, especially, the introduction of proportional representation" (Luebbert 1986: 53). In this framework, the metaphor of "translation" implied that the actions of political leaders simply reflected the underlying social and economic conflicts. The details of politics did not play a key role: cleavages had "precipitated" parties, and social and economic disputes "had given rise to the parties" (Luebbert 1986: 54).

In using such formulations, Luebbert understated the roles of specific political leaders. Although he hinted that individual choices mattered, his analysis emphasized patterns more than people. Luebbert asserted that parties used social cleavages to their advantage whenever that cleavage involved socioeconomic issues—as opposed to cleavages that concerned "constitutional, producer-consumer, cultural-ethnolinguistic, regional or center-periphery, ethical-religious, and foreign policy" issues.[1]

---

1. For instance, he stated that not all societal cleavages became lines of party opposition in every society. Which cleavages became politically relevant, he argued, "has depended on their relative intensity in the society at large, the historical sequences of mass mobilization, and considerations of organizational and electoral strategies, especially the payoffs of alliances

Parties also used cleavages whenever two cleavages reinforced each other (Luebbert 1986: 55).

Societal cleavages thus gave parties policy profiles, and then leaders struggled to maintain their positions of privilege on the basis of that profile. As stated in the book's closing paragraph, Luebbert (1986: 246) found an "almost complete absence of evidence that the skills, ideologies, and aspirations of individual politicians made any difference in the final coalitional outcome." In other words, the key to predicting which parties would form a coalition was knowing which issues party leaders needed to prioritize to retain their positions as leaders.

My own project was even more closely connected to Luebbert's second book, which he was writing as he advised me on my choice of dissertation topic. In his second book, *Liberalism, Fascism, or Social Democracy: Social Classes and the Political Origins of Regimes in Interwar Europe*, Luebbert (1991) noted that European countries that acquired liberal regimes by the outbreak of World War I—that is, the United Kingdom, France, and Switzerland—retained those regimes throughout the tumultuous years leading up to World War II. Those were the countries that developed neither social democratic regimes nor successful homegrown fascist movements. This observation set the stage for Luebbert's main argument, which sought to explain why some countries developed social democratic regimes, as in Scandinavia and Czechoslovakia, while others fell to fascism, as in Germany and Italy.

His central concern was working-class politics. Thus, the explanation for different political regimes focused principally on the national political coalitions that emerged out of a "fundamental historical transition: the emergence of the organized working class as a major contender in national politics," as David Collier and Lipset (1991: v) put it. The process of incorporating workers into national political regimes was a critical juncture *par excellence*: choices made as the franchise expanded and workers organized would shape party systems (Lipset and Rokkan 1967), coalition formation (Luebbert 1986), and even political regimes (Luebbert 1991).

FORMULATING THE FOCUS
ON RELIGION AND POLITICS

In advising me on the choice of a research question, Luebbert proposed that I investigate why liberal regimes were successfully established in some countries but not in others. He saw an opportunity to add crucial nuance to his argument by exploring the idea that "where liberal movements were successful before 1914, their appeal was

---

and mergers and the costs of splits and lost support" (Luebbert 1986: 55). In this passage, the terms "strategies," "payoffs," and "costs" suggested that leaders were making choices. These choices could of course be viewed fairly deterministically within some choice-theoretic frameworks, or they could be understood less deterministically as depending centrally on the skills of party leaders and/or somewhat idiosyncratic characteristics of specific countries.

reinforced by a religious cleavage" (Luebbert 1991: 6). He gave this advice just weeks before his death—a shock to everyone, as he was just thirty-two years old when he drowned in a white-water canoeing accident. His colleague Giuseppe Di Palma shepherded Luebbert's nearly completed manuscript to publication; he also became my advisor. Collier and Lipset wrote the preface to the resulting book.

Based on Luebbert's advice, it became my task to systematically account for the ways that religious conflicts yielded different political dynamics as liberals confronted closed hegemonies and sought popular support. The proposed study opened the possibility of reinforcing the conclusions of Lipset and Rokkan, as well as of Luebbert, that liberal movements could gain or lose supporters depending on the configuration of religious cleavages. At the same time, it might offer a rival perspective—for example, potentially challenging the argument that liberals took religious cleavages as political givens that they themselves could not influence.

My efforts to frame a research project on religion in nineteenth-century Europe coincided with new analytic challenges in the discipline of political science. Long-standing accounts of liberalism as a movement of rising middle classes seemed wedded to modernization theory. Such an approach came under strong attack in the 1970s and 1980s due to several shortcomings, among them failing to explain dictatorships in advanced societies such as Germany, Italy, Argentina, and Brazil. What could explain the evolution of liberalism in Europe? The literature no longer offered a convincing answer.

In the realm of real-world politics, moreover, religion had in fact not faded away, contrary to secularization theory's naïve prediction. By the 1990s, religious movements across the globe had aligned with revolution, democratization, and dictatorship. For example, Islamic clergy commanded a revolutionary regime in Iran; the Catholic Church had supported both dictatorship and democratization in Latin America, Iberia, Poland, and the Philippines; and Christian leaders in the United States crafted a new alliance with a resurgent Republican party. The political relevance of religion had thus been recast in many ways.

In this context, my new project on early episodes of liberalization promised novel insights into how religion shaped modern politics. The critical juncture approach changed the question from "Which factor is most important?" to "What happened first?" and "With what consequences?" Lipset and Rokkan's emphasis on the sequencing of formative moments opened the way to trace the impact of religion on politics over time.

HOW RELIGION SHAPED POLITICAL REGIMES

In the course of my research, a crucial insight began to emerge: the political significance of religion for the fate of liberal reform efforts changed as the franchise expanded. In the period of elite-dominated politics in the first three decades of the nineteenth century, clerical support for liberal reform hinged mainly on whether clerical authority would be curbed or enhanced in a reconfigured state. However, as mass political support became increasingly decisive for the success of parties in the

1870s and after, the middle classes and peasants weighed in as voters or potential voters. Liberal reform now challenged not just the role of clerical authority in the highest offices of the state, but also implicated clerical influence in other institutions, such as education and property rights.

The key was identifying who supported expanding (or reducing) the scope of clerical authority over nonreligious institutions. My research encompassed a fine-grained analysis of how particular political leaders and institutions shaped overall outcomes. Nonetheless, the overall style of the analysis shared the determinism of Luebbert's work.

In selecting cases for my project, like many scholars in the critical juncture tradition, I identified scope conditions that extended beyond a single country case, yet restricted the analysis to a small number of cases that were sufficiently similar. The analysis focused on liberal reform movements in nineteenth-century Europe, and especially on countries at the middle of a spectrum, where liberal reform was neither a foregone conclusion nor completely implausible. Thus, I examined Switzerland, Belgium, France, and Germany as "cases at the center of the distribution of liberal success and failure" (Gould 1999: 9).

Although it was restricted to these four cases, the study was also relevant to understanding the more prominent cases of success, notably the United Kingdom. It also yielded insight into countries where the prospects for liberal reform in the nineteenth century were dim, as in Southern and Eastern Europe. The case selection departed from the tendency in the literature on liberalism to focus on just one country at a time, or when comparisons were made, to emphasize contrasts between the two best-known cases, the United Kingdom and Germany. To understand why liberal reform ultimately failed in Germany, I argued, we should study other countries situated in the middle of the spectrum of likely success.

Drawing on a critical junctures approach, I focused on how a common process—the launching of liberal reforms—could evolve differently in comparable cases. I argued that the attempt by liberals to reform political regimes was a critical juncture in the four cases. I distinguished between two phases of the critical juncture, the first marked primarily by elite politics and the second by mass politics. I posited, in a nutshell, that each country's path through liberal reform was strongly shaped by the reaction of religious authorities to this common process. *Institutions* present at the onset of liberal reform, especially whether or not churches were incorporated into state institutions, influenced *reform dynamics*. Ultimately, the *outcomes* of these efforts differed across the cases: repeated failures in Germany, multiple successes in Switzerland, and checkered reforms in Belgium and France.

These alternative trajectories are summarized in Table 10.1. The Appendix presents an Annotated Table 10.1, in which over three dozen footnotes serve to clarify the meaning of categories and distinctions employed in the table. This version of Table 10.1 serves to illustrate a key point. Dozens of complex decisions stand behind the classification of cases shown in Table 10.1. As scholars strive for "best practices" in comparative-historical research, they should aim for transparency regarding these decisions. Annotated Table 10.1 seeks to move toward such transparency.

The Elite Phase

How should these contrasting patterns of success and failure be explained? Religion was a key factor.

My chapters on the elite phase encompassed the revolutions and attempted revolutions of 1830 and 1848, and concluded with the regimes that emerged in the 1850s. At the start of the nineteenth century, churches were incorporated into state institutions in Germany and France. Their religio-political regimes integrated religious and political power at the highest level such that neo-absolutist monarchs enforced religious conformity and high-ranking clergy occupied key state offices. As a result, only in Germany and France did liberals cast their programs as a challenge to both political *and* clerical authority. Where the church was incorporated into the state, clerical leaders viewed liberal reform as threatening. In France in particular, the Catholic Church had been deeply integrated into the pre-Revolutionary administration and had been a major landowner across much of the country, especially in the southeast. For these reasons, in both France and Germany high-ranking clergy staunchly opposed liberal reformers.

Table 10.1 Institutions, Reform Dynamics, and Outcomes: Elite Phase and Mass Phase

	1. Elite Phase			
	Germany (1815–1848)	France (1815–1848)	Belgium (1815–1846)	Switzerland (1815–1831)
1. Antecedent Conditions				
State and Church Institutions at Onset of Liberal Reform	Non-liberal, incorporated churches	Non-liberal, incorporated churches	Non-liberal, church not incorporated	Non-liberal, church not incorporated
1. Cleavage: Liberalism vs. Clerical Elite				
Liberal Policy toward Religious Authority	Attack Protestant and Catholic authority	Attack Catholic authority	Promote Catholic authority	Preserve Protestant and attack Catholic authority
1. Critical Juncture, Phase 1				
Clergy Response	Protestant and Catholic opposition	Catholic opposition	Catholic support	Protestant support and Catholic opposition
Liberal Reform Outcome	*Failed Reform*	*Failed Reform*	*Successful Reform*	*Successful Reform*

(continued)

Table 10.1 Institutions, Reform Dynamics, and Outcomes: Elite Phase and Mass Phase (*continued*)

	2. Mass Phase			
	Germany (1860–1914)	France (1852–1940)	Belgium (1847–1914)	Switzerland (1833–1874)
2. Antecedent Conditions				
Institutions at Onset of Second Liberal Reform	Monarchs sovereign	Emperor sovereign	Parliament sovereign	Parliament sovereign
2. Critical Juncture, Phase 2				
Liberal Policy toward Religious Authority	Preserve Protestant and attack Catholic authority	Attack Catholic authority	Attack Catholic authority	Preserve Protestant and attack Catholic authority
Clergy Response	Protestant toleration and Catholic opposition	Catholic opposition	Catholic opposition	Protestant support and Catholic opposition
2. Aftermath				
Provincial Middle-Class and Peasant Response	Protestants tolerate liberals and Catholics oppose liberals	Catholics support liberals	Catholics oppose liberals	Protestants support liberals and Catholics oppose liberals
2. Legacy				
Party Outcome	*Weak liberal parties: co-opted defeat of liberals*	*Strong liberal parties: victory of liberals (contested)*	*Weak liberal parties: conditional defeat of liberals*	*Strong liberal parties: supremacy of liberals*
Regime Outcome	*Authoritarian Regime*	*Constitutional Democracy (contested)*	*Constitutional Democracy*	*Constitutional Democracy*

By contrast, in Belgium and Switzerland, churches played only a limited role in the state and the rural economy. In neither case were churches significant landowners. The Catholic Church in Belgium, then the southern provinces of the Netherlands, was oppressed by its Protestant Dutch rulers. Belgian liberal reformers offered autonomy to the Catholic Church in a newly independent country. Switzerland lacked a strong federal state and its Catholic and Protestant churches were either allied to or established in the oligarchies ruling each canton. Here, liberal plans for political reform at a national level did not endanger clerical privileges in state administration.

Specifically, in these cases, liberal reform even held out the possibility for Protestant churches to achieve greater political supremacy. In Switzerland, liberal reformers were hostile toward the Catholic Church, but not toward the Protestant Church; as such, only the Catholic Church opposed the Swiss liberal reformers.

In sum, clergy supported liberal plans to reform political institutions only when such reform would enhance the scope of their authority.

Two alternative outcomes emerged. In both Belgium and Switzerland, liberal regimes were established with executives responsible to a legislature and a formal separation of church and state at the national level. By contrast, Prussia's governments depended mainly upon the Kaiser's support and France's governments depended upon that of Napoleon III. Crucially, neither ruler needed support from the legislature, and both integrated churches into their ruling apparatuses. The elite phase of liberal reform thus generated an even stronger contrast between the incorporated churches in Prussia and France and the church-state separation in Belgium and Switzerland.

The Mass Phase

In the context of these elite-dominated regimes, pressures for greater participation and mass franchise increased and brought new actors into the set of coalitional possibilities. Conservatives and liberals alike reached deeper into the urban and provincial middle classes, and into the peasantry. Politicians needed broad electoral support now that most of the adult male population was becoming eligible to vote, as was common throughout these cases in the 1870s and thereafter. I labeled this period the "mass phase" to signal the common process of expanding participation and inclusiveness in national politics.

The shared process yielded different coalitional possibilities in each case. A key factor shaping coalitions was how provincial middle classes and peasants responded to the specific economic and religious threats they faced. In France, middle classes and peasants feared both socialism and a revived Catholic Church, whereas their counterparts in Belgium—whose property did not derive from forced secularization of land—feared only socialism. In Prussia and France, monarchs seemed viable as checks against socialist-inspired expropriation, but not in Belgium or Switzerland, where neighboring powers checked the ambitions of would-be royal rulers.

The expansion of political participation thus reinforced a liberal regime in Switzerland, but strengthened the monarchy in Prussia. In Belgium, expanded suffrage brought a Catholic party to power that preserved parliamentary sovereignty and expanded clerical authority in education. In France, universal male suffrage rejected the presidential ambitions of generals and empowered radicals, such as Léon Gambetta, who declared clericalism to be the enemy of a constitutional republic. The expansion of participation in national politics, a quintessentially "modern" process, thus emboldened authoritarians in Prussia and republicans in France. In Belgium it buttressed Catholic constitutionalism, while in Switzerland it reinforced greater direct democracy. Liberals fared well when they had the support of newly enfranchised provincial middle classes and peasants, which enhanced their dominance in Switzerland and reversed their previous losses in France. Without such rural support, Belgian liberals lost their previously dominant position in Belgium and continued to be subservient to authoritarians in Germany. The mass phase of liberal reform created new and divergent outcomes in the four cases stemming from the religious implications of liberal reforms.

COMPETING EXPLANATIONS

The book sought to evaluate competing explanations for the successes and failures of liberalism. The historical scholarship on each country gave central attention to case-specific factors, including the personalities of political leaders and the outcomes actually experienced in a given country. Hence my book, like many works in comparative-historical analysis, faced a creative tension with other works of history. I argued for a greater comparability of explanatory factors than many historians found plausible given the diverse contexts of the four countries. Yet at the same time, I drew on these historians' very own work as basic sources of data.

I used a critical juncture framework and cross-national comparisons to generate insights that previous scholarship on individual countries did not offer. For instance, I found that liberals in Germany were well aware that established Lutheran churches encouraged support for monarchy; as a result, German liberals supported so-called free churches that incubated support for Enlightenment rationalism. I learned about these efforts in works of history, but previous assessments of German liberalism had downplayed their significance in favor of social structure (Dahrendorf 1967) and organized economic interests (Maier 1975). My book revealed that German liberals, at least before their fateful choice to emphasize economic liberalism over political liberty, knew that religion could be their ally only once it was differentiated from the state.

To take a different example, for some scholars of French politics, "republicans" were too popular to be liberal. Liberalism was supposed to be the distinctive attribute of the elite supporters of the Orléanist monarchy (Manent 1994). Yet scholars' excessive fealty to distinctions among liberals, republicans, and radicals obscured a key fact about France in the 1870s: a political movement advocating constitutional governance successfully attracted a mass following by activating concerns over the scope of a church's authority. My book's cross-case comparisons pointed to the liberal orientation of French republicans and even radicals.

With regard to modernization theory, which was commonplace in works by political scientists, I offered two responses to the argument that economic development accounted for liberalism. On the one hand, my case selection acknowledged that Europe's most economically developed country, Britain, provided the most hospitable setting for liberal reform, in contrast to the underdeveloped peripheral states in Southern and Eastern Europe. On the other hand, my book showed that levels of development in the middle-range could not account for differences between such key cases as France and Germany, much less between Belgium and Switzerland. Moreover, my analysis drew on revisionist historical scholarship on German history (Blackbourn and Eley 1984; Blackbourn and Evans 1991), not yet acknowledged in political science, that previous assessments of middle-class influence wrongly excluded Catholics by definitional fiat.

The final alternative explanation was the claim that Catholic political theology opposed liberalism, while Protestant political theology supported it. It simply did not bear sustained scrutiny to argue that national and regional religious elites conformed to uniform applications of doctrine. Protestant clergy supported direct democracy in Switzerland and opposed it in Germany, while Catholic clergy supported Belgian constitutionalism, but frequently sided with monarchists in France. Clerical elites, as well as members of churches, took stances on liberal reform mainly for local and institutional reasons—not based on their religious doctrines.

My book confirmed Luebbert's suggestion that religious cleavages provided crucial opportunities to Europe's most successful liberal movements. The book filled in key gaps in sustaining this argument across diverse cases, such as by explaining how the struggle against the Catholic Church in the 1870s could weaken liberal movements in Germany and Belgium but strengthen it in France and Switzerland. The German and Belgian fights against Catholicism alienated many middle-class voters who feared socialism but not the institutional power of the Church. At the same time, it bound together those who saw the Church as a threat to parliamentary sovereignty and the rural economy, as in France and Switzerland.

Like Luebbert, I argued that Lipset and Rokkan's framework could be used to explain not just party systems, but also the characteristics of the political regimes in which partisan competition took place. Political regimes are more short-lived than patterns of partisan support and opposition, which often survive interludes of authoritarianism. This analysis of liberal reform aimed squarely at a core goal of comparative politics, which is to understand the conditions for self-government.

CONCLUSION: THE STUDY OF RELIGION, THEN AND NOW

At the time I was doing research for my book in the 1990s, Lipset and Rokkan's 1967 work had already endured thirty years—an eternity in modern social science. Their work was a touchstone for almost all research on religion in comparative politics. They made religion relevant to this broad and exciting research agenda. As noted, the field had long been influenced by the often unacknowledged, yet widely shared, assumptions of secularization theory, with the idea that economic modernization would inevitably diminish the personal, social, and political importance of religion.

Potential successors to modernization theory—such as neo-Marxism and dependency theory—neither challenged long-standing assumptions about secularization nor provided useful ways to guide research on how religion shaped politics.

By contrast, Lipset and Rokkan contended that conflicts among different religions, and between religious and state authorities, created enduring legacies. Cleavages were conceived as boundaries between social groups that identified, on an ongoing basis, with one side or the other of old conflicts. As politics democratized and participation expanded in the nineteenth and early twentieth centuries, political parties formed with the objective of representing the interests of groups that were defined by these historically religious conflicts. Thus, long after modernization theory and its critique had become less salient for comparativists, Lipset and Rokkan endured as a valuable model for investigating the politics of religion.

Nearly two decades into the twenty-first century, scholars still face the challenge of explaining religion's role in politics. Islamist movements have thrived throughout Muslim-majority countries—in democratic or semi-democratic contexts such as Indonesia and Turkey, as well as repressive ones such as Egypt and Pakistan. In Europe, religious settlements that seemed firm and unchallenged have reemerged in highly contentious forms, as states and parties confront new religious heterogeneity.

In the original critical juncture formulation, the key role of religion was rooted in the past, given that the legacies of religious conflict endured for decades. My elaboration of the critical juncture analysis—while it similarly interpreted religion as embedded in historically derived institutions—emphasized that liberalizing movements could gain strength from religious leaders and movements that sought greater freedom and autonomy. This insight was crucial to understanding the divergent effects of Protestantism in Germany and Switzerland and Catholicism in France and Belgium. Religion has proven far more capable of renewal than most scholars of comparative politics previously allowed, making research on the political commitments of religious movements ever more pressing today.

Lipset and Rokkan's insights should be considered more relevant today than many scholars recognize. Yet several features of their work limit its appeal. Key terms were rooted in Western European events, such as the "Protestant Reformation" and the "French Revolution." In addition, Lipset and Rokkan favored a deterministic view of causality, and gave sparse attention to the details of how individual politicians attempted to assemble coalitions of supporters. My own research was similar to Lipset and Rokkan's in this regard. It focused on particular cases, in one region (Europe) and in one historical period (the nineteenth century). It also could be characterized as overly deterministic. Yet, for all of these limitations, Lipset and Rokkan's work helped my book show that religion was a key determinant of support for liberalism and of regime outcomes. Moreover, my research validated a general claim: that religion can have a decisive political impact when politicians threaten—or promise—to alter the scope of religious authority. And this lesson is certainly relevant today.

APPENDIX

Annotated Table 10.1 Institutions, Reform Dynamics, and Outcomes: Elite Phase and Mass Phase

Elite Phase				
	Germany (1815–1848)	*France (1815–1848)*	*Belgium (1815–1846)*	*Switzerland (1815–1831)*
1. Antecedent Conditions				
Catholic-Protestant Balance	Even split between Catholics and Protestants	Predominantly Catholic country; few Protestants	Predominantly Catholic country	Even split between Catholics and Protestants
National Political Regime	Catholic and Protestant Monarchies[1]	Catholic Monarchy[2]	Protestant Monarchy in the Netherlands[3]	Weak Oligarchies[4]
Church-State Relations	Incorporated Catholic and Protestant Churches[5]	Incorporated Catholic Church[6]	Non-incorporated Catholic Church[7]	Non-incorporated Catholic and Protestant Churches[8]
1. Cleavage: Liberalism vs. Clerical Elite[9]				
Liberal Policy toward Religious Authority	Attack Protestant and Catholic Churches[10]	Attack Catholic Church[11]	Promote Catholic Church[12]	Preserve Protestant and attack Catholic Churches[13]
1. Critical Juncture, Phase 1				
Clergy Supports or Opposes Liberals	Protestant and Catholic Clergy oppose[14]	Opposes[15]	Supports[16]	Protestant Clergy supports and Catholic Clergy oppose[17]
Fate of Liberal Reforms	Failed	Failed	Successful	Successful
1. Aftermath				
Resulting Church-State Relations	Established Protestant churches and more autonomous Catholic Church	Emperor allied with Catholic Church	Catholic Church more autonomous	Each canton has established Protestant or increasingly autonomous Catholic Church
Resulting National Political Regime	Monarch sovereign	Emperor sovereign[18]	Parliament sovereign	Parliament sovereign

(continued)

Annotated Table 10.1 Institutions, Reform Dynamics, and Outcomes: Elite Phase and Mass Phase (*continued*)

Mass Phase				
	Germany (1860–1914)	*France (1852–1940)*	*Belgium (1847–1914)*	*Switzerland (1833–1874)*
2. Antecedent Conditions				
Corresponding to Aftermath of Phase One	No effective constitutions in major states despite liberal reform attempts in 1840s	Monarch and constitutions fall to 1848 Revolution	Independence and constitution achieved 1830, Unionist governments in 1846	Liberal constitutions in most cantons in 1829–1831; Catholic secession suppressed in 1847; national constitution in 1848
2. Critical Juncture, Phase 2				
Liberal Policy toward Religious Authority	Protestant—preserve;[19] Catholic—attack[20]	Attack[21]	Attack[22]	Protestant—preserve;[23] Catholic—attack[24]
Response of Clergy	Protestant—toleration;[25] Catholic—opposition[26]	Opposition[27]	Opposition[28]	Protestant—support;[29] Catholic—opposition[30]
2. Aftermath				
Provincial Middle-Class and Peasant Response	Protestants—tolerate liberals;[31] Catholics—oppose liberals[32]	Support liberals[33]	Oppose liberals[34]	Protestants—support liberals;[35] Catholics—oppose liberals[36]
2. Legacy				
Years	1860–1914	1870–1940	1884–1914	1874–
Party Outcome	Co-opted defeat of liberals[37]	Contested victory of liberals	Conditional defeat of liberals[38]	Supremacy of liberals[39]
Regime Outcome	Authoritarian Regime[40]	Contested Constitutional Democracy[41]	Constitutional Democracy[42]	Constitutional Democracy[43]

1. Neo-absolutist Protestant monarchy in Prussia and Catholic monarchy in Austria in 1815. Prussia and Austria were member states of the German Confederation until the Austro-Prussian War of 1866.
2. Neo-absolutist Catholic monarchy.
3. Neo-absolutist, Protestant monarchy in the Netherlands, which was unified with Belgium until 1839.
4. Weak confederation of oligarchies, which were non-monarchical civilian governments that dominated the cantons.
5. Established Protestant churches that were under the direct control of the government. Allied Catholic Church that had a strong influence in state affairs.
6. The Catholic monarch was directly allied with the Catholic Church.

(*continued*)

Annotated Table 10.1 Institutions, Reform Dynamics, and Outcomes: Elite Phase and Mass Phase (*continued*)

7. The Catholic Church had no established administrative role in Belgian state functions after independence from the Netherlands in 1839.
8. Each canton had either an (A) established Protestant church that was tied to local institutions of power, or (B) allied Catholic church that had a strong influence in canton affairs.
9. Not all countries had cleavages. In Belgium, the liberals promoted the Catholic Church, and in return, the Church supported the liberals' goals. In Switzerland, the liberals experienced a cleavage with the Catholic Church, but not with the Protestant Church.
10. Liberals fostered Protestant dissent and supported separation from the Catholic Church.
11. Liberals attempted to curtail Catholic Church authority during the 1830 Revolution.
12. Liberals offered Catholic Church autonomy during the 1830 Revolution and afterwards once Belgium gained independence.
13. Liberals retained the Protestant Church's authority but curtailed the Catholic Church's authority.
14. The Protestant clergy accepted the conservative Pietists' direction and supported monarchs. The Catholic clergy allied with the monarchs. Both opposed the liberals.
15. The conservative Catholic clergy defeated the pro-liberal clergy of Lamennaisian movement, ally with monarch, aristocrats, and conservative deputies.
16. The Catholic clergy and the pro-church politicians supported Belgian independence and the liberal constitution.
17. The Protestant clergy aided the liberals, whereas the Catholic clergy seceded and sought alliance with the monarchs.
18. Authoritarian Empire of Louis Napoleon (1852–1870).
19. Liberals retain Protestant churches.
20. Liberals attempt to curtail Catholic Church authority.
21. Liberals criticize and curtail Church authority in education and other public institutions.
22. Liberals curtail Catholic Church authority through education law of 1879.
23. Liberals retain Protestant church authority.
24. Liberals attempt to curtail Catholic Church authority.
25. Prussia's Protestant clergy aids conservative parties.
26. Catholic clergy aids pro-Church party.
27. Clergy supports emperor, aristocrats, pretenders, Boulanger, and anti-Dreyfusards.
28. Clergy sponsors a boycott of state schools while promoting church schools and partisan organizing.
29. Clergy aids liberals.
30. Clergy aids pro-Church politicians.
31. Prussian Protestants support conservative parties.
32. Catholic Church accepts mobilization by Catholic party.
33. Peasants in southeast and provincial middle classes accept mobilization by Republicans and Radicals.
34. Catholics accept mobilization by pro-Church Catholic party.
35. Protestants support Radical party.
36. Catholics support Catholic party.
37. Weak liberal parties remain.
38. Weak Liberal Party forms in Parliament.
39. Strong liberal parties remain.
40. Liberals support national, economic, religious policies, but do not secure constitutional controls on executive power.
41. Republicans and Radicals dominate Third Republic (1870s–1940) despite repeated anti-systemic challenges.
42. Catholic party becomes majority party in 1884 and grants public educational authority to clergy, but otherwise retains liberal constitution.
43. Radicals dominate Protestant cantons and national government, but Catholic parties are strong in Catholic cantons.

BIBLIOGRAPHY

Blackbourn, David, and Geoff Eley. 1984. *The Peculiarities of German History: Bourgeois Society and Politics in Nineteenth Century Germany.* Oxford, UK: Oxford University Press.

Blackbourn, David, and Richard J. Evans (eds.). 1991. *The German Bourgeoisie: Essays on the Social History of the German Middle Class from the Late Eighteenth to the Early Twentieth Century.* London, UK: Routledge.

Collier, David, and Seymour Martin Lipset. 1991. "Preface." In Gregory M. Luebbert, *Liberalism, Fascism, or Social Democracy: Social Classes and the Political Origins of Regimes in Interwar Europe* (pp. v–vii). New York, NY: Oxford University Press.

Collier, Ruth Berins, and David Collier. 1991. *Shaping the Political Arena: Critical Junctures, the Labor Movement, and the Regime Dynamics in Latin America.* Princeton, NJ: Princeton University Press.

Dahrendorf, Ralph. 1967. *Society and Democracy in Germany.* New York, NY: Doubleday.

Gould, Andrew C. 1999. *Origins of Liberal Dominance: State, Church, and Party in Nineteenth-Century Europe.* Ann Arbor, MI: University of Michigan Press.

Lipset, Seymour M., and Stein Rokkan. 1967. "Cleavage Structures, Party Systems, and Voter Alignments: An Introduction." In Seymour M. Lipset and Stein Rokkan (eds.), *Party Systems and Voter Alignments: Cross–National Perspectives* (pp. 1–64). New York, NY: Free Press.

Luebbert, Gregory M. 1986. *Comparative Democracy: Policymaking and Governing Coalitions in Europe and Israel.* New York, NY: Columbia University Press.

———. 1991. *Liberalism, Fascism, or Social Democracy: Social Classes and the Political Origins of Regimes in Interwar Europe.* New York, NY: Oxford University Press.

Maier, Charles S. 1975. *Recasting Bourgeois Europe: Stabilization in France, Germany, and Italy in the Decade after World War I.* Princeton, NJ: Princeton University Press.

Manent, Pierre. 1994. *An Intellectual History of Liberalism.* Princeton, NJ: Princeton University Press.

11

Evaluating Critical Junctures in Latin America

Historical vs. Proximate Causes in the 1940s

Ruth Berins Collier

Critical juncture analyses make path-dependent arguments about the causal impact of historical causes. They are typically analytical constructs derived from qualitative small-N analysis and in a way that "fit" the cases under study. How then can one test such an argument against alternative explanations, particularly those regarding more proximate causes? The present analysis is intended to perform such a "test" by juxtaposing two explanatory perspectives, both of which account for class relations and regime outcomes in the Latin America in the 1940s: a critical juncture analysis and one focused on the impact of international events that could be expected to have a significant impact on the region.

The critical juncture perspective analyzed here focuses on internal trajectories in Latin America that starts with a period of major reform analyzed as labor incorporation, which occurred in the first part of the twentieth century (Collier and Collier 1991). This argument points to institutional changes that unfolded in a path-dependent sequence of two major periods of institutional change: (1) critical juncture, which occurred in distinct ways, each of which produced (2) a particular political reaction in its aftermath: Together, these produced a legacy, or institutional outcomes. Events in the 1940s are thereby understood in terms of the logic of unfolding sequential periods of critical juncture and aftermath.

The second explanatory perspective concerns the impact of international conjunctures, or a series of temporally proximate external "shocks," that occurred in the 1940s. Events surrounding World War II and the immediate postwar period reverberated in Latin American politics and have been seen as accounting for some of the changes in the region during that decade.

This chapter is a condensed and adapted version of Ruth Berins Collier (1993).

The decade of the 1940s thus provides a particularly good opportunity for juxta-posing historical and proximate explanatory frameworks, because international events generated strong pressures that were highly salient for the dynamics of regime and coalitional change in Latin America, at the same time that internal dynamics were playing out, rooted in the critical juncture of labor incorporation and its aftermath.

The analysis is based on a comparative analysis of four Latin American countries: Bra-zil, Chile, Mexico, and Venezuela.[1] They represent polar types of labor incorporation. In addition, they initiated labor incorporation in different decades, so that they "hit" the 1940s and the simultaneous influences of international events as, variously, they were experiencing one or both of the two causal steps laid out in the path-dependent analysis: the critical juncture itself and its aftermath. The analysis juxtaposes the way both per-spectives make predictions about a particular set of outcomes: class relations of conflict or collaboration, and regime opening, that is, democratization, or closing.

This chapter describes the predictions deriving from each explanatory perspective in turn and then analyzes the way in which they might be combined, teasing out a kind of "multivariate" analysis of historical and proximate causes on the basis of qualitative assessments. Case analysis indicates that the two arguments are comple-mentary: the historical causes can account for mistaken predictions of the proximate causes, yet the proximate causes had an impact and help explain variations of the timing and intensity of the steps set in motion by the critical juncture.

TWO EXPLANATORY PERSPECTIVES
ON CLASS RELATIONS AND REGIMES

The first explanatory perspective focuses on the causal importance of an historic trans-formation that occurred in Latin American countries in the first half of the twentieth century. With economic growth and the emergence of new classes (middle sectors and the working class) employed in new economic sectors, capital-labor relations became a major social cleavage as the new classes made new demands, often accompanied by social protest. The "resolution" was a multifaceted change involving a shift from a laissez-faire to an activist state; the legalization of unions and the development of state corporatism as a system of unionism and industrial relations for institutionalizing and regulating class conflict; and the introduction, sooner or later, of mass politics. This transition has been analytically treated as a critical juncture, dubbed "labor incorpora-tion" (Collier and Collier 1991). While much of this transition was common across cases, variation in type of labor incorporation established different political coalitions and had distinct legacies in terms of sequences of political change and regime dynam-ics, including patterns of labor protest and class conflict.

---

1. A few of the main sources used in the analysis of Brazil are Carone (1981), Chilcote (1974), Erickson (1977), Flynn (1978), French (1989), Harding (1973), Skidmore (1967), Rodrigues (1968), and Rodrigues (1966). On Chile, see Barría (1972), Drake (1978), Love-man (1988), Pike (1963), and Valenzuela (1976). On Mexico, see Fuentes Díaz (1959), Gar-rido (1984), Casanova (1982), and Medina (1978, 1979). On Venezuela, see Boeckh (1972), Ellner (1979), Fagan (1974), Martz (1966), and Powell (1971).

The second perspective is rooted in the proximate, international factors concerning relations among the major powers. The 1940s constituted a microcosm of the clash among the century's three great "isms," when the issues of war, international leadership, and global projection of power were central and when the content of and alignments surrounding these issues changed dramatically. Latin American developments in the 1940s are seen, in this account, in terms of the politics of the major powers as they waged World War II, then realigned themselves for the ensuing Cold War and established what became known as the postwar order.[2] Through a combination of diffusion, persuasion through the use of incentives or constraints, and imposition, international developments are seen as having had a dramatic impact within Latin America on domestic coalitions, patterns of labor mobilization and demobilization, and the transformation of national regimes.

Figure 11.1 presents the temporal intersection of these two perspectives. The critical juncture perspective focuses on a transition that unfolded at different chronological moments, according to domestic logics. The core of the argument is that different types of labor incorporation—state incorporation in Brazil and Chile, party incorporation in Mexico and Venezuela—led systematically to an aftermath as a period of reaction, and subsequently to a longer-term legacy that was different in cases of state and party incorporation. In contrast, the perspective that stresses proximate, international factors focuses on the impact of an exogenous shock that has synchronous effects on outcomes during the 1940s.

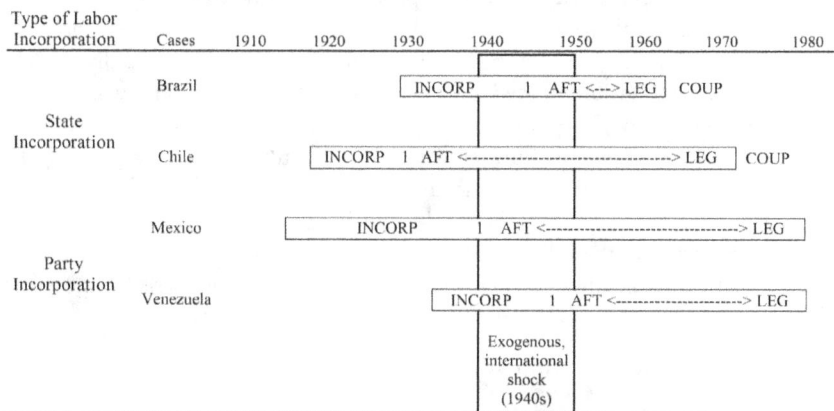

Figure 11.1 Historical Internal Trajectories and Proximate International Shocks: The Intersection of Two Analytic Perspectives. *Note:* INCORP = Labor incorporation; AFT = Aftermath; LEG = Legacy.

The present analysis will juxtapose the degree to which these two perspectives can account for the outcomes of class relations and regime opening or closing during the 1940s and discuss if they constitute rival or complementary explanations. The

---

2. This argument has been explored by Bethell and Roxborough (1988).

outcome of class relations will look more specifically at class coalitions and patterns of collaboration or conflict, particularly whether labor unions and left parties collaborated with other political and economic actors and the degree to which they engaged in strikes and other forms of protest and confrontation. The regime issues of democratic opening and closing include the advance or retreat of an unrestricted competitive electoral arena, the legalization or banning of Communist parties, the expansion or contraction of labor rights, government support of or hostility to union organization, and a change in policymaking toward greater or lesser responsiveness to and inclusion of lower-class interests.

HISTORICAL CAUSES AND INTERNAL TRAJECTORIES: LABOR INCORPORATION AS A CRITICAL JUNCTURE

According to the critical juncture perspective, the type of initial incorporation of labor marks a critical juncture that sets countries on a particular trajectory. A multifaceted transition in the nature of the state occurred, establishing the "new state," as it was literally called in Brazil. The new state featured the political incorporation of two new class actors: representatives of the middle sectors wrested political control and were incorporated into dominant ruling positions, and the working class was incorporated as a legitimate political actor represented by officially recognized unions.

The incorporation of labor was undertaken to address the "social question": how the state should respond to the rising level of worker protest against the dismal work conditions and exploitation of the laboring classes. The state response was a change from state repression to incorporation, in which the state established institutionalized channels for resolving and institutionalizing a new system of class bargaining. The form of labor incorporation varied, and the argument is that different types of labor incorporation produced distinct aftermaths and longer-term legacies. What follows provides an overview of the full thesis about labor incorporation as a critical juncture; subsequently the discussion will focus on the implications of this thesis for the 1940s.

Critical Juncture: Labor Incorporation

The project of labor incorporation was launched once the new middle sectors gained control of government. It contained many common features including the attempt to exert control over the working class and its protest. However, this was a time when crucial and divergent coalitional choices were made by the new middle-sector groups in power. Specifically, the choice was between a "populist" coalition with the lower classes and an "accommodationist" coalition with the traditional landed oligarchy. The key distinguishing trait between types of labor incorporation—state incorporation and party incorporation—concerned whether or not the labor movement would participate in multiclass political coalitions with the middle sectors and become affiliated to new, multiclass populist parties.

Everywhere, the common goal of the new governments was to control the working class. However, in some cases there was also a second goal: the mobilization of labor support. The incentive to mobilize labor support depended on middle-sector relations with the oligarchy and the difficulty the middle sectors had in establishing their own political dominance and consolidating a more activist, interventionist state. In each of the four cases considered here, political stalemate between the older and newer dominant classes prevented or stymied the middle-sector reform agenda.

Two solutions to the deadlock emerged and led to different incorporation projects. In Brazil and Chile, the military played a key role in breaking the political impasse and intervened to oversee the introduction of the new state. The authoritarian regimes that followed established a dominant accommodationist alliance between a relatively strong traditional oligarchy and the rising middle sectors, an alliance that excluded the popular sectors. In Mexico and Venezuela, the traditional oligarchies were relatively weak, and clientelist relations were eroding in their rural societies. Here an alternative strategy to overcome the deadlock was available in the form of middle-sector mobilization of labor and peasant support.

The political mobilization of popular-sector support is the crucial factor that distinguishes the two types of labor incorporation: state incorporation and party incorporation. In both, political leaders sought to use the resources of the state to respond to the rise in strikes and class conflict by controlling working-class unions and their activities. However, in cases of party incorporation, political leaders sought to control labor *and* win the political support of the working class—and, uniquely in Mexico and Venezuela, the peasantry as well. The political party became an important instrument of mobilization. State and party incorporation are thus distinguished by this difference in the balance between labor control and mobilization, as well as by the role of the political party in the incorporation project. The main characteristics of these two types of labor incorporation are outlined in Table 11.1 (see the rows on "Critical Juncture: Labor Incorporation").

In cases of state incorporation, organized labor was subjected to the greater constraints of a more control-oriented, corporative labor law, at the same time that it retained greater political autonomy since it was not affiliated to a governing, multiclass party. In the cases of party incorporation, sufficient benefits were offered to induce a major sector of the labor movement to cooperate with the state, and labor became politically incorporated in a multiclass alliance. Thus, the two types of incorporation produced quite different political alliances.

State Incorporation

State incorporation, in Brazil and Chile, was based on an accommodationist alliance consisting of an uneasy truce between the middle sectors and the oligarchy, focused on depoliticizing the working class and controlling the union movement. In Brazil, under Vargas, a highly elaborated labor law structured the system of trade union representation and provided explicit controls over unions with respect to strikes,

Table 11.1 State vs. Party Labor Incorporation: Contrasting Patterns of Change

Period	Type of Labor Incorporation	
	State Incorporation (Brazil and Chile)	Party Incorporation (Mexico and Venezuela)
	Pattern of Incorporation	
Critical Juncture: Labor Incorporation	Authoritarian regime	Electoral regime
	Accomodationist alliance	Populist alliance
	Depoliticization	Political mobilization
	Paternalistic benefits	Major concessions to labor
	No party or minimal party role	Populist party
	Dynamics at End of Incorporation	
Aftermath	No cross-class majority coalition; regime terminated in democratic opening	Cross-class majority coalition, but threatened by conservative reaction
	Failure to establish a centrist majority bloc	Transformation of majority coalition; reintegration of the right
	Stages: 1. Reactivation and repoliticization of labor 2. Creation of "populist" party and center-left coalition party 3. Failure and discrediting of "populism" and coalition politics: radicalization and polarization	Components: 1. Programmatic conservatization of populist party 2. Mechanism to limit political conflict 3. Exclusion of left from coalition 4. Retention of working class in coalition
Legacy		
Party System	Polarizing multiparty system	Integrative party system
Regime	Coup and long-term military rule	Hegemonic, stable regime

internal governance, and leadership selection. Independent and leftist unions were repressed and replaced with a state-sponsored and state-penetrated labor movement. With the emphasis on control, little or no political mobilization of the popular sectors occurred. Consequently, little effort was made to incorporate the popular sectors into a populist political party.

Chile, in the Ibáñez period, represents a variation on this theme. In this case a corporative labor law was not as fully elaborated, state-sponsored unions were never as widespread, and they did not survive the end of Ibáñez's presidency. Nevertheless, in broad outline the project was similar to that in Brazil, and quite different from that in other countries.

Party Incorporation

The pattern of party incorporation, in Mexico and Venezuela, was quite different. Because the politicization of the working class was an essential part of this strategy, incorporation involved integrating the labor movement politically and creating a broad multiclass coalition institutionalized in a political party, what would become the PRI (Institutional Revolutionary Party) in Mexico and AD (Democratic Action) in Venezuela. These parties institutionalized the populist alliance and channeled working-class political activity into support for the government. In addition to attracting the working-class vote, these parties established organizational links with labor unions, which became their core base of support.

The dynamics or logic of support mobilization meant that, compared to state incorporation, party incorporation involved more concessions and a stronger political position for the labor movement. Instead of being repressed, leftist and independent unions were tolerated or even became part of the governing coalition. A corporative labor code was promulgated, but it imposed fewer constraints on unions and union activity (Collier and Collier 1979: 974–76). The same kind of officialist, state-penetrated union movement was not established, even though mobilization induced the labor movement to support the government and, in receiving benefits from it, to become dependent on the state. In general, the adoption of a mobilization strategy entailed an increase in the political power of labor, since its very utility to the political leadership as a political resource depended on labor's strength.

In sum, the new state took two very different political forms, exhibiting different kinds of regimes and class relations. State incorporation occurred under a closed authoritarian regime and took on a decidedly anti-labor cast. By contrast, in cases of party incorporation, a cross-class coalition and patterns of class collaboration were forged and institutionalized in the political party in open, electoral regimes.

Aftermath

Each type of incorporation episode contained certain contradictions and internal dynamics that established a distinctive political agenda for the following period, the aftermath.

State Incorporation

The aftermath of state incorporation began when the authoritarian regimes that oversaw state incorporation became discredited and were terminated through democratic openings. The political reactivation and partisan affiliation of the labor movement thus became a key issue. The aftermath of party incorporation began with the conservative backlash against the progressive coalition in power and the reformist policies that had been necessary to entice labor to join a multiclass coalition. The key issue for the aftermath was to confront that opposition, which in most cases led to a military coup, and to create conditions that the right could accept.

The authoritarian regime that undertook state incorporation and its attempt to depoliticize labor meant that institutional channels for workers' political participation had not been established, partisan identities among workers had not been consolidated, and coalitions had not been formed between labor and other classes or political actors. Therefore, in relative terms, the working class was politically autonomous from governing parties (at the same time that it was highly constrained in the sphere of industrial relations).

With the democratic opening, working-class support was courted by both a revitalized left and middle-sector leaders, looking for electoral support. In Chile, Marmaduque Grove, Ibáñez's original co-conspirator of 1924, and Vargas in Brazil both sought to mobilize worker support through newly created "populist" parties, the Socialist Party and the PTB (Brazilian Labor Party), respectively. However, neither the middle sectors nor the working class could be united behind this effort, and both were divided in their partisan affiliations. The Communist Party continued to be strong among workers, and various parties of the center and right appealed to the middle sectors.

Because a mass, majoritarian cross-class party had not been forged during the incorporation period, the result was a highly fractionalized multiparty system, which required all parties to find coalition partners. However, even when reformist or center-right parties appealed to the working class in elections, once in power, they remained oriented toward an accommodationist *governing* coalition with conservative oligarchic groups, particularly given the continued influence of the oligarchy and its strength in parliament. As a result, an increasingly radicalized, non-collaborationist tendency emerged within the reformist parties and the union movements, a trend that was reinforced by a relatively powerful Communist Party that competed for working-class support. The result was growing polarization and the failure of what from a comparative perspective were belated, "populist" attempts and coalition politics more generally.

This trajectory unfolded in a series of steps: (1) conservative governments that protected established interests and confronted a newly activated labor movement led by the Communist party; (2) the creation of a would-be "populist" party, which never succeeded in governing on its own; and (3) a period of coalition politics led by the center or center-right, which was never willing to make sufficient concessions to workers. The result was increasing polarization and a failure of coalition politics. Prior to the elections of 1952 in Chile and 1960 in Brazil, the labor movement and those parties or tendencies that had attracted working-class support abandoned collaboration with the centrist parties. The aftermath periods ended with the collapse and discrediting of center-left coalition politics.

The outcome of state incorporation and its aftermath was thus a failure to create a strong, stable political center. Instead, polarization increased until a broad anti-left coalition supported a military coup in 1964 in Brazil and 1973 in Chile (see Aftermath, in Table 11.1).

Party Incorporation

Party incorporation unfolded quite differently. It produced a conservative reaction to the prolabor policies that had been necessary to forge class collaboration. In Venezuela a military coup deposed the incorporating AD government in 1948 and introduced a decade of repressive, counter-reformist rule, delaying the party-political adjustments until the return to civilian rule. In Mexico the same rightist opposition occurred, but the party managed to stay in power, electing in 1940 a more conservative successor to Cárdenas. In the aftermath, the main item on the agenda of the populist parties, immediately in Mexico and once civilian rule was restored in Venezuela, was to constitute a new centrist bloc that would not generate so much opposition; it would avoid polarization but continue to include labor while simultaneously bringing the bourgeoisie into the dominant political coalition (see Aftermath, in Table 11.1).

This effort had four components: a programmatic turn to the right; the establishment of conflict-limiting mechanisms to avoid polarization; the exclusion of the left; and the retention of the labor movement within the coalition. In Mexico, the mechanism employed was the strengthening of the one-party-dominant system through the restructuring of the PRI. In Venezuela, the mechanism was the functional equivalent: the party pact established between AD and COPEI (Social Christian Party), the main opposition party.

In sum, the aftermath of state incorporation saw political opening, an ultimately failed attempt to build a multiclass center, and increasing class conflict. By contrast, the aftermath of party incorporation was characterized by class collaboration and a more closed democratic regime, with the institutionalization of conflict-limiting mechanisms in the party system, specifically the one-party regime in Mexico and the party pact in Venezuela.

PROXIMATE CAUSES: THE INTERNATIONAL CONJUNCTURE OF THE 1940S

One might expect a number of external events in the 1940s to be reflected in Latin America along the two dimensions of class relations and regime that were also influenced by the historical argument. The relevant events are presented in Table 11.2.

Hypotheses

The expectation concerning the first dimension of anticipated change derives from the causal role of the Communist International's (Comintern) popular front policy, first adopted in the mid-1930s, abandoned in 1939 with the German-Soviet Pact, and renewed in a more accentuated form in 1941, with the German invasion of the Soviet Union. It advocated class collaboration, moderation of labor demands, and, at its most extreme, the dissolution of the Communist Party and no-strike pledges

Table 11.2 Key International Events in the 1940s

Year	Event
1939	German-Soviet Pact
1941	German invasion of Soviet Union
	Popular Front policy of Communist International (Comintern) restored
	Pearl Harbor
1943	Comintern disbanded
1944	D-Day
1945	V-E Day
	V-J Day
	UN Charter
1946	Iron Curtain speech
	Communist governments installed in Bulgaria and Romania
1947	Cominform founded
	Communist governments installed in Hungary and Poland
	Truman Doctrine
	Rio Treaty
	Taft-Hartley Act
1948	CIT (Confederación Inter-Americana de Trabajadores)/ORIT (Organización Regional Inter-Americana de Trabajadores)

for the duration of the war. One would expect to see reverberations of Comintern policy through its effect on Communist parties and their influence in labor movements throughout the region.

The spirit of multiclass solidarity and the advocacy of a reordered coalition to oppose fascism were not limited to the Communists. The advanced capitalist countries—particularly the United States—exerted a corresponding influence on capitalist classes and political organizations in Latin America. With the Japanese attack on Pearl Harbor and U.S. entry into the war, the U.S. strengthened ties to Latin America. Accordingly, noncommunist factions within the labor movement may have also been under pressure to pursue a more moderate course during the war effort, and Latin American governments and bourgeois parties may have been receptive to the Communist policy of collaboration.

Thus, given the paramount importance of the anti-fascist struggle, both the Comintern and the United States advocated broad coalitions and a cessation of labor protest and class struggle. One might expect that this strong advocacy by powerful and influential actors would be reflected in Latin America in the early 1940s.

The end of the war in 1945 brought an end to the rationale for political and class collaboration as Cold War rivalries replaced collaboration. To the extent that changes in European alliances were reflected within Latin American countries, one might further postulate the reemergence of the suspended reformist or radical political agendas, ideological polarization, and a renewal of class conflict and labor protest.

The second dimension has to do with democratization and political openings. The hypothesis is that the triumph of democracy over fascism in Europe led to a diffusion of democratic and reformist values throughout the world, including Latin America, a process which was reinforced by the UN charter.

In addition to diffusion, direct pressure was exerted by the United States for political liberalization and democratization. This effort began as early as 1943 and was sustained throughout 1944. By 1945 and the beginning of Cold War hostilities over the issue of democracy in eastern Europe, "it became even more imperative that the allies of the United States in Latin America were seen to be democratic" (Bethell and Roxborough 1988: 171–72). Starting in about 1944, one might predict a pattern of democratization and political opening in Latin America, and a period of reformist initiatives.

Though reformist democracy was sustained in the industrialized West, it might be hypothesized that it would not be sustained in Latin America because of other international developments. The turning point, presumably, occurred in the second half of 1946 or 1947 with the intensification of the Cold War, when the opposition to fascism was replaced with the opposition to communism. United States foreign policy subordinated the pro-democracy struggle to the fight against communism. Any ambiguities in dating the onset of this period seem to have been resolved by 1947. In that year, the Soviet Union established the Cominform to replace the dissolved Comintern and to reinstate Moscow's discipline over communist parties, and the United States announced the Truman Doctrine to contain communism and aid other governments in the anticommunist fight. Also, 1947 was the year of the Rio Treaty, a pact of hemispheric solidarity and mutual assistance, which in a sense brought the Cold War to the western hemisphere. In addition, it was the year in which the anticommunist battle was clearly brought into the labor arena, with the Taft-Hartley Act barring Communists from union leadership within the United States and the formation of a hemispheric, anticommunist labor confederation (ORIT, the Inter-American Regional Organization of Workers) under the auspices of the AFL (American Federation of Labor).

On this basis, we might hypothesize the existence of four partially overlapping periods.

H1. 1941–1945: A renewal of the popular front strategy, class cooperation, decline in strikes, and labor peace, following the greater level of class conflict and strikes predicted by the German-Soviet pact of 1939-41.

H2. 1944–1946: Democratization, political opening, and reformist initiatives.

H3. 1945–1948 (and beyond): Ideological polarization, greater class conflict, labor protest, and political opposition.

H4. From 1946/1947 on: Political closing, restored labor discipline, and a retreat from reformist politics.[3]

---

3. On these last two periods, see Bethell and Roxborough (1988).

The Empirical Evidence

To what extent, then, did these hypothesized phases actually occur in the four Latin American countries which concern us here?

H1: Multiclass Collaboration and Political Cooperation by the Left and Labor (1941–1945)

Multiclass collaboration occurred in all four countries. The Communist Party was influential among organized labor, which in all four cases pursued a policy of cooperation with the government and generally brought about a period of labor moderation in terms of industrial conflict. However, the cases exhibit some variation in the timing hypothesized by the international perspective.

The influence of the popular front policy was clearest in Chile. In the mid-1930s, the Communist, Socialist, and Radical Parties established a Popular Front that unified large segments of the working and middle classes. A Popular Front government under Radical leadership was elected in 1938, but contrary to internationally derived expectations, the coalition held together despite the German-Soviet Pact. The next Chilean elections were held in 1942, after the Comintern renewed the popular front policy in a more extreme form. Although the Chilean Popular Front per se was not renewed, the Communists and Socialists continued to collaborate with the Radical Party and even supported its more conservative presidential candidate and subsequently his government.

In Brazil, from 1941–1942, the Brazilian Communist Party (PCB) was suppressed and its leaders, including Luis Carlos Prestes, were imprisoned. However, policy changed in 1943, and, more consistent with international expectations, by 1945 the Vargas forces founded the Brazilian Labor Party (PTB) to mobilize labor support and struck a deal with the Communists, including an amnesty for Prestes and the legalization of the PCB. From its side, the PCB joined the PTB in supporting Vargas's presidential candidacy.

Like Chile, Mexico was also a particularly clear case of popular front collaboration, but, contrary to the international hypothesis, it also continued through the 1939–1941 period of the German-Soviet Pact. In the second half of the 1930s the Mexican Communist Party (PCM) turned from an anticollaborationist stance to one that supported the Cárdenas government (1934–1940). Under Cárdenas the Communists promoted the reorganization of the governing party (PNR, National Revolutionary Party, the predecessor of the PRI) in a way that would embody a popular front coalition. This collaboration continued in the 1940 election, a period of the German-Soviet Pact, when the PCM supported Avila Camacho, for whom it declared it would play the role of a "shock brigade" (North and Raby 1977: 51). After the German invasion of the Soviet Union the CTM (Confederation of Mexican Workers), the major national labor confederation, entered into pacts with business to promote labor peace, and in 1942 it renounced the use of the strike for the duration of the war.

Venezuela largely conforms to expectations. During the popular front period of the 1930s the Communists collaborated with the reformist opposition in an antigovernment front, which broke up with the Hitler-Stalin pact. With the renewed popular front policy in 1941, the PCV (Venezuelan Communist Party) began to collaborate with the government in a "marriage of convenience" (Betancourt 1979: 72). The following year it supported congressional candidates loyal to President Medina Angarita. Until 1944, the Communist Party was the dominant influence in the organized labor movement and was able to bring most of the organized working class into the coalition. The deviation from expectations comes from the reformist, AD (Democratic Action), which rejected collaboration with the government and remained in the opposition. AD was the dominant influence among the peasantry and the most important force in the working class after 1944.

H2: Political Opening and Reformist Initiatives (1944–1946)

Evidence for the hypothesized outcome during this second period is more mixed. Brazil and Venezuela both installed new democratic regimes and undertook reforms during this brief period. On the other hand, Mexico and to some extent Chile do not conform to the prediction.

In Brazil, a combination of international diffusion and direct pressure from the United States contributed to the downfall of the authoritarian Vargas government and the subsequent elections that inaugurated a new republic. In addition to the more open, competitive regime, a number of labor reforms were initiated during this transition. These began in 1943 when Vargas, already anticipating the impending regime change, sought to formulate a new political strategy by building a constituency among the working class. Concessions to labor, which continued until approximately 1946, included greater toleration of strikes, wage increases, the cancellation of the ideological oath (which had been a vehicle for barring political activists from union leadership), and the introduction of union elections, as well as the legalization of the Brazilian Communist Party (PCB) and political amnesty mentioned earlier.

Similarly, in 1945 Venezuela witnessed the advent of a more democratic government led by AD. However, the party's democratic agenda did not derive from the international conjuncture but had developed during the preceding decade in opposition. Further, a reformist opening had begun earlier under President Medina. Nevertheless, in addition to a regime change, 1945 marked a deepening of the commitment to reform, with respect to both the regime and labor policy under the AD government, including a new, much more favorable labor law, labor participation in government, increased wages, and the spread of collective bargaining.

Chile and Mexico fit the hypothesized pattern less well. While democratic rule had already prevailed in Chile for more than a decade, the 1944–1946 period was generally anti-reformist and exclusionary with respect to labor. The interim Duhalde government (1945–1946) was hostile to labor and repressed strikes and demonstrations led by the Communists. More in line with the international hypothesis, a change occurred briefly in 1946, when a new government under Gabriel González Videla became more closely aligned to labor and the Communist Party than previous governments and was not only elected with the support of the Communists, but also included them in the government.

Mexico's nonconformity to the expected pattern was considerably more marked, as the country moved toward regime closing, in a consistently anti-reformist, exclusionary direction. This period saw the tightening of authoritarian one-party dominance and greater control of labor. Real wages fell steeply, especially in the unionized industrial sectors, despite a record of economic growth. Unionization stagnated, and a change in labor law made it easier to dismiss workers and restricted the right to strike. The government also used a new law establishing a "crime of social dissolution" to persecute dissident union leaders. Changes in the party structure decreased the relative weight and influence of labor, culminating in the reorganization of the PNR into the PRI in January 1946, which further subordinated labor and concentrated power in central party organs. Also, in the beginning of 1946, a change in electoral law raised the requirements for the registration of political parties, insulating the dominant PRI from opposition challenges.

H3: New Combative Posture of Labor and the Left (Immediate Postwar Years)

On the whole, events in all four countries corresponded substantially to the prediction that heightened class conflict and political opposition would occur in the immediate postwar period as a result of the end of the Comintern's popular front policy and the onset of Cold War antagonisms.

This pattern was particularly evident in Brazil and Mexico. In Brazil, the period corresponded to the opening years of the Dutra government, when the re-politicization of the working class, which had begun in the last years of the Vargas presidency, intensified in both the party system and the sphere of industrial relations. In the newly opened political arena, parties with a base in the working class burst onto the scene with surprising electoral success. In the presidential and congressional elections of December 1945, the Communists won 10 percent of the national vote and pluralities in major industrial cities and a number of state capitals. The PTB fared comparably well, winning another 10 percent of the national vote, so that the two parties based in the union movement together received approximately 20 percent of the vote. This electoral mobilization was accompanied by a more militant political posture on the part of not only the Communists, but also the PTB.

Mexico also experienced heightened political and class conflict during this period. With the end of the war, the CTM split over the issue of continued collaboration with the government. Dissidents under Communist influence saw collaboration as a wartime expedient and were ready to resume a more militant, aggressive posture. Major splits occurred, resulting in two dissident confederations that favored a more combative and independent position and, at their height, probably constituted about 40 percent of the organized labor movement. The splits were mirrored in the political sphere, when Lombardo founded the PPS (Popular Socialist Party) as an opposition party based in the working class. Though the split of Lombardo from both the CTM and PRI is consistent with the hypothesis of greater working-class combativeness and leftist opposition in the immediate postwar period, the dominant labor confederation, the CTM, remained collaborationist.

In Chile and Venezuela, political collaboration continued along with a rise in class conflict. In Chile, the Communist Party did resume a more combative posture, and labor conflict rose significantly under its leadership. Further, the party's share of the vote in the 1947 municipal elections increased. However, despite this greater combativeness and opposition, the Communist Party supported the Radical Party candidate in the presidential elections of 1946 and participated in the new Radical government, despite having rejected participation in Radical-led governments under the popular front policy.

In Venezuela the hypothesized pattern was evident, but with a particular twist: the greater combativeness of labor took place with the blessing of the government. During the Trienio of 1945–1948, AD was in power, and AD-affiliated unions strongly supported and collaborated with the government. The Communist Party also commanded influence in the labor movement, and it too supported the progressive acts of the government. However, a dissident Communist group, the Machamiques, did not go along with this policy.

H4: Collapse of Reformist Initiative and Political Closing (from 1946–1947 on)

The hypothesis that the onset of the Cold War would reverberate in Latin America in the latter part of the 1940s is well corroborated by the evidence. In all four countries, the Communist Party was banned, and strong anti-labor measures were adopted. In addition, the reformist tide was reversed, and in some cases democratic regimes were overthrown.

In Chile, the democratic regime remained intact. Nevertheless, the government undertook a number of exclusionary, anti-reformist initiatives in response to both increased labor activity and Cold War antagonisms. In 1947 a new law drastically restricted rural unionization and outlawed strikes in the rural sector. President González Videla, who had come to power the year before, representing the left wing of the Radical Party, suddenly saw Communist subversion behind every strike and embarked on a vigorous anticommunist campaign. The Communists were ousted from the cabinet, and in 1948 a new Law for the Permanent Defense of Democracy proscribed the party.

Similarly, in Brazil, the electoral regime was maintained, but starting in mid-1946 the government reasserted control over the unions and oversaw a period of even greater retrenchment with respect to labor reforms. The government intervened in union elections, placing many unions under the direct control of the labor ministry and hardening its position on strikes. The law was changed to restrict strikes substantially, and the government frequently repressed them by force. At the same time the government moved directly against the Communists, reinstating the ideological oath to prevent them from assuming union leadership and ultimately banning Communist labor centrals, and, in 1947, the Communist Party.

Mexico also experienced an anti-reformist period of political closing in the late 1940s. In 1946, the government limited political opposition and strengthened one-party dominance. The party sphere was further restricted in 1949, when the Communist Party lost its registration. Once voluntary wartime collaboration had been superseded, the government employed coercive control to keep the unions in line and prevent the emergence of a more combative organized labor movement. From 1947 to 1949, the government responded to the new independence of labor with a series of interventions in union elections, adopting a pattern of action that came to be known as *charrismo*. In addition, Lombardo's new labor central, the UGOCM (General Union of Workers and Peasants of Mexico), was denied official recognition. By the end of the decade, the union movement was subordinated and leftists had been purged.

Venezuela represents the most dramatic case of political closing in the second half of the 1940s. In 1948 the coup by Pérez Jiménez and his co-conspirators overthrew the electoral regime and brought about an abrupt end to the period of reform under AD. The military regime, in power from 1948 to 1958, ushered in a period of severe political and labor repression. The initial years under Delgado Chalbaud were milder than the dictatorship subsequently established by Pérez Jiménez in 1950. Nevertheless, the initial junta moved quickly against AD and thereby against labor.

Summing Up

Table 11.3 presents a "score card" for the hypotheses derived from the impact of the international forces on domestic politics in Latin America. At this broad correlational level, the general hypothesis about the causal importance of the international conjuncture seems to hold up quite well, and events in Latin America, with exceptions, demonstrate substantial fit with the explanation focusing on external causes.

COMBINING PERSPECTIVES

Both analytic perspectives make predictions about class collaboration or conflict, and about regime opening or closing. Obviously, the social world is complex, and one should not expect monocausal explanations. Rather, the expectation would be that both sets of causes operated to some extent. How then might the two arguments be juxtaposed or combined?

Two points might be borne in mind. First, historical causes are arguments about particular sequences that follow from the logic embedded in the structural or institutional innovations founded in the critical juncture. Because the historical argument is inferred as a generalization from the cases, the existence of the sequences

Table 11.3 Proximate, International Influences

Hypotheses	Cases			
	Brazil	**Chile**	**Mexico**	**Venezuela**
About Class Relations				
H1. Class/Political Collaboration (1941–1945)	Yes (starting 1943/1945)	Partial (collaboration 1939–1941)	Partial (collaboration also 1939–1941)	Yes (but not AD)
H3. Labor and Left Combative (1945–)	Yes	Partial (political collaboration)	Partial (not the dominant labor confederation)	Partial (political collaboration)
About Regimes				
H2. Democratic Opening and Reformist Initiatives (1944–1946)	Yes	No (only briefly in 1946)	No	Yes
H4. Collapse of Reformist Initiatives and Political Closing (1946–1947)	Yes	Yes	Yes	Yes

"predicted" is not at issue. Rather, the question is how to account for the outcomes regarding key components of those sequences that may also be predicted from the proximate causes of the international events. Second, the historical argument predicts outcomes as trajectories or paths in a particular sequence; the proximate causes predict an outcome at a particular time. An historical argument predicts sequences but cannot account for the timing of these sequences or for many of the variations within the overall model in the legacy that ensues. By contrast, as we have seen, the proximate causes are quite rapidly changing causes and operate not only through international diffusion but also through immediate policy and pressure from particularly the United States and the Soviet Union. We have further seen that to a substantial degree, developments in Latin America correspond to these rapid changes.

Figure 11.2 presents the predictions of the two perspectives regarding greater class collaboration or conflict, and regime opening or closing. For the historical argument, the outcomes correspond to the two periods of the critical juncture of labor incorporation and the aftermath (see Figure 11.1). However, as discussed above, in historical arguments these are multifaceted phases that are seen as themselves "unfolding," so that although changes in class relations and regime are predicted *during* these phases, the figure is not meant to represent a more precise timing. Further, because the regimes during the incorporation periods in Brazil and Chile were authoritarian, the overt class conflict and the dynamics of political collaboration are sharply constrained and not relevant.

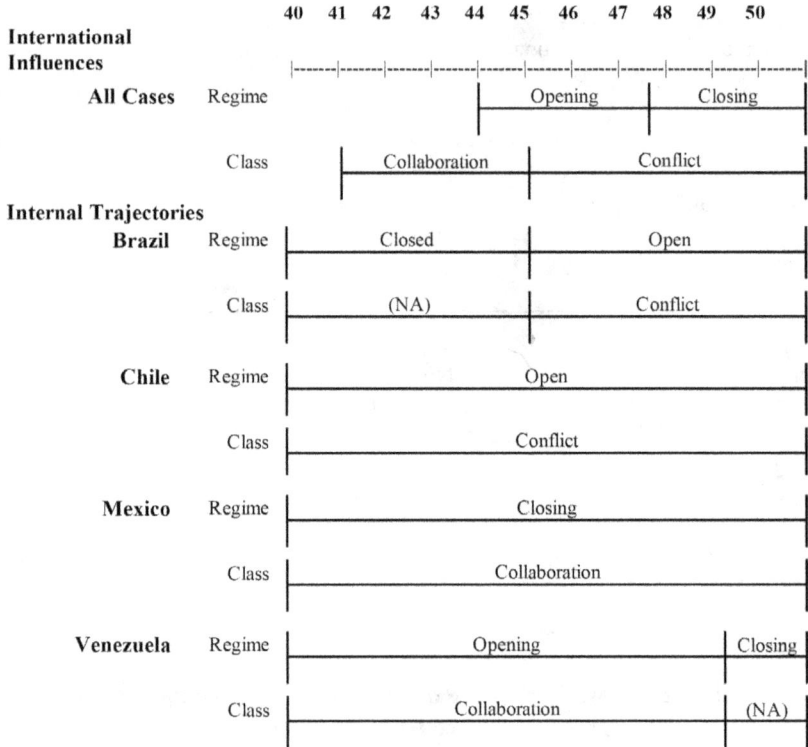

Figure 11.2 Timeline of Predictions: International Influences vs. Internal Trajectories. *Note:* NA: not applicable.

We might ask three questions, concerning whether the two perspectives present rival, contradictory, or complementary explanations. First, as rivals, which explanation prevails when the two perspectives make similar predictions? Are the proximate, international factors confounders that invalidate the historical argument? Second, as contradictory explanations, which prevails when they make different predictions? Does the historical argument account for the "mistakes" in the outcomes predicted by the proximate causes? Third, to what extent do the proximate causes help account for variations or specific details in the unfolding trajectories in the critical juncture argument that the historical causes themselves cannot account for?

Rival Explanations

The first question considers the two strands of analysis as rival explanations that account for the same outcome. It asks if the international events of the 1940s are really the causes of the outcomes attributed to internal dynamics from the critical juncture perspective.

As we have seen, the anticipated sequences of outcomes did occur according to paths outlined in the historical argument. The contrasts in timing between the two cases of state incorporation and between the two cases of party incorporation indicate that the proximate international events were not the causes of these sequences in regime and class collaboration (see Table 11.4). The historical steps occurred in different decades—and not only the incorporation and aftermath periods as a whole, but also the phases or subperiods of each. The fact that they are not synchronous supports the sequential argument about the unfolding of an internal political logic that can be traced back to the different types of labor incorporation, and it means that they are not the outcome of the proximate causes embedded in the international events argument.

Table 11.4 Timing of Key Developments

Developments	Timing of Developments, by Type of Labor Incorporation	
	State Incorporation	
	Brazil	Chile
Height of incorporation	1937–1943	1927–1931
Transition to aftermath	1943–1945	1931
Labor reactivation	1946–1950	1932–1938
"Populism" and coalition governments	1951–1960	1938–1948
Failure of coalitions; polarization	1961	1948
	Party Incorporation	
	Mexico	Venezuela
Height of incorporation (resolution of stalemate)	1934–1940	1945–1948
Transition to aftermath	1940	1948
Conservatization of populist party	1940–	1957/1958–
Conflict-limitation measures	1946	1957/58
Exclusion of left	1947–1948	1958–1962
Retention of labor support	1940–	1958–

Contradictory Predictions

The second question asks which explanation prevails when the two perspectives give contradictory predictions. Proximate causes had an influence in Latin America, and, as Table 11.3 shows, outcomes substantially corresponded to predictions based on external events. However, sometimes the expected outcomes deviated from those expected from the proximate causes. The deviations from the predictions of the events in the international conjuncture can often be explained in light of internal paths in the historical argument: when the two logics thus contradicted one another and pointed toward different outcomes, the historical causes took precedence.

Among the four countries considered, Brazil appeared to follow most closely the periodization suggested by international forces. Yet even in Brazil the deviations can be explained by internally driven logic. An example is the political opening that occurred at a time when the Cold War might have suggested a political closing. In 1950 a reformist opening began that could only be understood as an integral part of the aftermath of state incorporation—as part of the attempt to establish acceptable channels for the political participation of labor.

Venezuela, too, generally conforms to the periods predicted by the international perspective, with one main variation. In line with the hypothesized effects, labor protest increased dramatically in the immediate postwar years. However, the heightened protest was less a result of the end of popular front collaboration on the part of the Communist-influenced labor movement than a reflection of the new activism of AD unions, undertaken with the support of the Trienio government. This outcome must be understood in terms of the pattern of party incorporation and the mobilization of labor support that characterized it.

In Mexico the points of lack of conformity to international influences can be explained by the historical argument. The ongoing collaborationist position of the dominant labor movement even when the popular front period had ended must be understood as a result of the cross-class coalition cemented during party incorporation and the subsequent attempts to retain labor support. Similarly, instead of political opening and reform in 1944–1946, as expected from the international conjuncture, Mexico was moving in the opposite direction, exerting control over the labor movement and consolidating one-party dominance. These years corresponded to the aftermath of party incorporation and hence constituted a period of conservative reaction to the prior reformist period. In this case, the logics of the two perspectives are contradictory—the international conjuncture points to a period of reformism while the internal trajectory points to a period of anti-reformism—and of the two, the latter was more important in shaping politics in Mexico.

In Chile international influences became most visible in the relationship between the policy of the Comintern and the formation of the Chilean Popular Front in the mid-1930s, and in the subsequent coalitions among the Communist, Socialist, and Radical Parties in the 1940s. However, contrary to what would have been predicted, the Chilean Popular Front survived the German-Soviet Pact, and similar coalitions were reestablished for some time beyond the end of World War II, when international factors pointed to increased class conflict and protest. A wave of labor actions did occur after 1945, yet in some ways the shift to the politics of confrontation was limited, despite strong ties between a relatively strong, class-conscious labor movement and Marxist parties that might have suggested particular receptivity to the influence of international communism. In 1946, when Communist parties elsewhere in the region were returning to a confrontational posture, the Chilean party not only once again joined the governing coalition, but for the first time formally joined and participated in the government, something it had declined to do during the years of the Comintern's popular front policy, despite its collaboration. The various deviations from the expected patterns of the 1940s reflected the playing out of the attempts at coalition politics typical of the aftermath of state incorporation. In prior years, both the Communist and Socialist Parties had withdrawn and reentered coalitions with the Radicals; the Radical Party for its part had alternatively approached and distanced itself from the left and labor. It might be suggested, then, that although this type of center-left coalitional politics would ultimately be discredited, the final throes of this coalitional experimentation were still approaching by the end of the war, and the pattern continued, despite the international conjuncture of renewed political confrontation. However, the sudden government hostility to the Communist Party and its banning may reflect the onset of Cold War conflict.

Complementary Explanations

The third question considers the impact of the proximate factors as complementary to the perspective focusing on historical causes. It can be argued that while the sequence of steps unfolded according to the historical argument, the proximate causes of the 1940s may have affected the *timing, intensity,* and some *variation* of this unfolding. Let us consider each of the four cases in turn.

Brazil experienced a transition from an authoritarian incorporation period to a democratic aftermath period at a time that corresponds to the international triumph of democracies in World War II. Yet, there is evidence that some years before the Allied victory, Vargas had begun to anticipate a democratic opening, predating that predicted by international events. Nevertheless, direct or indirect influence may have been felt for democratic opening as the region, and especially Brazil (which joined the war effort) aligned with the U.S. after Pearl Harbor, and the actual regime change and its timing may have been influenced by the international climate favoring democratic opening.

International factors may also account for the particular intensity with which Brazil experienced certain phases of the aftermath period. The end of the popular front policy of international communism might help explain why Brazilian labor experienced an unprecedented and almost explosive reactivation during the immediate aftermath period (1945–1947). Similarly, it may also help explain the intensity of the conservative orientation in the early aftermath period as the Dutra government in 1947 cracked down on labor, reintroduced a number of *Estado Novo* (1937–1945) controls and restored the ban on the newly legalized Communist Party. This conservative reaction was stronger than that in Chile in the 1930s, which corresponds to the analytically comparable period in the historical argument.

The international factors may also have affected the distinct features of Chile's aftermath period, in particular the timing, long duration, and specific character of the coalition governments. In Chile, the coalitions of the aftermath period included the Communists and took the form of the Chilean Popular Front, a direct reflection of Comintern policy and the general international context of anti-fascist collaboration. Though the Chilean Popular Front itself was not sustained, subsequent broad, anti-fascist coalitions were continually reconstituted until the period of relative political closing with the onset of the Cold War. On the other hand, as mentioned, the abrupt change by President Videla, from alignment with to hostility to and banning of the Communist Party corresponds, to the heightening of the Cold War. In Brazil, by contrast, the entire coalitional period, during which the Communists had influence, corresponded to the Cold War, though the party itself was banned in 1947.

According to the internal trajectories thesis, the attempt during the aftermath of state incorporation to create a viable, multiclass political center ultimately failed. In Chile, however, coalition politics were discredited from the point of view of the left and the labor movement even more decisively than in Brazil. In Chile, in contrast to Brazil, the two dynamics coincided and reinforced each other: the onset of the Cold War and the region-wide move to proscribe the Communist Party coincided with the end of the aftermath period, when coalition politics were breaking down anyway under their own weight. This more decisive defeat in Chile may in turn have contributed to the stronger process of radicalization and polarization that subsequently occurred in Chile compared to Brazil.

In Mexico also, international factors may help explain some of the distinctive aspects of the aftermath period, in particular, why the conservative reaction to party incorporation was relatively mild, that is, why unlike in most countries the incorporating party was not ousted in a military coup but managed to stay in power. These distinctive features may have reflected the timing of the initial aftermath period during the Comintern's second and more extreme popular front policy favoring multiclass collaboration. During this period, as we have seen, most sectors were more open to collaboration in broad anti-fascist fronts, and the potential threat that labor seemed to pose was diminished by the policy of self-restraint in support of the war effort. Under these circumstances, labor proved more willing to acquiesce in the politically conservative trend and the unfavorable labor policies typical of the aftermath of party incorporation. Hence in Mexico international factors promoted political conservatism within the framework of institutional continuity, whereas in countries like Venezuela the aftermath period tended to coincide with the onset of the Cold War and the international period of political closing in the late 1940s.

Venezuela saw a nearly perfect coincidence of timing between the periods that derive from the two perspectives. Yet it is difficult to discern the way in which the international conjuncture may have colored the internal trajectory. The high point of party incorporation began in 1945, when a democratic, reformist regime was ushered in, coinciding with the complementary pressures deriving from international factors. Yet the timing itself seems more closely related to the particular situation within Venezuela, specifically, the breakdown of negotiations over the candidates for the upcoming elections, an episode which provoked the military coup that carried AD to power and initiated the incorporation period. However, AD's mobilization of the popular sectors and its adoption of democratic and reformist policies began earlier, in the mid-1930s during the popular front period, which may have exerted an influence.

The coup that terminated the Venezuelan incorporation period also coincided with international forces that were consistent with an anti-reformist hard line. However, accounts of Venezuelan politics do not refer to the impact of international forces, and the repression under the military government was much more clearly directed against AD than against the Communists; indeed, one of the Communist factions continued to collaborate with the government for a number of years. This evidence points in the direction of the stronger impact of internal factors (the conservative reaction to party incorporation) than of international factors (the anticommunism of the Cold War).

In sum, international factors may sometimes help to round out the picture and explain some of the variation in timing and intensity within patterns of change for which the internal argument does not systematically account.

CONCLUSION

This analysis has provided an attempt to juxtapose a critical juncture analysis to an alternate explanation. In a qualitative critical juncture analysis, a "problem" of causal inference may arise to the extent the argument is constructed to fit a small-N empirical base. In this case, there are no "mistakes." Confirming or strengthening the argument often takes the form of examining additional cases that did not form the original empirical base, often including cases that are "more dissimilar" (e.g., from a different region) to explore scope conditions. Another approach is that pursued here: juxtaposing different explanations for the outcomes the critical juncture argument claims to account for.

In juxtaposing explanations, one starts with degree of fit. The comparison is asymmetrical if restricted to the "original" cases with no "mistakes" on the critical juncture argument. We are left then with evaluating predictions on outcomes on which the critical juncture argument is correct but the alternate argument is wrong, and those on which both theories correctly predict the outcomes.

If there is substantial fit also on the alternate argument and the two make the same prediction, it would be difficult to argue that these are rival rather than complementary arguments, given the difficulty of disentangling the explanations and of preferring one and eliminating the other. The idea that they are instead complementary causes in a multivariate world could be further pursued by case study to determine if the alternate cause adds nuance of variation in the outcome. It should be noted that critical juncture analyses generally cannot account for timing, which, as here, the alternate case may help explain. One could also examine any cases of "mistakes" in the alternate argument to see if it makes sense to say that the critical juncture argument "blocks" its causal influence. On this basis one might argue that the critical juncture is the "stronger" explanation or takes precedence, but one remains with the conclusion that the two are complementary causes.

That is the conclusion of the present analysis in which I have looked jointly at two explanatory perspectives as they relate to labor politics and regime change in Latin America during the 1940s. Both perspectives contribute to our understanding; hence they should be viewed as complementary explanations. There is no question that the international events of the 1940s left a strong imprint on the political landscape of Latin America. Yet these events did not determine or deflect the unfolding of internal trajectories that were set in motion by the initial incorporation of labor. Rather, the internal trajectories perspectives can explain deviations from outcomes expected by the international conjunctures. However, the analysis does suggest that the international factors may help explain the distinctive coloration of the internal patterns by filling in some of the details and accounting in part for the timing and intensity of the steps as they unfolded in each country.

BIBLIOGRAPHY

Barría, Jorge. 1972. *El movimiento obrero en Chile*. Santiago: Ediciones de la Universidad Técnica de! Estado.

Betancourt, Rómulo. 1979. *Venezuela: Oil and Politics*. Boston, MA: Houghton-Mifflin.

Bethell, Leslie, and Ian Roxborough. 1988. "Latin America between the Second World War and the Cold War: Some Reflections on the 1945-8 Conjuncture." *Journal of Latin American Studies* 20(1): 167–89.

Boeckh, Andreas. 1972. "Organized Labor and Government under Conditions of Economic Scarcity: The Case of Venezuela." PhD dissertation, University of Florida.

Carone, Edgard. 1981. *Movimento operário no Brasil, 1945–1964*. São Paulo: DIFEL.

Casanova, Pablo González. 1982. *El estado y los partidos políticos en México*. Mexico City: Ediciones Era.

Chilcote, Ronald. 1974. *The Brazilian Communist Party*. New York, NY: Oxford University Press.

Collier, Ruth Berins. 1993. "Combining Alternative Perspectives: Internal Trajectories versus External Influences as Explanations of Latin American Politics in the 1940s." *Comparative Politics* 26(1): 1–29.

Collier, Ruth Berins, and David Collier. 1979. "Inducements versus Constraints: Disaggregating 'Corporatism.'" *American Political Science Review* 73(4): 967–86.

———. 1991. *Shaping the Political Arena: Critical Junctures, the Labor Movement, and the Regime Dynamics in Latin America*. Princeton, NJ: Princeton University Press.

Drake, Paul. 1978. *Socialism and Populism in Chile, 1932–1952*. Urbana, IL: University of Illinois Press.

Ellner, Steve. 1979. "Acción Democrática-Partido Comunista de Venezuela: Rivalry on the Venezuelan Left and in Organized Labor, 1936–1948." PhD dissertation, University of New Mexico.

Erickson, Kenneth. 1977. *The Brazilian Corporative State and Working-Class Politics*. Berkeley, CA: University of California Press.

Fagan, Stuart. 1974. "The Venezuelan Labor Movement: A Study in Political Unionism." PhD dissertation, University of California, Berkeley.

Flynn, Peter. 1978. *Brazil: A Political Analysis*. Boulder, CO: Westview.

French, John. 1989. "Industrial Workers and the Birth of the Populist Republic in Brazil, 1945–1946." *Latin American Perspectives* 16(3): 5–27.

Fuentes Díaz, Vicente. 1959. "Desarrollo y evolución del movimiento obrero a partir de 1929." *Revista de Ciencias Políticas y Sociales* 5(17): 325–48.

Garrido, Luis Javier. 1984. *El partido de la revolución institucionalizada*. Mexico City: Siglo XXI.

Harding, Timothy. 1973. "The Political History of Organized Labor in Brazil." PhD dissertation, Stanford University.

Loveman, Brian. 1988. *Chile: The Legacy of Hispanic Capitalism*. New York, NY: Oxford University Press.

Martz, John. 1966. *Acción Democrática: Evolution of a Modern Political Party in Venezuela*. Princeton, NJ: Princeton University Press.

Medina, Luis. 1978. *Del cardenismo al avilacamachismo: Historia de la revolución mexicana: 1940–1952* (Vol. 18). Mexico City: Colegio de México.

———. 1979. *Civilismo y modernización del autoritarismo: Historia de la revolución mexicana: 1940–1952* (Vol. 20). Mexico City: Colegio de México.

North, Liisa, and David Raby. 1977. "The Dynamic of Revolution and Counterrevolution: Mexico under Cárdenas, 1934–1940." *Latin American Research Unit Studies* 2(1).

Pike, Frederick. 1963. *Chile and the United States, 1800–1962*. Notre Dame, IN: University of Notre Dame Press.

Powell, John. 1971. *Political Mobilization of the Venezuelan Peasant*. Cambridge, MA: Harvard University Press.

Rodrigues, José Albertina. 1968. *Sindicato e desenvolvimento no Brasil*. São Paulo: Difusão Européia do Livro.

Rodrigues, Leôncio Martins. 1966. *Conflito industrial e sindicalismo no Brasil*. São Paulo: Difusão Européia do Livro.

Skidmore, Thomas. 1967. *Politics in Brazil,1930–1964*. New York, NY: Oxford University Press.

Valenzuela, J. Samuel. 1976. "The Chilean Labor Movement: The Institutionalization of Conflict." In Arturo Valenzuela and J. Samuel Valenzuela (eds.), *Chile: Politics and Society* (pp. 135–171). New Brunswick, NJ: Transaction Books.

12

Regime Transitions as Critical Junctures

Cultural Legacies of Democratization in Spain and Portugal

Robert M. Fishman

Transitions to democracy appear to offer a prime example of just the sort of critical juncture that has animated a large and important literature on historical causation and its implications for social science. After all, by definition, democratization involves highly consequential institutional change, thereby meeting the first major condition for the applicability of this framework in empirical analysis. Moreover, the overall universe of regime transitions includes enormous variation both in the historical circumstances surrounding macro-political transformation and the trajectories followed.[1] The process of democratization, that is to say the pathways followed, varies substantially across cases.[2] If the variation between transitions actually conditions important elements of political life in new democracies—and above all, if such an effect is found to endure long after democracy achieves consolidation—this phenomenon would stand as an important example of how critical junctures shape political life for long periods of time after they take place. Nonetheless, decades after the beginning of the ultimately global Third Wave of democratization in April 1974, there is still no scholarly consensus on whether pathways to democracy do indeed generate *distinctive* legacies.

This chapter owes a great deal to the scholarly leadership and generosity of David Collier and Gerardo L. Munck, for which I am grateful. Their comments and suggestions on several drafts have been invaluable. I am also grateful to those who offered feedback on an earlier draft presented at the 2019 APSA meetings and to a long list of colleagues and political actors whose support for my research has been essential.

---

1. Linz and Stepan (1978); O'Donnell et al. (1986); Huntington (1991); Mainwaing and Pérez-Liñán (2013); Weyland (2014).
2. Stepan (1986); Munck and Leff (1997); Collier (1999); Fishman (2019).

Early efforts to build a theoretically oriented literature on this point failed to produce intellectual closure or consensus.[3] Some eminent scholars have suggested that democratization instead offers a useful example of the causal process of *equifinality* in which *different pathways*, in this instance different types of transition, lead to the *same result* (Karl and Schmitter 1991). From that perspective, to the extent that democracies differ from one another, that variation is due not to the shape taken by democratization scenarios but instead to reasons that are unrelated to the road followed to this regime form: democratic transitions, in that view, lead simply to liberal representative democracies and afterwards other points of differentiation among free and representative systems may tend to produce variation in outcomes for reasons unconnected to the pathway followed to democracy. In this chapter, and in the long program of research that has culminated in my book, *Democratic Practice* (Fishman 2019), I return to this classic question, offering a new answer along with an analysis of the reasons why the literature has thus far failed to generate scientific closure. I show how transitions to free and representative political systems *can* put in place fundamentally divergent *cultural understandings* of democracy and, as a result, dissimilar forms of political practice that strongly condition the boundaries of inclusion in democratic polities. Indeed, I argue that precisely the sort of variation in democratic politics that can be induced by contrasts between national pathways to political freedom is, in turn, able to powerfully condition the capacity of democracies to attain the normative goal of full political equality among citizens.

I take up the search for enduring consequences of distinctive types of regime transition through an in-depth multi-method study of two democratization pathways and the outcomes they brought about in long-similar neighboring countries, Portugal and Spain. The adjacent countries of the Iberian Peninsula followed nearly polar opposite pathways of democratization in the 1970s—thus providing us with an extraordinary opportunity to examine how divergent forms of democratization may lead otherwise similar countries to develop in new and distinctive ways. In what follows I argue that the Iberian Peninsula's polar-opposite democratization scenarios of the 1970s put in place fundamentally different cultural understandings of democracy and as a result sharply dissimilar forms of "democratic practice." Portugal's post-revolutionary democratic practice has been inclusionary, opening up possibilities for the incorporation of protesters, socioeconomic marginals, and other outsiders into policy-making dynamics and processes of agenda setting. In contrast, Spain's institutionally segmented democratic practice has tended to exclude such groups from crucial political processes that take place during the long intervals between elections and the campaigns leading to them. I treat democratic practice as a crucial *intervening variable* that mediates between historical causes rooted in the critical juncture of transition pathways and *ultimate outcomes* such as distributional

---

3. Stepan (1986); Hagopian (1990); Karl (1990); Valenzuela (1992); Hunter (1997); Munck and Leff (1997).

and policy arrangements as well as cultural dispositions shaped by the two countries' educational systems. By identifying cultural legacies of the two transitions as a crucial intervening variable, I am able to account for enduring—indeed growing—differences between the neighboring cases that might largely elude observation were we to limit our analysis to the study of formal political institutions as such.[4]

Tarrow (2010) has argued that paired comparisons that involve the drawing of contrasts between two carefully chosen cases are especially useful for conceptual and theoretical development, and this chapter follows that approach, in pursuit of precisely those ends. There is ample reason to see paired comparisons as particularly valuable in exploratory studies within an area such as the thematic focus of this work, namely an in-depth examination of regime transitions, focused on the theoretical goal of establishing whether such processes of change constitute a critical juncture capable of inducing *new* patterns of enduring divergence between political systems. Nonetheless, clearly a pairing of two cases cannot fully capture all of the variation to be found in a large universe of cases such as the set of all countries that moved from authoritarianism to democracy during the Third Wave of democratization that began in Portugal in 1974. Thus, in what follows I also offer some methodological reflections, in which I take up the question of the generalizability of the argument presented here.

Before we turn to an examination of the enduring consequences of the Iberian Peninsula divergence in pathways to democracy, it is useful to first delineate basic features of the two transition scenarios.

THE CRITICAL JUNCTURE: TWO PATHWAYS TO DEMOCRACY

The Portuguese Case

Portugal's comprehensive process of change began on April 25, 1974, with a military coup—led by army captains, circumventing the institutional lines of command—that did much more than simply end a decades-old dictatorship. The Carnation Revolution launched by Portugal's "Captains of April" partially inverted existing social and political hierarchies while also initiating a comprehensive process of cultural renewal (Fishman 2019: Ch. 2). New forms of expression and practice emerged quickly in the revolutionary environment. In terms of actual political practice, the revolutionary transition scenario initiated by the captains' coup significantly widened the range of actors that would be participants and the breadth of their forms of political conduct, forging new ground rules for the operation of the political system. Activists demonstrating in the streets played a key supporting role

---

4. For a more elaborate version of the arguments presented here, along with full documentation and references, see Fishman (2019).

beginning on April 25, when they mingled with the insurgent army units engaged in confrontations with the defenders of the *Estado Novo* prior to the surrender of dictator Marcelo Caetano. As in all democratic transitions, the Portuguese pathway to political freedom involved institutional work elaborating the formal basis for the selection of power holders through competitive and free elections. However, much of the political, social, and cultural work of the country's transformation took place in venues, and involved forms of activity, that *challenged* institutional rules and boundaries. Enterprise and land occupations, large strikes waves, bottom-up purges, activist assemblies within the military and other institutions, widespread demonstrations, and new forms of cultural expression all played a role in shaping the country's pathway of change. This unusual transition scenario sent a clear and lasting *cultural* message to political actors within the country about the meaning of democracy and the definition of acceptable forms of political conflict.

Crucial elements of Portugal's transition scenario included the overturning of social and political hierarchies within a wide range of institutions and a thorough remaking of cultural structures and practices.[5] Those active in the revolution launched "bottom-up" purges of an extralegal nature within government ministries, schools, news media outlets, and private firms. Students and other erstwhile social subordinates participated in ousting those who had held hierarchically organized power during the long years of authoritarian rule. The very nature of the captains' coup of April 1974 that ended the long dictatorship of the *Estado Novo* challenged existing hierarchies, as it was led by middle-ranking officers whose actions in initiating and leading the democratizing coup involved disobedience to their hierarchical superiors within the military. The April 25 coup and its chief underlying cause—the country's then ongoing colonial wars in Africa (Bermeo 2007; Maxwell 1995)—quickly induced a classic "state crisis" within Portugal, a fundamental component of the conditions that Theda Skocpol's (1979) landmark contribution formulated as the basis for social revolution. The country's pathway to democracy involved much more than a simple "rupture" or clear break with the past.

Most social revolutions have failed to produce stable democratic institutions, but in Portugal the period of social revolution served as a conditioning factor for another crucial process that was historically simultaneous and politically interwoven with the revolution. Elections were called for April 25, 1975, precisely one year after the coup, and the assembly chosen by voters on that day was charged with writing a new democratic constitution. Social revolution and the forging of new representative democratic institutions occurred alongside one another in a process that left its mark both on social guarantees embedded in the new constitution and on a crucial cultural

---

5. In his pioneering theoretical formulation on revolutionary "events" and structural change, Sewell (1996) argues that cultural schema that shape practices and understandings in typically quite stable ways constitute "structures" that are subject to rapid and deep transformation in the context of extraordinary "events" such as revolutions.

factor: enduring understandings of democracy that have served to orient actors in the new system. Those enduring understandings and the forms of practice linked to them constitute the crucial intermediating variable that I emphasize, namely the cultural legacies of the Portuguese pathway to democracy.

The historical processes at play put in place a set of actors and of forms of joint action that was more broadly drawn and more inclusionary than in more conventional transition scenarios. In a telling remark that captures not only much of the substance of politics during the period, but also the mentalities that were forged by Portugal's Carnation Revolution, a prominent government minister during the revolutionary period, Mário Murteira, declared during an interview with a Portuguese journalist many years after the revolution that "several times when I was engaged in important conversations with [Prime Minister] Vasco Gonçalves in his office, we would go to the window to see those who were passing by in demonstrations. In the end and to a great extent we were more spectators in a grand popular movement than actors" (Silva et al. 2006: 105). Crucially, during the revolutionary period that served as the social backdrop for the drawing up of a new democratic constitution, those actively participating in street protests included previous social subordinates of all sorts: workers and peasants, the residents of low-income urban neighborhoods and others involved in overturning hierarchies or pushing forward demands for radical social change. Portugal's revolutionary path to democracy sent the message to political actors that the very meaning of democracy encapsulated within it a prominent place for the robust expression of political preferences by socially marginal and economically underprivileged actors.

The Spanish Case

In contrast, Spain's transition was essentially limited to redesigning institutional rules and procedures directly linked to the definition of the political regime itself. Following the death of longtime dictator Francisco Franco in November 1975, the political regime was fully transformed into a representative democracy in a process of change that was led by the successors to authoritarian power within the regime—under pressure from longtime opponents of authoritarian repression. Demonstrations, strikes, and other forms of mass political action helped to construct the broad assemblage of external pressures that sought to push regime elites toward democratization (Maravall 1978, 1982; Fishman 1990a; Radcliff 2011), but such popular pressures were effectively contained not only by the police, but also by a variety of fears and concerns that influenced the opposition. Workers and others within the democratic opposition internalized the view that democratization required, among other things, an element of restraint on their part (Fishman 1990a). The demands of labor in transition-era Spain developed in very different ways from revolutionary Portugal despite the remarkable fact that in the first moments of the two transitions the early demands of workers were virtually identical in the two neighboring cases (Durán Muñoz 2000).

Political elites in Spain explicitly elaborated the view that popular pressures outside official institutions constituted a dangerous threat to the essence of institutional life in the democratizing system. In April 1977 when the reformist Prime Minister Adolfo Suárez, a veteran politician from the Franco regime, legalized the Communist Party just over two months in advance of the first free elections of the post-Franco period, his public speech to the country explaining that move emphasized this point: "Sincerely, is it not preferable to count in the ballot boxes what otherwise we would have to measure on the poor basis of unrest in the streets?" (quoted by Linz and Stepan 1996: 97). In this formulation, the articulation of citizen preferences in the streets was framed as "unrest" and was posed as a more or less dangerous alternative to the political life centered on the counting of votes at election time. Furthermore, the effort of Suárez and other transition-era political leaders to erect a wall of meaning sharply separating the political life of representative institutions from the expression of citizen preferences in the streets was not limited to symbolic acts and discourse. The new democratic constitution written by the representatives freely elected in June 1977 explicitly prohibited in its Article 77 the presentation of petitions to the country's parliament by means of demonstrations. The Spanish pathway to democracy, like that of Portugal, was to hold large consequences for the way the new political system handled the relationship between representative institutions and expressions of citizen preferences outside their bounds, but those consequences were fundamentally dissimilar.

THE AFTERMATH: THE TRANSITION'S CODAS

In my book-length analysis of this theme in *Democratic Practice*, I find it necessary to introduce another important element into the analysis, one that strongly reaffirms the emphasis of Collier and Munck (2017) on the causal relevance of the *aftermath period* immediately following a critical juncture. I argue that in both cases after the end of the transitions as they are conventionally understood, crucial transition-era settlements were readjusted in processes that I refer to as the transitions' "codas." The readjustments of the two "codas" have proved highly important for the nature of the enduring legacies in both cases.

The crucial "coda" in the Spanish case was the 1982 reconfiguration of the party system five years after the first democratic elections in 1977. The most important change in the party system was the eclipse of the center-right governing party, the Unión de Centro Democrático (UCD), and its spatial replacement by a much more right-wing party, Alianza Popular, subsequently renamed the Partido Popular (PP). I argue that the change in the nature of the major right-of-center party conditioned the legacies of the transition. The UCD had insisted (along with other actors) on maintaining a sharp demarcation between representative institutions and expressions of citizen sentiments in the streets, but at the same time the UCD practiced inclusion *within* representative institutions, promoting dialogue among those elected to representative bodies. The UCD was an absolutely central actor in the transition. This center-right party expressed—and sought to promote—a relatively inclusionary reading of the transition's "ground rules," providing ample opportunities for discussion and accommodation among those present *within* formal representative institutions. This approach to handling the challenges of transition generated major internal tensions within the center-right, ultimately leading to the decline and collapse of the UCD—and the party's spatial replacement by a more right-wing party. The PP, in contrast, has frequently promoted exclusion even *within representative institutions* with unfortunate systemic consequences that are also at times manifested within elements of the Socialist Party. The transformation of the country's party system in 1982 accentuated the exclusionary tendencies in Spain's democratic practice.

In the Portuguese case, the transition's coda as I conceptualize it was the decision of the principal center-right and center-left parties to amend the Constitution in 1989, permitting the denationalization of the extensive revolution-era nationalizations of 1975. This large readjustment ended the system's formal commitment to the construction of socialism and transposed the social legacies of the revolution from the terrain of ownership in the economy to the welfare state arena. Beginning in 1990, just after the Portuguese transition's coda was put in place, the country's welfare state began to grow quickly with large consequences that are still increasing in magnitude. This transposition of the revolution's social commitments to the terrain of welfare state construction put in place a still ongoing process of development in the welfare state, a process that has provided new policy-making tools for exercising inclusion.

LEGACIES AND THEIR REPRODUCTION: DEMOCRATIC PRACTICE AND OTHER CULTURAL PHENOMENA

The new differences that emerged between these neighboring cases during the transitions were not limited to the formal institutions put in place at the time but crucially also encompassed the forging of highly dissimilar cultural assumptions and practices related to the very nature of democracy. The direct legacies bequeathed by the critical juncture of polar-opposite democratization scenarios are primarily cultural ones that condition how actors understand democracy and how they pursue their objectives in interaction with others. I conceive of the primary cultural legacy of transition pathways, that of nationally predominant forms of *democratic practice* (Fishman 2011: 236; 2019: 6–7), as an intervening variable that shows the marks of recent patterns of regime change and that in turn conditions important episodes of political contention and the myriad ultimate outcomes that such political interactions leave in their wake. Those ultimate outcomes may be thought of as more indirect legacies of the critical juncture.

Direct Legacies

During the Iberian Peninsula transitions political actors developed conceptions of democracy that delineated in one manner or another the connection between representative political institutions and the expression of citizen sentiments outside their bounds. Whereas Portuguese actors developed an understanding of democracy that sees these two political arenas as complementary to one another, Spanish political actors came to see the arenas of expression inside—and outside—formal representative institutions as being so thoroughly separate that they chose to erect both symbolic and tangibly physical barriers separating these two worlds of democratic politics. I formulate this difference as a matter of "democratic practice," constituted by a fundamental cross-case contrast in taken-for-granted assumptions and understandings about the nature of democracy that is, in turn, matched by related forms of conduct. As suggested above, democratic practice can be seen as an intervening variable that stands between the critical juncture of polar-opposite pathways to democracy and a long series of differences between the cases in policy and societal outcomes. Whereas Portuguese democratic practice has been inclusionary, making a space in democracy's decisive "conversations" for socioeconomically marginal actors, cultural "others," and demonstrators of various sorts, Spanish democratic practice has typically been segmented and often exclusionary, establishing clear and relatively impervious boundaries between power-holding institutions and political expression outside their bounds. And whereas Portugal's post-revolutionary democratic practice is relatively antihierarchical and inclusionary, Spain's post-transition democratic practice has contributed to the perpetuation of political hierarchies and exclusions.

A decisive element of nationally predominant forms of democratic practice concerns the form taken by interactions between protest movements and elected political power-holders, a point on which the two Iberian Peninsula cases are quite different. However, the patterns of democratic practice that have predominated in Portugal and Spain in the four-plus decades following their transitions to democracy also involve major elements of cross-case contrast on other matters. These matters include the handling of participatory institutional initiatives such as those involved in participatory budgeting, and forms of practice found in secondary institutions—such as the school system and the news media—that hold special importance for the functioning of democracy. I argue that the forms of practice found in these components of democratic life hold large consequences for the degree of inclusion characterizing a democratic polity and, as a result, for the degree to which democracies genuinely attain the normative goal of full political equality between citizens—especially in the long intervals of time between elections. It is precisely in the long interludes of democratic life between election campaigns that the crucial challenges of policy making and agenda setting are handled. The way in which free and representative systems treat those matters in turn holds large consequences for the attainment of political equality. Yet, if the impact of democratic practice on those two crucial processes holds special significance, we are still left with the question about what type of phenomenon democratic practice is. In the discussion that follows I offer a brief explanation of what it means to suggest that democratic practice is primarily a cultural phenomenon and of how this phenomenon should be differentiated from institutional matters.

The culturally rooted understandings of democracy and related forms of political conduct that I refer to as democratic practice are in certain crucial respects quite different from the strictly institutional parameters of democratic life. The cultural phenomena emphasized here are wider in their possible breadth of relevance than specifically institutional guidelines for political action but significantly less binding. After all, even informal institutions tend to rely on enforcement mechanisms that punish those who fail to adhere to institutional expectations (Helmke and Levitsky 2006). Cultural inputs on political conduct involve the internalization of cognitive frameworks but lack the clear rules and the enforcement mechanisms of institutions (Fishman 2019: Ch. 1). A distinctive scholarly payoff of this study's comparative design is the way in which it serves to delineate the considerable relevance of strictly cultural dynamics and legacies.

The contrast between Portugal and Spain in the actual conduct of political actors is evident in several ways: in interactions between representative institutions and demonstrators; in actions that take place within the bounds of representative institutions, particularly with regard to the acceptance of all present as legitimate participants; in the introduction and consolidation—or evisceration—of innovative participatory institutions; in some indicators captured by survey research such as the subjective political efficacy of ordinary citizens; and in ongoing practice within two key secondary institutions—the educational system and the news media (Fishman 2019: Ch. 3), both of which hold great significance for democracy's vitality. In all of these settings the difference in actual forms of conduct between the two Iberian Peninsula cases is often substantially greater than one would expect on the basis of formal institutional rules or design. Portuguese power-holders view demonstrators in the streets as relevant political actors and often provide them with a hearing on matters ranging from housing policy to labor market regulation and anti-crisis economic measures. That hearing may take the form of direct face-to-face conversation or the more indirect form of interchange through public statements directed toward the citizenry at large. In contrast, Spanish institutional power-holders tend to shield themselves from the voices of protest articulated in the streets. Whether demonstrations dealt with the housing needs of immigrants and the poor, the concern of truckers over rising fuel costs, or the broadly posed opposition of large movements to austerity policies, officeholders in the neighboring democracies have handled protest in remarkably different ways. Similar types of cross-national difference between the cases are to be found in the official handling of participatory initiatives such as participatory budgeting and on other matters mentioned above.

In making the key analytical distinction between culture and institutions, broadly construed, I draw on key works by cultural sociologists including those such as Patterson (2014) and Lizardo (2017), who incorporate within their understanding of culture its "nondeclarative" components. I argue that, unlike the clear (if at times only tacit) rules of institutions, the cultural orientations shaping predominant forms of democratic practice are rather general. Lacking the enforcement sanctions of clearly established rules, their effect may be somewhat less constant—with some exceptions to general patterns as a result of this absence and as a reflection of the repertoire-like range of cultural "matter" shaping conduct—but the scope of their relevance is broader and more all-encompassing than in the case of explicit rules with their clear boundaries of applicability. Indeed, I argue that the general assumptions about democratic politics that I emphasize shape countless forms of conduct, including those manifested in circumstances that actors may have never expected to encounter.

Mechanisms of Reproduction

This claim raises the question of how cultural legacies can be sustained over time, a question that concerns what are called the *mechanisms of reproduction* in the critical juncture framework (Collier and Collier 1991: 31, 35–37) and that deserves mention here, even though it cannot be taken up in depth due to space limitations. Most students of culture assume that cultural legacies need to be reproduced if they are to survive, and thus it is important to ask how and why the cultural perspectives on democracy that were put in place by the Iberian Peninsula transitions have managed to persist. This question raises the large theoretical theme of change and persistence in cultures, an issue on which the cases of Portugal and Spain offer much evidence and numerous lessons (Fishman 2019: Ch. 7). Both conscious efforts and structural factors (Sewell 1996) help to determine whether cultural patterns will be reproduced or changed.

In the case of Portugal, the enormous collective efforts devoted to annual commemorations of the Carnation Revolution—both inside formal institutions, for example in the annual special session of the parliament on remembering "April," and in civil society-led endeavors in the streets—serve to underscore how cultural work *matters*. In the case of Spain, the efforts of some actors to transform the culture of politics have run up against the structural impediments imposed by the inescapable fact that democratic practice is inherently relational and in that sense cannot be easily altered by any one actor that attempts to achieve change unilaterally. Portugal's extensive program of annually commemorating the revolution, telling its story and reflecting on its meaning for the contemporary country, has regularly involved the country's political elite, as well as a wide range of civil society organizations and activists in often creative efforts to remember the revolution, reflect on its enduring relevance, and celebrate its legacies. Once a year political and social actors exchange perspectives on the memory of "April" and the importance of its lessons. In the parliament, in other institutional venues, and in the streets this important work is carried out every year. Shared opportunities for broad interchange on the memories and meaning of the democracy's revolutionary origins stand as a robust mechanism, sustaining the cultural legacies of April 25, 1974, which are delineated in this chapter. In the Spanish case, numerous efforts to bring about cultural change in the country's understanding and practice of democracy have encountered a formidable obstacle—limiting their success and in that way reproducing existing legacies of the country's pathway to democracy. Democratic practice necessarily involves interchange and interaction between political forces and for that reason, the desire of one actor to change the pattern of broader relationships in the polity can fully succeed only if it is matched by a willingness of others to share in the desired transformation.

To a large degree Portuguese democratic practice has been broadly accepted by the country's sociopolitical actors—a state of affairs that the active program of commemorations has successfully sought to reproduce. In Spain, efforts to alter the often-exclusionary practices of the country's democracy have led to cultural conflict over the nature of acceptable democratic behavior but not to system-wide transformation. Movements such as the 15-M mobilizations of 2011, and parties such as Podemos, have attempted to reconceptualize the polity's bounds of inclusion, but their impact on existing actors has been weaker than they would like. The intrinsic difficulty of fundamentally changing democratic practice—given its relational or interactive nature—has left Spain with a contested yet still segmented model of democratic practice rather than comprehensive and consensual change. Both the conscious cultural work of many Portuguese actors engaged in commemoration and the structural impediments on changing the relational—or interactive—nature of democratic practice in Spain have tended to reproduce the cultural legacies put in place by the 1970s Iberian Peninsula transitions.

ADDITIONAL LEGACIES: POLITICAL INCLUSION AND SOCIAL POLICY

The Iberian divide in democratic practice leads in turn to considerable cross-case variation in two key processes that carry large implications for the attainment of robust forms of political equality, namely agenda setting and policy making. These two processes, which take place largely during the long expanses of time between the institutionally defining feature of Schumpeterian democracy—free and competitive elections with universal adult suffrage (for citizens)—are of essential importance in the pursuit of a complete Dahlian understanding of political equality (Dahl 1998; 2006), and I argue that in both cases Portuguese democracy attains the ideal of robust political equality more fully than Spanish democracy as a result of the cultural assumptions and related forms of practice put in place by the transitions to democracy of the 1970s. The list of ultimate outcomes that is conditioned by this contrast is a long one, including the difference in predominant forms of macroeconomic policy making and in institutional behavior in the finance sector that has generated persistently higher unemployment in Spain; cross-case contrasts in housing policies; and, in the conduct of elected officeholders on related matters, the practice and effects of the two educational systems and the conduct of the news media in the two cases—to mention only some relevant areas in which the effects of the Iberian divide in political inclusion can be found (Fishman 2019: Ch. 4). Many of these outcomes were already in place when I initially formulated this set of theoretical claims, and partly for that reason I have also examined more recent evidence that has emerged after the initial development of this perspective. Specifically, after the theory had been developed, I added as test cases the political handling of the Great Recession and its aftermath in the two country cases (Fishman 2019: Ch. 5), and the handling in Spain of Catalan demands for a referendum on independence (Fishman 2019: Ch. 6).

The politics of economic crisis offers strong confirmation of the utility of the democratic practice approach and in fact suggests that differences between the cases may actually grow over time as the impact of their divergent forms of democratic practice influences the handling of an ever-growing list of challenges. Multiple data sources show that Portugal has actually diminished distributional inequality during the crisis whereas Spanish policies during the same period have led to a substantial in-crease in inequality (Perez and Matsaganis 2018; Fishman 2019: Chs. 5 and 8). This point of differentiation is especially significant for social science analysis because in conventional ideological terms the identity of the governments in power in the two countries was the same for all but a few months in between 2005 and 2015 when this crucial distributional divergence emerged. Socialists were in power in both countries when the economic crisis first developed and in both cases those governments were replaced by right-wing governments elected in 2011. Although Portuguese policy makers have had to deal with the "head winds" created by lingering effects of a major negative "critical antecedent," namely the historically late introduction of universal access to education in the mid-1950s, two decades before the ultimate demise of the *Estado Novo*, the country now has the lowest poverty rate in southern Europe and better distributional outcomes than Spain on several crucial indicators. This critical antecedent in the historical expansion of access to education initially limited the impact of tendencies put in place by the critical juncture of polar-opposite transi-tion pathways, but with time this countervailing factor waned in significance. If we turn to crucial measures of what democratic governments actually did, in Portugal both taxation and welfare state spending are higher than in Spain as a proportion of GDP, and educational spending—a key marker of progressive social commitments by governments—is proportionally significantly higher (Fishman 2019: Ch. 4).

Crucially, the analysis presented in *Democratic Practice* shows that the single most important mechanism responsible for the major distributional divergence between the cases during the economic crisis years is directly related to the cultural legacies left in place by the two countries' polar-opposite pathways to democracy. In the fall of 2012 right-wing governments in both countries were confronted by major waves of social protest in opposition to their austerity policies. In Portugal government officeholders reversed course on a major piece of legislation with large distributional consequences, directly citing the importance of paying heed to the voices of pro-testers. The government's proposal, which would have directly reallocated several percentage points of the country's GDP from employees to employers (thereby accentuating inequality), was withdrawn after the center-right president and prime minister explicitly chose to modify the policy in response to large-scale protests. In other cases, austerity policies of the Portuguese government were blocked by decisions of the country's Constitutional Court but the single most important instance of an austerity initiative being abandoned was driven by the government's sensitivity to protest. In Spain at roughly the same time in the fall of 2012 the right-wing government responded to anti-austerity protests by criminalizing certain forms of protest and by reaffirming its policy perspectives (Fishman 2019: Ch. 5). The cross-national contrast in democratic practice generated divergent distributional tendencies.

METHODOLOGICAL CONSIDERATIONS

Antecedent Conditions

One possible objection to the usefulness of this comparative design—and the conclusions that it generates—concerns the genuine breadth of the two cases' similarity before the critical juncture, when they followed nearly polar-opposite pathways to democracy in the 1970s, that is, in terms of the *antecedent conditions* of the posited critical juncture (Collier and Munck 2017: 3–5).

Antecedent Conditions as Rival Hypotheses

To assess whether antecedent conditions might be a source of rival hypotheses, several points of contrast in the antecedent conditions of the Iberian Peninsula neighbors deserve to be mentioned: the juxtaposition of multiple national identities in Spain with the unitary national identity of Portugal, the depth and length of the Spanish Civil War of 1936–1939 in contrast with the relatively brief Portuguese mini-civil wars of that country's early twentieth century First Republic, the survival of elements of the Portuguese colonial empire until the demise of the *Estado Novo* on April 25, 1974, and pre-democratization differences between the two cases in their economic and educational profiles. I argue that these differences in antecedent conditions are sufficient in magnitude to prevent us from conceptualizing the pairing as a pure or perfect natural experiment, yet not so large in magnitude as to undermine the theoretical usefulness of the two-way contrast.

To focus on just one example, in the Spanish case, the Civil War of 1936–1939 is often seen as a factor that strongly conditions contemporary Spanish politics, and clearly there is something to this claim. However, I add two crucial points to the standard emphasis of many analysts on legacies of the Civil War. First, Portugal also had mini-civil wars during its early twentieth century First Republic. And secondly, I argue that collective memories of the Spanish Civil War were actually shaped in part by the politics of the country's post-Franco transition. The left shifted its perspective on memories of the War and the Republic as a result of the political judgment that it was necessary to do so in order to reach and consolidate democracy in a country in which the authoritarian regime never suffered a debilitating "crisis of failure." A factor that some analysts have seen as a precondition for Spain's transition—the cultural rethinking of the Civil War in ways that promoted reconciliation instead of reasserting virtues of the defeated Second Republic—was at least in some measure a consequence of the Spanish pathway to democracy, as the most important work on historical memory of the Civil War has shown (Aguilar 1997; Aguilar and Payne 2018).

It is important to note that the early twentieth-century democratic experiences of Spain and Portugal—prior to the two countries' decades-long experience of repressive authoritarian rule—were both characterized by sharp sociopolitical conflict. Many fundamental features of political life in this earlier period were quite similar in the two countries. Later, after decades of authoritarian rule in the two cases, the initial demands of working-class movements were deeply similar in the preliminary phase of transition, as the important work of Durán Muñoz (2000) shows. Indeed, nothing in the pattern of democratic life—and pro-democracy mobilization—of the two countries before the critical juncture of the 1970s fits the post-1970s contrast between inclusionary democratic practice in Portugal and institutionally segmented democratic practice in Spain. The Iberian divide in political inclusion put in place by the critical juncture of the 1970s transitions to democracy was historically new.

Antecedent Conditions as Critical Antecedents

In addition to considering antecedent conditions as a source of rival hypotheses, differing prior conditions could be considered "critical antecedents" (Slater and Simmons 2010: 889), that is, antecedents that "shape the choices and changes that emerge during critical junctures in causally significant ways." The Portuguese effort to maintain its colonial holdings in Africa is a key conditioning factor that could be conceptualized as a critical antecedent in the Portuguese case. Indeed, the colonial question powerfully conditioned the Carnation Revolution itself but not the legacies of transition within Portugal. However, this distinctive feature of Portugal does not undermine my argument about the impact of Portugal's mode of transition to democracy. Rather, bringing in the role of Portugal's colonial endeavors simply adds substance to the argument, specifying a crucial precondition for Portugal's revolution.

Antecedent Conditions as the Baseline against Which Change Is Assessed

Finally, antecedent conditions could "represent a 'base line' against which the critical juncture and the legacy are assessed" (Collier and Collier 1991: 30). One such example, as noted earlier in this chapter, is the delayed introduction of universal access to education only two decades before the demise of authoritarian rule in Portugal. This factor created, in a sense, strong headwinds for the post-revolutionary system's pursuit of social inclusion. The underlying structure of educational inequality that was put in place by this antecedent condition made crucial types of social progress more difficult than would have otherwise been the case, but ultimately with a large commitment to public education the Portuguese system has largely overcome those headwinds. Thus, drawing attention to this distinctive feature strengthens rather than weakens my argument: by showing the low base line from which Portugal started, it bolsters the case that the change introduced by Portugal revolutionary pathway to democracy was significant. Indeed, even though Portugal and Spain differ in terms of some antecedent conditions, these differences do not significantly diminish the explanatory force of the cross-case divergence between the Iberian countries in their transition pathways. The contrast between the Iberian Peninsula cases in the breadth of inclusion that characterizes their democratic practice is a historically new point of divergence that emerged only after the democratic transitions of the 1970s.

Scope Conditions

A second possible objection concerns the comparative range of applicability of lessons derived from the contrasts between two unusual cases, in the terminology most widely used in comparative work, the *scope conditions* of the lessons to be drawn from this paired comparison. Although a number of democratic transitions during the global Third Wave of democratization have moved forward through more or less revolutionary dynamics (della Porta 2016), most of those cases were essentially political revolutions; the broadly social character of Portugal's democratizing revolution stands as a highly unusual pathway to democracy. Spain's largely regime-initiated transition is also historically unusual in both the guiding role of incumbent elites and the magnitude of formal continuities that were permitted to remain in place. This question of the comparative applicability of lessons derived from this pairing deserves somewhat lengthier treatment here. It is only fair to assess the theoretical usefulness of a comparison that quite intentionally magnifies the variation between cases in the mode of transition to something rather close to the maximum possible range of differentiation in democratization scenarios.

No two-case comparison can fully capture all the forms of variation that differentiate between regime transition scenarios, but that does not necessarily mean that paired comparisons are inadequate for drawing out wide-ranging implications. Scholars of democratization have formulated a number of useful—but quite different—typologies of democratization pathways, each of these formulations rooted in important insights about elements of genuine differentiation between scenarios of transition.[6] I argue that transition pathways even within the small three-way set of south European cases that began the Third Wave in Portugal, Greece, and Spain during the 1970s should be seen to rest on not one but two major dimensions of variation. I briefly broaden the scope of comparison to these three cases to highlight this point.

---

6. See citations in footnotes 1, 2, and 3.

Whereas Greece and Portugal both moved from authoritarian dictatorships to democracy through interventions by the military that abruptly ended anti-democratic rule in two clear instances of *"ruptura"* with the past, Greece shared with Spain the continuity of state institutions and state power in the context of regime change (Fishman 1990b). On one dimension, the Greek case approximated Portugal, yet on the other the Greek case was far more similar to Spain. Of the three cases, only Portugal experienced a classic Skocpolian state crisis and with it an overturning of social and political hierarchies accompanied by the forging of new cultural patterns and practices deeply conditioned by the pervasive challenge to hierarchies. This pattern of differentiation yields two dimensions of variation between the three countries in the enduring legacies of transition: whereas Portuguese and Greek political actors were "disencumbered" by the swift break with the authoritarian past, freeing them to pursue political objectives without fear of inducing a resurgence of authoritarian rule, Spanish political actors were constrained throughout the transition by their concern that militant tactics and expansive objectives might strengthen the still very relevant advocates of a return to dictatorship. Yet in Greece as in Spain the transition was essentially limited to political changes; social hierarchies and cultural phenomena failed to undergo the comprehensive transformation experienced in revolutionary Portugal. In the post-transition period, Greek democratic practice has taken a form quite different from the patterns predominating in the Iberian Peninsula cases, and analysts of this third case have linked predominant forms of political conflict to the country's recent political past (see references in Fishman 2019: 221–23)—just as I argue for the cases of Portugal and Spain. The pattern of differentiation on two separate dimensions of regime transformation in the south European cases of transition during the 1970s has yielded three quite different predominant forms of democratic practice.

Thus, the two-way contrast between Portugal and Spain is not intended to provide the basis to theoretically lay out all of the dynamics at work linking the universe of all cases of democratization to enduring legacies. The Iberian Peninsula contrast establishes the possible space for divergence following a democratizing critical juncture, but it offers no guarantees that all meaningful differences between cases in their pathway to democracy will generate equivalently large distinctive legacies. The divergence between the Iberian Peninsula cases following their remarkably different pathways to democracy is intended to establish the *capacity* of transition scenarios to leave in their wake powerful cultural legacies. This key point, in turn, serves as the basis for elaborating causal processes and mechanisms capable of linking the critical juncture of transition scenarios to long-enduring consequences, but it is not intended to provide a comprehensive set of predictions about the magnitude of such effects likely to be encountered in other cases. Instead, this chapter's central claim is intended to help motivate in-depth work on other cases and contextually sensitive large-N comparisons as well.

If transition pathways potentially hold the ability to generate cultural legacies shaping democratic life, that effect should be observable in the in-depth study of these two cases, which experienced near polar-opposite forms of democratizing change. The research discussed here has amply supported that expectation. But the contrast with Greece serves as a warning about the great difficulty of formulating generalizations intended to explain patterns of variation in multiple cases without the sort of case-sensitive comparative research that Ragin (1987, 2008) and others advocate. Thus, much of the comparative value of this paired comparison lies in its ability to identify rather broad types of causal dynamics that researchers should search for. There is no assumption advanced here that the causal dynamics in other cases will directly mirror those of either the Spanish or Portuguese pattern. Indeed, this chapter's multidimensional view of variation within the universe of democratic transitions suggests just the reverse: namely that the types of legacies left in place by transition pathways are likely to constitute a quite complex set of patterns. The findings presented here should be seen as an instance of causal process and causal mechanism observation, not as an effort to reproduce what data set observations do (Brady and Collier 2010).

CONCLUSION: TOWARD CONSENSUS?

By way of conclusion, it is useful to briefly consider reasons why the literature on this theme has found it difficult to delineate clear and enduring consequences of transition scenarios capable of eliciting widespread consensus among social scientists. I suggest that one key factor in the absence thus far of scholarly consensus on this theme is the typical focus of critical junctures work on institutional legacies. This focus has proved quite useful in numerous studies and for a considerable range of purposes, but in the instance of democratization scenarios the case for centering our attention exclusively on institutional legacies seems very much open to question. One factor to consider is the presence of considerable transnational pressures in favor of institutional isomorphism—especially on matters related to democracy itself and basic legal guarantees. Once countries become democracies they are, in most cases, subject to external pressures to adhere to certain international or regional institutional expectations. Additionally, bottom-up processes within new democracies should be expected to shape the definition of new institutions at least to some degree, even in polities that are less disposed toward inclusion than the Portuguese case emphasized here. Such bottom-up processes may be shaped to a large extent by structural features of the countries in question and other matters unrelated to transition pathways. Thus, a great deal of variation across cases in the design of new institutions should be expected to reflect the impact of causal forces unrelated to a country's pathway to democracy.

However, if transnational or supranational institutions and dynamics can shape the design of new formal institutions within national cases, it seems much less likely that they can be expected to reconfigure cultural dispositions and practices in those cases. Cultural change cannot be achieved as an automatic result of legislative measures or treaty obligations; it requires cultural work by civil society actors and other historically complex conditions, such as those that are put in place by macro-historical processes of the type emphasized here. For theoretical reasons, it makes good sense to expect the major enduring legacies of transition scenarios to be cultural ones, and this is exactly what my research shows. Thus, my argument focuses on culturally rooted approaches to political life that shape an ongoing succession of outcomes, in interaction with other causal dynamics—and not on one unchanging package of institutional outcomes dating from the regime transitions.

Another key explanation for the lack of scholarly consensus on enduring legacies of transition scenarios concerns the way we choose to operationalize the independent variable, namely differences across cases in the pathway followed to democracy. I offer a suggestion on this matter that is borrowed from Durkheim. Although for most purposes, I strongly prefer Weber to Durkheim as a methodological guide, on the matter of formulating typologies Durkheim's approach proves highly useful here. He argues classically in *Suicide* that the typological differences that should be seen as "real social facts" are those that generate clear causal consequences. From this perspective, it is only research on the enduring consequences of divergent pathways to democracy that can establish *which* typologies are actually useful for this purpose. Some typologies of transition pathways may be very useful for specifying distinctive challenges of democratization itself without really being helpful for spotting enduring consequences of transition scenarios. The perspective of Weber is also helpful; it argues that ideal types such as typologies are not correct or incorrect, as such, but only more or less *useful*. Thus, there is ample reason to think that typologies that are highly fruitful for the study of transitions themselves may not be equally relevant for the effort to delineate consequences of transition pathways.

The argument advanced here (and summarized in Table 12.1) is not that all differences between regime transition pathways generate distinctive consequences, but instead that *some* differences between democratization scenarios do so in a very powerful manner. The implications of this research suggest ways in which the critical junctures perspective can be extended to terrains in which it has seldom been applied. But in a broader sense, instead of generating predictive expectations for the overall universe of post-transition democracies, this research establishes the existence of a terrain of variation—namely cultural understandings of democracy and related forms of practice—that merits much new work. New questions more than new predictions are the most important implication of this work for the study of post-transition democracies. The paired comparison of the two Iberian Peninsula transitions to democracy generates valuable new findings on causal processes and mechanisms through which the critical juncture of democratization pathways can exert a major enduring impact on important features of democratic life. The contrasts between Portugal and Spain show us *how* regime transitions can powerfully condition the breadth of democratic inclusion—well beyond what is fully reflected in the design of formal institutions.

Table 12.1 Legacies of Democratic Transitions in Portugal and Spain: Inclusionary vs. Institutionally Segmented Democratic Practice

Summary of Argument	As a legacy of their markedly different democratic transitions in the 1970s, Portugal and Spain developed fundamentally different cultural understandings of democracy and its bounds of inclusion, resulting in divergent forms of democratic practice.	
	Portugal's revolutionary transition left a legacy of *inclusionary democratic practice*, with representative institutions that are more receptive to actors and forms of conduct located outside those institutions.	
	Spain's regime-initiated transition left a legacy of *institutionally segmented democratic practice* that strictly separates actors located within representative institutions from actors and forms of conduct located outside their bounds.	
	These contrasting legacies had important ultimate consequences. Portugal's higher level of political inclusion ultimately led to better social and policy outcomes: a more robust welfare state, more effective poverty reduction, certain types of enhanced cultural capacities, and lower unemployment, despite the country's lower level of development at the time of the transitions.	
Antecedent Conditions	Remarkable persistence of authoritarian regimes for three decades after World War II.	
	The contrast that later emerged between the post-transition democracies Portugal vs. Spain is historically new, and has no precedent among the antecedent conditions.	
	Portugal	**Spain**
Dynamics of change leading up to critical juncture	• **Authoritarianism to Democracy:** Rupture brings about an inversion within the military hierarchy, state crisis, and a large role for students, workers, and other activists.	• **Authoritarianism to Democracy:** Institutional reform, ultimately fully democratizing the political system, initiated by elements of the authoritarian regime under pressure from the opposition. Institutional sources of power reaffirmed during transition.
Defenders vs. Opponents of Authoritarian Regime	• **Regime Transition Begins:** Carnation Revolution by "Captains of April," April 25, 1974—Army captains led coup that circumvented institutional lines of command.	• **Regime Transition Begins:** Franco's death on November 20, 1975; successors to authoritarian power within regime led democratization under pressure from mass political action.
Protesters vs. Political Authorities	• **Protesters:** Activists as well as members of marginalized groups, such as workers, peasants, and residents of low-income neighborhoods. Protesters effectively overturned hierarchies in many social settings.	• **Protesters:** Activists play significant yet limited role. Democratic opposition to authoritarian regime, especially by organized labor groups. Protestors feared pushing too hard, and thus showed restraint with demands especially after first elections in 1977.

(continued)

Table 12.1 Legacies of Democratic Transitions in Portugal and Spain: Inclusionary vs. Institutionally Segmented Democratic Practice (*continued*)

Critical Juncture	Revolutionary Transition	Regime-Initiated Transition
Mode of Democratic Transition in 1970s	• Middle-ranking military officers launched coup against the dictatorship, disobeying superiors and undermining existing hierarchies. • Activists played key role, assisting rebelling military officers in confrontations with defenders of regime. • Students and activists ousted supporters of regime from ministries, schools, media outlets, and private firms, while also articulating demands for social change. • Social revolution and forging of new representative institutions occurred simultaneously.	• Regime-led transition to democracy. • Mass push for democratization, but labor exercised restraint. Franco's successors implement democratic reforms. • Elements of legal and symbolic continuity between authoritarian regime and the new democracy. • Government officials and other key political actors viewed popular pressure from outside official institutions as thoroughly distinct from and potentially a threat to those institutions.
Aftermath	**Shaping the Political Terrain of Inclusion**	**Reinforcing Exclusion** Even within representative Institutions
"Coda" of Transition	• Amendment of constitution in 1989 by center-right and center-left parties. • Ended formal commitment to socialism. • Shifted legacies of revolution from economic arena of enterprise ownership to welfare state construction.	• 1982 reconfiguration of the party system, five years after first democratic elections in 1977. • Right-wing Alianza Popular (ultimately renamed Partido Popular) spatially replaced UCD. UCD had promoted demarcation between popular pressure and representative institutions but exercised inclusion within political institutions' bounds, whereas Partido Popular often promoted exclusion even within representative institutions.
Legacy: Democratic Practice	**Inclusionary**	**Institutionally Segmented**
Prevailing Form of Democratic Practice	• Revolutionary (bottom-up) path to democracy occurred simultaneously with the forging of new democratic institutions, creating new and enduring understandings of inclusive democracy. • Actors inside formal institutions acknowledge and interact with democratic practice that takes place outside those institutions.	• Democratic practice that takes place outside the formal representative institutions is kept separate from the democratic practice that takes place inside those institutions. • Change in the identity of the major right-wing party reinforced and furthered the legacy of exclusion, even within representative bodies.

(continued)

Table 12.1 Legacies of Democratic Transitions in Portugal and Spain: Inclusionary vs. Institutionally Segmented Democratic Practice (*continued*)

Level of Political Inclusion	• More inclusive of socially marginalized groups. • Protesters seen by institutional power-holders as an important part of Portuguese political life. Protesters may engage in direct or tacit negotiations with elected officials. • Widespread interest in participatory institutions such as participatory budgeting, often supported even by center-right. • Participatory institutional practices in key secondary institutions, e.g., schools and news media.	• Less inclusive of socially marginalized groups. • Protesters typically not seen as relevant political actors: new democratic constitution prohibited citizens from using demonstrations to petition the parliament. Use of police barriers to prevent demonstrators from accessing parliament. • Instances of opposition to participatory institutions such as participatory budgeting even within parties of the left. • Hierarchical institutional practices often found in secondary institutions such as school system and news media.
Further Consequences of Legacy	**High Level of Inclusion Yields More Comprehensive Social Policy**	**Lower Level of Inclusion Yields More Limited Social Policy**
Institutional Outcomes	• Power-holders provide demonstrators a hearing on matters ranging from housing policy to labor market regulation and anti-crisis measures. • During Euro crisis government modified austerity policies due to protest in 2012.	• Housing policy relatively impervious to bottom-up pressures from protesters. Economic policy less focused on employment creation, with consequence of chronically high unemployment. • Sharp expansion of inequality during Euro crisis, with government impervious to popular pressures to restrict austerity measures.
Responses to Recession	• Decline in distributional inequality during crisis that began with Great Recession. • Taxation, and state spending for welfare and education, higher than in Spain.	• Responded to anti-austerity protests in 2012 and 2013 by criminalizing certain forms of protest and reaffirming government's basic policies.
Social and Political Outcomes	• **Unemployment:** Lower for most of the post-authoritarian period. • **Welfare State (all policy areas except unemployment):** Ultimately more effective at reducing poverty: initially higher relative poverty rate, but by 2005, lower than Spain.	• **Unemployment:** Persistently higher for most of the post-authoritarian period. • **Welfare State (all policy areas except unemployment):** More welfare state development in 1980s, but stagnated beginning in the 1990s. Welfare state was less effective than Portugal's at reducing poverty.

BIBLIOGRAPHY

Aguilar Fernández, Paloma. 1997. "La amnesia y la memoria: las movilizaciones por la amnistía en la transición a la democracia." In Manuel Pérez Ledesma and Rafael Cruz (eds.), *Cultura y movilización en la España contemporánea* (pp. 327–57). Madrid: Alianza Editorial.

Aguilar Fernández, Paloma, and Leigh A. Payne. 2018. *El resurgir del pasado en España: fosas de víctimas y confesiones de verdugos*. Madrid: Editorial Taurus.

Bermeo, Nancy. 2007. "War and Democratization: Lessons from the Portuguese Experience." *Democratization* 14(3): 388–406.

Brady, Henry E., and David Collier (eds.). 2010. *Rethinking Social Inquiry: Diverse Tools, Shared Standards* (2nd ed.). Lanham, MD: Rowman & Littlefield.

Collier, David, and Gerardo L. Munck. 2017. "Building Blocks and Methodological Challenges: A Framework for Studying Critical Junctures." *Qualitative and Multi-Method Research* 15(1): 2–9.

Collier, Ruth Berins. 1999. *Paths toward Democracy: The Working Class and Elites in Western Europe and South America*. New York, NY: Cambridge University Press.

Collier, Ruth Berins, and David Collier. 1991. *Shaping the Political Arena: Critical Junctures, the Labor Movement, and the Regime Dynamics in Latin America*. Princeton, NJ: Princeton University Press.

Dahl, Robert A. 1998. *On Democracy*. New Haven, CT: Yale University Press.

———. 2006. *On Political Equality*. New Haven, CT: Yale University Press.

della Porta, Donatella. 2016. *Where Did the Revolution Go? Contentious Politics and the Quality of Democracy*. New York, NY: Cambridge University Press.

Durán Muñoz, Rafael. 2000. *Contención y Transgresión: Las Movilizaciones Sociales y el Estado en las Transiciones Española y Portuguesa*. Madrid, Spain: Centro de Estudios Políticos y Constitucionales.

Fishman, Robert M. 1990a. *Working-Class Organization and the Return to Democracy in Spain*. Ithaca, NY: Cornell University Press.

———. 1990b. "Rethinking State and Regime: Southern Europe's Transition to Democracy." *World Politics* 42(3): 422–40.

———. 2011. "Democratic Practice after the Revolution: The Case of Portugal and Beyond." *Politics & Society* 39(2): 233–67.

———. 2019. *Democratic Practice: Origins of the Iberian Divide in Political Inclusion*. Oxford, UK: Oxford University Press.

Hagopian, Frances. 1990. "'Democracy by Undemocratic Means'? Elites, Political Pacts, and Regime Transition in Brazil." *Comparative Political Studies* 23(2): 147–70.

Helmke, Gretchen, and Steven Levitsky (eds.). 2006. *Informal Institutions and Democracy: Lessons from Latin America*. Baltimore, MD: The Johns Hopkins University Press.

Hunter, Wendy. 1997. *Eroding Military Influence in Brazil: Politicians against Soldiers*. Chapel Hill, NC: University of North Carolina Press.

Huntington, Samuel P. 1991. *The Third Wave. Democratization in the Late Twentieth Century*. Norman, OK: University of Oklahoma Press.

Karl, Terry L. 1990. "Dilemmas of Democratization in Latin America." *Comparative Politics* 23(1): 1–21.

Karl, Terry L., and Philippe Schmitter. 1991. "Modes of Transition in Latin America, Southern and Eastern Europe." *International Social Science Journal* 128(2): 269–84.

Linz, Juan J., and Alfred Stepan (eds.). 1978. *The Breakdown of Democratic Regimes*. Baltimore, MD: The Johns Hopkins University Press.

Linz, Juan J., and Alfred Stepan. 1996. *Problems of Democratic Transition and Consolidation: Southern Europe, South America and Post-Communist Europe*. Baltimore, MD: The Johns Hopkins University Press.

Lizardo, Omar. 2017. "Improving Cultural Analysis: Considering Personal Culture in Its Declarative and Nondeclarative Modes." *American Sociological Review* 82(1): 88–115.

Mainwaring, Scott, and Aníbal Pérez-Liñán. 2013. *Democracies and Dictatorships in Latin America: Emergence, Survival, and Fall*. New York, NY: Cambridge University Press.

Maravall, José María. 1978. *Dictatorship and Political Dissent: Workers and Students in Franco's Spain*. London, UK: Tavistock.

———. 1982. *The Transition to Democracy in Spain*. New York, NY: St. Martin's Press.

Maxwell, Kenneth. 1995. *The Making of Portuguese Democracy*. New York, NY: Cambridge University Press.

Munck, Gerardo L., and Carol Skalnik Leff. 1997. "Modes of Transition and Democratization: South America and Eastern Europe in Comparative." *Comparative Politics* 29(3): 343–62.

O'Donnell, Guillermo, Philippe Schmitter, and Laurence Whitehead (eds.). 1986. *Transitions from Authoritarian Rule: Prospects for Democracy*. Baltimore, MD: The Johns Hopkins University Press.

Patterson, Orlando. 2014. "Making Sense of Culture." *Annual Review of Sociology* 40: 1–30.

Perez, Sofia A., and Manos Matsaganis. 2018. "The Political Economy of Austerity in Southern Europe." *New Political Economy* 23(2): 192–207.

Radcliff, Pamela Beth. 2011. *Making Democratic Citizens in Spain: Civil Society and the Popular Origins of the Transition, 1960–78*. Basingstoke, UK: Palgrave Macmillan.

Ragin, Charles. 1987. *The Comparative Method: Moving Beyond Qualitative and Quantitative Strategies*. Berkeley, CA: University of California Press.

———. 2008. *Redesigning Social Inquiry: Fuzzy Sets and Beyond*. Chicago, IL: University of Chicago Press.

Sewell, William H. 1996. "Historical Events as Transformations of Structures: Inventing Revolution at the Bastille." *Theory and Society* 25(6): 841–81.

Silva, Manuela et al. 2006. *Memorias de Economistas*. Lisboa, Portugal: Exame.

Skocpol, Theda. 1979. *States and Social Revolution*. New York, NY: Cambridge University Press.

Slater, Dan, and Erica Simmons. 2010. "Informative Regress: Critical Antecedents in Comparative Politics." *Comparative Political Studies* 43(7): 886–917.

Stepan, Alfred. 1986. "Paths toward Redemocratization: Theoretical and Comparative Considerations." In Guillermo O'Donnell, Philippe Schmitter, and Laurence Whitehead (eds.), *Transitions from Authoritarian Rule: Comparative Perspectives* (pp. 64–84). Baltimore, MD: The Johns Hopkins University Press.

Tarrow, Sidney. 2010. "The Strategy of Paired Comparison: Toward a Theory of Practice." *Comparative Political Studies* 43(2): 230–59.

Valenzuela, J. Samuel. 1992. "Democratic Consolidation in Post-Transitional Settings: Notion, Process and Facilitating Conditions." In Scott Mainwaring, Guillermo O'Donnell, and J. Samuel Valenzuela (eds.), *Issues in Democratic Consolidation: The New South American Democracies in Comparative Perspective* (pp. 57–104). Notre Dame, IN: Notre Dame Press.

Weyland, Kurt. 2014. *Making Waves: Democratic Contention in Europe and Latin America since the Revolutions of 1848*. New York, NY: Cambridge University Press.

13

Leninist Extinction?

Critical Junctures, Legacies, and the Study of Post-Communism

Danielle N. Lussier and Jody LaPorte

In the thirty years since communist systems began to unravel and ultimately collapse across Eurasia, scholarship examining cases from the region has made important contributions to comparative politics, advancing our knowledge of the prospects for democratization and democratic survival (Bunce 2003, 2016; Fish 2005; Levitsky and Way 2010), economic transformation (Gaddy and Ickes 1998; Greskovits 1998; Stark and Bruszt 1998; Bunce 1999; Orenstein and Haas 2005; Gans-Morse 2017), party development and party systems (Kitschelt et al. 1999; Grzymała-Busse 2002; Hale 2006; Rohrschneider and Whitefield 2009), political attitudes and trust (Howard 2003; Pop-Eleches and Tucker 2011, 2017), and numerous other outcomes. A common theme that unites explanatory frameworks across all of these topics is the rich and nuanced manner in which historically located explanatory variables have been considered alongside more proximate causes. As we argued in an earlier overview of this literature (LaPorte and Lussier 2011), "there is hardly any outcome of interest in eastern Europe and Eurasia that has not been linked in some way to the legacies that a respective country inherited from communism." Indeed, as several scholars have noted, the very concept of "postcommunism" assumes that the arrival and demise of communism across the geographic span of Eurasia are critical junctures.

In spite of all the attention scholars of postcommunist political outcomes give to historical causes, there is no overarching consensus about the role of a singular communist legacy in affecting change in the region. Additionally, arguments about historical legacies are not limited to those originating in the communist period (Kotkin and Beissinger 2014; Wittenberg 2015; Simpser et al. 2018). Historical events that precede communism—and likely inform the structures and practices of the communist regimes that exercised power in the twentieth century—have commanded scholarly attention, as have the potential legacies that originate at various points during communist rule. Similarly, the swift end of communism across Eurasia and its replacement with a broad range of political and economic arrangements in the 1990s may have generated enduring legacies that affect contemporary outcomes. Indeed, given that three decades have passed since the end of communism, arguments about legacies have also considered whether variation in twenty-first century political and economic outcomes can be traced back to the political and economic transformations of the late 1980s and 1990s (Hanson 2017).

Much of the scholarship invoking historical legacies in the postcommunist region takes the structure of a critical juncture argument, positing that the arrival of or departure from communism in the region was a rupture that created discontinuity that would not have otherwise occurred. Moreover, the postcommunist scholarship that addresses historical causes in a rigorous way recognizes that correlational patterns between past and present are insufficient evidence to accept that a legacy is a causal effect of some earlier event. Indeed, to the extent that a consensus has emerged within the scholarship on postcommunist societies, it is that for a legacy argument to bear causal weight, it must be contextually specific, empirically verifiable, and demonstrated with clearly specified causal mechanisms that show how a legacy of a distant cause endures over time, sometimes even several decades.

In many instances, the empirical burden needed to substantiate how critical the rise or fall of communism is to a particular outcome has not been sufficiently discharged. While a number of important scholarly works that invoke the role of historical legacies in the postcommunist region are methodologically rigorous and have succeeded at clearly establishing a causal chain between a historical variable and an outcome of interest, in many instances the relative roles of a hypothesized critical juncture and its antecedent conditions are underspecified, particularly when used to explain broad, macro-level variation in the political and economic regimes that currently exist in the lands of formerly communist Eurasia. Indeed, we agree with Waldner (see Chapter 7) that scholars working with historically located causal models need to further develop a qualitative analogue to the maxim that "correlation does not equal causation." Moreover, along the lines suggested by Waldner, we suggest that the critical juncture framework, when thoughtfully applied to comparative-historical work that employs qualitative approaches for the identification of causal mechanisms and processes, can help assess the relative causal weight of precommunist, communist, and postcommunist influences, allowing for a more productive and fruitful assessment of the role of historical variables on macro-level change in the region.

The critical juncture framework offers some valuable tools for bringing the study of historical legacies from precommunist and communist eras into closer dialogue with explanatory frameworks from other regions. Collier (see Chapter 1) models critical juncture-driven change as a five-step process. First, analysts must identify the *antecedent conditions*, i.e. the stable, preexisting circumstances and "diverse features of economy, society, and politics" that provide a starting point for institutional change (Collier, in Chapter 1). These antecedent conditions are a source of rival hypotheses for explaining the outcomes attributed to a subsequent critical juncture. The second phase is a *cleavage* or *shock*, which creates the conditions necessary for a critical juncture to emerge. These events disrupt an otherwise continuous state of affairs, generating space for institutional innovation to occur. Third is the *critical juncture* itself, defined as a major episode of institutional innovation. The fourth component is the *mechanisms of production*, which refers to the means by which the legacy emerges, which may be straightforward or may involve a complex reactive (and, in some cases, counter-reactive) sequence. Fifth, these processes produce a *legacy*, i.e. the durable, stable institutions and the mechanisms by which they are reproduced.

The central question we address in this chapter is, what is the role of critical junctures in the study of communist legacies? While there is a natural affinity between the study of historical legacies in the postcommunist world and causal analyses situated in the critical juncture framework, in practical terms there is often limited cross-pollination of models across the two traditions, leading to differences in how concepts and causal processes are understood. The ubiquity of legacy-based arguments—both rigorous and oversimplified—in nearly all political science work covering postcommunist cases dictated the terms of scholarly discussion on the region for much of the past three decades. Competing explanations for a broad array of outcomes frequently revolve around different views of the causal weight of communist inheritances or variables that are independent of the communist experience. However, analytical frameworks that address the competing force of historical versus more proximate causes, as well as the conditions under which they are activated, are rarely used. In this chapter, we reconstruct several dimensions of this rich literature through the lens of critical junctures with the goal of trying to develop a more precise understanding of arguments about communism's causal force made in the literature.

Our goal in this chapter is to take up Waldner's charge and use the critical junctures framework to advance a discussion of the conceptual and causal role of legacies in the study of postcommunist outcomes. First, we briefly contextualize the paradigm of historical legacies in the study of postcommunism, showing how what was initially understood as a negative, constant inheritance from the past that would likely counteract an optimistic view about the political and economic transformation introduced with the end of communism has evolved into narrower, more precise arguments. Second, we discuss the concept of legacy and outline the different ways the concept is used in the causal frameworks employed by scholars of postcommunism, namely as effects of distant causes, some of which might be resistant to shock and others that persist after a critical juncture. Third, we shift our discussion to address the specific relationship between legacies and causality. We take three exemplary works of postcommunist scholarship and examine them against the steps of the critical juncture framework: antecedent conditions, cleavage, potential critical juncture, mechanisms of production, and possible legacy. Ultimately, this exercise challenges the assumption that the rise or fall of communism alone constitute critical junctures. Rather, we find evidence of more complex causal relationships that comprise a mix of evidence for the causal force of critical junctures, as well as rivaling antecedent conditions, and their combined causal power. Further, this exercise advances methodological discussions about the challenges of evaluating historical causes. We demonstrate that the task of identifying the connections between antecedent conditions, a potential critical juncture, and a possible legacy compels a scholar to identify causal mechanisms while also considering how "critical" a particular juncture is to the outcome at hand, thereby leading to more circumspect conclusions. More broadly, in our view, the critical juncture framework provides a fairly elaborate way to consider the possible causal sequences that connect putative explanatory and outcome variables and weigh them against competing explanations. Moreover, this framework offers a useful tool for assessing individual studies and aggregating the findings across a body of literature.

THE LEGACIES PARADIGM IN POSTCOMMUNIST STUDIES

The scholarship on "legacies" emerging from work on postcommunism finds its origins in Jowitt's 1992 *New World Disorder: The Leninist Extinction*, in which Jowitt famously described "the Leninist legacy," or the "inheritance" Eastern Europe received from an extensive period of Leninist rule. Among the various attributes that Jowitt ascribed to this legacy were personalism in place of individualism, the absence of a shared public identity as citizens, and fragmented societies incapable of developing frameworks for collective action, which, he cautioned, may lead to demographic and political fragmentation throughout the region. Jowitt's articulation of the Leninist legacy sought to moderate the contemporary discussion of the probable political and economic trajectories of former communist regimes that did not fully consider the countervailing causal force of these factors. The democratic transitions of Poland and Hungary, which appeared to serve as almost textbook models of elite pacting, as well as the relatively swift and peaceful discarding of Leninist regimes across the region in 1989–1991, cast Eastern European cases into a broader democratization framework that emphasized the more proximate and contingent causal forces of transition experiences, early elections, and institutional design.[1] Jowitt's focus on the inheritance of Leninism sought to quell the temptation to look at the economic and political developments in the region as if occurring on a *tabula rasa*.

Jowitt sought to describe a syndrome and an approach to understanding the localized context of politics in the former communist world. He did not conceptualize "legacy" as a variable, but rather as a parameter that posed meaningful constraints on

---

1. In a 2015 overview of research on postcommunist politics, Ekiert (2015) suggested that three paradigms have shaped approaches to studying the region over the past three decades: the "communist legacy/liability paradigm," the "transition to democracy paradigm," and "new historicism as a paradigm." Of particular relevance to us is the connection between the first and third approaches.

the range of potential outcomes formerly communist regimes could reasonably expect to achieve in the process of building new institutions. Other scholars, however, seized on his terminology, broadening it to include "legacies" that could vary across space and time. In effect, the syndrome Jowitt described was broken down into numerous constituent parts that were defined in terms of a scholar's specific research question. In many respects, the shift from "legacy" to "legacies" was logical for both methodological and empirical reasons. Methodologically speaking, a "legacy" as a syndrome is essentially a parameter, understood as a constant, or only as a variable that separates communist and noncommunist countries in the broadest of terms. Moreover, it was a very general parameter. It was abundantly clear to any scholar working on the region that a host of factors that were bundled into a Leninist legacy differed both across and within specific communist countries. As such, treating communist history as a parameter that was uniform across cases could lead to faulty research designs, assumptions, and conclusions. From an empirical perspective, if Leninism varied across contexts, it needed to be measured in a more nuanced way, and a starting point would be to disaggregate it into smaller, more empirically valid segments.

As Kotkin and Beissinger (2014) have suggested, Jowitt's understanding of the Leninist legacy was normatively charged—it assumed a collection of negative attributes that served to drag down what was largely seen as a normatively positive process of political opening. The lack of an empirically neutral understanding of the potential impact of historical variables on postcommunist macro-level outcomes contributed at times to overestimation and under-specification of the causal weight of communist-era influences. Legacy effects were frequently taken to be accurate on relatively weak grounds. Scholars observing an outcome that appeared puzzling because it did not conform to theoretical expectations about political and economic outcomes might argue that the visible association between some present phenomenon and its communist predecessor was evidence of the persistent impact of communism. Much of this work lacked precision, with murky understandings of what comprised a "legacy," and how one might identify and measure its impact. For example, when surveying the state of the literature a decade ago, we found that only 8 texts in a sample of 400 scholarly works that advanced arguments about historical causal processes in the postcommunist region offered an explicit definition of "legacy" (LaPorte and Lussier 2011: 642). In our earlier work we also distinguished three different ways that scholars of postcommunism placed "legacies" into a causal framework: (1) as an outcome to be explained; (2) as a factor effecting change directly; and (3) as a variable that moderates a proximate causal factor, thereby shaping an outcome indirectly (LaPorte and Lussier 2011: 641–42).

As analysis of communist inheritances has evolved in the twenty-first century, scholars have increasingly developed explanatory models in value-neutral ways with sharpened empirical precision (Grzymała-Busse 2002; Howard 2003; Pop-Eleches and Tucker 2017). These works frequently seek to understand the causal force of communism on other outcomes of interest. They also place the potential role of precommunist legacies into sharper focus by giving more attention to identification and measurement (see, for example, Wittenberg 2006; Darden and Grzymała-Busse 2006), raising important questions about whether the lived communist experience was as transformative of social and political institutions as was often assumed. They also advanced the literature on historical legacies in the postcommunist region by moving away from broad macro-level theorizing, and by focusing on narrower, and specific, outcomes.

Methodological sophistication has not always been accompanied by theoretical clarity, however. On the one hand, this more rigorous, value-neutral work is marked by renewed methodological attention to rigorous qualitative and multi-method approaches, yielding valuable contributions to scholarly analyses of causal processes in the postcommunist region. On the other hand, the lack of a shared framework for identifying, measuring, and comparing historical legacies in postcommunist scholarship has limited our ability to answer broader questions about the causal force of communism on political, economic, and social outcomes across Eurasia. As the next section will elaborate, a lack of consensus among postcommunist scholars about what constitutes a legacy hinders our ability to aggregate the findings of a broad field of research and integrate them into the broader field of comparative scholarship.

WHAT IS A LEGACY?

There are several challenges for integrating the study of communism's rise, fall, and legacy into critical juncture frameworks. A significant challenge involves conceptual clarification: scholars who advance historical arguments to explain variation in postcommunist outcomes employ the concept of "legacy" in several different ways, making communication across studies difficult. Several scholars of postcommunist outcomes adopt the language of critical junctures largely as a periodization scheme without adopting the theoretical approach to critical junctures advanced by scholars operating within the tradition of historical institutionalism.

As a starting point for bringing causal arguments involving postcommunist cases into dialogue with the critical juncture framework, we first need to clarify concepts and terms. More concretely, we need to acknowledge a lack of agreement across scholars about the meaning and usage of common terms. In particular, three different understandings of the term "legacies" are in use, and differences in the way this concept is employed has, at times, meant that scholars working in different traditions are talking past each other. The mismatch in terminology is consequential because different understandings of the same concept cloud our ability to understand a key component of causal arguments.

Legacies as Effects of Distant Causes

The broadest understanding of "legacies" takes an expansive view of historical arguments, viewing legacies as independent of critical junctures, shocks, or ruptures.

Simpser et al. (2018: 421) advance the idea of a "legacy argument" as one that "describes a source of influence in the past, empirically identifies its causal effect on a contemporary outcome, provides evidence that the hypothesized causal mechanisms are indeed at work across at least one macropolitical regime divide, and attempts to rule out alternative explanations." According to these scholars, "legacy arguments can be explicated without reference to" critical junctures (Simpser et al. 2018: 422). They advocate for a broad understanding of a legacy argument as a way to transcend complementary research traditions that frequently operate in silos. As such, they essentially move "legacies" up Sartori's (1970) ladder of generality, reducing the concept's intension as intimately connected to a critical juncture to thereby increase its extension to a broader range of cases. In doing so, Simpser et al. (2018: 422) identify that three transmission mechanisms—coalitions, institutions, and cognitions—"collectively dominate the field of legacy research." They further note that cognitions and formal institutions can "exist in a relationship of mutual causation" (Simpser et al. 2018: 428), which appears to us as similar to Stinchcombe's (1968: 103) self-replicating causal loop. Simpser et al.'s view of a legacy argument is represented in the causal path diagram in Figure 13.1. Implicit in their understanding of legacy arguments is the idea of causation involving a connection between some variable exerting force in an earlier period on an outcome measured in a later period, which we represent with two boxes. The arrow connecting the two boxes symbolizes the transition mechanisms connecting the historical variable and outcome.

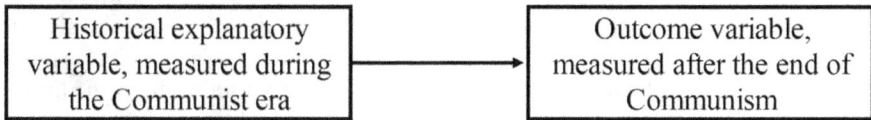

Figure 13.1 Legacies as Effects of Distant Causes

Legacies as Effects of a Distant Cause That Is Resistant to a Shock

A second understanding of "legacies" views them as historical causes that are resistant to a potential critical juncture. In this conception, a legacy is a causal factor that *endures through* a rupture or discontinuity (in this case, the collapse of communism), not one that emerges as a product of a critical juncture. While this understanding of a legacy is less intimately attached to the causal role of a juncture, it nevertheless presumes some form of rupture, exogenous shock, or discontinuity that can reasonably be expected to engender long-term change. In contrast to the understanding of "legacy" in the critical juncture framework, this view of legacies does not necessarily distinguish between the explanatory power of legacies and other antecedent conditions that might precede a rupture and exert causal force on the outcome of interest *independent of* a rupture or shock. In an attempt to clarify the distinction between legacy variables and other historical causes, Wittenberg (2015) suggests that a communist legacy necessarily requires that the phenomenon appeared in both the communist and postcommunist periods. If those criteria are met, and the analyst can identify a credible causal mechanism, then the postcommunist outcome can be called a "legacy" of communism. In common scholarly usage, a communist legacy frequently refers to a feature of communism that persisted through its collapse, and continued to exist in the postcommunist era, with causal effect, such as the weakness (or nonexistence) of independent labor unions. We note that this concept is different from the understanding that a "legacy" of communism has in the context of the critical juncture framework, as the latter denotes a legacy of the rise of communism, while usage among postcommunist scholars more often refers to the "durable causal relationship between past institutions and policies on subsequent beliefs, long beyond the life of the regimes, institutions, and policies that gave birth to them" (Kotkin and Beissinger 2014: 7).

Figure 13.2 represents a causal path diagram depicting this understanding of legacy. This diagram is slightly more nuanced than that depicted in Figure 13.1, demonstrating that the use of "legacy" in this context is further down Sartori's ladder of generality than that of Simpser et al.'s "legacy argument." Yet it, too, is rather general. The first box in the diagram refers to the formal institutions of the communist system, as well as the informal practices that developed in response to these institutions. The second box specifies the end of communism as creating some form of rupture or discontinuity that can reasonably be expected to change the causal course of an outcome of interest. The third box displays the legacy as the continuation of communist-era institutions and practices. The middle box reveals one of the general challenges presented by much of the work invoking communist legacies in the post-communist region: a failure to separate out the end of communism from the initiation of what comes after it. The broader study of legacy variables on postcommunist outcomes regularly conflates the cleavage or shock that precedes a hypothesized critical juncture with the juncture itself. In other words, the end of communism was not determinative of any outcomes that followed it. Rather, it loosened constraints and heightened contingency—albeit to varying degrees across communist successor

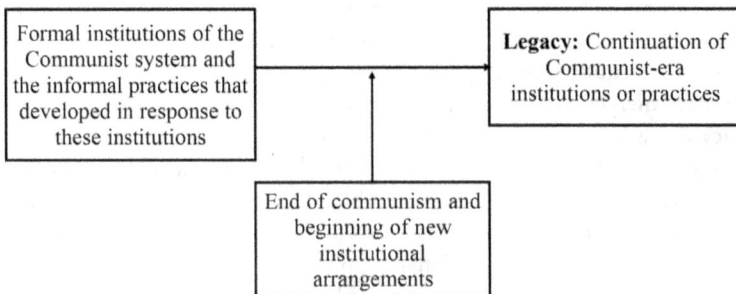

Figure 13.2 Legacies as Effects of a Distant Cause That Is Resistant to a Shock

states—for new institutions and practices to take form. Inattentiveness to the non-determinative relationship between the end of communism and the beginning of what happened after communism limits our ability to aggregate and assess the broad range of findings attributed to so-called legacies of communism.

Legacies as the Persistent Effect of a Critical Juncture

Lastly, the comparative historical tradition commonly defines legacies as the "durable, stable institutions" that emerge from a critical juncture (Collier and Munck 2017: 3). In this view, critical junctures *produce* legacies—and, indeed, the presence of a legacy is a central criterion for determining whether a critical juncture occurred. As Collier and Collier (1991: 30) write, "If the explanatory hypothesis proves to be false—that is, the hypothesized critical juncture did not produce the legacy—then one would assert that it was not, in fact, a critical juncture." For example, the central argument in Collier and Collier's (1991) *Shaping the Political Arena* concerns how different modes of labor incorporation produced distinct patterns of accommodation and conflict between unions, parties, and national regimes. The initial incorporation of the labor movement thus constitutes the critical juncture. The relevant legacy is the new coalitional relationships and party systems that emerged from the incorporation of the labor movement, which stood in sharp contrast to the political coalitions that existed before the critical juncture. In the longer term, these coalitional relationships—institutionalized in the form of party systems—created greater or lesser capacity within each national regime to accommodate new political challenges and avoid or succumb to bureaucratic authoritarianism. This conceptualization of "legacies" demands connection to a critical juncture as a definitional attribute.

Figures 13.3a and 13.3b depict causal path diagrams for a postcommunist outcome using the language and logic of the critical juncture framework. These paths represent a more complex causal relationship than those portrayed in Figures 13.1 and 13.2. The two diagrams share the same conceptual understanding of "legacy," but differ in the values and events depicted in the first three boxes in the diagram. For Figure 13.3a, the antecedent conditions on the left-hand side are the same as those articulated in the first box of Figure 13.2: the formal and informal institutions of communism. The second and third boxes, however, distinguish between the shock of the collapse of formal communist institutions and the *potential* critical juncture that arises when new reforms, coalitions, or other institutional arrangements come into being after the formal institutions of communism are abandoned. We emphasize the word "potential" in this diagram, as the question about whether the period following the collapse of communist institutions comprises a new critical juncture is an empirical one beyond the scope of the current discussion. The fourth box describes the modes by which a legacy of such a potential critical juncture could be reproduced, namely via institutions and cognitions. The final box describes the legacy as enduring institutions and practices that might emerge out of the juncture *after* the collapse of communism. While this figure attempts to demonstrate how a critical juncture argument could be applied to a postcommunist outcome of interest, the legacy depicted in the final box is generally not what postcommunist scholars have in mind when they think of "legacies" that became visible following the end of communism. Rather, thinking back to the path diagram in Figure 13.2, for most scholars of postcommunism, the outcome of interest is the persistence of communist-era institutions or cognitions in spite of the shock or rupture posed by the end of communism.

Figure 13.3b illustrates a causal path that reflects an understanding of the term "communist legacy" that can be shared by both postcommunist scholars and those maintaining fidelity to a critical juncture framework. In this depiction, the antecedent conditions described in the first box are the formal institutions and informal practices present in countries at the time that communist rule was initiated. The cleavage or shock revealed in the second box comprises the specific social and political cleavages that gave rise to communist rule or the imposition of it in the aftermath of war. The potential critical juncture in the third box is the formation of formal communist institutions. As in Figure 13.3a, the modes of reproduction of a potential legacy are institutions and cognitions. Lastly, the legacy in the final box can be described as the continuity of communist practices following the collapse of communist rule.

Figure 13.3b is not simply a longer temporal version of the causal pathway described in Figure 13.3a. Rather, the two diagrams can be viewed as rival hypotheses elaborated through a critical juncture framework to explain outcomes that are mea-

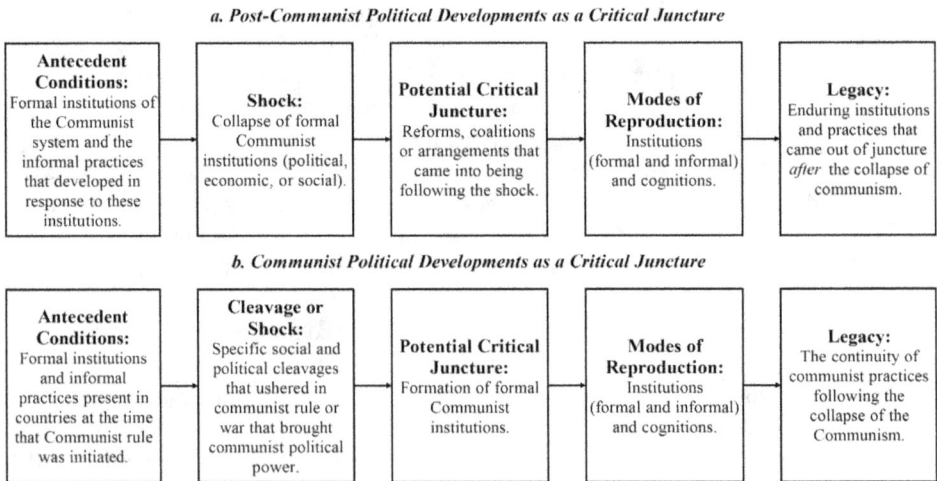

a. Post-Communist Political Developments as a Critical Juncture

| Antecedent Conditions: Formal institutions of the Communist system and the informal practices that developed in response to these institutions. | Shock: Collapse of formal Communist institutions (political, economic, or social). | Potential Critical Juncture: Reforms, coalitions or arrangements that came into being following the shock. | Modes of Reproduction: Institutions (formal and informal) and cognitions. | Legacy: Enduring institutions and practices that came out of juncture *after* the collapse of communism. |

b. Communist Political Developments as a Critical Juncture

| Antecedent Conditions: Formal institutions and informal practices present in countries at the time that Communist rule was initiated. | Cleavage or Shock: Specific social and political cleavages that ushered in communist rule or war that brought communist political power. | Potential Critical Juncture: Formation of formal Communist institutions. | Modes of Reproduction: Institutions (formal and informal) and cognitions. | Legacy: The continuity of communist practices following the collapse of the Communism. |

Figure 13.3 Legacies as the Persistent Effect of Critical Junctures

sured in the postcommunist era. Several differences are apparent between the causal processes depicted in the two figures. Most significantly, the shocks and critical junctures that are hypothesized to produce lasting legacies are quite distinct. In the thirty years that scholars have been studying the aftermath of communism, it has become increasingly apparent that there are a number of outcomes that can be explained with the causal path in Figure 13.3b, speaking to the resilience of legacies that arose from the critical juncture of communism's formation in the region. The number of lasting legacies that can be traced using Figure 13.3a, however, is unclear, in part because we may be too close temporally to when the potential critical juncture took place.

The distinction between the different conceptual understandings of legacies described in Figures 13.1–13.3 is more than semantic; it reflects different judgments about causal processes, the force of antecedent conditions, and the significance of discontinuity or rupture on outcomes, as well as the intersection of structure and agency. Consider, for example, applying the different conceptual approaches to Howard's (2003) influential analysis of the weakness of civil society in postcommunist Europe. Howard attributes the relative weakness of associational life in postcommunist countries to three factors: 1) a legacy of mistrust of organizations carried over from the communist era; 2) the persistence of friendship networks that have substituted the functions often undertaken by civic associations; and 3) disappointment with the postcommunist experience. The empirical analysis on which this argument rests nests both statistical analysis of survey data and extensive in-depth interviews within a cross-case research design, allowing for process tracing to identify and connect causal mechanisms to broader correlational patterns. The structure of Howard's analysis meets the criteria outlined by Simpser et al. to be called a "legacy argument." Yet, because legacy arguments are classified based on relatively general criteria, knowing that Howard is making a "legacy argument" is insufficient for assessing the argument or comparing it to alternate accounts of the weakness of civil society, either in postcommunist Europe or other regions.

The first two of Howard's variables are considered examples of legacies in their standard framing by most postcommunist scholars, as described and depicted in Figure 13.2. Mistrust of institutions and tight, insular friendship networks were features of society that arose in the communist era as a response to conditions specific to the communist experience, yet persisted after the conditions that gave rise to them no longer existed. They may be enduring patterns of thinking or behavior carried over from the communist experience, but would not be accurately described as "legacies" as depicted in Figure 13.3a in accordance with the critical juncture framework. Rather, in accordance with the causal process outlined in Figure 13.3a, mistrust in organizations might be viewed as an antecedent condition that hindered the development of civil society after the rupture of communism's collapse permitted the development of non-state organizations. Similarly, the persistence of friendship networks could be understood as a "constant cause" that weakens social investment in associational life on an ongoing basis. In a rival interpretation, however, Howard's variables of mistrust and the persistence of friendship networks could be viewed as a legacy of communism as represented in Figure 13.3b, having emerged in response to the structure of formal Communist institutions and persisting after the collapse of these institutions. In short, while Howard's dependent variable—the weakness of associational life in postcommunist Europe—is measured after the collapse of communism, his historical independent variables do not appear to be legacies of the end of communism as a critical juncture, although they might qualify as legacies of the arrival of communism as a critical juncture. This is an important distinction because, as Collier and Munck (2017) note, antecedent conditions and constant causes are common sources of rival hypotheses to critical juncture accounts. Thus, in comparative historical analysis, the causal significance of critical junctures is exercised through the legacies they create.

As the example of Howard's analysis suggests, our ability to integrate findings from individual studies—even those that are attentive to the theoretical, methodological, and empirical complexities of historical variables—is limited without shared frameworks for aggregation and evaluation. The limitations are compounded when we consider the broad range of macro-level outcomes for which historical variables are hypothesized to exert a causal force in the region, such as the variation in political regimes and economic systems that arose after communism. This limitation is particularly consequential since "legacies" frequently play the role of a *causal* variable in explanatory frameworks of postcommunist outcomes of interest.

APPLYING THE CRITICAL JUNCTURE FRAMEWORK

With the goal of bringing further clarity to the discussion of postcommunist legacies and developing a strategy for determining whether scholarship is making compatible or competing arguments, it is necessary to identify a common language and framework that we can use to establish a dialogue across works that emphasize a variation of relationships between historical causes and outcomes. We believe the critical juncture framework can provide a valuable analytical tool for this purpose. Within the critical juncture framework, Collier and Munck (2017: 2) define a critical juncture as "(1) a major episode of institutional innovation, (2) occurring in distinct ways, (3) and generating an enduring legacy." This definition provides some conceptual guideposts for identifying a critical juncture, which can be useful in considering the different ways that historical variables might exert causal force. For one, critical junctures are understood as periods of institutional fluidity, when multiple paths of action are open or available. To this end, Mahoney (2000: 513) notes that "[c]ritical junctures are characterized by the adoption of a particular institutional arrangement from among two or more alternatives. These junctures are 'critical' because once a particular option is selected it becomes progressively more difficult to return to the initial point when multiple alternatives were still available." Such moments are preceded by cleavages, which could be between social forces or configurations of empowered elites, or through a macro-scale event that creates a shock (Collier and

Munck 2017). Second, critical junctures are marked by institutional innovation. Finally, the post-juncture step that is necessary for a juncture to be defined as "critical" is the reproduction of an enduring legacy. Once a particular option is selected, it becomes locked in, generating path-dependent outcomes that become increasingly resistant to change. In their words, "no legacy, no critical juncture" (Collier and Munck 2017: 6). In short, within the framework outlined by Collier and Munck, a cleavage or shock triggers the critical juncture.

Collier and Munck (2017) discuss several debates active within the study of critical junctures, some of which are particularly relevant to the study of postcommunist outcomes. First, as Waldner has argued (see Chapter 7), the ontological and empirical attributes assigned to the properties of antecedent conditions and the idea of contingency are often ambiguous. While logically coherent and plausible within the realm of individual studies, the breadth by which these elements of the critical juncture framework have been interpreted and applied varies so extensively as to make meaningful adjudication across macro-historical explanations impossible. As Waldner suggests, in its purest form, a critical juncture is not dependent on specific antecedent conditions. Rather, the critical juncture causes the stable legacy. According to Waldner, one of the challenges we encounter in assessing critical juncture arguments is navigating through the murkiness in specifications of the relationship between the purported antecedent conditions, critical juncture, and legacy. In our view, clarity over the causal force of a legacy is further obscured when the legacy is used to explain another outcome, which frequently occurs in scholarship on postcommunism. Waldner posits four possible scenarios in which antecedent conditions, hypothesized critical junctures, and purported legacies could be related.[2] The process of considering how a causal argument travels along each path can help strengthen the validity of causal claims.

In the first scenario, which Waldner (2018) describes as "the front-door path," antecedent conditions shape a critical juncture, which creates a stable legacy. This path depicts the classic critical juncture account. A second scenario adds what Waldner describes as "the backdoor path," in which an antecedent condition hypothesized to shape a critical juncture actually directly causes the outcome, independent of the purported juncture. In this scenario, antecedent conditions act as rival hypotheses to the critical juncture. In the third scenario, both the "front-door" and the "backdoor" paths are operative, suggesting that the antecedent condition both shapes the critical juncture and directly impacts the outcome of interest. Lastly, it is possible that no direct or indirect relationship between an antecedent condition and a legacy exists, in which case the hypothesized association is spurious. We believe that this approach to considering the logic of causal relationships can help bring greater coherence to the study of historical legacies in the postcommunist region.

---

2. We list the scenarios here in a slightly different order than presented by Waldner (2018).

A second active debate within the study of critical junctures involves identification of mechanisms of production and reproduction, which are frequently underspecified. Collier and Munck (2017: 6) note that while mechanisms of production generate a legacy following a critical juncture, it is mechanisms of reproduction that account for a legacy's stability. Mechanisms of reproduction are self-reinforcing (Collier and Munck 2017: 7) and are distinct from a stable, constant cause that is continuously operative. As such, mechanisms of reproduction are similar to the three levels of analysis we observe legacies operating on in studies of postcommunist outcomes: institutional, attitudinal, and behavioral (LaPorte and Lussier 2011: 646–48). While legacies can operate at any of these levels, the strongest legacies appear to depend on one or more of these mechanisms to endure. Generally speaking, reactive sequences rely on the presence of some form of institutions that incentivize particular behaviors that contribute to a legacy's self-replication. The role of institutions is frequently invoked by causal language that emphasizes increasing returns, stickiness, or lock-in effects. Formal institutions alone rarely engender self-replicating processes, however. Rather, they help facilitate particular attitudinal and behavioral responses to institutional innovations, establishing self-reinforcing patterns of thought and action that are independent from formal institutional structures.[3] In thinking specifically about legacies of communism, the development of the formal political, economic, and social institutions of the communist state in turn fostered a host of micro-level behavioral and attitudinal responses on the part of both elites and citizens. Much of the most interesting work on communist legacies has sought to understand the enduring nature of these attitudinal and behavioral responses to formal institutions that are no longer in existence.

Bearing in mind these considerations, we suggest that the five-step process outlined by Collier and Munck can be drawn upon productively as a framework to consider the causal force of historical variables, the extent to which shocks or cleavages create discontinuity in macro-level political, economic, and social conditions. Employing the five-step process more broadly, not only to validate causal claims about the role of a critical juncture, but also to mediate competing arguments about the extent to which outcomes of interest are constrained or contingent upon historical or contemporaneous processes, may also be fruitful.

To demonstrate how the critical juncture framework could be applied to compare historical causal accounts, it is necessary to shift our discussion from the abstract and apply it to specific scholarly arguments. In the remainder of this section, we draw on three exemplary works of scholarship on postcommunist outcomes that invoke communist-era legacies as a primary part of their causal argument. All three studies under examination are highly regarded among scholars of the postcommunist region, praised

---

3. This latter mechanism is similar to what Simpser et al. call "cognitions."

for their conceptual, theoretical, and empirical rigor, as well as the thoughtful atten-tion they pay to alternative explanations. Moreover, while all three works fit into the canon of work on communist legacies, none cast their arguments as critical juncture accounts. We outline each of the scholarly arguments in terms of the critical juncture framework in an attempt to more clearly understand the varying roles of antecedent conditions, legacies emerging from critical junctures, and rival explanatory factors that shape the outcomes of interest, asking in each instance whether the causal argument made by the scholars depends—even implicitly—on a critical juncture. It is not our intention to explicate the strengths and weaknesses of these specific works, or remark on the validity of the causal claims made by their authors. Rather, the purpose of this exercise is to demonstrate how a critical juncture framework could be applied pro-ductively to consider the relative causal force of historical legacies on postcommunist political outcomes and provide a platform for the findings from this literature to be in closer dialogue with each other and broader comparative historical work. Specifically, we reveal three ways antecedent conditions that came into being prior to or during communism have been rigorously demonstrated to affect postcommunist outcomes, rendering these arguments as simplified causal path diagrams (see Figures 13.4–13.6). In doing so, we are moving from the conceptual discussion of the previous section to an exercise in theoretical reconstruction and clarification that can serve as a starting block for aggregation and integration of work framed around communist legacies.

In the interest of being ontologically and methodologically inclusive in our lan-guage, we have altered box labels in our figures to differ slightly from the Collier-Munck framework with the goal of applying it to broader hypothesis testing. The language "antecedent conditions" remains in the furthest left-hand box, denoting the historical conditions that are hypothesized to obtain at t_0 and exert causal power at a later t_1. The second box is where a *potential* critical juncture is considered. The fourth box is where a *possible* legacy would occur if a critical juncture is present. We add the language "possible" and "potential" to the second box to resist any temptation at post-hoc searching for junctures or legacies that are not actually pres-ent. In the language of the critical juncture framework, the outcome in the fourth box would be a "legacy," if, indeed, a critical juncture created a new, stable institution. In the more general usage of legacies that is often employed independent of critical junctures as described in Figures 13.1 and 13.2, this box is simply the outcome that is measured at some point, t_1, which is after the end of communism. If the role of the possible legacy in the argument is that of a causal variable that affects a further outcome, we add another box for that outcome to the diagram. For simplicity's sake, we are omitting cleavages or shocks from the diagrams in Figures 13.4–13.6, refer-ring the reader instead to the cleavages and shocks elaborated in Figure 13.3. To be clear, the labeling of specific attributes of these arguments as antecedent conditions, potential critical juncture, and possible legacy is ours and is strictly one interpreta-tion of these arguments. The scholars themselves might not share this view of their work.[4] Our goal is to encourage a disciplined dialogue by examining where critical junctures might be present (even implicitly) and the degree to which historical causal relationships rely on them.

Scenario I. Causal Claim with Isolated Front-Door Path

The first example is Wittenberg's (2006) *Crucibles of Political Loyalty: Church Institutions and Electoral Continuity in Hungary*. In this study, Wittenberg exploits within-country variation to thoroughly explicate the path between the antecedent condition of precommunist patterns of political support and his outcome of interest—the persistence of these political loyalties through the upheaval of communism. While Wittenberg does not make direct reference to critical junctures or legacies, *Crucibles of Political Loyalty* is an example of the genre of postcommunist scholarship that invokes historical causes for postcommunist outcomes (consistent with the use of legacies depicted in Figure 13.1). The causal argument in this study hinges on a particular aspect of the communist experience: the generation of localized conflicts between clergy and Communist Party branches. These conflicts—which were a product of the institutionalization of communism—engendered "local church-based social networks" (Wittenberg 2006: 13) that served to transmit the precommunist political loyalties of a subset of the population into the postcommunist era. In other words, political loyalties in the postcommunist era would not have persisted absent the church communities that emerged in response to the rise of communism. Wittenberg describes the pre- and postcommunist political continuity at the center of the study as "path dependent," identifying the socializing experience of participating in these Catholic Church communities as the mechanism of reproduction. Catholicism's insistence on salvation only through the Church emboldened Catholic clergy to engage in opposition to maintain some institutional autonomy from the state, and these local parish communities in turn had a socializing effect on the values (or "cognitions") that are revealed in the continuity between pre- and postcommunist political loyalties.

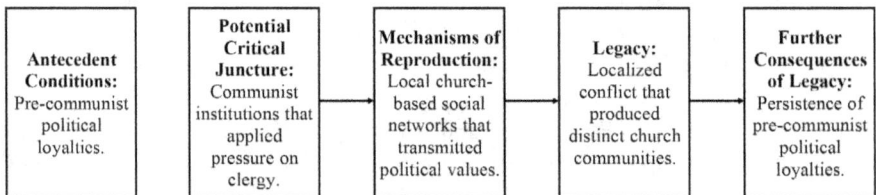

Antecedent Conditions: Pre-communist political loyalties.	Potential Critical Juncture: Communist institutions that applied pressure on clergy.	Mechanisms of Reproduction: Local church-based social networks that transmitted political values.	Legacy: Localized conflict that produced distinct church communities.	Further Consequences of Legacy: Persistence of pre-communist political loyalties.

Figure 13.4 Applying the Critical Juncture Framework to Wittenberg's *Crucibles of Political Loyalty*

---

4. In order to distinguish between the language used specifically by the authors whose work we are citing and our own labels, we have placed language taken directly from their texts in quotation marks.

Is this causal argument dependent on a critical juncture? The answer to this question depends on relatively subjective criteria about the temporal boundaries of the juncture, as well as whether the element that is "critical" has a direct or indirect causal bearing on the outcome being explained. The outcome under investigation in Wittenberg's study is not simply the distribution of partisan support in Hungary's postcommunist elections, but rather the political continuity of loyalties that persist in spite of the major discontinuity of the communist experience. Wittenberg's research question rests on the assumption that such continuity across the transformative experience of communism is puzzling—an assumption most postcommunist scholars would share. The localized conflicts that give rise to semi-autonomous church communities were themselves a legacy of the arrival of Communist institutions. While this legacy operates as an explanatory rather than outcome variable in Wittenberg's study, the arrival of communism as a critical juncture that produces the specific path church communities travel to postcommunism is implied.

This perspective is diagramed in Figure 13.4. Wittenberg employs a multi-method approach that builds on statistical evidence to establish pre- and postcommunist consistency in political loyalties and analysis of archival material to identify and explicate his causal mechanism. This research design effectively demonstrates that the antecedent conditions that are frequently the rival hypotheses in legacy arguments are truly unrelated to the critical juncture that produces the legacy of local church-based networks. This example might be viewed as a "pure" critical juncture argument in which antecedent conditions play no operative role on the critical juncture or the legacy, which, in turn, serves as the explanatory variable for the persistence of political loyalties. The clear separation of antecedent conditions from the legacy closes off the possibility of a "backdoor" path weakening the causal impact of the critical juncture, isolating the causal effect through the "front-door" path.

Scenario II. Causal Claim with Front-Door Path and Measured Backdoor Path

The second example is *Communism's Shadow: Historical Legacies and Contemporary Political Attitudes*, by Pop-Eleches and Tucker (2017). This ambitious work is among the most theoretically rigorous and methodologically self-conscious examples of scholarship on historical legacies in postcommunist societies. The authors' overall premise is to distinguish both conceptually and empirically between "living through communism" and "living in postcommunist countries" to determine which of these phenomena better explains variation in a variety of postcommunist political attitudes. While Pop-Eleches and Tucker do not explicitly define legacies in their work, their usage of the term is consistent with the model of "legacies as effects of a distant cause that is resistant to a shock," described above and diagramed in Figure 13.2. Yet their interest is not in explaining why the legacy exists, but rather measuring it accurately to test its impact as a causal variable on a separate outcome (postcommunist attitudes).

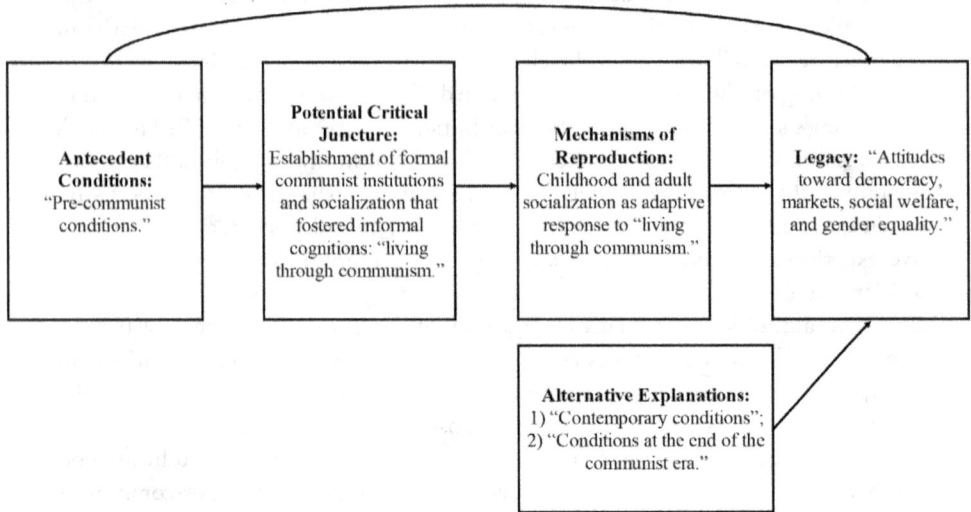

Figure 13.5 Applying the Critical Juncture Framework to Pop-Eleches and Tucker's *Communism's Shadow*

The authors do not make explicit reference to the arrival of communism as a critical juncture that created an enduring legacy of specific institutional, attitudinal, or behavioral effects that shape attitudes after the end of communism. Rather, drawing on the language of experimental research, they consider the process of "living through communism" as a "treatment" that "was of a long and continuous duration" (Pop-Eleches and Tucker 2017: 282). As such, their framing implies that the legacy they are interested in did arise from a critical juncture. The mechanisms of reproduction of this legacy are embedded in the concept of "living through communism," which views both childhood and adult political socialization as part of the embodied experience of all individuals holding political attitudes. In explicating their theoretical argument and testing it empirically, Pop-Eleches and Tucker take into consideration a number of rival hypotheses. One set of alternate explanations involves the effects of antecedent conditions that could shape both the nature of communist rule as well as later attitudes, setting up both front-door and backdoor paths. A second set of explanations considers the socioeconomic and political conditions that were present both at the time of communism's collapse and at the time attitudes were measured. Pop-Eleches and Tucker aim to carefully parse out the differential impact of these potential sources of variation in order to improve measurement of the legacy of living through communism.

Figure 13.5 offers an example of how the argument explicated in *Communism's Shadow* might be elaborated using the critical juncture framework. Pop-Eleches and Tucker take seriously the role of antecedent conditions, measuring both their impact on how "living through communism" itself varied across different countries (the "front-door path"), as well as their potential direct effect on attitudes independent of the critical juncture (the "backdoor path"). While Pop-Eleches and Tucker find support for antecedent conditions and alternative explanations having an independent effect on their outcome, they find strong evidence that the impact of "living through communism" dwarfs the overall effects of other causes. In short, Pop-Eleches and Tucker provide compelling evidence for the strength of communist legacies on postcommunist attitudes, and the persuasiveness of their argument rests heavily on the lengths they take to measure and account for rival explanations and validate their causal claims.

Scenario III: Causal Claim with Two Front-Door Paths

The final example is Grzymała-Busse's (2002) *Redeeming the Communist Past: The Regeneration of Communist Parties in East Central Europe*, which examines the survival of communist parties following the introduction of competitive, democratic elections. In contrast to the previous two examples, Grzymała-Busse's work directly engages two potential critical junctures, both the introduction of communist institutions and the introduction of democratic institutions following the collapse of communism. As such, her analysis is consistent with the understanding of legacy elaborated by linking both parts of Figure 13.3 together. Grzymała-Busse locates the political resources communist parties developed under communist regimes as central to understanding whether they survive democratic competition or die out.

The causal diagram rendered in Figure 13.6 elaborates this complex argument in somewhat simplified form, eliminating a few boxes for ease of presentation. First, we leave out antecedent conditions to the first potential critical juncture as Grzymała-Busse (2002: 24) argues that "the configurations of parties and electorates prior to World War II" had no significant influence on communist parties' "structures and practices" in East-Central Europe. As Figure 13.6 demonstrates, the legacy of the first critical juncture—the formation of communist parties—essentially serves as the antecedent conditions for the second potential critical juncture, the transition from communist to democratic rule.

Figure 13.6 Applying the Critical Juncture Framework to Grzymała-Busse's *Redeeming the Communist Past*

Are both critical junctures essential to this causal argument? Similar to Witten-berg's study of persistent loyalties, Grzymała-Busse's research question of communist successor parties becomes a puzzle to be explained precisely because the demise of communism in East-Central Europe renders the survival of communist parties unexpected. As such, the first critical juncture is explicated fully in her argument, and Grzymała-Busse goes to considerable length to locate the mechanisms of re-production within the communist era as evidence of the legacy of "portable skills" and "usable pasts" that subsequently shaped postcommunist political competition. Yet, because the survival of communist parties would not even be an outcome meriting explanation outside of circumstances of communist collapse, the second critical juncture of introducing new political institutions becomes a necessary, if somewhat implicit part of the argument. The mechanisms of reproduction for the second legacy are similar to the first in that they are concentrated in elite political resources, made manifest primarily in their patterns of behavior and organizational practices. Grzymała-Busse (2002: 58–59) argues that these organizational practices conditioned the critical juncture of transition by determining "the pace of the regime collapse, and the degree to which the transition was negotiated and gradual." Thus, the second legacy depicted in Figure 13.6—the survival of communist parties—is a product of two critical junctures, both of which followed "front-door" paths between the antecedent conditions and the legacy.

DISCUSSION

The elaboration of these three examples highlights both the complexity of commu-nist legacy explanations, as well as the potential contribution of the critical juncture framework for facilitating a clearer dialogue across studies. Table 13.1 summarizes the points of comparison across the three examples just discussed. Several general observations are worth noting. First, all arguments are conditional on a critical juncture producing a stable legacy, even if indirectly. All of these studies place some causal force on variables that originate in the communist era and are at least partly dependent on formal communist structures for shaping their strength and form. The studies by Wittenberg and Grzymała-Busse explore dependent variables that are themselves rooted in the puzzling persistence or survival of partisan attachments that we would have expected to be upended by the discontinuity of communism's arrival or demise. All three examples persuasively demonstrate that the historical relation-ships at the center of their arguments are not spurious.

Nevertheless, our investigation raises valuable questions about the centrality of critical junctures to the ultimate outcome of interest. While it is possible to identify a potential critical juncture in each of these accounts, it is often difficult to pinpoint the boundaries of the juncture. Wittenberg's account is generally not concerned with the institution of communism, but rather with the resolution of local conflicts that emerged as a result of it. If the local conflicts had originated from a different

Table 13.1 Summary of Causal Arguments in Figures 13.4–13.6

Author/Work	Antecedent Conditions	Potential Critical Juncture	Mechanisms of Reproduction	Legacy
Wittenberg (2006)	Precommunist political loyalties	Emergence of communist institutions	Local church-based social networks that transmitted political values	Localized conflicts that produced church communities, which in turn fostered the persistence of precommunist political loyalties
Pop-Eleches and Tucker (2017)	Precommunist conditions	Emergence and continuation of communist institutions	Childhood and adult socialization as adaptive response to "living through communism"	Postcommunist political attitudes
Grzymała-Busse (2002)	L1: Precommunist conditions/L2: elite resources developed under communism	L1: Formation of communist parties/L2: transition to democratic rule	Elite political resources in forms of elite recruitment, policy formation, negotiation	Survival of communist parties

source, would the other elements in Wittenberg's causal argument have changed? The outcome in Grzymała-Busse's study is measured relatively soon after the critical juncture of the introduction of multi-party elections, providing a clearer temporal boundary on the juncture, but also limiting the extent to which we can consider her outcome a stable legacy. Pop-Eleches and Tucker do not conceptualize the arrival of communism as a uniform critical juncture, but rather integrate it into their model as an unfolding process, which itself could vary over time. As such, is it reasonable to consider "living through communism" as the cause of a stable legacy? In short, while communism's arrival is central to all of these arguments, either in the form of producing a stable legacy that, in turn, exerts causal force on another outcome of interest, or in the form of antecedent conditions that shape a later critical juncture, our understanding of its "criticalness" remains rather general and blunt.

Third, it is difficult to separate the potential critical juncture from the mechanisms of causal reproduction. All three of the studies rely to some degree on both institutional mechanisms of reproduction (settlement churches, multi-party systems, schools, and workplaces) as well as attitudinal and behavioral responses to those institutions. In all instances, the causal accounts do not hinge on the arrival or end of communism as a macro-level variable, but rather emphasize the ways in which institutions or patterns of behavior responded to its arrival. In other words, some aspect of what Pop-Eleches and Tucker conceive of as "living through communism," whether in the creation of specific formal institutions or in the development and practice of behavioral adaptations to these institutions, is the mechanism of repro-duction in each of these works.

These examples suggest that while the critical juncture framework can assist in disciplining causal arguments and placing them in dialogue with each other, the boundaries of a critical juncture and the interplay between a macro-political juncture and its more micro-level manifestations would benefit from further theorization, particularly when applied to postcommunist outcomes.

CONCLUSION

As desirable as it might be to attribute specific macro-level political, economic, or social outcomes to a particular pathway taken when communism arrived or collapsed across Eurasia, this chapter has demonstrated that the study of historical legacies in formerly communist countries challenges the idea of a universal critical juncture that explains postcommunist outcomes. Rather, the application of historical legacies as explanatory variables in postcommunist outcomes comprises a broad range of practices. Although a number of excellent studies have advanced our methodologi-cal expectations of the identification work necessary to make a convincing legacy argument, as well as our substantive knowledge of causal processes at work in the region, on the whole, we lack good tools to aggregate, compare, and augment legacy arguments. While not all historical variables become causally relevant only through a critical juncture argument, we believe that the critical juncture framework offers a valuable tool to think through the potential causal paths that might connect tempo-rally distant causes and effects.

The central debate in the study of postcommunist politics is whether contem-porary outcomes have their origins in the communist past or in developments that arose in the 1990s. As we outlined in Figures 13.1–13.3 and in the examples pre-sented in Figures 13.4–13.6, the critical juncture framework can be productively ap-plied by scholars as a tool for more deeply investigating the causal processes at work in a legacy argument. In doing so, the application of the critical juncture framework helps to address a particularly insidious methodological point in work on postcom-munism as well as historical arguments more generally: How to separate out the influence of antecedent conditions versus the causal force of a critical juncture? We suggest that by focusing attention on identification not only of causal mechanisms, but also of antecedent conditions, possible shocks and cleavages, and potential critical junctures, the critical juncture framework helps to outline the problem in a productive way. At the same time, and in the opposite vein, scholars have largely overlooked the interplay between antecedent conditions and the dynamics of critical junctures. The debate is often cast as an either-or proposition—that is, it was either lingering effects of communism or it was the decisions undertaken during the transition that produce these outcomes.

As we show through the examples in Figures 13.4–13.6, by working through the steps of identifying not only the modes of reproduction, but also the antecedent conditions, the potential critical juncture, and possible legacies, analysts can better determine whether the perceived continuities between a historical factor observed at t_0 and an outcome observed at t_1 are: 1) an enduring legacy caused by a critical juncture operating through a "front-door path"; 2) an enduring legacy caused by a critical juncture operating through a "front-door" path in which antecedent conditions also exert independent (though weaker) effects on the legacy; or 3) an enduring legacy caused, sequentially, by two critical junctures. This exercise can also help prevent scholars from falling into post-hoc identification and justification of "critical" junctures that are not actually causal forces at work, but rather a convenient form of periodization (such as the end of communism).

Analyzing several exemplary works of scholarship on postcommunist legacies through the lens of the critical juncture framework offers valuable insights into the study of postcommunist phenomena as well. First, it is clear that communism's shadow—to borrow the phrase of Pop-Eleches and Tucker—stands over a range of attitudes and behaviors that regulate micro-level political, economic, and social outcomes. While the communist-era institutions that engendered specific mechanisms of reproduction of a communist legacy have largely crumbled, the "cognitions" of reproduction have frequently persisted. Moreover, it appears as though the end of communism, in and of itself, did not always create conditions of discontinuity in thought or behavior. Nevertheless, there is evidence that the 1990s served as a potential critical juncture for the development of new institutions that could engender lasting legacies, or combine with cognitions that have persisted through the end of communism to help explain the length and duration of its shadow. Lastly, the frequent identification of individual-level attitudes and behaviors as mechanisms of reproduction for communism's shadow raises important questions about the empirical limitations scholars face in building verifiable causal accounts of communist legacies. It is difficult (if not impossible) to determine when such cognitions became stable across a broad enough cross section of society to be operative as a causal mechanism. As a result, while scholars might have good reason to hypothesize that a causal variable in their explanatory framework is likely a legacy of communism, it might be impossible to verify that empirically.

In closing, walking examples through the steps of a critical juncture framework challenges analysts to make their assumptions transparent. Holding ourselves and others to these standards of rigor will reduce overgeneralizations and allow some of the thoughtful and innovative work being done on communist-era continuities to have a greater impact on the comparative politics canon.

BIBLIOGRAPHY

Bunce, Valerie. 1999. "The Political Economy of Postsocialism." *Slavic Review* 58(4): 756–93.

———. 2003. "Rethinking Recent Democratization: Lessons from the Postcommunist Experience." *World Politics* 55(2): 167–92.

———. 2016. "The Drivers of Diffusion: Comparing 1989, the Color Revolutions, and the Arab Uprisings." In Eitan Y. Alimi, Avraham Sela, and Mario Sznajder (eds.), *Popular Contention, Regime and Transition: Arab Revolts in Comparative Global Perspective* (pp. 115–33). Oxford, UK: Oxford University Press.

Collier, David, and Gerardo L. Munck. 2017. "Building Blocks and Methodological Challenges: A Framework for Studying Critical Junctures." *Qualitative & Multi-Method Research* 15(1): 2–9.

Collier, Ruth Berins, and David Collier. 1991. *Shaping the Political Arena: Critical Junctures, the Labor Movement, and Regime Dynamics in Latin America*. Princeton, NJ: Princeton University Press.

Darden, Keith, and Anna Grzymała-Busse. 2006. "The Great Divide: Literacy, Nationalism, and the Communist Collapse." *World Politics* 59(1): 83–115.

Ekiert, Grzegorz. 2015. "Three Generations of Research on Post Communist Politics—A Sketch." *East European Politics and Societies* 29(2): 323–37.

Fish, M. Steven. 2005. *Democracy Derailed in Russia: The Failure of Open Politics*. New York, NY: Cambridge University Press.

Gaddy, Clifford G., and Barry W. Ickes. 1998. "Russia's Virtual Economy." *Foreign Affairs* 77(5): 53–67.

Gans-Morse, Jordan. 2017. *Property Rights in Post-Soviet Russia: Violence, Corruption, and the Demand for Law*. New York, NY: Cambridge University Press.

Greskovits, Béla. 1998. *The Political Economy of Protest and Patience: East European and Latin American Transformations Compared*. Budapest, Hungary: Central European University Press.

Grzymała-Busse, Anna M. 2002. *Redeeming the Communist Past: The Regeneration of Communist Parties in East Central Europe*. New York, NY: Cambridge University Press.

Hale, Henry E. 2006. *Why Not Parties in Russia? Democracy, Federalism, and the State*. New York, NY: Cambridge University Press.

Hanson, Stephen E. 2017. "The Evolution of Regimes: What Can Twenty-Five Years of Post-Soviet Change Teach Us?" *Perspectives on Politics* 15(2): 317–27.

Howard, Marc Morjé. 2003. *The Weakness of Civil Society in Post-Communist Europe*. New York, NY: Cambridge University Press.

Jowitt, Ken. 1992. *New World Disorder: The Leninist Extinction*. Berkeley, CA: University of California Press.

Kitschelt, Herbert, Zdenka Mansfeldova, Radoslaw Markowski, and Gabor Toka. 1999. *Post-Communist Party Systems: Competition, Representation, and Inter-Party Cooperation*. New York, NY: Cambridge University Press.

Kotkin, Stephen, and Mark R. Beissinger. 2014. "The Historical Legacies of Communism: An Empirical Agenda." In Mark R. Beissinger and Stephen Kotkin (eds.), *Historical Legacies of Communism in Russia and Eastern Europe* (pp. 1–27). New York, NY: Cambridge University Press.

LaPorte, Jody, and Danielle N. Lussier. 2011. "What Is the Leninist Legacy? Assessing Twenty Years of Scholarship." *Slavic Review* 70(3): 637–54.

Levitsky, Steven, and Lucan A. Way. 2010. *Competitive Authoritarianism: Hybrid Regimes after the Cold War.* New York, NY: Cambridge University Press.

Mahoney, James. 2000. "Path Dependence in Historical Sociology." *Theory and Society* 29(4): 507–48.

Orenstein, Mitchell A., and Martine R. Haas. 2005. "Globalization and the Development of Welfare States in Central and Eastern Europe." In Miguel Glatzer and Dietrich Rueschemeyer (eds.), *Globalization and the Future of the Welfare State* (pp. 130–52). Pittsburgh, PA: University of Pittsburgh Press.

Pop-Eleches, Grigore, and Joshua A. Tucker. 2011. "Communist Legacies, and Political Values and Behavior: A Theoretical Framework with an Application to Political Party Trust." *Comparative Politics* 43(4): 379–408.

———. 2017. *Communism's Shadow: Historical Legacies and Contemporary Political Attitudes.* Princeton, NJ: Princeton University Press.

Rohrschneider, Robert, and Stephen Whitefield. 2009. "Understanding Cleavages in Party Systems: Issue Position and Issue Salience in 13 Post-Communist Democracies." *Comparative Political Studies* 42(2): 280–313.

Sartori, Giovanni. 1970. "Concept Misformation in Comparative Politics." *American Political Science Review* 64(4): 1033–53.

Simpser, Alberto, Dan Slater, and Jason Wittenberg. 2018. "Dead but Not Gone: Contemporary Legacies of Communism, Imperialism, and Authoritarianism." *American Review of Political Science* 21: 419–39.

Stark, David, and Lázló Bruszt. 1998. *Postsocialist Pathways: Transforming Politics and Property in East Central Europe.* New York, NY: Cambridge University Press.

Stinchcombe, Arthur L. 1968. *Constructing Social Theories.* New York, NY: Harcourt, Brace, and World.

Waldner, David. 2018. "Critical Junctures and Qualitative Causal Inference." Paper presented at the Annual Meeting of the American Political Science Association, Boston, September 2, 2018.

Wittenberg, Jason. 2006. *Crucibles of Political Loyalty: Church Institutions and Electoral Continuity in Hungary.* New York, NY: Cambridge University Press.

———. 2015. "Conceptualizing Historical Legacies." *East European Politics and Societies and Cultures* 29(2): 366–78.

IV

SUBSTANTIVE APPLICATIONS II

Neoliberalism and Political Parties

14

Temporal Distance, Reactive Sequences, and Institutional Legacies

Reflections on Latin America's Neoliberal Critical Junctures

Kenneth M. Roberts

One of the enduring debates in the study of critical junctures concerns the role of historical hindsight in accounts of institutional change (Collier and Munck 2017). Such debates are perhaps inevitable, as critical juncture approaches do not simply argue that a major institutional change or discontinuity has occurred; they argue that such changes have durable legacies that "lock in" or get reproduced over time (Pierson 2000), differentiating cases that experienced a critical juncture in distinct ways. So conceived, a critical juncture account of institutional change, even where major discontinuities are readily apparent, is necessarily tentative or incomplete in the absence of *some* measure—admittedly ill-defined—of temporal distance to assess longer-term institutional legacies and their patterns of reproduction (Capoccia and Kelemen 2007; Boas Chapter 17; Kaufman Chapter 18).

The dilemma, however, as Tarrow (2017: 9) suggests, is that political "earthquakes" sometimes transpire that raise "the possibility of recognizing critical junctures as they occur." As conceived by Tarrow, these earthquakes—such as a major terrorist attack, acute economic crises, a regime breakdown, the outbreak of civil or international warfare, or massive social protest—may constitute a major break with the past. They can reset the coordinates for political behavior, transform the actors on the political stage, alter the issues and policies under political contestation, and trigger profound, and often immediate, institutional changes. Even when the ultimate institutional legacies of such earthquakes remain indeterminate, political actors may recognize that the game has changed, and a new political era has dawned.

Tarrow's dilemma, and the attendant challenge of identifying and explaining divergent long-term legacies, were paramount in my own work on party system transformations during Latin America's neoliberal critical junctures (Roberts 2014).

Indeed, these challenges largely accounted for multiple rewrites of the manuscript across two decades of fitful research that began with the recognition that a political earthquake had occurred—namely, the collapse of state-led development in the debt crisis of the 1980s. Although I recognized that that earthquake was highly disruptive for traditional party systems in Latin America, I could not fully comprehend its institutional *legacies* across the full range of cases until greater temporal distance provided new forms of analytical leverage.

Greater temporal distance was needed because initial institutional changes and party system configurations produced by the critical juncture of neoliberal reform—the near-universal policy response to the collapse of state-led development—did not necessarily hold. They were not, in other words, enduring, self-reinforcing institutional legacies in a number of countries. As Ruth Berins Collier and David Collier (1991: 37) noted in their path-breaking study of critical junctures, changes introduced during a critical juncture may vary in their levels of institutionalization and stability, in part because a critical juncture "is a polarizing event that produces intense political reactions and counterreactions." Mahoney (2000: 526) suggests that such conflict-induced chains of reactions and counterreactions, or what he labels "reactive sequences," are "marked by backlash processes that can *transform* and perhaps *reverse* early events" (emphasis in the original).[1] Although these sequences "typically give way to more stable final outcomes" that entail "the formation of new institutional patterns," these outcomes can be "far removed from the original critical juncture" (Mahoney 2001b: 114–15). Consequently, as Collier and Collier (1991: 37) argue, "the crystallization of the legacy" of a critical juncture "does not necessarily occur immediately, but rather may consist of a sequence of intervening steps that respond to these reactions and counterreactions."

Such reactive sequences in response to neoliberal reform were not fully anticipated in my initial assessment of Latin America's political earthquake, and their final outcomes, or legacies, were surely unrecognizable during the critical juncture itself. In a number of countries these outcomes only crystallized in response to a series of interconnected events that unfolded in the aftermath period, following the adoption of neoliberal programs of austerity and structural adjustment. Reactive sequences, therefore, weighed heavily on the institutional legacies that I ultimately sought to explain.

How, then, can critical juncture approaches address such political earthquakes and identify the patterns of institutional change they unleash, especially when these earthquakes take place in the recent past? This chapter suggests that an essential

---

1. Collier and Collier (1991) and Mahoney (2001a: 5; 2001b: 115) locate the timing of these reactions and counterreactions at somewhat different points in a critical juncture analysis, but they concur on their basic political logic and transformative effects. Both see reactions as a political backlash against policy and institutional reforms adopted during a critical juncture, and both believe reactive sequences play a major role in the production of institutional legacies.

starting point is the analytical disaggregation of different stages and components of a critical juncture account, some of which are identifiable during the initial earthquake, but others of which unfold sequentially over a longer span of time and are only recognizable with the benefit of at least some historical hindsight. Illustrative examples of such analytical disaggregation are drawn from research on critical junctures in institutional development in Latin America.

DISTINGUISHING CRISES FROM CRITICAL JUNCTURES

I have a feeling we're not in Kansas anymore.
—Dorothy (*The Wizard of Oz*)

Two essential hallmarks distinguish critical junctures from other models of institutional change—namely, the discontinuous character and the enduring quality of the institutional transformations they produce. Major institutional discontinuities, or breaks with the past, differentiate a critical juncture from the more gradual and incremental patterns of change analyzed in the work of Thelen (2004) and Mahoney and Thelen (2010). Enduring institutional legacies, on the other hand, distinguish critical junctures from more fluid patterns of "chronic instability" (Bernhard 2015) or "serial replacement" (Levitsky and Murillo 2014), whereby institutional disruption and change do not produce a new, self-reinforcing institutional equilibrium.

These two defining features endow critical junctures with the basic attributes of a punctuated equilibrium in institutional development (see Krasner 1988; and Chapters 1 and 5 of this volume). In short, they make critical junctures watershed moments or major turning points that demarcate different institutional configurations, or even different political eras. Discontinuity and endurance are, however, analytically distinct components of a process of institutional change, and they are operationally independent of each other. It is their joint occurrence that constitutes a critical juncture; incremental changes, by contrast, tend to be durable but not discontinuous, while serial replacement introduces changes that are often discontinuous but not enduring. Tarrow's dilemma lies in the fact that the joint occurrence of discontinuity and endurance is not necessarily simultaneous. The discontinuity or break with the past may occur prior to the emergence of the new institutional configuration—or equilibrium—that gets reproduced over time. That is especially the case where highly contentious reactive sequences occur during the interval between the point of institutional rupture and the onset of a new equilibration and institutional reproduction.

Such intervals and reactive sequences were clearly present in Collier and Collier's (1991) analysis of labor-incorporating critical junctures during the early stages of industrialization in the first half of the twentieth century in Latin America. In their account, critical junctures were defined by diverse party- and state-led efforts to recognize and legalize labor unions and construct class-based forms of interest intermediation. In all eight of the countries they studied, however, the process of labor incorporation "produced a strong political reaction, and in most countries this reaction culminated in the breakdown of the national political regime under which the incorporation policies had been implemented" (Collier and Collier 1991: 8). These conservative reactions, in turn, produced their own counterreactions such that "the ultimate legacy of incorporation commonly entailed outcomes quite divergent from the goals of the leaders of the original incorporation period" (Collier and Collier 1991: 8). In a number of cases, significant time intervals elapsed—what they characterized as an "aftermath" period—between the end of the incorporation process and the onset of the institutional "heritage" (Collier and Collier 1991: 752–53).

Since Collier and Collier wrote their book nearly half a century (or more, depending on the case) following the critical junctures they studied, they benefited from a substantial degree of temporal distance to analyze what transpired in those reactive sequences and to assess their longer-term effects. The historical hindsight afforded by this temporal distance was surely integral to their ability to identify and explain the institutional legacies of critical junctures spawned by the onset of mass politics in Latin America.

Both substantively and methodologically, my own book (Roberts 2014) built explicitly on the foundations laid by Collier and Collier in an effort to explain the party system effects of Latin America's tumultuous, crisis-strewn transition from state-led development to market liberalism during the waning decades of the twentieth century. The starting point for my research was the recognition that the institutional legacies of the labor-incorporating critical junctures studied by Collier and Collier—including classical populism, corporatism, and import substitution industrialization—had run their course and been eclipsed by a new era whose defining features were political and economic liberalism. My research sought to explain how the debt crisis and market-based structural adjustment policies in the 1980s and 1990s had undermined the labor-based modes of political representation studied by Collier and Collier, thoroughly transforming party systems in the region. This economic transition, I argued, generated a new critical juncture that realigned Latin America's social, economic, and political fields.

Briefly stated, my central argument was that the crisis-induced transition from state-led development to market liberalism programmatically aligned and stabilized party systems where market reforms were imposed by conservative political actors and resisted by a major party of the left in opposition. By contrast, this transition de-aligned and destabilized those countries where structural adjustment policies were adopted by traditional center-left or labor-based populist parties. Under this latter, de-aligning pattern, party systems converged around variants of market liberalism that left them highly susceptible to destabilizing reactive sequences as societal resistance to market orthodoxy intensified in the post-adjustment era. This societal resistance found expression in extra-systemic outlets, given that institutional channels in established party systems were lacking. These outlets ranged from mass social protest to mass electoral protest, culminating in the demise of mainstream party systems and the rise of new left-populist or "movement" parties.

That argument, however, was hardly present—and perhaps not imaginable—when I first began work on this project in the mid-1990s. It only emerged through a series of false starts, missteps, and detours as I sought to understand divergent political reactions and counterreactions to the market liberalization process. Indeed, the argument required that I think more systematically about strategic choices to support and oppose market reforms, and the impact of these choices on the alignment or de-alignment of national party systems. In the end, it took me the better part of two decades to publish the book, given the challenges of identifying generalizable sequences and causal processes across a wide range of national experiences.

The primary stumbling block I faced was, in fact, Tarrow's dilemma, as I began research when it was clear that the old order had broken down in much of the region, but the new order was still in gestation. The Collier and Collier volume was published at the apogee of the so-called "Washington Consensus" in Latin America (Williamson 1990), at a time when every country in the region had responded to the debt crisis by initiating ambitious market reform programs. When I first read their book, labor movements had been dramatically weakened by economic crises, market restructuring, and (in some cases) military repression, while labor-based parties were in retreat or climbing aboard the neoliberal bandwagon. In that context, I had little doubt that the political heritage bequeathed by the process of labor incorporation had been eclipsed across the region. The debt crisis, as I saw it, was a political earthquake that broke with the past—a watershed moment of economic upheaval that shifted Latin America's political coordinates and inaugurated a new political era.

As Tarrow put it, I had recognized a critical juncture while it was happening—or, at least, so I thought. In reality, I was about to discover that it is much easier to recognize that the old order has been broken—i.e., that discontinuity has occurred—than it is to identify the new order that replaces it. Even harder is explaining how that new order came to be—what Collier and Collier (1991: 30–31, 37) call the "mechanisms of production" that configure the new institutional order and generate its legacy. Neither the *genesis* of this new order nor its *reproduction* over time could be explained with the analytical tools I employed at the outset of the project.

To identify such mechanisms of production, it was essential to make an analytical distinction between the *crisis*—i.e., the collapse of state-led development in the debt crisis of the 1980s—and the *critical juncture* of neoliberal reform. As David Collier (see Chapter 1) warns, there is a danger in conflating the cleavage, shock, or crisis that *triggers* a critical juncture with the critical juncture itself. Whereas the former may be attributable to deep structural strains or even exogenous forces (such as an international financial shock), the latter involves "an episode of institutional innovation," and therefore important elements of political agency, choice, and contingency. Although a shock or crisis may thoroughly disrupt an established institutional order and preclude its reproduction, it does not on its own generate the institutional innovation. As Kaufman (2017: 16) aptly notes, "not all crises . . . necessarily constitute critical junctures." The shock or crisis alone cannot provide a full account of institutional discontinuity, as discontinuity involves both a break with the past and a transition to something new.

The dangers of conflation were readily apparent in my initial efforts to explain how the combination of an exogenous shock (the international debt crisis) and endogenous strain (the exhaustion of import substitution industrialization) posed severe threats to party systems embedded in Latin America's state-centric matrix of development. Following the basic logic of retrospective voting models (Fiorina 1981; Lewis-Beck 1990; Roberts and Wibbels 1999), I assumed that more disruptive and destabilizing party system effects were largely a function of the severity of economic crises. Via backwards induction, I then attributed cross-national variation in the severity of economic crises to distinct "antecedent conditions" that were in place prior to the onset of the debt crisis—namely, the differences between "elitist" and "labor-mobilizing" party systems and the broader developmental matrices in which they were embedded. Simply put, more severe economic crises and political turmoil occurred in countries with labor-mobilizing party systems and ambitious state-led development models. I thus saw the collapse of state-led development as leading to the demise of labor-based modes of political representation and the revival of elitist or oligarchic forms of political domination (Roberts 2002).

Consequently, in my initial account, party system upheaval during the period of economic crisis and reform was largely predetermined by what existed beforehand. Strategic choices and political alignments regarding policy and institutional reforms during the transition period played little or no explanatory role. Indeed, I failed to identify anything that was really "critical" about the "juncture" itself that was decisive for explaining party system outcomes; the locus of causal attribution, so to speak, lay in the distant past. Institutional discontinuities—a break with the past—were surely recognizable during this period of upheaval, but what I thought of as a critical juncture did not yet have the analytical structure of a critical juncture account.

That analytical structure only developed as I struggled to understand dynamics of party system change that could not be accounted for by antecedent properties and the relative severity of economic crises—explanatory factors that left behind a high degree of unexplained variance in party system outcomes. Party system dynamics, in fact, were heavily conditioned by the strategic choices and alignments of political actors as they managed economic crises and imposed ambitious neoliberal structural adjustment policies on often reluctant societies. By analytically separating the critical juncture of policy and institutional reform from the crisis that brought it on, it became evident that what happened *in the juncture itself* was critical for understanding what came next. As seen below, the basic distinction between the crisis and the critical juncture was essential for providing analytical leverage to understand political reactions and counterreactions to the market reform process, as well as the impact of those reactive sequences on longer-term institutional legacies.

REACTIVE SEQUENCES AND THE PRODUCTION
OF INSTITUTIONAL LEGACIES

The crisis consists precisely in the fact that the old is dying and the new cannot be born; in the interregnum a great variety of morbid symptoms appears.

—Antonio Gramsci (1971: 276).

In the recent Latin American experience, some of the most important institutional changes in party systems played out not during the crisis-induced critical juncture of structural adjustment, but rather in the aftermath or post-adjustment period. These changes were, in essence, delayed effects that were only identifiable with a measure of temporal distance from the critical juncture itself. They were, however, heavily conditioned by divergent political alignments within national critical junctures. The delayed effects only unfolded when societal resistance to market liberalization strengthened—in the classic Polanyian sense (Polanyi 1944)—and Latin America began to "turn left" politically at the turn of the century. Divergent institutional trajectories—the legacies of these critical junctures—were not fully identifiable, therefore, until the region had gone through a series of "reactive sequences" in the early aftermath period that were driven by this societal resistance to market orthodoxy. Only with this greater temporal distance was it possible to chart the full range of variation on the outcome of interest—party system transformation—and develop a causal explanation that was not severely truncated.

By affording opportunities to observe reactive sequences, this greater temporal distance also shifted the locus of causal attribution in my theoretical argument. Cross-national comparisons suggested that the strength and character of reactive sequences were influenced but not predetermined by antecedent properties; they were, instead, heavily conditioned by political alignments around the process of structural adjustment *during* the critical juncture itself. "Critical antecedents" may have predisposed cases to experience the critical juncture in particular ways (Slater and Simmons 2010), but an important element of political contingency—the configuration of political actors in support of and opposition to the market reform process—was decisive for understanding the impact of critical junctures on institutional change. It was these alignments that made the juncture truly critical, even where its effects were delayed and its institutional outcomes were only identifiable in the aftermath period. In the framework introduced by Riedl and Roberts in Chapter 6, Latin America's neoliberal critical junctures had both "activating" and "generative" components, and the balance between these components varied across cases.

What was it about these alignments, then, that made them so crucial for shaping the reactive sequences of the post-adjustment era? Structural adjustment either aligned or de-aligned party systems programmatically, depending on whether conservative actors directed the process of market reform and whether a major party of the left was available to channel societal resistance to market orthodoxy. This societal resistance strengthened as Latin American economies stabilized, defeated hyperinflationary pressures, and entered the post-adjustment era by the latter half of the 1990s (Yashar 2005; Silva 2009). As Mahoney states (2001b: 115): "Actor resistance to prevailing institutions is often the initial force that launches a reactive sequence." Indeed, where institutions persist "by virtue of the support of a small elite, reactive sequences may be launched when subordinate groups mobilize against the established arrangements."

Such patterns of mobilization by subordinate groups opposed to market orthodoxy weighed heavily on political dynamics in the aftermath or post-adjustment period, shaping and reshaping the institutional legacies of neoliberal critical junctures. This mobilization, however, played out differently in party systems that had been aligned or de-aligned during the critical juncture of market reform. Reactive sequences were moderated where conservative-led reforms aligned party systems programmatically, stabilized partisan competition, and channeled societal resistance toward institutionalized leftist parties. In countries like Brazil, Chile, and Uruguay, these parties strengthened and won national elections in the post-adjustment era, leading to relatively moderate "left turns" and institutionalized democratic alternations in office (see Figure 14.1). Critical junctures that aligned party systems programmatically, therefore, generated relatively stable institutional equilibria at an early stage of the process, with durable legacies for the post-adjustment era. Indeed, they had many of the attributes of Mahoney's (2000: 508) path-dependent, "self-reinforcing sequences" characterized by "the formation and long-term reproduction of a given institutional pattern." Subtle shifts in the electoral balance among rival parties naturally occurred across election cycles, but the major actors remained in place for a generation to come.

	Cases	
	Brazil, Chile, Uruguay	Venezuela, Ecuador, Bolivia, Argentina
Critical Juncture	*Aligning*	*De-aligning*
	Conservative-led neoliberal reforms	Neoliberal reforms adopted by populist or center-left parties
	Major party of the left in opposition	No major party of the left in opposition
	↓	↓
Reactive Sequences	Electoral strengthening of established left party	Mass social and electoral protest
		Partial or complete party system breakdown
	Stabilize partisan competition along left–right axis	Rise of new populist or movement alternative on left flank of party system
	↓	↓
Institutional Legacies	Moderate left turn;	Radical left turn;
	Institutionalized partisan competition, alternation in office	Restructuring of programmatic competition along a populist/anti-populist cleavage, asymmetrical rebuilding of party system

Figure 14.1 Neoliberal Critical Junctures in Latin American Party Systems

In countries like Venezuela, Ecuador, Bolivia, and Argentina, however, where traditional center-left or populist parties implemented structural adjustment policies, the critical juncture de-aligned party systems programmatically. In so doing, it made them vulnerable to highly disruptive reactive sequences driven by social and electoral protest against market orthodoxy, culminating in the partial or complete collapse of traditional party systems and the rise of more radical alternatives on their left flank. Programmatically de-aligned party systems, therefore, were an unstable institutional equilibrium in the post-adjustment era, one that was predicated on the ongoing political fragmentation and demobilization of popular sectors. The social and political mobilization of these sectors in the aftermath period generated powerful reactive sequences that broke down, transformed, and at least partially reconstituted representative institutions around a new central sociopolitical cleavage. These cleavages restructured partisan and programmatic competition, with a major left-of-center party forged by populist figures in Venezuela and Ecuador, mass movements in Bolivia, and leftist currents within Argentine Peronism facing off against organizationally fluid center-right blocs. Reactive sequences in the aftermath period thus transformed party systems and produced more polarized institutional legacies that were very different from the initial outcomes of the critical junctures themselves, when mainstream parties had all converged around variants of neoliberal orthodoxy.

In short, reactive sequences produced electoral shifts to the left across much of Latin America in the aftermath period, but they spawned very different types of "left turns" in aligned and de-aligned party systems. Notably, these reactive sequences of the post-adjustment era were analogous to those analyzed by Collier and Collier (1991) in the aftermath of labor incorporation, but they pushed in the opposite direction. Where labor-incorporating critical junctures pushed political systems to the left, reactive sequences were triggered by right-wing actors who pulled political systems back in a more conservative direction. In my study, by contrast, critical junctures entailed the political exclusion or marginalization of labor and popular sectors, moving politics in a rightward direction. Reactive sequences, therefore, involved a rearticulation of popular sectors—albeit with organized labor playing a diminished role—and a strengthening of new or established leftist alternatives, depending on the alignment or de-alignment of party systems around the process of market liberalization.

In some ways, it might have been more consistent with Collier and Collier's (1991) analysis to treat the turn of the century "left turn" and its reincorporation of popular sectors as the new critical juncture (see Rossi 2015, 2017; Silva and Rossi 2018). The conditioning of this "left turn" and the reactive sequences that produced it by political alignments during the process of market reform, however, led me to identify this earlier period as the decisive juncture for the break with the past and the onset of new, path-dependent patterns of institutional change. In other respects, my analysis closely paralleled that of Collier and Collier. In particular, both of our works saw reactive sequences to critical junctures as being integral to the structuring of party systems along a left–right axis of programmatic contestation that cleaved elite and popular blocs—in my case, following the neoliberal convergence of the late twentieth century. The (re)construction of that axis, or sociopolitical cleavage, was the most important institutional legacy of neoliberal critical junctures, and to date it has endured even as the "left turn" faded and conservative actors returned to the forefront across much of the region.

In my work, that reconstruction occurred—albeit belatedly—even in the cases of party system de-alignment that exited the critical juncture with unstable institutional equilibria.[2] In the cases of programmatic alignment, the central axis crystallized in Uruguay and Chile by the late 1980s and in Brazil by the mid-1990s; by contrast, in the cases of de-alignment, it took the popular mobilizations and reactive sequences of the late 1990s and early 2000s to reconstruct a central axis in Venezuela, Argentina, Bolivia, and Ecuador. In these latter cases, Boas's (2017: 20) hypothesis that "populist vs. anti-populist cleavages might emerge out of unstable equilibria" is fully consistent with my own account of how reactive sequences pushed back against the initial post-adjustment political order and produced the longer-term institutional legacies of neoliberal critical junctures. My account thus relies heavily on two basic insights from Collier and Collier (1991: 37) and Mahoney (2001b: 114–15) regarding the institutional legacies of critical junctures: (1) the understanding that institutional legacies do not necessarily crystallize during the critical juncture itself; rather, it may take a series of intervening steps or reactive sequences *conditioned* by the critical juncture to produce them, and (2) the recognition that these long-term institutional legacies may depart significantly from the initial institutional order bequeathed by the critical juncture.

Clearly, some measure of temporal distance is required to identify reactive sequences and assess their impact on institutional production and reproduction. The question remains, however, whether sufficient temporal leverage exists—not to mention adequate levels of institutional reproduction—to identify institutional legacies in contemporary Latin America that are attributable to neoliberal critical junctures (Capoccia and Kelemen 2007: 360–63; Boas Chapter 17; Kaufman Chapter 18). In the absence of such legacies, there is no basis to claim that the regionwide transition to neoliberalism in the 1980s constituted a new critical juncture in Latin America's political development. Instead, that transition could be treated as a temporary disruption or deviation, or perhaps as the onset of a "long-term disequilibrium, where old behaviors have changed, but no stable new patterns have emerged" (Kaufman 2017: 29).

Collier and Collier (1991: 34) recognized that the institutional legacies of critical junctures vary considerably in their stability and duration, with some critical junctures producing "a political dynamic that prevents or mitigates against stable

---

2. Peru was the primary exception with its fluid pattern of serial populism, rather than the more polarizing forms of left-wing populism that reconstructed a central sociopolitical cleavage in countries like Venezuela, Bolivia, Ecuador, and Argentina.

patterns." Nevertheless, the competitive axes and institutional legacies identified above have demonstrated a relatively high degree of resiliency in Latin America, especially in comparison to the region's turbulent recent past. Corruption scandals, new episodes of financial crises, and internal partisan factional divisions have surely taken their toll and exerted corrosive effects on contemporary party systems. They have not, however, erased the central sociopolitical cleavages between major center-left parties and their conservative rivals that have structured democratic contestation in Chile, Uruguay, and Brazil for a quarter of a century or more. Neither have they erased the central cleavages between left-populist or movement parties and their center-right opponents in Venezuela, Bolivia, Ecuador, and Argentina—alignments that are now well into their second decade. Leadership successions, divisions, and alternations in office will inevitably occur, but it is difficult to envision new political orders emerging anytime soon—whether democratic or authoritarian—that are not structured by a central cleavage between supporters and opponents of *Chavismo* in Venezuela or the MAS (Movement Towards Socialism) in Bolivia. As I argued in my book (Roberts 2014: 264), the reactive sequences that spawned Chávez's populist project in Venezuela created "a profound sociopolitical cleavage that is likely to be a durable axis of competition whether or not *Chavismo* holds onto power, much like the cleavages forged by Peronism in Argentina and *Sandinismo* in Nicaragua." The same can surely be said of Bolivia, given the deep roots of the MAS in mass social movements that triggered the reactive sequences of the early 2000s (Anria 2018).

In short, where neoliberal critical junctures did not institutionalize a left–right sociopolitical cleavage in the party system, reactive sequences in the post-adjustment era tended to construct such a cleavage in a more polarizing and sometimes less organized form—but not necessarily a less durable form. New forms of party-building were arguably less prevalent in neoliberal critical junctures than they were in the earlier, labor-incorporating critical junctures studied by Collier and Collier (1991). Where traditional party systems broke down during neoliberal critical junctures or their aftermath periods, rebuilding was often an asymmetrical process, occurring on one side of the cleavage—typically the more "popular" or left side of the divide, with the exception of Peru—before the other.

As Levitsky et al. (2016: 8–21) suggest, however, political polarization and conflict are often the inspiration and the foundation for successful party-building projects. It follows, then, that highly polarizing reactive sequences in the aftermath of neoliberal reforms eventually culminated in party-building processes in the cases outlined above. The sequential timing and organizational expression of the cleavage construction process may have varied across cases, but it was a consistent overarching pattern in response to the breakdown of the neoliberal policy consensus in the post-adjustment era. The polarized institutional legacies produced by reactive sequences, however, were not fully identifiable in the midst of the critical juncture itself; they required a measure of temporal distance to be accounted for theoretically.

CONCLUSION: EMPLOYING CRITICAL JUNCTURES APPROACHES

Critical junctures produce institutional changes that are discontinuous and durable. A principal challenge faced by scholars who study critical junctures, however, is that the legacies of these institutional changes do not necessarily crystallize in the short term. Scholars can often recognize that an old order has broken down or been eclipsed before they can identify, much less explain across a range of similarly situated cases, what has taken its place. It is, then, intrinsically difficult, if not impossible, to develop a complete critical juncture argument in the midst of the juncture itself.

Although a measure of temporal distance is required to fully account for the institutional legacies of critical junctures, it may still be possible for scholars to employ insights from the analytical toolkit of critical juncture approaches to assess watershed periods of institutional change whose legacies are still on the horizon. This toolkit, in other words, need not be restricted to analyses of the distant past. Recent institutional "shocks" are intrinsically interesting and important for scholars to study, and critical juncture approaches provide analytical tools to conceptualize their antecedent or baseline conditions, identify the exogenous or endogenous strains that disrupt the established order, and examine patterns of change and continuity in institutional forms. The toolkit is especially useful for analyzing the strategic behavior and choices of actors around contested processes of policy or institutional reform. It may also be capable of sketching alternative institutional scenarios or pathways that could logically unfold in the aftermath period.

As this chapter suggests, an essential starting point is to analytically distinguish the crisis or shock that triggers a critical juncture from the policy and institutional changes that mark the juncture as critical. A crisis or shock may disrupt the old order, but it is major policy or institutional change that establishes the "break point" for institutional discontinuity. This initial component of a critical juncture approach is amenable to contemporaneous recognition and analysis, particularly regarding the strategic alignments, behavior, and decision-making processes of key actors who introduce or resist major policy and institutional reforms.

If institutional discontinuity is identifiable in the short term, however, the durability of new institutional configurations, by definition, is not. Indeed, as Collier and Collier (1991) and Mahoney (2000, 2001a, 2001b) suggest, the initial institutional "outcomes" of a critical juncture do not necessarily persist over time. Some critical junctures implant new institutional forms that lock in and reproduce themselves by means of self-reinforcing or increasing returns processes. Such institutional forms *could* be identifiable in the midst of a critical juncture, but their reproduction over time and the mechanisms that account for them would require greater temporal distance to assess.

More problematic, however, are cases in which initial institutional outcomes generate complex reactive sequences in an aftermath period, including the mobilization of social and political actors opposed to the new institutional order. These reactive sequences are conditioned by critical junctures, but they are capable of altering or redirecting the institutional pathways that emerge from those junctures. In so doing, they produce institutional legacies that may diverge sharply from those in place at the end of the critical juncture itself.

Such legacies cannot be examined empirically without a measure of temporal distance from the critical juncture. Even in the absence of historical hindsight, however, the critical juncture toolkit may help a scholar anticipate the possibility—indeed, the probability—of future political backlashes and theorize the potential actors and conflicts that are most likely to generate reactive sequences. In so doing, it may be possible to compare and contrast the short-term institutional outcomes of different cases that experience a critical juncture and assess their relative susceptibility to disruptive reactive sequences in an aftermath period. There may be reasons, for example, to believe that some institutional arrangements are more likely to spawn organized resistance than others, or that some new institutional equilibria are more solidly grounded and resilient in the face of future challenges than others. A critical juncture approach, therefore, could help to generate working hypotheses that structure the analysis of reactive sequences and institutional change or reproduction in the aftermath period.

In short, critical juncture approaches provide analytic tools for assessing the political consequences of Tarrow's earthquakes—even where they have only recently occurred—so long as the analyst is cognizant of these tools' limitations. In the absence of temporal distance, critical juncture approaches can fruitfully analyze institutional discontinuity, but not the reactive sequences and long-term legacies that it produces. It is precisely this discontinuity, however—a sharp break with the past—that distinguishes a critical juncture from more incremental forms of institutional change (Thelen 2004; Mahoney and Thelen 2010; see also Chapter 6 of this volume). Models of the latter are undoubtedly appropriate for explaining many patterns of institutional change that involve the layering of new rules on top of the old, adjustments in the application of existing rules, or even the progressive displacement of old rules by new ones (see Mahoney and Thelen 2010: 16–17). These types of incremental change, however, are different from those that are abrupt and dramatic—what Mahoney and Thelen (2010: 16) characterize as the "rapid, sudden breakdown of institutions and their replacement with new ones."

Such patterns of breakdown and replacement in temporally constrained periods are the hallmarks of critical junctures, and their dynamics are best understood through the analytical lens of a critical juncture approach. Incremental models of change could be usefully applied to the study of party system adaptation during the transition to neoliberalism in a number of Latin American countries at the "low" end of systemic change, such as in Honduras, Paraguay, and Uruguay. They would provide little analytical leverage to explain what happened in the "earthquake" cases like Venezuela, Bolivia, and Ecuador, however, where systemic breakdowns and replacements occurred not only at the level of party systems, but also at the level of national political regimes.

A critical juncture approach not only sheds light on such patterns of breakdown and replacement, but may also provide insights as to why the regionwide economic transition generated more disruptive political shocks in some countries than in others. In short, it may help to explain why some countries experienced only incremental changes in party systems, whereas others were traumatized by the breakdown and re-founding of entire political orders. When studying a wide range of cases subjected to similar environmental challenges, therefore, it may be counterproductive to treat incrementalist and critical juncture approaches as rival or mutually exclusive models of institutional change; scholars would do well to consider how they may complement and mutually enrich each other by identifying the conditions and causal mechanisms associated with distinct patterns of change.

BIBLIOGRAPHY

Anria, Santiago. 2018. *Movements, Party, and Power: The Bolivian MAS in Comparative Perspective.* New York, NY: Cambridge University Press.

Bernhard, Michael. 2015. "Chronic Instability and the Limits of Path Dependence." *Perspectives on Politics* 13(4): 976–91.

Boas, Taylor C. 2017. "Potential Mistakes, Plausible Options: Establishing the Legacy of Hypothesized Critical Junctures." *Qualitative and Multi-Method Research* 15(1): 18–20.

Capoccia, Giovanni, and R. Daniel Kelemen. 2007. "The Study of Critical Junctures: Theory, Narrative, and Counterfactuals in Historical Institutionalism." *World Politics* 59(3): 341–69.

Collier, David, and Gerardo L. Munck. 2017. "Building Blocks and Methodological Challenges: A Framework for Studying Critical Junctures." *Qualitative and Multi-Method Research* 15(1): 2–9.

Collier, Ruth Berins, and David Collier. 1991. *Shaping the Political Arena: Critical Junctures, the Labor Movement and Regime Dynamics in Latin America.* Princeton, NJ: Princeton University Press.

Fiorina, Morris P. 1981. *Retrospective Voting in American National Elections.* New Haven, CT: Yale University Press.

Gramsci, Antonio. 1971. *Selections from the Prison Notebooks of Antonio Gramsci,* edited by Quintin Hoare and Geoffrey Nowell Smith. New York, NY: International Publishers.

Kaufman, Robert R. 2017. "Great Transformations but no Critical Junctures? Latin America in the Twenty-First Century." *Qualitative & Multi-Method Research* 15(1): 16–17.

Krasner, Stephen D. 1988. "Sovereignty: An Institutional Perspective." *Comparative Political Studies* 21(1): 66–94.

Levitsky, Steven, James Loxton, and Brandon Van Dyck. 2016. "Introduction: Challenges of Party-Building in Latin America." In Steven Levitsky, James Loxton, Brandon Van Dyck, and Jorge I. Domínguez (eds.), *Challenges of Party-Building in Latin America* (pp. 1–48). New York, NY: Cambridge University Press.

Levitsky, Steven, and María Victoria Murillo. 2014. "Building Institutions on Weak Foundations: Lessons from Latin America." In Daniel Brinks, Marcelo Leiras, and Scott Mainwaring (eds.), *Reflections on Uneven Democracies: The Legacy of Guillermo O'Donnell* (pp. 189–213). Baltimore, MD: Johns Hopkins University Press.

Lewis-Beck, Michael S. 1990. *Economics and Elections: The Major Western Democracies.* Ann Arbor, MI: University of Michigan Press.

Mahoney, James. 2000. "Path Dependence in Historical Sociology." *Theory and Society* 29(4): 507–48.

———. 2001a. *The Legacies of Liberalism: Path Dependence and Political Regimes in Central America.* Baltimore, MD: Johns Hopkins University Press.

———. 2001b. "Path-Dependent Explanations of Regime Change: Central America in Comparative Perspective." *Studies in Comparative International Development* 36(1): 111–41.

Mahoney, James, and Kathleen Thelen. 2010. "A Theory of Gradual Institutional Change." In James Mahoney and Kathleen Thelen (eds.), *Explaining Institutional Change: Ambiguity, Agency, and Power* (pp. 1–37). New York, NY: Cambridge University Press.

Pierson, Paul, 2000. "Increasing Returns, Path Dependence, and the Study of Politics." *American Political Science Review* 94(2): 251–67.

Polanyi, Karl. 1944. *The Great Transformation: The Political and Economic Origins of Our Time.* New York, NY: Farrar and Rinehart.

Roberts, Kenneth M. 2002. "Social Inequalities without Class Cleavages: Party Systems and Labor Movements in Latin America's Neoliberal Era." *Studies in Comparative International Development* 36(4): 3–33.

———. 2014. *Changing Course in Latin America: Party Systems in the Neoliberal Era.* New York, NY: Cambridge University Press.

Roberts, Kenneth M., and Erik Wibbels. 1999. "Party Systems and Electoral Volatility in Latin America: A Test of Economic, Institutional, and Structural Explanations." *American Political Science Review* 93(3): 575–90.

Rossi, Federico. M. 2015. "The Second Wave of Incorporation in Latin America: A Conceptualization of the Quest for Inclusion Applied to Argentina." *Latin American Politics and Society* 57(1): 1–28.

———. 2017. *The Poor's Struggle for Political Incorporation: The Piquetero Movement in Argentina.* New York, NY: Cambridge University Press.

Silva, Eduardo. 2009. *Challenging Neoliberalism in Latin America.* New York, NY: Cambridge University Press.

Silva, Eduardo, and Federico M. Rossi (eds.). 2018. *Reshaping the Political Arena in Latin America: From Resisting Neoliberalism to the Second Incorporation.* Pittsburgh, PA: University of Pittsburgh Press.

Slater, Dan, and Erica Simmons. 2010. "Informative Regress: Critical Antecedents in Comparative Politics." *Comparative Political Studies* 43(7): 886–917.

Tarrow, Sidney. 2017. "The World Changed Today! Can We Recognize Critical Junctures When We See Them?" *Qualitative and Multi-Method Research* 15(1): 9–11.

Thelen, Kathleen. 2004. *How Institutions Evolve: The Political Economy of Skills in Germany, Britain, the United States, and Japan.* New York, NY: Cambridge University Press.

Williamson, John. 1990. "What Washington Means by Policy Reform." In John Williamson (ed.), *Latin American Adjustment: How Much Has Happened?* (pp. 7–20). Washington, DC: Institute for International Economics.

Yashar, Deborah J. 2005. *Contesting Citizenship in Latin America: The Rise of Indigenous Movements and the Postliberal Challenge.* New York, NY: Cambridge University Press.

15

A New Critical Juncture?

Analyzing Party System Transformation in South American Politics

Samuel Handlin

The post–Cold War era in South America witnessed a momentous transformation of regional party systems. Established parties broke down in many countries. New party system configurations that subsequently emerged exhibited great variation, especially with respect to their degree of political polarization. Looking upon these developments, Kenneth Roberts and I both wrote comparative historical analyses that examined this period of party system change, underlined variation in newly emergent institutional configurations, and explored the causes of that variation (Roberts 2014; Handlin 2017). We both saw a *potential* critical juncture. From that common starting point, however, we drew a number of different conclusions and made different analytic choices. Roberts theorized that the political dynamics of neoliberal reform decisively shaped subsequent patterns of party system development and explicitly utilized the critical juncture framework to structure this analysis. In contrast, I focused attention on the occurrence of state crises and patterns of left-wing coalition-building as drivers of party system variation but opted not to deploy the critical juncture framework.

I use this chapter to reflect on some of these decisions and what they might tell us about critical juncture analysis. To provide a frame of reference for the discussion, I begin with a concise summary of the argument of my book. The rest of the chapter discusses the two analytic choices made by Roberts and me, how these choices differ, and some implications for critical juncture analysis.

The first choice regards the causal role of antecedent conditions and contingency in our arguments. Antecedent conditions play a relatively minor role in Roberts's argument, which hinges on the contingent choices of political actors during market reform. In my argument, contingency plays virtually no role, with antecedent coalitions powerfully shaping party system divergence. Two analytic points are drawn. First, the contrast provides a useful illustration of the pitfalls of making contingency a definitional attribute of critical junctures, an argument made by David Collier (see Chapter 1). Were contingency to be a definitional attribute, we would have to conclude that Roberts was analyzing a critical juncture but that my book, examining the same set of divergent institutional patterns and offering an alternative explanation based on different theoretical motivations, was not. This seems both unnecessarily limiting and potentially quite counterproductive for the research agenda into critical junctures. Further, a consideration of the two books allows us to view several different ways in which antecedent conditions can bear on causal processes during potential critical junctures. By doing so, I attempt to build on Slater and Simmons's (2010) notion of "critical antecedents" by identifying distinct ways in which such antecedents operate and clarifying several different roles antecedent conditions may play in critical juncture arguments.

The second analytic choice involved determining whether or not to utilize the critical juncture framework at all. As Roberts (Chapter 14) has indicated, he was planning a critical juncture analysis even when first conceiving of his project, having decided early on that the analytic advantages of using the framework outweighed any potential concerns about the length and endurance of legacies. In contrast, I decided not to use the critical juncture framework, in part because I was uncomfortable doing so at such short temporal range. Our alternative approaches raise several important issues for critical juncture analysis. For one, must we see enduring legacies to infer the occurrence of critical junctures? I argue that we can (and often should) utilize the critical juncture framework with a falsificationist mindset, in that we may apply the framework as a tool to help test a hypothesis that a critical juncture occurred. But to ultimately make the inference that a critical juncture occurred, we do need to perceive an enduring legacy, since this is a definitional attribute of the phenomenon.

What criteria should we apply to determine whether legacies have lasted long enough to be considered enduring? I suggest that one useful exercise involves an explicit comparison of the length of legacies versus the length of (hypothesized) critical junctures, given the common assumption among scholars that the former should be relatively long compared to the latter. Going through this exercise for my book produces two observations. The average legacy length (as could be perceived at the time of publication) was actually shorter than the average critical juncture length. However, we can also see substantial variation across the cases in my book in this legacy-to-critical-juncture ratio. When scholars are faced with this situation, a reasonable alternative might be to treat the subset of cases with more clearly enduring legacies as providing potentially strong evidence for the occurrence of a critical juncture, while treating cases with relatively short legacies as providing more limited and speculative evidentiary value.

STATE CRISES, LEFT-WING POLITICS, AND PARTY SYSTEM TRANSFORMATION IN SOUTH AMERICA

Critical juncture analyses typically begin with a shock or crisis that disrupts the status quo and creates the possibility of significant institutional innovation and change (Collier and Munck 2017: 3, 5–6). While not utilizing the critical juncture framework, my book does posit the occurrence of a "triple shock," a trio of macro-political processes during the 1980s and early 1990s that disrupted established patterns of sociopolitical representation and competition. First and foremost, democracy spread across the region, opening the political arena once again to popular contestation and mobilization but also spawning new expectations regarding the functioning of government and the meaning of citizenship. In contexts marked by weak states, these expectations often led to disappointment, as pathologies such as corruption, particularism, and inefficiency continued to plague state institutions in most countries. Second, the end of the Cold War entailed a seismic shift in the international environment. While this exogenous shock was not a major factor undermining established patterns of party politics in South America, it greatly conditioned the strategic and programmatic choices of a category of political actors—the Latin American left— whose actions would be central to shaping new patterns of party politics.

The final part of the "triple shock" was that market reform swept through South America, generating political turmoil and, often, substantial popular backlash. Liberalization concentrated heavy losses on interest groups that had benefited from the more protected import substitution industrialization (ISI) model, decimated institutions of popular representation like labor unions, and exacerbated poverty and inequality among the general population, at least in the short term. And the difficult politics of adjustment frequently led politicians to implement reforms by surprise or to embrace strange bedfellow coalitions, alienating citizens in the process.

An important contrast between my book and that of Roberts is that my analysis treats these market reform dynamics as part of a shock whereas his work considers them integral to a critical juncture. In my view, market reform helped disrupt established patterns of political representation but did not determine subsequent variation in party system reconfiguration. In his view, market reform not only played a disruptive role, but the political choices made during the reform period decisively shaped subsequent party system variation.

Critical Juncture? Modes of Left Incorporation into Evolving Party Systems

South American party systems were reconfigured after this triple shock. The essential question in most countries involved how ascendant left-wing parties and movements would enter and be integrated into party systems. With the exception of Chile, left parties and movements were relatively marginal players in electoral politics during the Cold War era, struggling to make inroads during periods of democracy and often harshly repressed under authoritarian rule. The triple shock favored the political

ascendance of the left for several reasons. The end of the Cold War catalyzed reinvention and moderation on the left while also easing fears of left-wing government
among conservative parties and business interests. The economic dislocations of
the "lost decade" and subsequent neoliberal reforms also generally favored the left,
which was well suited to channel popular discontent and address demands for greater
redistribution. And the left's new emphasis on reimagining state-society relations was
particularly well suited to capitalizing on popular dissatisfaction with the pathologies of dysfunctional states. This confluence of conditions made the rise of left-wing
parties and movements nearly inevitable in most countries. However, the way that
rise occurred differed greatly across countries and this difference proved highly consequential for the broader reorientation of national party systems.

Across the eight South American countries on which my book focuses, the political left was integrated into politics in three different ways during the 1990s and early
2000s, with consequent implications for variation in the nature of evolving national
party systems.[1] These three modes of integration were differentiated along two dimensions, as shown in Table 15.1. In three countries, the left parties that eventually
came to power in the twenty-first century were insiders, left parties established well
prior to this period that then fought within institutional channels to solidify their
position as the major party player to the left of center. In five other countries, the
major left parties that eventually came to power were led by political outsiders who
emerged during the 1990s or early 2000s, forged new parties and movements, and
won the presidency. The second dimension involved the radicalization of the left.
In five countries, the left came to power promising to work within established institutional channels and backing relatively moderate economic programs that worked
within (rather than challenged) the broad contours of the neoliberal model. In three
others, the left came to power promising sweeping institutional changes via constitutional reform and pushing an economic program that rejected market liberalism
in important ways.

While political actors—especially those on the left—undertook strategic calculations and choices that directly produced these modes of left party integration, those
processes were themselves powerfully driven by two more contextual variables (see
Table 15.1).[2] The first variable is the occurrence (or not) in the aftermath of the triple

---

1. Argentina and Colombia are the two major South American countries not included in
this chapter and my broader work on this topic. As discussed at greater length in Handlin
(2017), the rationale for the case selection was not that party system outcomes in Argentina
and Colombia failed to conform to the predictions of the theory regarding the causal logic of
the critical juncture (which they largely do). Rather, these two cases possess highly idiosyncratic features—respectively, the remarkably durable and amorphous Peronist movement and
a civil war involving the left—that powerfully conditioned how the left turn unfolded, setting
them off from the rest of the region in important ways.

2. I lack the space in this format to provide the detailed scores of these variables and a
discussion of their measurement. For more information, see Appendix A of Handlin (2017)
and the relevant discussions in Chapter 2.

Table 15.1 Reanalyzing *State Crisis in Fragile Democracies*: Is the Critical Juncture Framework Productive?

Country	Bolivia, Ecuador, Venezuela	Brazil, Chile, Uruguay	Paraguay, Peru
Antecedent Conditions			
a. State strength	Weak, highly prone to experiencing state crisis.	Strong in Chile and Uruguay, not prone to state crisis. Medium in Brazil, facilitating ability of state reformers to improve institutional performance during 1990s and therefore avoid prolonged state crisis.	Weak, highly prone to experiencing state crisis.
b. Infrastructure of left-wing politics	Robust, parties and/or social movements of the left are important political actors during the late 1980s and early 1990s.	Robust, parties and/or social movements of the left are important political actors during the late 1980s and early 1990s.	Parties and social movements of the left are either very weak (Paraguay) or decimated under autocratic rule (Peru).
Transformative Shock			
a. Regionwide triple shock		Spread of democratic politics Embrace of liberalizing market reforms End of the Cold War	
Critical Juncture			
a. Fate of extant major left-wing parties.	Fail amid popular rejection of political status quo and factional strife.	Successfully entrench themselves as moderate factions win out.	Do not exist.
b. Coalitional logic for left outsiders.	Build new movements on the left.	Blocked by extant left-wing parties.	Forge alliances with centrist actors.
c. Mode of incorporation of left into evolving party systems	Radical outsiders	Pragmatic insiders	Pragmatic outsiders
Legacy: New Party System Trajectory			
a. Level of polarization	Highly polarizing	Weakly polarizing	Weakly polarizing
b. Institution-alization of left bloc	Moderate	High	Low
c. Fate of legacy since book's publication	Largely consistent in Venezuela and Bolivia, attenuation of polarization in Ecuador.	Consistent in Uruguay, rise in polarization in Brazil, upheaval on the left in Chile.	Consistent in terms of low institutional-ization; fluidity facilitated uptick in polarization in Peru.

shock—roughly the late 1980s to early 2000s—of prolonged "state crises," a term borrowed from Guillermo O'Donnell's (1993) seminal analysis of the phenomenon. State crises tended to undermine established political parties, including those on the left, and to create opportunities for political outsiders. State crises involved two dimensions. First, states were weak, marked by inefficiency and corruption and highly partial in their delivery of goods and treatment of citizens. Second, mass publics became strongly disenchanted with the functioning of basic state institutions. While the former was a longstanding feature of many South American countries, the latter became particularly likely in the post–Cold War era as the failures of democracy to solve state pathologies and the socioeconomic dislocations of the neoliberal age spurred mass discontent. In this sense, state crises required more than state weakness to break out, but their occurrence was only likely where the antecedent condition of state weakness was present.

The second explanatory variable represents another antecedent condition, the infrastructure of left-wing political mobilization—parties of the left and overtly left-wing social movements—that existed in each country as the post–Cold War period began. In some countries, a human and organizational infrastructure of relevant left-wing parties, activists, anti-neoliberal social movements, and voters accustomed to leftist political mobilization was in place. In other countries, many if not all of these components simply did not exist. The existence (or not) of a reasonably strong political left entailed different landscapes of actors facing the challenges of the post–Cold War period, particularly the occurrence (or not) of state crisis.

Alternative combinations of these two binary variables (state crisis, strong left) led to different ways in which the rising political left was integrated into party systems, through two principal mechanisms. The first was only relevant for those countries where a strong political left existed at the end of the Cold War. In Bolivia, Venezuela, and Ecuador, state crises undermined the attempts of moderate factions to consolidate the extant left parties (MIR [Revolutionary Left Movement] in Bolivia, MAS [Movement for Socialism] and LCR [Radical Cause] in Venezuela, PSE [Ecuadorian Socialist Party] and FADI [Broad Left Front] in Ecuador) as pragmatic insiders. A systemic orientation met disfavor with voters and moderate leaders on the left faced destructive internal challenges from radical factions emboldened by the crisis atmosphere. In contrast, the lack of state crisis in Chile and Uruguay, or the avoidance of a prolonged state crisis more narrowly in Brazil, facilitated the consolidation of extant left parties (PS [Socialist Party] in Chile, FA [Broad Front] in Uruguay, PT [Workers' Party] in Brazil) as pragmatic insiders, as voters reacted positively to systemic strategies and behavior and factional discord was quelled by the inability of radical factions to articulate an alternative path to electoral viability.

The second mechanism related to the prospects of political outsiders on the left and the coalitional logic of those outsiders if they emerged. Where state crises did not occur, outsiders were effectively blocked in Chile and Uruguay or, in the case of Brazil, disappeared from the political landscape over the course of the 1990s as state crisis was narrowly avoided. Where state crises occurred, ground was particularly fertile for the rise of political outsiders in general, including those on the left. The strategic and coalitional logic of outsiders on the left, however, hinged critically on whether or not they emerged in contexts marked by a robust infrastructure of left-wing political mobilization. In contexts largely barren of left-wing political infrastructure, such as Paraguay and Peru (after the reign of Alberto Fujimori), outsiders on the left were forced to seek allies and coalition partners from among established centrist forces, creating incentives to attenuate anti-establishment rhetoric and moderate anti-neoliberal appeals. The rising left therefore coalesced around pragmatic outsiders. In contexts in which a much more robust infrastructure of left-wing party organization, activists, social movements, and voters already existed, as in Bolivia, Ecuador, and Venezuela, outsiders on the left built new movements on top of that infrastructure and had little need to seek centrist, systemic allies. This situation incentivized the adoption of a more polarizing platform and the rising left took the form of radical outsiders.

Legacy? New Party System Configurations

Disparate modes of left integration produced distinct institutional legacies in the form of party system configurations that institutionalized alternative patterns of contestation and conflict.[3] To a substantial degree, the most important differences in party systems emerged at the close of the critical juncture itself, as almost definitional consequences of different modes of left party integration. But some aspects of party system legacies only fully consolidated after predictable political reactions that followed the left's ascent to power. This section summarizes these legacies while also providing some brief comments on their fate since the publication of my book.

Party system divergence occurred along two dimensions. Most centrally to the overall argument, party systems varied significantly in their levels of polarization, understood as the left–right ideological differentiation among component parties and considered in terms of both distance (the spread of the distribution) and intensity (the incidence of cooperation between major opposing camps).[4] Levels of polarization in Bolivia, Ecuador, and Venezuela came to far surpass polarization anywhere else on the continent. Further, party systems also differed significantly in the institutionalization of the left bloc, varying from very high in Brazil, Chile, and Uruguay (where pragmatic insiders rose to power) to moderate in Bolivia, Ecuador, and Venezuela (where ambitious new party building enterprises were launched by left

---

3. My book also explores divergent political regime dynamics as part of the legacy. For purposes of brevity and maintaining the contrast with Roberts and our analysis of party systems, I do not discuss regime implications here.

4. See Appendix B of Handlin (2017) for polarization scores for each case and detailed discussions of conceptualization and measurement.

outsiders), to very low in Paraguay and Peru (where those left parties that brought presidents to power fell apart after their terms in office).[5]

In Brazil, Chile, and Uruguay, where established center-left parties successfully entrenched dominant positions, left–right programmatic competition was institutionalized within party systems but bounded by a common adherence to the broad contours of the neoliberal model among those parties that had the largest congressional representation and competed for the presidency. Further, competition exclusively among insiders was conducive to pragmatic deal-making and compromise, such that the intensity of polarization tended to be very low by regional standards. The integration of established left parties also meant that the left bloc within party systems would be highly stable and institutionalized, helping anchor party systems that were highly institutionalized in the aggregate. These patterns—bounded polarization amid relatively high levels of institutionalization and stability—had emerged during the critical juncture period but were reinforced by the arrival to power of left parties. Recent years, however, have seen these legacies begin to erode in certain respects, especially with a sharp uptick in polarization in Brazil attending the rise of Jair Bolsonaro and major challenges to the institutionalized left bloc in Chile from new left-wing parties and movements.

The rise of radical outsider movements on the left transformed party systems in Bolivia, Ecuador, and Venezuela into highly polarizing configurations, in which radical left majoritarian parties faced off against opposition blocs that loosely united various center-right and right-wing forces. High polarization was already present in the initial elections in which the left won the presidency. Once the left took power and embarked on transformational projects, polarization became even more acute as opponents began to defensively coordinate, such that party competition revolved around two antagonistic blocs proposing very different political programs. Party systems also were characterized by moderate institutionalization on the left. Radical left movements sought broad social and political transformations that required holding power over the long run across different levels of government, which created incentives for strengthening parties. The polarized atmosphere also contributed to the forging of partisan identities while a stranglehold on the state offered patronage resources to facilitate party building. The partial institutionalization of left blocs was not mirrored on the other side of the spectrum. Opposition parties tended to be electorally unstable (as opposition voters tired of parties that could not win and cycled among them) and to struggle to build strong organizations while being cut off from state power. Party systems came to be marked by an imbalance in institutionalization

---

5. The variant institutionalization of left parties is not conceptualized as a major dimension of party system divergence in my book, which focuses heavily on polarization. I give additional emphasis to this dimension in this chapter because it can be viewed as an important aspect of the legacy and because doing so helps shine light on important issues related to the institutionalization of durable legacies.

favoring the left. These party system legacies have remained largely stable in more recent years in Bolivia and Venezuela, despite big political upheavals in both countries in other regards. In Ecuador, the uneven institutionalization of the party system remains while the level of polarization was attenuated by the moderation of Alianza País under the leadership of Lenín Moreno.

The third party system trajectory, represented by Paraguay and Peru, involved relatively low levels of polarization and very weak levels of institutionalization on the left. Given that the left was a non-factor in electoral politics in the years immediately before the emergence of Lugo and Humala, in Paraguay and Peru respectively, polarization could only increase with outsider entrance. But the programmatic compromises necessary for these left outsiders to compete for power applied bounds to the level of distance polarization in party competition while the pragmatic necessity of forging alliances with systemic actors outside the left applied limits to the intensity of contestation. These cases still experienced some very controversial episodes, particularly the impeachment of Lugo on largely trumped-up charges. But levels of polarization did not match the consistently uncompromising politics of Bolivia, Ecuador, and Venezuela. Paraguay and Peru were also characterized by very low levels of institutionalization of left blocs within party systems. Since Lugo and Humala challenged for power without being able to build movements on top of a substantial left-wing infrastructure, they ran highly personalistic candidacies with little grassroots organization. Further, once they were in office, the modest programmatic ambitions of the two presidents disincentivized long-term investments in party building, while modest levels of polarization provided little impetus for the forging of strong party identities. Neither Lugo's Patriotic Alliance for Change nor Humala's Peruvian Nationalist Party lasted as major partisan vehicles after their respective leaders' terms in office. Instead, new and relatively noninstitutionalized parties and movements emerged on the left to take their place. This pattern contrasted with trends on the right. While the Peruvian party system was highly fluid overall, party building within the Fujimorista bloc was most successful. In Paraguay, the longstanding Colorados and PLRA (Authentic Radical Liberal Party) weathered Lugo's rise and remained fixtures in the party system. Party systems were therefore marked by an imbalance in institutionalization that favored the right. These party system legacies have persisted with respect to the low institutionalization of the left bloc, but this fluidity also creates the possibility of sharp upticks in polarization if new left outsiders emerge with more radical orientations, as occurred in Peru in 2021.

ANALYTIC DILEMMAS AND THE
CRITICAL JUNCTURE FRAMEWORK

This section presents some reflections on two analytic choices made in this project, how they differed from those made by Roberts, and what this might reveal about the use of critical juncture analysis. In broad strokes, Roberts and I perceived the same potential critical juncture. Using David Collier and Gerardo Munck's (2017: 2) definition, we both identified a "major episode of institutional innovation" (a period in which South American party systems experienced great change) that occurred in "distinct ways" and that produced a clear—if not clearly enduring—legacy (party systems that differed in their level of polarization and institutionalization). However, we developed very different arguments regarding the causes of the institutional variation that emerged out of the critical juncture, including the role of antecedent conditions in shaping events and the level of contingency involved, and also made different analytic choices regarding how and whether to utilize the critical juncture framework.

Contingency and Antecedent Conditions

One area of divergence between my analysis and that of Roberts regards our treatment of antecedent conditions and their effect on outcomes. This difference is particularly notable given that we are analyzing nearly the same institutional outcomes and roughly the same period in which those outcomes were generated. Nevertheless, Roberts concluded that the contingent decision of political actors drove outcomes whereas I found that inherited structural conditions were decisive. The contrast between the studies provides a good illustration of an argument by David Collier (see Chapter 1) in his critique of contingency as a definitional attribute of critical junctures: scholars will often disagree about the contingency involved in a major episode of institutional innovation and these disagreements are often rooted in different theoretical approaches.

In Roberts's work, party system trajectories are decisively shaped by the political orientations of market reformers and their opponents. Where conservative parties implement reforms and labor-based or left parties consistently oppose neoliberalism, party systems stabilize around this left–right competitive axis. Where labor-based or left parties join market reform coalitions, in contrast, party systems become highly unstable, as such actions alienate supporters and open up possibilities for outsider entrants, especially radical outsiders on the left that can channel anti-neoliberal sentiment. As such, Roberts's work draws upon and operates within a variety of economistic theoretical traditions. These include spatial theories of party competition that view electoral contests as largely programmatic, with the competitive space defined mainly by economic and distributive issues. It also works within a broad tradition in the analysis of Latin American politics that has emphasized the political centrality of conflicts over distribution and redistribution and, more specifically, has highlighted the process and aftermath of neoliberal reforms as central to understanding contemporary democratic politics in the region.

In contrast, in my book party system trajectories are most decisively shaped by the occurrence or not of state crises. Where such crises were avoided, established partisan insiders tended to consolidate, as mass publics had reason to throw the bums out en masse, and outsiders found little oxygen. Where such crises occurred, populations became highly disenchanted with status quo parties and turned to outsiders, who opportunistically lambasted the system. This argument works within a very different set of state-centric theoretical traditions, particularly a broad tradition in the analysis of Latin American politics that has emphasized how state pathologies shape the operation of democratic institutions, generating popular alienation and coloring the experience of citizenship.

The weight placed on contingency in our two arguments flows from these alternative theoretical orientations. Theory centered on redistributive conflict and competition on the left–right spectrum lends itself to a focus on agency: politicians and parties make programmatic choices and, as citizens and other political actors respond, those choices have far-reaching consequences. But theory centered on the pathologies of weak states lends itself to an emphasis on structure and highly constrained agents. Politicians do not choose to work in a context of functional or dysfunctional state institutions and are largely incapable of changing them.

Were contingency a definitional attribute of critical junctures, we would have to conclude that Roberts's work was analyzing a critical juncture whereas mine, examining the same novel and contrasting institutional outcomes and posing an alternative explanation for their generation, was not. This seems both somewhat nonsensical and potentially counterproductive for the research agenda on critical junctures. If we embrace the contingency criterion, scholars looking to use the critical juncture framework will be incentivized to favor certain kinds of theoretical explanations over others: they certainly would not want to make largely immutable state characteristics too central to their explanatory frameworks. Further, it would limit the ability of critical juncture analysis to serve as a vehicle for scholars to advance and contrast rival explanations of important outcomes.

A conceptualization of critical junctures that removes contingency as a defining attribute also opens the way for fruitful analysis of the many ways in which antecedent conditions can impact events during the critical juncture and, therefore, limit or eliminate contingency. Slater and Simmons (2010) helpfully distinguish "critical antecedents"—prior conditions that combine with causal forces within the critical juncture to produce an outcome—from other antecedent conditions that do not have such effects. Similarly, Riedl and Roberts (see Chapter 6) distinguish between "activating" critical junctures, in which antecedent conditions weigh heavily on outcomes, and "generative" critical junctures, in which choice plays a more decisive role. A logical avenue for building upon those insights is to distinguish some ways in which antecedents exert influence within the critical juncture. Illustrations from Roberts's (2014) book and my own can help demonstrate some of this variety (see Figure 15.1).

Even when high degrees of contingency exist within critical junctures, antecedent conditions might still favor one outcome over others, increasing the probability of a certain path or paths being taken—for example, by throwing up barriers to certain strategies or by making certain political choices more or less costly—without determining or strictly precluding any option. As such, they are neither necessary nor sufficient for any particular outcome within the critical juncture. An example of this kind of antecedent condition in Roberts's (2014) analysis is whether party systems prior to the critical juncture were labor mobilizing or elitist. Key actors within labor mobilizing party systems, especially labor-based parties, faced greater difficulties adapting to the neoliberal era and, therefore, these systems were more prone to disruption and volatility during the critical juncture. As Roberts (Chapter 14) notes in his reflections on critical juncture analysis, in his book this factor "predisposed cases to experience the critical juncture in particular ways" but exerted only a modest impact when compared to the contingent choices of political actors in the process of market reform.

Some antecedent conditions are necessary for certain outcomes or sets of outcomes, but not sufficient for determining a specific outcome. An example from my book is the antecedent condition of state weakness. Since full-blown state crises only occurred where states were weak, and state crises drove the emergence and success of political outsiders, the antecedent condition of a weak state was effectively necessary for outsider politics. Yet state weakness was not sufficient for determining either kind of outsider outcome. Specific outcomes in the presence of such an antecedent condition

		Necessity	
		No	**Yes**
Sufficiency	**No**	Labor-mobilizing party systems are more likely than elite-led party systems to experience dealignment in Roberts (2014), but are neither necessary nor sufficient for this outcome.	State weakness is necessary for outsider politics in Handlin (2017), but does not define which kind of outsider trajectory is taken.
	Yes		When a strong left-infrastructure is combined with state weakness in Handlin (2017), the two are individually necessary and jointly sufficient for a highly polarizing party system led by radical outsiders.

Figure 15.1 Varieties of "Critical Antecedents" in Roberts and Handlin

rest on other variables and processes, with one possibility being the choices of political actors. In the abstract, we can easily envision a causal pattern in which a critical antecedent pushes a case toward a subset of possible trajectories, then the contingent choices of actors determine which path among the narrower subset is taken.

The two books do not offer any examples of a third logical pattern, critical antecedents that are sufficient but not necessary for a particular outcome. Some more consideration of whether other critical juncture studies can provide examples of this type is merited (and planned for the future).

A fourth type of pattern involves both necessity and sufficiency. While there is no single antecedent condition that fits this bill in the two books, the two antecedent conditions of state weakness and a strong infrastructure of left-wing politics might be viewed as individually necessary and jointly sufficient, such that their combination belongs in this box. Whereas state weakness was necessary for outsider politics but not sufficient for any specific outcome, the addition of a strong infrastructure of left-wing politics makes the combination sufficient for radical outsiders and a highly polarizing party system. Whereas the top left cell allows the most room for contingency and agency, the bottom right cell effectively eliminates it.

Using the Critical Juncture Framework and Identifying an "Enduring" Legacy

Most scholars utilizing the critical juncture framework do so to examine events in the distant past, with the benefit of substantial historical hindsight. Using the framework to analyze events at relatively short temporal distance raises some additional complications, especially related to the assessment of legacies. Scholars may be unsure about their ability to discern and characterize the legacy of a hypothesized critical juncture. Even when they feel relatively confident in doing so, they may worry whether a legacy characterized in one way today might be disrupted tomorrow, inviting a reappraisal. Indeed, as we saw in the last section, some important changes have occurred within just the last few years to the South American party system legacies examined by myself and Roberts (2014). Since the two of us made different choices regarding whether and how to utilize the critical juncture framework at short temporal range, some reflection upon these decisions may be useful.

It is useful to draw an analytic distinction between two choices. The first is whether or not to utilize the critical juncture framework at all, particularly when dealing with relatively recent events. We need not perceive enduring and stable legacies *a priori* to answer this question in the affirmative. Rather, we should be willing to utilize the critical juncture framework with a falsificationist mindset, to test the hypothesis that a critical juncture occurred. But there may also be other good reasons not to deploy the critical juncture framework—with all of its associated terminology and its particular way of organizing comparative historical analysis—if we are unsure how suited our comparative analyses will be to this particular tool. For example, in my case, the bulk of my empirical research and theoretical interest related to explaining the emergence of cross-national divergence, which I did in substantial detail across many cases. But I possessed neither the empirical information nor the 50,000 extra words from my publisher that would have been necessary to analyze legacy periods—e.g., mechanisms of production and reproduction, potential complex reactive sequences—with the same careful attention to detail. In sum, scholars will typically have to balance many different scholarly objectives when deciding whether or not to use the critical juncture framework. Working at close temporal range and being unsure about whether enduring legacies can be perceived can make such decisions more complex, but these concerns should not themselves rule out use of the framework.

If scholars do decide to utilize the critical juncture framework, however, they will need to establish criteria for determining whether a legacy has persisted long enough to be considered enduring. Despite the significant body of methodological research devoted to the critical juncture framework, relatively little attention has been paid to developing or even debating systematic criteria for determining the existence of an enduring legacy. Boas (Chapter 17) emphasizes that legacies must have crystalized enough for scholars to score them *a priori* in a clear and consistent manner. While this seems like a productive starting point, it leaves open the question of endurance. A legacy could crystalize, or "freeze" in the language of Lipset and Rokkan (1967), for a brief period of time without lasting long enough to be considered truly enduring.

One plausible starting point for assessing legacy endurance is to compare the length of legacies to the length of critical junctures that hypothetically spawned them. Scholarship on critical junctures often stresses that the former must be relatively long compared to the latter. For example, Cappoccia and Kelemen (2007: 348) state that "the duration of the juncture must be brief relative to the duration of the path-dependent process it instigates." This assumption is also built into concepts like "punctuated equilibrium" often associated with critical juncture analysis, which invokes a relatively short period of flux that is followed by a lengthier period of relative stability. If lengthy periods of flux are followed by short respites of institutional continuity, it is hard to justify calling the former critical junctures. Following Kaufman (2017), a term like "great transformations" may be more appropriate for capturing patterns of change in which huge upheavals occur that produce distinctive outcomes, but these outcomes are either unstable or quickly upended by some other transformative process.

While there is no unarbitrary value for the legacy-to-critical juncture length ratio that would justify considering a legacy enduring, explicitly making this comparison may still be useful as a heuristic. To use my own work as an example, had I utilized the critical juncture framework, a reasonable approach would have been to consider the critical juncture to have opened in each case with the first year of post–Cold War democratic rule (at which point the left was clearly faced with the dilemma of how to compete for power through institutional channels in a changed milieu) and to have ended with the ascension of a major left party or candidate to executive power (at which point the direction of the left had crystalized in each case). We can then compare the length of critical junctures to the length of legacies at the time of my book's publication in 2017. Table 15.2 displays this information for the eight cases analyzed in my study.

Table 15.2 Length of Critical Junctures and Legacy Periods as My Book Went to Press

Country	Opening of Critical Juncture	Closing of Critical Juncture	Length of Critical Juncture	Legacy Length
Venezuela	1990	1998	8	19
Chile	1990	1999	9	18
Brazil	1990	2002	12	15
Uruguay	1990	2004	14	13
Bolivia	1990	2005	15	12
Ecuador	1990	2006	16	11
Paraguay	1992	2008	18	9
Peru	1990	2011	21	6

Several observations about this data might be highlighted. First, legacies on average were slightly shorter in duration (12.87 years) than critical junctures (13.87 years) at the time of my book's publication. Had I used the framework, this would have undermined the case for inferring the occurrence of a critical juncture (at least at that point in time): while there is no objective threshold for how long legacies must last on average to be considered enduring, it seems reasonable that the legacy mean should be longer than the average critical juncture. Notably, it seems likely that the legacy-to-critical juncture length ratio would be higher for Roberts's (2014) study. Critical junctures are shorter in his analysis, closing with the end of neoliberal reform in each country (rather than with the rise of the left to power), so legacies begin earlier and are relatively longer. As such, he may have a stronger case for inferring that a critical juncture occurred when using this benchmark. In any event, this comparison of legacy length to critical juncture length is not intended to constitute a final word, justifying the inference of a critical juncture or not. However, it might serve as one helpful benchmark for thinking about how we conceptualize patterns of continuity and change and draw inferences about them.

A second observation is that there is substantial variation among the countries. It is common in this line of research to find significant variation in the length of critical junctures and legacies. The ratios of legacy length to critical juncture length, however, are much more unusual. In Venezuela, the legacy had already lasted nearly two-and-half times the length of the critical juncture. Had this been the case for all countries in the study, or had it been a comparison of only Venezuela and Chile, the case for declaring a critical juncture would seem stronger. In Peru, in contrast, the legacy had lasted less than a third the length of the critical juncture. In practice, this was hardly more than a single presidential electoral cycle.

These contrasts raise the question of how scholars should proceed when some cases appear to be marked by enduring institutional legacies, including cases with starkly contrasting outcomes, yet other legacies are still far too young to be considered enduring. One approach would be to determine that the contrasts within the case universe in general simply weren't stable enough to infer the occurrence of a critical juncture. Another possibility might be to simply draw more nuanced conclusions. We might claim certain case contrasts, marked by enduring and divergent legacies, offered strong evidence for the inference of a critical juncture, while other cases in the universe provided more indeterminate evidence, with their younger legacies seemingly following the same trajectories but not having endured long enough to provide strong confirmation. Thinking along these lines—that different cases within a universe might provide different levels of support for the overall inference of a critical juncture occurring—is likely a useful approach in critical juncture analysis in general. But it may be particularly essential when deploying the framework at close temporal range.

CONCLUSION

This chapter offered a few reflections from the perspective of someone who wrote a comparative historical analysis of relatively recent events and grappled with the question of whether or not to utilize the critical juncture framework, ultimately deciding against that choice. After summarizing the argument of my book explaining party system transformation in contemporary South America, the chapter highlighted two analytic choices and how they differed from those made by Roberts (2014) in his work: How much causal weight to give to antecedent conditions vis-à-vis contingent choices within a critical juncture and whether and how to deploy the critical juncture framework at close range, particularly in relation to the issue of legacies.

This comparison between the analytic choices of two scholars looking at roughly the same hypothetical critical juncture suggests that we should not be overly rigid in specifying when a critical juncture argument should or should not be utilized. A definition of critical junctures that insists on a very high degree of contingency would have ruled out my project, given the powerful role of antecedent conditions in the argument. A definition with a very restrictive insistence on legacy length might have ruled out Roberts's (2014) project from using the framework, which he clearly put to good analytic use in his impressive book. Ultimately, the critical juncture framework is a tool for structuring comparative historical analysis: Scholars may reasonably come to different decisions regarding how and whether to use it and the study of critical junctures will remain most vibrant if, within reason, we afford them that flexibility.

BIBLIOGRAPHY

Capoccia, Giovanni, and R. Daniel Kelemen. 2007. "The Study of Critical Junctures: Theory, Narrative, and Counterfactuals in Historical Institutionalism." *World Politics* 59(3): 341–69.

Collier, David, and Gerardo L. Munck. 2017. "Building Blocks and Methodological Challenges: A Framework for Studying Critical Junctures." *Qualitative and Multi-Method Research* 15(1): 2–9.

Collier, Ruth Berins, and David Collier. 1991. *Shaping the Political Arena: Critical Junctures, the Labor Movement, and the Regime Dynamics in Latin America.* Princeton, NJ: Princeton University Press.

Handlin, Samuel. 2017. *State Crisis in Fragile Democracies: Polarization and Political Regimes in South America.* Cambridge, UK: Cambridge University Press.

Kaufman, Robert R. 2017. "Great Transformations but no Critical Junctures? Latin America in the Twenty-First Century." *Qualitative & Multi-Method Research* 15(1): 16–17.

Lipset, Seymour M., and Stein Rokkan. 1967. "Cleavage Structures, Party Systems, and Voter Alignments: An Introduction." In Seymour M. Lipset and Stein Rokkan (eds.), *Party Systems and Voter Alignments: Cross-National Perspectives* (pp. 1–64). New York, NY: Free Press.

Mahoney, James. 2001. "Path Dependent Explanations of Regime Change: Central America in Comparative Perspective." *Studies in Comparative International Development* 36(1): 111–41.

O'Donnell, Guillermo. 1993. "On the State, Democratization and Some Conceptual Problems: A Latin American View with Glances at Some Postcommunist Countries." *World Development* 21(8): 1355–69.

Roberts, Kenneth M. 2014. *Changing Course in Latin America: Party Systems in the Neoliberal Era.* New York, NY: Cambridge University Press.

Slater, Dan, and Erica Simmons. 2010. "Informative Regress: Critical Antecedents in Comparative Politics." *Comparative Political Studies* 43(7): 886–917.

Soifer, Hillel David. 2012. "The Causal Logic of Critical Junctures." *Comparative Political Studies* 45(12): 1572–97.

16

A Fourth Critical Juncture?

Party Politics in Contemporary Chile

Timothy R. Scully

The Chilean party system has been a legacy of three fundamental social and political watersheds in the nineteenth and twentieth centuries. At each watershed, *two-sided* cleavages generated a *tripartite* configuration of parties. Thus, two poles emerged representing antagonistic positions with respect to a fundamental axis of cleavage, and a politically significant center occupied the space between them. In a comparative Latin American framework, this political configuration is distinctive since it resembles more closely patterns in some Western European party systems.

Working in the tradition of Lipset and Rokkan (1967), and Collier and Collier (1991), I argued in my book *Rethinking the Center* that these three watersheds were driven by generative cleavages that yielded critical junctures, shaping and reshaping the national party system and creating institutional patterns that endured for long periods of time (Scully 1992).

This chapter extends my earlier analysis by asking whether—in the wake of (1) authoritarian rule and the neoliberal economic model adopted in the 1970s and 1980s under Pinochet, (2) the economic and social transformations resulting from the subsequent dramatic economic growth experienced in Chile under the democratic governments after the Pinochet period, and (3) the consequential institutional changes such as those resulting from the 2015 electoral formula as well as the electoral tremors unleashed by the elections of November 2017 and May 2021—a fourth critical juncture has again reshaped the party system. To provide a baseline for analyzing this new episode, I present a brief overview of the criteria for identifying critical junctures, along with a synoptic summary of the three prior episodes.

In the present framework, a critical juncture is interpreted not solely based on the scope and intensity of conflict involved—for example class or religious conflict—but also on whether it generates an enduring legacy. According to standard criteria, in observing a critical juncture we expect to identify a fundamental new conflict and line of cleavage, followed by change in the key issues around which parties cluster and over which they compete. The party system shifts on its axis, and this new line of cleavage cuts across the electorate. Change also occurs in the identity of parties, the party attachments of voters, and the attitudes and predispositions of party identifiers. As we have argued previously, party identities and attachments are reproduced over time by the crystallization around the new constellation of cleavage patterns of powerful "political sensibilities," even "subcultures" derived from family traditions, social networks, and narratives that anchor voter identities and preferences (Valenzuela et al. 2018: 142). And, given the distinctive trajectory of the political center in Chile, one must likewise ask: What happens to the political center? Given that each of these three prior cleavages in a sense bifurcated the existing political system, how and why did a stable center party emerge each time? How is it reproduced or transformed?

Overall, we rely on these criteria and questions to judge whether a presumed fourth critical juncture indeed generated a distinctive legacy that reconfigured party alliances for years to come. And to reiterate, affirmation of this legacy provides the basis for concluding that the *juncture* is indeed *critical*. To foreshadow the central argument, since the underlying cleavage structure of the contemporary party system remains rooted in religion and class, the Pinochet period *per se* did not represent a new critical juncture. While there exist significant indications of disjuncture with the pre–1973 party system, there is not yet evidence for a well-defined, enduring legacy.

THREE CRITICAL JUNCTURES IN CHILE

Against this standard for evaluating a critical juncture, we delineate three such episodes.

First, in the mid-nineteenth century, the clerical–anticlerical cleavage produced a political "space" between the contending parties at opposing ends of the spectrum, the anti-clerical Radicals versus the Conservatives. The dispute between these two contending factions centered around a profound divide between those who sought to elevate the role of the republican state in providing critically important services such as health, education, and birth registries, versus those who wished to retain these functions in the hands of the Catholic Church. By avoiding identifying themselves directly with either side of the dispute, the Liberal Party established itself as a non-ideological, pragmatic center that came to serve as a coalitional fulcrum, periodically occupying the presidency. The result was a well-institutionalized party system that persisted for more than five decades.

Second, in the initial decades of the twentieth century a new, defining axis of political opposition emerged. We observed the emergence of an organized working class and the corresponding rise of worker–owner conflict in the modern sector—i.e., in urban areas and modernized export enclaves, above all mining. In this context, two major new parties appeared on the left, the Socialist and Communist Parties.

The Radical Party, like the pragmatic Liberals before them, established itself as the mediating center party, playing the role of broker between the right and the left and periodically holding the presidency. This pattern persisted for roughly four decades.

Third, in the mid-twentieth century another dimension of class conflict emerged, between an organized peasantry and the elite of the traditional rural sector. This conflict generated a blood feud between the forces of the conservative Catholic right and a newly energized, progressive Catholic political movement, the *Falange Nacional*, which described itself as "*mas allá de derecha e izquierda*" (i.e., "beyond the right and the left"). This political group, which became the Christian Democratic Party (PDC), represented a different kind of center party, which inserted itself into the middle position of the political spectrum. In contrast to the previous pragmatic center parties, the PDC represented a *positional* center as it related to the central axis of class conflict in the urban and rural sectors. The PDC represented a positional center party rather than a pragmatic one in that it advanced an uncompromising ideological position with regard to the predominant line of cleave, class, opposed to the Conservative right and opposed to the Marxist left, drawing inspiration from the wider tradition of Catholic social thought that comprised the wellspring of Christian Democratic parties in many countries.

Whereas for the first two critical junctures the duration of the legacy is well established, the duration of this third critical juncture remains an open question. How long has this third constellation of parties and party identities persisted? How enduring have the symbolic, social, cultural, religious, programmatic, and ideological subcultures that resulted from the underlying religious and class cleavages been in retaining their salience for shaping predispositions within the electorate? How has the political center, in this case the Christian Democratic Party—and the party system at large—fared over time under these changed circumstances? Has the Chilean party system undergone a fourth critical juncture? For example, did the Pinochet dictatorship, as some have argued, leave an enduring and distinctive party legacy, one defined by a democracy versus authoritarianism cleavage? If the answer to that question is yes, then the legacy of the third critical juncture may have lasted less than two decades, until the coup in 1973. If the answer is no, then it is possible that the legacy of the third critical juncture still persists today, having thereby lasted six decades, but interrupted for sixteen and a half years by the political hiatus created by the dictatorship.

According to the interpretation advanced in this chapter, the longstanding cleavages that have defined the cultures and subcultures that shape the basic morphology of the party system, that is religion and class, remain salient, though salient in an ever-evolving way. And in that sense, the Pinochet period *per se* did not represent a critical juncture. At the same time, however, the substance of what these cleavages represent have undergone important transformations over the decades that followed the Pinochet period. In addition, significant transformations in institutions such as changing electoral formulas, combined with a resulting political landscape characterized by increased party fragmentation, heightened electoral volatility and voter dispersion, represent important elements of discontinuity with the preexisting party system. But the absence of a clearly defined, enduring set of party legacies suggests that it is premature to invoke a critical juncture framework.

A FOURTH CRITICAL JUNCTURE?

The Pinochet coup of 1973 set in motion dramatic change. Pinochet launched a highly repressive authoritarian regime, accompanied by the suppression of political parties that anchored the preexisting party system and an assault on the political organizations of the working class and the left—in both the urban and rural sectors. This period likewise saw a fundamental transformation of the Chilean political economy: a wide-ranging neoliberal reform, partial dismantling of the state-centric model of development, and an opening of the Chilean economy to global competition. In terms of the magnitude of sectoral and class conflict, as well as the scope of policy innovation, this new episode is certainly equivalent to the second and third critical junctures discussed above.

Several questions should be considered here: Was this a critical juncture in the sense that it fundamentally restructured the party system, uprooting the deeper political sensibilities and subcultures that historically served as guideposts that set the underlying boundaries of voter identities? Alternatively, were the specific effects of the authoritarian interlude on the party system itself less profound and less permanent—such that the critical juncture framework does not fit here? Or, are there other institutional factors at work, such as the introduction of voluntary voting, and the reintroduction of a modified D'Hondt proportional representation system, that are rearticulating the dynamics of the party system in fundamental ways?

Writing two-and-a-half decades ago, from the perspective of the early 1990s, I expressed skepticism that the Pinochet episode, despite the scope and depth of the transformations that the regime effectuated, represented a new critical juncture. In my concluding chapter in *Rethinking the Center*, I argued that "for a critical juncture to occur, the changes experienced by the party system during a specified period of time must be lasting, that is, they must endure well beyond the period of transformation. . . . As a result, any conclusions . . . must necessarily remain tentative" (Scully 1992: 191). Within that framework of caution, I suggested that despite the "significant change as a consequence of the experience of authoritarianism, it is unlikely that a new generative cleavage has reorganized the basic contours of the political landscape" (Scully 1992: 191).

Today, thirty years later, it is productive to revisit this question of a fourth critical juncture. With the benefit of hindsight, we can now examine the *political* legacy of the Pinochet, and post-Pinochet, years as this hypothesized legacy has played out since 1990, during the more than two-and-a-half decades of competitive democratic politics. This assessment must be carried out with care, because persuasive arguments have been made both for and against the claim that the underlying cleavages around which parties derive their identities and organize electoral politics have been transformed in fundamental ways, leaving an enduring legacy.[1] Further, as will become clear, the analysis is made more complex by substantial social and economic transformations resulting from the extraordinary expansion of the economy, widespread secularization, as well as incremental institutional changes that have occurred *within* this thirty-year period, especially visible in the results of the most recent elections of 2017 and May 2021.

ARGUMENTS FOR A NEW CRITICAL JUNCTURE

Several analysts have argued that major changes took root in Chilean politics specifically as a result of the Pinochet interlude. These scholars suggest that the Pinochet period generated a distinctive legacy in the form of a new party system, and correspondingly that it was indeed a critical juncture.

They argue that the new party system was characterized by two key features. First, as a result of the Pinochet dictatorship, the prior tripartite division of left, center, and right had been transformed into two contending blocs, the Alliance on the right and the *Concertación* on the center-left, and it appeared that the center was no longer a basic force in Chilean politics. Second, these scholars argue that a fundamental shift in the underlying cleavages also occurred. The baseline for this shift rested upon earlier patterns of religious and class cleavages—including a profound left–right division on issues of political economy and public policy. By contrast, they argued that the post-dictatorship period saw a shift to an "authoritarian versus democratic cleavage" (Tironi and Agüero 1999; Torcal and Mainwaring 2003).

These two dimensions of change first became clearly evident in the national plebiscite of 1988, which was the precipitating event for the transition to a democratic regime. A *yes* vote mandated that Pinochet remain in power for an additional eight-year term, whereas a *no* mandated that he step down the following year. The vote for the *no* became a rallying cry for the opposition, which dramatically won the plebiscite: 56 percent no versus 44 percent yes.

Obviously, the 1988 plebiscite was a one-time event, rather than an ongoing electoral cycle. Yet at the very onset of the transition to democracy it was a key moment in restructuring political conflict. First of all, parties that had previously aligned themselves along a *left versus right* political economy spectrum now regrouped around the choice presented by the plebiscite: *Pinochet versus anti-Pinochet*. Second, given the binary, *yes-no* structure of the plebiscite, it provided no opportunity for a centrist alternative. This was the first of many steps through which the Christian Democrats were drawn into an enduring electoral and subsequently a governing alliance with the parties of the secular left.

---

1. The debate over this argument is complex and ongoing. For some of the key contributions to this debate, see the references in Valenzuela et al. (2018).

The proponents of the view that the party system had become redefined by the democratic-authoritarian cleavage cited as evidence a 1995 *Latinobarometro* survey, which revealed a striking divergence across the political spectrum. Voters who identified with center and left parties strongly preferred democracy: 75 percent for both the PDC and the Party for Democracy (PPD). By contrast, relatively few voters who identified with right-wing parties preferred democracy: only 17 percent for the Union of Independent Democrats (UDI), and 36 percent for National Renewal (RN) (Torcal and Mainwaring 2003: 76). This, they argued, represented a stunning contrast between the two opposing positions.[2]

Along with this dramatic contrast among party identifiers, these analysts argued that the right had undergone a fundamental transformation. In the 1969 election for the lower chamber (the last election before Allende's electoral victory), the right won 20 percent of the electorate; after the plebiscite of 1988, the right doubled its vote share to over 40 percent. Some of its parties were new—in particular UDI—having been created by allies of the Pinochet government with the goal of preserving its legacy (Loxton 2016: 6–7). UDI developed new linkages to a variety of different constituencies. While it initially had strong ties to elites and business leaders, it subsequently sought to secure broader support from the popular sectors through a variety of strategies including clientelist practices (Luna 2010: 343–53).

Coalitional relationships on the center-left were also transformed.[3] The campaign for the 1988 plebiscite yielded a marked reduction in the historical enmity between the Christian Democrats, on the one hand, and the parties of the secular left on the other. The left parties, and in particular the Socialist party, many of whose members had formerly adopted a stance opposed to representative democracy, and had considered the Christian Democrats to be class enemies, adopted a more moderate stance, and embraced democracy (Torcal and Mainwaring 2003: 81–82).[4] During the 1988 plebiscite, there was a change in political tone and a tendency towards moderation, which remained an ongoing feature among longer-standing Chilean parties (Boas 2016: Ch. 2). This moderation stood in stark contrast to the more ideological and

---

2. The wording of the questions posed by the 1995 survey may lead to problems with the interpretation of these data, but the findings, even if exaggerated, certainly point to a wide breach between the two positions. For my view on the salience of the democratic-authoritarian cleavage, see Valenzuela et al. (2007) and Valenzuela et al. (2018).

3. It should be noted that other factors unrelated to the critical juncture also played a role in the transformation of the left. The collapse of the Soviet Union of course had a dramatic effect on communist parties throughout the world, and was very significant for the Chilean left. Another factor was indirectly related to the Pinochet experience. Many of Chile's political leaders lived in exile in both Eastern and Western Europe, contributing to an increased commitment to the democratic component of democratic socialism. See Lagos (2013: 390), Ortega Frei (1992), and Walker (1990).

4. Walker (1990) provides a full account of the gradual transition of the Socialist party toward representative, procedural democracy.

polarizing appeals made by the left prior to 1973. The result was an entente between the Christian Democrats and parties of the left that crystallized as a center-left coalition, the *Concertación*. The formation and duration for nearly thirty years of this coalition between parties of the secular left and the religiously oriented center was unprecedented, and represented an alliance that only the profoundly traumatic experience of the Pinochet regime could have forged (Munck and Bosworth 1998: 480–82).

The Christian Democrats' alliance with the secular left, which dominated Chilean politics from the beginning of the democratic transition until the elections of 2017, had important implications for the normative positions adopted (or perhaps it is better to say side-stepped) by this party. The very nature of this alliance between the more religiously oriented progressive Christian Democrats and the secular left increasingly meant that perspectives advanced by the parties in the *Concertación* coalition on issues such as divorce and abortion became necessarily more complex. An unmistakable *izquierdización* ("turn to the secular left"), occurred within the Concertation alliance when Michelle Bachelet returned from her stint at the United Nations in New York, and became especially acute when she regained the presidency in 2013. During the second Bachelet government, more secular and leftist elements of the *Concertación* gained a predominant voice within the governing alliance.

For many among the PDC rank and file and party notables, a watershed moment was reached in 2014 when the leftist members of the alliance embraced the Communist Party within the coalition, a move that appeared to some to violate the longstanding anti-communist stance of the PDC, and defined the party from its very inception. As we shall see below, this resulted in defections by numerous PDC supporters, many of whom shifted their support to rightist parties, particularly *Renovación Nacional* (RN). Under the leadership of Sebastián Piñera, who comes from a long family tradition of Christian Democrats, RN deftly moved to the center, advancing programmatic positions traditionally put forward by the PDC, especially as they pertained to sensitive religious values issues, and occupied the centrist political space previously claimed by the PDC.[5] From the standpoint of some PDC party loyalists, the decades-long governing and electoral alliance with parties of the secular left threatened to undermine the PDC's core identity, resulting in what Noam Lupu (2016: Ch. 1) has termed corrosive "brand dilution."[6] The steady decline in the PDC vote share, from 1993 to 2021, represents a significant marker of party system discontinuity. One indication of the decline of the centrist option as a preferred party

---

5. It is noteworthy that the advertisements designed to promote Sebastián Piñera's presidential bid were replete with countless images of the recently deceased and enormously popular former PDC president Patricio Aylwin, the first democratically elected president after the Pinochet regime.

6. For the Christian Democratic Party, the departures of party notables such as Mariana Aylwin, Soledad Alvear, and Gutenberg Martínez were particularly damaging to party morale and identity.

option is captured in longitudinal survey data reported by the Centro de Estudios Públicos. Whereas in 2005 there existed an 85 percent probability that a person who located him or herself at the center of the ideological spectrum identified with a particular political party, by 2014 that figure had fallen to 35 percent (Bargsted and Somma 2018: 217–18) Whether or not the PDC, and the political centrist option that it represented, can recover electorally, especially in light of its dismal performance in the May 2021 elections, remains an open question.[7]

THE CONSEQUENCES OF THE CHANGING ELECTORAL SYSTEM

The binomial electoral law that went into effect in 1989 was a driving force in shaping the electoral and coalitional dynamics that came to characterize the party system after the Pinochet period. The consequences of the law were not accidental. Indeed, some analysts such as Daniel Pastor maintain that the binomial system reflected a deliberate effort on the part of the Pinochet government to reshape the party system (Pastor 2004: 28).

This unusual electoral system was carefully designed by Pinochet loyalists to achieve two key goals. The first was to strengthen the right in the national legislature, giving it the capacity to veto constitutional reforms that might have weakened the prerogatives of the Pinochet loyalists, as well as to block other policy initiatives advanced by the center-left. Given the results of the 1988 plebiscite, if the electoral system had instead employed a simple plurality formula (with single-member districts), it was thought that rightist parties would have had a more difficult time winning seats, since the results of the plebiscite suggested that they could only mobilize about 40 percent of the electorate (Siavelis 1997: 657). By creating a system in which two seats were in play in each district, in order to win both seats a party needed to double the vote share of its nearest competitor. This meant that a runner-up party needed only 33 percent of the vote to win the second seat in a given district.

The law's second goal was to offer strong incentives in favor of a bimodal distribution of the electoral landscape. By limiting candidate lists to only two per district, the binomial rules provided a powerful incentive to group party alliances into two large coalitions. The resulting bimodal pattern of competition led some observers to view electoral politics through the lens of a contest between two large multiparty coalitions, rather than between the parties that formed them. This electoral formula played a key role in eroding the political center, both by weakening the Christian Democrats and by creating a bimodal coalitional imperative in which the PDC had

---

7. For a thoughtful discussion of the implosion of party identification experienced by the PDC, and its electoral consequences, see Navia and Osorio (2015).

no alternative but to form an alliance either with the right or the left. Operating as an independent center was not an electorally viable option. Given this choice, and given the recency of the authoritarian experience, an alliance with the right for the PDC was out of the question.

The actual representational consequences of the binomial electoral system produced fewer distortions than predicted, however. Though critics argued that it was designed to increase the legislative representation of the right, the real effect in terms of the apportionment of seats was rather negligible (Polga-Hecimovich and Siavelis 2015; Valenzuela et al. 2018). The parties of the *Concertación* alliance remained remarkably cohesive during elections in 1989 and 1993, winning majorities in the lower house while the right fell short of what it had expected. However, because the nine senators who were appointed for the 1990–1998 period were all sympathetic to the military regime, the right was able to block meaningful reforms to the constitution that would have weakened their own position (Siavelis 1997: 657–58).

Again, the biggest electoral loser in the binomial system was the Christian Democrats. This system created coalitional dynamics that tended to overrepresent smaller parties that formed part of the two large electoral coalitions, imposing a greater cost on the PDC in terms of lost representation and local party activation. The electoral decline experienced by the PDC is unprecedented among major Chilean parties in the period between 1989 and 2017. Whereas in the parliamentary elections of 1989 the PDC garnered 1.8 million votes, in the 2017 elections they attracted the support of a third of that total, or 617,000 votes. The PDC's decline has been even more precipitous in municipal elections. As my colleagues and I have argued, a central reason for the PDC's electoral decline "is due to its alliances [within the *Concertación* governments] with the secular left, especially from 2014 when the Communist party entered the coalition, isolating the party like no other in the matrix of symbolic positioning that buttresses the party system, thereby limiting its ability to obtain occasional electoral support from the soft vote of its coalition partners" (Valenzuela et al. 2018: 145).[8] These factors, along with weak PDC party leadership, growing secularization, and the greatly eroded institutional legitimacy of the Chilean Catholic Church due to the clerical abuse crisis, all combined to weaken the underlying electoral support of the PDC.

Another major consequence of the binomial system was its contribution to a growing crisis of representation. Under the binomial formula, the party system was in one important sense stable, given the low levels of volatility in the national vote share of the two contending party blocs. Yet, some analysts argued that the parties that made up the two coalitions appeared to have diminishing levels of legitimacy and rootedness in society, as well as weak grassroots organizations (Luna and Altman

---

8. See also Walker (2018) for a description of the divisive effects upon the PDC of the *izquierdización* of the *Concertación* alliance during the second Bachelet government.

2011: 3).[9] Electoral rules increasingly gave party elites, not voters in party primaries, control over candidate selection. The creation of electoral lists was dictated by pact-making, horse-trading, and backroom deals. Over time, the electoral rules promoted conflict among the parties comprising coalitional blocs, rather than between them. As we shall see below, this growing elite-driven character of Chilean party politics and resulting crisis of representation almost certainly contributed to the explosive electoral success of the secular leftist *Frente Amplio* coalition, which secured more than 20 percent of the vote in the 2017 parliamentary elections.

According to some analysts, the elitist character of Chilean democracy led to wide-spread disaffection with the traditional parties, and Luna (2016: 129–30) reports a significant crisis of representation that is reflected in a number of surveys. Trust in political and representative institutions reached an all-time low in 2021, with parties registering a mere 2 percent, Congress 8 percent, and the government 9 percent (Centro de Estudios Públicos 2021). Perhaps the most telling sign of the crisis of representation being experienced by Chile's traditional party elites was reflected in the striking success of non-party-affiliated independent candidates in the May 2021 elections for Chile's Constitutional Assembly. Independents garnered 48 of the 155 seats, or 31 percent of the seats. Most alarmingly, voter alienation from the political process was further reflected in the abysmally low voter turnout of 41 percent. These trends marked a significant departure from the past, when party politics was characterized by intense engagement and identification from the grassroots.

In 2015 the binomial system, long opposed ideologically by the center and left, was finally rescinded when fragmentation in the right enabled smaller parties to achieve the four-sevenths majority needed in both houses of congress (Campos 2009). The key vote to reach that majority in the Senate was provided by three independent senators.[10] The new 2015 electoral law introduced an open-list proportional representation system using a modified d'Hondt formula. This was much like the law that had been in effect before 1973. Twenty-eight House districts were created wherein magnitudes changed from two seats per district to districts whereby between 3 and 8 seats were available to be filled, depending on the population of the district. Correspondingly, 15 Senate districts were created with between 2 and 5 seats available. That meant that, whereas between 1989 and 2013 it was necessary to obtain at least 33 percent of the vote to gain a seat, in 2017 it was only necessary to secure 25 percent of the vote to obtain a seat. Furthermore, the total number of seats in both houses of Congress was expanded, from 120 to 155 in the Chamber of Deputies, and

---

9. Luna and Altman (2011) derive their figure to characterize the Chilean party system as "uprooted" from a 2010 LAPOP (Latin American Public Opinion Project) poll, which generated an excessively low estimate of the number of Chileans who identified with parties, asking "At this moment, do you sympathize with a political party?" Party identities are meant to refer to considerably longer-term attachments. See Valenzuela et al. (2018: 140).

10. For a thorough description of the intricate interparty negotiations that led to the 2015 electoral reform, see Gamboa and Morales (2016).

from 38 to 50 in the Senate. All parties could present lists with one more candidate than there were seats to be filled. As a result, each party coalition, which under the previous electoral law could present 120 total candidates nationally, could now put forward 183 candidates nationally.

The result of replacing the previous D'Hondt binomial formula with the new D'Hondt formula represented a significant discontinuity in the party system, which became apparent in the 2017 presidential and congressional elections.[11] In the absence of the powerful incentives to form two multiparty coalitions provided by the binomial system, the bimodal electoral dynamics that had been in place since 1989 virtually disappeared. Instead, the result was widespread party fragmentation and vote dispersion. The simple fact that 8 presidential candidates competed in the first round, and 9 multiparty lists of electoral coalitions competed for seats, provides a striking contrast with the relatively stable bimodal competitive dynamics that had formerly characterized the party system. The number of parties that won votes increased from 15 in 2013 to 26 in 2017. Moreover, 16 of those 26 parties obtained representation in the Chamber of Deputies. For comparison's sake, the historical average from 1932 to 2017 for the number of parties holding seats in the House is 11.1 parties. Only in the elections of 1932 and 1953 did a greater number of parties obtain representation in the House.

In the 2017 elections, Chile's four major parties saw their vote shares decline. Whereas the vote share of the top four parties from 1932 to 2017 averaged 69.4 percent, in 2017 that figure declined to 53.8 percent. Again, only in the elections of 1932 (52.7 percent), and 1953 (49.5 percent), did the major parties receive fewer votes. Employing the Laakso and Taagepera index to measure the effective number of parties, the effective number of both electoral and legislative parties reached their highest point since 1949, with more than 10 relevant parties competing in elections and more than 7 relevant parties represented in Congress. In 2017, only three parties, RN, UDI, and the PDC, received more than 10 percent of the total vote.

Another consequence of the adoption of a broader proportional representation formula, and the resulting lower threshold for successfully gaining seats, was the emergence of a loosely coupled secular-leftist coalition called the *Frente Amplio*, a driving factor in the erosion of the traditional parties' electoral support in 2017. An additional modification contained within the new electoral legislation reinforced this lower threshold with a new provision, which lowered the number of signatures required to form a new party to only 0.25 percent of the number of votes in the previous election, and led to the proliferation of small new parties formed around regional political notables, much like what occurred in Chile in the 1940s. Eschewing the identity of a formal party, the *Frente Amplio* "*movimiento*" brought a number of these smaller parties together with younger voters frustrated with what they viewed

---

11. For a very forceful argument advancing the perspective that the 2017 election resulted in a fundamental change in the Chilean party system, see Bunker (2018).

as the political machinations of the parties in the *Concertación* alliance. Concentrated in the Metropolitan Region of Santiago and Valparaíso, the *Frente Amplio* coalition seized upon the growing disaffection with the parties that had comprised the *Concertación* and tapped into a secular-leftist largely anti-party sentiment within the electorate, and as such took votes primarily from the Communists and Socialists, and to a lesser extent from the Radical Party and the PPD. The electoral success of the *Frente Amplio* was repeated in the May 2021 elections, when they gained 16 seats in the Constitutional Assembly, and won surprising electoral upsets in major urban areas such as Valparaíso and Viña del Mar. However, despite these successes, there are reasons to doubt the institutional coherence or the longer-term viability of this internally fragmented coalition of convenience. That said, there can be no doubt that the suddenness of the electoral surge and popularity of the *Frente Amplio*, especially among younger voters, introduces a major political "wild card" into the party system, and thus poses a major challenge to the future prospects of the traditional parties. But, viewed more positively, the improved incentives for the formation and electoral success of smaller parties and independent candidates provided by the 2015 electoral formula gave social actors, who had previously lacked meaningful representation, a new impulse to engage in the political process.

As my colleagues and I predicted in earlier work, the adoption in 2012 of universal and automatic voter registration combined with voluntary voting resulted in significant declining levels of turnout (Valenzuela et al. 2018: 157–58). In fact, with only 46.7 percent of registered voters going to the polls in the 2017 elections and, as was noted earlier, 41 percent in May 2021, Chile's level of turnout ranks among the lowest in South America. To place this declining turnout in Chile within a broader longitudinal context, voter turnout in first-round presidential elections in Chile has fallen by 40 percent, from 87 percent in 1989 (when registration was voluntary but voting was mandatory) to 47 percent in 2017. Of further concern is the recent increase in null and blank votes cast in the 2017 election, which rose from a regional average of 6–7 percent in the 2013 election to 10–11 percent in the 2017 elections, potentially signaling dissatisfaction with party offerings.[12]

As further foreseen, the 2012 adoption of voluntary voting led to a significant increase in electoral volatility. As my colleagues and I argued, the adoption of voluntary voting would "create even more variation in the composition of legislatures and councils given the small margin of victory in many contests, as many voters who are aligned with different segments of opinion feel differently motivated, given the

---

12. A more likely explanation for the significant increase in null and blank votes is the sheer increase in the complexity of the ballot due to the explosion of the number of candidates up for election in any given district. Whereas in 2013 there were 470 candidates for the lower house, in 2017 there were 960. Between 1989 and 2013, the average number of lower-house candidates numbered around 8 per district, in 2017 that number rose to 34, sharply increasing the cost of information for voters. In some districts there were over 50 candidates from which voters had to choose! See Morales (2018: 244–45, 255).

circumstances of the moment, to show up at the voting booth" (Valenzuela et al. 2018: 158). The resulting increase in volatility has been striking. Whereas from 1989 to 2005, the average electoral volatility in House elections was 13.9 percent, from 2013 to 2017 period, volatility reached 21.2 percent. (Most of this added volatility was due to what Mainwaring et al. (2016) termed "extra-system electoral volatility," i.e., when the percentage of votes from one or more established parties are captured by a new party, as opposed to within-system electoral volatility, when votes are exchanged between established parties.) The sharp increase in extra-system volatility in 2017, from an average during the 1989–2005 period of 2.9 percent to 8.9 percent in the 2013–2017 period, provides further evidence of increasing dissatisfaction with preexisting party options. Overall, this suggests a significant change in the structure of party competition.

ARGUMENTS FOR CONTINUITY

Notwithstanding these telling indicators of discontinuity within the party system, there exists evidence of important elements of continuity in terms of the fundamental axes of cleavage that provide the underlying political sensibilities that define voter identities, suggesting that the Pinochet period *per se* did not constitute a critical juncture. By the second decade of the twenty-first century, the party legacies of authoritarian rule had largely been eroded. Moreover, most institutional protections put in place by the authoritarian regime, such as the appointed senators, were eliminated by 2005, and Pinochet, who had been designated as senator for life, stepped down in 2002, and died under house arrest in 2006. Even the parties of the right supported the elimination of most of the protective institutions created by the outgoing military regime. Moreover, revelations of corruption during the Pinochet period further discredited the authoritarian regime, and multiple surveys have shown a broadly negative assessment of Pinochet himself. As we have argued, the electoral dynamics that characterized the party system between 1989 and 2017 were driven largely by the imperatives of the binomial electoral formula. The two contending blocs became, in fact, coalitions of convenience, and the parties that constituted these blocs have—notwithstanding the dynamics of coalitional formation—by and large retained their distinctive identities.

While the legacy of authoritarian rule surely cast a shadow over party politics during the 1990s and into the early 2000s, increasingly Chilean voter proclivities appeared to continue to reflect a resonance with the earlier cleavage lines of class and religion. Along with my co-authors, I have argued that the deep and long-standing political, social, and ideological subcultures and predispositions that derive from earlier underlying religious and class cleavages still provide "a general sense of [voter] self-placement within the scaffolding of party system divisions" (Valenzuela et al. 2018: 141).

The central argument for continuity rests on the claim that the two earlier lines of fundamental cleavage, religion and class, continue to be major forces shaping the underlying morphology of the party system. At the same time, making a claim for the continued salience of religion and class does not overlook the profound social and economic transformations experienced by Chile over the past few decades. Nor does it suggest that the specific manner in which the issues that define these decisive cleavages have not experienced substantial changes themselves in terms of how they are experienced or have become articulated in contemporary Chile. The cultural, economic, and social contexts have changed profoundly since the return to democracy.

In terms of religion, like most countries in the region, Chile is undergoing a persistent and unprecedented process of secularization. Whereas in 2006, 12 percent of the Chilean population reported practicing no religion, by 2020 that figure had risen to 36 percent, with an outsized percentage of those claiming to practice no religion among the young (Latinobarómetro 2020). In addition, levels of trust in the Catholic Church, which continues to be the reported religious identity of the majority of Chileans, have plummeted, both among Catholics as well as within the broader population. By 2020, trust in the Catholic Church among Chileans had fallen to just 31 percent, the lowest by a considerable margin in the region (Latinobarómetro 2020). These broader contextual trends have undoubtedly reshaped how religious issues are experienced and get translated into the political arena, contributing to the electoral implosion of the PDC and a shift in the evangelical vote to the less secular parties of the right.[13]

A similar set of observations needs to be made about the underlying structure of class in Chile. Whereas the earlier instantiations of the class cleavage were driven by the relations between worker-owner, and peasant-landholder, the social structure of contemporary Chile is much more complex and variegated. No longer a "third-world country," Chile needs to be viewed today as an upper-middle-income country. With the highest per capita GDP in the region in 2019 of over $ 24,000 per year, Chile has made significant progress in reducing inequality and has succeeded in a rather dramatic reduction in poverty. Whereas in 2012, 22.2 percent of the population lived in poverty, and 8.1 percent lived in extreme poverty, by 2015 those figures had been reduced to 11.7 percent and 3.5 percent, respectively (ECLAC 2018; World Bank 2018). As a result of these transformations, contemporary Chile is characterized by significant emerging aspirational middle sectors of society. Take, for example, the fact that in 2013, 30 percent of Chileans considered themselves "middle class," but by 2018 that figure had risen to 37 percent (Latinobarómetro 2018). Or take also the fact that as recently as 2013, seven out of every ten students enrolled in higher education in Chile are first-generation students (Walker 2013: 191). This new set of middle sectors are perhaps not best understood as an emergent

---

13. These figures come from the Bicentenario Survey conducted by the Department of Sociology of the Catholic University in Chile, 2018; similar figures are reported in Latinobarómetro (2018).

new "class." Rather, given the fact that they are characterized by an extreme heterogeneity of cultural, social, and political interests, these new social actors lack both the identity of, and the homogeneity of, a class. Politically, this growing set of social actors has demonstrated a very high degree of heterogeneity in terms of party vote; they vote across the party spectrum. Appealing successfully to the emerging aspirational middle sectors in Chile and in other more economically advanced countries in Latin America reveals the continued salience of social class, and comprises what Ignacio Walker has termed the central electoral challenge of the times: the challenge of "the New Social Question in Latin America" (Walker 2013: 191–214; see also Foxley and Stallings 2016).

A further indicator of underlying system continuity can be discerned in the results of the unusually disruptive 2017 elections. Despite the exceptional degree of vote dispersion and party fragmentation, driven in large part by the adoption in 2015 of the proportional representation formula and other changes in the representation formula that are discussed above, the seven principal Chilean parties (as we define them in Valenzuela et al. 2018: 137) still obtained 68 percent of the parliamentary vote in 2017. Though admittedly lower than the vote share of the principal parties before and after the dictatorship (which historically averaged nearly 80 percent in parliamentary elections), it is arguably still within the expected range. And in comparison with other Latin American and European party systems, even with the important changes in the representation formula described in the foregoing, the principal parties' 68 percent vote share reflects a relatively high degree of party system continuity. Indeed, the principal parties that had previously constituted the *Concertación* alliance and that comprised the major electoral coalitions in the 2017 parliamentary elections, *Chile Vamos* on the right and *la Fuerza de la Mayoría* and *Convergencia Democrática* on the center-left, each still captured roughly one-third of the vote in a majority of the regions in the country.

The ideological tendencies that define these seven principal parties continue to be the two historic axes of differentiation, religion and class. The secular-leftist side of the spectrum continues to be anchored by parties such as the Communists and the Socialists that draw their symbols and trace their ancestry back to the formative decades of the labor movement. The loosely coupled coalition of parties and voters in the *Frente Amplio* are the most recent manifestation of new formations on the mostly secular-leftist side of the ideological spectrum. It is perhaps worth remembering that smaller parties and movements have presented candidates, though not in the same numbers as in 2017 and May 2021, since 1989, and even in parliamentary elections, capturing between 10 and 25 percent of the vote. A secular versus religious difference over value-laden issues such as marriage, abortion, and education policy remains deeply salient. Finally, the old split between the social Christians and traditionalist Conservatives is still reflected in the differences between the more socially progressive Christian Democrats and the more socially conservative parties of the right, in particular UDI. This set of party subcultures bears resemblance to the party system in place before 1973.

A relatively strong sense of ideological self-identification among voters—along with a degree of intergenerational continuity in party identities—can also be discerned in contemporary Chilean politics. It is a mistake to think that, in the past, voters identified more intensely with parties; indeed, within a complex multiparty system, voters have always had low levels of identification with specific parties (Valenzuela et al. 2018). Again, these identities are best understood, rather than in terms of specific party labels, by their subcultural sensibilities along the original axes of cleavage: religion and class. In a 2013 survey, socioeconomic and religious factors strongly influenced voters' attachments to parties, while attitudes toward regime type shifted decisively in favor of democracy for all voters. In addition, on a spectrum of closeness to the Church and to the rich, voters were able to locate parties with accuracy. This suggests a deeply embedded social rootedness of parties that is often overlooked.[14]

The results of the 2017 parliamentary elections revealed that the bimodal dynamics characteristic of electoral politics from 1989 to 2013 was almost entirely a by-product of the coalitional imperatives imposed by the binomial electoral system. With its elimination, the two contending electoral blocs that had their origins in the 1988 plebiscite experienced a very different set of electoral challenges. In fact, it can be argued that the so-called democratic-authoritarian cleavage was largely a reflection of this bimodal electoral imperative. In the more than twenty-five years for which data are available, well over half of Chileans surveyed have nearly always responded affirmatively to the question "In Chile only democracy is preferable to any other form of government." In 2018, that figure was 58 percent, ranking it fourth-highest in Latin America and tied with Argentina (and nearly equal to Costa Rica at 63 percent, and Uruguay, at 61 percent) (Latinobarómetro 2018). In 2020, in response to the question, "It doesn't matter to me if a non-democratic government were to come to power as long as it resolves the problems," less than 30 percent of Chileans responded affirmatively, the lowest by far in the region (Latinobarómetro 2020). I argue with my co-authors that, during the 1973 crisis and in its aftermath, the key defining conflict for the right was not a dispute over the value of democracy itself, or an advocacy of an authoritarian regime, but rather a profound dispute over fundamental principles involving socioeconomic policies advanced especially by the Allende government (Valenzuela et al. 2018: 146–57).

ASSESSMENT

Assessing whether or not a fourth critical juncture has occurred to redefine the underlying cleavages that underpin the party system in Chile and generate a new

---

14. The 2013 survey was designed and undertaken by Valenzuela et al., and is the most recent survey that is available that asks the kind of questions that identify these underlying features of the party system. See Valenzuela et al. (2018).

set of parties defined by these new identities requires a nuanced interpretation of ongoing change. With the introduction of proportional representation and other changes in the representation formula in 2015, the bimodal distribution of the electorate that characterized party competition since 1989, largely a product of the binomial formula, disappeared in the 2017 presidential and parliamentary elections. It is not likely to reappear any time soon. The crisis of representation noted by various scholars that resulted largely from the elite-centered horse-trading politics driven by the coalitional imperatives provided by the binomial formula, and the growing disaffection with and eroding electoral support of, the traditional parties, represent unmistakable signs of discontinuity with the former party system. The exceptional party fragmentation that resulted in the 2017 elections, combined with higher levels of voter volatility and lower levels of voter turnout, are also indications that important changes are occurring at the level of the party system. The fact that non-party-affiliated independents emerged in the May 2021 electoral contest as the largest political force in the country argues forcibly for change over continuity. This, combined with the emergence of a Communist Party-*Frente Amplio* alliance as a hegemonic political force on the left, with a weakened center-left represented by the *Lista del Apruebo*, and a PDC that bit the dust electorally, further reinforces that view. All of this, set in a broader context of a majority of politically unengaged voters who do not see the value of even turning up at the polls, redounds to the argument of change over continuity.

Nonetheless, I argue that these shifts, as important as they are, do not necessarily constitute an enduring and fundamental change in the underlying subcultures and predispositions that define different segments of the Chilean electorate. Rather, the essential morphology of parties continues to reflect the long-standing divisions in society along religious and class lines. As we have argued, these divisions were created, and recreated, by the three critical junctures of the mid-nineteenth and twentieth centuries. That said, it is essential to recognize the different ways these earlier lines of cleavage manifest themselves given the depth of the cultural, economic, and social transformations experienced by Chile over the past several decades. The searing winds of secularization and the crisis of confidence in the Catholic Church have deeply impacted how religious issues, though still salient, become translated into party politics. Values-related issues such as women's equality, protection of the environment, the rights of indigenous peoples, and greater access to abortion are high on the list of those who campaigned successfully in the May 2021 elections.

Though a profoundly changed electoral landscape has emerged, it is important not to overstate the discontinuities. The parties of the right in *Chile Vamos* still managed to win 37 seats in the Constitutional Assembly, or 24 percent of all seats. The parties of the *Lista del Apruebo* consisting of the parties of the former *Concertación* obtained 25 seats, or 16 percent of the seats. In all, party-affiliated candidates won 90 seats, or 58 percent of the seats, and therefore hold the largest single bloc in the Constitutional Assembly. In the highly contested gubernatorial elections of May 2021, the first of their kind in Chile, the traditional center-left parties of the former

Concertación, aligned in the *Unidad Constituyente,* won 10 of the 16 governorships, including the Metropolitan Region of Santiago, securing 47.5 percent of the votes cast nationally. The *Frente Amplio*/Communist Party alliance captured the leadership of two regions with nearly 30 percent of the national vote, while the right aligned in *Chile Vamos* was able to capture only one governorship, with 13.5 percent of the vote. Independents again displayed a degree of strength, capturing three governorships, with 10.4 percent of the vote. Though with the lowest voter turnout on record at 20 percent, it is important not to draw definitive conclusions from the results of the regional elections. Still, the remarkable persistence of deep-seated political subcultures with origins long before 1973 suggests that the criteria for identifying a new critical juncture, in terms of a new generative cleavage, have not been met—at least not yet.

But these claims of continuity need to be made with a great deal of humility and tentativeness. It is certainly telling that the degree of party fragmentation, voter dispersion, and electoral volatility that resulted in the elections of 2017 and May 2021 has not been seen since 1932 and 1953. These two dates, perhaps not coincidentally, correspond nearly exactly with two earlier critical junctures, wherein the class cleavage in the urban and subsequently the rural sector came to redefine the cleavage lines of Chilean party competition. There are clearly powerful new social forces at work in Chilean society, perhaps made no more visibly manifest than in the explosion of social protests across the country in October 2019, which served as the catalyst for the overwhelming majority of Chilean voters calling for a new constitution. But as other authors in this volume have made abundantly clear, it is essential not to be too hasty when invoking a new critical juncture. Two elections, even as disruptive as the 2017 and May 2021 elections were, cannot serve as the basis for a definitive conclusion. By early 2021, the forces of fluidity and disequilibrium at work on the political landscape had made prediction nearly impossible. For example, even at the time of this writing, the Chilean Congress was deliberating a provision to reinstate mandatory voting, a potentially salutary institutional change that almost certainly would have profound implications for future elections.[15] If this measure had been implemented in time for the presidential and parliamentary elections of November and December 2021, it would undoubtedly have had profound implications for a

---

15. The challenge of building an argument that incorporates a long-term historical perspective, in the absence of adequate hindsight to evaluate the legacy of a hypothesized critical juncture, can be illustrated in my experience in presenting this analysis at the 2021 Congress of the Latin American Studies Association (LASA). On the one hand, a key strand of the study extends back to the nineteenth century. On the other hand, the panel was on a Thursday. In Chile, the previous Saturday saw an electoral outcome crucial to my analysis, and the intervening Monday witnessed the first step in a key initiative—involving compulsory voting—that could transform electoral dynamics in a way that was likewise critical for my interpretation. All of this places in dramatic relief the juxtaposition of research on critical junctures and a focus on current events.

broad array of electoral dynamics within the party system. This is but one example of the difficulty of determining the presence of a critical juncture without the benefit of a long enough time horizon.

To conclude, some further observations should be made about the importance of historical distance in evaluating critical junctures and their legacies. These observations are relevant as a general comment on the study of critical junctures, thereby making a connection with other chapters in this part of the volume. They also contribute to interpreting the Chilean case by placing it in comparative perspective.

Two distinctive challenges emerge in analyzing Chile: the imperative of adopting a long time horizon and the problem of false positives. Thus, it can readily be argued that key observations needed in evaluating the legacy of the hypothesized critical juncture can only be made in the years after 2015—following a full twenty-five years of competitive democratic politics, and after fully assessing the consequences of the changes in the representation formula, and the depth of the crisis of representation that appear to be reshuffling the contemporary Chilean electoral landscape in important ways. Researchers must be patient in waiting for the evidence to come in. Further, for scholars seeking to demonstrate that the Chilean party system has definitively changed, this delay in the emergence of crucial evidence substantially increases the risk of a *false positive*. There is a danger of incorrectly confirming the hypothesis of change, simply because the relevant evidence for continuity is not yet available. In the critical juncture framework, this chapter has cautiously argued for the hypothesis of continuity, recognizing that in the coming years, further evidence must be critically evaluated to determine whether fundamental change has in fact produced an enduring legacy.

BIBLIOGRAPHY

Bargsted, Matías, and Nicolás M. Somma. 2018. "La cultura política, diagnóstico y evolución." In Carlos Huneeus and Octavio Avendaño Pavez (eds.), *El sistema político de Chile* (pp. 193–224). Santiago, Chile: LOM Ediciones.

Bernhard, Michael. 2015. "Chronic Instability and the Limits of Path Dependence." *Perspectives on Politics* 13(4): 976–91.

Boas, Taylor. 2016. *Presidential Campaigns in Latin America: Electoral Strategies and Success Contagion.* New York, NY: Cambridge University Press.

Bunker, Kenneth. 2018. "La elección de 2017 y el fraccionamiento del sistema de partidos en Chile." *Revista Chilena de Derecho y Ciencia Política* 9(2): 204–29.

Campos, Javiera. 2009. "El sistema electoral binominal: duro de matar." In Patricio Navia Lucero, Mauricio Morales Quiroga, and Renato Briceño Espinoza (eds.), *El genoma electoral chileno: dibujando el mapa genético de las preferencias políticas en Chile* (pp. 33–53). Santiago, Chile: Ediciones Universidad Diego Portales.

Centro de Estudios Públicos. 2021. Encuesta especial CEP, April 2021.

Collier, Ruth Berins, and David Collier. 1991. *Shaping the Political Arena: Critical Junctures, the Labor Movement and Regime Dynamics in Latin America.* Princeton, NY: Princeton University Press.

ECLAC. 2018. *Social Panorama of Latin America 2017*. Santiago, Chile: United Nations.

Foxley, Alejandro, and Barbara Stallings (eds.). 2016. *Innovation and Inclusion in Latin America: Strategies to Avoid the Middle Income Trap*. New York, NY: Palgrave Macmillan.

Gamboa, Ricardo, and Mauricio Morales. 2016. "Chile's 2015 Electoral Reform: Changing the Rules of the Game." *Latin American Politics and Society* 58(4): 126–44.

Hunter, Wendy. 1997. "Continuity or Change? Civil-Military Relations in Democratic Argentina, Chile, and Peru." *Political Science Quarterly* 112(3): 453–75.

Lagos, Ricardo. 2013. *Mi vida. De la infancia a la lucha contra la dictadura. Memorias I*. Santiago, Chile: Penguin Random House.

Latinobarómetro. 2018. *Informe Latinobarómetro 2018*. Santiago de Chile: Corporación Latinobarómetro.

———. 2020. *Informe Latinobarómetro 2020*. Santiago de Chile: Corporación Latinobarómetro.

Lipset, Seymour M., and Stein Rokkan. 1967. "Cleavage Structures, Party Systems, and Voter Alignments: An Introduction." In Seymour M. Lipset and Stein Rokkan (eds.), *Party Systems and Voter Alignments: Cross-National Perspectives* (pp. 1–64). New York, NY: Free Press.

Loxton, James. 2016. "Authoritarian Successor Parties Worldwide: A Framework for Analysis." Kellogg Institute for International Studies *Working Paper* # 411. Notre Dame, IN: University of Notre Dame.

Luna, Juan Pablo. 2010. "Segmented Party-Voter Linkages in Latin America: The Case of the UDI." *Journal of Latin American Studies* 42(2): 325–56.

———. 2016. "Chile's Crisis of Representation." *Journal of Democracy* 27(3): 129–38.

Luna, Juan Pablo, and David Altman. 2011. "Uprooted but Stable: Chilean Parties and the Concept of Party System Institutionalization." *Latin American Politics and Society* 53(2): 1–28.

Lupu, Noam. 2016. *Party Brands in Crisis: Partisanship, Brand Dilution, and the Breakdown of Political Parties in Latin America*. New York, NY: Cambridge University Press.

Mahoney, James. 2000. "Path Dependence in Historical Sociology." *Theory and Society* 29(4): 507–48.

Mainwaring, Scott, Carlos Gervasoni, and Annabella España-Najera. 2016. "Extra- and Within-System Electoral Volatility." *Party Politics* 23(6): 623–35.

Morales, Mauricio. 2018. "Elecciones y participación en Chile, 1988–2017." In Carlos Huneeus and Octavio Avendaño Pavez (eds.), *El sistema político de Chile* (pp. 225–57). Santiago, Chile: LOM Ediciones.

Munck, Gerardo L., and Jeffrey Bosworth. 1998. "Patterns of Representation and Competition: Parties and Democracy in Post-Pinochet Chile." *Party Politics* 4(4): 471–93.

Navia, Patricio, and Rodrigo Osorio. 2015. "It's the Christian Democrats' Fault: Declining Political Identification in Chile, 1957–2012." *Canadian Journal of Political Science/Revue canadienne de science politique* 48(4): 815–38.

Ortega Frei, Eugenio. 1992. *Historia de una alianza: el Partido Socialista de Chile y el Partido Demócrata Cristiano. 1973–1988*. Santiago, Chile: CED-CESOC.

Pastor, Daniel. 2004. "Origins of the Chilean Binominal Election System." *Revista de Ciencia Política* 24(1): 38–57.

Polga-Hecimovich, John, and Peter Siavelis. 2015. "Here's the Bias! A (Re-) Reassessment of the Chilean Electoral System." *Electoral Studies* 40: 268–79.

Roberts, Kenneth M. 2014. *Changing Course in Latin America: Party Systems in the Neoliberal Era*. New York, NY: Cambridge University Press.

Scully, Timothy R. 1992. *Rethinking the Center: Party Politics in Nineteenth- and Twentieth-Century Chile*. Stanford, CA: Stanford University Press.

Siavelis, Peter. 1997. "Continuity and Change in the Chilean Party System: On the Transformational Effects of Electoral Reform." *Comparative Political Studies* 30(6): 651–74.

Tironi, Eugenio, and Felipe Agüero. 1999. "¿Sobrevivirá el nuevo paisaje político chileno?" *Estudios Públicos* 74: 151–58.

Torcal, Mariano, and Scott Mainwaring. 2003. "The Political Recrafting of Social Bases of Party Competition: Chile, 1973–95." *British Journal of Political Science* 33(1): 55–84.

Valenzuela, J. Samuel, Timothy R. Scully, and Nicolás Somma. 2007. "The Enduring Presence of Religion in Chilean Ideological Positionings and Voter Options." *Comparative Politics* 40(1): 1–20.

Valenzuela, J. Samuel, Nicolás Somma, and Timothy R. Scully. 2018. "Resilience and Change: The Party System in Redemocratized Chile." In Scott Mainwaring (ed.), *Party Systems in Latin America: Institutionalization, Decay, and Collapse* (pp. 135–63). New York, NY: Cambridge University Press.

Visconti, Giancarlo. 2021. "Reevaluando la tesis del desplome." *Centro de Investigación Periodística*. Santiago: Chile. May 22, 2021.

Walker, Ignacio. 1990. *Socialismo y democracia: Chile y Europa en perspectiva comparada*. Santiago, Chile: CIEPLAN-Hachette.

———. 2013. *Democracy in Latin America: Between Hope and Despair*. Notre Dame, IN: University of Notre Dame Press.

———. 2018. *La Nueva Mayoría. Reflexiones sobre una derrota*. Santiago, Chile: Catalonia.

———. 2021. "Otro país." *El Mostrador*, Santiago, Chile.

World Bank. 2018. *World Development Report 2018*. Washington, DC: World Bank.

17

Potential Mistakes, Plausible Options

Establishing the Legacy of Hypothesized Critical Junctures

Taylor C. Boas

When I was studying at Berkeley in the first decade of the 2000s, a recurring question was whether the shift to neoliberalism constituted a "new critical juncture" for Latin American politics. In graduate seminars, we frequently debated the political consequences of neoliberal reforms and how to make sense of the ensuing transformations of party systems and political representation. Meanwhile, others outside of Berkeley were pursuing similar themes. Most prominently, Kenneth Roberts began developing the "new critical juncture" argument in detail, both in a 2002 article and also in the draft book manuscript—circulating *samizdat*-style among Berkeley graduate students at the time—that eventually became *Changing Course in Latin America* (Roberts 2002, 2014).

In exploring critical junctures, we sought to ask big questions about substantively important outcomes in Latin American politics, but also to answer these questions through a careful application of the comparative method. And while I enjoyed debating the *new* critical juncture question in seminars and hallway conversations, I had significant doubts at the time as to whether it could be answered in a similarly definitive fashion as Collier and Collier (1991) had done for the *old* one. My concern centered on the inherent difficulties in analyzing recent or ongoing transformations with a method and theoretical model that presupposes temporal distance from the events in question. Looking at the panorama of Latin American politics and party systems several years later, I think many of these misgivings were justified.

In this essay, I reflect upon the challenges of using the critical juncture framework to analyze the political- and party-system consequences of the shift to neoliberalism in Latin America. I do so primarily by examining the work of Roberts (2002, 2014). I should state at the outset that I consider *Changing Course in Latin America* to be a masterful analysis of the transformation of Latin American party systems over the past several decades, as well as a careful application of the critical juncture framework, which is often invoked much more casually. Moreover, as both Roberts's book (2014) and his contribution to this book (see Chapter 14) make clear, we agree on the importance of hindsight in developing a critical juncture argument.

Yet I would urge caution in applying the critical juncture framework in cases where it is uncertain whether a definitive legacy has emerged. Absent a clear dividing line between the hypothesized legacy and the present day, one risks making an analytical mistake. That is, the outcome being explained might ultimately prove to be just one step in a larger sequence of reactions and counterreactions to the critical juncture. One need not take this theoretical framework off the table when analyzing contemporary transformations, especially in arguments about sequential critical junctures, where only the most recent in a series of branching points lies close to the present. Yet in all cases, scholars should characterize arguments about recent critical junctures as hypotheses that must await the passage of time to be fully evaluated.

THE IMPORTANCE OF TEMPORAL DISTANCE

Collier and Collier (1991: 29) define a critical juncture as "a period of significant change, which typically occurs in distinct ways in different countries (or in other units of analysis) and which is hypothesized to produce distinct legacies." A critical juncture argument thus constitutes a causal hypothesis linking a major societal transformation to a temporally distant dependent variable that represents the culmination of a process of change, not merely something that happened along the way.

Connecting the critical juncture and legacy by means of process-tracing is necessary for evaluating this hypothesis. In order to advance a critical juncture argument, therefore, one needs to specify the legacy *a priori* and describe how countries vary with respect to this legacy. Doing so is crucial not only for establishing that there are distinct legacies produced by the critical juncture, but also for connecting cause and effect.

Given the need to score cases on the outcome when applying a critical juncture framework, it is essential to adopt specific criteria for identifying the end of the legacy, while also remaining open to some ambiguity about its duration (Collier and Collier 1991: 33–34). Collier and Collier had the advantage of a clear analytical endpoint for five of their cases: coups in the 1960s and 1970s that ushered in long-term military rule and fundamentally interrupted party system dynamics. More generally, however, the change in Latin America's economic environment brought on by the debt crisis and neoliberal reform radically altered the conditions that had facilitated the class compromises of the incorporation period and underlain party system dynamics throughout the legacy. In Mexico, Colombia, and Venezuela, therefore, Collier and Collier were able to argue that the legacy had sufficiently crystalized by the 1980s to allow for analysis, despite important elements of continuity in these countries' subsequent party system development.

The critical junctures framework is typically used to make arguments about causal processes that are hypothesized to play out over long periods of time, so extended analytical time horizons are crucial. The point of departure for a critical juncture is typically a cleavage or crisis that calls into question the political status quo. Yet the critical juncture is analytically distinct from this cleavage or crisis, and it is often temporally removed as well. The emergence of the legacy may also be temporally removed from the critical juncture itself. This is particularly true if "the critical juncture is a polarizing event that produces intense political reactions and counterreactions." These are intervening steps that constitute the "mechanisms of production" of the legacy one seeks to analyze (Collier and Collier 1991: 37).

In the conclusion to *Shaping the Political Arena*, and in their Authors' Note in the 2002 edition, Collier and Collier (1991: 772–74; 2002: xv) pose the question of a new critical juncture for Latin American politics stemming from the collapse of the state-centric economic model and the ensuing shift to neoliberalism. Though this economic transformation had many distinct causes, and the height of neoliberal reform happened at different times in different places, for the purpose of analysis we can identify the 1982 debt crisis as playing a key role in the move toward reform efforts in many countries, and in placing the issue on the table in others.

Given the timing of neoliberal reform, contemporary efforts to develop a "new critical juncture" argument face major challenges. Across the eight cases in *Shaping the Political Arena*, the average onset of the reform period was the year 1921, or seven decades prior to the book's publication (Collier and Collier 1991: 164). If Collier and Collier had attempted to assess the long-term impact of labor incorporation in the 1940s or 1950s, they would have fundamentally mischaracterized the outcome in most countries. Even if the analyst is convinced that political transformations play out on a faster scale in the contemporary period, analyzing the political legacy of a neoliberal critical juncture only two to three decades after the debt crisis implies a significant challenge. Characterizing this legacy and scoring cases on the dependent variable are obviously difficult when one may be in the midst of the reactions and counterreactions that are producing the legacy itself.

Temporal distance is helpful not only for applying the critical junctures framework, but also for making available the sort of data and scholarly sources that are routinely used for comparative-historical analysis. Writing a half-century after the events in question, Collier and Collier drew upon a massive bibliography of country-specific monographs covering various historical episodes. Work of this sort takes time to produce, and less of it will be available to present-day scholars analyzing a more recent transformation.[1] In sum, the lack of temporal distance between the period of neoliberal reform and the present raises serious challenges in assessing the outcome that is being analyzed, and in judging whether it will endure.

---

1. The problem is compounded by the fact that new methodological trends and changing standards in comparative politics have made the single-country dissertation based on extensive fieldwork less common than it was a generation ago.

Taylor C. Boas

ASSESSING THE LEGACY
OF A NEW CRITICAL JUNCTURE

These reflections on temporal distance have implications for assessing Roberts's work. In the first published formulation of his argument, Roberts (2002) maintains that the critical juncture stemming from the 1982 debt crisis fundamentally altered labor-mobilizing party systems by undermining their class-based character, trans-forming them into something much more similar to their elitist counterparts. The result, Roberts argues, is a "re-oligarchization" of politics, in which party competition across the region revolves around individual politicians and patronage networks that do little to promote class identities.

This re-oligarchization of politics is an accurate characterization of what Roberts treats as the legacy of the neoliberal critical juncture—the landscape of Latin American party systems at the time. Yet as Roberts acknowledges in his contribution to this book, and as his 2014 book makes abundantly clear, the year 2002 in no way constituted the end point of the party system legacy of neoliberal reform. On the contrary, the early 2000s marked the beginning of a series of reactions to neoliberalism that brought left-wing, class-mobilizing parties to power in much of Latin America, fundamentally altering the political landscape that had prevailed at the turn of the millennium (Levitsky and Roberts 2011).

Moreover, while the re-oligarchization of politics had involved growing similarities among previously diverse party systems, Roberts (2014) identified distinct, divergent trajectories that depended on the type of party implementing neoliberal reform. His argument may be summarized concisely: where conservative parties led these reforms and a strong left party could provide consistent opposition, party systems stabilized along a programmatic axis of competition—as exemplified by Brazil. Where leftist opposition to conservative-led reform was weak, or where independents or labor-based parties themselves were the ones to implement such reforms, the major players in the political system all converged on support for neoliberalism, opening the door to social protest, populist challenges from the left, and high electoral volatility—as exemplified by Venezuela. In these latter cases, Roberts argues, the party system legacy of the new critical juncture was an unstable equilibrium, given the polarizing "reactive sequences" (Mahoney 2000) spawned by neoliberal reform.

How confidently can we conclude that the ultimate party system legacy of neoliberal reform is as Roberts (2014) describes it? Was there a reason for greater certainty in 2014 than in 2002? As noted above, Collier and Collier (1991) had a strong basis for arguing that the legacy of labor incorporation had crystalized by the time of their analysis: long-term military rule interrupted party system dynamics in five of eight countries; and an exogenous shock, the debt crisis, fundamentally altered state–society relations in all of them. In the present era, by contrast, we may still be in the midst of ongoing change. Political competition throughout the region continues to be driven by reactions and counterreactions to neoliberal reform and its conse-quences, as the campaign rhetoric of left-wing candidates has often made abundantly clear. As a result, we should inherently exercise more caution when analyzing the legacy of new critical junctures compared to events that occurred in the distant past. In other words, reactive sequences that had yet to begin in 2002 are clearly in play, but we cannot be certain that they have concluded.

Indeed, developments since 2014 suggest that stable patterns of competition might still emerge in some of the party systems where Roberts (2014) had identified unstable equilibria. One possible scenario is seen in the emergence of Republican Proposal (PRO) in Argentina in the 2000s and the election of Mauricio Macri in 2015. Here, Peronism's left turn under the Kirchners encouraged once-fragmented (or authoritarian-inclined) conservative forces to unify in order to take on a powerful incumbent (Monestier 2019). While the future is quite uncertain, party competition in Argentina might eventually stabilize around a populist versus anti-populist axis. Indeed, there is historical precedent for such a transformation. Peronism in Argentina and Democratic Action (AD) in Venezuela were highly disruptive to prior patterns of political competition; "unstable equilibrium" would have been an apt description of Venezuelan politics in the late 1940s and of Argentine politics for several decades at mid-century. Yet both of these new populist movements anchored their party systems going forward, generating durable patterns of competition.

Developments since 2014 have also called into question Roberts's characterization of Brazil and Chile as cases whose legacy involves stable competition between a neoliberal right and a reformist left. Since 2014, both countries have seen the rise of political outsiders—President Jair Bolsonaro in Brazil, and the numerous independents elected to Chile's constitutional convention in 2021—that have severely challenged established parties on both sides of the ideological spectrum. "Unstable equilibrium" might eventually be an apt term for characterizing politics in these countries, especially if Brazil's Workers' Party (PT) cannot find a viable successor to former president Luiz Inácio Lula da Silva, which could open the door to populist challenges from the left as well as the right.

The hypothesis that Argentine party competition is stabilizing around a programmatic axis while Chile and Brazil fall into unstable equilibria may ultimately prove to be wrong. But critical juncture analysis works best when there is little need for such speculation. If researchers have a strong basis for arguing that a definitive legacy has emerged, they are in a better position to conclusively score the outcome and assess the consequences of a new critical juncture.

STUDYING CRITICAL JUNCTURES
BEFORE THE DUST SETTLES

If critical juncture analysis is best applied with the benefit of hindsight, what are scholars analyzing more contemporary transformations to do? I argue that this framework can be used productively to study recent events as long as scholars approach the task with appropriate humility, positing critical junctures in more hypothetical terms. Roberts's analysis makes clear that, even without a strong basis for arguing that a definitive legacy has emerged, one can use the framework productively to rule out other competing models of change. Even in 2002, before the dust had settled, it was evident that the party system consequences of neoliberal reform qualified as an instance of significant, discontinuous change with distinct, immediate consequences across countries. The debt crisis and demise of the protectionist model of industrialization raised new political questions that were not merely an outgrowth of dynamics from the 1970s. Party systems had converged on more elitist forms as of 2002 with the counterreactions to "re-oligarchization" yet to occur, but the *paths* that different countries took to this outcome clearly differed cross-nationally.

In other words, some key criteria for a critical juncture were satisfied. Although Roberts could not yet specify a definitive political legacy of neoliberal reform, the evidence at least did not falsify a critical juncture hypothesis. Thus, he could rule out claims that this transformation did not constitute a critical juncture, which might have been made either on the grounds that change was merely incremental or that it occurred in a similar fashion across countries (Roberts 2002).

Scully's (1992) analysis of Chile is another example of how the critical juncture framework can be used productively to pose hypotheses about contemporary transformations. In his book, Scully analyzes a series of critical junctures that reshaped the Chilean party system, the most recent of which occurred in the 1950s. While his analysis of all three critical junctures benefited from decades or more of hindsight, he also addresses the hypothesis that a cleavage stemming from opposition or loyalty to the Pinochet regime might generate a fourth critical juncture in the contemporary era. In his contribution to this volume (see Chapter 16), Scully is able to return to this question—now with three additional decades of hindsight—to argue more definitively against the notion of a fourth critical juncture in Chile.

Scully's work highlights a context, the analysis of *sequential critical junctures*, in which this framework can be employed productively as long as one is appropriately tentative in characterizing recent transformations. In a series of sequential critical junctures, the legacy of a first transformation serves as the antecedent condition for the next one. Scully's (1992) book examines sequential critical junctures in Chile brought on by changing forms of class conflict. Lipset and Rokkan's (1967) analysis of European party systems also examines sequential critical junctures, as does Ikenberry (2001 and Chapter 3) in his study of major wars and world order, and the question of a new critical juncture in Latin America implicitly invokes this notion as well. When studying a series of transformations that may be considered critical junctures, it makes sense to use this model to analyze historical as well as more contemporary processes of change, as long as one is appropriately cautious in characterizing recent events. Abandoning the framework entirely because one lacks hindsight on the most recent in a series of changes would seem to be throwing the baby out with the bathwater.

A practical suggestion flows from this discussion. Rather than waiting decades to justify delving into questions of a "new critical juncture," my suggestion is that, if a definitive legacy has not yet crystallized, scholars can nonetheless pose and examine hypotheses about critical junctures as long as their conclusions about recent transformations are appropriately tentative. In the short to medium term, there is ample opportunity to debate alternative explanations about antecedent conditions and constant causes, and to look for evidence of both reactive and self-reinforcing sequences (Collier and Collier 1991: Ch. 1). Doing so will surely lay the groundwork for subsequent, more conclusive research on critical junctures and their legacies.

BIBLIOGRAPHY

Collier, Ruth Berins, and David Collier. 1991. *Shaping the Political Arena: Critical Junctures, the Labor Movement and Regime Dynamics in Latin America*. Princeton, NJ: Princeton University Press.

———. 2002. *Shaping the Political Arena: Critical Junctures, the Labor Movement, and Regime Dynamics in Latin America*. Notre Dame, IN: University of Notre Dame Press.

Ikenberry, G. John. 2001. *After Victory: Institutions, Strategic Restraint, and the Rebuilding of Order after Major Wars*. Princeton, NJ: Princeton University Press.

Levitsky, Steven, and Kenneth M. Roberts (eds.). 2011. *The Resurgence of the Latin American Left*. Baltimore, MD: Johns Hopkins University Press.

Lipset, Seymour M., and Stein Rokkan. 1967. "Cleavage Structures, Party Systems, and Voter Alignments: An Introduction." In Seymour M. Lipset and Stein Rokkan (eds.), *Party Systems and Voter Alignments: Cross-National Perspectives* (pp. 1–64). New York, NY: Free Press.

Mahoney, James. 2000. "Path Dependence in Historical Sociology." *Theory and Society* 29(4): 507–48.

Monestier, Felipe. 2019. "The Successful Building of a Conservative Party in Argentina." *European Review of Latin American and Caribbean Studies* 108: 175–191

Roberts, Kenneth M. 2002. "Social Inequalities without Class Cleavages in Latin America's Neoliberal Era." *Studies in Comparative International Development* 36(4): 3–33.

———. 2014. *Changing Course in Latin America: Party Systems in the Neoliberal Era*. New York, NY: Cambridge University Press.

Scully, Timothy R. 1992. *Rethinking the Center: Party Politics in Nineteenth- and Twentieth-Century Chile*. Stanford, CA: Stanford University Press.

18

Critical Junctures and Contemporary Latin America

A Note of Caution

Robert R. Kaufman

The debt crisis and neoliberal reforms of the 1980s and 1990s are commonly viewed as watersheds in the political economy of Latin America, but the region has been jolted virtually continuously by a succession of shocks in the twenty-first century as well: the Great Recession; the rise of China as a critical source of investment and as a *demandeur* of Latin American exports; and the challenges to global democracy posed by the political tremors in the European Union and the severe dysfunction of democratic politics in the United States. Indeed, the most salient feature of the early twenty-first century has been the destabilization of economic and political relationships and institutions that had been pillars of the world order since the end of World War II.

What are the implications of these shocks for understanding change in Latin America? Do they herald the onset of new critical junctures? In addressing this question, it is important to note Ruth Berins Collier and David Colliers' word of caution (1991: 772–74) at the end of their masterwork on critical junctures and their legacy. They observe that the global shock of the Great Depression did less to reshape the political arena than is commonly thought. The critical junctures that *they* identify—the challenges to oligarchical domination and the incorporation of labor organizations into the political system—were a product of domestic conflicts that came at widely different points in time.

One lesson to draw about the current period is that not all crises—whether international or domestic—necessarily lead to new and enduring institutional equilibria. The turmoil that we are now experiencing in the international system may usher

My thanks to David Collier and Gerardo L. Munck for their trenchant critiques and very helpful suggestions on earlier drafts.

in lasting social and political transformations in some societies and have relatively limited effects in others. To make matters even more complicated, a divergence in paths may conceivably have less to do with "critical" breaks with the past than with differences in antecedent social and political conditions that shape whether and how such breaks occur.

The question of how to identify critical junctures and sort through their causal effects has been a subject of debate both within the larger scholarly community and in this volume. It is especially challenging when we are dealing not with a single public policy or institution, but with broad systemic changes. The landmark works in this more "macro" comparative tradition—for example, Collier and Collier (1991) and Roberts (2014)—must take into account a much wider range of causal variables. This, in turn, increases the difficulty of identifying two necessary features of a critical juncture: a) whether the change in question represents a significant break from antecedent conditions, and b) whether it has long-term consequences going forward.

How do we determine whether a change represents a significant break with past conditions? How, in other words, do we avoid the trap of "infinite regress?" (Mahoney 2000: 527). A widespread view is that critical junctures occur when crises generate a temporary relaxation of structural and institutional constraints and expand opportunities for actors to choose alternative courses of actions (e.g., Capoccia and Kelemen 2007). However, as Collier (2020) argues, sorting through the relative importance of "choice" versus "constraint" risks leading investigators down an analytic rabbit hole. There are, he suggests, other more manageable criteria for identifying possible critical junctures—and their causal importance in generating new paths of change.

The most straightforward criterion is the determination of whether institutions that grow out of potential critical junctures—for example, the political incorporation of labor organizations in Collier and Collier (1991)—constitute "novel" departures from past practices. A second criterion—"differentiation"—is whether different responses to similar crises generate diverging paths of political change. Again, a classic example is Collier and Collier's (1991) analysis of how various modes of labor incorporation shaped different patterns of political cleavage.

These approaches provide useful alternatives to insisting on "choice" as a necessary feature of critical junctures and have the advantage of lining up well with much of the existing research using a critical juncture framework. But there may be other approaches as well. In the ongoing turmoil of the twenty-first century, exogenous shocks can conceivably generate new political forces that interact with, and decisively alter, the old equilibrium. The interaction between "old" and "new" causal factors in turn can potentially produce outcomes that differ markedly from ones that would have occurred with either factor by itself—and thus can constitute another way in which "critical" breaks with the past can be caused, and can be identified.

Exogenous shocks, as I noted in the introduction, may not necessarily produce new critical junctures. But in the current moment, they have certainly shaken up both national institutions and the international system in which they are nested. And as David Collier reminds us (see Chapter 1), a focus on cleavages, crises, and shocks did play a major role in Lipset and Rokkan's seminal work (1967) in the critical juncture tradition, as well as in important work by Mazzuca on state formation in Latin America (see Chapter 9) and by Scully (1992 and Chapter 16) on Chile. The twenty-first century has been marked by comparable shocks, including the decline of organized labor, the emergence of identity politics, and the transformation of linkages to the world economy, among many other things.

Contemporary changes in political identities, resources, and incentives have expanded the range of possible outcomes beyond what might have been expected from antecedent conditions alone. And whatever the consequence of such changes, it is not likely that they can be usefully explained in terms of the agency of the political actors. New cleavages and correlations of power are likely to be the products of many determinants beyond their control.

The ultimate test of whether these changes constitute critical junctures, however, hinges on whether we can identify long-term effects, and we gain the greatest traction in confronting this question when we have the advantage of ample historical hindsight. Hindsight, to be sure, does not elide the theoretical importance of specifying the mechanisms of reproduction that sustain a legacy over time. But empirically, as Capoccia and Kelemen (2007: 360–63) argue, we should expect critical junctures to provide "temporal leverage"—that is, the duration of the impact should be substantially longer than the critical juncture itself. Collier and Collier's (1991) analysis meets this criterion. The incorporation periods that they identify stretch over one or two decades during the first half of the twentieth century, but the resulting legacy stretched until at least the 1980s. In this volume, on the other hand, Roberts, Handlin, Scully, and Boas (see Chapters 14–17) have each grappled in highly innovative ways with the substantial challenge of identifying critical junctures within a shorter time frame.

As these authors suggest, even when a change seems important in the short-term, the effects may not be enduring. In hindsight, for example, there is not much evidence for the once widely held view that pact-making in democratic transitions would affect the future stability of new democratic regimes.[1] Similarly, in attempting to make sense of the still unfolding and highly confusing changes of the twenty-first century, we cannot be sure if they will generate long-term legacies, if they will be altered by new shocks, or even whether they might return to an older equilibrium.

So, what are the alternatives in dealing with all the explosive changes going on around us?

---

1. On the other hand, Fishman (see Chapter 12) has persuasively argued that a different kind of legacy, involving political culture, definitely was established in the aftermath of the democratic transitions in Spain and Portugal in the 1970s.

One option is to adopt a more restricted "meso" approach,[2] concentrating, for example, on relatively limited institutional arenas such as legislatures or judicial and criminal justice systems, or on specific policies such as those related to pensions, health, or education. Even taking into account the possibility of spillover effects, a critical juncture with respect to one institution or policy may not constitute a fundamental change in others. This offers a variety of analytical opportunities relevant to the current period. Some institutions—such as those mentioned above—may have reached a new equilibrium, while others may still be in flux.

Additional strategies will conceivably be necessary for dealing with macro-level changes. In grappling with the long-term implications of contemporary crises, for example, it is obviously important to assess the durability of the institutional legacies generated by previous transformations and the mechanisms of reproduction that might allow them to survive. Scully (see Chapter 16) and Valenzuela et al. (2018) address this issue in their examination of the extent to which underlying, tripartite cleavages within the Chilean party system were altered by the trauma of the Pinochet dictatorship and the imposition of the binomial electoral system. Similarly, the current turmoil in Brazil offers new opportunities to explore both Roberts's (2014) claim that the debt crisis generated enduring political alignments, and Handlin's (2017) focus on shorter-term changes in party behavior.

The identification of continuities that persist in such systems despite the turmoil would be an indication that the older legacy nevertheless persists. On the other hand, although a discovery of substantial discontinuities would not in itself indicate the onset of a new critical juncture, it would clearly indicate the fading effects of the previous one. Either way, there is traction to be gained by examining the extent to which political actors are significantly constrained by electoral choices made in earlier decades.

A focus on incremental change may also be useful for understanding how other institutions adapt to contemporary disequilibria. Especially important in this regard is the work on layering and conversion outlined in Mahoney and Thelen (2010: 15–16) and Streeck and Thelen (2005: 18–29): "the introduction of new rules on top of or alongside existing ones" and "the changed enactment of existing rules due to their strategic redeployment."

The concepts of layering and conversion can, for example, be important tools for understanding how some freely elected governments in Latin America—as well as in the European Union and Turkey—have slid backward toward "competitive authoritarian" regimes, maintaining the outward forms of constitutional democracy while dismantling the horizontal constraints on their power and restricting the spaces for effective electoral oppositions. Competitive authoritarianism is hardly new in Latin America, but the fecklessness of democracies in the twenty-first century has opened

---

2. For a classic example of such a "meso" approach, see David (1985) on the economics of QWERTY.

the way to widespread "backsliding" across the region—pushed by populists of both the left and right who gain elective office by stoking conflicts between the "virtuous people" and the "corrupt elites" (Mudde and Kaltwasser 2017). Venezuela, Ecuador, Bolivia, and Nicaragua became increasingly authoritarian through this route during the 2000s and 2010s, and democratic institutions have come under siege in Brazil, Mexico, Peru, and El Salvador, among other countries. What distinguishes "backsliding" in these cases from other forms of democratic regress is that authoritarianism emerges incrementally and from "within," rather than through military coups or other sudden shocks (Bermeo 2016; Haggard and Kaufman 2021).

Notwithstanding these disturbing trends, however, it is important to recognize that in many important respects we may be living in an era characterized neither by critical junctures nor incremental change, but by a long-term disequilibrium in which there are deep changes in institutions but no stable new patterns of behavior (Brinks et al. 2019). In the twenty-first century, Latin America's political landscape has been transformed by neoliberalism, and by the emergence of new cleavages around gender, ethnicity, sexual orientation, and religion. Party systems once thought to be relatively durable have been severely shaken, most recently in Chile and El Salvador, and new parties, populist politicians, and social movements have emerged throughout the region. And, as just noted, broader issues of political democracy and development remain in play.

But as of now, it is difficult to imagine how current struggles over such questions might generate durable new "paths," like the ones identified by Ruth Berins Collier and David Collier or by Kenneth Roberts. Our approach to these uncertainties must certainly be framed by the kind of systematic theoretical engagement we find in the contributions of Roberts, Handlin, Scully, and Boas (see Chapters 14–17). But as is clear in their own careful research, it also calls for some humility: an empirical mapping of changes and continuities within and across countries, an identification of the relevant actors, and an analysis of the factors that condition their goals, resources, and short-term impact.

BIBLIOGRAPHY

Bermeo, Nancy 2016. "On Democratic Backsliding." *Journal of Democracy* 27 (1): 5–19.

Brinks, Daniel M., Steven Levitsky, and Maria Victoria Murillo. 2019. *Understanding Institutional Weakness: Power and Design in Latin American Institutions.* New York, NY: Cambridge University Press.

Capoccia, Giovanni, and R. Daniel Kelemen. 2007. "The Study of Critical Junctures: Theory, Narrative, and Counterfactuals in Historical Institutionalism." *World Politics* 59(3): 341–69.

Collier, David. 2020. "What Is a Critical Juncture? Contingency Should Not Be a Defining Attribute." University of California, Berkeley.

Collier, Ruth Berins, and David Collier. 1991. *Shaping the Political Arena: Critical Junctures, the Labor Movement and Regime Dynamics in Latin America.* Princeton, NJ: Princeton University Press.

David, Paul A. 1985. "Clio and the Economics of QWERTY." *American Economic Review* 75(2): 332–37.

Fishman, Robert M. 2019. *Democratic Practice: Origins of the Iberian Divide in Political Inclusion.* Oxford, UK: Oxford University Press.

Haggard, Stephan, and Robert R. Kaufman. 2021. *Backsliding: Democratic Regress in the Contemporary World.* New York, NY: Cambridge University Press.

Handlin, Samuel. 2017. *State Crisis in Fragile Democracies: Polarization and Political Regimes in South America.* New York, NY: Cambridge University Press.

Lipset, Seymour M., and Stein Rokkan. 1967. "Cleavage Structures, Party Systems, and Voter Alignments: An Introduction." In Seymour M. Lipset and Stein Rokkan (eds.), *Party Systems and Voter Alignments: Cross-National Perspectives* (pp. 1–64). New York, NY: Free Press.

Mahoney, James. 2000. "Path Dependence in Historical Sociology." *Theory and Society* 29(4): 507–48.

Mahoney, James, and Kathleen Thelen. 2010. "A Theory of Gradual Institutional Change." In James Mahoney and Kathleen Thelen (eds.), *Explaining Institutional Change: Ambiguity, Agency, and Power* (pp. 1–37). New York, NY: Cambridge University Press.

Mudde, Cas, and Cristóbal Rovira Kaltwasser. 2017. *Populism: A Very Short Introduction.* Oxford, UK: Oxford University Press.

Roberts, Kenneth M. 2014. *Changing Course in Latin America: Party Systems in the Neoliberal Era.* New York, NY: Cambridge University Press.

Scully, Timothy R. 1992. *Rethinking the Center: Party Politics in Nineteenth- and Twentieth-Century Chile.* Stanford, CA: Stanford University Press.

Streeck, Wolfgang, and Kathleen A. Thelen. 2005. "Introduction: Institutional Change in Advanced Political Economies." In Wolfgang Streeck and Kathleen Thelen (eds.), *Beyond Continuity: Institutional Change in Advanced Political Economies* (pp. 1–39). Oxford, UK: Oxford University Press.

Valenzuela, J. Samuel, Nicolás Somma, and Timothy R. Scully. 2018. "Resilience and Change: The Party System in Redemocratized Chile." In Scott Mainwaring (ed.), *Party Systems in Latin America: Institutionalization, Decay, and Collapse* (pp. 135–63). New York, NY: Cambridge University Press.

V

CONCLUSION

19

The Power and Promise of Critical Juncture Research

Gerardo L. Munck

The development of historically oriented social sciences has motivated many sociologists, political scientists, and economists since the 1960s, and interest in this project has grown in the twenty-first century. Within this collective endeavor to understand how history matters, one of the distinctive ways of incorporating temporality is provided by the critical juncture tradition, the focus of this volume.

The volume has shown how researchers are working on all three aspects of the research tradition: its theoretical framework, research methods, and substantive questions. It has demonstrated how many traditional practices continue to be useful, and also that innovation is needed to improve the framework and methods used in this research. It has highlighted how substantive contributions are the driving force of this tradition and continue to offer the clearest indications of its vitality. In various ways, it has provided evidence that research on critical junctures has been and remains a vibrant tradition in the social sciences.

To conclude this volume, this chapter turns to two tasks. First, it discusses some of the key reasons why critical juncture research is valuable and should be encouraged. (For brief discussions of several works that exemplify the value of this research tradition, see Appendix IV.) Second, it dispels some common misconceptions about research on critical junctures. Discussions about this research regularly invoke ideas that are questionable. And these misconceptions are costly, usually because they unjustifiably treat some trait as necessary to inquiry in this tradition and as a consequence reduce the scope of investigations or limit the tools possibly used in research. Thus, this chapter clarifies what critical junctures research is not, that is, what traits should not be treated as necessary aspects of this research. Relatedly, it shows that important avenues for future research are opened up when questionable views are discarded.

WHY CRITICAL JUNCTURE RESEARCH IS VALUABLE

Critical juncture research has several distinctive features that make it a valuable tradition. Some works exemplify these virtues better than others. Some of these qualities are not exclusive to this tradition. Nonetheless, the following four features are part of the reason why this tradition should be supported and continued.

A Focus on Big, Substantive Questions

Research on critical junctures focuses on what Tilly (1984) calls "big structures" and "large processes," such as the development of capitalist economies, the formation of national states, the democratization of political regimes, the secularization of culture, and the shaping of international (political and economic) orders (see also Skocpol 2003). It seeks to understand why such structures—which affect the lives of people around the world—emerge, endure, and are replaced. It tackles many key problems facing the social sciences.

Providing good answers to big, substantive questions is challenging. But they are answerable. Indeed, relying on existing theoretical ideas and methods, researchers have made considerable progress in both developing interesting, insightful answers to big questions and in evaluating the validity of these answers.

Research on critical junctures has focused more on some structures and processes than others (see Appendix III). We have dozens of studies on the state, political regimes, political parties, and economic development. We even have dozens of studies on the impact of colonialism on economic development. Yet considerably fewer studies focus on culture and the international system. And only a few studies address racial domination and virtually none patriarchal domination. These gaps are important and should be noted. However, they are less a reflection of some intrinsic limitation of critical juncture research than an opportunity for future research.

A Recognition of Qualitative Breaks

Research on critical junctures places the focus on key changes in the evolution of societies that involve qualitative breaks or discontinuities.

Qualitative distinctions play a key role in the social sciences. They are the basis for commonly used and enduring typologies that distinguish among types of state (empires, city states, modern states); international order (balance of power, hegemonic, constitutional); public administration (patrimonial, bureaucratic); political regime (democracy, dictatorship); mode of economic production (ancient, feudal, capitalist); and society (hunting-and-gathering, agricultural, industrial, postindustrial).

Moreover, such qualitative distinctions lie at the heart of critical juncture research. This research adapts the idea that *natura facit saltus* (nature makes jumps). It rejects the universal validity of a continuist conception of change—that is, it heeds Moore's (1966: 519–21) advice to question the view that "all differences can be reduced to quantitative differences." And it focuses centrally on the task of understanding why these types of order emerge, endure, and come to an end.

Quantitative distinctions are key. For example, democracies can be more or less democratic, capitalist economies can be more or less market-oriented, and public administrations can be more or less patrimonial. And explaining such differences is important. Nonetheless, quantitative distinctions do not erase qualitative distinctions. What is more, the attempt to understand quantitative differences before a solid understanding of qualitative differences has been developed is likely to prove fruitless. Thus, this research is valuable because it keeps the focus on basic distinctions and avoids the unjustified tendency to treat all differences as differences of degree.

A Sense of Temporal Depth

Critical juncture research brings a historical perspective to bear on the study of societies. More specifically, it relies on several temporal concepts and is attuned to the temporal dimension of reality and not just the spatial one (Moore 1974; Abbott 2001; Pierson 2004; Grzymała-Busse 2011; Falleti and Mahoney 2015; Kreuzer forthcoming).

A concern with *timing* makes researchers interested in critical junctures ask not just if some event occurs, but also when. Being sensitized to the concept of *tempo* or *pace* makes them consider how quickly events unfold. An interest in *duration* makes them examine how long a certain state of affairs lasts. A focus on *sequence* makes them wonder in what order events happen. Attention to the more comprehensive concept of *path* or *trajectory* makes them probe whether changes are frequent or episodic, gradual or abrupt, and involve short-term or long-term evolutionary patterns.

Thus, critical juncture research helps to counteract the tendency in the social sciences to abstract from and ignore the full texture of temporality. One fundamental way to learn about the social world is by comparing spatially distinct units through what is conventionally called cross-sectional analysis. However, a social science that is based only on such analysis is an impoverished social science. And critical juncture research routinely goes to considerable length to add historical nuance to the social sciences and, most distinctively, offers a corrective to the common tendency to concentrate on the short-term by exploring the historical sources of the contemporary world.

An Expansive Vision of Theory

Critical juncture research is part of a larger social science agenda that focuses on temporality. Thus, it is not the only approach that makes use of temporal concepts, addresses how history matters in a systematic manner, and studies historical causation. However, this research stands out in terms of its reliance on a recognizable and tested theoretical framework.

This framework has been debated and refined over many decades. It has been elaborated more than other frameworks used in historically oriented social science research; indeed, its synthesis of key ideas about how to study both social order and change is unrivalled. And its use in numerous research projects shows that, even though the framework is not a finished work and has been amended over time, it works in practice.

More specifically, the critical juncture framework is a key asset in two ways. First, the reliance on a relatively established framework helps to make knowledge about critical junctures and their legacies cumulative. Kuhn's (1970 [1962]: 148–50) claim that knowledge only cumulates within a paradigm and that knowledge produced in different paradigms is incommensurable is an exaggeration. However, research that uses a shared framework is more obviously comparable. For example, research on critical junctures and parties in Western Europe has shown that the reliance on a common language and set of ideas is one of the factors behind the steady gains in knowledge made since the work by Lipset and Rokkan (1967; see Bartolini and Mair 1990; Karvonen and Kuhnle 2001; Bartolini 2000, 2005; Caramani 2004, 2015; Hooghe and Marks 2017).

Second, this framework provides the general ideas for theorizing about social order and change in an analytically rigorous yet expansive manner. It calls on researchers to address questions of statics and dynamics, to consider historical causes, to take into account the impact of structural factors and of actors, and to theorize both endogenous and exogenous factors. Indeed, just to take the last point, this framework nudges scholars to avoid focusing narrowly on internal relations within a system (e.g., seeking a political explanation for political outcomes) and to explore rather how different spheres in society (the economic, political, and cultural spheres) affect each other and how societies are affected by other societies (Rokkan 1970: 57–60; Skocpol 1979: 19–33; Tilly 1990: 5–16; Rueschemeyer et al. 1992: Ch. 3).

In brief, critical juncture research is valuable because it draws on a framework for theorizing about the social world that counters the tendency to ignore history, to treat all problems as problems of statics, and to overly rely on reductionism. Indeed, in contrast to many contemporary approaches to theory in the social sciences, the vision that inspires research on critical junctures is well grounded and ambitious.

WHAT CRITICAL JUNCTURE RESEARCH IS NOT

Beyond making a positive case for the value of critical juncture research, it is also key to dismiss mistaken views that limit the potential of this research tradition. The community of researchers working on critical junctures is large and has different views about what makes a study a critical juncture study. Critics also have their views about what these researchers do and should do. And the diversity of views and exchanges about this research is largely a source of strength.

However, some claims about critical juncture research are erroneous and costly— they reduce the scope of this research and limit the tools researchers can use. Indeed, what follows identifies six such claims, makes a case for rejecting or revising them, and, most importantly, shows how the agenda and possibilities of critical juncture research are expanded when these misconceptions are rejected. It is key that the power and promise of critical juncture research are not curtailed due to flawed views about the theory and methods used in this tradition.

A Critical Juncture Is Not a Change in an Entire System

Research on critical junctures seeks to understand the big picture. It focuses on system change, on the change *of* a system—systemic or structural change—rather than change *within* a system—reformist or incremental change. But a critical juncture never is—and never could be—the change of an entire system. And thus the critical juncture framework can be used to study changes that fall short of being big or total revolutions.

More specifically, critical juncture research usually focuses on subsystems of a social system—the political, economic, or cultural subsystems—and treats other social systems (i.e., countries) as part of the environment. Moreover, rather than study entire subsystems, studies in this field routinely focus on one part of a subsystem (e.g., parts of the political subsystem, such as the state, the political regime, or public policy), or even parts of these parts (e.g., "partial regimes," such as the party system or the popular interest regime, or "policy subsystems") (Collier and Chambers-Ju 2012: 565; Baumgartner and Jones 2009). Even studies of the international system actually focus on one subsystem of the international system—usually the political or the economic—or one part of one subsystem.

Thus, the commitment of critical juncture research to consider the big picture does not lead it to focus on—let alone only on—changes in whole countries or total transformations of an entire system, an impossibly limiting scope condition. Indeed, it is important to recognize that, even though this research focuses on big changes, the scope of this research tradition is broad.

A Critical Juncture Is Not the Only Way in Which Change Occurs

The critical juncture framework is an ambitious synthesis of ideas. However, it offers a partial theory of social order and change that does not profess to subsume other frameworks. Research that draws on this framework does not claim that all causes are distal causes, let alone distal causes that produce historical legacies, or that proximate causes do not operate alongside critical junctures. Furthermore, research that draws on this framework does not claim that all causes involve rapid discontinuous changes, or even that there is a necessary trade-off between discontinuous and continuous change.

As Collier and Collier (1991: 9, 27) underscore, "some political change . . . may . . . occur incrementally. However, other aspects of political change . . . may be more discontinuous" and "the effect of the critical juncture is . . . commonly . . . intertwined with other processes of change." Indeed, many works in this tradition explicitly acknowledge that forms of incremental change, such as layering, occur alongside discontinuous changes (Collier and Collier 1991: 11–12; Scully 1992: 172–73; Bartolini 2005: Ch. 7; Baumgartner and Jones 2009; Ekiert and Ziblatt 2013). Further, even authors who argue rather forcefully for discontinuous change assign a role to gradual change (Kuhn 1970 [1962]: 49, 69–74, 83; Moore 1966: 4, 104–05, 505–06).

Thus, the critical juncture framework is a partial, rather than a complete and unified, framework. It does not claim that various kinds of causes are unimportant or that approaches that focus on proximate causes or incremental change should necessarily be considered rival approaches that shed no light on the social world. It does not even claim that big changes can only occur through critical junctures. That is, this framework more modestly focuses on one kind of cause, which is seen as one among many other kinds of causes. And it does not cease to be a useful framework simply because much change is driven by proximate factors or is incremental.

A dialogue about how best to combine the study of big, discontinuous change and gradual change in particular is needed. We only have some vague ideas about how to integrate the study of these two kinds of change (see, however, Levitsky and Murillo 2014; Gerschewski 2021; and Riedl and Roberts in Chapter 6). Yet the basis for such a dialogue has to be the recognition that critical juncture research does not claim that all outcomes can be explained, let alone fully, in terms of critical junctures, and actually treats discontinuous and incremental change as complementary in principle.

A Critical Juncture Is Not an Uncaused Cause

Agency plays an important role in causal analysis. Social actors have the freedom to choose among externally given alternatives. They have the power to control conditions. They also have the power to create new conditions. Thus, outcomes are never fated, never predetermined by conditions. Outcomes always *may* occur; they never *must* occur, they never are inevitable.

However, social action is never entirely unconditioned, freedom is never total. And agency can never be a first cause, an uncaused cause (Hodgson 2004: 54–62; Bunge 2009: Chs. 4, 7, and 8). Thus, the view that critical junctures necessarily involve a "contingent occurrence that cannot be explained on the basis of prior historical conditions [or] prior events" (Mahoney 2000: 507–09, 511, 513; see also Bernhard 2015: 978) is problematic.

This conception of a critical juncture is much cited but, fortunately, never strictly enforced. Nonetheless, its negative implications deserve to be noted.

First, this conception would lead to the exclusion of most—and possibly all—of the events treated as critical junctures in the literature. If critical junctures are only contingent events in an *epistemic* sense, i.e., they are only events that cannot be explained on the basis of prior historical conditions in light of existing theory, this conception would presumably disqualify many big changes that have been treated as critical junctures. The exclusion would obviously apply to critical junctures that have been explained in structural-historical terms (e.g., Lipset and Rokkan 1967; Collier and Collier 1991). But it would also apply to critical junctures that are explained in terms of a combination of structural-historical factors and agency that account for actors' choices in terms of prior conditions and events (e.g., Grzymała-Busse 2002; Mazzuca 2021).

If critical junctures are only contingent events in an *ontological* sense, i.e., they are only events that cannot be explained on the basis of prior historical conditions because agency is uncaused and "contingent events" make "all the difference" (García-Montoya and Mahoney 2020: 2), the problem is even greater. Indeed, since agents are always historically conditioned, if to different degrees, and every turning point is historically conditioned by antecedent conditions, this field of study would have no referents.

Second, this conception of a critical juncture would foreclose, by definitional fiat, what is one of the most interesting questions in this research, i.e., how structural (endogenous and exogenous) factors and agency interact to produce critical junctures. This research has led to some fruitful conceptual innovations (Slater and Simmons 2010; Soifer 2012). It has also yielded some of the most nuanced substantive arguments in the literature on critical junctures, such as Mazzuca's (2021: 186, Ch. 6) explanation of state formation in Argentina in terms of a "set of antecedent conditions" and the "free agency and political creativity" of political leaders. Thus, the loss would be great.

In short, critical junctures are not necessarily fully contingent events or, more precisely, causes unaffected by antecedent conditions. Indeed, the claim that agency can cause outcomes but be uncaused is unwarranted. And critical junctures research is not limited to instances where causes are supposedly uncaused by past conditions.

A Critical Juncture Does Not Produce Only Institutional Legacies

There is an affinity between the study of critical junctures and of institutions. Critical juncture research was initially closely linked with a rejection of societal determinism and an interest in political institutions, understood as rules that structure social interactions (Lipset and Rokkan 1967; Sartori 1969: 207–14; North 1990; Collier and Collier 1991: 10–12). Moreover, this research was part of the "institutional turn" in the social sciences (Thelen 1999, 2004; Orren and Skowronek 2004: Ch. 3; Fioretos et al. 2016), and many of the better-known works in this field focus on changes in institutions and institutional legacies (Lipset and Rokkan 1967; Collier and Collier 1991; Acemoglu and Robinson 2012).

Nonetheless, research on critical junctures does not focus exclusively on political institutions. Substantive research explores other institutions, giving considerable attention to economic institutions, such as property rights, access to education, and slavery (North 1990: Ch. 6; Acemoglu and Robinson 2012: Ch. 3). Additionally, this research has rightly focused on noninstitutional features of social systems. For instance, studies have explored territorial boundaries and physical space (Mazzuca

2021), the relationship between classes and the state (Mahoney 2001: 6–11; Chibber 2003: 45), public policies (Baumgartner and Jones 2009), and cultural norms (Wittenberg 2006; Mitterauer 2010; Nunn and Wantchekon 2011; Voigtländer and Voth 2012; Peisakhin 2015; Acharya et al. 2018; Fishman 2019).

Thus, it is not correct to claim that critical juncture research is necessarily linked with institutional analysis. Relatedly, definitions of critical junctures and historical legacies framed exclusively in terms of institutional change and stability are mistaken. In other words, it is important to avoid overly restrictive definitions that are limited to institutions, or even more narrowly to political institutions, and to explicitly acknowledge the broader aspects of social life that can be studied with the critical juncture framework.

A Critical Juncture Does Not Produce Only Divergent Legacies

There is also an affinity between the study of critical junctures and the idea that a critical juncture involves a change or choice that puts countries or other units on divergent paths. The idea that critical junctures produce divergent legacies is nearly unanimously endorsed in theoretical works. For example, scholars note that a critical juncture "typically occurs in distinct ways in different countries" (Collier and Collier 1991: 20, 27–29, 36, 38–39) and posit that "divergence across cases" is a "distinct feature" of critical junctures (Soifer 2012: 1573). Relatedly, a recurring idea is that of "branching points" (Kurtz 2013: 8–9, 36, 42), "forking paths" (Roberts 2014: 6), "divergent pathways" (Fishman and Lizardo 2013: 213), and "divergent development paths" (Acemoglu and Robinson 2012: 57).

Moreover, the emphasis on divergent outcomes has a strong rationale. Part of the impetus for research on critical junctures was the desire to provide an alternative to a unilinear model of social change, which was viewed as a weakness of the neo-evolutionism of Parsons and modernization theorists in the 1960s, precisely by drawing attention to divergent paths (Moore 1966: 4, 159; Tilly 1975: 21; 1984: 10–12, 41–50; 1990: 11–13). And insisting on the need to avoid a unilinear model of change is as valid today as in the 1960s (Mazzuca and Munck 2020: 7–8).

However, attention to divergence should not blind scholars to other options. It is conventional in evolutionary biology to consider, alongside the possibility of divergent evolution or speciation (i.e., the divergence of species), the converse idea of convergent evolution or speciation reversal (i.e., the merger of distinct lineages) (Mahner and Bunge 1997: 240–43; Mayr 2001: 245–49). Moreover, even though some social scientists express resistance to the concept of convergent paths (Pempel 1998: 3–4; Thelen 2004: 1–2; Streeck and Thelen 2005: 1, 5), a similar idea has been considered in the literature on critical junctures.

Rokkan (1970: 113) posits that critical junctures sometimes lead to divergent paths and other times to convergent paths, and Sabel and Zeitlin (1985: 162–63) claim that they can generate a "tendency to uniformity" and the reduction of diversity (see also Tilly 1984: 43–50). Moreover, scholars provide various examples of such convergence. Sabel and Zeitlin (1985) study how mass production in industry came to eliminate alternatives. In turn, Tilly (1990: 5) theorizes why the "great variation over time and space in the kinds of states" found in Europe was reduced, and European states "eventually converge[d] on different variants of the national state."

Additionally, yet another option is that a group of countries (or some other unit) that undergoes a critical juncture (e.g., they experience communism) are put on the same path. In this scenario, their path would differ from the one they followed prior to the critical juncture and from the path followed by countries that did not go through a similar experience. However, as a group, the legacy of the critical juncture would not make them more or less diverse. Rather, they will have changed course as a group (for examples, see Pop-Eleches and Tucker 2017 and Acharya et al. 2018).

It is important to recognize that these versions of paths are consistent with the critical juncture framework, and that there is no reason to restrict its applicability to outcomes that entail divergent paths. History shows that societies have followed divergent, convergent, and parallel paths (Sanderson 1995: 4, 379–86). And scholars should be open to the possibility that critical junctures can increase diversity, decrease diversity, or not alter diversity.

Critical Juncture Research Is Not Wedded to One Methodological Tradition

Critical juncture research has also been strongly associated with qualitative methods. And again, this partnership was well justified in the 1960s and continues to be warranted today. The fruitfulness of these methods has increased. In recent decades, theories have given more attention to the specification of causal mechanisms. At the same time, the contribution of process tracing—a key tool in qualitative research—to the study of mechanisms has been clarified (Collier 2011; Waldner 2012; Bennett and Checkel 2015). The importance of qualitative research to the study of critical junctures is well established.

However, the critical juncture tradition is not necessarily tied to one method or another. It uses the same methods as the broader social sciences; that is, it does not have its own methods. And the contributions of quantitative history, a recent innovation, are a welcome development.

Thus, the methods used in critical juncture research are another area where a dialogue among researchers that work in different methodological traditions would be fruitful. Such a dialogue can draw on a literature that offers a variety of options regarding the integration of research using qualitative and quantitative methods (Brady and Collier 2010; Dunning 2012; Waldner 2012; Beach and Pedersen 2016; Seawright 2016). However, it is also clear that the basis for such a dialogue must be a recognition that critical juncture research can and should draw on different methods and that no single methodological tradition offers all the answers to the important methodological challenges faced in historically oriented research.

FINAL WORDS

The assumption that patterns of the current world can be explained by causes in the recent past—an assumption called presentism or short-termism—is pervasive in the social sciences. And this assumption has several negative consequences. It does not allow us to distinguish events and changes that are consistent with the normal fluctuations of social life from significant changes. It blinds us to the deep roots of key problems in the social world. It prevents us from understanding the present and thinking about strategies to address the world's problems. Thus, the development of a historically oriented social sciences is a central mission of the social sciences.

This volume has sought to contribute to this mission. It has strived to demonstrate the power and promise of critical juncture research. It has suggested that this research tradition is not self-contained and benefits from dialogue with, and critical scrutiny from, the larger community of scholars engaged in historically oriented research. It has also pointed out some pitfalls that should be avoided, some doors that should not be closed, and some steps that should be taken to ensure the continued progress of the research tradition.

BIBLIOGRAPHY

Abbott, Andrew. 2001. *Time Matters: On Theory and Method*. Chicago, IL: University of Chicago Press.

Acemoglu, Daron, and James A. Robinson. 2012. *Why Nations Fail: Origins of Power, Poverty and Prosperity*. New York, NY: Crown.

Acharya, Avidit, Matthew Blackwell, and Maya Sen. 2018. *Deep Roots: How Slavery Still Shapes Southern Politics*. Princeton, NJ: Princeton University Press.

Bartolini, Stefano. 2000. *The Political Mobilization of the European Left, 1860–1980: The Class Cleavage*. New York, NY: Cambridge University Press.

———. 2005. *Restructuring Europe. Centre Formation, System Building, and Political Structuring Between the Nation State and the European Union*. Oxford, UK: Oxford University Press.

Bartolini, Stefano, and Peter Mair. 1990. *Identity, Competition and Electoral Availability: The Stabilisation of European Electorates 1885–1985*. New York, NY: Cambridge University Press.

Baumgartner, Frank R., and Bryan D. Jones. 2009. *Agendas and Instability in American Politics* (2nd ed.). Chicago, IL: University of Chicago Press.

Beach, Derek, and Rasmus Brun Pedersen. 2016. *Causal Case Studies: Foundations and Guidelines for Comparing, Matching and Tracing*. Ann Arbor, MI: University of Michigan Press.

Bennett, Andrew, and Jeffrey Checkel (eds.). 2015. *Process Tracing: From Metaphor to Analytic Tool*. New York, NY: Cambridge University Press.

Bernhard, Michael. 2015. "Chronic Instability and the Limits of Path Dependence." *Perspectives on Politics* 13(4): 976–91.

Brady, Henry E., and David Collier (eds.). 2010. *Rethinking Social Inquiry: Diverse Tools, Shared Standards* (2nd ed.). Lanham, MD: Rowman & Littlefield.

Bunge, Mario. 2009. *Causality and Modern Science* (4th ed.). New Brunswick, NJ: Transaction Publishers.

Caramani, Daniele. 2004. *The Nationalization of Politics: The Formation of National Electorates and Party Systems in Western Europe*. New York, NY: Cambridge University Press.

———. 2015. *The Europeanization of Politics: The Formation of a European Electorate and Party System in Historical Perspective*. New York, NY: Cambridge University Press.

Chibber, Vivek. 2003. *Locked in Place: State-Building and Late Industrialization in India*. Princeton, NJ: Princeton University Press.

Collier, David. 2011. "Understanding Process Tracing." *PS: Political Science & Politics* 44(4): 823–30.

Collier, Ruth Berins, and Christopher Chambers-Ju. 2012. "Popular Representation in Contemporary Latin American Politics: An Agenda for Research." In Peter Kingstone and Deborah J. Yashar (eds.), *Routledge Handbook of Latin American Politics* (pp. 564–78). New York, NY: Routledge.

Collier, Ruth Berins, and David Collier. 1991. *Shaping the Political Arena: Critical Junctures, the Labor Movement, and the Regime Dynamics in Latin America*. Princeton, NJ: Princeton University Press.

Dunning, Thad. 2012. *Natural Experiments in the Social Sciences: A Design-Based Approach*. New York, NY: Cambridge University Press.

Ekiert, Grzegorz, and Daniel Ziblatt. 2013. "Democracy in Central and Eastern Europe One Hundred Years." *East European Politics and Societies* 12(1): 90–107.

Falleti, Tulia G., and James Mahoney. 2015. "The Comparative Sequential Method." In James Mahoney and Kathleen Thelen (eds)., *Advances in Comparative-Historical Analysis* (pp. 211–39). New York, NY: Cambridge University Press.

Fioretos, Orfeo, Tulia G. Falleti, and Adam Sheingate. 2016. "Historical Institutionalism in Political Science." In Orfeo Fioretos, Tulia G. Falleti, and Adam Sheingate (eds.), *The Oxford Handbook of Historical Institutionalism* (pp. 3–28). New York, NY: Oxford University Press.

Fishman, Robert M. 2019. *Democratic Practice: Origins of the Iberian Divide in Political Inclusion*. Oxford, UK: Oxford University Press.

Fishman, Robert M., and Omar Lizardo. 2013. "How Macro-Historical Change Shapes Cultural Taste: Legacies of Democratization in Spain and Portugal." *American Sociological Review* 78(2): 213–39.

García-Montoya, Laura, and James Mahoney. 2020. "Critical Event Analysis in Case Study Research." *Sociological Methods and Research*. doi:10.1177/0049124120926201

Gerschewski, Johannes. 2021. "Explanations of Institutional Change. Reflecting on a 'Missing Diagonal.'" *American Political Science Review* 115(1): 218–33.

Grzymała-Busse, Anna M. 2002. *Redeeming the Communist Past: The Regeneration of Communist Parties in East Central Europe*. New York, NY: Cambridge University Press.

———. 2011. "Time Will Tell? Temporality and the Analysis of Causal Mechanisms and Processes." *Comparative Political Studies* 44(9): 1267–97.

Hodgson, Geoffrey M. 2004. *The Evolution of Institutional Economics: Agency, Structure and Darwinism in American Institutionalism*. New York, NY: Routledge.

Hooghe, Liesbet, and Gary Marks. 2017. "Cleavage Theory Meets Europe's Crises: Lipset, Rokkan, and the Transnational Cleavage." *Journal of European Public Policy* 25(1): 109–35.

Karvonen, Lauri, and Stein Kuhnle (eds.). 2001. *Party Systems and Voter Alignments Revisited*. New York, NY: Routledge.

Kreuzer, Marcus. Forthcoming. *The Grammar of Time: Using Comparative Historical Analysis to Study the Past*. New York, NY: Cambridge University Press.

Kuhn, Thomas S. 1970 [1962]. *The Structure of Scientific Revolutions* (2nd ed.). Chicago, IL: University of Chicago Press.

Kurtz, Marcus. 2013. *Latin American State-Building in Comparative Perspective: Social Foundations of Institutional Order*. New York, NY: Cambridge University Press.

Levitsky, Steven, and María Victoria Murillo. 2014. "Building Institutions on Weak Foundations: Lessons from Latin America." In Daniel Brinks, Marcelo Leiras, and Scott Mainwaring (eds.), *Reflections on Uneven Democracies: The Legacy of Guillermo O'Donnell* (pp. 189–213). Baltimore, MD: Johns Hopkins University Press.

Lipset, Seymour M., and Stein Rokkan. 1967. "Cleavage Structures, Party Systems, and Voter Alignments: An Introduction." In Seymour M. Lipset and Stein Rokkan (eds.), *Party Systems and Voter Alignments: Cross-National Perspectives* (pp. 1–64). New York, NY: Free Press.

Mahner, Martin, and Mario Bunge. 1997. *Foundations of Biophilosophy*. New York, NY: Springer-Verlag.

Mahoney, James. 2000. "Path Dependence in Historical Sociology." *Theory and Society* 29(4): 507–48.

———. 2001. *The Legacies of Liberalism: Path Dependence and Political Regimes in Central America*. Baltimore, MD: Johns Hopkins University Press.

Mayr, Ernst. 2001. *What Evolution Is*. New York, NY: Basic Books.

Mazzuca, Sebastián. 2021. *Latecomer State Formation. Political Geography and Capacity Failure in Latin America*. New Haven, CT: Yale University Press.

Mazzuca, Sebastián L., and Gerardo L. Munck. 2020. *A Middle-Quality Institutional Trap: Democracy and State Capacity in Latin America*. New York, NY: Cambridge University Press.

Mitterauer, Michael. 2010. *Why Europe? The Medieval Origins of Its Special Path*. Chicago, IL: University of Chicago Press.

Moore, Jr., Barrington. 1966. *Social Origins of Dictatorship and Democracy: Lord and Peasant in the Making of the Modern World*. Boston, MA: Beacon Press.

Moore, Wilbert E. 1974. *Social Change* (2nd ed.). Englewood Cliffs, NJ: Prentice-Hall, Inc.

North, Douglass C. 1990. *Institutions, Institutional Change and Economic Performance*. New York, NY: Cambridge University Press.

Nunn, Nathan, and Leonard Wantchekon. 2011. "The Slave Trade and the Origins of Mistrust in Africa." *American Economic Review* 101(7): 3221–52.

Orren, Karen, and Stephen Skowronek. 2004. *The Search for American Political Development*. New York, NY: Cambridge University Press.

Peisakhin, Leonid. 2015. "Cultural Legacies: Persistence and Transmission." In Norman Schofield and Gonzalo Caballero (eds.), *The Political Economy of Governance: Institutions, Political Performance and Elections* (pp. 21–39). Basel, Switzerland: Springer.

Pempel, T.J. 1998. *Regime Shift: Comparative Dynamics of the Japanese Political Economy*. Ithaca, NY: Cornell University Press.

Pierson, Paul. 2004. *Politics in Time: History, Institutions, and Social Analysis*. Princeton, NJ: Princeton University Press.

Pop-Eleches, Grigore, and Joshua Tucker. 2017. *Communism's Shadow: Historical Legacies and Contemporary Political Attitudes*. Princeton, NJ: Princeton University Press.

Riedl, Rachel Beatty. 2014. *Authoritarian Origins of Democratic Party Systems in Africa*. New York, NY: Cambridge University Press.

Roberts, Kenneth M. 2014. *Changing Course in Latin America: Party Systems in the Neoliberal Era*. New York, NY: Cambridge University Press.

Rokkan, Stein, with Angus Campbell, Per Torsvik, and Henry Valen. 1970. *Citizens, Elections, and Parties: Approaches to the Comparative Study of the Processes of Development*. New York, NY: David McKay.

Rueschemeyer, Dietrich, Evelyne Huber Stephens, and John D. Stephens. 1992. *Capitalist Development and Democracy*. Chicago, IL: University of Chicago Press.

Sabel, Charles F., and Jonathan Zeitlin. 1985. "Historical Alternatives to Mass Production: Politics, Markets and Technology in Nineteenth-Century Industrialization." *Past and Present* 108: 133–76.

Sanderson, Stephen K. 1995. *Social Transformations: A General Theory of Historical Development*. Oxford, UK: Blackwell.

Sartori, Giovanni. 1969. "From the Sociology of Politics to Political Sociology." *Government and Opposition* 4(2): 195–214.

Scully, Timothy R. 1992. *Rethinking the Center: Party Politics in Nineteenth- and Twentieth-Century Chile*. Stanford, CA: Stanford University Press.

Seawright, Jason. 2016. *Multi-Method Social Science. Combining Qualitative and Quantitative Tools*. New York, NY: Cambridge University Press.

Skocpol, Theda. 1979. *States and Social Revolution*. New York, NY: Cambridge University Press.

———. 2003. "Doubly Engaged Social Science: The Promise of Comparative Historical Analysis." In James Mahoney and Dietrich Rueschemeyer (eds.), *Comparative Historical Analysis in the Social Sciences* (pp. 407–28). New York, NY: Cambridge University Press.

Slater, Dan, and Erica Simmons. 2010. "Informative Regress: Critical Antecedents in Comparative Politics." *Comparative Political Studies* 43(7): 886–917.

Soifer, Hillel David. 2012. "The Causal Logic of Critical Junctures." *Comparative Political Studies* 45(12): 1572–597.

Streeck, Wolfgang, and Kathleen A. Thelen. 2005. "Introduction: Institutional Change in Advanced Political Economies." In Wolfgang Streeck and Kathleen Thelen (eds.), *Beyond Continuity: Institutional Change in Advanced Political Economies* (pp. 1–39). Oxford, UK: Oxford University Press.

Thelen, Kathleen. 1999. "Historical Institutionalism in Comparative Politics." *Annual Review of Political Science* 2: 369–404.

———. 2004. *How Institutions Evolve: The Political Economy of Skills in Germany, Britain, the United States and Japan*. New York, NY: Cambridge University Press.

Tilly, Charles. 1975. "Reflections on the History of European State-Making." In Charles Tilly (ed.), *The Formation of National States in Western Europe* (pp. 3–83). Princeton, NJ: Princeton University Press.

———. 1984. *Big Structures, Large Processes, Huge Comparisons*. New York, NY: Russell Sage Foundation.

———. 1990. *Coercion, Capital, and European States, AD 990–1990*. Oxford, UK: Basil Blackwell.

Voigtländer, Nico, and Hans-Joachim Voth. 2012. "Persecution Perpetuated: The Medieval Origins of Anti-Semitic Violence in Nazi Germany." *Quarterly Journal of Economics* 127(3): 1339–92.

Waldner, David. 2012. "Process Tracing and Causal Mechanisms." In Harold Kincaid (ed.), *The Oxford Handbook of Philosophy of Social Science* (pp. 65–84). Oxford, UK: Oxford University Press.

Wittenberg, Jason. 2006. *Crucibles of Political Loyalty: Church Institutions and Electoral Continuity in Hungary*. New York, NY: Cambridge University Press.

Appendix I

Conceptions of a Critical Juncture
and Cognate Terms

This appendix presents conceptions of critical junctures and cognate terms, such as punctuated equilibrium and path dependence, offered by authors who provide explicit definitions of these concepts. The table below provides an overview and comparison of these definitions, showing the extent of agreement and disagreement regarding what attributes are included or excluded from a definition of a critical juncture.

The definitions compared in the table are as follows:

Acemoglu and Robinson (2012: 106–07, 110, 332): "During critical junctures, a major event or confluence of factors disrupts the existing balance of political or economic power in a nation. . . . The outcomes of the events during critical junctures are shaped by the weight of history, as existing economic and political institutions shape the balance of power and delineate what is politically feasible. The outcome, however, is not historically predetermined but contingent. . . . The outcome of political conflict is never certain, and even if in hindsight we see many historical events as inevitable, the path of history is contingent. Nevertheless, once in place . . . institutions tend to create a . . . circle, a process of . . . feedback, making it more likely that these institutions will persist and even expand. . . . Once a critical juncture happens, the small differences that matter are the initial institutional differences that put in motion very different responses. . . . Even if small institutional differences matter greatly during critical junctures, not all institutional differences are small, and naturally, larger institutional differences lead to even more divergent patterns during such junctures."

Arthur (1989: 177, 128; 1994: 27, 112–13, 188): In a dynamic approach, "historical 'small events' . . . and chance circumstances . . . are not averaged away and 'forgotten' . . . they may decide the outcome." Furthermore, "once an outcome (a dominant technology) begins to emerge it becomes progressively more 'locked in.'" "Increasing returns can cause the economy gradually to lock itself in to an outcome not necessarily superior to alternatives, not easily altered, and not entirely predictable in advance." "Under increasing returns . . . the process becomes path-dependent." "Exit from an inferior equilibrium in economics depends very much on the source of the self-reinforcing mechanism. It depends on the degree to which the advantages accrued by the inferior 'equilibrium' are reversible or transferable to an alternative one. . . . Where coordination effects are the source of lock-in, often advantages are transferable."

Bernhard (2015: 978): "Critical junctures are concentrated periods where actors have a high degree of independence from structural and environmental constraints in pursuing their preferences in institutional design. Though multiple options may be available to actors at each juncture, once a particular set of decisions are made, possibilities are foreclosed and paths of development are locked in. . . . critical junctures [lead] to new configurations of institutions characterized by path dependence." Indeed, "critical junctures are 'critical' because they generate path dependence. . . . Agency and contingency are linked in critical junctures. . . . Contingency means that more than one outcome exists thus precluding structural determination." Following critical junctures, "contingency collapses and paths previously open at critical junctures are no longer 'available.'"

Bulmer and Burch (1998: 605): "Critical junctures create branching points at which institutional development moves on to a new trajectory or pathway which is then followed incrementally until a new critical moment arises, a new critical juncture follows and a new direction is taken." Critical junctures are "moments when the fundamentals of institutions change" and which bring about "an alteration in the quality of the institution itself. These periodic alterations, while not wholly breaking with the past, are sufficiently novel to be considered as significant. They may amount to sudden, dramatic transformations involving new structures, procedures or a change in the underlying principles of administration. Alternatively, they may amount to an incremental transformation when separate and emerging patterns crystallize and become established as a coherent whole which is distinctly different from that which previously existed. A novel institutional feature, once thus initiated, is thereafter likely to develop along the broad lines laid down at its inception." Critical junctures "may be generated by forces external to the institution . . . or by internal factors." "In theory, at each critical moment the opportunities for institutional innovation are at their widest. Conversely, at each such moment, various alternative pathways are not taken—either because they were considered and rejected or actors were not aware of them or did not give credence to them."

Table AI.1. Definitions of Critical Juncture, Compared

Panel A

Authors	Attributes of the Critical Juncture				
	Critical junctures are only macro-level changes or large-scale events.	Critical junctures are discontinuous or rapid changes.	Critical junctures are changes of institutions.	Critical junctures are changes only or mainly of political institutions.	Critical junctures are moments of contingency; structure is not important.
Acemoglu and Robinson (2012)	×		✓	×	?
Arthur (1989, 1994)	×			×	✓
Bernhard (2015)			✓		✓
Bulmer and Burch (1998)	✓	✓	✓		
Calder and Ye (2010)		✓	✓	✓	✓
Capoccia and Kelemen (2007; Capoccia 2016)					
Collier and Collier (1991)	✓	✓	✓	×	✓
David (1985)	×		×		×
Ekiert (1996)	✓	✓	✓	×	✓
Gerring (2012)			✓		✓
Greer (2008)	×	✓	✓	×	✓
Hacker (2002)	✓		✓	×	
Hogan (2006)	✓	✓	✓		
Ikenberry (2016)	✓	✓	✓	✓	
Katznelson (2003)	✓		✓	×	×

(continued)

Table AI.1. Definitions of Critical Juncture, Compared (*continued*)

Panel A

Authors	Attributes of the Critical Juncture				
	Critical junctures are only macro-level changes or large-scale events.	Critical junctures are discontinuous or rapid changes.	Critical junctures are changes of institutions.	Critical junctures are changes only or mainly of political institutions.	Critical junctures are moments of contingency; structure is not important.
Krasner (1984, 1988)	x	√	√		
Kuhn (1970 [1962])	√	√	x	x	
Lieberman (2003)	√		√	√	
Mahoney (2000, 2001)	√	√	√	x	√
Martin (2015)	√	√	√	x	
Martin and Sunley (2006)	√	√	x	x	x
Pempel (1998)		√	√		
Pierson (2004)	x		√	x	x
Roberts (2014)		√	√		√
Rokkan (1970, in Flora 1999)	√		√		
Sabel and Zeitlin (1985)		√	x	x	x
Scully (1992)	√	√			
Slater (2010, Slater and Simmons 2010)					x
Soifer (2012)		√			x
Thelen (1999, 2004)			√	√	
Weingast (2005)	√	√			x
Yashar (1997)	√	√	√	x	

Legend: √ = Yes; x = No; ? = Unclear; Empty cell = the attribute is not addressed.

(*continued*)

Table AI.1. Definitions of Critical Juncture, Compared (*continued*)

Panel B

Attributes of the Legacy of the Critical Juncture

Authors	Critical junctures are changes that produce a historical legacy.	Critical junctures produce divergent legacies.	Critical junctures can produce convergent legacies.	Critical junctures produce or reproduce legacies only through path dependence.	Critical junctures reproduce legacies through reactive sequences.	Critical junctures produce legacies deterministically, not probabilistically.	Critical junctures offer partial explanations.
Acemoglu and Robinson (2012)	√	√				x	
Arthur (1989, 1994)	√			x		x	
Bernhard (2015)	√			√		√	
Bulmer and Burch (1998)	√	√					
Calder and Ye (2010)	√			√			
Capoccia and Kelemen (2007; Capoccia 2016)	?	x		√			
Collier and Collier (1991)	√	√			x	x	√
David (1985)	√			√			
Ekiert (1996)	√	√		√			
Gerring (2012)	√			√			
Greer (2008)	√			√		x	
Hacker (2002)	√			√		x	
Hogan (2006)	√			x			
Ikenberry (2016)	√			√			
Katznelson (2003)	√						

(*continued*)

Table A1.1. Definitions of Critical Juncture, Compared (*continued*)

Panel B

Attributes of the Legacy of the Critical Juncture

Authors	Critical junctures are changes that produce a historical legacy.	Critical junctures produce divergent legacies.	Critical junctures can produce convergent legacies.	Critical junctures produce or reproduce legacies only through path dependence.	Critical junctures reproduce legacies through reactive sequences.	Critical junctures produce legacies deterministically, not probabilistically.	Critical junctures offer partial explanations.
Krasner (1984, 1988)	√			x			
Kuhn (1970 [1962])							
Lieberman (2003)	√	√		√			
Mahoney (2000, 2001)	√	√		√	√	√	
Martin (2015)	√			√			
Martin and Sunley (2006)	√					x	
Pempel (1998)	√			√			
Pierson (2004)	√	√		√		x	
Roberts (2014)	?	√		√	?		
Rokkan (1970, in Flora 1999)	√	√	√				
Sabel and Zeitlin (1985)	√		√			x	
Scully (1992)	√						
Slater (2010, Slater and Simmons 2010)	√	√				x	
Soifer (2012)	√	√					
Thelen (1999, 2004)	√	√		x		x	
Weingast (2005)	√						
Yashar (1997)	√						

Legend: √ = Yes; x = No; ? = Unclear; Empty cell = the attribute is not addressed.

Calder and Ye (2010: 42–43, 45–48): "A critical juncture [is] a historical decision point at which there are clear alternative paths to the future. Specifically, for a decision point to be a critical juncture, certain defining features are both necessary and sufficient: . . . A. There usually exists a crisis that calls the legitimacy of current arrangements into serious question . . . B. Crisis breeds stimulus for change . . . C. There is intense time pressure on the parties involved. . . . At a critical juncture, decision-makers are clearly faced with enormous uncertainty, and simultaneous time pressure to decide . . . crisis-driven decision-making [is] often dramatic and discontinuous." Critical junctures are moments of "profound contingency. . . . Existing institutions are important contextual elements of a critical juncture. Yet because of the distinctive, indeterminate nature of such potential turning points . . . institutions by definition cannot determine the outcome of such a critical juncture." "Critical junctures are . . . central in institution-building and institutional change. . . . Institutional development at critical junctures has inevitable discontinuity from a historical perspective. . . . The structural product of [a] critical-juncture [new institutions] . . . is stabilized, codified, and in turn itself shapes the future . . . until another crisis occurs at a subsequent critical juncture."

Capoccia and Kelemen (2007: 341, 343, 348, 352; Capoccia 2016: 103, italics removed): Critical junctures are "relatively short periods of time during which there is a substantially heightened probability that agents' choices will affect the outcome of interest . . . choices during the critical juncture trigger a path-dependent process that constrains future choices. . . . Structural fluidity and heightened contingency . . . are the defining traits of critical junctures." "Change is not a necessary element of a critical juncture." Moreover, because "the concept of critical juncture . . . needs to be defined independently from its empirical consequences . . . the reference to 'divergence' as a defining element of critical junctures [is] problematic." "The concept of 'critical junctures' is an essential building block of historical institutionalism." But it "can be invoked in order to interpret all sorts of developmental processes."

Collier and Collier (1991: 11, 20, 27–29, 36–39): "A critical juncture may be defined as a period of significant change, which typically occurs in distinct ways in different countries (or in other units of analysis) and which is hypothesized to produce distinct legacies." Critical junctures are "a type of discontinuous political change . . . which . . . consists of macro transformation [that] . . . 'dislodge[s]' older institutional patterns." "Some critical junctures . . . may entail considerable discretion, whereas with others the presumed choice appears deeply embedded in antecedent conditions." Moreover, "the effect of the critical juncture is . . . commonly . . . intertwined with other processes of change." Thus, the explanation of outcomes in terms of critical junctures "are probabilistic and partial"; critical junctures "make certain outcomes more likely, but not inevitable." "The period of continuity [following a critical juncture] . . . is explained by . . . mechanisms of reproduction . . . processes that reproduce the legacy of the historical cause." However, "the crystallization of the legacy does not necessarily occur immediately [after a critical juncture], but rather may consist of a sequence of intervening steps that respond to these reactions and counterreactions." Thus, "it is useful to distinguish between the mechanisms of the *reproduction* and the *production* of the legacy."

David (1985: 332): "A *path-dependent* economic sequence of economic changes is one in which important influences upon the eventual outcome can be exerted by temporarily remote events, including happenings dominated by chance elements rather than systematic forces. . . . In such circumstances, 'historical accidents' can neither be ignored nor reality quarantined for the purpose of economic analysis; the dynamic process itself takes on an essentially historical character."

Ekiert (1996: xi, xiv): Critical junctures are "momentous political events" that set "in motion unique, long-term, path-dependent developments" and produce "cross-national differences."

Gerring (2012: 418): A critical juncture is "a type of causal relationship in which a contingent moment determines a longer trajectory, that is, a period of path-dependence in which that trajectory is maintained and perhaps reinforced (through 'increasing returns')."

Greer (2008: 219–21): "A critical juncture [is] a moment at which decisions are highly contingent but, once taken, will shape politics and policy for the future. . . . A critical juncture is characterized by a high degree of contingency, multiple possible trajectories, and a high likelihood that the results will prove self-perpetuating. . . . Critical junctures are times at which the ordinary incrementalism of politics is temporarily replaced by uncertainty and the possibility of significant change, which will later stabilize and return to incrementalism. . . . The decisions taken in this fluid situation will shape future policy because of . . . path dependence. . . . At some time in the past, those involved made decisions and investments that set them along one trajectory. Now, even if they wish they were on a different trajectory, their existing investments bind them to it. . . . [S]mall decisions about institutions and policy tools taken at one time can have a major influence over what is possible and realistic in the future."

Hacker (2002: 58–59): "Critical junctures represent moments of political opportunity when significant new policy departures may be put in place or when the forces for change are strong enough to cut into the ongoing path-dependent development of an existing policy and alter its trajectory. . . . What all these critical moments have in common is their fundamental impact on subsequent historical dynamics. . . . Advocates of the concept of critical junctures sometimes link the idea to the notion of path dependence. Yet the two concepts are not identical. Path dependence suggests why the effects of critical junctures may be so profound and enduring. It does not necessarily explain why critical junctures occur, nor does it necessarily imply—as the idea of critical junctures does—that . . . big historical events have big historical consequences. . . . In fact, path dependence implies that seemingly 'small' events or choices may also have big eventual effects."

Hogan (2006: 664): "A critical juncture [is] an event, prior to which a range of possibilities must exist, but after which these possibilities will have mostly vanished. . . . [T]wo separate elements are required for a critical juncture. First, it is necessary to identify the generative cleavage. . . . Second, the change must be significant, swift and encompassing. . . . [A] critical juncture will not be defined by the assumption that it initiates a path-dependent process. Non-path-dependent processes can result in institutional stability, and path dependence is less common than previously believed."

Ikenberry (2016: 540–43): Critical junctures are "rare moments" when "polities pass through founding moments . . . that fix in place basic political orientations and institutions . . . During critical junctures, [actors have] choices to make. . . . At least when it comes to overarching . . . rules and institutions, change tends to be episodic rather than continuous and incremental. Institutional structures, once established, can be difficult to change even when underlying social forces continue to evolve. . . . [T]he rules and institutions . . . once put in place, do tend to persist, at least until a subsequent disruption shatters the old rules and institutions and opens up a new moment of order building. . . . [A] path dependence logic is . . . evident."

Katznelson (2003: 282–83, 291): Critical junctures are "periods of large-scale change . . . [during which] actors . . . redefine situations, provide solutions, and create institutional results, some of which then endure for extended periods to reshape boundaries, naturalize outcomes, redistribute power, and provide new contexts for solving problems." Critical junctures are "times when the advantages of the status quo are broken, thus conducing an uncommon range of choice. . . . In such circumstances, many constraints on agency are broken or relaxed and opportunities expand so that purposive action may be especially consequential." However, "even at such times, the conditions under which . . . [agents] operate are not simply of their own making." "Path dependence comes into play only . . . after critical junctures have performed their work."

Krasner (1984: 225, 240, 242–43; 1988: 81, 83): Punctuated equilibriums are "short bursts of rapid institutional change followed by long period of stasis . . . New structures originate during periods of crisis. . . . Political change follows a branching model. . . . But once institutions are in place they can assume a life of their own . . . once a critical choice has been made it cannot be taken back. . . . [O]nce a path is taken it canalizes future developments. . . . A number of mechanisms can contribute to institutional persistence and inertia. One factor is the ability of an institution to alter its environment. . . . Institutions may also persist because they follow path-dependent patterns of development. Path-dependent patterns are characterized by self-reinforcing positive feedback. Initial choices, often small and random, may determine future historical trajectories. Once a particular path is chosen, it precludes other paths, even if these alternatives might, in the long run, have proven to be more efficient or adaptive." Punctuated equilibrium can be contrasted to "a slow, continuous process of change. . . . In a world characterized by punctuated equilibrium there is more uncertainty and chance."

Kuhn (1970 [1962]: 1, 6, 49, 64, 85, 92, 13, 139, 150): "Scientific revolutions" or "paradigm shifts" are "major turning points," "relatively sudden and unstructured event[s]" and "non-cumulative developmental episodes in which an older paradigm is replaced in whole or in part by an incompatible new one." Scientific revolutions "can be small . . . as well as large," but they "occur all at once (though not necessarily in an instant) or not at all." Scientific revolutions are contrasted to "linear . . . cumulative . . . piecemeal [or] incremental" change. A scientific revolution has an "impact" and is "consequential" in that it changes the "view of the field [of knowledge], its methods, and its goals." "Once it has achieved the status of paradigm, a scientific theory is declared invalid only if an alternative candidate is available to take its place." But there is "considerable resistance to paradigm change."

Lieberman (2003: 13–14): "A critical juncture . . . is the historical period during which a wide range of . . . alternatives and possibilities [regarding some issue] . . . are considered . . . by national political elites." A critical juncture "concludes when a definition is ultimately specified in crucial legal documents, typically including the constitution, various laws, and national policies. . . . Subsequently, the distinguishing characteristics of the critical juncture—that is, the different ways in which [an issue] gets defined—tend to cast a long shadow on the future, even once the initial conditions have changed. The institutions that remain and endure set in motion path-dependent processes."

Mahoney (2000: 507–09, 2001: 11, 268): "Critical junctures" are "branching points" or moments "when historically contingent selection processes lead to abrupt changes and set countries on enduring paths of development. . . . A path-dependent approach emphasizes how actor choices create institutions and structures, which in turn shape subsequent actor behaviors, which in turn lead to the development of new institutional and structural patterns . . . path dependence characterizes specifically those historical sequences in which contingent events set into motion institutional patterns or event chains that have deterministic properties. The identification of path dependence therefore involves both tracing a given outcome back to a particular set of historical events, and showing how these events are themselves contingent occurrences that cannot be explained on the basis of prior historical conditions." Path dependence involves "two dominant types of sequences . . . *self-reinforcing sequences* characterized by the formation and long-term reproduction of a given institutional pattern . . . [or] *reactive sequences* [that] are chains of temporally ordered and causally connected events."

Martin (2015: 19, italics removed): "Discontinuous punctuated equilibrium models view change as occurring at moments of major upheaval, dramatically transforming institutions, and establishing new paths for future political trajectories. . . . In punctuated equilibrium models of change, strategic choices at critical junctures establish policy legacies for future action and define the new normal. Moments of economic and political upheaval permit a broad repertoire of response and early outcomes are unpredictable. Yet the resolution of political conflicts at critical junctures creates enduring path dependencies through lock-in effects and feedback processes. . . . Institutions created at critical junctures have subsequent reinforcing mechanisms."

Martin and Sunley (2006: 401–03, 407–08): "Path dependence . . . would seem to subscribe to a particular view of evolution that is very close to biology's notion of 'punctuated equilibrium.' In the latter, evolution is a periodic or episodic process, whereby phases of relative stability are 'punctuated' by critical junctures wherein major shocks cause system-wrenching change that then establishes a new phase of relative stability or slow change." "Path dependence is a probabilistic and contingent process: at each moment in historical time the suite of possible future evolutionary trajectories (paths) of a technology, institution, firm or industry is conditioned by (contingent on) both the past and the current states of the system in question, and some of these possible paths are more likely or probable than others. The past thus sets the possibilities, while the present controls what possibility is to be explored, which only becomes explained *ex post*." "Early decisions reverberate through history, closing alternative paths and validating a particular path." However, "processes of path destruction and new path creation are always latent in the process of path dependence."

Pempel (1998: 3–4): "'Punctuated equilibrium' is the term often used to characterize such mixtures of long continuities followed by dramatic shifts . . . breaks with the past [or] sudden shifts. . . . Even the most 'stable' countries, having followed the most consistent patterns for sustained periods of time, periodically lurch onto paths quite at odds with the one long traveled. Following such deviations, similarities to the past are less striking than are the breaks from it. Path-dependent equilibrium is periodically ruptured by radical change, making for sudden bends in the path of history."

Pierson (2004: 19, 27, 49, 51–52): "'Critical junctures' generate . . . divergent [and] . . . persistent paths of . . . development. Although analyses invoking the language of 'critical junctures' sometimes focus on large-scale, dramatic events, those qualities are neither necessary nor sufficient to generate path-dependent dynamics. In fact, the point in path-dependent analyses is that 'causes' may often seem relatively small compared with their effects. . . . What makes a particular juncture 'critical' is that it triggers a process of positive feedback. . . . A critical feature of path-dependent processes is the relative 'openness' or 'permissiveness' of early stages in a sequence compared with the relatively 'closed' or 'coercive' nature of later stages. . . . Although sometimes these junctures are treated as highly contingent or random, generally analysts seek to generate convincing explanations for why one path rather than another was chosen. . . . Nothing in path-dependent analyses implies that a particular alternative is permanently 'locked in' following the move onto a self-reinforcing path. Identifying self-reinforcing processes does help us to understand why organizational and institutional practices are often extremely persistent—and this is crucial, because these continuities are a striking feature of the social world. Asserting that the social landscape can be permanently frozen is hardly credible, however, and that is not the claim. Change continues, but it is bounded change—until something erodes or swamps the mechanisms of reproduction that generate continuity. . . . Path-dependent processes will often be evident not only at the level of individual organizations or institutions but at a more macro level that involves configurations of complementary organizations and institutions."

Roberts (2014: 42–45): Critical junctures "are periods of crisis or strain that existing policies and institutions are ill-suited to resolve. As such, they challenge the reproduction of existing institutions and generate powerful pressures for policy and/or institutional changes that are (a) abrupt; (b) discontinuous; and (c) path dependent." "Critical junctures produce institutional outcomes that condition what follow in their wake. . . . [D]urable consequences . . . are the hallmark of critical junctures." However, "critical junctures . . . need not re-align or re-equilibrate [institutions] in every case, much less generate durable new ones to take the place of the old." Moreover, "a critical juncture might produce a durable legacy of de-institutionalization rather than institutional lock-in." Critical junctures "produce divergent outcomes across a range of cases that are subjected to similar pressures for change." "Critical junctures are characterized by high levels of uncertainty and political contingency . . . [and] are not structurally determined." The "outcomes of the critical juncture become crystallized through self-reinforcing feedback mechanisms . . . or [are] modified through the 'reactive sequences' triggered by social or political resistance. . . . Reactive sequences may reinforce some outcomes, producing linear legacies of institutional continuity, but they may corrode or destabilize others and generate a legacy of ongoing institutional change or fluidity."

Rokkan (1970), as summarized by Flora (1999: 36–37): "[C]ritical junctures are periods of radical change . . . at critical junctures . . . basic decisions are made . . . which then are frozen over long periods of time." Moreover, Rokkan (1970: 113, italics removed) states, critical junctures sometimes generate "developments in divergent directions" and other times bring "systems closer to each other."

Sabel and Zeitlin (1985: 162–63): "Relatively short periods of growing . . . diversity punctuate longer periods dominated by a tendency to uniformity. During the brief interludes of openness, accumulated technical knowledge creates the possibility of divergent breakthroughs. At these branching points the diversity of political circumstances moves technology down correspondingly different paths. But competition eliminates some of these experiments and bends others towards a common goal. . . . [T]he logic of the dominant paradigm becomes so compellingly self-evident that competing lines of innovation become almost inconceivable . . . The tendency towards uniformity is only reversed when some combination of developments in the market and in the capacity to control nature make it economically feasible to disregard the sunk costs and technically plausible to strike out in new directions."

Scully (1992: 11–12): A critical juncture is "a period of profound and enduring change. . . . Rather than approaching political change as an essentially incremental phenomenon . . . [the critical juncture] approach tends to view it as discontinuous. Closely allied to Arthur Stinchcombe's concept of a 'historical cause,' . . . once a historical cause results in a specific outcome, the pattern that is established reproduces itself without requiring the recurrence of the original cause."

Slater (2010: 55; Slater and Simmons 2010: 888, 890, italics removed): "critical junctures can . . . be defined as periods in history when variation in a specified causal force pushes multiple cases onto divergent long-term pathways . . . or pushes a single case onto a new political trajectory that diverges significantly from the old. . . . Divergence . . . [is] a defining feature of critical junctures." Though "the methodological literature is divided over whether contingency and choice are defining attributes of critical junctures . . . the importance of choice and contingency . . . [are] an empirical question."

Soifer (2012: 1573, 1577, 1579–80, 1593): Critical junctures are a "type of historical moment" that can be characterized as "punctuated change" rather than "incremental change," and "what makes a juncture *critical* is that the outcomes generated in one historical moment persist over time. . . . The distinct feature of a historical juncture with the potential to be critical is the loosening of the constraints of structure to allow for agency or contingency to shape divergence from the past, or divergence across cases." However, "divergence rather than contingency" is key to a definition of a critical juncture; agnosticism "about the relative importance of agency and contingency in the critical juncture" is justified because "we can imagine moments of heightened contingency that are not critical junctures."

Thelen (1999: 387–88; 2004: 8, 31, 34): Critical junctures are "crucial founding moments of institutional formation that send countries along broadly different developmental paths." "At critical junctures, old institutions are not necessarily dismantled and replaced, but often either recalibrated or 'functionally reconverted' in part or in whole." After critical junctures, "institutions continue to evolve in response to changing environmental conditions and ongoing political maneuvering but in ways that are constrained by past trajectories." "It is not sufficient to view institutions as frozen residue of critical junctures, or even as 'locked in' in the straightforward sense that path dependence arguments adapted from the economics literature often suggest. In politics, institutional reproduction can be partly understood in terms of the increasing returns effects to which this literature has drawn our attention—but only partly. . . . [I]nstitutional survival often involves active political renegotiation and heavy doses of institutional adaptation, in order to bring institutions inherited from the past into line with changes in the social and political context." In other words, "positive feedback effects . . . help explain important institutional continuities over time. . . . [But] versions of a path-dependent argument that paint a deterministic picture of institutional 'lock in'" should be rejected.

Weingast (2005: 164–66, 171): A critical juncture is a "discontinuous political change . . . [a] massive change. . . . A critical juncture occurs when a major dislocation occurs in society, such as when people abandon previous views and come to hold new ones sufficiently different that the direction of politics transforms radically." In a critical juncture "the role of structure is important [and] contingency is important."

Yashar (1997: 235): A critical juncture is "a discontinuous process" during which "actors attempt to resolve politically salient conflicts . . . and, in the process, consolidate new political, economic, and social institutions. Thereafter, these institutions sustain a historical legacy by shaping as well as constraining subsequent action and discourse. The ability of actors to transform these institutions fundamentally occurs infrequently."

REFERENCES

Acemoglu, Daron, and James A. Robinson. 2012. *Why Nations Fail: Origins of Power, Poverty and Prosperity*. New York, NY: Crown.

Arthur, W. Brian. 1989. "Competing Technologies, Increasing Returns, and Lock-In by Historical Events." *Economic Journal* 99(394): 116–31.

———. 1994. *Increasing Returns and Path Dependence in the Economy*. Ann Arbor, MI: University of Michigan Press.

Bernhard, Michael. 2015. "Chronic Instability and the Limits of Path Dependence." *Perspectives on Politics* 13(4): 976–91.

Bulmer, Simon, and Martin Burch. 1998. "Organising for Europe: Whitehall, the British State and the European Union." *Public Administration* 76(4): 601–28.

Calder, Kent, and Min Ye. 2010. *The Making of Northeast Asia*. Stanford, CA: Stanford University Press.

Capoccia, Giovanni. 2016. "Critical Junctures." In Orfeo Fioretos, Tulia G. Falleti, and Adam Sheingate (eds.), *The Oxford Handbook of Historical Institutionalism* (pp. 89–106). New York, NY: Oxford University Press

Capoccia, Giovanni, and R. Daniel Kelemen 2007. "The Study of Critical Junctures: Theory, Narrative, and Counterfactuals in Historical Institutionalism." *World Politics* 59(3): 341–69.

Collier, Ruth Berins, and David Collier. 1991. *Shaping the Political Arena: Critical Junctures, the Labor Movement, and the Regime Dynamics in Latin America*. Princeton, NJ: Princeton University Press.

David, Paul A. 1985. "Clio and the Economics of QWERTY." *American Economic Review* 75(2): 332–37.

Ekiert, Grzegorz. 1996. *The State against Society: Political Crises and Their Aftermath in East Central Europe*. Princeton, NJ: Princeton University Press.

Flora, Peter. 1999. "Introduction and Interpretation." In Peter Flora (ed.), *State Formation, Nation-Building, and Mass Politics in Europe: The Theory of Stein Rokkan* (pp. 1–91). Oxford, UK: Oxford University Press.

Gerring, John. 2012. *Social Science Methodology: A Unified Framework*. New York, NY: Cambridge University Press.

Greer, Scott L. 2008. "Choosing Paths in European Union Health Services Policy: A Political Analysis of a Critical Juncture." *Journal of European Social Policy* 18(3): 219–31.

Hacker, Jacob S. 2002. *The Divided Welfare State: The Battle over Public and Private Social Benefits in the United States*. New York, NY: Cambridge University Press.

Hogan, John. 2006. "Remoulding the Critical Junctures Approach." *Canadian Journal of Political Science* 39(3): 657–79.

Ikenberry, G. John. 2016. "The Rise, Character, and Evolution of International Order." In Orfeo Fioretos, Tulia G. Falleti, and Adam Sheingate (eds.), *The Oxford Handbook of Historical Institutionalism* (pp. 738–52). New York, NY: Oxford University Press.

Katznelson, Ira. 2003. "Periodization and Preferences: Reflections on Purposive Action in Comparative Historical Social Science." In James Mahoney and Dietrich Rueschemeyer (eds.), *Comparative Historical Analysis in the Social Sciences* (pp. 270–303). New York, NY: Cambridge University Press.

Krasner, Stephen D. 1984. "Approaches to the State: Alternative Conceptions and Historical Dynamics." *Comparative Politics* 16(2): 223–46.

———. 1988. "Sovereignty: An Institutional Perspective." *Comparative Political Studies* 21(1): 66–94.

Kuhn, Thomas S. 1970 [1962]. *The Structure of Scientific Revolutions* (2nd ed.). Chicago, IL: University of Chicago Press.

Lieberman, Evan S. 2003. *Race and Regionalism in the Politics of Taxation in Brazil and South Africa*. New York, NY: Cambridge University Press.

Mahoney, James. 2000. "Path Dependence in Historical Sociology." *Theory and Society* 29(4): 507–48.

———. 2001. *The Legacies of Liberalism: Path Dependence and Political Regimes in Central America*. Baltimore, MD: Johns Hopkins University Press.

Martin, Cathie Jo. 2015. "Negotiation and the Micro-Foundations of Institutional Change." In Fredrik Engelstad and Anniken Hagelund (eds.), *Cooperation and Conflict the Nordic Way: Work, Welfare, and Institutional Change in Scandinavia* (pp. 17–34). Berlin: De Gruyter.

Martin, Ron, and Peter Sunley. 2006. "Path Dependence and Regional Economic Evolution." *Journal of Economic Geography* 6(4): 395–437.

Pempel, T.J. 1998. *Regime Shift: Comparative Dynamics of the Japanese Political Economy*. Ithaca, NY: Cornell University Press.

Pierson, Paul. 2004. *Politics in Time: History, Institutions, and Social Analysis*. Princeton, NJ: Princeton University Press.

Roberts, Kenneth M. 2014. *Changing Course in Latin America: Party Systems in the Neoliberal Era.* New York, NY: Cambridge University Press.

Rokkan, Stein, with Angus Campbell, Per Torsvik, and Henry Valen. 1970. *Citizens, Elections, and Parties: Approaches to the Comparative Study of the Processes of Development.* New York, NY: David McKay.

Sabel, Charles F., and Jonathan Zeitlin. 1985. "Historical Alternatives to Mass Production: Politics, Markets and Technology in Nineteenth-Century Industrialization." *Past and Present* 108: 133–76.

Scully, Timothy R. 1992. *Rethinking the Center. Party Politics in Nineteenth- and Twentieth-Century Chile.* Stanford, CA: Stanford University Press.

Slater, Dan. 2010. *Ordering Power: Contentious Politics and Authoritarian Leviathans in Southeast Asia.* New York, NY: Cambridge University Press.

Slater, Dan, and Erica Simmons. 2010. "Informative Regress: Critical Antecedents in Comparative Politics." *Comparative Political Studies* 43(7): 886–917.

Soifer, Hillel David. 2012. "The Causal Logic of Critical Junctures." *Comparative Political Studies* 45(12): 1572–597.

Thelen, Kathleen. 1999. "Historical Institutionalism in Comparative Politics." *Annual Review of Political Science* 2: 369–404.

———. 2004. *How Institutions Evolve: The Political Economy of Skills in Germany, Britain, the United States and Japan.* New York, NY: Cambridge University Press.

Weingast, Barry R. 2005. "Persuasion, Preference, Change, and Critical Junctures: The Microfoundations of a Macroscopic Concept." In Ira Katznelson and Barry R. Weingast (eds.), *Preferences and Situations: Points of Intersection Between Historical and Rational Choice Institutionalism* (pp. 129–60). New York, NY: Russell Sage Foundation.

Yashar, Deborah J. 1997. *Demanding Democracy: Reform and Reaction in Costa Rica and Guatemala, 1870s–1950s.* Stanford, CA: Stanford University Press.

Appendix II

Glossary of Terms Used in Critical Juncture Research

activating critical juncture. Term introduced by Riedl and Roberts, in this volume, to designate a **critical juncture** that is strongly affected by **antecedent conditions**. Contrast with **generative critical juncture**.

aftermath. A concept of the **critical juncture framework** introduced by Collier and Collier (1991: 37) to designate the period between a **critical juncture** and a **legacy** characterized by a series of "reactions and counter reactions." It is important to distinguish the aftermath from the critical juncture and the legacy. The aftermath is a period during which the immediate outcome of a critical juncture is contested and can either by rolled back or accepted, possibly with some adjustment. In contrast, during the legacy, the outcome of a critical juncture is treated as the status quo, and what is at stake is whether the new status quo is reproduced over time or not. See **mechanisms of production**.

agency. In the social sciences, agency is the power of actors to counteract necessity and make their own history. Theories that emphasize agency seek to recognize that actors have an independent role in causation and are alternatives to theories that rely on various forms of determinism—such as **structural determinism**, **historical determinism**, and **path-dependent determinism**. See **contingency** and **self-determination**.

antecedent conditions. In general terms, an antecedent condition is a state of affairs that precedes another particular state of affairs. In the context of the **critical juncture framework**, an antecedent condition has a more specific meaning: it is the condition that stands prior to a posited critical juncture.

Antecedent conditions can play different roles in critical juncture analysis. They are a source of factors that explain the way in which critical junctures occur, as in the case of **critical antecedents**. They are a source of **rival hypotheses** for explaining the outcome attributed to a critical juncture. They offer a "base line against which the critical juncture and its legacy are assessed" (Collier and Collier 1991: 30). Finally, as stressed by Waldner, in this volume, antecedent conditions can be a source of a **backdoor path**. See **activating critical juncture** and **critical antecedents**.

antecedents, critical. See **critical antecedents**.

approaches to causation. There are different approaches to causation that offer alternative ways of understanding causation. Some of the most prominent current approaches to causation are the difference-making approach, which focuses squarely on the idea of **causal effect**, and the production approach, which highlights the importance of a **causal mechanism** in a causal account. See **difference-making approach to causation, production approach to causation**, and **potential outcomes approach to causation**.

backdoor path. Concept introduced by Pearl (2000). A backdoor path between two variables X and Y, where X is a symbol for a cause and Y is a symbol for an effect, is any path from X to Y that starts with an arrow pointing to X (Z → X) rather that out of X (X → Y). Backdoor paths generally indicate a common cause of X and Y, that confounds the effect of X on Y. See **front-door path**.

backdoor path bias. Term used by Waldner, in this volume, to refer to the bias introduced in the estimation of a causal effect that does not take into consideration and correct for noncausal sources of association due to a **backdoor path**.

behavioral path dependence. Term introduced by Acharya, Blackwell, and Sen (2018) to refer to a form of path dependence in which persistence is reinforced by behavioral properties (e.g., attitudes, norms, and beliefs). Contrast with **institutional path dependence**.

causal chain. An ordered sequence of events in which one event in the chain is the cause of the next. In a causal chain, what is first an effect becomes a cause in the next step in the chain. A **causal cycle** and a **causal series** are two kinds of causal chain.

causal cycle. Term introduced by Bunge (2009: 132, 155) to designate a **causal chain** characterized by a **persistent effect**. It offers a way to give precision to the structure of the **causal explanation** of a historical **legacy** and to distinguish these explanations, characteristic of critical juncture research, from arguments about historical causation that posit a concatenation of causes that do not involve a persistent effect. The idea is similar to that of **self-replicating causal loop**. Contrast with **causal series**.

causal effect. A causal effect of X on Y is the difference in Y when X is present and operative and when X is not present and operative. Contrast with **causal mechanism**.

causal explanation. An account of some fact that shows that a cause generates an effect and how a cause generates an effect. A causal explanation based on claims about a **causal effect** and a **causal mechanism** is deeper and fuller than a causal explanation based solely on a claim about a **causal effect**. Contrast with **prediction**.

causal inference. The process of drawing conclusions about causal relations.

causal loop, self-replicating. See **self-replicating causal loop**.

causal mechanism. A process connecting a variable X and a variable Y. Some scholars treat a causal mechanism as an intervening variable. Others treat causal mechanisms as something distinct, a process at a lower level of organization than the outcome variable Y. In this second view, an explanation that specifies a causal mechanism is not the same as one that relies on variables at the same level of organization, and hence an explanation based on mechanisms is different from, and cannot be reduced to, an explanation based only on the idea of a **causal effect**.

causal mechanism, change. See **change causal mechanism**.

causal mechanism, stabilizing. See **stabilizing causal mechanism**.

causal process observation (CPO). A term proposed by Collier, Brady, and Seawright (2010: 184) to refer to "an insight or piece of data that provides information about context or mechanism and contributes a different kind of leverage in causal inference." Adding precision to the idea of causal process observations, Mahoney (2010) distinguishes between independent variable CPOs, that provide "data concerning the existence of posited causes"; mechanism CPOs, that provide "data concerning posited intervening events and processes"; and auxiliary outcome CPOs, that provide "data concerning posited auxiliary outcomes." In a further development, Dunning (2012: Ch. 7) distinguishes between model-validation CPOs, "knowledge about causal process that support or invalidate core assumptions of causal models," and treatment-assignment CPOs, "pieces or nuggets of information about the process by which units were assigned to treatment and control conditions in a natural experiment." Contrast with **data set observations**.

causal series. Term introduced by Bunge (2009: 132, 155) to designate a **causal chain** in which no cause-effect pair repeats itself and which causes a **long-term effect** but not a **persistent effect**. Contrast with **causal cycle**.

causation, approaches to. See **approaches to causation**.

causation, reciprocal. See **reciprocal causation**.

cause. An event that generates another event or, more precisely, a change in some property (X) of a thing that produces a change in some property (Y) of a thing.

cause, constant. See **constant cause**.

cause, distal. See **distal cause**.

cause, historical. See **historical cause**.

cause, proximate. See **proximate cause**.

cause, uncaused. See **uncaused cause**.

change causal mechanism. Term introduced by Munck, in this volume, to designate a **causal mechanism** that produces change. Change causal mechanisms play a role in explaining why social orders come to an end and new orders are created. See **stabilizing causal mechanism**.

change, immanent. See **immanent change**.

cleavage. A key concept in the **critical juncture framework**. Cleavages are lines that divide groups. Cleavages that are commonly studied in research on critical junctures include the center-periphery, church-state, land-industry, and owner-worker cleavages. Critical junctures are routinely seen as growing out of a fundamental societal or political cleavage. See **shock**.

comparative historical analysis. An approach in the study of the social sciences, launched in the 1960s, that bridges sociology and political science, as well as history, and is distinctly concerned with understanding the historical origins of social outcomes.

conditions, antecedent. See **antecedent conditions**.

conditions, productive. See **productive conditions**.

confounding variable. A variable that influences both the posited cause and effect (Z → X, Z → Y, where X is a symbol for a cause and Y is a symbol for an effect). An estimate of the causal effect of X on Y that does not correct for the effect of Z is said to suffer from confounding bias.

constant cause. Term introduced by Stinchcombe (1968: 101) to designate causes that operate on an ongoing basis, for example year after year, and produce the same effect only inasmuch as the cause recurs. Hypotheses about constant causes are common **rival hypotheses** to **critical juncture hypotheses**. Synonym for **proximate cause**. Contrast with **distal cause** and **historical cause**.

contingency. In critical juncture research, contingency is understood to mean different things. (1) A contingent outcome is one that cannot be predicted on the basis of existing knowledge. (2) A contingent outcome is one that does not necessarily follow from antecedent conditions. (3) A contingent outcome is one that is not determined by antecedent conditions and involves, rather, an unconditioned choice by actors. Moderate versions of contingency provide a salutary corrective to various forms of determinism that deny a role to **agency** (e.g., **structural determinism**, **historical determinism**, and **path-dependent determinism**). Extreme versions of contingency treat agency as an **uncaused cause**, an unjustified claim. See **activating critical juncture** and **generative critical juncture**. See also **self-determination**.

continuism. The assumption that differences, and hence all changes, entail differences of degree within a continuum and never differences in kind. Also known as **degreeism**.

continuous change. A kind of change that occurs along some continuum that represents variation in one property. Continuous change is contrasted to **discontinuous change**.

convergent paths. The idea that the path of evolution of a group of countries (or some other unit) makes them more similar over time. Contrast with **divergent paths**, **parallel paths**, and **unilinear path**.

conversion. Term introduced by Thelen (2003, 2004: 36) to designate a kind of **incremental change**, in which "the adoption of new goals or the incorporation of new groups into the coalitions on which institutions are founded . . . drive a change in the functions these institutions serve or the role they perform" (see also Streeck and Thelen 2005: 26–29).

crisis. A term that is occasionally used as a synonym for a **shock**, an event the triggers a **critical juncture**.

critical antecedents. Term introduced by Slater and Simmons (2010) to designate factors or conditions preceding a critical juncture that combine in a causal sequence with factors operating during that juncture to produce a legacy. A critical antecedent is a distinctive kind of **antecedent condition.**

critical juncture. The key concept in the **critical juncture framework.** A critical juncture is (1) a major episode of innovation that (2) generates an enduring **legacy.** More elaborately, a critical juncture is (1) a rapid **discontinuous change** at the **macro** level, and (2) a **distal cause** that generates a historical **legacy** or, more precisely, has a **persistent effect** via a **causal cycle,** i.e., a causal chain that includes a **self-replicating causal loop.**

Although some definitions of a critical juncture are framed in terms of the change and persistence of an **institution,** critical junctures are not limited to institutions. Similarly, although some definitions of a critical juncture hold that a critical juncture necessarily involves differentiation and **divergent paths,** critical junctures can increase diversity, decrease diversity, or not alter diversity.

Some scholars consider **contingency** to be a defining feature of critical junctures. However, treating contingency as a defining feature of a critical juncture unjustifiably excludes potential critical junctures from consideration and forecloses, by definitional fiat, theorizing about the variable role of structural-historical factors and agency in critical junctures. See **activating critical juncture** and **generative critical juncture.**

critical juncture, activating. See **activating critical juncture.**

critical juncture framework. The conceptual framework that synthesizes the key concepts used in critical juncture research. This framework draws on the work by Lipset and Rokkan (1967) and has evolved with the contribution of multiple scholars, including Collier and Collier (1991). The fundamental aim of the critical juncture framework is to address the impact of **discontinuous change;** that is, it is not a general model of change. And its five key parts are the **antecedent conditions,** the **cleavage** or **shock,** the **critical juncture,** the **aftermath,** and the **legacy.**

There is considerable overlap between this framework and **punctuated equilibrium** models. Some of these concepts, or similar concepts, are part of other frameworks used in the study of social change and order, such as the strand of the **new institutional economics** influenced by North (1990). Research using this framework is also closely related to research in the traditions of **comparative historical analysis** and **historical institutionalism.**

critical juncture, generative. See **generative critical juncture.**

critical juncture hypotheses. The central hypothesis about critical junctures focuses on the way a **critical juncture** generates a **legacy.** For example, in *Shaping the Political Arena,* Collier and Collier (1991) posit that differences in the mode of labor incorporation led to differences in the subsequent party system and political regime dynamics. Critical junctures hypotheses can also address why a critical juncture occurs in different ways. For example, Collier and Collier (1991) argue that the power of the oligarchy determined the mode of labor incorporation.

Thus, the central hypotheses in the literature on critical junctures concern the causes and consequences of critical junctures.

critical juncture, sequential. See **sequential critical juncture**.

critical transitions. A term used by Alston, Melo, Mueller, and Pereira (2016: 1, 5) to designate "historical periods when the powerful organizations in a country shift from one set of beliefs about how institutions (the formal and informal rules of the game) will affect outcomes to a new set of beliefs." The authors contrast this idea to that of a critical juncture, which they see as conveying "the notion of a shock in the more distant past to which rulers and citizens reacted with less understanding of all that was involved and a weaker notion of what could possibly be done." Although the concept of critical transition places an emphasis on changes in beliefs and opportunities, it is consistent with the concept of **critical juncture**.

data set observation (DSO). A term proposed by Collier, Brady, and Seawright (2010: 184) "to refer to observation in the sense of a row in a rectangular data set." Contrast with **causal process observation (CPO)**.

degreeism. See **continuism**.

design, research. See **research design**.

design-based inference. Term that designates research in which control over confounding variables is mainly sought through choices pertaining to the design of research rather than through ex post adjustment using parametric statistical models. Examples of design-based inference are **instrumental variable design** and **regression discontinuity design**. See **research design**. Contrast with **model-based inference**.

determination, self-. See **self-determination**.

determinism, historical. See **historical determinism**.

determinism, path-dependent. See **path-dependent determinism**.

determinism, structural. See **structural determinism**.

difference-making approach to causation. An approach to causation that reduces the concept of causation to that of **causal effect** and either disregards or treats as secondary the idea of **causal mechanism**. Within this approach, an event is a cause of some effect if in the absence of the event the effect would not have occurred. One of the key strands within the difference-making approach to causation is the **potential outcomes approach to causation**. Contrast with **production approach to causation**.

discontinuous change. A kind of change that involves the introduction of some new property and hence of **qualitative novelty**. Synonym for **synoptic change**. Discontinuous change is contrasted to **continuous change**.

displacement. Term used by Streeck and Thelen (2005: 19), based on Orren and Skowronek (2004), to designate a kind of **incremental change** in which "new models emerge and diffuse which call into question existing, previously taken-for-granted organizational forms and practices." In contrast, Kuhn (1970 [1962]) uses the term to designate a discontinuous kind of change.

distal cause. In the context of historical analysis, a distal cause is a cause that is temporally distant, that is, an event that happened decades or centuries before its ultimate effect. A distal cause can have a **persistent effect** or a **long-term effect**. Synonym for **historical cause**. Contrast with **constant cause** and **proximate cause**.

divergent paths. The idea that the path of evolution of a group of countries (or some other unit) makes them more different over time. Contrast with **convergent paths**, **parallel paths**, and **unilinear path**.

drift. Term introduced by Hacker (2005: 45) to designate a kind of **incremental change** in which "a shift in the context of policies . . . significantly alters their effects" (see also Streeck and Thelen 2005: 24–26).

dynamics, social. See **social dynamics**.

effect, long-term. See **long-term effect**.

effect, persistent. See **persistent effect**.

endogenous change. Change that is a consequence of an **endogenous factor**. See **immanent change**.

endogenous factor. A source of change that originates within the affected system. Contrast with **exogenous factor**.

endogenous variable. A variable in a causal model whose value is dependent on the states of other variables in the model. Relatedly, a causal model is said to have a problem of endogeneity when an explanatory variable is correlated with the error term. Endogeneity may be due to measurement error, omitted variables, or reverse causality (when an "effect" determines a "cause"). An estimate of the causal effect of X on Y that does not correct for endogeneity is said to suffer from endogeneity bias. Contrast with **exogenous variable**.

exclusion condition. An **instrumental variable** is said to satisfy the exclusion condition when the instrument affects the outcome exclusively via its effect on the main explanatory variable. See also **relevance condition**.

exhaustion. Term introduced by Streeck and Thelen (2005: 29) to designate a kind of **incremental change** in which institutions break down in a gradual rather than an abrupt way.

exogenous change. Change that is a consequence of an **exogenous factor**.

exogenous factor. A source of change that originates outside the affected system. See **exogenous shock**. Contrast with **endogenous factor**.

exogenous shock. A sudden change in some **exogenous factor** that induces a change in the affected system.

exogenous variable. A variable in a causal model whose value is independent from the states of other variables in the model. Contrast with **endogenous variable**.

experiment, natural. See **natural experiment**.

experimental research. Research that relies on experimental data, that is, data that is collected by a researcher who controls the assignment of treatment to subjects. Contrast with **observational research**.

explanation, causal. See **causal explanation**.

externalism. The view that factors from outside some system (e.g., economic factors in an account of the political system) are the key source of change. In its extreme version, externalism denies any role to internal factors. Contrast with **internalism.**

framework, theoretical. See **theoretical framework.**

front-door path. Concept introduced by Pearl (2000). Two variables X and Y are said to have a front-door path when there is a "mediator" (M) between two variables X and Y, and when there are no confounders between X and M and between M and Y, and there is no path from X to Y other than through M. See **backdoor path.**

generative critical juncture. Term introduced by Riedl and Roberts, in this volume, to designate a critical juncture characterized by a high degree of **contingency,** such that outcomes are largely a product of actor choices and strategic behavior during the critical juncture itself. Contrast with **activating critical juncture.**

gradualism. Change that unfolds slowly, in increments. A weak version of gradualism emphasizes the virtues or ubiquity of gradual or **incremental change** and contrasts gradual change to **discontinuous change** or **synoptic change.** A strong version of gradualism claims that all change is gradual or incremental and hence assumes **continuism** or **degreeism.**

hindsight. The ability to study events after they have happened. A distinctive methodological issue in critical juncture research concerns how much hindsight is needed before a claim that an event was a critical juncture can be adequately verified.

historical cause. A broad concept used to refer to causes that occurred in a distant past. In the critical juncture framework, the term historical cause is used, more specifically, for a cause that has a distinct causal structure: the original cause is held to have an effect, even without the recurrence of the original cause, because it triggers what Stinchcombe (1968: 103) calls a **self-replicating causal loop.** Synonym for **distal cause.** Contrast with **constant cause** and **proximate cause.**

historical determinism. The view that the course of history is predetermined and that actors cannot alter it. Similar to **path-dependent determinism** and **structural determinism.**

historical institutionalism. An approach in the study of the social sciences that is distinctly concerned with understanding the historical origins of institutional arrangements.

historical legacy. See **legacy.**

hypotheses, critical juncture. See **critical juncture hypotheses.**

hypotheses, rival. See **rival hypotheses.**

immanent change. A change that is purely driven by an **endogenous factor** or factors.

increasing returns. Term introduced by Arthur (1989, 1994) to designate the idea that gains associated with the introduction of some novelty get "locked in" and endure over time through a feedback effect, which reinforces the initial gains. See **path dependence**.

incremental change. A kind of change, also called gradual change, that is contrasted to the **discontinuous change** involved in critical junctures. The literature distinguishes, in turn, between various forms of incremental change, such as **conversion**, **displacement**, **drift**, **exhaustion**, and **layering**. Contrast with **discontinuous change** and **serial replacement**.

infinite regress, problem of. In the context of historically oriented causal analysis, the problem of infinite regress arises when the analyst is not able to offer a credible criterion for cutting into the flow of history and thus constantly pushes back the analysis to earlier events.

institution. Scholars offer many definitions of institutions, and some are very expansive, including policies and cultural issues. For example, definitions of institutions sometimes include rules, conventions, codes of behavior and norms, the nation's normative social order, regulations and policies, as well as standard operating practices. The most common and conventional view is that institutions are rules, whether formal or informal, that structure the actions and interactions of actors. Although the term "institutions" is frequent used as shorthand for political institutions, it also covers economic and cultural institutions.

institutional path dependence. Term introduced by Acharya, Blackwell, and Sen (2018) to refer to a form of path dependence in which persistence is reinforced by formal institutions. Contrast with **behavioral path dependence**.

instrumental variable. In regression analysis, instrumental variables or instruments are variables that are correlated with an explanatory variable (X) and uncorrelated with the error term (e). Instrumental variables are used to confront the problem of omitted-variable bias and the simultaneity bias (due to reserve causation) in estimations of causal effects. Instruments need to fulfill two crucial conditions: the **relevance condition** and the **exclusion condition**.

instrumental variable designs. Research designs that rely on an **instrumental variable**.

intercurrence. Term introduced by Orren and Skowronek (2004: 113) to designate the relationship among institutions and to highlight that coordination among institutions is "inherently problematic" and "cannot be assumed."

internalism. The view that factors of the system (e.g., political actors and relationships in an account of the political system) are the key source of change. In its extreme version, internalism denies any role to external factors. Contrast with **externalism**.

layering. Term introduced by Schickler (2001) to designate a kind of **incremental change** in which new rules are introduced on top of or alongside existing ones (see also Streeck and Thelen 2005: 22–24).

legacy. A key concept in the **critical juncture framework**. A legacy, also commonly referred to as a historical legacy, is an enduring, self-perpetuating effect of a critical juncture that persists for a substantial period of time. Hypotheses about critical junctures are centrally about legacies. In short: no legacy, no critical juncture. Legacies are usually explained in terms of **mechanisms of reproduction**, a **self-replicating causal loop**, or **path dependence**.

Critical juncture research frequently identifies more than one legacy, which can be distinguished with labels such as "legacy" and "further consequences of [the] legacy," or "direct legacy" and "additional legacies." Thus, in the case of Collier and Collier's (1991: 752–53) work, the party system is the "legacy" and regime stability is a "further consequence of [the] legacy."

long-term effect. An effect that has a temporally distant cause but that does not persist over time. Contrast with **persistent effect**.

macro. In the social sciences, the term macro is commonly used to designate **social systems** as opposed to the most basic component of social systems, persons. However, what may be regarded as macro in one context (e.g., the state) may be treated as micro in another (e.g., in a discussion of the global order). A macro-level property can also be defined as a property that is not possessed intrinsically by a unit. Contrast with **micro**.

macro-reductionism. The assumption that societies are wholes that cannot be analyzed in terms of their parts or components. See **micro-reductionism**.

mechanism, causal. See **causal mechanism**.

mechanisms of production. The mechanisms through which a **legacy** is generated are called the **mechanisms of production**, and are distinguished from the **mechanisms of reproduction** that account for the ongoing stability of the legacy.

mechanisms of reproduction. In contrast to the **mechanisms of production** that generate the **legacy**, mechanisms of reproduction account for its stability. Mechanisms of reproduction are routinely spelled out in terms of a **self-replicating causal loop** or **path dependence**.

method. A well-specified repeatable procedure for doing something.

micro. In the social sciences, the term micro is commonly used to designate the most basic component of **social systems**, persons. A micro-level property can also be defined as a property that is possessed intrinsically by a unit. Contrast with **macro**.

micro-reductionism. The assumption that social outcomes are always explainable in terms of processes at the micro-level of organization of society and that macro-level entities cannot determine action. See **macro-reductionism**.

model-based inference. Term that designates research in which control over confounding variables is mainly sought through the statistical adjustment of potential confounders. Contrast with **design-based inference**.

models of change. **Incremental change** and **discontinuous change** are basic models of institutional change. The relationship between these two models of change is central to the discussion about how critical junctures fit within a general model of change.

multi-method approach. Research that relies on more than one **method** to study a problem. It is frequently used to designate research that relies on methods from more than one of the three big families of methods: qualitative, quantitative, and experimental.

natural experiment. A kind of experiment in the real world "in which some process of random or *as-if* random assignment places cases in alternative categories of the key independent variable" (Dunning 2010: 281). Natural experiments are generally sought as a way of addressing confounding, which occurs when an extraneous factor is associated with both a posited cause (X) and a posited effect (Y). Common natural experiments are **instrumental variable designs** and **regression discontinuity designs**. See **design-based inference**.

new institutional economics. An approach in the discipline of economics, launched in the 1990s by scholars influenced by North (1990), that gives centrality to the study of institutions and specifically political institutions.

nonrecurring causes, problem of. In the context of historically oriented causal analysis, the problem of nonrecurring causes concerns the challenge of establishing a link between cause and effect when the cause is a **distal cause** that has ceased to recur.

novelty, qualitative. See **qualitative novelty**.

observational research. Research that relies on observational data, that is, data that is collected by a researcher who does not control the assignment of treatment to subjects. Contrast with **experimental research**.

paradigm shift. Term introduced by Kuhn (1970 [1962]: 66, 104, 150) to designate a **critical juncture** in the field of knowledge.

parallel paths. The idea that the path of evolution of a group of countries (or some other unit) does not alter their diversity. Contrast with **convergent paths**, **divergent paths**, and **unilinear path**.

path dependence. Term introduced by David (1985: 332) to designate a "sequence of . . . changes [in] . . . which important influences upon the eventual outcome can be exerted by temporally remote events, including happenings dominated by chance elements rather than systematic forces." Closely tied to the concept of path dependence is the idea that "small fortuitous events" can affect the path that is followed and have large consequences (Arthur 1994: 5). See **increasing returns**.

Arguments about path dependence are routinely used to spell out the **mechanisms of reproduction** of the **legacy** of critical junctures. However, although causal chains that involve "reactive sequences" are frequently treated as a kind of path dependence (Mahoney 2000), these causal chains do not explain the persistence of a legacy and hence are not suitable ways to specify mechanisms of reproduction.

path dependence, behavioral. See **behavioral path dependence**.

path dependence, institutional. See **institutional path dependence.**

path-dependent determinism. The view that **path dependence** places countries (or other units) on a certain path that actors cannot alter. Similar to **historical determinism** and **structural determinism.**

path, unilinear. See **unilinear path.**

paths, convergent. See **convergent paths.**

paths, divergent. See **divergent paths.**

paths, parallel. See **parallel paths.**

permissive conditions. Term introduced by Soifer (2012) to designate a causal condition that operates during a critical juncture, marks the loosening of constraints on agency or contingency, and makes change possible. See **productive causes.**

persistent effect. An effect that persists over time and hence accounts for the **legacy** of a **critical juncture.** See **self-replicating causal loop.** Contrast with **long-term effect.**

potential outcomes approach to causation. An approach to causation that is a part of the **difference-making approach to causation** and combines a counterfactual and manipulation view of causation. Although the philosophy of science distinguishes between two broad classes of approaches to causation, many proponents of this approach to causation claim to have subsumed all views on causation and provided a unified theory of causation. Contrast with **production approach to causation.**

prediction. A forecast of some future or some unknown state of the world. Predictions do not require a claim about a **cause.** Contrast with **causal explanation.**

presentism. The assumption that all effects have a temporally **proximate cause,** that is, that the current state of the world can be explained fully by reference to causes in the recent past. It is also called short-termism.

process tracing. Process tracing is the examination of diagnostic pieces of evidence, commonly evaluated in a temporal and/or explanatory sequence, with the goal of supporting or overturning alternative causal hypotheses. Process tracing is a fundamental tool in qualitative analysis and, more broadly, is commonly seen as a method uniquely suited to the study of **causal mechanisms.**

production approach to causation. An approach to causation that holds that a cause produces an effect through a **causal mechanism** that connects cause and effect. Contrast with **difference-making approach to causation.**

productive conditions. Term introduced by Soifer (2012) to designate a causal condition, which operates during a critical juncture and, in the presence of **permissive conditions,** produces outcomes that endure once the permissive conditions disappear. See **permissive causes.**

proximate cause. Cause that is temporally proximate to an effect. Synonym for **constant cause.** Contrast with **distal cause** and **historical cause.**

punctuated equilibrium. A concept introduced by Eldredge and Gould (1972) to characterize a model of biological evolution that involves rare and rapid change. This model of change stands in opposition to the model of change known as phyletic **gradualism,** which sees evolution as involving slow and gradual changes. The contrast between punctuated equilibrium and phyletic gradualism is similar to the contrast between **discontinuous change** and **incremental change**.

qualitative diagnostics. Qualitative tools that are used to supplement the main tools used to infer causal relations. In some cases, qualitative research is used to check an assumption made in quantitative research.

qualitative novelty. A change involving the introduction of a new property. A qualitative novelty marks a before and after, and provides a basis for solving the **problem of infinite regress**. Synonym for **discontinuous change**.

quantitative diagnostics. Quantitative tools that are used to supplement the main tools used to infer causal relations. Commonly, these quantitative tools are used to address the assumptions made in quantitative research.

quantitative history. A tradition in the testing of historical arguments that relies on quantitative methods.

reciprocal causation. The effect of two causes on each other. The **self-replicating causal loop** used to explain the **legacy** of a **critical juncture** is an example of reciprocal causation.

reductionism. The view that certain objects can be fully reduced to other, more basic ones. Common examples of reductionism are **macro-reductionism** and **micro-reductionism**. Economicism, the claim that economic factors are the ultimate source of change of all aspects of society, is another example of reductionism.

regression discontinuity designs. Research designs that relies on a cutoff or threshold above or below which an intervention is assigned. A desired characteristic of such designs is that it allows researchers to treat the intervention as exogenous.

relevance condition. An **instrumental variable** is said to satisfy the relevance condition when the instrument is significantly correlated with the main explanatory variable. See also **exclusion condition**.

research design. A strategy to integrate the various parts of the study. In discussions of methodology, research design is commonly used in a narrow sense to designate the design options that have different implications for the ability of a research to draw causal inferences. See **design-based inference**, **model-based inference**, **instrumental variable design**, and **regression discontinuity design**.

rival hypotheses. Hypotheses that differ from, and compete with, the hypothesis favored in a given research project. The most basic rival hypotheses to **critical juncture hypotheses** are ones that posit that a critical juncture introduces no change, or that the outcome that is hypothesized to be a **legacy** of a critical juncture can be explained by a **constant cause** or an **antecedent condition** that directly affects the outcome. Two critical juncture hypotheses could also be rival hypotheses (e.g., that poor economic performance in Latin America is a legacy of colonialism or of state formation).

selection bias. Bias in estimating a causal relationship introduced by the selection of units (e.g., individuals, groups, countries) in a nonrandom manner.

self-determination. The impact of actors on social processes, which is contrasted to causal determination by factors or conditions external to actors. An analysis of self-determination is a way to address the role of **agency** and to counter various forms of determinism such as **structural determinism**, **historical determinism**, and **path-dependent determinism**.

self-replicating causal loop. Term introduced by Stinchcombe (1968) to specify the structure of the historical causes analyzed in critical juncture research. In a self-replicating causal loop, "an *effect* created by causes at some previous period *becomes a cause of that same effect* in succeeding periods" (103). For example, whatever the origin of some institution might be, the institution could strengthen certain actors who subsequently support the institution. The idea is similar to that of a **causal cycle**.

sequential critical juncture. A sequence of critical junctures. An example of sequential critical junctures is provided by Scully (1992), who studies how critical junctures in Chile in the mid-nineteenth century, the initial decades of the twentieth century, and the mid-twentieth century reshaped the political party system. One of the distinctive features of the analysis of back-to-back critical junctures is that the legacy of one critical juncture becomes part of the antecedent conditions for the next critical juncture.

serial replacement. Term introduced by Levitsky and Murillo (2013) to designate frequently occurring **discontinuous changes**, which they contrast to both critical junctures, which they characterize as rare discontinuous changes, and to **incremental change**.

shock. A possible trigger or precipitating event of a critical juncture. See **cleavage** and **crisis**.

social dynamics. The study of how and why a society (or some other unit) changes over time. It is supplemented by the study of **social statics**.

social statics. The study of how and why order is maintained in a society (or some other unit). It is supplemented by the study of **social dynamics**.

social systems. A complex object composed of multiple interrelated components. Systems can include subsystems. For example, in the social sciences, the political regime is a subsystem of the state, and the state is a subsystem of the international system.

stabilizing causal mechanism. Term introduced by Munck, in this volume, to designate a **causal mechanism** that accounts for the continuation or reproduction of a social order. Stabilizing causal mechanisms play a role in explaining why social orders endure. See **change causal mechanism**.

statics, social. See **social statics**.

structural determinism. An explanation based only on structural factors and that ignores or discounts the role of agency. Similar to **path-dependent determinism** and **historical determinism**.

synoptic change. Change that happens in a short period of time. In the literature on critical junctures, it is sometimes used as a synonym of **discontinuous change** and contrasted with **incremental change**.

systems, social. See **social systems**.

temporality. A fundamental concept in the social sciences. Basic concepts of temporality include **discontinuous change**, **continuous change**, **incremental change**, **convergent paths**, **divergent paths**, **parallel paths**, and **unilinear path**. Concepts of temporality that are part of causal arguments include **historical cause**, **constant cause**, **proximate cause**, **distal cause**, **persistent effect**, **long-term effect**, **legacy**, and **path dependence**.

theoretical framework. A kind of theory. It is a set of very general ideas that have been systematized and that are used to develop theories of a narrower scope. For example, the critical juncture theoretical framework can be used to develop theories about state capacity, democracy, and party systems.

turning point. Term used by Kuhn (1970 [1962]: 6) as a synonym for **discontinuous change** and elaborated by Abbott (1997).

uncaused cause. A **cause** that is not conditioned by any prior cause. The history of the sciences shows that the search for uncaused causes is futile. Also called a first cause or prime mover.

unilinear path. The idea that countries (or some other unit) evolve along one single path. Contrast with **convergent paths**, **divergent paths**, and **parallel paths**.

REFERENCES

Abbott, Andrew. 1997. "On the Concept of Turning Point." *Comparative Social Research* 16: 85–105.

Acharya, Avidit, Matthew Blackwell, and Maya Sen. 2018. *Deep Roots: How Slavery Still Shapes Southern Politics*. Princeton, NJ: Princeton University Press.

Alston, Lee J., Marcus André Melo, Bernardo Mueller, and Carlos Pereira. 2016. *Brazil in Transition: Beliefs, Leadership, and Institutional Change*. Princeton, NJ: Princeton University Press.

Arthur, W. Brian. 1989. "Competing Technologies, Increasing Returns, and Lock–In by Historical Events." *Economic Journal* 99(394): 116–31.

———. 1994. *Increasing Returns and Path Dependence in the Economy*. Ann Arbor, MI: University of Michigan Press.

Bunge, Mario. 2009. *Causality and Modern Science* (4th ed.). New Brunswick, NJ: Transaction Publishers.

Collier, David, Henry E. Brady, and Jason Seawright. 2010. "Sources of Leverage in Causal Inference: Toward an Alternative View of Methodology." In Henry E. Brady and David Collier (eds.), *Rethinking Social Inquiry: Diverse Tools, Shared Standards* (2nd ed.; pp. 161–99). Lanham, MD: Rowman & Littlefield.

Collier, Ruth Berins, and David Collier. 1991. *Shaping the Political Arena: Critical Junctures, the Labor Movement, and the Regime Dynamics in Latin America*. Princeton, NJ: Princeton University Press.

David, Paul A. 1985. "Clio and the Economics of QWERTY." *American Economic Review* 75(2): 332–37.

Dunning, Thad. 2010. "Design-Based Inference: Beyond the Pitfalls of Regression Analysis?" In Henry E. Brady and David Collier (eds.), *Rethinking Social Inquiry: Diverse Tools, Shared Standards* (pp. 273–311). Lanham, MD: Rowman & Littlefield.

———. 2012. *Natural Experiments in the Social Sciences: A Design-Based Approach*. New York, NY: Cambridge University Press.

Eldredge, Niles, and Stephen Jay Gould. 1972. "Punctuated Equilibria: An Alternative to Phyletic Gradualism." In Thomas J. M. Schopf (ed.), *Models in Paleobiology* (pp. 82–115). San Francisco, CA: Freeman-Cooper.

Hacker, Jacob S. 2005. "Policy Drift: The Hidden Politics of US Welfare State Retrenchment." In Wolfgang Streeck and Kathleen Thelen (eds.), *Beyond Continuity: Institutional Change in Advanced Political Economies* (pp. 40–82). Oxford, UK: Oxford University Press.

Kuhn, Thomas S. 1970 [1962]. *The Structure of Scientific Revolutions* (2nd ed.). Chicago, IL: University of Chicago Press.

Levitsky, Steven, and María Victoria Murillo. 2013. "Building Institutions on Weak Foundations: Lessons from Latin America." *Journal of Democracy* 24(2): 93–107.

Lipset, Seymour M., and Stein Rokkan. 1967. "Cleavage Structures, Party Systems, and Voter Alignments: An Introduction." In Seymour M. Lipset and Stein Rokkan (eds.), *Party Systems and Voter Alignments: Cross–National Perspectives* (pp. 1–64). New York, NY: Free Press.

Mahoney, James. 2000. "Path Dependence in Historical Sociology." *Theory and Society* 29(4): 507–48.

———. 2010. "After KKV: The New Methodology of Qualitative Research." *World Politics* 62(1): 120–47.

North, Douglass C. 1990. *Institutions, Institutional Change and Economic Performance*. New York, NY: Cambridge University Press.

Orren, Karen, and Stephen Skowronek. 2004. *The Search for American Political Development*. New York, NY: Cambridge University Press.

Pearl, Judea. 2000. *Causality: Models, Reasoning, and Inference*. New York, NY: Cambridge University Press.

Schickler, Eric. 2001. *Disjointed Pluralism: Institutional Innovation and the Development of the U.S. Congress*. Princeton, NJ: Princeton University Press.

Scully, Timothy R. 1992. *Rethinking the Center. Party Politics in Nineteenth- and Twentieth-Century Chile*. Stanford, CA: Stanford University Press.

Slater, Dan, and Erica Simmons. 2010. "Informative Regress: Critical Antecedents in Comparative Politics." *Comparative Political Studies* 43(7): 886–917.

Soifer, Hillel David. 2012. "The Causal Logic of Critical Junctures." *Comparative Political Studies* 45(12): 1572–597.

Stinchcombe, Arthur L. 1968. *Constructing Social Theories*. New York, NY: Harcourt Brace.

Streeck, Wolfgang, and Kathleen A. Thelen. 2005. "Introduction: Institutional Change in Advanced Political Economies." In Wolfgang Streeck and Kathleen Thelen (eds.), *Beyond Continuity: Institutional Change in Advanced Political Economies* (pp. 1–39). Oxford, UK: Oxford University Press.

Appendix III

Bibliography of Substantive Research on Critical Junctures

This bibliography includes works in the critical juncture tradition, including also studies that—while not explicitly framed as studies of critical junctures—adopt a similar approach to comparative historical analysis. It demonstrates the remarkable range of substantive topics addressed by critical juncture studies, along with other works of comparative-historical analysis that are closely akin to the critical juncture tradition. The bibliography is organized as follows:

1. States and State Capacity (Including Order and Civil War)
2. Political Regimes and Democracy
3. Political Parties and Party Systems
4. Economic Development (Economic Growth, Inequality)
5. Public Policy and Government Performance (Social Policy, Welfare State, Varieties of Capitalism)
6. Culture (Language, Religion, Racism)
7. International Relations (Colonialism, Independence, Global Norms)
8. Miscellaneous Political and Social Developments

1. STATES AND STATE CAPACITY (INCLUDING ORDER AND CIVIL WAR)

Acemoglu, Daron, and James A. Robinson. 2019. *The Narrow Corridor: States, Societies, and the Fate of Liberty.* New York, NY: Penguin.

Bartolini, Stefano. 2005. *Restructuring Europe: Centre Formation, System Building, and Political Structuring Between the Nation State and the European Union.* Oxford, UK: Oxford University Press.

Besley, Timothy, and Marta Reynal-Querol. 2014. "The Legacy of Historical Conflict: Evidence from Africa." *American Political Science Review* 108(2): 319–36.

Boone, Catherine. 2003. *Political Topographies of the African State: Territorial Authority and Institutional Choice*. New York, NY: Cambridge University Press.

Cappelen, Christoffer, and Jason Sorens. 2018. "Pre-Colonial Centralisation, Traditional Indirect Rule, and State Capacity in Africa." *Commonwealth & Comparative Politics* 56(2): 195–215.

Centeno, Miguel A., and Agustín Enrique Ferraro (eds.). 2013. *State and Nation Making in Latin America and Spain: Republics of the Possible*. New York, NY: Cambridge University Press.

Eck, Kristine. 2018. "The Origins of Policing Institutions: Legacies of Colonial Insurgency." *Journal of Peace Research* 55(2): 147–60.

Ertman, Thomas. 1997. *Birth of the Leviathan: Building States and Regimes in Medieval and Early Modern Europe*. New York, NY: Cambridge University Press.

Gennaioli, Nicola, and Ilia Rainer. 2006. "The Modern Impact of Precolonial Centralization in Africa." *Journal of Economic Growth* 12(3): 185–234.

Green, Elliott. 2012. "On the Size and Shape of African States." *International Studies Quarterly* 56(2): 229–44.

Herbst, Jeffrey. 2000. *States and Power in Africa: Comparative Lessons in Authority and Control*. Princeton, NJ: Princeton University Press.

Hui, Victoria Tin-Bor. 2005. *War and State Formation in Ancient China and Early Modern Europe*. New York, NY: Cambridge University Press.

Javid, Hassan. 2011. "Class, Power, and Patronage: Landowners and Politics in Punjab." *History and Anthropology* 22(3): 337–69.

Kurtz, Marcus. 2013. *Latin American State-Building in Comparative Perspective: Social Foundations of Institutional Order*. New York, NY: Cambridge University Press.

Lange, Matthew. 2009. *Lineages of Despotism and Development. British Colonialism and State Power*. Chicago, IL: University of Chicago Press.

Lange, Matthew, and Dietrich Rueschemeyer (eds.). 2005. *States and Development: Historical Antecedents of Stagnation and Advance*. New York, NY: Palgrave.

López-Alves, Fernando. 2000. *State Formation and Democracy in Latin America, 1810–1900*. Durham, NC: Duke University Press.

Mann, Michael. 1986. *The Sources of Social Power* Vol. 1: *A History of Power from the Beginning to A.D. 1760*. New York, NY: Cambridge University Press.

Mattingly, Daniel. 2017. "Colonial Legacies and State Institutions in China: Evidence from a Natural Experiment." *Comparative Political Studies* 50(4): 434–63.

Mazzuca, Sebastián. 2021. *Latecomer State Formation. Political Geography and Capacity Failure in Latin America*. New Haven, CT: Yale University Press.

Migdal, Joel S. *Strong Societies and Weak States: State-Society Relations and State Capabilities in the Third World*. Princeton, NJ: Princeton University Press.

Mukherjee, Shivaji. 2018a. "Colonial Origins of Maoist Insurgency in India: Historical Institutions and Civil War." *Journal of Conflict Resolution* 62(10): 2232–74.

———. 2018b. "Historical Legacies of Colonial Indirect Rule: Princely States and Maoist Insurgency in Central India." *World Development* 111: 113–29.

North, Douglass C., John Joseph Wallis, and Barry R. Weingast. 2009. *Violence and Social Orders: A Conceptual Framework for Interpreting Recorded Human History*. New York, NY: Cambridge University Press.

Poulos, Jason. 2018. "Building State Capacity through Public Land Disposal: An Application of RNN-Based Counterfactual Prediction." Unpublished paper, University of California. Berkeley.

Ray, Subhasish. 2018. "Beyond Divide and Rule: Explaining the Link between British Colonialism and Ethnic Violence." *Nationalism and Ethnic Politics* 24(4): 367–88.

———. 2019. "History and Ethnic Conflict: Does Precolonial Centralization Matter?" *International Studies Quarterly* 63(2): 417–31.

Rogers, Clifford. 1993. "The Military Revolutions of the Hundred Years' War." *The Journal of Military History* 57(2): 241–78.

Skocpol, Theda. 1979. *States and Social Revolution.* New York, NY: Cambridge University Press.

Skowronek, Stephen. 1982. *Building a New American State: The Expansion of National Administrative Capacities, 1877–1920.* New York, NY: Cambridge University Press.

Slater, Dan. 2010. *Ordering Power: Contentious Politics and Authoritarian Leviathans in Southeast Asia.* New York, NY: Cambridge University Press.

Soifer, Hillel David. 2015. *State Building in Latin America.* New York, NY: Cambridge University Press.

Spruyt, Hendrik. 1994. *The Sovereign State and Its Competitors: An Analysis of Systems Change.* Princeton, NJ: Princeton University Press.

Tilly, Charles. 1990. *Coercion, Capital, and European States, AD 990–1990.* Oxford, UK: Basil Blackwell.

Vogler, Jan P. 2019. "Imperial Rule, the Imposition of Bureaucratic Institutions, and Their Long-Term Legacies." *World Politics* 71(4): 806–63.

Waldner, David. 1999. *State-Building and Late Development.* Ithaca, NY: Cornell University Press.

Young, Crawford. 1994. *The African Colonial State in Comparative Perspective.* New Haven, CT: Yale University Press.

———. 2004. "The End of the Post-Colonial State in Africa? Reflections on Changing African Political Dynamics." *African Affairs* 103(410): 23–49.

———. 2012. *The Postcolonial State in Africa: Fifty Years of Independence, 1960–2010.* Madison, WI: University of Wisconsin Press.

Ziblatt, Daniel. 2006. *Structuring the State: The Formation of Italy and Germany and the Puzzle of Federalism.* Princeton, NJ: Princeton University Press.

2. POLITICAL REGIMES AND DEMOCRACY

Acemoglu, Daron, Simon Johnson, James A. Robinson, and Pierre Yared. 2008. "Income and Democracy." *American Economic Review* 98(3): 808–42.

Albertus, Michael, and Victor Menaldo. 2018. *Authoritarianism and the Elite Origins of Democracy.* New York, NY: Cambridge University Press.

Angrist, Michele Penner. 2006. *Party-Building in the Modern Middle East.* Seattle, WA: University of Washington Press.

Bentzen, Jeanet Sinding, Jacob Gerner Hariri, and James A. Robinson. 2019. "Power and Persistence: The Indigenous Roots of Representative Democracy." *The Economic Journal* 129(618): 678–714.

Bernhard, Michael, Christopher Reenock, and Timothy Nordstrom. 2004. "The Legacy of Western Overseas Colonialism on Democratic Survival." *International Studies Quarterly* 48(1): 225–50.

Blaydes, Lisa, and Eric Chaney. 2013. "The Feudal Revolution and Europe's Rise: Political Divergence of the Christian and Muslim Worlds before 1500 CE." *American Political Science Review* 107(1): 16–34.

Capoccia, Giovanni. 2005. *Defending Democracy: Reactions to Extremism in Interwar Europe.* Baltimore, MD: Johns Hopkins University Press.

Clark, Janine A., and Marie-Joëlle Zahar. 2014. "Critical Junctures and Missed Opportunities: The Case of Lebanon's Cedar Revolution." *Ethnopolitics* 14(1): 1–18.

Collier, Ruth Berins, and David Collier. 1991. *Shaping the Political Arena: Critical Junctures, the Labor Movement, and the Regime Dynamics in Latin America.* Princeton, NJ: Princeton University Press.

della Porta, Donatella. 2016. *Where Did the Revolution Go?: Contentious Politics and the Quality of Democracy.* New York, NY: Cambridge University Press.

della Porta, Donatella, Massimiliano Andretta, Tiago Fernandes, Eduardo Romanos, and Markos Vogiatzoglou. 2018. *Legacies and Memories in Movements: Justice and Democracy in Southern Europe.* New York, NY: Oxford University Press.

Denk, Thomas, and Sarah Lehtinen. 2019. "The Legacy of Initial Regimes and Democratization in New States." In *State-Formation and Democratization: A New Classification* (pp. 109–38). New York, NY: Palgrave Macmillan.

Downing, Brian M. 1992. *The Military Revolution and Political Change.* Princeton, NJ: Princeton University Press.

Ekiert, Grzegorz. 1996. *The State against Society: Political Crises and Their Aftermath in East Central Europe.* Princeton, NJ: Princeton University Press.

Ekiert, Grzegorz, and Stephen E. Hanson (eds.). 2003. *Capitalism and Democracy in Central and Eastern Europe: Assessing the Legacy of Communist Rule.* New York, NY: Cambridge University Press.

Ekiert, Grzegorz, and Daniel Ziblatt. 2013. "Democracy in Central and Eastern Europe One Hundred Years." *East European Politics & Societies* 12(1): 90–107.

Ertman, Thomas. 1997. *Birth of the Leviathan: Building States and Regimes in Medieval and Early Modern Europe.* New York, NY: Cambridge University Press.

Ferrara, Federico. 2015. *The Political Development of Modern Thailand.* New York, NY: Cambridge University Press.

Frye, Timothy. 2010. *Building States and Markets after Communism: The Perils of Polarized Democracy.* New York, NY: Cambridge University Press.

García-Ponce, Omar, and Léonard Wantchékon. 2017. "Critical Junctures: Independence Movements and Democracy in Africa." Unpublished paper, May 2017.

Gould, Andrew C. 1999. *Origins of Liberal Dominance: State, Church, and Party in Nineteenth-Century Europe.* Ann Arbor, MI: University of Michigan Press.

Hariri, Jacob G. 2012. "The Autocratic Legacy of Early Statehood." *American Political Science Review* 106(3): 471–94.

Heilbrunn, John R. 2014. "Historic Paths: Colonialism and Its Legacies." In *Oil, Democracy, and Development in Africa* (pp. 37–74). New York, NY: Cambridge University Press.

Howlett, Michael. 2009. "Process Sequencing Policy Dynamics: Beyond Homeostasis and Path Dependency." *Journal of Public Policy* 29(3): 241–62.

Huber, Evelyne. 1989. "Capitalist Development and Democracy in South America." *Politics and Society* 17(3): 281–352.

Ishiyama, John. 2015. "Regime Legacies and Governance in Post-Communist States." *Taiwan Journal of Democracy* 11(2): 1–24.

Jalal, Ayesha. 1995. *Democracy and Authoritarianism in South Asia: A Comparative and Historical Perspective*. New York, NY: Cambridge University Press.

Jamal, Amal, and Anna Kensicki. 2016. "A Theory of Critical Junctures for Democratization: A Comparative Examination of Constitution-Making in Egypt and Tunisia." *The Law & Ethics of Human Rights* 10(1): 185–222.

Javid, Hassan. 2011. "Class, Power, and Patronage: Landowners and Politics in Punjab." *History and Anthropology* 22(3): 337–69.

Jones-Luong, Pauline. 2002. *Institutional Change and Political Continuity in Post-Soviet Central Asia*. New York, NY: Cambridge University Press.

Jowitt, Ken. 1992. "The Leninist Legacy." In Ken Jowitt, *New World Disorder: The Leninist Extinction* (pp. 284–305). Berkeley, CA: University of California Press.

Karl, Terry Lynn. 1990. "Dilemmas of Democratization in Latin America." *Comparative Politics* 23(1): 1–21.

———. 1997. *The Paradox of Plenty: Oil Booms and Petro-States*. Berkeley, CA: University of California Press.

LeBas, Adrienne. 2011. *From Protest to Parties: Party-Building and Democratization in Africa*. New York, NY: Oxford University Press.

Lipset, Seymour M., and Jason Lakin. 2004. "Part III. Hemispheric Divide: The United States and Latin America." In *The Democratic Century* (pp. 241–407). Norman, OK: University of Oklahoma Press.

López-Alves, Fernando. 2000. *State Formation and Democracy in Latin America, 1810–1900*. Durham, NC: Duke University Press.

Luebbert, Gregory M. 1991. *Liberalism, Fascism, or Social Democracy: Social Classes and the Political Origins of Regimes in Interwar Europe*. New York, NY: Oxford University Press.

Loveman, Brian. 1993. *The Constitution of Tyranny: Regimes of Exception in Spanish America*. Pittsburgh, PA: University of Pittsburgh Press.

Lowi, Miriam R. 2009. *Oil Wealth and the Poverty of Politics: Algeria Compared*. New York, NY: Cambridge University Press.

Mahoney, James. 2001. *The Legacies of Liberalism: Path Dependence and Political Regimes in Central America*. Baltimore, MD: Johns Hopkins University Press.

———. 2013. "Militarization without Bureaucratization in Central America." In Miguel A. Centeno and Agustín Enrique Ferraro (eds.), *State and Nation Making in Latin America and Spain: Republics of the Possible* (pp. 203–24). New York, NY: Cambridge University Press.

Mamdani, Mahmood. 1996. *Citizen and Subject: Contemporary Africa and the Legacy of Late Colonialism*. Princeton, NJ: Princeton University Press.

Møller, Jørgen. 2017. "Medieval Origins of the Rule of Law: The Gregorian Reforms as Critical Juncture?" *Hague Journal on the Rule of Law* 9(2): 265–82.

Montinola, Gabriella R. 2012. "Change and Continuity in a Limited Access Order: The Philippines." In Douglass C. North, John Wallis, Barry Weingast, and Steven Webb (eds.), *In the Shadow of Violence: Politics, Economics and the Problems of Development* (pp. 149–97). New York, NY: Cambridge University Press.

Moore, Jr., Barrington. 1966. *Social Origins of Dictatorship and Democracy: Lord and Peasant in the Making of the Modern World*. Boston, MA: Beacon Press.

North, Douglass C., John Joseph Wallis, and Barry R. Weingast. 2009. *Violence and Social Orders: A Conceptual Framework for Interpreting Recorded Human History*. New York, NY: Cambridge University Press.

Pop-Eleches, Grigore. 2007. "Historical Legacies and Post-Communist Regime Change." *Journal of Politics* 69(4): 908–26.

Söyler, Mehtap. 2015. *The Turkish Deep State: State Consolidation, Civil-Military Relations and Democracy*. New York, NY: Routledge.

Subrahmanyam, Gita. 2006. "Ruling Continuities: Colonial Rule, Social Forces and Path Dependency in British India and Africa." *Commonwealth & Comparative Politics* 44(1): 84–117.

Tsui, Lin. 2016. "Institutional Legacies and Political Transition in Central Asia." *Taiwan Journal of Democracy* 12(1): 93–123.

Tudor, Maya. 2013. *The Promise of Power: The Origins of Democracy in India and Autocracy in Pakistan*. New York, NY: Cambridge University Press.

van Eerd, Jonathan. 2017. *The Quality of Democracy in Africa: Opposition Competitiveness Rooted in Legacies of Cleavages*. New York, NY: Palgrave.

Yashar, Deborah J. 1997. *Demanding Democracy: Reform and Reaction in Costa Rica and Guatemala, 1870s–1950s*. Stanford, CA: Stanford University Press.

Young, Crawford. 1994. *The African Colonial State in Comparative Perspective*. New Haven, CT: Yale University Press.

———. 2004. "The End of the Post-Colonial State in Africa? Reflections on Changing African Political Dynamics." *African Affairs* 103(410): 23–49.

———. 2012. *The Postcolonial State in Africa: Fifty Years of Independence, 1960–2010*. Madison, WI: University of Wisconsin Press.

3. POLITICAL PARTIES AND PARTY SYSTEMS

Angrist, Michele Penner. 2006. *Party Building in the Modern Middle East*. Seattle, WA: University of Washington Press.

Arriola, Leonardo R. 2013. *Multiethnic Coalitions in Africa: Business Financing of Opposition Election Campaigns*. New York, NY: Cambridge University Press.

Bartolini, Stefano. 2000. *The Political Mobilization of the European Left, 1860–1980: The Class Cleavage*. New York, NY: Cambridge University Press.

———. 2007. *Restructuring Europe: Centre Formation, System Building, and Political Structuring between the Nation State and the European Union*. Oxford, UK: Oxford University Press.

Bartolini, Stefano, and Peter Mair. 1990. *Identity, Competition and Electoral Availability: The Stabilisation of European Electorates 1885–1985*. New York, NY: Cambridge University Press.

Burnham, Walter Dean. 1970. *Critical Elections and the Mainsprings of American Politics*. New York, NY: Norton.

———. 2016. "The Current Realignment of US Politics Means That the Outcome in November Could Be Anyone's Guess." LSE US Centre (blog). https://blogs.lse.ac.uk/usappblog/2016/05/27/the-current-realignment-of-us-politics-means-that-the-outcome-in-november-could-be-anyones-guess/.

Caramani, Daniele. 2004. *The Nationalization of Politics: The Formation of National Electorates and Party Systems in Western Europe*. New York, NY: Cambridge University Press.

————. 2015. *The Europeanization of Politics: The Formation of a European Electorate and Party System in Historical Perspective*. New York, NY: Cambridge University Press.

Collier Ruth Berins. 1992. *The Contradictory Alliance: State-Labor Relations and Regime Change in Mexico*. Berkeley, CA.: University of California at Berkeley.

————. 1993. "Combining Alternative Perspectives: Internal Trajectories versus External Influences as Explanations of Latin American Politics in the 1940s." *Comparative Politics* 26(1): 1–29.

Collier, Ruth Berins, and Christopher Chambers-Ju. 2012. "Popular Representation in Contemporary Latin American Politics: An Agenda for Research." In Peter Kingstone and Deborah J. Yashar (eds.), *Routledge Handbook of Latin American Politics* (pp. 564–78). New York, NY: Routledge.

Collier, Ruth Berins, and David Collier. 1991. *Shaping the Political Arena: Critical Junctures, the Labor Movement, and the Regime Dynamics in Latin America*. Princeton, NJ: Princeton University Press.

della Porta, Donatella, Joseba Fernández, Hara Kouki, and Lorenzo Mosca. 2017. *Movement Parties against Austerity*. Cambridge, UK: Polity.

Geddes, Barbara. 1995. "A Comparative Perspective on the Leninist Legacy in Eastern Europe." *Comparative Political Studies* 28(2): 239–74.

Gould, Andrew C. 1999. *Origins of Liberal Dominance: State, Church, and Party in Nineteenth-Century Europe*. Ann Arbor, MI: University of Michigan Press.

Grzymała-Busse, Anna M. 2002. *Redeeming the Communist Past: The Regeneration of Communist Parties in East Central Europe*. New York, NY: Cambridge University Press.

Hooghe, Liesbet, and Gary Marks. 2017. "Cleavage Theory Meets Europe's Crises: Lipset, Rokkan, and the Transnational Cleavage." *Journal of European Public Policy* 25(1): 109–35.

Kalyvas, Stathis N. 1998. "From Pulpit to Party: Party Formation and the Christian Democratic Phenomenon." *Comparative Politics* 30(3): 293–312.

Karvonen, Lauri, and Stein Kuhnle (eds.). 2001. *Party Systems and Voter Alignments Revisited*. New York, NY: Routledge.

Kenny, Paul D. 2017. *Populism and Patronage: Why Populists Win Elections in India, Asia, and Beyond*. Oxford, UK: Oxford University Press.

Key, V. O., Jr. 1955 "A Theory of Critical Elections." *Journal of Politics* 17(1): 3–18.

————. 1959. "Secular Realignment and the Party System." *Journal of Politics* 21(2): 198–210.

Kitschelt, Herbert. 1995. "Formation of Party Cleavages in Post-Communist Democracies: Theoretical Propositions." *Party Politics* 1(4): 447–72.

Kitschelt, Herbert, Kirk Hawkins, Juan Pablo Luna, Guillermo Rosas, and Elizabeth Zechmeister. 2010. *Latin American Party Systems*. New York, NY: Cambridge University Press.

Kitschelt, Herbert, Zdenka Mansfeldova, Radoslaw Markowski, and Gabor Toka. 1999. *Post-Communist Party Systems: Competition, Representation, and Inter-Party Cooperation*. New York, NY: Cambridge University Press.

Kreuzer, Marcus. 2009. "How Party Systems Form: Path Dependency and the Institutionalization of the Post-War German Party System." *British Journal of Political Science* 39(4): 669–97.

Lipset, Seymour M., and Stein Rokkan. 1967. "Cleavage Structures, Party Systems, and Voter Alignments: An Introduction." In Seymour M. Lipset and Stein Rokkan (eds.), *Party Systems and Voter Alignments: Cross-National Perspectives* (pp. 1–64). New York, NY: Free Press.

Lust, Ellen, and David Waldner. 2016. "Parties in Transitional Democracies: Authoritarian Legacies and Post-Authoritarian Challenges in the Middle East and North Africa." In Nancy Bermeo and Deborah J. Yashar (eds.), *Parties, Movements, and Democracy in the Developing World* (pp. 157–89). New York, NY: Cambridge University Press

Mair, Peter. 1997. *Party System Change: Approaches and Interpretations*. Oxford, UK: Clarendon Press.

———. 2001. "The Freezing Hypothesis. An Evaluation." In Lauri Karvonen and Stein Kuhnle (eds.), *Party Systems and Voter Alignments Revisited* (pp. 27–44). New York, NY: Routledge.

Mayhew, David R. 2002. *Electoral Realignments: A Critique of an American Genre*. New Haven, CT: Yale University Press.

Riedl, Rachel Beatty. 2014. *Authoritarian Origins of Democratic Party Systems in Africa*. New York, NY: Cambridge University Press.

———. 2018. "Institutional Legacies: Understanding Multiparty Politics in Historical Perspective." In Nic Cheeseman (ed.), *Institutions and Democracy in Africa: How the Rules of the Game Shape Political Developments* (pp. 41–60). New York, NY: Cambridge University Press.

Roberts, Kenneth M. 2014. *Changing Course in Latin America: Party Systems in the Neoliberal Era*. New York, NY: Cambridge University Press.

Rokkan, Stein. 1999. *State Formation, Nation-Building, and Mass Politics in Europe*. New York: Oxford University Press.

Rokkan, Stein, with Angus Campbell, Per Torsvik, and Henry Valen. 1970. *Citizens, Elections, and Parties: Approaches to the Comparative Study of the Processes of Development*. New York, NY: David McKay.

Rossi, Federico M. 2015. "The Second Wave of Incorporation in Latin America: A Conceptualization of the Quest for Inclusion Applied to Argentina." *Latin American Politics and Society* 57(1): 1–28.

———. 2017. *The Poor's Struggle for Political Incorporation: The Piquetero Movement in Argentina*. New York, NY: Cambridge University Press.

Scully, Timothy R. 1992. *Rethinking the Center: Party Politics in Nineteenth- and Twentieth-Century Chile*. Stanford, CA: Stanford University Press.

Shefter, Martin. 1994. *Political Parties and the State: The American Historical Experience*. Princeton, NJ: Princeton University Press.

Shyu, Huo-Yan. 2011. "Taiwan's Democratization and the Freezing of the Party System." In Liang Fook Lye and Wilhelm Hofmeister (eds.), *Political Parties, Party Systems and Democratization in East Asia* (pp. 257–90). Singapore: World Scientific.

Silva, Eduardo. 2009. *Challenging Neoliberalism in Latin America*. New York, NY: Cambridge University Press.

Silva, Eduardo, and Federico M. Rossi (eds.). 2018. *Reshaping the Political Arena in Latin America: From Resisting Neoliberalism to the Second Incorporation*. Pittsburgh, PA: University of Pittsburgh Press.

Sundquist, James L. 1983. *Dynamics of the Party System: Alignment and Realignment of Political Parties in the United States*. Washington, DC: Brookings Institution Press.

Ufen, Andreas. 2012. "Party Systems, Critical Junctures, and Cleavages in Southeast Asia." *Asian Survey* 52(3): 441–64.

————. 2013. "Lipset and Rokkan In Southeast Asia: Indonesia in Comparative Perspective." In Dirk Tomsa and Andreas Ufen (eds.), *Party Politics in Southeast Asia: Clientelism and Electoral Competition in Indonesia, Thailand, and the Philippines* (pp. 40–61). New York, NY: Routledge.

Wittenberg, Jason. 2006. *Crucibles of Political Loyalty: Church Institutions and Political Continuity in Hungary*. New York, NY: Cambridge University Press.

4. ECONOMIC DEVELOPMENT
(ECONOMIC GROWTH, INEQUALITY)

Acemoglu, Daron, Davide Cantoni, Simon Johnson, and James A. Robinson. 2011. "The Consequences of Radical Reform: The French Revolution." *American Economic Review* 101(7): 3286–307.

Acemoglu, Daron, Camilo García-Jimeno, and James A. Robinson. 2012. "Finding Eldorado: Slavery and Long-Run Development in Colombia." *Journal of Comparative Economics* 40(4): 534–64.

Acemoglu, Daron, Simon Johnson, and James A. Robinson. 2001. "The Colonial Origins of Comparative Development: An Empirical Investigation." *American Economic Review* 91(5): 1369–401.

————. 2002. "Reversal of Fortune: Geography and Institutions in the Making of the Modern World Income Distribution." *Quarterly Journal of Economics* 117(4): 1231–294.

Acemoglu, Daron, and James A. Robinson. 2012. *Why Nations Fail: Origins of Power, Poverty and Prosperity*. New York, NY: Crown.

Akee, Randall, Miriam Jorgensen, and Uwe Sunde. 2015. "Critical Junctures and Economic Development. Evidence from the Adoption of Constitutions among American Indian Nations." *Journal of Comparative Economics* 43(4): 844–61.

Akyeampong, Emmanuel, Robert H. Bates, Nathan Nunn, and James A. Robinson (eds.). 2014. *Africa's Development in Historical Perspective*. New York, NY: Cambridge University Press.

Alston, Lee J., Marcus André Melo, Bernardo Mueller, and Carlos Pereira. 2016. *Brazil in Transition: Beliefs, Leadership, and Institutional Change*. Princeton, NJ: Princeton University Press.

Bandopadhyay, Sanghamitra, and Elliott Green. 2013. "Precolonial Political Centralization and Contemporary Development in Uganda." *Economic Development and Cultural Change* 64(3): 471–508.

Banerjee, Abhijit, and Lakshmi Iyer. 2005. "History, Institutions and Economic Performance: The Legacy of Colonial Land Tenure Systems in India." *American Economic Review* 95(4): 1190–213.

Bockstette, Valeri, Areendam Chanda, and Louis Putterman. 2002. "States and Markets: The Advantage of an Early Start." *Journal of Economic Growth* 7(4): 347–69.

Boone, Catherine. 1994. "States and Ruling Classes in Postcolonial Africa: The Enduring Contradictions of Power." In Joel Migdal, Atul Kohli, and Vivienne Shue (eds.), *State Power and Social Forces: Domination and Transformation in the Third World* (pp. 108–40). New York, NY: Cambridge University Press.

Bruhn, Miriam, and Francisco Gallego. 2012. "Good, Bad, and Ugly Colonial Activities: Do They Matter for Economic Development?" *Review of Economics and Statistics* 94(2): 433–61.

Chanda, Areendam, and Louis Putterman. 2005. "State Effectiveness, Economic Growth, and the Age of States." In Matthew Lange and Dietrich Rueschemeyer (eds.), *States and Development: Historical Antecedents of Stagnation and Advance* (pp. 69–91). New York, NY: Palgrave MacMillan.

Chibber, Vivek. 2003. *Locked in Place: State-Building and Late Industrialization in India.* Princeton, NJ: Princeton University Press.

Coatsworth, John H. 1998. "Economic and Institutional Trajectories in Nineteenth-Century Latin America." In John H. Coatsworth and Alan M. Taylor (eds.), *Latin America and the World Economy Since 1800* (pp. 23–54). Cambridge, MA: Harvard University Press.

Dell, Melissa. 2010. "The Persistent Effects of Peru's Mining Mita." *Econometrica* 78(6): 1863–903.

Diamond, Jared. 1997. *Guns, Germs and Steel: The Fate of Human Societies.* New York, NY: Norton.

———. 2010. "Intra-Island and Inter-Island Comparisons." In Jared Diamond and James A. Robinson (eds.), *Natural Experiments of History* (pp. 120–41). Cambridge, MA: The Belknap Press of Harvard University Press.

Dincecco, Mark, and Mauricio Prado. 2012. "Warfare, Fiscal Capacity, and Performance." *Journal of Economic Growth* 17(3): 171–203.

Egnal, Marc. 1996. *Divergent Paths: How Culture and Institutions Have Shaped North American Growth.* New York, NY: Oxford University Press.

Engerman, Stanley L., and Kenneth L. Sokoloff. 1997. "Factor Endowments, Institutions, and Differential Paths of Growth among New World Economies." In Stephen Haber (ed.), *How Latin America Fell Behind: Essays on the Economic History of Brazil and Mexico, 1800–1914* (pp. 260–304). Stanford, CA: Stanford University Press.

———. 2012. *Economic Development in the Americas since 1500: Endowments and Institutions.* New York, NY: Cambridge University Press.

Feyrer, James, and Bruce Sacerdote. 2009. "Colonialism and Modern Income: Islands as Natural Experiments." *The Review of Economics and Statistics* 91(2): 245–62.

Fishman, Robert M. 2010. "Rethinking the Iberian Transformations: How Democratization Scenarios Shaped Labor Market Outcomes." *Studies in Comparative International Development* 45(3): 281–310.

Foa, Roberto Stefan. 2017. "Persistence or Reversal of Fortune? Early State Inheritance and the Legacies of Colonial Rule." *Politics and Society* 45(2): 301–24.

Gerschenkron, Alexander. 1962. *Economic Backwardness in Historical Perspective: A Book of Essays.* Cambridge, MA: Belknap Press of Harvard University Press.

Grosjean, Pauline. 2011. "The Institutional Legacy of the Ottoman Empire: Islamic Rule and Financial Development in South Eastern Europe." *Journal of Comparative Economics* 39(1): 1–16.

Heilbrunn, John R. 2014. "Historic Paths: Colonialism and Its Legacies." In *Oil, Democracy, and Development in Africa* (pp. 37–74). New York, NY: Cambridge University Press.

Hjort, Jonas. 2010. "Pre-Colonial Culture, Post-Colonial Economic Success? The Tswana and the African Economic Miracle." *Economic History Review* 63(3): 688–709.

Hough, Jerry F., and Robin Grier. 2015. *The Long Process of Development: Building Markets and States in Pre-Industrial England, Spain, and Their Colonies*. New York, NY: Cambridge University Press.

Huillery, Elise. 2009. "History Matters: The Long-Term Impact of Colonial Public Investments in French West Africa." *American Economic Journal: Applied Economics* 1(2): 176–215.

Iyer, Lakshmi. 2010. "Direct versus Indirect Colonial Rule in India: Long-Term Consequences." *Review of Economics and Statistics* 92(4): 693–713.

———. 2015. "The Long-Run Consequences of Colonial Institutions." In Latika Chaudhary, Bishnupriya Gupta, Tirthankar Roy, and Anand V. Swamy (eds.), *A New Economic History of Colonial India* (pp. 117–39). New York, NY: Routledge.

Jedwab, Remi, Edward Kerby, and Alexander Moradi. 2017. "History, Path Dependence and Development: Evidence from Colonial Railways, Settlers and Cities in Kenya." *The Economic Journal* 127(603): 1467–94.

Karl, Terry Lynn. 1997. *The Paradox of Plenty: Oil Booms and Petro-States*. Berkeley, CA: University of California Press.

Kohli, Atul. 2004. *State-Directed Development: Political Power and Industrialization in the Global Periphery*. New York, NY: Cambridge University Press.

Lange, Matthew K. 2004. "British Colonial Legacies and Political Development." *World Development* 32(6): 905–22.

———. 2009. *Lineages of Despotism and Development British Colonialism and State Power*. Chicago, IL: University of Chicago Press.

Lange, Matthew, and Dietrich Rueschemeyer (eds.). 2005. *States and Development: Historical Antecedents of Stagnation and Advance*. New York, NY: Palgrave.

LaPorta, Rafael, Florencio Lopez-de-Silanes, and Andrei Shleifer. 2008. "The Economic Consequences of Legal Origins." *Journal of Economic Literature* 46(2): 285–332.

LaPorta, Rafael, Florencio Lopez-de-Silanes, Andrei Shleifer, and Robert W Vishny. 1998. "Law and Finance." *Journal of Political Economy* 106(6): 1113–155.

Lee, Alexander. 2017. "Redistributive Colonialism: The Long Term Legacy of International Conflict in India." *Politics and Society* 45 (2): 173–224.

———. 2019. "Land, State Capacity, and Colonialism: Evidence From India." *Comparative Political Studies* 52(3): 412–44.

Lee, Alexander, and Kenneth A. Schultz. 2012. "Comparing British and French Colonial Legacies: A Discontinuity Analysis of Cameroon." *Quarterly Journal of Political Science* 7(4): 365–410.

Levine, Ross, Chen Lin, and Wensi Xie. 2017. "The Origins of Financial Development: How the African Slave Trade Continues to Influence Modern Finance." *NBER Working Papers* 23800.

Mahoney, James. 2003. "Long-Run Development and the Legacy of Colonialism in Spanish America." *American Journal of Sociology* 109(1): 50–106.

———. 2010. *Colonialism and Postcolonial Development: Spanish America in Comparative Perspective*. New York, NY: Cambridge University Press.

Maloney, William F., and Felipe Valencia Caicedo. 2016. "The Persistence of (Subnational) Fortune." *The Economic Journal* 126(598): 2363–401.

Maseland, Robert. 2018. "Is Colonialism History? The Declining Impact of Colonial Legacies on African Institutional and Economic Development." *Journal of Institutional Economics* 14(2): 259–87.

Michalopoulos, Stelios, and Elias Papaioannou. 2013. "Pre-Colonial Ethnic Institutions and Contemporary African Development." *Econometrica* 81(1): 113–52.

———. 2016. "The Long-Run Effects of the Scramble for Africa." *American Economic Review* 106(7): 1802–48.

Mitterauer, Michael. 2010. *Why Europe? The Medieval Origins of its Special Path.* Chicago, IL: University of Chicago Press.

North, Douglass C., William R. Summerhill, and Barry R. Weingast. 2000. "Order, Disorder, and Economic Change: Latin America vs. North America." In Bruce Bueno de Mesquita and Hilton Root (eds.), *Governing for Prosperity* (pp. 17–58). New Haven, CT: Yale University Press.

North, Douglass C., and Barry W. Weingast. 1989. "Constitutions and Commitment: The Evolution of Institutional Governing Public Choice in Seventeenth-Century England." *Journal of Economic History* 49(4): 803–32.

Nunn, Nathan. 2007. "Historical Legacies: A Model Linking Africa's Past to Its Current Underdevelopment." *Journal of Development Economics* 83(1): 157–75.

———. 2008. "The Long-Term Effects of Africa's Slave Trades." *Quarterly Journal of Economics* 123(1): 139–76.

———. 2010. "Shackled to the Past: The Causes and Consequences of Africa's Slave Trade." In Jared Diamond and James A. Robinson (eds.), *Natural Experiments of History* (pp. 142–84). Cambridge, MA: The Belknap Press of Harvard University Press.

Nunn, Nathan, and Nancy Qian. 2011. "The Potato's Contribution to Population and Urbanization: Evidence from a Historical Experiment." *Quarterly Journal of Economics* 126(2): 593–50.

Oto-Peralías, Daniel, and Diego Romero-Ávila. 2016. "The Economic Consequences of the Spanish Reconquest: The Long-Term Effects of Medieval Conquest and Colonization." *Journal of Economic Growth* 21(4): 409–64.

———. 2017a. "Historical Frontiers and the Rise of Inequality: The Case of the Frontier of Granada." *Journal of the European Economic Association* 15(1): 54–98.

———. 2017b. *Colonial Theories of Institutional Development: Toward a Model of Styles of Imperialism.* Cham, Switzerland: Springer.

Pierce, Lamar, and Jason A. Snyder. 2018. "The Historical Slave Trade and Firm Access to Finance in Africa." *The Review of Financial Studies* 31(1): 142–74.

Piketty, Thomas. 2020. *Capital and Ideology.* Cambridge, MA: Harvard University Press.

Przeworski, Adam, with Carolina Curvale. 2008. "Does Politics Explain the Economic Gap between the United States and Latin America?" In Francis Fukuyama (ed.), *Falling Behind: Explaining the Development Gap between Latin America and the United States* (pp. 99–133). New York, NY: Oxford University Press.

Robinson, James A. 2008. "The Latin American Equilibrium." In Francis Fukuyama (ed.), *Falling Behind: Explaining the Development Gap Between Latin America and the United States* (pp. 161–93). New York, NY: Oxford University Press.

Soto-Oñate, David. 2015. "The Historical Origins of Regional Economic Inequality in Spain: The Cultural Legacy of Political Institutions." In Norman Schofield and Gonzalo Caballero (eds.), *The Political Economy of Governance: Institutions, Political Performance and Elections* (pp. 79–111). Basel, Switzerland: Springer.

Spolaore, Enrico, and Romain Wacziarg. 2013. "How Deep Are the Roots of Economic Development?" *Journal of Economic Literature* 51(2): 325–69.

Vu, Tuong. 2010. *Paths to Development in Asia: South Korea, Vietnam, China, and. Indonesia.* New York, NY: Cambridge University Press.

Waisman, Carlos H. 1987. *Reversal of Development in Argentina: Postwar Counter-Revolutionary Policies and Their Structural Consequences.* Princeton, NJ: Princeton University Press.

Williamson, Jeffrey G. 2015. "Latin American Inequality: Colonial Origins, Commodity Booms or a Missed Twentieth-Century Leveling?" *Journal of Human Development and Capabilities* 16(3): 324–41.

Zysman, John. 1994. "How Institutions Create Historically Rooted Trajectories of Growth." *Industrial and Corporate Change* 2(1): 243–83.

5. PUBLIC POLICY AND GOVERNMENT PERFORMANCE (SOCIAL POLICY, WELFARE STATE, VARIETIES OF CAPITALISM)

Baldwin, Peter. 1999. *Contagion and the State in Europe, 1830–1930.* New York, NY: Cambridge University Press.

Ban, Cornel. 2016. *Ruling Ideas: How Global Neoliberalism Goes Local.* Oxford, UK: Oxford University Press.

Baumgartner, Frank R., and Bryan D. Jones. 2005. *The Politics of Attention: How Government Prioritizes Problems.* Chicago, IL: University of Chicago Press.

———. 2009. *Agendas and Instability in American Politics* (2nd ed.). Chicago, IL: University of Chicago Press.

Baumgartner, Frank R., Christian Breunig, Christoffer Green-Pedersen, Bryan D. Jones, Peter B. Mortensen, Michiel Neytemans, and Stefaan Walgrave. 2009. "Punctuated Equilibrium in Comparative Perspective." *American Journal of Political Science* 53(3): 602–19.

Bell, Stephen, and Hui Feng. 2021. "Rethinking Critical Juncture Analysis: Institutional Change in Chinese Banking and Finance." *Review of International Political Economy* 28(1): 36–58.

Boushey, Graeme. 2012. "Punctuated Equilibrium Theory and the Diffusion of Innovations." *Policy Studies Journal* 40(1): 127–46.

———. 2013. "The Punctuated Equilibrium Theory of Agenda Setting and Policy Change." In Eduardo Araral, Scott Fritzen, Michael Howlett, M. Ramesh, and Xun Wu (eds.), *Routledge Handbook of Public Policy* (pp. 138–52). New York, NY: Routledge.

Calder, Kent E. 1988. *Crisis and Compensation: Public Policy and Political Stability in Japan, 1949–1986.* Princeton, NJ: Princeton University Press.

Caraway, Teri L., Maria Lorena Cook, and Stephen F. Crowley (eds.). 2015. *Working through the Past: Labor and Authoritarian Legacies in Comparative Perspective.* Ithaca, NY: Cornell University Press.

Cashore, Benjamin, and Michael Howlett. 2007. "Punctuating Which Equilibrium? Understanding Thermostatic Policy Dynamics in Pacific Northwest Forestry." *American Journal of Political Science* 51(3): 532–55.

Crouch, Colin. 1993. *Industrial Relations and European State Traditions.* Oxford, UK: Oxford University Press.

Desai, Manali. 2003. "From Movement to Party to Government: Why Social Policies in Kerala and West Bengal Are So Different." In Jack Goldstone (ed.), *States, Parties, and Social Movements* (pp. 170–96). New York, NY: Cambridge University Press.

Donnelly, Paul, and John Hogan. 2012. "Understanding Policy Change Using a Critical Junctures Theory in Comparative Context: The Cases of Ireland and Sweden." *Policy Studies Journal* 40(2): 324–50.

Esping-Andersen, Gøsta. 1990. *The Three Worlds of Welfare Capitalism.* Cambridge, UK: Polity.

Flynn, Matthew B. 2015. *Pharmaceutical Autonomy and Public Health in Latin America: State, Society, and Industry in Brazil's AIDS Program.* New York, NY: Routledge.

Frye, Timothy. 2010. *Building States and Markets after Communism: The Perils of Polarized Democracy.* New York, NY: Cambridge University Press.

Gal, John, and David Bargal. 2002. "Critical Junctures, Labor Movements and the Development of Occupational Welfare in Israel." *Social Problems* 49(3): 432–54.

Gourevitch, Peter. 1986. *Politics in Hard Times: Comparative Responses to International Economic Crises.* Ithaca, NY: Cornell University Press.

Greer, Scott L. 2008. "Choosing Paths in European Union Health Services Policy: A Political Analysis of a Critical Juncture." *Journal of European Social Policy* 18(3): 219–31.

Hacker, Jacob S. 1998. "The Historical Logic of National Health Insurance: Structure and Sequence in the Development of British, Canadian, and US Medical Policy." *Studies in American Political Development* 12(1): 57–130.

———. 2002. *The Divided Welfare State: The Battle over Public and Private Social Benefits in the United States.* New York, NY: Cambridge University Press.

Hall, Peter A. 1993. "Policy Paradigms, Social Learning, and the State: The Case of Economic Policymaking in Britain." *Comparative Politics* 25(3): 275–96.

Hicks, Alexander. 1999. *Social Democracy and Welfare Capitalism: A Century of Income Security Politics.* Ithaca, NY: Cornell University Press.

Hogan, John. 2005. "Testing for a Critical Juncture: Change in the ICTU's Influence over Public Policy in 1959." *Irish Political Studies* 20(3): 23–43.

Hogan, John, and Brendan K. O'Rourke. 2015. "The Critical Role of Ideas: Understanding Industrial Policy Changes in Ireland in the 1980s." In John Hogan and Michael Howlett (eds.), *Policy Paradigms in Theory and Practice: Discourses, Ideas and Anomalies in Public Policy Dynamics* (pp. 167–88). Basingstoke, UK: Palgrave.

Karch, Andrew. 2013. *Early Start: Preschool Politics in the United States.* Ann Arbor, MI: University of Michigan Press.

Kato, Junko. 2003. *Regressive Taxation and the Welfare State: Path Dependency and Policy Diffusion.* New York, NY: Cambridge University Press.

Lieberman, Evan S. 2003. *Race and Regionalism in the Politics of Taxation in Brazil and South Africa.* New York, NY: Cambridge University Press.

Lieberman, Robert C. 2002. "Political Institutions and the Politics of Race in the Development of Modern Welfare States." In Bo Rothstein and Sven Steinmo (eds.), *Restructuring the Welfare State: Political Institutions and Policy Change* (pp. 102–28). New York, NY: Palgrave.

———. 2005. *Shaping Race Policy: The United States in Comparative Perspective.* Princeton, NJ: Princeton University Press.

Lynch, Julia. 2006. *Age in the Welfare State: The Origins of Social Spending on Pensioners, Workers, and Children.* New York, NY: Cambridge University Press.

Marriott, Lisa. 2010. *The Politics of Retirement Savings: A Trans-Tasman Comparison.* Sydney, Australia: CCH Publishing.

Martin, Cathie Jo, and Duane Swank. 2012. *The Political Construction of Business Interests: Coordination, Growth, and Equality.* New York, NY: Cambridge University Press.

Martinez-Diaz, Leonardo. 2009. *Globalizing in Hard Times: The Politics of Banking-Sector Opening in the Emerging World.* Ithaca, NY: Cornell University Press.

Mayes, Rick. 2004. *Universal Coverage: The Elusive Quest for National Health Insurance.* Ann Arbor, MI: University of Michigan Press.

Miguel, Edward. 2004. "Tribe or Nation? Nation Building and Public Goods in Kenya versus Tanzania." *World Politics* 56(3): 327–62.

Nunn, Amy. 2009. *The Politics and History of AIDS Treatment in Brazil.* New York, NY: Springer.

Pempel, T.J. 1998. *Regime Shift: Comparative Dynamics of the Japanese Political Economy.* Ithaca, NY: Cornell University Press.

Putnam, Robert D., with Robert Leonardi and Raffaella Nanetti. 1993. *Making Democracy Work: Civic Traditions in Modern Italy.* Princeton, NJ: Princeton University Press.

Sabel, Charles F., and Jonathan Zeitlin. 1985. "Historical Alternatives to Mass Production: Politics, Markets and Technology in Nineteenth-Century Industrialization." *Past and Present* 108: 133–76.

Sabel, Charles F., and Jonathan Zeitlin. (eds.). 1997. *World of Possibilities: Flexibility and Mass Production in Western Industrialization.* New York, NY: Cambridge University Press.

Skocpol, Theda. 1992. *Protecting Soldiers and Mothers: The Political Origins of Social Policy in the United States.* Cambridge, MA: Harvard University Press.

Stark, David, and László Bruszt. 1998. *Postsocialist Pathways: Transforming Politics and Property in East Central Europe.* New York, NY: Cambridge University Press.

Steinmo, Sven. 1993. *Taxation and Democracy: Swedish, British and American Approaches to Financing the Modern State.* New Haven, CT: Yale University Press.

St John, Taylor. 2018. *The Rise of Investor-State Arbitration: Politics, Law, and Unintended Consequences.* Oxford, UK: Oxford University Press.

Thelen, Kathleen. 2004. *How Institutions Evolve: The Political Economy of Skills in Germany, Britain, the United States and Japan.* New York, NY: Cambridge University Press.

Ward, Tom. 2018. "Critical Junctures and the Department of Finance: From DPS to DPER?" *Irish Political Studies* 33(1): 68–87.

Wimmer, Andreas. 2016. "Is Diversity Detrimental? Ethnic Fractionalization, Public Goods Provision, and the Historical Legacies of Stateness." *Comparative Political Studies* 49(11): 1407–45.

6. CULTURE (LANGUAGE, RELIGION, RACISM)

Acharya, Avidit, Matthew Blackwell, and Maya Sen. 2016. "The Political Legacy of American Slavery." *Journal of Politics* 78(3): 621–41.

———. 2018. *Deep Roots: How Slavery Still Shapes Southern Politics.* Princeton, NJ: Princeton University Press.

Dixon, R.M.W. 1997. *The Rise and Fall of Languages.* New York, NY: Cambridge University Press.

Erk, Jan. 2005. "Sub-State Nationalism and the Left-Right Divide: Critical Junctures in the Formation of Nationalist Labour Movements in Belgium." *Nations and Nationalism* 11(4): 551–70.

Fishman, Robert M. 2019. *Democratic Practice: Origins of the Iberian Divide in Political Inclusion.* Oxford, UK: Oxford University Press.

Fishman, Robert M., and Omar Lizardo. 2013. "How Macro-Historical Change Shapes Cultural Taste: Legacies of Democratization in Spain and Portugal." *American Sociological Review* 78(2): 213–39.

Fontana, Nicola, Tommaso Nannicini, and Guido Tabellini. 2017. "Historical Roots of Political Extremism: The Effects of Nazi Occupation of Italy." IZA Discussion Paper No. 10551.

Grosfeld, Irena, and Ekaterina Zhuravskaya. 2015. "Cultural vs. Economic Legacies of Empires: Evidence from the Partition of Poland." *Journal of Comparative Economics* 43(1): 55–75.

Guiso, Luigi, Paola Sapienza, and Luigi Zingales. 2016. "Long-Term Persistence." *Journal of the European Economic Association* 14(6): 1401–36.

Hartz, Louis, with contributions by Kenneth D. McRae et al. 1964. *The Founding of New Societies: Studies in the History of the United States, Latin America, South Africa, Canada, and Australia.* New York, NY: Harcourt, Brace and World.

Kuipers, Nicholas. 2018. "The Long-Run Consequences of The Opium Farms on Ethnic Animosity in Java." Unpublished paper, University of California, Berkeley.

Kuru, Ahmet T. 2007. "Passive and Assertive Secularism: Historical Conditions, Ideological Struggles, and State Policies toward Religion." *World Politics* 59(4): 568–94.

———. 2009. *Secularism and State Policies toward Religion: The United States, France, and Turkey.* New York, NY: Cambridge University Press.

Kuru, Ahmet T., and Alfred Stepan (eds.). 2012. *Democracy, Islam and Secularism in Turkey.* New York: Columbia University Press.

Laitin, David D. 1992. *Language Repertoires and State Construction in Africa.* New York, NY: Cambridge University Press.

Laitin, David D., Joachim Moortgat, and Amanda Lea Robinson. 2012. "Geographic Axes and the Persistence of Cultural Diversity." *PNAS (Proceedings of the National Academy of Sciences)* 109(26): 10263–68.

Lerner, Hanna. 2014. "Critical Junctures, Religion, and Personal Status Regulations in Israel and India." *Law & Social Inquiry* 39(2): 387–415.

Lowes, Sara, Nathan Nunn, James A. Robinson, and Jonathan L. Weigel. 2017. "The Evolution of Culture and Institutions: Evidence from the Kuba Kingdom." *Econometrica* 85(4): 1065–91.

Lupu, Noam, and Leonid Peisakhin. 2017. "The Legacy of Political Violence across Generations." *American Journal of Political Science* 61(4): 836–51.

Marx, Anthony W. 1998. *Making Race and Nation: A Comparison of the United States, South Africa, and Brazil.* New York, NY: Cambridge University Press.

Mazumder, Soumyajit. 2018. "The Persistent Effect of U.S. Civil Rights Protests on Political Attitudes." *American Journal of Political Science* 62(4): 922–35.

McNamee, Lachlan. 2020. "Colonial Legacies and Comparative Racial Identification in the Americas." *American Journal of Sociology* 126(2): 318–53.

Nunn, Nathan, and Leonard Wantchekon. 2011. "The Slave Trade and the Origins of Mistrust in Africa." *American Economic Review* 101(7): 3221–52.

Oto-Peralías, Daniel. 2015. "The Long-Term Effects of Political Violence on Political Attitudes: Evidence from the Spanish Civil War." *Kyklos* 68(3): 412–42.

Peisakhin, Leonid. 2015. "Cultural Legacies: Persistence and Transmission." In Norman Schofield and Gonzalo Caballero (eds.), *The Political Economy of Governance: Institutions, Political Performance and Elections* (pp. 21–39). Basel, Switzerland: Springer.

Rinscheid, Adrian, Burkard Eberlein, Patrick Emmenegger, and Volker Schneider. 2019. "Why Do Junctures Become Critical? Political Discourse, Agency, and Joint Belief Shifts in Comparative Perspective." *Regulation and Governance* 14(4): 653–73.

Rozenas, Arturas, Sebastian Schutte, and Yuri Zhukov. 2017. "The Political Legacy of Violence: The Long-Term Impact of Stalin's Repression in Ukraine." *The Journal of Politics* 79(4): 1147–61.

Straus, Scott. 2015. *Making and Unmaking Nations: War, Leadership, and Genocide in Modern Africa*. Ithaca, NY: Cornell University Press.

Voigtländer, Nico, and Hans-Joachim Voth. 2012. "Persecution Perpetuated: The Medieval Origins of Anti-Semitic Violence in Nazi Germany." *Quarterly Journal of Economics* 127(3): 1339–92.

Wittenberg, Jason. 2006. *Crucibles of Political Loyalty: Church Institutions and Electoral Continuity in Hungary*. New York, NY: Cambridge University Press.

7. INTERNATIONAL RELATIONS (COLONIALISM, INDEPENDENCE, WAR, GLOBAL NORMS)

Ancelovici, Marcos. 2014. "Globalization and the Politics of Trade Union Preferences in France." In Peter A. Hall, Wade Jacoby, Jonah Levy, and Sophie Meunier (eds.), *The Politics of Representation in the Global Age: Identification, Mobilization, and Adjudication* (pp. 75–99). New York, NY: Cambridge University Press.

Bulmer, Simon, and Martin Burch. 1998. "Organising for Europe: Whitehall, the British State and the European Union." *Public Administration* 76(4): 601–28.

Buzan, Barry, and George Lawson. 2014. "Rethinking Benchmark Dates in International Relations." *European Journal of International Relations* 20(2): 437–62.

———. 2015. "Twentieth-Century Benchmark Dates in International Relations: The Three World Wars in Historical Perspective." *Journal of International Security Studies* 1(1): 39–58.

Calder, Kent, and Min Ye. 2004. "Regionalism and Critical Junctures: Explaining the 'Organization Gap.'" *Journal of East Asian Studies* 4(2): 191–226.

———. 2010. *The Making of Northeast Asia*. Stanford, CA: Stanford University Press.

Cioffi-Revilla, Claudio. 1997. "The Political Uncertainty of Interstate Rivalries: A Punctuated Equilibrium Model." In Paul F. Diehl (ed.), *The Dynamics of Enduring Rivalries* (pp. 64–97). Urbana, IL: University of Illinois Press.

Dashwood, Hevina S. 2012. *The Rise of Global Corporate Social Responsibility: Mining and the Spread of Global Norms*. New York, NY: Cambridge University Press.

Diamond, Jared. 1997. *Guns, Germs and Steel: The Fate of Human Societies*. New York, NY: Norton.

Disdier, Anne-Célia, and Keith Head. 2008. "The Puzzling Persistence of the Distance Effect on Bilateral Trade." *Review of Economics and Statistics* 90(1): 37–41.

Djelic, Marie-Laure, and Sigrid Quack. 2007. "Overcoming Path Dependency: Path Generation in Open Systems." *Theory and Society* 36(2): 161–86.

Domínguez, Jorge I. 1980. *Insurrection or Loyalty: The Breakdown of the Spanish American Empire*. Cambridge, MA: Harvard University Press.

———. 2017. "The Wars of Independence in Spanish America as a Point of Inflection." *Qualitative and Multi-Method Research* 15(1): 26–28.

Druckman, Daniel. 2001. "Turning Points in International Negotiation: A Comparative Analysis." *The Journal of Conflict Resolution* 45(4): 519–44.

Druckman, Daniel, and Mara Olekalns. 2013. "Punctuated Negotiations: Transitions, Interruptions, and Turning Points." In Mara Olekalns and Wendy L. Adair (eds.), *Handbook of Research on Negotiation* (pp. 332–56). Cheltenham, UK: Edward Elgar Publishing.

Firmin-Sellers, Kathryn. 2000. "Institutions, Context, and Outcomes: Explaining French and British Rule in West Africa." *Comparative Politics* 32(3): 253–72.

Hanrieder, Tine. 2015. "The Path-Dependent Design of International Organizations: Federalism in the World Health Organization." *European Journal of International Relations* 21(1): 215–39.

Hanrieder, Tine, and Michael Zürn. 2017. "Reactive Sequences in Global Health Governance." In Orfeo Fioretos (ed.), *International History and Politics in Time* (pp. 93–116). Oxford, UK: Oxford University Press.

Ikenberry, G. John. 2001. *After Victory: Institutions, Strategic Restraint, and the Rebuilding of Order after Major Wars*. Princeton, NJ: Princeton University Press.

———. 2016. "The Rise, Character, and Evolution of International Order." In Orfeo Fioretos, Tulia G. Falleti, and Adam Sheingate (eds.), *The Oxford Handbook of Historical Institutionalism* (pp. 738–52). New York, NY: Oxford University Press.

Krasner, Stephen D. 2017. "The Persistence of State Sovereignty." In Orfeo Fioretos (ed.), *International History and Politics in Time* (pp. 39–58). Oxford, UK: Oxford University Press.

Nwankwo, Cletus Famous. 2018. "Brexit: Critical Juncture in the UK's International Development Agenda?" *Open Political Science* 1(1): 16–19.

Sikkink, Kathryn. 2017. "Timing and Sequencing in International Politics: Latin America's Contributions to Human Rights." In Orfeo Fioretos (ed.), *International History and Politics in Time* (pp. 231–50). Oxford, UK: Oxford University Press.

Smith, Benjamin. 2018. "Comparing Separatism across Regions: Rebellious Legacies and Contentious Politics in Africa, Asia, and the Middle East." In Ariel Ahram, Patrick Köllner, and Rudra Sil (eds.), *Comparative Area Studies: Methodological Rationales and Cross-Regional Applications* (pp. 168–84). Oxford, UK: Oxford University Press.

Solingen, Etel, and Wilfred Wan. 2016. "Critical Junctures, Developmental Pathways, and Incremental Change in Security Institutions." In Orfeo Fioretos, Tulia G. Falleti, and Adam Sheingate (eds.), *The Oxford Handbook of Historical Institutionalism* (pp. 553–71). New York, NY: Oxford University Press.

Thies, Cameron G. 2001. "An Historical Institutionalist Approach to the Uruguay Round Agricultural Negotiations." *Comparative Political Studies* 34(4): 400–28.

Vetterlein, Antje, and Manuela Moschella. 2016. "Self-Reinforcing and Reactive Path-Dependency: Tracing the IMF's Path of Policy Change." In Thomas Rixen, Lora Viola, and Michael Zuern (eds.), *Historical Institutionalism and International Relations* (pp. 143–64). Oxford, UK: Oxford University Press.

Weingast, Barry R. 2005. "Persuasion, Preference, Change, and Critical Junctures: The Microfoundations of a Macroscopic Concept." In Ira Katznelson and Barry R. Weingast (eds.), *Preferences and Situations: Points of Intersection between Historical and Rational Choice Institutionalism* (pp. 129–60). New York, NY: Russell Sage Foundation.

Wunderlich, Jens Uwe. 2020. *European And East Asian Regionalism: Critical Junctures and Historical Turning Points*. New York, NY: Routledge.

Yoshimatsu, Hidetaka. 2014. *Comparing Institution-Building in East Asia: Power Politics, Governance and Critical Junctures*. Basingstoke, Hampshire: Palgrave.

8. MISCELLANEOUS POLITICAL AND SOCIAL DEVELOPMENTS

Al-Rodhan, Nayef R. F., Graeme P. Herd, and Lisa Watanabe. 2011. *Critical Turning Points in the Middle East: 1915–2015.* New York, NY: Palgrave.

Abernethy, David B. 2000. "Legacies." In *The Dynamics of Global Dominance: European Overseas Empires, 1415–1980* (pp. 363–86). New Haven, CT: Yale University Press.

Allen, Daniel. 2010. "New Directions in the Study of Nation-Building: Views through the Lens of Path Dependence." *International Studies Review* 12(3): 413–29.

Barany, Zoltan, and Ivan Volgyes (eds.). 1995. *The Legacies of Communism in Eastern Europe.* Baltimore, MD: Johns Hopkins University Press.

Beissinger, Mark R., and Stephen Kotkin (eds.). 2014. *Historical Legacies of Communism in Russia and Eastern Europe.* New York, NY: Cambridge University Press.

Broschek, Jörg. 2013. "Between Path Dependence and Gradual Change: Historical Institutionalism and the Study of Federal Dynamics." In Arthur Benz and Jörg Broschek (eds.), *Federal Dynamics: Continuity, Change, and the Varieties of Federalism* (pp. 93–116). Oxford, UK: Oxford University Press.

Charrad, Mounira M. 2001. *States and Women's Rights: The Making of Postcolonial Tunisia, Algeria, and Morocco.* Berkeley, CA: University of California Press.

De Juan, Alexander, and Jan Henryk Pierskalla (eds.). 2017. "The Comparative Politics of Colonialism and Its Legacies." A special issue of *Politics & Society* 45(2).

Diamond, Jared, and James A. Robinson. (eds.). 2010. *Natural Experiments of History.* Cambridge, MA: The Belknap Press of Harvard University Press.

della Porta, Donatella. 2020. "Protests as Critical Junctures: Some Reflections towards a Momentous Approach to Social Movements." *Social Movement Studies* 19(5–6): 556–75.

Fioretos, Orfeo (ed.). 2017. *International History and Politics in Time.* Oxford, UK: Oxford University Press.

Glaeser, Edward L., and Andrei Shleifer. 2002. "Legal Origins." *Quarterly Journal of Economics* 117(4): 1193–229.

Ju, Chang Bum, and Shui-Yan Tang. 2011. "Path Dependence, Critical Junctures, and Political Contestation: The Developmental Trajectories of Environmental NGOs in South Korea." *Nonprofit and Voluntary Sector Quarterly* 40(6): 1048–72.

Kenny, Paul D. 2015a. "The Origins of Patronage Politics: State Building, Centrifugalism, and Decolonization." *British Journal of Political Science* 45(1): 141–71.

———. 2015b. "Colonial Rule, Decolonisation and Corruption in India." *Commonwealth and Comparative Politics* 53(4): 401–27.

LaPorte, Jody, and Danielle N. Lussier. 2011 "What Is the Leninist Legacy? Assessing Twenty Years of Scholarship." *Slavic Review* 70(3): 637–54.

Lessa, Francesca. 2013. *Memory and Transitional Justice in Argentina and Uruguay: Against Impunity.* Basingstoke, UK: Palgrave Macmillan.

Magnusson, Lars, and Jan Ottosson (eds.). 2009. *The Evolution of Path Dependence.* Northampton, MA: Edward Elgar.

Mamdani, Mahmood. 2001. *When Victims Become Killers: Colonialism, Nativism, and the Genocide in Rwanda.* Princeton, NJ: Princeton University Press.

Paulson-Smith, Kaden, and. Aili Mari Tripp. 2021. "Women's Rights and Critical Junctures in Constitutional Reform in Africa (1951–2019)." *African Affairs* 120(480): 365–89.

Pop-Eleches, Grigore, and Joshua Tucker. 2017. *Communism's Shadow: Historical Legacies and Contemporary Political Attitudes*. Princeton, NJ: Princeton University Press.

Rast, Joel. 2009. "Critical Junctures, Long-Term Processes: Urban Redevelopment in Chicago and Milwaukee, 1945–1980." *Social Science History* 33(4): 393–426.

Steinmo, Sven, Kathleen Thelen, and Frank Longstreth (eds.). 1992. *Structuring Politics: Historical Institutionalism in Comparative Analysis*. New York, NY: Cambridge University Press.

Tsai, Kellee. 2006. "Adaptive Informal Institutions and Endogenous Institutional Change in China." *World Politics* 59(1): 116–14.

Villalon, Leonardo, and Phillip Huxtable (eds.). 1998. *The African State at a Critical Juncture: Between Disintegration and Reconfiguration*. Boulder, CO: Lynne Rienner.

You, Jong-Sung. 2015. *Democracy, Inequality and Corruption: Korea, Taiwan and the Philippines Compared*. New York, NY: Cambridge University Press.

Appendix IV

Examples of Critical Juncture Research

This appendix offers a brief discussion of eight books that exemplify critical juncture research. These books illustrate the kind of arguments that are a trademark of this research tradition. They also help to convey the contributions critical juncture research has made to multiple fields of research over several decades.

These books, as all research on critical junctures, contribute to the knowledge about subject matters that are of interest to scholars who use a variety of approaches. And no attempt is made here to show what critical juncture research has contributed to specific fields of research relative to other approaches. Nonetheless, these examples serve the more modest purpose of showing that critical juncture research has made significant contributions to several fields, in some instances even opening up whole new avenues for research. Thus, they make a prima facie case for the value of this tradition.

Revolutions, Democracy, and Dictatorship. Moore (1966) accounts for political regime outcomes in the 1930s and 1950s in terms of variation in the type of revolution (the critical juncture) experienced by countries decades and even centuries earlier. Bourgeois revolutions in England, France, and the United States led to democracy; revolutions from above in Germany and Japan to fascism; and peasant revolutions in Russia and China to communism. Moore also explains why different types of revolution occurred as a result of the extent of commercialization of agriculture, class coalitions, and the autonomy of classes. This work offered a strong critique of the assumption of unilinear evolution used in the then-dominant modernization theory and propelled research on the historical origins of political regimes and the class basis of democracy.

Revolutions and Party Systems. Lipset and Rokkan (1967) argue that party systems in Western Europe took shape in the 1920s and maintained the same contours for several decades after, and that the shape of Europe's party system can be explained in terms of the impact of four critical junctures. Three early critical junctures—the Reformation–Counterreformation struggle, the national revolution, and the industrial revolution—led to considerable divergence in party systems. A fourth, later critical juncture—the Russian Revolution—led to a convergence of party systems. This work helped to focus research on the cleavages that underlie party systems around the world and launched a strand of scholarship on the historical origins of party systems in Europe and other regions of the world.

Political Culture and the Performance of Democratic Governments. Putnam (1993) posits that the relative performance of democratic governments within Italy in the late twentieth century can be explained in terms of a critical juncture in the twelfth and thirteenth centuries that led to divergent traditions of civil engagement. Where the tradition of civic community was strong—in Northern-Central Italy—regional government performed better (e.g., in delivering public goods in the fields of agriculture, housing, and health) than where no such civic tradition existed, as in Southern Italy. Putnam's work initiated a strand of research on social capital and its consequences in various fields within political science, while also drawing attention to the path-dependent nature of political culture.

Public Policy and Policy Monopolies. Baumgartner and Jones (1993, 2009) argue that the making of public policy in the United States is stable over long periods during which policy monopolies—the dominance of public policy by the same group of policymakers and organizations—remain unchallenged. In turn, this equilibrium is disrupted when new ideas about policy problems are proposed and when momentum for change grows through a feedback effect. Eventually, a new policy monopoly gets established. Baumgartner and Jones's book reshaped the study of public policy in the field of American politics, providing an alternative to rational choice accounts that stress equilibrium in decision-making and to incrementalist accounts that stress that policy changes in small steps. It also was used as a model for studies beyond the United States.

Political Institutions and Economic Development. Acemoglu and Robinson (2012) explain differences in economic development around the world in the early twenty-first century in terms of critical junctures in the seventeenth and eighteen centuries (e.g., the Glorious Revolution in England) that put countries on different paths. Countries that adopted inclusive political and economic institutions grew over the long run. In contrast, countries that adopted extractive political and economic institutions did not prosper over the long run. This work offered an alternative explanation to modernization theory's account of the association between economic development and democracy, and contributed to the recognition in economics of the role of political institutions (as opposed to geography or culture) and the debate about the historical origin of economic prosperity and poverty.

Authoritarian Rulers and Party Institutionalization in Democracies. Riedl (2014) explains differences in party system institutionalization in sub-Saharan Africa in terms of the critical juncture of democratic transitions. Where democratic transitions are controlled by authoritarian incumbents, party system institutionalization is relatively high. Where democratic transitions are not controlled by authoritarian incumbents, party system institutionalization is relatively low. The different ways in which democratic transitions occurred is explained in terms of a key antecedent condition: the power accumulation strategy of authoritarian rulers. Where local notables were incorporated into authoritarian regimes, democratic transitions were controlled. Where authoritarian rulers replaced local notables with newly created organizations and parties, democratic transitions were not controlled. In turn, the persistence of the party system outcomes that emerged from democratic transitions is explained in terms of various mechanisms of reproduction: the isomorphic competitive pressures embodied in the rules of the game, the forms of party organization, and the competitive strategies that shape party and voter behavior. This work underscored that rule construction is an historical process and helped to spur a line of research on the authoritarian origins of political parties in democracies.

Slavery, Community Norms, and Racism. Acharya, Blackwell, and Sen (2018) argue that racial political attitudes in the United States South in the early twenty-first century can be explained in terms of a critical juncture, the end of slavery in the U.S. South. Where the emancipation of slaves threatened white political and economic power, white elites promoted anti-black sentiment. In contrast, when whites lived in places where slavery was not central, anti-black sentiment was lower. Additionally, they argue that white racial hostility was passed on from generation to generation through two mechanisms of reproduction: formal institutions such as Jim Crow laws, and family socialization and community norms. This work introduced the idea of behavioral path dependency, demonstrated how political attitudes persist over time, and made a strong case that an explanation of present-day political beliefs must invoke historical causes.

State Formation and State Capacity. Mazzuca (2021) explains differences in state capacity in terms of the critical juncture of state formation. State formation in early modern Europe was war-led, which forced state-builders to eliminate peripheral potentates, a key obstacle to the development of state capacity. In contrast, state formation in Latin America in the mid-nineteenth century was trade-led, and this induced state builders to appease peripheral patrimonial rulers. Thus, in Europe, state formation and state-building—the development of state capacity—coincided. However, in Latin America, state formation undermined state-building, and the survival of patrimonial rulers in the periphery and the design of territorial governance institutions ensured the persistence of weak states. This work introduced political geography as a key dimension of a theory of state formation; it also contributed to comparative state formation by offering one of the first cross-regional studies of state formation.

BIBLIOGRAPHY

Acemoglu, Daron, and James A. Robinson. 2012. *Why Nations Fail: Origins of Power, Poverty and Prosperity.* New York, NY: Crown.

Acharya, Avidit, Matthew Blackwell, and Maya Sen. 2018. *Deep Roots: How Slavery Still Shapes Southern Politics.* Princeton, NJ: Princeton University Press.

Baumgartner, Frank R., and Bryan D. Jones. 1993. *Agendas and Instability in American Politics.* Chicago, IL: University of Chicago Press.

———. 2009. *Agendas and Instability in American Politics* (2nd ed.). Chicago, IL: University of Chicago Press.

Lipset, Seymour M., and Stein Rokkan. 1967. "Cleavage Structures, Party Systems, and Voter Alignments: An Introduction." In Seymour M. Lipset and Stein Rokkan (eds.), *Party Systems and Voter Alignments: Cross-National Perspectives* (pp. 1–64). New York, NY: Free Press.

Mazzuca, Sebastián. 2021. *Latecomer State Formation: Political Geography and Capacity Failure in Latin America.* New Haven, CT: Yale University Press.

Moore, Jr., Barrington. 1966. *Social Origins of Dictatorship and Democracy: Lord and Peasant in the Making of the Modern World.* Boston, MA: Beacon Press.

Putnam, Robert D., with Robert Leonardi and Raffaella Nanetti. 1993. *Making Democracy Work: Civic Traditions in Modern Italy.* Princeton, NJ: Princeton University Press.

Riedl, Rachel Beatty. 2014. *Authoritarian Origins of Democratic Party Systems in Africa.* New York, NY: Cambridge University Press.

Index

Acemoglu, Daron, 39, 41, 46, *49,* 57, 58, 61, *187,* 189, 194, 197, 456

Acharya, Avidit, *49,* 420, 457

activating critical juncture, 15, 86, 89, 91, 140, 145, *145,* 146, 148, 323, 343, 419; and antecedent conditions, 343; defined, 419. *See also* generative critical juncture

Africa: colonialism in West, 58; party system change in, 140, 146–47; punctuated equilibrium in, 149; weak institutional environment in sub-Saharan, 152, 153

aftermath, 13, *229, 234, 235;* Brazil democratic, 259–60; Chile period of, 260; of communism, 299; conflation with legacy, 8, 121–22; in critical junction framework, *38,* 42–43, 48, 142; in critical juncture research, *49;* defined, 42, 419; Latin America political reaction in, 239, 325; Mexico period of, 260; modeled as a causal series, 118n14; of neoliberal reforms, 342; Portugal and Spain Great Recession, 276; and mechanisms of production, 291, 375; potential occurrence of, 42; reactions and counterreactions pattern, 42; as reactive sequence, 42, 146, 318, 323–25, 329; of democratic transitions, 270–71, *284*

agency, 8–9, 14, 15, 111, 119, 123, 124, 166, 343, 419; causal role of, 126, 126n26, 394; and contingency, 126, 129, 130, 143–44, 164, 345; critical junctures and expanded, 164; importance of, 143–44; and path dependence, 9; political, 143, 321, 383; as political opportunity, 63; and social theory, 125–26; and structure, 125–26, 127–29, *129,* 164, 299, 395; as uncaused cause, 394–95. *See also* determinism; structure

Americas: colonization of, 13, 58; Europe discovery of, 53; Great Britain colonial expansion in, 57; indigenous peoples in, 13, 58, 59; Spain trading activities in, 57. *See also* Latin America; North America; South America

antecedent conditions, 6n21, 7; as background similarities, 43, *44,* 45; as baseline for change assessment, 142, 278–79; causal significance of, 144; of colonialism, *54,* 59–61; and contingency, 145; as critical antecedents, 43, *44,* 45–46, *173,* 278; in critical junction framework, *38,* 43–46, 48; in critical juncture research, *49;* defined, 43, 419; democracy and institutional credibility, 73–75; as descriptive context, 43–45, *44;* as

459

About the Contributors

Taylor C. Boas is Associate Professor of Political Science at Boston University. His research examines electoral politics, public opinion, and political behavior in Latin America, focusing on topics such as accountability, campaigns, religion, and the mass media. He is author of *Presidential Campaigns in Latin America: Electoral Strategies and Success Contagion* (Cambridge University Press, 2016). His articles have been published in the *American Journal of Political Science, Journal of Politics, World Politics, Journal of Theoretical Politics*, and *World Development*.

Ruth Berins Collier is Heller Professor of Political Science at the University of California, Berkeley. Her work encompasses comparative and historical research on popular participation and the dynamics of national political regimes in Latin America, Africa, and Western Europe. She is co-author of *Shaping the Political Arena: Critical Junctures, the Labor Movement, and the Regime Dynamics in Latin America* (with David Collier; Princeton University Press, 1991, reissued in 2002), which won the Best Book Prize of the APSA Comparative Politics Section. She is author of *Regimes in Tropical Africa: Changing Forms of Supremacy, 1945–1975* (University of California Press, 1982); *The Contradictory Alliance: State-Labor Relations and Regime Change in Mexico* (IIS, University of California Press, 1992); *Paths toward Democracy: The Working Class and Elites in Western Europe and South America* (Cambridge University Press, 1999); and co-editor of *Reorganizing Popular Politics: Participation and the New Interest Regime in Latin America* (Pennsylvania State University Press, 2009).

David Collier is Chancellor's Professor Emeritus at the University of California, Berkeley. His scholarly contributions were recognized in 2014, when he received the Johan Skytte Prize, the preeminent international award in the discipline of political science. At Berkeley, he served as Department Chair and Chair of the Center for

Latin American Studies. His research focuses on democracy and authoritarianism, Latin American politics, comparative-historical analysis, and methodology. Collier's books include *Shaping the Political Arena: Critical Junctures, the Labor Movement, and the Regime Dynamics in Latin America* (with Ruth Berins Collier; Princeton University Press, 1991, reissued in 2002), which won the Best Book Prize of the APSA Comparative Politics Section and is a pioneering work in the field of critical junctures and comparative historical analysis. His co-edited methodological work includes *Rethinking Social Inquiry: Diverse Tools, Shared Standards*, 2nd expanded edition (Rowman & Littlefield, 2010); *Statistical Models and Causal Inference: A Dialogue with the Social Sciences* (Cambridge University Press, 2009); *Concepts and Method in Social Science: The Tradition of Giovanni Sartori* (Routledge, 2009), and *The Oxford Handbook of Political Methodology* (Oxford University Press, 2008). Within the American Political Science Association, he has served as President of the Organized Section for Comparative Politics, Vice President of the Association, and founding President of the Organized Section for Qualitative and Multi-Method Research. Collier is an elected Fellow of the American Academy of Arts and Sciences and of the American Association for the Advancement of Science. His more recent awards, along with the Skytte Prize, include the 2014 Frank J. Goodnow Award for Distinguished Service to Political Science and the American Political Science Association.

Robert M. Fishman, Conex-Marie Curie Professor of Political Science and Sociology at Madrid's Carlos III University, is a comparativist who works on democracy and democratic practice, politics and culture, consequences of inequality, and the Euro crisis. Fishman's books include *Working-Class Organization and the Return to Democracy in Spain* (Cornell University Press, 1990); *Democracy's Voices: Social Ties and the Quality of Public Life in Spain* (Cornell University Press, 2004), winner in 2005 of Honorable Mention for Best Book in Political Sociology; *The Year of the Euro: The Cultural, Social, and Political Import of Europe's Common Currency* (University of Notre Dame Press, 2006), co-edited with Anthony Messina; and *Democratic Practice: Origins of the Iberian Divide in Political Inclusion* (Oxford University Press, 2019).

Andrew C. Gould is Associate Professor of Political Science at the University of Notre Dame. His published works have been in the subfields of religion and politics, the political economy of decision-making, and qualitative research methods. Gould is author of *Origins of Liberal Dominance: State, Church, and Party in Nineteenth-Century Europe* (University of Michigan Press, 1999); and co-editor of *Europe's Contending Identities: Supranationalism, Ethnoregionalism, Religion, and New Nationalism* (Cambridge University Press, 2014), and *The Rise of the Nazi Regime: Historical Reassessments* (Westview Press, 1986). His articles appeared in the *Annual Review of Political Science*, *West European Politics*, *Studies in Comparative International Development*, and the *Review of Politics*.

Samuel Handlin is Associate Professor of Political Science at Swarthmore College. His research focuses on the comparative politics of developing countries, with a regional emphasis on Latin America and a substantive focus on democracy, authoritarianism, and electoral politics. He is the author of *State Crisis in Fragile Democracies: Polarization and Political Regimes in South America* (Cambridge University Press, 2017) and the author/editor of *Reorganizing Popular Politics: Participation and the New Interest Regime in Latin America* (Pennsylvania State University Press, 2009). His work has also been published in numerous academic journals.

G. John Ikenberry is the Albert G. Milbank Professor of Politics and International Affairs at Princeton University in the Department of Politics and the Woodrow Wilson School of Public and International Affairs. His research focuses on liberal international relations theory, the global order, and United States foreign policy. His books include *Reasons of State: Oil Politics and the Capacities of American Government* (Cornell University Press, 1988); *After Victory: Institutions, Strategic Restraint, and the Rebuilding of Order after Major Wars* (Princeton, 2001), winner of the 2002 Robert L. Jervis and Paul W. Schroeder Prize for the best book on international history and politics; *Liberal Leviathan: The Origins, Crisis, and Transformation of the American System* (Princeton University Press, 2011); and *A World Safe for Democracy: Liberal Internationalism and the Crises of Global Order* (Yale University Press, 2020). His articles have been published in the *American Political Science Review*, *World Politics*, *International Organization*, *International Security*, and *Foreign Affairs*. Ikenberry is an elected member of the American Academy of Arts and Sciences.

Robert R. Kaufman is Distinguished Professor of Political Science at Rutgers University. His research focuses on comparative democratization, economic reform, and social policy. He is co-author (with Stephan Haggard) of *Backsliding: Democratic Regress in the Contemporary World* (Cambridge University Press, 2021); *Dictators and Democrats: Elites, Masses, and Regime Change* (Princeton University Press, 2016), winner of the Best Book Award from the Comparative Democratization Section of the American Political Science Association 2017, and finalist for the 2017 Woodrow Wilson Foundation Award of the American Political Science Association; *Development, Democracy, and Welfare States: Latin America, East Asia, and Eastern Europe* (Princeton University Press, 2008); and *The Political Economy of Democratic Transitions* (Princeton University Press, 1995), winner of the Luebbert Prize for the best book in comparative politics in 1995, awarded by the Comparative Politics Section of the American Political Science Association.

Jody LaPorte is the Gonticas Fellow in Politics and International Relations at Lincoln College, University of Oxford. Her research investigates the dynamics of politics and policy-making in nondemocratic regimes, with a regional focus on post-Soviet Eurasia. Her current book manuscript examines the politics of highly corrupt regimes. She has published articles in *Comparative Politics, Political Research Quarterly, Post-Soviet Affairs,* and *Slavic Review.*

Danielle N. Lussier is Associate Professor of Political Science at Grinnell College. Her research focuses on democratization, political participation, and religion and politics, with geographic expertise on postcommunist Eurasia and Indonesia. She is the author of *Constraining Elites in Russia and Indonesia: Political Participation and Regime Survival* (Cambridge University Press, 2016) and *The Many Faces of Political Islam,* 2nd edition (with Mohammed Ayoob, University of Michigan Press, 2020). Her research has also been published in the *Journal of Democracy, Religion & Politics, Problems of Post-Communism, Post-Soviet Affairs,* and *Slavic Review.* Lussier is developing a book manuscript on the role of houses of worship in the political lives of Muslims and Christians in Indonesia.

Sebastián L. Mazzuca is Assistant Professor of Political Science at Johns Hopkins University. His work focuses on state formation, regime change, and economic development. He is author of *A Middle-Quality Institutional Trap: Democracy and State Capacity in Latin America* (with Gerardo Munck; Cambridge University Press, 2020); and *Latecomer State Formation: Political Geography and Capacity Failure in Latin America* (Yale University Press, 2021). His articles have been published in the *American Political Science Review,* the *American Journal of Political Science, Comparative Politics, Studies in International Comparative Development, Journal of Democracy, Hispanic American Historical Review,* and the *Oxford Handbook of Political Science.*

Gerardo L. Munck is Professor in the Department of Political Science and International Relations at the University of Southern California (USC). His books include *Authoritarianism and Democratization: Soldiers and Workers in Argentina, 1976–83* (Penn State University Press, 1998); *Regimes and Democracy in Latin America* (Oxford University Press, 2007); *Passion, Craft, and Method in Comparative Politics* (with Richard Snyder; Johns Hopkins University Press, 2007); *Measuring Democracy: A Bridge between Scholarship and Politics* (Johns Hopkins University, 2009); *A Middle-Quality Institutional Trap: Democracy and State Capacity in Latin America* (with Sebastián Mazzuca; Cambridge University Press, 2020); and *Latin American Politics and Society: A Comparative and Historical Analysis* (with Juan Pablo Luna; Cambridge University Press, forthcoming, 2022). He is currently completing a book manuscript on the evolution of knowledge about the social world, entitled *How Advances in the Social Sciences Have Been Made: The Study of Democracy and Democratization since 1789.* His articles have been published in the *Annual Review of Political Science, World Politics, Comparative Politics,* and *Comparative Political Studies.* The awards he has received include the 2003 Award for Conceptual Innovation in Democratic Studies, of the International Political Science Association (IPSA) Committee on Concepts and Methods (C&M) and the Facultad Latinoamericana de Ciencias Sociales (FLACSO), Mexico; and the Frank Cass Prize for Best Overall Article in *Democratization* in 2016.

Rachel Beatty Riedl is Professor in the Department of Government at Cornell University. Her research interests include institutional development in new democracies, local governance and decentralization policy, and authoritarian regime legacies, with a regional focus in sub-Saharan Africa. She is author of *Authoritarian Origins of Democratic Party Systems in Africa* (Cambridge University Press, 2014), winner of the Best Book Award from the African Politics Conference Group of the American Political Science Association 2014 and Honorable Mention, Best Book Award of the Comparative Democratization Section of the APSA 2015; and *From Pews to Politics: Religious Sermons and Political Participation in Africa* (with Gwyneth McClendon; Cambridge University Press, 2019). Her articles have been published in *American Behavioral Scientist, Journal of Politics, Comparative Political Studies, Studies in Comparative International Development*, and *African Affairs*.

Kenneth M. Roberts is Richard J. Schwartz Professor in the Department of Government at Cornell University. His research is devoted to the study of political parties, populism, and labor and social movements. He is author of *Deepening Democracy? The Modern Left and Social Movements in Chile and Peru* (Stanford University Press, 1998); and *Changing Course in Latin America: Party Systems in Latin America's Neoliberal Era* (Cambridge University Press, 2014), winner of the Best Book Award from the Comparative Democratization Section of the American Political Science Association 2016. He is co-editor of *The Diffusion of Social Movements: Actors, Mechanisms, and Political Effects* (Cambridge University Press, 2010); *The Resurgence of the Latin American Left* (Johns Hopkins University Press, 2011); and *When Democracy Trumps Populism: European and Latin American Lessons for the United States* (Cambridge University Press, 2019). His research has been published in a number of scholarly journals, including *American Political Science Review, Annual Review of Political Science, World Politics, Comparative Political Studies, Comparative Politics, Studies in Comparative International Development, Politics and Society*, and *Latin American Politics and Society*.

James A. Robinson is University Professor at the Harris School of Public Policy, University of Chicago. His research, in the field of political and economic development, addresses the factors that are the root causes of conflict, and explores the underlying relationship between poverty and the institutions of a society and how institutions emerge out of political conflicts. He is co-author (with Daron Acemoglu) of *Economic Origins of Dictatorship and Democracy* (Cambridge University Press, 2006), winner of the Woodrow Wilson Foundation Award and the William Riker Prize of the American Political Science Association; *Why Nations Fail: The Origins of Power, Prosperity, and Poverty* (Crown, 2012), winner of the Eccles Prize of the Columbia Business School and chosen as one of the *Washington Post's* top 10 books of the year for 2012, one of the *Economist* and *Financial Times's* "Best Books of 2012," one of the *Christian Science Monitor's* 15 Best Books of 2012, and one of *Businessweek's* "Best Books of 2012, According to Business Leaders"; and *The Nar-*

row Corridor: States, Societies, and the Fate of Liberty (Penguin, 2019), one of the *Financial Times*'s "Best Books of 2019." He is co-editor of *Natural Experiments of History* (Harvard University Press, 2010); *The Role of Elites in Economic Development* (Oxford University Press, 2012); and *Africa's Development in Historical Perspective* (Cambridge University Press, 2014). His articles have been published in *American Economic Review, Quarterly Journal of Economics, Econometrica, American Political Science Review*, and the *Annual Reviews of Political Science*. Robinson is an elected Fellow of the American Academy of Arts and Sciences.

Rev. Timothy Scully is a Professor of Political Science and a faculty fellow of the Helen Kellogg Institute for International Studies as well as the Nanovic Institute for European Studies at the University of Notre Dame. His research and graduate teaching focuses on comparative political institutions, especially political parties. He is author of *Rethinking the Center: Party Politics in Nineteenth- and Twentieth-Century Chile* (Stanford University Press, 1992) and five coauthored volumes: *Building Democratic Institutions: Party Systems in Latin America* (Stanford University Press, 1995); *Christian Democracy in Latin America: Electoral Competition and Regime Conflicts* (Stanford University Press, 2003); *El Eslabón Perdido: Familia, Bienestar, y Modernización en Chile* (Taurus, 2006), *Creencias e Ilusiones: la Cohesión Social de Los Latinoamericanos* (Santiago, Uqbar Editores, 2008), and *Democratic Governance in Latin America* (Stanford University Press, 2010). He has served the University of Notre Dame as Senior Associate Provost and Executive Vice President, and currently serves as a Fellow and Trustee. He is founder of the Alliance for Catholic Education (ACE), where he currently supports the ACE mission in a variety of ways. He has been recognized with several awards, including the United States Presidential Citizen's Medal, the Simon Prize for Social Entrepreneurship, and the Seton Award for Catholic Education.

Sidney Tarrow is Emeritus Maxwell Upson Professor of Government at Cornell University. His research focuses on social movements, contentious politics, and legal mobilization. Tarrow's books include *Peasant Communism in Southern Italy* (Yale University Press, 1967); *Between Center and Periphery: Grassroots Politicians in Italy and France* (Yale University Press, 1977); *Democracy and Disorder: Protest and Politics in Italy, 1965–1974* (Oxford University Press, 1989); *Dynamics of Contention* (with Doug McAdam and Charles Tilly, Cambridge University Press, 2001); *The New Transnational Activism* (Cambridge University Press, 2006); *Power in Movement: Social Movements and Contentious Politics*, 3rd edition (Cambridge University Press, 2011); *War, States, and Contention. A Comparative Historical Study* (Cornell University Press, 2015); and *Movements and Parties: Critical Connections in American Political Development* (Cambridge University Press, 2021). Tarrow is a fellow of the American Academy of Arts and Sciences and has been President of the Comparative Politics section of the APSA and of the Conference Group on Italian Politics.

David Waldner is Associate Professor in the Department of Government and Foreign Affairs at the University of Virginia. His research focuses on the causes of different forms of state formation and the consequences of variations in state-building trajectories for economic development and democratization. He also addresses questions about theories of comparative politics, qualitative methods, and the philosophy of science. He is author of *State Building and Late Development* (Cornell University Press, 1999); and *Rethinking the Resource Curse* (with Benjamin Smith; Cambridge University Press, 2021). His two current book projects are *Democracy and Dictatorship in the Post-Colonial World* and *The Philosophy of Social Science Methods*. His work has been published in the *Annual Review of Political Science, Security Studies*, and *The Oxford Handbook of Philosophy of Social Science*.